BLUE SMOKE

BLUE SMOKE

THE LOST DAWN OF NEW ZEALAND POPULAR MUSIC 1918-1964

CHRIS BOURKE

AUCKLAND UNIVERSITY PRESS

For Claire, Lynn and Rosemary, for music and memories.

First published 2010

Auckland University Press
University of Auckland
Private Bag 92019
Auckland 1142, New Zealand
www.auckland.ac.nz/aup
www.bluesmoke.net.nz

© Chris Bourke

ISBN 978 1 86940 455 0

National Library of New Zealand Cataloguing-in-Publication Data
Blue smoke : the lost dawn of New Zealand popular music, 1918-1964 /
Chris Bourke.
Includes bibliographical references and index.
ISBN 978-1-86940-455-0
1. Popular music—New Zealand—History and criticism. I. Title.
781.630993—dc 22

Publication is kindly assisted by the International Association of Music Libraries
Archives and Documentation Centres (New Zealand), the Lilburn Trust and

The author offers grateful thanks to the National Library of New Zealand for a research fellowship in 2006
and the University of Waikato for its Writer in Residence award in 2008, which enabled *Blue Smoke* to be completed.

Brief passages of this book have appeared in the author's contributions to *The Dictionary of
New Zealand Biography*, the *New Zealand Listener* and the *Turnbull Library Record*.

Picture research by the author.

Thanks are due to the following publishers for permission to quote from songs still in copyright: 'Maori Battalion Marching Song' by
Anania Amohau and J. Thompson (Musical Import Co. Ltd); 'Tea at Te Kuiti' by Kenneth Stopford Avery (Mushroom Music Pty Ltd);
'Monde Marie' by Peter Cape (Gladwen McIntyre); 'Rocky Mountain Lullaby' by Rex Franklin (Rex Franklin); 'Land of the Long
White Cloud' by Sam Freedman and Sam Karetu, 'Haere Mai' and 'I'll Serenade a Star' by Sam Freedman; 'Love in a Fowl House'
by Garner Wayne (Viking Seven Seas NZ Ltd, P.O. Box 152, Paraparaumu); 'Poi Poi Twist' by Rim D. Paul (Rimini D. Paul);
'Tomo Mai' by Henare Waitoa (Waitoa family); 'My Old Man's an All Black' by Gerald Kereti Merito (Essex Music Australia Pty Ltd).

Previous page: Rehearsing in Auckland in the early 1940s are four members of Cliff Russell's Civic Wintergarden big band.
From left: guitarist Gordon Hall, drummer Bruce McDonald, bass player Thomson Yandall and saxophonist Niel Randrup. Bennie Gunn collection

Book design: Katrina Duncan
Cover design: Spencer Levine

Printed by 1010 Printing Ltd, China

CONTENTS

Tai Paul and his Pohutu Boys were Rotorua's leading dance band in the 1950s. Pictured at their regular dance in the Ohinemutu meeting house of Tamatekapua, c. 1953, are (L-R) Pat Montague, guitar; Vic Bartholomew, piano; Alf Brown, saxophone; Margaret Henderson, vocalist; Don McKenzie, drums; Tai Paul, saxophone; Angus Douglas, vocalist and guitar; Teddy Walker, saxophone; Oscar Maika, bass; and Napi Walker, trumpet. John Scott Studios, Rotorua

PREFACE

Blue Smoke is a history of New Zealand popular music in the days before rock'n'roll. I felt there was a gap, not in the market but in our understanding: how we got from Alfred Hill's 'Waiata Poi' to Rim D. Paul's 'Poi Poi Twist' seemed to be a mystery.

For my purposes, 'popular music' is a genre, not a description. Also popular in this period – the mid-twentieth century – were brass bands, bagpipers and choirs. But they are hardly mentioned in this book, which looks at the evolution of modern popular music as an industry: the changes in musical fashions, technology and social mores. This popular music keeps evolving, and is usually heavily affected by overseas influences. Songs are the currency, although during this period almost all were written by foreigners. But this era leads to a time when our own original songs become commonplace, rather than restricted to hobbyists or nationalistic folk singers.

Popular music is not pure: there is no holy grail of authenticity. It has an element of the marketplace that will never satisfy the folklorists in the field, though some songs become so popular that they almost become folk songs. The working title of this book, *Blue Smoke Gets in Your Eyes*, seemed to capture both worlds (but would have created a new 'mondegreen': a misheard lyric). That and the final title referred to 'Blue Smoke', the song that was pivotal to the creation of a recording industry in New Zealand. The segue to Jerome Kern's song acknowledged the overwhelming international presence. Popular music is something old, new, borrowed and blue – and eventually something *ours*.

The period covered shows a shift in influence, from Britain to America. Technological changes were also crucial: new styles arrived quickly through radio and records, and these developments are examined for their effects on music-making. With each new style of music comes a reaction, from a musical or civic establishment disturbed by possible shifts in the social order. But this book is a music history before it is a social or cultural history. It concentrates on the people who made music and their connections, the changes to the way the music sounded, how it was created and enjoyed. I wanted to describe how the baton keeps getting passed on, and the characters, locations and innovations that shaped our own musical world. For much of this period, jazz was at its peak as a form of popular music, breaking out of the dance halls. But the book needed to be more than a history of jazz in New Zealand: it needed to explore the other genres that became part of the popular music industry. Country, Hawaiian and middle-of-the-road pop are all part of the mix before – and during – the arrival of rock'n'roll.

The Howard Morrison Quartet in particular needed more extensive treatment than it has (appropriately) received in other music histories. Otherwise, the years since Johnny Devlin brought the news from Gonville have been well covered, by John Dix in *Stranded in Paradise* and in many works that seminal

book has inspired. The colonial period has also been discussed, by John Mansfield Thomson and Angela Annabell and others. Musical theatre has been explained by Peter Downes and Peter Harcourt, and Maori music has been the life's work of Mervyn McLean.

I have written *Blue Smoke* not because of what I knew, but because of what I wanted to know. It isn't supposed to be an encyclopaedia: there are areas that didn't fit my parameters. The worlds of variety and community singing are discussed only as they affected popular music; brass bands are occasionally mentioned as a training ground for jazz musicians; musical theatre has already been covered elsewhere and, despite its huge popularity, its influence quickly waned.

There is room for more discussion of these genres, and the other topics covered in this book, and I hope – as happened with *Stranded in Paradise* – it will encourage students and historians to explore further.

Two influences that converged a long time ago initiated *Blue Smoke*. At its heart is a desire to hear the war stories my mother never told. As a young adult in Wellington during the 1940s, Claire Kennedy experienced the Second World War on the home front: the rationing, the tragedy and the music. Afterwards, hearing the music provoked sadness, not nostalgia. Years later she would occasionally drop kernels of detail about that period. For music fans, she hinted, the visit of the Artie Shaw band in 1943 was as exciting as the arrival of the Beatles. The Wellington Swing Club was the place where the jazz musicians mingled with their audience, in the Nimmo's Building across the road from the city's smartest club, the Majestic Cabaret on Willis Street.

But the book really began in 1981 as an undergraduate essay that nurtured an interest in New Zealand popular music of this era. Studying music history at Victoria University, I sometimes felt like a gatecrasher at a funeral. Thirty years ago, popular music wasn't on the curriculum; I had just missed an experimental course briefly offered in the mid-1970s. There were plenty of quality books on jazz and pop on the library shelves, but no records: the genre was never discussed. The music we studied was almost exclusively in the European tradition, from plainchant to the most challenging of contemporary music. There was a healthy concentration on New Zealand music, though, and with Douglas Lilburn still a presence on campus, and leading younger composers such as Jack Body and Ross Harris on the staff, one quickly became aware of the strength of the music we produced ourselves.

Each year, the ethnomusicology lecturer Allan Thomas sent his students out on a field exercise, to emulate Alan Lomax or other seekers of song. His musical vision was all-inclusive, from gamelan orchestras to whistling. I decided to interview pianists who had mastered blues and boogie woogie in their youth (my hidden agenda was to learn to play in those styles). It was a total joy, thanks to the enthusiasm of family friends such as Jim Walker and Henk Knottenbelt. They never needed much persuasion to perform at parental gatherings. Jeanette Walker suggested I contact Ray Harris, the long-serving jazz reviewer at the *Listener*.

Ray came to the party, and then some. He explained how he learnt boogie woogie, but described much more: musical Wellington in the 1940s and 1950s, the characters, the locations, the social scene. This wasn't a milieu in which revered violinist Alex Lindsay played only in string quartets, he also mixed with the jazzers.

In 2003 Allan Thomas asked me to write a paper for a musicological conference. The topic was 'Jazz in New Zealand during the Second World War'. I found that there was almost nothing on the written record. All I knew were the unreliable anecdotes and myths that I had picked up over the years, and in the limited time I had, all I could offer was not a paper but a proposal: 'Notes towards a history of jazz in New Zealand'. This was an untapped field, I said at the conference: here are some leads, some themes. Talk to these people while they are still alive.

Luckily, someone was present who knew much more about the topic. Dennis Huggard is an Auckland archivist who became a jazz aficionado as a teenager during the Second World War. In the course of his lifetime, he has assembled a staggering collection of clippings, acetates, commercial discs and tape recordings – mostly jazz, but also of other forms of popular music. He has compiled and published thorough and useful discographies of New Zealand labels such as Tanza and Stebbing. Dennis is the researchers' saviour: generations of New Zealand music historians will be grateful for his efforts and generosity. For the last 20 years the other person committed to keeping this music alive has been Jim Sutton, whose big-hearted *Nostalgia* programme on ZB celebrates the musicians rather than wallows in the past.

In 2005 I felt the need to begin the book I had suggested at the musicology conference. There seemed to be an urgency,

to collect the stories and information from participants who were now appearing in the 'deceased' columns with increasing regularity. In 2006, the National Library awarded me its annual research fellowship. This allowed me to dive into the archives and spend months searching through microfilm, periodicals and a few manuscripts. Most importantly, it enabled me to connect with Dennis and to interview as many of the musicians as I could. They ranged from Gerry Merito – my youngest, at 68 – to Jim Gower, then 94. Sadly, Gerry and several others have now passed away.

Most of the book was written while at the University of Waikato, as the English Department's writer-in-residence in 2008. There, I connected with Sarah Shieff (who knew Chips Healy) and three former colleagues in the Music Department, William Dart, Martin Lodge and Ian Whalley (who was taught piano by Bill Hoffmeister). All provided encouragement and practical help.

Music is about connecting the dots, and there is rarely ever more than one step of separation. My former *Listener* colleague Tom McWilliams led to Jim Warren, whose jazz reviews for *Playdate* Tom edited in the 1960s. Jim's sharp memories go back before the 1930s; he was a participant as well as an observer, of band leaders such as Ted Croad and Chips Healy, and his entrepreneurial nephew Phil Warren.

I would like to have covered more regional music-making – local heroes such as Taranaki's Colin King, the West Coast's Rene Jacobs – but the more detours from State Highway One, the longer the journey. Luckily, many local music scenes have already compiled their own histories. Also, the development of songwriting is only touched upon. Gordon Spittle's *Counting the Beat* covers this field, while the prolific output of hobby songwriters is a thesis in waiting.

The exploration of this period has confirmed what I always suspected. New Zealand musicians were not isolated from international developments, but remarkably current and equally proficient. We may have followed overseas styles, but we brought our own creativity to the music. New Zealand after hours was an exciting world; it didn't close at six o'clock, it opened up.

ACKNOWLEDGEMENTS

To research and write this book, I have relied on the generosity and tolerance of family, friends, librarians and institutions. I must thank the National Library of New Zealand for awarding me their research fellowship in 2006, and the University of Waikato for allowing me to be their writer in residence in 2008 (partly funded by Creative New Zealand). Most of all, I am grateful for several stalwarts who became the backbone of this project: Sarah Shieff, Peter Downes, Dennis and Rene Huggard, Tom McWilliams, Jim Sutton, Jim Warren and Redmer Yska. Ray Harris and Allan Thomas have been quietly supportive since 1981.

Thanks especially to the people I interviewed, for their memories and patience: Dale Alderton, Bernie Allen, Jack Baker, Bob Barcham, Doug Caldwell, Lew Campbell, Jim Carter, Les Cleveland, Ray Columbus, Johnny Devlin, Colin Dorsey, Frank Douglas, Johnny Douglas, Peter Downes, Pat Dugan, Rex and Noelene Franklin, Justin du Fresne, Frank Gibson Jnr, Thérèse Gore, Jim Gower, Bennie Gunn, Rocky Don Hall, Ray Harris, Ron Haywood, Tony Hopkins, Monty Julian, Bruce Kaplan, Ruma Karaitiana, Joan Kennett, Colin King, Trevor King, Julian Lee, Laurie and Alwyn Lewis, Alan Loney, Mac McKenzie, Murray Marbeck, Ann Marston, Max McCauley, Colin and Nola McCrorie, Pat McMinn and Niel Randrup, Bruce Morley, Mike Nock, Bill Patterson, Calder Prestcott, Dalvanius Prime, Don Richardson, Murdoch Riley, John and Ann Shears, Reo Sheirtcliffe, Jimmy Sloggett, Eldred Stebbing, Murray Tanner, Merv Thomas, Dave Van Weede, Harry Voice and Jim Warren. Geoffrey Totton shared the notes of interviews he did with jazz musicians in the mid-1980s.

Friends who have provided advice and support are: Clare Avery, John Baker, Matiu Baker, Arthur Baysting, Nick Bollinger, Michael Brown, Rod Bryant, Bev Cameron, Murray Cammick, Kate Camp, Jean Clarkson, Roy Colbert, Michael Colonna, Grant Gillanders, Stephen Hamilton, Richard Hardie, Judy Haswell, Vicki Hughes, Mel Johnston, Robyn Langwell, Simon Lynch, David McGill, Bruce Morley, Lucy Orbell, Neill Pickard, Graham Reid, Ross Somerville, Bryan Staff, Julie Starr, Stephen Stratford, Marama Warren and Georgina White.

My extended family provided accommodation, meals and encouragement (though my mother did say, near the end, 'I hope someone's interested'): Nick Bevin and Judith Vickerman; Penny Bieder and Barry Fraser; Claire, Mary Anne, Tim and Sam Bourke; Roy and Christine Colbert; Prue Dashfield; Devta Doolan; Chris and Maxine Green; Michael and Jane Howley; Glenn Jowitt; Paul Kennedy and Callie Blood; Mark and Gemma Kennedy; Dianne Moffatt; and Phil and Heather Walker. For offering me stints as a house-sitter, thanks to Peter and Diane Beatson; Ian and Robert Cross; Mary, Pat and Paul Duignan; Fiona Hill; and Rosemary Norman.

The transcribing team seemed to enjoy their arduous task: Hilary Bevin, Sylvia Bevin, Elizabeth Cottrell, Libby Giles, Lynn McKenzie, Catherine Perry and Graham Reid.

The support of colleagues at Radio New Zealand was crucial throughout: Mark Cubey, Mark Hector, Kim Hill, John Howson, David Knowles, Alison Lloyd-Davies, Gavin McGinley, Liisa McMillan, Amelia Nurse, John Pilley, John Roberts and Haydn Sherley. For their archive interviews, thanks to Warwick Burke, Caitlin Cherry, Jerome Cvitanovich, Eric Frykberg, Jack Perkins and Jim Sullivan. At RNZ Sound Archives: John Kelcher, Rachel Lord, Karen Neill and Blair Parkes.

But thanks in particular to the librarians who so often went the extra mile. Infofind, the RNZ reference library, has been like a second home for 25 years: thanks to Yvonne Boland, Anne Buchanan, Emma Hart and Yumi Nagafuchi. At Auckland City Libraries, thanks to Kate de Courcy, Keith Giles, Marilyn Portman and Jenny Whalley; at the Hocken, Dunedin: David Murray; the splendid New Zealand collection at the University of Waikato Library; the Christchurch Public Library; and Archives New Zealand.

At the Alexander Turnbull Library and National Library: Chris Anderson, Peter Attwell, Cathy Bentley, Margaret Calder, Penny Carnaby, Jocelyn Chambers, Mary Cobeldick, David Colquhoun, Walter Cook, Linda Evans, Roger Flury, Glenda Gale, Gillian Headifen, Peter Ireland, Tim Lovell-Smith, Barbara Lyon, Merryn McAulay, Joan McCracken, Keith McEwing, Shaun McGuire, Sean McMahon, John Mohi, Brendan O'Brien, Jill Palmer, Philip Rainer, David Retter, Lynette Shum, Colleen Slater, Kevin Stewart, Danny Sue, John Sullivan, Amy Watling and Kirsty Willis.

At the University of Waikato, thanks to Athena Chambers, Dellie Dellow, William Faramond, Mark Houlahan, Kirstine Moffat and Sarah Shieff at the English Department; at the Music Department, William Dart, Martin Lodge, Ian Whalley; and Roy Crawford, Geoff Lealand and Dan Zirker.

Photos came from many sources, but especially generous were Bernie Allen, Jane Burke, Fay Burns, Costa Christie, Roy Colbert, Michael Colonna, David Dell, Peter Downes, Adam Gifford, Thérèse Gore, Bennie Gunn, Ron Haywood, Dennis Huggard, Joan Kennett, Bruce King, Trevor King, Marise McDonald, Mac McKenzie, Pat McMinn, Rangi Parker, Chris Prowse, Murdoch Riley, RNZ Sound Archives, Warren Rod, Dave Ross, Gordon Spittle, Bryan Staff, Merv Thomas, Ans Westra, Jim Warren and Redmer Yska.

Finally, it was the team at Auckland University Press who turned a ream of A4 into an elegant, inviting book. Thanks to Sam Elworthy for his exuberance and vision, Ginny Sullivan for careful editing, Katrina Duncan and Spencer Levine for their empathetic design, Christine O'Brien, Vani Sripathy and Anna Hodge.

Recorded on DECCA No. X1094, George Nepia, also ASTOR Recording, Aloha Orchestra and Nuhaka Trio

1918-1929

New Zealanders have never been 'a people without songs'. When the pioneering settlers emigrated, they carried with them instruments and leather-bound volumes of their favourite sheet music. Upon arriving, they found vigorous music-making among Maori: haka, karanga, poi, waiata. Maori musicians were quick to adopt European instruments and form their own bands, and their music-making was heavily influenced by Christianity.

The appropriation went both ways. Pakeha composers such as Alfred Hill borrowed Maori themes for songs or larger works, while Maori songwriters wrote lyrics to foreign melodies. Some, like 'Now is the Hour', almost became indigenous folk songs. Local songwriting was popular, much of it amateur and self-published, although some songs – 'On the Ball', 'Invercargill' and 'God Defend New Zealand' – lasted and travelled. New Zealand was visited by many international shows and performers, and sent musical ambassadors abroad.

But the increased globalisation encouraged by the First World War did change the path of New Zealand music. The combination of a new, provocative style of popular music and dancing with the new media of recorded sound, film and radio altered the soundscape. Silent movies employed armies of musicians to perform an eclectic repertoire, serving as a training ground for the noisy changes in popular music.

How did this new music differ? Its dance tempos weren't 'strict' like the waltzes and valetas. The musicians frequently improvised, and the instruments were often in unconventional combinations. Exuberance eclipsed politesse. The music played during the 1920s dance craze was called jazz. Brash, with syncopated rhythms, the style kept evolving.

How was the new music disseminated? Recordings were widely available before the First World War, but the industry escalated in the years following. Technological developments hastened the jazz age: improved electric recordings, swifter distribution from Australia. The rapid spread of radio brought music into a growing number of homes and new nightclubs based on American models revolutionised the dance scene.

The biggest change – in New Zealand and other British colonies – was that the United States became the dominant influence. In the decade after the end of the First World War, New Zealand musicians and their audiences no longer turned so devotedly towards the distant 'home' they had just defended.

Opposite: 'Beneath the Maori Moon', written by Auckland music teacher and composer Walter Smith, recorded by former All Black George Nepia in 1936. This edition was published by J. E. Jenkins, Auckland, 1950. B-K 477-cover, Alexander Turnbull Library, Wellington

Ted Marchant and his Kit Kat Dance Band in 1927, the year they made their debut on 2YA. They were a drawcard at Wellington's Evans Bay Yacht Club and a favourite for government department balls. From left are V. Shepherd (drums and effects), Ted Marchant (violin, soprano saxophone), W. Ashworth (saxophone and clarinets), W. Pearce (piano) and D. Henderson (banjo). S. P. Andrew. F-18413-1/1, Alexander Turnbull Library, Wellington

ONE

Welcome to the Jazz Age

1918: PEACE IN RAG TIME

New Zealand's dance halls were silent when the First World War finally came to an end. Due to a telegraphic error, the first murmurs that the war was over were heard a few days early, on 8 November 1918. The timing could not have been worse: just as everyone wanted to rush into the streets to dance, to sing and to cheer, the government wanted the public to stay home.

An influenza epidemic was sweeping the country, swiftly causing hundreds of deaths. Only two days before the 'false armistice', the acting chief health officer Dr Joseph Frengley ordered that public halls and places of entertainment shut for at least a week. Race meetings and many church services were cancelled.[1] On 11 November, the government invoked Section 18 of the Public Health Act and closed all theatres, dance halls, schools and other public gathering places. 'These ranged from band practices and lodge meetings to such delights as the Seatoun Social Club Fancy Dress and Masquerade Dance.'[2]

Once the 'false armistice' rumour took hold, however, the citizenry ignored the government and did not stay at home. 'As if by magic Queen Street just filled with people', an eyewitness recalled. 'It was one mass of laughing, crying, coughing and obviously sick people.' Threepenny flags suddenly cost one shilling, yet they were carried 'by

every man, woman and child and there was a great noise, joy bells ringing, drums playing, tin cans being beaten, and people shouting hurrah! Until they were hoarse.'

The national anthem 'God Save the Queen' was sung 'over and over again, while attempts to sing "Rule Britannia" were limited to the chorus, the only section known by the public'.[3]

When the official news arrived on 12 November, Christchurch ignored the warnings and huge crowds of sneezing and coughing people gathered in the square. The cathedral bells rang out, brass bands performed, and 'it was a noisy and festive day'. Dunedinites also hit the streets, for a procession, speeches, singing and band music in the Octagon.[4]

In Wellington, a fusillade of cannon fire announced the peace at 9.00 am, 'then pandemonium broke loose – every whistle, hooter, syren [sic] and, in fact, any noise producing instrument within a radius of 10 miles shrieked out the downfall of the enemy'.[5] The 'gayest and most delightful of cheerily disordered processions' trooped through the streets, and groups of young men upped the cacophony by parading 'with musical instruments and tin cans (that were the reverse of musical)'.[6] At Stewart Dawson's corner, the Waterside Workers' Band played popular songs of a patriotic bent, and the choruses of well-known songs ('in which the crowd joined with great vigour').

'With blaring toy trumpets, rattles, cymbals, tin-cans, and every imaginable musical instrument that could be promptly secured, the crowds – filling the full width of the street – drifted noisily but ever so gladsomely to the Town Hall.'[7] There, speeches by the Prime Minister William Massey and the Finance Minister Joseph Ward received a refrain of 'Hearts of Oak' from the band. Privately, however, there were murmurings that Massey and Ward were responsible for the influenza epidemic. Both had recently returned from an overseas trip on the *Niagara*, which was not quarantined when it berthed in Auckland. Although these suspicions have since been proved to be unfounded, at the time many citizens responded sardonically by turning the First World War song 'Mademoiselle from Armentières' into a subversive chant: 'Old Bill Massey brought the flu, parlez vous/a pity he didn't get it too . . .'.[8]

Music, like a virus, respects no borders. The swift travel and growing internationalism – albeit in the cause of war – that enabled the influenza epidemic to cause havoc worldwide were typical of the technological developments that would make the twentieth century a time of extreme and rapid change. Popular music was a conspicuous example; so powerful were the new media of recordings, cinema and radio that they drove rather than reflected the innovations.

Popular music had been an industry for decades, with sheet music, instruments and live performance as its media. Besides the theatre, singing in the home – accompanied by a piano or a variety of other instruments – was one of the most common ways by which songs were disseminated. But after the First World War, the dominant share of the home entertainment market was taken over by record players.

The 1930s Depression would also contribute to the decline in domestic music-making, with record players and radios being more affordable than pianos in a straitened economy. John MacGibbon suggests another reason for this change:

> Comparisons can be odious and singing around the family piano started to become a demoralising experience for fumbling amateurs. When do-it-yourself was the only way

to have music in the home, people were prepared to 'have a go' and audiences, many of whom knew little better anyway, welcomed it. Embarrassment would have been a particular problem from about 1908, when the quality of reproduction had improved enough for the gramophone to be regarded as a serious musical instrument.[9]

When the war began in 1914, rampant patriotism became the prevailing spirit. This was audible in the proliferation of jingoistic songs, and visible in the large number of public concerts taking place. In Wellington, there were as many as eight concerts a night, recalled the sportscaster Winston McCarthy: 'Anyone with pretensions to singing or instrument playing was in demand . . . . everyone wanted to put on concerts to raise funds for the troops.' McCarthy was a child singer, renowned for his impersonation of Harry Lauder, and he estimated that he performed at 400 wartime patriotic concerts. 'As I was only 10 when the war ended, I must have had the constitution of an ox to have stood up to that. Mind you, they were patriotic concerts only. In addition there would be Irish concerts, Scottish concerts, the Orphans, the Savage Club, the Jewish Club (how the old man got accepted there I don't know), Charlie's Aunt Club and so on.' McCarthy had a good voice and a Scottish accent, said the *Dominion*, 'and a wink that is effective at a mile. In "Roamin' in the Gloamin'" he simply wrecked the audience with the force of his irresistibly comic personality.'[10]

The war made many marks on music in New Zealand. Riding the wave of patriotism, amateur songwriters tried to create a hit that expressed loyalty to the cause and support to the troops. Among the dozens that were published – many by vanity presses – were 'The Call of the Fernleaf', 'Good Old New Zealand', 'Sons of New Zealand' and 'The New Zealand Marseillaise'. Business dealings with enemy countries ceased, so in 1916, while imports of recordings and music-making machinery from Britain remained static, there was a large increase from the US that meant the two countries were now equals in the New Zealand market.[11] Piano sales dropped slightly, and one of the most successful hire-purchase piano firms was forced to change its name. The Dresden Piano Company was a high-profile business founded in Dunedin in 1881, and during the war its ascending sales graph was halted only by its unfortunate Germanic name. In 1915 Dresden rebranded itself the Bristol Piano Company, with advertisements emphasising that the shareholders and directors

TOWN HALL, WELLINGTON, N.Z.

Souvenir Programme

KIA ORA   H.M.S. PHILOMEL   KIA ORA

TE TOA (TO ARMS)

IN AID OF THE NAVY LEAGUE

WEDNESDAY AND THURSDAY, APRIL 4th and 5th, 1917.

'When Britain Really Ruled the Waves' was among the items performed at two variety concerts at the Wellington Town Hall in April 1917, although the image on the programme suggests cultural imperialism can go both ways. Experienced vaudeville performers and a 'lusty chorus' from the crew of the British naval vessel HMS *Philomel* shared the stage with local artists such as Teresa McEnroe and Hamilton Hodges, raising funds for the Navy League. The grand finale was a choral rendition of 'Motherland'. Ladies of Wellington provided a selection of sweetmeats, wearing 'their best frocks to sell them'.
Eph-B-VARIETY-1917-01-title, Alexander Turnbull Library, Wellington

New Zealanders had been quick to take to the new medium, recorded sound. The first demonstration of a phonograph in New Zealand was in 1879, just two years after it had been invented by Thomas Edison. Although the *Lyttelton Times* described 2000 Cantabrians experiencing 'Edison's wonderful phonograph speak, sing, laugh, whistle, and play Levy's cornet solos', the sound was primitive.[14] It was not until 1890 that the audience at a Dunedin exhibition could appreciate the possibilities. A local singer, John Jago, made a demonstration recording on site. A year later, a Professor Archibald displayed a phonograph in Wellington, 'A crude and raucous thing it was, though still wonderful', recalled T. Lindsay Buick.[15]

In the first years of the twentieth century, a new industry quickly developed, with companies such as Gramophone, Edison and Columbia establishing distribution agencies in New Zealand. Retail outlets included the Begg's and Dresden stores, and phonographs could soon be bought in provincial centres as well. In 1901 a chain called the Talkeries was established, specialising in discs, which would soon outsell – and supersede – Edison cylinders. In 1905 its Wellington branch advertised that 15,000 discs had been imported and 'record concerts' were to be held to give the public the opportunity to hear the mechanised music. As more discs were recorded featuring famous singers such as Nellie Melba, Enrico Caruso and Harry Lauder, these concerts became common events at this and other Talkeries branches in Christchurch, Auckland and New Plymouth.[16]

By 1911 New Zealand's record distribution and retailing industry was sufficiently sophisticated that, during the visit of US brass-band leader John Philip Sousa, his recordings were available for sale; in the next few years New Zealand welcomed tours by John McCormack, Clara Butt, Harry Lauder and Peter Dawson, all of whom were recording stars. Advertisements in their programmes reminded their audiences that their discs were available for sale in nearby stores.[17]

The first New Zealander to make a commercial recording is said to have been John Prouse. Born in Wellington in 1856, Prouse recorded twelve songs while on a visit to Britain in June 1905, six of which were released by the Gramophone and Typewriter Company.[18] Other New Zealand singers who recorded overseas include Frances Alda, singing with Caruso in the US in 1910; and Rosina Buckman, who recorded Alfred Hill's 'Waiata Poi' in England in 1914. The earliest to lay down a significant

were all British born and bred. Begg's in Wellington exhorted its customers to buy 'British Pianos for British Homes'.[12]

Despite the war, records still managed to be imported into New Zealand, with patriotic products such as 'Good Old New Zealand', 'Sons of New Zealand' and 'The March of the Anzacs' among them. On 18 July 1919, eight months after the war ended, the same *Dominion* that featured the news of a peace treaty with Germany contained an advertisement from the distributors Bannatyne and Hunter. It announced they had records available of 'popular songs, dance hits, opera, orchestral and band selections, still at pre-war prices'. It also invited the women of Wellington to buy record players for when their relatives in the forces returned.[13]

body of work was the tenor Ernest McKinlay, who was also one of the first artists to be recorded at the Sydney studio opened by Columbia in 1926. With resident pianist, Gil Dech, as accompanist, McKinlay recorded ballads and Maori songs that sold well in New Zealand; in the international career that followed, he always featured Maori songs in his repertoire, and published them in a songbook.[19]

McKinlay, born in Dunedin in 1889, got his career break in the grimmest of circumstances. He was serving in France as part of the ambulance corps of the New Zealand Division after the Battle of the Somme, when the decision was made to assemble an entertainment unit for troops returning from the front. As an amateur singer and participant in camp concerts, McKinlay became one of ten 'Kiwis' who gave regular shows dressed in Pierrot costumes. They performed light classical songs, operetta excerpts, straight songs, ballads and even ragtime items, with high production standards under difficult circumstances; they even featured a female impersonator. The Kiwis were one of several New Zealand entertainment troupes that emerged during the war, others being the Tuis, the Dinks and the New Zealand Pierrots. During the post-war occupation of Germany, members of the Pierrots formed the basis of the Diggers, an entertainment troupe that toured internationally and lasted until the 1930s.[20] Led by New Zealander Pat Hanna, the Diggers concentrated on theatre and comedy rather than music, but they had some fine singers in their ensemble. Stealing the show, however, was their 'he-lady', Stan Lawson, whose cross-dressing talents appealed to a New Zealand reviewer during a 1921 tour: 'Stan cannot sing, but he can put the jazz numbers over with rare vitality and aplomb, without ever forgetting the Flossie touch.'[21]

The *Niagara* has been unfairly blamed for bringing in-fluenza to New Zealand – it actually travelled ahead of the disease. But it was the carrier of another sort of epi-demic: in the 1920s, this fast-moving mail steamer would play a pivotal role in disseminating a new style of music to the country. Word of this music – with its strange name, jazz – had been filtering south as the First World War came to a close.

Before the war, going to a dance meant 'indulging in a sedate activity' that had changed little since colonial times. In rural halls and at debutantes' balls, dance cards would offer the schottische, the valeta, the barn dance and, 'for the more adventurous, the lancers and quadrilles'.[22]

This cosy, chaperoned ritual began to change in 1916 with the invention of the foxtrot, which immediately became popular worldwide. The first recorded foxtrot arrived quickly in New Zealand, a banjo and piano piece called 'Beets and Turnips'.[23] To 'strict tempo' orchestras and dancers, it was as though rhythms were being released from the 'tyranny of the bar line'.[24] Ragtime had been popular in New Zealand as early as 1901, when a variety show audience at the Federal Theatre in Wellington left whistling 'Tell It To Me', a ragtime song performed by Harry Thomas.[25] Before the war, albums of ragtime sheet music were available, and the popularity of Irving Berlin's rags is apparent from his prominence in advertisements placed by Wellington's Anglo-American Music Store ('the Dominion's cheapest').[26]

By 1917 a new word – 'jazz' – was mentioned by visiting American entertainers, and the word itself, let alone the music, had risqué connotations. Australia had its own jazz bands before the war finished. In mid-1918, vaudeville entrepreneur Ben Fuller advertised London singer Belle Sylvia appearing at Sydney's National with 'Australia's First Jazz Band': 'See that crazy drummer, see that dippy fiddler, see that perky pianist. You can't keep your seats while the Jazzers Jazz.'[27]

Like an imported pest, in the last months of the war jazz began to spread throughout New Zealand: the word, if not the music. At first it was a catch-all that meant something modern and exciting or, in a musical context, something unfamiliar, cacophonous, abrasive and even uncivilised.

One of the earliest reports to use the word was definitely not positive and was almost certainly inaccurate. It was probably an Australian sub-editor having a joke at New Zealand's expense. On 11 June 1918, Waikato police raided a Maori gathering in Mercer to arrest seven men who had failed to report for their medical examinations prior to being conscripted. A large group of Maori had gathered to discuss the conscription issue, and the meeting had been going on for two or three weeks.

The police were expected. Escorting them onto the marae was 'a bevy of Maori girls, a number of whom were equipped with brass band instruments, from which they produced music of a somewhat uncertain tune'. As the police approached the first to be arrested – Te Raungaanga Mahuta, a brother of the Maori King – he was surrounded by these women, who placed a flag in front of him 'as if to protect him'.[28] News of the incident reached Sydney, where the *Sun* report was headlined MAORI MAIDS' JAZZ BAND![29]

Jazz was an international phenomenon, and New Zealanders were quickly caught up in it on both sides of the globe. In 1919 a New Zealand songwriter was having success in London with his ragtime song 'The Mad Jazz Razz'. Lance-Corporal Ivor Weir was still in the army, as a pianist with the Diggers' Pierrot Troupe. Formerly the pianist at Everybody's theatre in Christchurch, Weir was 23, already had half a dozen hit songs to his name and was desperately awaiting his discharge so that he could enjoy his triumph. He wrote 'without boasting' to a friend in New Zealand: 'Every big London restaurant I enter, I always hear the orchestra play my ragtime song . . . it's a big success everywhere.'[30]

In August that year, the *Dominion* announced that a group of prominent Wellington instrumentalists had formed a 'jazz' band and a concert was imminent. Rehearsals – using sheet music imported from the United States – produced the 'weirdest effects imaginable'. The paper doubted whether 'such queer noises can be termed music', but whatever the noise was, it had the power 'to make people dance to its quaint rhythms and amazing pauses'.[31]

Four days later, there was another Wellington outbreak, during the Gay Gambols' Saturday night concert at the Grand Opera House. With the song 'Hey, Ruba' – 'a rural jazz' – the Wellington Performing Musicians' Orchestra introduced 'the clang and clatter of the modern trap-drummer's varied appurtenances in rythmical [*sic*] association'.

The concert's highlight was the song of the season, the seductive 'Missouri Waltz' (by Americans John Eppel and J. R. Shannon). Considered a failure when it was first published in the United States five years earlier, the song was now so ubiquitous in Wellington that without it 'no modern entertainment would be complete. It haunts one in the home, the dance room, the vaudeville, the parks and the theatre.'[32]

What was this thing called jazz? In its earliest appearances, what was publicised as a jazz band was likely to be a dance band made up of instruments that were not usually played together, with startling percussion effects. In addition, these bands played music for new sorts of dances. 'Dance bands were those bands which played the newest "jazz" and popular music from America', writes UK historian James Nott. 'They played the foxtrot and the quickstep, not the valeta or the polka. There were few, if any, real "jazz" bands on the American model, although there were many who called themselves such.'[33]

Australian jazz historian Bruce Johnson says that besides the novelty and theatrical aspects of the bands labelled 'jazz', to musicians and their audiences in the 1920s the most distinguishable feature would have been rhythm: 'aggressive, disordered. We must recall the rhythmic conventions which preceded this African-inflected fashion – the undisturbed regularity of the waltz, the pride of the Erin, the gypsy tap.' Johnson makes the point that, in the decades since jazz emerged, our ears have become so attuned to rhythmic invention that it is now difficult for us 'to retrieve sympathetically the disrupted impression created by syncopation. This was the most widely recognised musical innovation in jazz.'[34]

The war had not cut New Zealand off from the influence of overseas popular music, of any kind. Vaudeville, music theatre and silent movies flourished; recordings and sheet music continued to arrive. Some performers still managed to visit; among them, early in the war, were Harry Lauder, Peter Dawson and Miss Dorothy Harris, the 'acknowledged queen of ragtime'.[35]

In 1918, as the war drew to a close, audiences welcomed Ada Reeve – later dubbed 'the Vera Lynn of World War I'[36] – and Gladys Moncrieff in her first tour as the headline act. In June, Auckland could offer a wealth of international entertainment. Depending on one's predilection, there were classical organ recitals at the Town Hall, and vaudeville seasons at Fuller's Opera House with Tom Haverly's Irish Players, or at the King's with the Merrymakers. The latter event included the 'gripping drama' *For England and Honour*, Omah the Hindoo Illusionist and a ragtime song competition. The Fisk Jubilee Singers – a world-famous troupe of African-American gospel singers – performed a season at the Town Hall's concert chamber. This was 'an entertainment that has seldom been surpassed', said the *New Zealand Herald*, '. . . coon songs that are almost classical, and operatic excerpts.'[37] Alternatively, silent films starring Billie Burke and Charlie Chaplin ('the Prime Minister of mirth') were screening at the Tivoli and Westend.[38]

But the films were not silent. Pit orchestras had been around almost as long as theatre itself, and the popularity of the cinema gave hundreds of musicians work that required skills of improvisation, spontaneity and a broad repertoire of material from all genres. Unbeknownst to the musicians accompanying silent movies, within a decade they would be made redundant, but they had served the perfect apprenticeship for the shifts in popular music in the 1930s.

THE SOUND OF SILENTS

Charlie Chaplin has been stood up. His little tramp has fallen in love with a saloon girl, and has invited her to dinner. But she hasn't arrived, so he entertains himself by making the bread rolls dance. The film is *The Gold Rush*, and in 1925 the era of the silent film is at its peak. If bread rolls are to dance, Chaplin needs music.

Watching the screen in Wellington's De Luxe theatre, conductor L. D. Austin doesn't miss his cue. At the wave of his baton the orchestra strikes up a familiar foxtrot: 'I Am Only Dreaming'. The tune is perfect for Chaplin's scene. 'It might have been written for it', Austin recalled. 'We were never stuck for the right music, we played all kinds. But we never used jazz.'[39]

Whether in a pit band or an orchestra, the musicians who accompanied silent films introduced a wide variety of music to audiences in the 1910s and 1920s. Many prominent New Zealand musicians served an apprenticeship in the challenging environment of the cinema pit band. Among them were Edgar Bendall, leading dance-band pianist in Auckland for 50 years; Llewellyn Jones, composer of *Maori Rhapsody*; and Alfred Marbeck, founder of Marbeck's record store. Around New Zealand, the pianists became local stars.[40]

New Zealanders had quickly become regular cinema-goers after the first picture show had been presented in Auckland on 13 October 1896.[41]

Early gimmicks to provide films with an audio accompaniment were crude. The title character in the 1904 film *She Would Sing* was a woman who liked to sing, but couldn't, in any recognisable key or pitch. To illustrate this, Fred Mills, manager of the Empress, in Auckland – who had performed comic songs with the Brescians – stood behind the screen and warbled in falsetto when required. He imitated any instruments being played by using a kazoo.[42]

Cinema magnate Henry Hayward first visited New Zealand as a variety show violinist in 1905, then immigrated and founded his own chain of picture theatres (his nephew Rudall was the pioneering film director).

He set a new standard in cinemas when he opened the Lyric on Symonds Street, Auckland, in 1911. On the roof, Auckland's first flashing sign announced, 'Hayward's Pictures'. The theatre was carpeted, the seats were armchairs and in the pit was a real novelty that boosted the theatre's popularity: an all-female orchestra of about twenty players. Another Hayward's theatre, the Adelphi in Wellington, had an all-female quintet.[43]

In 1914 Hayward's Pictures presented artists such as the flautist Signor A. P. Truda leading a Wellington orchestra accompanying epics that included *The Last Days of Pompeii*. Historian J. M. Thomson has written, 'Many kinds of music were re-scored, adapted and then classified by genre in catalogues, so that Schubert's *Unfinished* Symphony might appear as a "light, flowing agitato" and Beethoven overtures might be suitable for tree-felling, aeroplane dives, or cannibal island escapes.'[44]

By 1916 more people were attending the motion pictures each week than went to church; a year later Parliament was told that 550,000 film tickets were sold every week in New Zealand, at a time when the total population of the country was only double that.[45] Combinations of instrumentalists ranged from a solo pianist – especially in the provinces – to small orchestras in grand palaces such as Wellington's De Luxe (later re-named the Embassy).

The solo silent pianist needed a broad repertoire and adaptability. Violet Capstick was the leading cinema pianist in Timaru. Born in 1884, she made her debut in 1908 at the Theatre Royal, playing solo before eventually being joined by an 'orchestra' of eight. She also worked at Begg's, demonstrating sheet music to the customers: songs such as 'Schooldays', 'Smartie' and 'Goodbye, Little Yellow Bird'. She built up a large range of music that was useful for her film work. 'When I began with the orchestra there was no orchestral music for these films at all. I just had to supply everything from the sheet music that I had bought at Begg's.' Another pianist, Freddie Chapman, helped her write band arrangements.[46]

Regular picture-goers made requests whether they suited the film or not, particular favourites being 'Maori Maiden', 'The Rosary' and the overture to *Poet and Peasant*. But it was Capstick's task to find appropriate music, such as 'hearts and flowers' melodies for sad scenes, which brought out the handkerchiefs in the stalls. Another Timaru pianist who played for silent films, Margaret Fahey, recalled: 'For love scenes, there was always Schubert and

Pianist, conductor and critical iconoclast L. D. Austin led the renowned cinema orchestra at Wellington's De Luxe theatre (later called the Embassy), accompanying silent films in the mid-1920s. RNZ Infofind; 1/4-020145-F, Alexander Turnbull Library, Wellington

Chopin, and I don't know what we would have done without "William Tell" for storms.'[47]

Sound effects were also created – rain by shaking dried peas in a tin, horses' hooves with half-coconut shells, the sea using rough sandpaper – and sometimes by the audience itself. During a Pathé newsreel showing the Welsh Guards on a march, Capstick segued to 'Men of Harlech' and found the returned soldiers in the back rows whistling and stamping their feet in time. She kept raising the pitch by a third until they couldn't reach the top note. 'There was a sudden lull with the audience and a roar of laughter broke out all over the theatre.'[48]

The work was demanding, emotionally as well as physically, for solo pianists, band members and conductors. Auckland dance-band trumpeter Vern Wilson regularly sat in with silent film orchestras on his nights off. 'The pianist was looking at the film all the time, making sure you could cut off when there was a love scene or it was getting raucous. You'd have to throw down your music and get on with something else. You played right through the film, from beginning to end. The only rest you got was when there was a love scene on. Either you were

playing quiet music or, with a cowboy movie, they'd be galloping.'[49]

The music, which was changed monthly to keep it fresh, was eclectic: classical, popular songs, waltzes and the occasional foxtrot. 'There was plenty of music to pick from without worrying about the modern stuff', said Wilson. The classical pieces would be well known, and if there was an Irish film, fifes would be brought out. The theatres featured the best musicians available, as they needed to be adaptable and to be good sightreaders.

Holding court at Wellington's De Luxe was the doyen of New Zealand silent film music: pianist, conductor, composer and critic L. D. Austin, whose long life spanned an era of popular music. Born in London in 1877, the year Edison invented the phonograph, he died in 1967, the year the Beatles released *Sgt Pepper's Lonely Hearts Club Band*. Trained in London and Europe, he spent two years in Australia before immigrating to New Zealand in 1910. He brought classical music to the masses within a popular wrapping. A 1913 screening of *The Brand of Cain* at the People's Picture Palace in Wellington opened with a Chopin waltz and concluded with Handel's 'Largo in G'.[50]

Austin's film music career peaked when he was appointed the musical director of a fourteen-piece orchestra in Wellington's De Luxe cinema, which opened in 1924. 'Its acoustics were simply wonderful', he said in 1957. 'You'd have sworn there was an orchestra of 30 or 40.' Opening night featured *The Ten Commandments*, and it was only because the film's American producers were present that Austin's orchestra performed the music provided rather than his own score. Within two weeks, he said, 'I'd gradually substituted the original music and cut out the American score. Nobody ever knew.'[51]

Austin became the highest paid musician in the country, but the De Luxe orchestra's glory days were short-lived: after two years the theatre installed a Wurlitzer organ so the musicians became redundant. Austin headed for Dunedin and the Octagon Picture Theatre, but the era of silent film orchestras was rapidly drawing to a close.

Despite working in such a popular art form as film, Austin was disdainful of most popular music and any contemporary serious music that did not conform to his rigid standards. His own compositions, and tastes, were romantic: he idolised Chopin and thought good chamber music finished with Brahms. His criticism could be 'trenchant and provocative', but historian John Thomson prefers to describe Austin as 'obsessionally retrogressive'.[52]

He maintained his prominence through journalism – for 37 years he was music critic of Dunedin's *Evening Star* – and countless barbed but elegant Letters to the Editor of publications around the country. He abhorred modernism, in art or music, and among his targets were the Beatles, Benjamin Britten, Douglas Lilburn and Picasso. 'When you get to my age', Austin said on his ninetieth birthday, 'you can afford to be a little intolerant.'

WILL YOU, WON'T YOU, JOIN THE DANCE?
In the sedate Wellington suburb of Thorndon, the scholar Edward Tregear had a problem. He couldn't get to sleep. It was 1920, and across the road from his house in quiet, dead-end Goring Street, a neighbour had opened a dance school. Among its pupils was Iris Wilkinson, a schoolgirl who later became known as the writer Robin Hyde. But it wasn't the dance classes that bothered Tregear, it was the noises late at night when the school became The Cabaret: a venue that played 'jazz'.[53]

Tregear went to see Pat Lawlor, then a reporter at *Truth*, and asked him 'to attack the nocturnal gaieties' taking place at Wellington's first cabaret. According to Lawlor, it was founded by a prominent prohibitionist who wanted to create an exclusive club; the joining fee was ten guineas. But since the Cabaret had first opened, the neighbours' peace had been 'blasted o' nights with the happenings at the dance hall. Bedlam reigned until the small hours with the din of jazz music, the shouts of dancers, the popping of corks and the noise of motor cars.'[54]

The club was managed by Theo Trezise, a former member of the First World War entertainment troupe the Kiwis, and now a dance instructor and drama producer. Publicity photos of him in exotic poses and costumes suggest he saw himself as Wellington's Valentino. Certainly, he was flamboyant, and *Truth* responded with several alliterative headlines to its salacious story about the 'Gay Goings on in Goring Street', with the 'Householders Hot Over Highborn Hullabaloo' as the revellers enjoyed their 'Mirth, Motors and Maledictions'. Lawlor considered this to be 'the beginning of the era of barbarous jazz bands, the grinding orchestrations of motor gears and motor horns on nightly joy rides – a new age of ungodly noises'. So it was no wonder that Tregear – a friend of Seddon and Ballance and a 'peaceful, cultured Victorian gentleman' – sold up and spent the rest of his retirement in Picton. Wellington in the jazz age was too noisy.[55]

For most of the early 1920s, the word 'jazz' was used more as an all-purpose adjective than as a noun. It helped give a modern tinge to products ranging from hair cream to health tonics, but it is debatable how close the music was to real jazz. Were the syncopated rhythms more emphasised than ragtime, was there more improvisation – or just more chaos? As in Britain, the local bands were taking their lead from gramophone records and pianists from piano rolls, changing existing styles by bringing together unusual combinations of instruments, with the percussionist adding exotic effects from anything at hand: 'cowbells, pistol shots and other noises, musical and unmusical'.

These novelty effects – especially those imitating farmyard animals – were a prominent feature of early 'jazz' bands of the 1920s. They were often all that differentiated an alleged jazz band from a traditional dance orchestra: an ability to swing and improvise was not yet common, or understood.[56] 'Not all dance music was jazz', said Auckland musician Spike Donovan, 'and not all dance musicians were jazz men either. They were usually in the minority.'[57]

The *Dancing Times* in Britain gamely came up with a definition for a true 'Jazz Band'. It needed five instruments, 'namely the clarinet (playing violin parts), the cornet, the trombone, a "snappy" drummer, and a ragtime player'. While plenty of bands called themselves jazz bands, most were novelty bands until the arrival of the Original Dixieland Jazz Band (ODJB) in Britain.[58]

Very few people yet realised that true jazz required spontaneous improvisation, and that the reliable beat of a dance-band drummer was different to the energetic drive of a jazz drummer.[59]

Advertisements including the scarlet word soon began appearing in many parts of New Zealand. In January 1921, Timaru heard the new music when local photographer and musician Havelock Williams formed a band to play at dances to celebrate the arrival of the New Year. Using the buzzword as an eye-catching headline, the *Timaru Herald* advertised 'jazz' dance lessons with a teacher visiting from London, while Williams – punning on a recent hit by Irving Berlin – touted for gigs:

EVERYBODY'S JAZZING NOW
They must have the
WILLIAMS PROFESSIONAL JAZZ BAND
Full Jazz Effects. All Professional Players.
9th Engagement since formation in January.

Timaruvians were given an explanation by the newspaper: 'The cacophony of the American Jazz was slow in catching on in New Zealand, its peculiar syncopation, eerie effects, and tonal shocks being just not traditional enough for the dominion ear, but now that the newness of the craze has gone the jazz has taken South Canterbury by storm, and in the words of the song, "Everybody's Doing It Now".'[60]

The *Timaru Herald*'s reporter was remarkably astute, even explaining the reference to Irving Berlin's hit. As a port town, Timaru had access to other cultures and fashionable imports. Also, Williams's work as a commercial photographer often took him to the tourist areas of the South Island, or caused him to mix socially with the smart set. When combined with the Wellington reports in *Truth* and the *Dominion*, the Timaru account suggests that jazz arrived quickly and simultaneously in various areas of the country.

Light classical pianist Henry Shirley remembered live jazz appearing in Auckland in the winter of 1922, when local vaudeville drummer Bob Adams formed a group that some claim was the city's first jazz band. Shirley was briefly a member that year, and had just written '1921', a film music overture. However, the blurring of memory and fact make the actual date uncertain. Late in life, Adams said he formed the band when aged seventeen, which would put the date at 1916 or 1917. More reliable is the recollection of Spike Donovan, who had the keenest interest in history among his dance-band peers. He said Adams formed his band at 'about the end of World War One', and that it performed often at Government House, Auckland, when Lord Jellicoe was governor-general (1920–24).[61] However, the significance is not in the timing, but in the more convincing evidence that the music they played was in fact jazz.

The first jazz band to record anywhere in the world was the white New Orleans group the Original Dixieland Jazz Band, whose debut 'Livery Stable Blues' was released in the US in March 1917. Two years later the group arrived in Britain to a 'tumultuous reception' and soon began a nine-month residency at London's Hammersmith Palais.[62]

Shirley recalled that the ODJB records got to New Zealand shortly after Adams formed his band, and this gives another clue to the date. In 1922 Shirley worked in the warehouse of A. H. Nathan's, the agents for Columbia, where he could listen to the latest records while packing them. Because the ODJB records had been a hit in the States, Nathan's was sent a large shipment, 'But no one would buy them. Customers recoiled from this first impact of the hideous noise from New Orleans. To amuse visitors we would sometimes play them "Barnyard Blues" – it was like all the roosters in the world crowing together.'[63]

Nathan's threw away the records that did not sell, but some of the ODJB discs made their way south and caused a stir in Wellington at a dance class attended by a young Arthur Pearce, who up till then had been enjoying musical comedies. At the class, ritualised group dances such as the gay gordons were giving way to American innovations such as the foxtrot, the Black Bottom and the Charleston, and the new, spirited and raucous music of the ODJB immediately caught the ear of the young man. 'The sounds Arthur heard completely overrode his concentration on the body movements.' Asking who the band was, Pearce was told it was a new American import by the Original Dixieland Jazz Band; at this moment his musical tastes expanded and he was on his way to becoming an international jazz expert and hugely influential broadcaster.[64]

Magic, Mirth and Melody: Walter Smith

Walter Smith, bringing his mandolin skills to Hawke's Bay after twenty years in Utah, c. 1915. Kia Ngawari Trust

Two prominent musicians are credited with founding Auckland's first jazz band: Walter Smith and Robert Adams. As a music teacher and songwriter, Smith would have the most influence on the city's popular music-making. George Snow, who was crafting guitars in Auckland in the 1920s, said that Smith did more for jazz and for popularising string instruments than anyone else in the city. 'He claimed that jazz music of the 1920s and 1930s was the greatest music of the era and that it taught young people rhythm.'[65]

Smith (Ngati Kahungunu) was born in Nuhaka, a small town in northern Hawke's Bay, on 11 May 1883. When he was ten years old he accompanied his uncle and aunt to Salt Lake City, Utah, as part of a contingent of nine Maori Mormon missionaries. While attending school there, he showed his aptitude for music, and took lessons for the guitar, banjo and mandolin. According to his niece Dinah Greening, the church authorities wanted to send him to Germany to study the violin, but an interim stint as a shepherd at Rexburg, Idaho, changed his musical direction. He contracted a severe case of rheumatism, which confined him to bed for three years. During this time, he continued learning the guitar, banjo and mandolin, this time from C. D. Schettler, a highly regarded US music teacher and guitarist. Smith spent hours every day practising, then went to Brigham Young University at Provo, Utah, to continue his recovery, and to study music and 'commercial training'. In addition to his other instruments, he became proficient at the Spanish and steel guitar, ukulele, cello-banjo and bass.

He then became a professional musician, joining Ed Montgomery's Royal Hawaiian Quintette to tour the US from coast to coast. During the tour, he met Ida Mae Haley of Oakland, California, marrying her in Salt Lake City on 11 May 1910. He also wrote and published his song 'My Beautiful Isle of the Sea'.

Smith then toured with his own group, the Hawaii-Maorian Quintette – an early gig was at the Utah Hotel in Salt Lake City – performing the Hawaiian music then in vogue. Among the people he met during the quintet's travels were William F. Cody (Buffalo Bill), John Philip Sousa, Jack Johnson, Sir Maui Pomare and Queen Liliuoakalai of Hawaii.[66]

A musical group from the Maori Agricultural College, c. 1918, with their teacher Walter Smith second from left, playing guitar lap style. Kia Ngawari Trust

The church called him back to New Zealand in 1913 with his wife to take up a mission at the Maori Agricultural College, a Mormon institution near Hastings, Hawke's Bay. Among his pupils was Sidney David Kamau who became an accomplished saxophonist. While teaching there, Smith formed a string orchestra, brass band and choirs. At special parades, he would conduct the brass band while mounted on a white Arabian horse. After five years the couple moved to Auckland, buying a home at 16 Turner Street, opposite Myers Park on Queen Street.

Smith began a long career as the leading stringed-instrument teacher in Auckland. The business quickly outgrew his home, and he began teaching from a studio in the Lewis Eady building. He also bought a saxophone and taught himself to play it. His niece Dinah said Smith was only the second man to own one in New Zealand, after Bert Kingsley, who later led his own saxophone quartet.[67] Smith also added the clarinet to his list of instruments.

Auckland nightlife in the early 1920s offered silent movies, theatre, vaudeville and dance halls. Walter Smith and his various bands were very much at the centre of this. Rush-Munro – later famous as a boutique ice cream manufacturer in Hastings – opened a milkbar/cabaret on Karangahape Road, and Smith supplied the five-piece jazz band, which included Rush-Munro's son Lew on piano.[68] The milkbar was small, but the tables dancers sat at between items gave it a modern feel. On nearby Queen Street the Dixieland Cabaret had afternoon sessions but in the evenings its functions were private,[69] so the casual Dixieland dancers would head up the road to Rush-Munro's. From 8.00 pm until midnight, six days a week, patrons at the milkbar/cabaret were entertained by sentimental parlour ballads including 'Say It With Music', 'Avalon', 'Margie' and the jaunty 'Dardanella'. Smith's band also played at venues such as dance halls, the university and the Town Hall.[70]

Walter Smith's Jazz Band, c. 1927. From left: unknown trombone, trumpet and saxophone players, Sidney David Kamau (clarinet), Dinah Greening (banjo), Marjorie Greening (piano) and Walter Smith (saxophone). Dennis Huggard collection

Left: An invitation to hear Walter Smith's Aloha Jazz Band in Newmarket, December 1927. Dennis Huggard collection

Below: Walter Smith and his Smart Set Maori Entertainers promised pretty melodies and magic tricks. MS-Papers-0151-37b-01 2, Alexander Turnbull Library, Wellington

With another of his ensembles, the Click-Clack Band, Smith did a long stint at the Click-Clack Cabaret, above the Rialto cinema in Newmarket (1YA broadcast the band performing in a live, Saturday-night relay from the club on 20 August 1927).[71] An invitation to hear Walter Smith's Aloha Jazz Band at the Click-Clack for a function later that year in honour of his pupil Sid David Kamau is inscribed, 'Come along to a big tangi . . . plenty eat'un, plenty drink'un – go home – plenty sleep'un.'[72]

On New Year's Eve, 1929, Smith provided the music at the Moulin Rouge, in the Tudor cinema, Remuera, after the film *Bare Knees* had finished ('Dedicated to the Auckland Flappers, God bless 'em – and dress 'em'). Until 1.00 am into 1930, Smith and His Merry Syncopators played old and new favourites at the 'Carnival Jazz' ball which, as a diversion, included the novelty acrobatic dance duo Pic and Alf.[73]

The many musical combinations Smith formed testify to his versatility, as a bilingual advertising flyer exclaims:

Smith organised large string bands featuring his pupils on guitars, mandolins, banjos and ukuleles, performing his arrangements of overtures such as *William Tell* and *Poet and Peasant*. As the Aloha Orchestra, 60 players took the stage for charity in the Auckland Town Hall. 'Every time they played there, the place was packed', said former pupil Jimmy Higgot.[74] All band members were dressed completely in white, and in the front row one musician would have a giant bass banjo on his knee. This massive instrument – the drumhead had a diameter of nearly a metre – was especially made for Smith using a bass drum and the fingerboard and tuning pegs from a double bass. It helped balance the treble-dominant sound of the orchestra. There were also ten-stringed 'harp guitars', which had the strings away from the body of the guitar, but the lead instruments were mandolin and steel guitar.[75]

Smith bought his niece Marge Greening a saxophone and clarinet, and she became the first female saxophonist in New Zealand. (Elsie Nixon, whose father ran a tearooms/outdoor cabaret in Mission Bay, was the second.) 'Uncle Walter was a very lovable character, generous [although] he could have been a wealthy man', recalled Marge's sister Dinah, who played banjo and violin.[76] Both Dinah and Marge quickly became proficient players and joined their uncle's jazz band (Marge's first instrument was piano), as well as the all-women band he formed, the Gala Girls. Another woman musician he nurtured was Pearl Gibbs, who for thirteen years was his 'pupil, professional artist and assistant teacher'. Smith wanted her to play a harp in his orchestra. Harps were scarce, and Smith could only find a dilapidated model in a second-hand furniture

As Auckland's leading stringed-instrument teacher for nearly 40 years, Walter Smith organised large groups of his pupils to give annual concerts. Note the homemade bass banjo to the far right, made using a drumhead and the neck from a double bass. Dennis Huggard collection

shop, its frame damaged and strings broken. After refurbishing the harp, he taught himself how to play it – then Gibbs.

As the banjo went out of favour, US guitar-makers eased the transition by making four-string guitars with banjo tuning. But, in the days before amplification, acoustic guitars could not cut through the sound of a big band. Eventually, recalled Donovan, 'Smith's reign was over. He kept on teaching but he was less active. He'd had a good run with his dance band, his radio band and so forth, and he was getting on in years . . . but he did everything that was worthwhile for a while around town.'[77]

Among Smith's songs are 'Dear Old Maoriland', 'Maori Eyes', 'Kia Ngawari' and 'Let There Be Light'. A song he dedicated to the 1924 All Blacks, 'On!! New Zealand', received an enthusiastic response at its premiere performance by the visiting Dixie Jubilee Singers at the Auckland Town Hall on 5 January 1925. However, its melody was later said to be borrowed from the US university song 'On Wisconsin'.[78]

But his most famous song is 'Beneath the Maori Moon'. Published as a waltz in 1922, it was recorded in 1936 by former All Black fullback George Nepia for Decca in England, when he was playing rugby league there. (Nepia was Smith's cousin and grew up in Nuhaka. Although not a Mormon, he had attended the Maori Agricultural College.) 1ZB's Maori announcer Lou Paul also recorded the song in the 1930s, backed by Ted Croad's Band ('and His

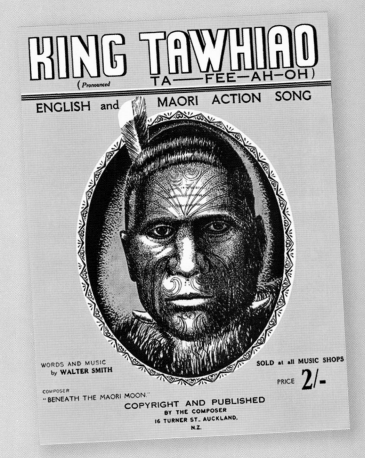

In 1939, 'King Tawhiao' and 'Beneath the Maori Moon' were recorded by Maori broadcaster Lou Paul (Uramo Paora). Walter Smith published 'King Tawhiao' himself. Sheet Music Archive of NZ

Maori Maidens') at Beacon Studios in Auckland. Smith himself recorded the song in the early 1950s with his Aloha Orchestra and Nuhaka Trio, and it was revived by Don McGlashan in 1992 for the film *Absent Without Leave*.

The lyrics of 'Beneath the Maori Moon' are corny ('Beneath the Maori moon, on a silvery night in June . . .'), but the shift to a foxtrot in the bridge section lifts it from languor: 'We'll change the rhythm of this little song/We'll give it the boogy woogy swing . . .'.

When a reporter called on Smith in 1952, he was practising arias and overtures on his favourite instrument, the Spanish guitar. 'The robust body, the clear eyes and strong voice belied his 68 years. Still with a trace of American accent he said, "I sure wish I could find a pupil interested enough to tackle this work. But it's cowboy and boogie today."' Not that he minded. 'It's all music, and music is in my blood.'[79]

Biff, Bang and Wallop: Bob Adams

Bob Adams was the doyen of New Zealand percussionists. He became a professional musician at the age of fifteen, playing for silent movies. Nearly 70 years later he was still performing, in the orchestra for a Christmas pantomime.

He was born in 1899 to an Auckland family respected in music circles. An early memory was witnessing the visit of John Philip Sousa to Auckland in 1911. Adams's father Samuel played many instruments, taught music and had an instrument shop on Symonds Street. Every year the pupils of Samuel Adams would give a concert in the Auckland Town Hall concert chamber. At these, Bob would play xylophone in his father's orchestra, although drums were his passion.

At fifteen he joined the silent film orchestra at the Princess Theatre, Queen Street, earning £3/10 a week. By the early 1920s, he formed a jazz band that was popular for the leading balls, including those at Government House.

Adams's band was the first jazz band in New Zealand, according to Henry Shirley, briefly the pianist in the band, in 1921 or 1922. Bass player Spike Donovan also gave Adams, rather than Walter Smith, the credit for having

the first jazz band in Auckland,[80] though trumpeter Vern Wilson put in a bid for the band he was playing in at the Dixieland Cabaret on Queen Street from April 1922. 'It depends on what you call jazz', said Donovan, '. . . [but] it seems pretty clear that jazz hit Auckland very early in the 1920s and we never recovered from it.'[81]

Adams's jazz band had seven players, including two women, pianist Rita Sullivan and violinist Freda Hunter. 'Like most of the original jazz bands they went in heavily for noise – and rather coarse noises at that', said Donovan. Looking back in 1971, Adams concurred: 'We used to give a bit of biff, bang, wallop, and the dancers were in their element.'[82]

Shirley recalled that –

Nobody in Auckland really knew what jazz sounded like, but according to reports the drummer had to make a din like all hell let loose. So Bob placed himself in the centre of the stage and made a tremendous uproar on a collection of drums, gongs and cymbals and a variety of other articles such as cow bells, motorcar horns and beer bottles.

With the rest of the band sitting around him, they specialised in the newly arrived foxtrot and one-steps of the 'How ya gonna keep em down on the farm?' variety, trombone and piano enjoying themselves immensely as they improvised fancy slides and basses.[83]

Adams was also one of the first popular musicians and players to take up the saxophone, though his fellow musicians joked he could only play one tune on it, 'Oh By Jingo! Oh By Gee! (You're the Only Girl for Me)' from the 1919 musical *Linger Longer Letty*. 'When Bob played it as an entr'acte the crowd when mad', said Chips Healy, later band leader at the Civic Wintergarden.[84]

In 1920 Fullers Vaudeville hired Adams for its orchestra pit at the Opera House; he played there until it burnt down five years later. Tickets were 2/6 in the dress circle, or one shilling in the gallery. No expense was spared, with lavish costumes and scenery, and up to 50 showgirls on stage. 'We had some fun in those days', he said. 'The management was a bit straight about audience participation, but on certain nights we used to invite anyone who thought he had a talent to come up on the stage . . . . Well, jeering and booing – and cabbages thrown on the stage – it was real fun.'[85]

Fullers built the St James Theatre as a replacement, although to Adams the atmosphere was never the same.

The Bob Adams Jazz Band of 1922. From left: F. Hunter (trombone), R. Edwards (bass), R. Adams (saxophone, percussion), C. Adams (cornet), A. Harris (cornet), Rita Sullivan (piano), Freda Hunter (violin). The dog on the bass drum is unnamed. *New Zealand Herald*, neg. A67.

Fullers persisted with vaudeville until talkies took over. In 1930 the film *Gold Diggers of Broadway* (1929) was 'the death knell of the vaudeville era', said Adams.[86]

But he stayed with musical theatre, based at His Majesty's and working in J. C. Williamson productions and playing in dance bands. He was in demand as an all-rounder, a master of the drums but also adept at the xylophone, vibes and the marimba. His equipment took up 'three-quarters of the pit', said Donovan, but 'he was a most excellent performer on what we called tuned percussion'. Adams was also a master of special aural effects in the productions.

'He had a good sense of humour, and he always kept us amused in the pit', said Donovan. 'We'd get him talking and he was a scream . . . pushing down tobacco in his pipe and saying, "Did I ever tell you about the time . . .". We

used to get ourselves set for a good laugh.' If the pianist Betty Isaacs was present, the story-telling would turn into a double act. 'They were a very funny cross-talk team.' Musicians always knew when Adams was at His Majesty's: he kept his big Essex car chained to a lamp-post on Durham Street, and the flower-vase on the dashboard would be jammed with fresh cigarettes.

After the Second World War, Adams declined a seat in the fledgling National Orchestra, not wanting to leave Auckland. 'He was very versatile . . . and he wasn't a musical snob', said Donovan, who remembered Adams as the only musician he played with who never made a mistake.[87]

Ten years before Adams died in 1981, he was asked how he saw the future for show business. 'Television', he replied. 'Say what you like, it is first-rate entertainment.'[88]

DANCING AT THE DIXIE

Jazz and be happy!
By a remarkable, simple, new method YOU can now master all the latest 'Jazz' Dances in the seclusion of your own room – without music or partner – without anyone knowing you are learning.
If you can walk – you can 'Jazz'[89]

For Auckland's smart set, there was only one place to be seen on 11 April 1922: at the corner of Queen and Waverley Streets, for the grand opening of the city's first large-scale cabaret.[90] Called the Dixieland, the extravagance of the venue could only have been achieved by the visionary, stylish – and rich – entrepreneur who developed it. Dr Frederick Rayner and his wife Ethel had emigrated from Canada in 1900; she was a well-travelled heiress, he was a dentist with business savvy and energy. Rayner made a fortune in Auckland, founding the American Dental Parlours, which specialised in high-turnover 'painless' tooth extraction and replacement with dentures. He launched the Hippodrome Picture Company

that evolved into the Amalgamated chain, milled vast tracts of West Coast kauri and subdivided Piha, then built a mansion on the slopes of Mt Eden. He also owned a lodge, with launch, at Lake Rotoiti. His launch was called *Moose*, and both houses were named Moose Lodge and decorated – like the Dixieland – with his deer trophies.[91]

Having seen American nightlife first hand, Rayner was keen to introduce the latest ideas in entertainment to his adopted city. Advertisements prior to the Dixieland's opening emphasised that this glitzy venture was taking place in the jazz age: 'You'll hear the latest Jazz Music as it should be.' In the evenings, the music was provided by the Southern Dixieland Band, an Australian group directed from the piano by Arthur Frost, formerly of the Tivoli cabarets. Each afternoon *thé dansants* – tea dances – were on offer, served by 'picturesque waitresses' to the strains of the band; patrons could take part in the jazz dancing and enjoy the vocal items that were performed using a megaphone. Inside the Dixieland were chandeliers, quality fittings, tables that could be booked in advance, and couches on raised platforms from which guests could watch the dancing that took place on a 3000-square-foot sprung dance floor.

The Southern Dixieland Band arrived from Australia in 1922 to entertain Auckland's smart set at the Dixieland Cabaret on Queen Street, and recruited local trumpeter Vern Wilson. From left: Ces (Pop) Little (saxophone), Fred Swanberg (trombone), Aby Green (drums), Vern Wilson and Arthur Frost (piano and leader). Dennis Huggard Archive, F- 90428-35mm-7, Alexander Turnbull Library, Wellington

To familiarise patrons with the new steps of jazz dancing, tuition classes were available, also in cinema acting and dramatic art: 'The lists are filling like wildfire.' The dance tutors were Miss M. Julian, 'direct from London and Paris'; and Del S. Foster, from the United States, who was also the Dixieland's first manager. If one's confidence did not extend to public classes, an opportunistic publisher offered free mail-order dance instruction booklets: 'Master "Jazzing" in your spare time . . . to be able to Dance – and Dance well – should be every person's desire who loves to be happy.'[92]

Foster, a former J. C. Williamson employee, had already introduced Aucklanders to the American style of cabaret by hiring the Town Hall and placing tables and chairs around the dance floor. He also repositioned the musicians so that they were directly facing the dancers, rather than the pianist at stage left. 'I want you to let them know you're here', Foster told Vern Wilson, who played trumpet in the eight-piece band. The success of this event led to a partnership with Rayner to develop the large Queen Street building into the Dixieland; it was 'the largest cabaret outside of America', claimed Foster.[93]

The new venue quickly attracted the loyal support of Auckland's dancers, and for good reason. Besides the splendid dance floor, the *New Zealand Observer* praised the Dixieland's 'exceedingly talented orchestra with a repertoire of the latest and most distinctive in jazz music'.[94]

It was the Dixieland that popularised jazz in Auckland, said Wilson. He joined the Southern Dixieland Band, which had arrived without a trumpet player. Then aged eighteen, Wilson recalled it being 'A hectic start in life, they were solid drinkers. And I was very young, I didn't smoke or drink. I was sober waiting for 12 o'clock. I learnt how to drink later on.'

There were only soft drinks available – and the city's first fresh orange juicer – but the laxity shown towards patrons smuggling in their own alcohol helped encourage customers. 'The liquor brought a lot of people in, carrying sackfuls of booze into their cubicles. It didn't cause any problems with the police, and it helped make the jazz popular.'

Regular dances were established all around the city. As part of Ernie Beacham's Melody Boys, Wilson would bus out as far as Otahuhu or Titirangi. In town, Edgar Bendall led the band at the Masonic Hall on Belgium Street; there

Hello, sailor: in the 1920s Ernie Beacham's Melody Boys employed many leading Auckland dance-band musicians. Beside him are, from left, Vern Wilson, Alf 'Chips' Healy, Vic Clark, J. F. Meyers, Bunny Cannan, George Wallace and George McGrath. Dennis Huggard Archive, 35mm-90427-4, Alexander Turnbull Library, Wellington

was also the Druids' Hall, the Gaiety and the Railway Social Hall. Later would come two venues on the harbour's edge at Point Chevalier: the Yacht Club and, from 1925, a second Dixieland.

At Milford, on Auckland's North Shore, the Picturedrome opened three days before Christmas in 1922. The cinema screened silent movies in the evening, then turned into a dance hall. The manager, Laurie Speedy, had the transformation well organised: 'A gang of youths would swing into action. One group would slide the theatre seats to the sides . . . another group would sprinkle damp sawdust about to keep down the dust when the floor was swept with very wide brooms. While all this activity was going on the musicians would be tuning up and patrons were congregating in the foyer and the forecourt, all keen to start dancing.' During the week, the dance floor was given an extra polish by Speedy, driving around the room in his small Calcott car while towing sacks weighed down by local boys.

When the band began playing, the crowd outside finished their ice creams and the dance session would commence; on a big night the room might hold a thousand people. Although the music was advertised as jazz, 'it was not jazz in the modern sense of the word. It was a saxophone-dance band with a variety of other instruments.'[95]

From their bandstands, musicians watched the dances change as social mores evolved and acceptable behaviour broadened. The dance diet at the Dixieland was mostly jazz, though 'if someone asked for a maxina, we'd oblige', trumpeter Vern Wilson recalled. At old-time dances, older crowds stayed with old-time dancing, even when 'they introduced a jazz dance into an old-time dance: a one-step was considered a version of a jazz dance. In the old-time dancing, there was a foot between the dancers, but in the jazz age you could really grab hold of a girl and lean on her.'[96] An evening would begin with a fast Viennese waltz; once jazz arrived, this changed to a slow waltz, which also closed proceedings. And in between,

> . . . [there were] different dances, no set programme. A one-step after the waltz, the valeta, maxina, gay gordons, three-step, Latin American and the lancers. Most popular were the waltz-type dances. The valeta always filled the floor. Some were a bit intricate and there weren't that many who could follow it. But those who could were experts. There would be non-stop dancing, there was just enough time to put the music away and then off you would go again. There were no real breaks between dances until supper.

While older couples preferred the traditional, strict-tempo dances, the modern jazz dances attracted the young. Wilson was bemused by their popularity: 'When you look at it, it's quite monotonous, jazz dancing. Just the waltz, the foxtrot and the one-step. That's all there would be all night, just the three types, plus one or two novelties.'[97]

MORAL LAXITY

As the popularity of the new dance styles and venues increased, the press was quick to label it a 'dance craze'. Inevitably, a backlash followed – people were having too much fun – and a committee got involved. In 1922 there was a flurry of discussion about the propriety of dancing, and the activity was considered by the Board of Health's Committee on Venereal Disease. Their report said the moral laxity that leads to promiscuity was caused by many factors, and among the more minor mentioned were:

> . . . the modern dress of women, which was stated to be in certain cases sexually suggestive, and certain modern forms of dancing. There appear some grounds to suppose that dances conducted under undesirable conditions contribute to sexual immorality, but the Committee sees no reason to condemn dancing generally because the coincident conditions under which it has been or is conducted in some cases have contributed to impropriety.[98]

Among those who gave evidence was Dr P. Clennel Fenwick who, despite approving of dancing as a healthy amusement and exercise, argued that 'jazz and other kinds of dancing at present in vogue are in my opinion most unhealthy'. If this activity was to fall from fashion, much unhealthy sexual excitement would be avoided, he said, telling the committee that a 'lady patrol' was needed, with police powers under the Social Hygiene Act.

The Christchurch *Press* ridiculed Fenwick's remarks. 'The trouble, we suspect, is the name: "Jazz" suggests riotousness and license.' Modern dances were no more pernicious than older styles, the editorial said, hoping that the committee didn't recommend that dances should only occur 'under the supervision of some elderly policeman armed with power to arrest anyone whose style does not remind him of his own early days'.[99]

To the establishment, it seemed as if the spread of jazz was threatening, but it was a phenomenon promoters were happy to exploit and customers clamoured to be part of. In 1924 Dunedin's Empire Theatre held a 'Jazz Week', screening a film, *How to Dance the Fox Trot*, which showed all the steps in slow motion. Although the film was silent, the Dixieland Jazz Band was on stage to provide the accompaniment.[100]

There was no shortage of decadent stories to enflame critics of the 1920s 'dance craze'. In 1923 a young Wellington man's decline into dishonesty was said to have come about through 'a mania he developed for attending dance saloons and entertaining young women in town'.[101] The most lurid account of the new hedonism came, not unexpectedly, when *Truth* reported on the appearance of Frederick Rayner in an Auckland court on a charge of permitting his second Dixieland Cabaret at Point Chevalier to be used for the consumption of alcohol, although it was unlicensed. Two constables, with their female partners, attended a charity ball incognito and witnessed Auckland's smart set at its less-than-smart. They were 'mixing champagne and cocktails in cuddle cubicles'.

Setting aside the relish with which *Truth* described the patrons ('young jazz weeds, dashing sheiks, effeminate nincompoops and frivolous flappers'), the constables' evidence reflected conservative contemporary mores and presented the dance scene as decadent and unruly. Although alcohol was not sold at the club, it was openly being consumed: besides being able to smell it, the constables could read the labels on bottles left on tables while people danced. Waitresses asked if they wanted to rent 'spot glasses' for the evening, a service offered because glasses were often stolen. Patrons were 'under the influence', and the atmosphere was 'very lively', especially after 11.00 pm. The young women could hardly hold themselves upright: they had 'gone at the knees' and were clinging to the necks of their partners.

The judge, Hunt SM, enjoyed himself at Rayner's expense – especially his claim that the Dixieland served the elite of Auckland – and then convicted him and imposed the maximum penalty. Rayner and his manager were fined £20 each, and Hunt declared that anyone bringing liquor into the establishment would also face the maximum fine: £5. 'This is one of the most mischievous occupations or businesses one could possibly have in a comparatively small place like this. I am of the opinion that it should be stopped.'[102]

JAZZ AMBASSADORS

A new style of popular culture and recreation had arrived, and, if authorities felt threatened, their fear was equally felt by the musical establishment. When the New Zealand-born soprano Rosina Buckman returned for a tour in 1922 after a twelve-year absence, she was concerned that there had been so little progress made in local music-making; it seemed to her to be at a standstill. Young people appeared to have no interest in it, she despaired: 'Perhaps it is the jazz that is upsetting the standards. Jazz is good in the right place, but everything now is jazz, and I do not think its influence is good.' Australia's experience was being replicated: the jazz craze had swept right through both countries, and an appreciation of higher standards was being lost.

What was needed, said Buckman, was a good school of music, like Sydney's conservatorium, led by a first-class musician, 'preferably a Britisher, who would make it his business to do all to advance British music. We have had enough of our musical academies being run by foreigners.'[103]

Already, the overseas influence was pervasive, through the importation of the latest jazz records, local bands wanting to play in the new styles and initiatives such as Rayner's cabaret. With radio still in its infancy, live performance and direct contact were essential means of transmission.

An early foray came in 1923 when ex-US Navy musician Dick Richards 'breezed' into Wellington and attached himself to a band at St Francis Hall near Parliament; his 'stomp arrangements stirred up a sensation amongst local enthusiasts'. Richards, a banjo player 'in eccentric style', joined the Ambassador Musical Trio with pianist Frank Andrews and Jack Maybury on sax. Andrews was billed as a jazz specialist and 'Australasian King of the Ivories'; he would intersperse his seven different interpretations of 'The Prisoner's Song' with a musical monologue.[104]

In the same year, a musician with a more lasting impact on the dance scene came from Australia. Linn Smith's Royal Jazz Band was popular on the Australian vaudeville circuit in the 1920s, making its name at Sydney's Tivoli. The *Fuller News* described this 'high-voltage crew of musicians, who tumble into gay and gladsome jazz with an artistic finish. At times they are dreamy, but never draggy, and they make a chop suey of the foxtrot, whilst retaining time and melody. Their grotesque trombone warbling and waltz oddities are the real thing in stimulating, seductive jazz.'[105]

Linn Smith's Royal Jazz Band broke down musical prejudice during their visits to New Zealand, which began in 1923. From the Tivoli circuit in Australia, they could make 'chop suey of the foxtrot, whilst retaining time and melody'. From left: Brassey Allen (drums), Tom Coghlan (trumpet), Paul Jeacle (saxophone), Linn Smith (piano), Sam De Tinge (trombone), Cliff Clarke (banjo). *NZ Theatre and Motion Picture*, January 1925

Smith's band visited New Zealand several times in the 1920s, starting in November 1923 as part of a vaudeville show at Fuller's Opera House, Auckland. The *New Zealand Observer* wrote that Smith's Jazz Band 'dispenses gloom-dispelling music with a vivacity that at times becomes strenuous – to the artists – but which the audience thoroughly enjoys'.[106] One reviewer, expecting 'a triumph of blare', enjoyed their humour but came away surprised by the 'subdued' tone of a quintet that had 'gripped Auckland and Wellington'.[107] Most of the musicians played solos that 'go with a swing', Smith himself performing a left-handed piano piece. For two years in the mid-1920s, the Royal Jazz Band also toured Australia and New Zealand as the Hells Bells Jazz Band in the J. C. Williamson shows *Good Morning, Dearie* and *Kid Boots*, at which 'audiences roared themselves hoarse for more "Bow Wow Blues" and "Yes! We Have No Bananas"'.[108]

The visit of Bert Ralton's Savoy Havana Band in late 1924 gave New Zealand its first extended demonstration of the new music as it had evolved from its roots. The band's name indicated its varied pedigree: although an attraction at one of London's leading hotels, Ralton and several of his musicians were Americans with experience in San Francisco, New York and Cuba. Ralton himself had performed with George Gershwin in 1920.

The Savoy Havana Band came to New Zealand as part of a vaudeville show, after performing in its own right for over a year in Sydney and Melbourne. The band's visit began in Auckland on 6 December 1924 and continued to Wellington and Christchurch in early 1925.[109]

Pre-publicity trumpeted that Ralton's group was acclaimed by critics as London's best jazz band and was the favourite dance band of HRH the Prince of Wales. 'At enormous expense . . . their presence in Auckland is London's loss.' Opening night, to a crowded house at His Majesty's Theatre, received a rave review in the *New Zealand Herald*. Their performance was far from a 'wearisome succession of sickly syncopations', and a tribute not just to the cleverness of the musicians but to the 'prevalence and popularity of jazz – jazz music, jazz rhythm and the jazz spirit'. Many in the audience were already familiar with the band's hit records, and any concerns that a seven-piece dance band would be upstaged by the vaudeville acts that had preceded it were quelled.

Such sceptics were quickly disillusioned. From the first crash of the cymbals the band was master of the situation, setting the feet tapping with a sprightly fox trot, appealing to the emotions with haunting, mysterious refrains of Eastern origin, and then soothing the sense with a slowly played, dreamy waltz. It was dance music in excelsis.

They played the latest foxtrots, medleys of Hawaiian melodies, Scottish songs and well-known plantation airs. 'Dominating all, and infusing it with laughter and good spirits, was the joyous personality of Bert Ralton . . . . if he were the spirit incarnate of jazz he could not better fill the role.' The audience stayed in their seats demanding an encore, and was 'rewarded with a dashing rendering of the new foxtrot hit, "Horsey, Keep Your Tail Up!" with Bert Ralton gyrating round the stage mounted on a ridiculous-looking dummy horse'.[110]

Above and below: Bert Ralton, 1925: the American who gave New Zealand its first demonstration of jazz, as played at the source. Bert Ralton's Savoy Havana Band offered 'dance music in excelsis' during its New Zealand visit in summer 1924–25. *Bothamley collection/Peter Downes*

Only two years after his New Zealand tour, Ralton died of a gunshot wound while on safari in South Africa (showing his 'characteristic cheeriness' right to the end, he played the ukulele as he was taken on a stretcher to hospital).[111] But his band had an impact on New Zealand music in several ways. It gave the country its widest exposure to live jazz yet, and Ralton contributed a footnote to New Zealand music by segueing his recording of the hit foxtrot 'Yaaka Hula Hickey Dula' into a piece called 'Maori–Hula Medley': this included a reference to 'Pokarekare'.[112] A member of the Savoy Havana Band also encouraged the career of New Zealand's first international jazz musician, Abe Romain.

SEA BLUES

In the early 1920s, before radio became a significant medium, New Zealand connected with the outside world by ship. It was not just meat and dairy products being exported to the Northern Hemisphere, but musicians along for the voyage to perform for the passengers. They returned with sheet music, band arrangements, hit records in the latest styles – and overseas musicians. Most of the ships visiting New Zealand were English, but one of the most crucial in the evolution of the country's popular music belonged to the locally owned Union Steam Ship Company. With their red and black funnels, the 'greyhounds' of the Union fleet were the mail boats on the Pacific run: Auckland, Sydney, Suva, Vancouver, San Francisco were their regular ports of call. The most famous – and the fastest – was RMS *Niagara*, 13,000 tons of luxury. For land-based musicians, working on the *Niagara* seemed a dream job.

In 1922 the pianist leading the *Niagara* band was Edgar Bendall, a man who would become synonymous with Auckland dance bands over the next 50 years. Bendall was born in Birmingham, and began his career on the *Niagara* in 1917, at the age of twenty. By 1922 *terra firma* called, and he offered the job to young Auckland pianist Henry Shirley. The *Niagara* was willing to discharge Bendall from his contract if he found a good replacement, he explained to Shirley. The pay was £15/16 per month, plus tips, and the ship departed at 8.00 pm that night: 'So you'll have to make up your mind smartly.'

Shirley recalled that he could hardly find enough breath to say 'Yes'. He had to recruit a pianist to take over his cinema job, join the Seaman's Union, sign papers, acquire his uniforms – winter blues and summer whites – and say

his farewells. That night he discovered what he had let himself in for. As soon as the *Niagara* left the shelter of the Hauraki Gulf, he became dreadfully seasick:

> There was no question of staying in my bunk next day. Without a pianist there could be no orchestra. Being a steward as well as a musician I had saloon duty to do . . . . from the other side of the salon came a roar of abuse – the head waiter was a Cockney with no patience for the fumblings of beginners – 'Don't drop them effing forks!' He had the manner and vocabulary of an old-style Sergeant Major and musician-stewards were his favourite target.[113]

The musicians were expected to play during all meals, and morning and afternoon teas. As musical director Shirley also had to write arrangements and programmes. Every morning his trumpeter Dick Symons was required to sound a reveille to wake the passengers. At night, Symons played popular tunes such as 'Because', 'O Sole Mio' or – for a tip – a request. 'It was possible to double one's earnings by means of tips, plus a collection made at the end of each voyage. Many wealthy and famous people crossed the Pacific in the *Niagara*. So it was not surprising that some good musicians were attracted by a steady £8 a week . . . very good wages in 1922.' Among the musicians were Henry Engel and his cousin Carl Hellriegel, who would later be foundation violinists in New Zealand's National Orchestra.

On board the *Niagara*, said Shirley, 'it is hard to believe that such a combination of instruments playing both dance and straight music could produce a very musical sound. Yet I remember a compliment we received from an American gentleman who handed us a $5 note for what he called a "fine performance" of Mozart's *Magic Flute*.' After visiting Fiji, Hawaii and Vancouver – and putting up with the autocratic senior steward, storms, a heatwave and agonising swollen legs – Shirley decided to leave the *Niagara* in Sydney and go to England. He had £60 in his pocket, and a steerage ticket to Southampton was £36.[114]

Meanwhile, Edgar Bendall was beginning his long career as the doyen of the Auckland dance bands. He formed his most famous band in the early 1920s, Edgar Bendall's Collegians, which featured a quartet of leading players who would all have prominent jazz careers in Australia: Dick and Ted McMinn on sax and banjo, saxophonist Maurie Gilman and trumpeter Jimmy Gussey.[115] The drummer, Johnny Madden, was just sixteen

SAX EXPORT

In Theo Trezise's noisy Goring Street Cabaret in the early 1920s, the music was provided by Charles Dalton's Orchestra. Among them was a teenage violin player called Abe Romain, who was also learning the saxophone. Although some patrons at the Cabaret 'suggested the harbour as a suitable place for him to throw it in to', recalled local musician Jack McEwen, it was on the saxophone that Romain would become renowned.[116]

Born in Wellington in 1905, Adrian August Bussy de Saint-Romain was the son of a French-Mauritian father who stowed away to Australia and then settled in New Zealand. From the age of ten, Romain was encouraged towards a career in music, although it was not taught at his high school, St Patrick's College. He was formally trained in the violin and clarinet, and, while travelling with a J. C. Williamson show, a vaudeville musician gave him pointers on the saxophone. He especially enjoyed the dance music introduced to him by a girlfriend in a Wellington record shop: discs by Paul Whiteman, Ted Lewis and the Original Dixieland Jazz Band.

While still a teenager, Romain went to sea as a musician and bellboy on the *Tahiti*, which steamed between New Zealand and San Francisco, enabling him to see live jazz and buy the latest records. It was when performing at Trezise's Cabaret that he changed his first name to Abe: 'he could not stand the effeminate way the manager said Adrian'.[117]

Emigrating to Australia early in the 1920s, Romain's long career there included stints in bands – or leading them – at the top clubs such as Ambassadors and the Trocadero. Heading the bill at Ambassadors right through 1924 was Bert Ralton's Savoy Havana Band. When the band went to New Zealand, its star trumpeter Eddie Frizelle stayed behind in Sydney and persuaded Romain that he should get some experience further afield.

Romain left for England in 1930 and his overseas sojourn was a jazzman's dream. As lead saxophonist of Jack Hylton's hugely successful band he made extensive tours of Europe, performed for royalty, recorded with Hylton and the Harry Roy band, and took part in the first live broadcasts from Britain to the US. As part of

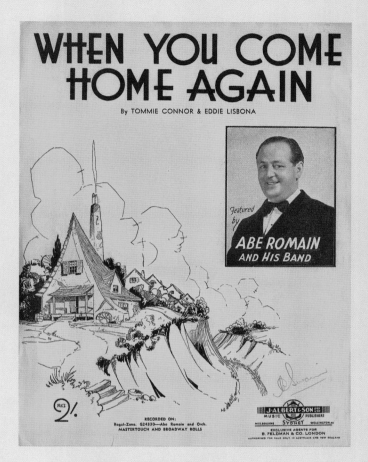

Visits home were rare for Abe Romain, who became a star in Australia after playing with Louis Armstrong at his London debut in 1932. Chris Bourke collection

Hylton's band, Romain accompanied Louis Armstrong when he made his London debut at the Palladium in July 1932. He was now a committed expatriate; returning to Sydney in 1940, he remained there until his death in 1994, staying active as one of Sydney's top musicians until the mid-1950s.

In 1932, the year that Romain backed Armstrong, the New Zealand column in the *Australian Music Maker* made a comment that would later become very familiar: 'Phar Lap was born and bred in New Zealand as was Abe Romain, who is now with Jack Hylton's orchestra. Abe is claimed in England as an Australian.'[118]

Edgar Bendall was the doyen of Auckland dance-band pianists for 50 years. His band the Collegians nurtured many key musicians. Seen here in 1925 they were (L-R): Edgar Bendall, Maurie Gilman, Dick McMinn, Stew Dawkins, Jack Evans, Johnny Madden, Jim Gussey and Ted McMinn. Dennis Huggard Archive, PAColl-9492-10, Alexander Turnbull Library, Wellington

when he began playing with Bendall's Collegians in 1924; the pair would be playing together 40 years later. Bendall gave up shortly before he died in 1977, aged 80, while Madden's career lasted into the 1980s.[119]

On Auckland's Waitemata Harbour just after midday on 11 August 1925, a puff of white smoke was followed by the thunderous boom of cannon. In response came the crack of heavy artillery from Devonport's North Head. This military salute marked the arrival of the first jazz bands direct from the United States.[120]

Thousands of New Zealanders gathered around the shoreline to greet the second coming of the American 'great white fleet'. It was an even greater armada from the United States Navy than the visiting fleet of 1908; this time large flotillas simultaneously visited Wellington,

Lyttelton and Port Chalmers. With Auckland hosting eight battleships and several other support vessels, 12,000 officers and crew streamed into the city. Hundreds attended concerts, rugby games, race meetings, functions and parties, and saw Rudall Hayward's new feature film, *Rewi's Last Stand*, billed as 'the only way to see the great Maori race'.[121]

Each of the battleships had its own military band, many members of which also played in the ships' orchestra and jazz and dance bands. The *New Zealand Herald*'s entertainment columns quickly advertised the appearance on shore of many of the ships' jazz bands. The Dixieland Cabaret got in early, with several nights honouring the visit of the fleet, mostly themed around the ships: *California, New Mexico, Colorado, Mississippi, West Virginia*. The cabaret also advertised for 'a number of girls of good address wanted as dancing partners' at its afternoon soirées. There were outdoor performances, and cinemas secured naval bands for concerts between films: the *USS Mississippi*'s ten-piece jazz band – 'the pick of Uncle Sam syncopators' – appearing at the Strand, and the *USS New Mexico* jazz band at the Westend.

Hundreds of sailors who could not make the last launch back to their ships bedded down in a shed on Prince's Wharf. The wharf also hosted a dance for those who were not invited to the official ball at the Town Hall; well into the night, Walter Smith's Orchestra entertained 500 men 'who had no lack of partners'. And for the naval musicians who wanted to entertain themselves, local firms advertised fleet-week specials, including the musical instrument store Meltzer Bros, where Hawaiian ukuleles were on offer from 19/6, and steel guitars from £3/19/6.[122]

The civic pride at being able to host such a large contingent of glamorous Americans is obvious. But the 1925 'great white fleet' visit was a pivotal Jazz Age phenomenon, with the appropriate soundtrack. Even the exclusive Auckland Club's 'at home' was serenaded by Bendall's jazz band. As the fleet readied itself for departure, the *New Zealand Observer* commented: 'The American officers and men-o'-warsmen seem to be so badly smitten with the jazz craze that the bands are in danger of being asked to work overtime, and no doubt they would have to were it not for the invention of the gramophone.'[123]

RADIO WAVES

'Hello My Dearie' is an unlikely way to start a revolution. This light-hearted 1918 song, among others, launched New Zealand's first radio programme on 17 November 1921; it would bring the world into people's homes, and a world of music. Dr Robert Jack, professor of physics at the University of Otago, had been experimenting with radio transmission for several months: he was now ready to transmit outside of the laboratory. With the necessary approvals from the Post and Telegraph Department, he broadcast a programme of musical items using records supplied by a local music store, with a microphone placed inside the horn of a gramophone. At first, he began each broadcast with a five-minute buzzer to give the few people with radio sets time to tune in. Jack later attempted live music, including a recital by the matron of Knox Theological College, his future wife Isabella Manson.[124]

Jack was quickly followed by Charles Forrest in Wellington, a radio parts merchant who began broadcasting music and talk in February 1922, from a studio in the multi-storey building owned by his business partner, Hope Gibbons. The first person to sing over the radio in New Zealand did so from this studio, said Forrest. Her name was Violet Gyles, and she performed unaccompanied. Forrest also claimed other milestones: the first male singer broadcast (local picture theatre manager Tony Wood) and the first dance band (H. J. Tutschka and His Dance Band).[125] Shortly afterwards, he had competition from Arthur McClay, who broadcast from his parents' house in Newtown, using an antenna strung between two tall pine trees. For live music items he used the piano in his parents' lounge.[126]

Local radio stations were soon established in many centres. An early adopter was Morton Coutts of Taihape, who launched 2AQ in 1922. By March 1923, he was able to make a pioneering live broadcast of a Diggers' concert from the Town Hall.[127] The transmission range of the amateur stations could be freakishly vast. Coutts had listeners in Russell to the north, Cromwell in the south and in Sydney. Jack's transmissions reached Auckland.[128] In Wellington, on 11 August 1922, McClay's station broadcast the P&T Engineers' Social and Sports Club dance live-to-air from a Kent Terrace hall. Later the Presbyterian Bible Class hired the ferry *Duchess* for a shipboard dance while cruising Wellington harbour, to music broadcast from the city.[129]

Although the first radio stations were private, from the beginning the government was involved. The Post and Telegraph Department policed the airwaves, which hitherto had been used for Morse code. During the war, the airwaves were monitored for communications, and in peacetime they were needed for the safety of ships at sea, so there were concerns about who could receive radio signals. The earliest radio owners needed to apply for a licence, supplying references, a circuit diagram of their receiver, a three-shilling stamp and a form signed before a JP – and they had to swear on the Bible that they would not disclose any secrets they might accidentally hear.[130]

At first, advertisements were banned, though limited sponsorship was permitted. The music store Begg's showed initiative in Wellington when it paid for the phrase 'Yes! We have no bananas' to be mentioned often on air. Listeners were puzzled until the release of the song that became the biggest hit of the 1923–24 dance season, and the most irritating since 1912, when Irving Berlin's 'Everybody's Doin' It Now' took ragtime to the world.[131]

Bill Huggins monitors the signal of 1YA, at the station's studio in Scots Hall, Auckland, in 1925. *RNZ Sound Archives*

SOUTH SEAS EXHIBITIONISTS

New Zealand's cultural links with the world were accelerating. This was reflected by an entertainment event on a scale that the country had never seen before. The New Zealand and South Seas International Exhibition opened in Dunedin on 17 November 1925. The scale of the endeavour captured the public's imagination. The exhibition occupied 65 acres of the reclaimed Lake Logan, with twelve acres set aside for international pavilions and New Zealand exhibitors; an amusement park took up another 25 acres. A temporary Festival Hall held 2500 people, and a sports arena boasted a 3000-seat grandstand. Attendances far surpassed expectations: in the six months the exhibition was open, it drew 3,200,498 visitors from throughout the country, many people going several times.

The star musical attraction was the Argyll and Sutherland Highlanders Band, which had been brought out from Britain for the duration of the exhibition at a cost of £30,000. Their conductor was F. J. Ricketts, a dapper showman who composed the well-known march 'Colonel Bogey' using the pseudonym Kenneth J. Alford. While at the exhibition he wrote two pieces with the name 'Dunedin'. One was a serious composition, a march that entered the brass band repertoire. The other 'Dunedin' was not supposed to last beyond the exhibition, but was a great success: it was a burlesque that combined a medley of tunes associated with the event plus sound effects imitating the noises that reverberated from the amusement park.[132]

Music at the exhibition was dominated by the socially sanctioned genres: bagpipe and brass bands, choirs conducted by the upright Victor Galway and H. Temple White, light classical orchestral concerts, opera recitals, musicals, and soloists such as Clara Butt and her husband Kennerly Rumford.

But a leading dance band was also brought out from Britain; led by Manuel (Manny) Hyman, it was to have a lasting effect on local dance music. After performing at the exhibition every night for six months, Hyman's band stayed on in Dunedin to play at the Oriental Caves cabaret, and two years later they played at the Adelphi in Wellington. When Hyman's band returned to London, it was hired by the Savoy.[133]

A popular singing star also emerged. Ellen Dempster was born in England and had come with other singers to perform at a music publisher's stall in the Australian court. Thousands of visitors enjoyed her renditions of songs such as 'The Lonely Road', 'Sad Little Eyes' and 'I Gave You All', and many left with copies of the sheet music to play at home. According to Walter Sinton, who attended the exhibition as a teenage percussionist in a military band, 'The Lonely Road' was the most popular of all these songs: 'The road seems long and lonely/when your luck's all upside down . . .'. After having won the hearts of Dunedinites, Dempster contracted an illness and, just weeks after the exhibition closed, died aged 30 without returning home. Her headstone at Anderson's Bay reads: 'The Exhibition Singer. End of the Lonely Road'.[134]

One of the most popular attractions at the South Seas Exhibition was the Columbia Graphophone Company's display of the latest gramophones and records. Technological developments in entertainment helped replace the sombre, austere post-war atmosphere with an exuberant acceptance of the modern. The country's embrace of the 78 rpm disc for entertainment accelerated with the improvement in quality after electrical recordings began in 1925. Before this, musicians performed in front of a large metal horn, and the sounds they made were transferred to a needle directly cutting into a master disc. Playback was essentially the same process in reverse, using a gramophone with a horn as the speaker. With the invention of the valve, microphones could be powered by electricity, enhancing fidelity and widening the sound spectrum considerably.[135]

These advances – and a lift in prosperity – led to a boom in the sales of discs and gramophones, and by the mid-1920s, most New Zealand homes owned a player. In Wellington, during May 1926, the New Zealand branch of His Master's Voice (HMV) sold 3064 gramophones, which ranged from a portable at £11 to a large cabinet model at £67.[136] That year, 'O Come All Ye Faithful' – the

first electric recording available in New Zealand – sold 4000 copies. Other initiatives improved stock supplies to New Zealand and assisted local recording. In 1926, outside Sydney, the Gramophone Company opened a modern HMV pressing plant at Erskineville (eclipsing the plant Brunswick built in 1924), and Columbia opened a recording studio and pressing plant at Homebush. In the same year, the Gramophone Company in England established His Master's Voice (New Zealand) Ltd, where they had been represented by E. J. Hyams since 1910.[137]

Once recording and manufacturing were possible in Australia, there seemed to be no limit to the number and variety of discs available in New Zealand. The record industry could get overseas hits onto the market swiftly, and take advantage of artists' tours by simultaneously putting discs into record stores while they were visiting. Most significantly, no longer would New Zealand musicians have to travel all the way to Britain to record, as Alfred Hill and Ernest McKinlay had done. In 1925 HMV demonstrated the possibilities during a visit to the UK by William Massey, the New Zealand Prime Minister. They recorded a speech he gave about the British Empire, made the discs in Australia and put them on sale several days after his death in May 1925. On the B-side was Peter Dawson – the Australian bass-baritone – singing 'God Defend New Zealand'.[138]

In the 1920s, public demonstrations of the player piano were popular, and given a human dimension by pianists who would join the 'mechanical marvel' in a duet, and singers who would use it as an accompanist. While the instrument could also be played as a normal piano, it was another factor in the decline of domestic music-making, writes piano historian John MacGibbon. 'Reading one Lewis Eady advert from 1922, you might think there had never been music in homes before player pianos came along: "How cheerless were the long evenings; how we all used to bury ourselves in books and paper; what a dull, dismal time we had – until – the Player Piano came!"'

The instrument had been around since 1898, and at its peak in 1923 approximately half of the 200,000 pianos made worldwide were player pianos. They were not cheap: in 1928 Lewis Eady's in Auckland offered a slightly used Williams Pla-Ola for £165. In the late 1920s, the instrument lost its main advantage over gramophone records: the quality of reproduction. The mechanical player pianos had a much superior sound to recordings made acoustically, and piano rolls could reflect the subtle

On 3 August 1928, the *Radio Record* celebrated the first birthday
of New Zealand's 'super-power station', Wellington's 2YA.
Inside, letter writers grumbled that using the 2YA Orchestra to
perform jazz was deplorable and degrading. RNZ Infofind

dynamics of a piece and the idiosyncrasies of the performer
(who was often a celebrated pianist, such as George
Gershwin, James P. Johnson or Rachmaninov).[139] Once
recordings were made electrically, things changed.

By 1925 only 4702 people held radio listening licences
in New Zealand, but the medium was enough of a force to
make it necessary to bring in new regulations that prepared
for its future growth. The government determined
that four 500-watt stations – one in each of the main
centres – would get broadcast rights for non-commercial
broadcasting, funded by a proportion of the licence fee.
Other stations could continue, but were disadvantaged by
restrictions on advertising and their broadcast hours. The
Radio Broadcasting Company (RBC) was contracted to
run the four stations, and by trial and error – the medium
was too new for any real expertise to exist – it developed
management structures and programming philosophies
that would shape New Zealand's public radio service.

'Music became the mainstay of programming', writes
radio historian Patrick Day. 'Regulations permitted only
a small proportion of recorded music. For some time

there was a willing flood of singers, musicians and other
performers keen to be on the air.' At first, this was done for
free: it was a novelty. But the RBC soon found that airtime
was an insatiable consumer of talent and the novelty wore
off. Staff improvised with recordings, player pianos, even
reading from the newspaper. Programming was shaped by
'availability rather than quality'. It was not until 1928 that
it became policy that artists should be paid.[140]

When radio began, musicians acted as its patrons,
rather than the other way around. 'If the talkies had been
in existence in those days Lord knows what we would
have done, as picture theatre orchestras were our chief
stand-bys', recalled a 1YA pioneer. There was little in it
for the musicians – the programmer only had 22/6 an hour
to spend on programmes, and there were restrictions on
the number of records played. In addition, 'artists in those
days were not paid for their first performance over the air.
It was amazing the number of "first appearances" that the
programme organiser brought before the microphone.'[141]

Bands had been performing modern dance and light
music on radio almost since its inception. Relays over
ordinary phone lines enabled live broadcasts from outside
the studio. As early as 1924, Basil Bird's dance band
broadcast every Saturday from the Columbian Cabaret
in Kilbirnie, Wellington (the studio technicians were
powerless when, just beneath the microphone, a fight
broke out between two dancers and the band had to lift
its volume).[142] Stations would take a relay from cinema
orchestras, as they performed lengthy overtures before
the feature. Soon, professionals such as Walter Smith's
Click-Clack Band and Ted Marchant's Kit Kat Band were
regularly heard from their cabarets, as well as curiosities
such as the Island Bay Mouth-Organ Boomerang Band
and Barry Ingall's Hawaiians. The South Seas Exhibition
provided the RBC with an early showcase as well, with
many of its performances being broadcast. From the
late 1920s, the RBC employed musical groups on a
retainer as a way of controlling their standards; advisory
committees were set up, and arrangements were made with
the Australasian Performing Right Association to fulfil
copyright payments.[143]

A curious first occurred on 3 December 1925, when
a trans-Tasman link enabled a new song to be taught via
broadcast from Dunedin, and performed on a Sydney
stage the following night. From a studio in the south of
New Zealand, songwriter Neal McBeath recited the words
and then sang the melody to his song 'Canberra' into

the microphone; Manuel Hyman's Cabaret Dance Band also performed the song, to demonstrate its arrangement. Across the Tasman, transcribers and music copyists took notes, and the next night the vaudeville star Ella Shields sang the song at Sydney's Tivoli theatre.[144]

VAUDEVILLIAN VISITORS

'The greatest rival of the theatre today is the dancing germ and not the kinema, which is having as bad a time as the theatre.' Prompter, entertainment columnist of the *New Zealand Observer*, was quoting a report on the British scene in 1923. Yet New Zealand theatre, musicals and vaudeville thrived through the 1920s. The column was surrounded by advertisements for the latest productions visiting from London and Australia. Once here, they shared eclectic bills with New Zealand performers.

In Dunedin in the early 1920s, there was a wealth of entertainment available, of all kinds: brass bands, choral and classical concerts, festivals of Shakespearean plays and Gilbert and Sullivan operettas, vaudeville – and curiosities such as Olympic champion Annette Kellerman diving into a tank on the stage of the King's Theatre. In Auckland, vaudeville still ruled at His Majesty's and Fuller's Opera House.[145]

For decades, the Fuller's circuit had been 'dissipating the megrims' through New Zealand.[146] The company presented vaudeville and revue shows six nights a week in the four main centres, with matinees on Wednesdays and Saturdays. Fuller's also toured its shows through the provinces. Besides the actors, jugglers and clowns featured in Fuller's revues, regular musical acts included singer Anita Green, violinist Sidney Clark and influential Christchurch banjoist Louis Bloy.

In the 1920s, music hall and its more polished sibling vaudeville remained popular, while simultaneously evolving into variety shows, revues and cabaret. However, their appeal faded with the growing appeal of other cheap forms of entertainment: cinema, radio and the increasingly popular dance halls.[147]

Musical theatre could involve a lavish, touring produc-tion, and early in the 1920s New Zealand received many of the big shows not long after their overseas debuts: *Cairo*, Jerome Kern's *Sally* – one of the first 'dancing' musicals – and *Sybil* starring Gladys Moncrieff. The most spectacular attraction in 1921 was the national tour of the hit London musical *Chu Chin Chow*, with its lavish costuming,

multi-coloured staging and energetic dancing. 'The complications and convolutions of the plot defy analysis but there were plenty of good tunes', recalled Brian Salkeld.[148]

Music hall performers from overseas often visited New Zealand. In April 1922, one of the last great music hall stars arrived: Ella Shields, of 'Burlington Bertie from Bow' fame. A dark comment on the British class system, this rhyming ballad was an evergreen and its cross-dressing mockney singer was born an American.[149]

Shields was brought to New Zealand by Australian promoter Harry G. Musgrove. His 'first invasion of New Zealand as an entrepreneur' was a 1921 tour by Wilkie Bard, master of the tongue-twister and parody songs. Bard was given his surname because of his resemblance to Shakespeare; his big hit was 'She Sells Sea-Shells on the Sea-Shore', which started the vogue for tongue-twisters. According to Musgrove, he was paid the largest fee ever received for an Australasian tour (£400 per week, which shocked Dunedin), but his success opened the door for other British performers, such as Shields, who now saw rich pickings in the region.[150]

Besides Fuller's, the most prominent promoters bringing acts to New Zealand were the Australian firms J. C. Williamson's and J. & N. Tait. In 1924 J. C. Williamson's established its own vaudeville troupe, the Entertainers, who received rave reviews during their season at His Majesty's in Auckland: 'There are no duds in the company, no wading through a morass of mediocrity to gain an oasis of real talent.'[151] Acting for promoter E. J. Carroll, Wellington advertising pioneer Leo Du Chateau brought acts such as Harry Lauder and the Hawaiian Troubadours.[152]

New Zealanders regularly complained about the calibre of their vaudevillian visitors, unaware that they were often seeing the best performers, on their way up. Asking 'Where Are the Mummers of Yester Year?' in 1921, the *NZ Theatre and Motion Picture* found that the mummers – music hall performers – who had been to New Zealand now populated the best West End stages. And in 1924 the magazine commented on a glut of quality vaudeville shows touring New Zealand, thanks to J. C. Williamson's hostile takeover of Tivoli Theatres Ltd; both companies had been enthusiastically booking artists to compete with each other and now Williamson's had to fulfil the contracts.[153]

Fresh local acts emerged at amateur trials held in Auckland picture theatres during the early 1920s. Each week, crowds filled venues such as the King's, Empress, Westend, Britannia – and especially the Hippodrome

1927: WAIATA MAORI

In the fledgling Dominion's songbook, Maori writers were strongly represented. Among the songs to find wide and lasting appeal early in the century were Princess Te Rangi Pai's 'Hine E Hine'; Paraire Tomoana's 'E Pari Ra' and 'Hoki Hoki'; 'Pokarekare' (usually attributed to Tomoana);[154] and 'Po Atarau' ('Now is the Hour'), whose Maori lyrics were written in 1926 by Maewa Kaihau to an Australian melody.[155] For years, anthropologists and ethnomusicologists had been endeavouring to get Maori music and oral culture on to wax cylinders. But with international recording companies searching for material that was both exotic and marketable, it is no surprise that Maori dominated the first commercial recording ventures: in the late 1920s, the recording industry was turning its gaze towards New Zealand's indigenous music.

The Parlophone company said it wanted to record singers in all countries likely to be of interest to its buyers, 'irrespective of the cost entailed thereby'. Altruism may have been at the forefront of the company's press statements, but Parlophone was interested in the popular, not the pure. That meant a Westernised hybrid of waiata and Tin Pan Alley.[156]

Some anthropologists, such as Johannes Andersen, marvelled at the way Maori were 'always given to song', with something appropriate for all occasions – love songs, war songs – despite the limited melodic range of their music. 'The fact is', he wrote in 1928, 'the Maori had no such thing as melody as we know it. He had no tune apart from the words. The words were the important thing, and the words were sung more or less in the natural speech tones':

> It is well known how readily the Maori took to our music, and how he excels in it; so that he enjoys two kinds of music: ours in addition to his own. An intermediate form has sprung up, too; European tunes taken by the Maori and altered slightly in melody and in tune, so that they are neither the one nor the other, but are extremely pleasing both to Maori and to European; and it is these tunes that often are regarded as Maori music, and are referred to as Maori music. Songs like Alfred Hill's 'Waiata Poi' have used Maori rhythm, but not Maori melody . . .[157]

As the composer of 'Waiata Poi' – and a Pakeha – Hill could not be considered a purist. Yet after hearing a Rotorua concert party in 1939 he lamented that 'much of what was precious in Maori music was being rapidly lost'. It was being neglected and evolving into something Hawaiian, 'complete with guitar, ukulele and Maori words set to a Hawaiian tune'.[158] However, the early commercial recordings of Maori popular music do not just record what was happening to Maori music and how it was changing; they were also much loved and very successful. They emerged from the Western, classical tradition of which Hill approved.

Ohinemutu, near Rotorua, is where the recording of popular music in New Zealand began. In 1927 a recording team from Parlophone's Australian branch visited Rotorua during the tour of New Zealand by the Duke and Duchess of York (later to become King George VI and the Queen Mother). The technicians took the opportunity to record some Maori music while they were there, using portable acoustic equipment. In February 1927, in the small Tinohopu meeting house at Ohinemutu, they recorded Ana Hato – an untrained, twenty-year-old soprano – singing sixteen songs. For some of the songs, she was accompanied by her cousin, baritone Deane Waretini, by pianist Te Mauri Meihana, or by a chorus, likely to be the singers who became the Rotorua Maori Choir. The songs were already favourites for Maori and Pakeha; among them were 'Hine E Hine', 'Pokarekare', 'E Pari Ra', 'Hoki Hoki Tonu Mai', 'Po Atarau' and Alfred Hill's 'Waiata Poi'. They became New Zealand's first commercial recordings, and some of the most successful, selling widely domestically and around the world; their recording of 'Pokarekare' is credited with accelerating its popularity throughout New Zealand.[159]

Tourism played a key role in Hato's career. Born Ana Matawhaura Hato (Tuhourangi/Ngati Whakaue) in 1906, she began singing at Whakarewarewa School, encouraged by the headmaster's wife, Mrs Banks. As a child, Hato dived for pennies at Whakarewarewa village with her friends and gave impromptu performances. 'Everybody sang, from the time we were kids', remembered Kuru Waaka of Tuhourangi. 'The particular quality of Arawa singing is because of the tourism: singing, singing, singing, every day. Tuhourangi were quick to realise if you sing a song or poke your tongue out, you'd get a penny.' Hato's

Opposite: Ana Hato (right) and Deane Waretini made the first commercial recordings in New Zealand, when an Australian mobile unit visited Rotorua with the Duke and Duchess of York. Twenty years later, their Parlophone discs were still selling. Peter Downes collection

voice shone through, and from the age of sixteen she was being asked to give solo recitals and to perform at official functions. In about 1925, Hato was chosen to visit Australia with a small concert party from Whakarewarewa, and quickly became the star at their appearances.[160]

Two years after the Yorks visited Rotorua, Parlophone invited Hato and Waretini over to Sydney for more recordings. This time they were made electrically, and among the nine discs – with backing of piano, violin and cello – they re-visited several songs from the 1927 session. These were Hato's last published recordings in her lifetime, although in 1950 the duo recorded several songs by an Auckland composer, E. H. Cross, which remained unreleased for nearly 50 years.

The Parlophone discs were a big success in New Zealand and Australia, and remained in the catalogue for more than two decades. Hato travelled widely, giving concerts and radio broadcasts, and making ceremonial, charity and patriotic appearances. She became a guide at Whakarewarewa, and is credited with being 'the Maori who taught "Now is the Hour" to Gracie Fields' during her 1946 visit.[161] Hato died of breast cancer in 1953, aged only 47.

She was remembered for her good works and strong faith, but most of all for her music. Hato loved parties, which always became singalongs, especially if her close friend the songwriter Tuini Ngawai was visiting from the East Coast. Ngawai would bring her guitar and Deane Waretini his ukulele. 'You heard some singing!', her niece

Bubbles Mihinui reminisced. 'Nobody in Whaka closed their windows when they had parties!'[162]

Another historic recording took place at the Tinohopu meeting house in 1930, when the pianist/arranger Gil Dech visited with technicians from the Columbia Graphophone Company in Sydney. The company had often been told about the quality of Maori singing in Rotorua, with American tourists especially wanting to buy recordings – but none existed.

The Columbia technicians built portable recording equipment in Sydney and, once they arrived at Ohinemutu, set up a studio inside the meeting house. Blankets and carpets were hung from the ceiling and over windows and walls to deaden the echo, and the porch became a control room. Unlike the 1927 Ana Hato/Deane Waretini sessions, these were electric recordings, cut into wax discs 30 mm thick, and then taken back to Sydney where master discs were made out of copper. The 'Maori Recording Expedition' sessions took place over twelve days in April, and the first discs were released in June 1927.[163]

Dech kept the choir's own harmonies in the arrangements, but when they sang in unison he wrote separate parts and taught them to the individual singers. He also conducted the choir: 'At first they were amused at the Pakeha standing up in front of them waving his arms about. The great difficulty was to get everyone to take it seriously and give their undivided attention to the conductor.'[164]

Most of the choir were Ngati Whakaue, and among the soloists were the contralto Mere Amohau and soprano Te Mauri Meihana (also known as Molly Mason, she played piano for Hato and Waretini in the 1927 recordings). One of the youngest choir members was Kahu, the mother of Howard Morrison, then aged seventeen. Thirty sides were recorded – Maori folk songs, love ballads, hymns, stick-game songs, welcomes and farewells – and, wrote ethnomusicologist Mervyn McLean, 'all in the European idiom'. They were released on 78 rpm discs, and re-released on album several times: they kept selling over the next 35 years.[165]

Te Mauri Meihana commented on the eclectic tastes of Maori, all influencing their music as it was being sung in 1937. Church music was just the beginning, she said; Maori also enjoyed swing, sea shanties, Victorian ballads, music hall ditties, opera and jazz. 'Each in its turn has left its sign and impress upon our music. But we have kept the Maori spirit intact. The yearning for the past; the lament for the days and times that are no more.'

PARLOPHONE

POKAREKARE
(Alfred Hill)   (Speed 78)
ANA HATO & DEANE WARETINI
With Violin, 'Cello and Piano
Accompaniment
(Recorded in Australia)

A 2801
(A 413-1)

MADE IN AUSTRALIA

CHAPPELL & CO LTD SYDNEY

Although Johannes Andersen thought 'Hine E Hine' was the most beautiful Maori melody he had heard, Meihana said: 'My grandfather would have dismissed it with one word – "Pakeha!" – his expression I leave you to imagine. That song has the sadness and mystery of Maori music; but for a closer approach to the original Maori, I would ask you to listen to Mere Amohau singing "Takutu Ranga Ake".'[166]

Parlophone was quick to follow up its success with Ana Hato and Deane Waretini with more recordings by Maori. 'Everybody with a gramophone these days is "talking Maori"', reported the *Levin Daily Chronicle* in July 1930. The small town paper had reason to be proud: a Maori trio from nearby Otaki had just released two 78 rpm discs. The Tahiwis had travelled to Sydney on the *Ulimaroa* especially to record for Parlophone, accompanied by Australian musicians. It was just a month after the Rotorua Maori Choir sessions.[167]

Henare, Hinehou and Weno Tahiwi were siblings from a distinguished family in which all eight children were musical. Their father Rawiri Rota Tahiwi had helped form the Otaki Maori Brass Band in 1891, and several of his sons followed him into the band. Among them was his eldest, Kingi Tahiwi, who became renowned as a translator and songwriter. He wrote both words and music, using a five-string banjo or a piano.

Henare, a baritone, had been a bugler in the First World War. Hinehou, a mezzo-soprano, sang at silent movies and was a member of a country and western group. Weno, also a mezzo, trained with H. Temple White and could play classical piano exquisitely or 'rattle the keys' for any request. But how the trio came to make the recordings is unknown. Kingi was unable to go with them and was reluctant to let his sisters travel to Sydney without a chaperone – even though their brother Henare had been a Maori All Black, he was also known for his rakish charm. 'They got on the boat and took off anyway', said Hinehou's daughter Horiana Joyce. 'When they finally came home again, Kingi really roasted them – amongst other things for what they did with some of his lyrics!'[168]

The Tahiwis stayed in Sydney a month and recorded 22 sides of traditional and newly written Maori songs, including several by Kingi such as 'Puru Taitama' and 'Mapu Kau'. The arrangements make it clear that Parlophone intended these recordings for the popular market: the trio was accompanied by instruments such as piano, violin, guitar, cello and trombone. Although sung

Henare, Hinehou and Weno Tahiwi were siblings from a distinguished Otaki family that travelled to Sydney in 1930 and recorded 22 Maori and contemporary popular songs; among them was 'Happy Days Are Here Again'. Alexander Turnbull Library, Wellington

in the Maori language, authenticity was not an issue; most were suitable for parlour recitals. 'Waiata Maori' is an art song, arranged by Alfred Hill like a miniature cycle with shifts in tempo, references to other melodies and even a haka. Princess Te Rangi Pai wrote 'Aroha', and 'Tawhaki' was by prolific Dunedin songwriter D. S. Sharp. Unique among the recordings is 'A Poi Dance', a hillbilly two-step instrumental with Henare on a harmonica, backed by a piano and violin.

The trio also recorded four recent pop songs that were currently being heard in cinemas: a jaunty 'Happy Days Are Here Again', and the laments 'Somebody Might Like You', 'South Sea Rose' and 'Should I?' A few days' break in the recordings suggests the Tahiwis learnt these songs while in Sydney.

On their return, the trio appeared at a concert in Wellington's Grand Opera House, the audience insisting on many encores.[169] The Tahiwis often performed together – although rarely as the complete trio – and the influence of the family continued for many years after they made their recordings. They were dedicated contributors to community music-making, for church, charity or marae. Kingi's influence was especially felt as a songwriter ('Kapiti' was a succinct history of the island); as a Maori rugby stalwart; and as the founder of the Ngati Poneke Young Maori Club, which gave many morale-boosting concerts during the war, and became a social and musical nurturing ground for Maori in Wellington.

– to watch unknown performers display their talents. 'Vaudeville lovers followed their favourites from theatre to theatre', wrote theatre historian Frank Broad. 'Judging was done mostly by the audiences until the finals, when one had to be early to get a seat.' From these talent quests, the person who achieved the longest career was probably Jack Reilly. At the age of sixteen he conquered his nerves to sing in a contest at the King's with Ernie (Red) Beacham's band. He won, and continued to win most contests he entered. For the next decade – when he could get away from his job as a baker – Reilly performed as a comic singer throughout the North Island. As part of a duo, or in his family act *The Reilly Show*, his career lasted into the early 1960s.[170]

A regular in the audience at Fuller's Christchurch shows in the early 1920s was Eddie Hegan, aspirant entertainer. As a teenager, every Monday night he would be in the Opera House stalls to watch a variety show, the format of which rarely varied: six vaudeville acts in the first half, a revue in the second. 'A revue then was really a potted musical comedy, complete with ballet girls, singers, dancers and a featured comedian. It had a well-defined plot and quite elaborate dressing, scenery and lighting.'[171]

'I never saw a really bad one', recalled Hegan, who regarded George Wallace as the greatest act of the era. With Chaplinesque pathos, he broke the rules of comedy and succeeded. He would interrupt a rollicking sketch with a sentimental song he had written himself, then, just as the audience adjusted its mood, he would swing back to broad humour. 'He had many imitators, including his own son. All were pale copies.'[172]

Hegan joined a local semi-professional company, the Kiwi Sunshine Players.[173] It was the perfect start to his career. 'There were no stars, everybody had to "feed" everybody else, besides doing their own specialty single . . . . the show moved at a lightning pace. From opening chorus to finale everybody moved, fast!' In a two-hour programme, there might be ten costume changes. The troupe carried – and operated – its own footlights and curtains, travelling each night from Christchurch on an old bus. They would arrive half an hour before show time, set the stage and lights, and the curtain would go up at 8.00 pm. 'As always in country towns, any entertainment in the local hall was followed by a dance, which we were expected to attend, so very often it would be after two in the morning before we started on the way home.'[174]

Within a couple of years, Hegan got his break into the big time: a tour on the Fuller's circuit. He found himself sharing a bill alongside well-known acts such as the male impersonator Nellie Kolle. An Australian singer and comedian who had been visiting New Zealand since the First World War, in 1919 she offered a popular 'stunt at the piano, with serious stuff and ragtime'.[175]

Kolle's act hardly changed for over 30 years. Her audiences knew all the songs and loved singing along. Her show-stopper was 'Fill 'Em Up It Is My Birthday', which she was often pressured to repeat several times before the curtain could come down.

A crucial character on any bill was the singer of comic songs, a legacy from music hall. For them, songwriters produced material that worked in the theatre but was rarely taken up by the public; publishers made new comic songs available to professional performers free of charge. The songs could be parodies or tongue-twisters, and cover topics such as food, misplaced nostalgia, petty bureaucracy, and advice to young women or to henpecked husbands.

> A comic singer would begin his act with a couple of these songs, then go into a line of patter (which is where the 'stand-up comic' of today evolved from) and finish with a comic medley. The medleys were something special and consisted of bits of up to 20 songs all cunningly melded together to tell a story . . . . it was the material which was funny and carried the performer. They were helped, too, by the fact that audiences still liked baggy trousers and funny suits, although the red nose was slowly disappearing.[176]

Musicians and singers were usually guest starts in vaudeville and revues. A 1927 programme for a J. C. Williamson production at the Grand Opera House, Wellington, gives an idea of the breadth in a vaudeville show. The billing emphasised the international acts on offer: Swedish acrobats, an English comedienne, French 'clay modellers in vaudeville', a fashion show 'direct from New York' and orchestral items. While the eleven-piece orchestra tuned up, the audience could peruse the advertisements for a snapshot of musical fashions. The distributors Bannatyne and Hunter offered the latest and best dance records on Columbia, 'the only electric-recorded record with silent surface'. Among them, as a foxtrot, was 'Bye Bye, Blackbird', and as a waltz, 'The Prisoner's Song'. For those impressed by the saxophones heard during the evening, the instruments were available from Turner's Music Stores on Willis Street: 'Earn big money in the coming Winter'.

The star attraction closing the show was American 'singing conductor' Henry Santry and His World Famous Orchestra, whose repertoire included 'Where'd You Get Those Eyes?' and 'When the Red, Red Robin Comes Bobbin', Along'. All were available – as sheet music or on record – at Begg's.[177]

Earlier in the 1920s, Bathie Stuart, a former member of Pollard's juvenile opera company, returned to the stage in Auckland after her husband died in the influenza pandemic. Her show *Bathie Stuart and Her Musical Maids* combined vaudeville acts and films; for its sequel, *Bathie Stuart and Her Maori Maids*, Stuart recruited four Maori women from Rotorua who taught her Maori songs, poi dances and haka (Ana Hato was a member of this quartet for a time).[178] For decades afterwards while living in the US, Stuart featured these items in her role as unofficial promoter of tourism to New Zealand. When she left New Zealand in 1921 'to try her fortune on the English stage', the *NZ Theatre and Motion Picture* commented: 'With plenty of talent, not much voice, uncommon good looks, a distinctly original specialty, and a shrewd business head, Miss Stuart should do well.'[179]

Stuart's use of film as a prelude to the vaudeville in *Musical Maids* was a common device from the earliest days of cinema. Initially, when talkies arrived in 1929, Fuller's hoped to continue to include live acts as part of the attraction, while simultaneously converting their theatres to cinemas. But Benjamin Fuller could see the demise of the medium that had made him wealthy. Watching a film one night from the wings, he had said to his performers, 'That fellow up there on the screen is going to take your place some day. No kicks from him. He doesn't want to know when he is going to get a rise, when he's going to finish a tour, or ask, "When do we go back to Australia?"'[180]

BROADCAST NEWS

At 8.00 pm on 16 July 1927, the chimes of the Wellington General Post Office rang out to a much wider audience than usual. They were the first notes heard on 2YA, the jewel in RBC's operation, with the largest transmitter in the country. During his speech on opening night, Prime Minister Gordon Coates said that the Wellington station's 5000 watts made it ten times more powerful than those in the other centres, and the second most powerful in the Empire. In case of a national emergency, 2YA could theoretically communicate to the entire country.[181]

We play free for charity: Wellington's J.G.T. Banjo, Mandolin and Guitar Club was formed by Mr J. G. Turner in 1895. The 1924 band seen here was led by Miss Jean Turner. *NZ Theatre and Motion Picture*, January 1924

Billy Hart, New Zealand's first recorded crooner, as pictured in the *Radio Record* in September 1927, just prior to moving to Australia. S. P. Andrew (Bothamley collection/Peter Downes)

Then, it was on with the show, with a variety that reveals the breadth of musical talent, from the class of 1927. The programme favoured brass bands, light classical vocalists, instrumental soloists and chamber groups. Besides the Petone Maori Variety Entertainers singing 'Pokarekare' and Alfred Hill's 'Waiata Poi', the only concession to contemporary popular music was J. W. Goer's Hawaiian Steel Guitar Trio. 'God Save the King' brought down the imaginary curtain in 2YA's Grand Studio on Waring Taylor Street.[182]

While light classics and sentimental favourites from the 'mother country' dominated the music programming, modern dance music was regularly included. Often labelled 'jazz' but usually up-tempo foxtrots, it fulfilled the programmers' desire to make radio listening an interactive experience. Hoping that listeners at home would roll back the rugs in their parlours, 2YA devoted the evening of 26 August 1927 to a 'special jazz programme', with Allen's Dance Orchestra playing live-to-air from 8.00 pm until shutdown at 11.00 pm. It was an arduous evening for the

orchestra, who performed 23 pieces, all foxtrots except for three waltzes. To give the band – and those at home – a rest, their items were interspersed by solo singers and comedy acts. It was a bold move by the RBC: many in the audience were anti-dance music, yet it was the dancers who were irritated by the interruptions. In rural areas, some had organised public balls to take advantage of the live broadcasts. The dancers were especially outraged by the 10-minute break in which 2YA broadcast a lecture on the parliamentary system.[183]

Broadcasting live music every evening – of varying styles and qualities – made for dull radio, however, and in 1928 the RBC decided to coordinate its programming among its four urban stations. Each night, they would take turns offering a different style: while one played light opera, another could offer comedy, brass bands, talks or dance music. Listeners could tune in to RBC's other stations to satisfy their tastes. 'Saturday night would be uniformly "vaudeville" and Sunday just as uniformly sacred.'[184]

This policy made sense, although radio receivers were too primitive to pick up distant stations reliably yet. But that year listeners had begun to enjoy the benefit of electric pickups. No longer was music broadcast using a microphone aimed at a large gramophone horn; it now travelled through an electric stylus directly to the transmitter. The scratchy 78 was less apparent. The amount of recorded music on the air immediately increased, as did transmission hours.[185]

The technological advances altered the music itself, in the dance halls and on record. Lower frequency instruments were heard more successfully: tubas could be replaced by string basses, and eventually guitars would replace banjos. Electric microphones allowed vocalists with dance bands to drop their megaphones, and to stop shouting in the studio. A new style of singing emerged: crooning.[186]

Wellington baritone Billy Hart was one of the first New Zealand singers to learn how to use a microphone. It could enhance a performance but required a different approach: one could sing quietly, almost whisper, and the microphone would pick up every nuance. Accompanying himself on piano, the charismatic Hart became widely popular from his broadcasts on 2YA from 1927. He was then invited by HMV Australia to come to Sydney and make recordings of 'When You Come to the End of Your Day' and a film theme, 'South Sea Rose'.[187]

The theatres needed to keep pace with technology as well. Vaudeville peaked in the mid-1920s, but would remain popular for another decade. The young were attracted by the glamour of the cinema, so the vaudeville audience became more middle-aged. But the influence of vaudeville continued as entertainment evolved. The comic elements of community singing had links to music hall, and the early days of commercial radio relied on performers groomed in vaudeville. Also, many of the first real jazz musicians heard by New Zealanders came as part of a package vaudeville show, among them the bands of Bert Ralton and Linn Smith.

The new music was infiltrating the old order; when the musical comedy *Kid Boots* toured in 1925, it received rave reviews. Set around the most contemporary of sports – golf – this production was 'on a scale of Williamson magnificence, even to the inclusion of a real jazz band in the ballroom scene', reported the *NZ Theatre and Motion Picture*.[188]

The word 'jazz' may have attracted the publicity and the new styles of dancing much social opprobrium, but in the second half of the 1920s the big player in entertainment was cinema. Such was the exhibitors' confidence in the medium that large picture palaces began to be built around the country: Wellington's De Luxe; Dunedin's Empire and Regent; and Auckland's the Civic. Although films were the main event, these theatres continued to provide work for musicians and entertainers, often themed to tie in with the film.[189]

Competition was strong: every major cinema in town had its own orchestra, while Dunedin's Regent added a bonus, a performance by the Tom Katz saxophone band. Wearing blackface while dressed in comic bellboy uniforms and playing every saxophone in the instrument's family, the Katz band was famous for its virtuosic playing, humorous routines and intricate marching. Over at Fuller's, the George Ward Revue Company proudly stated its relevance: on the bill was the pioneering Australian jazz-band leader, trombonist Dave Meredith, with his band the Melody Five. They were advertised as 'six musicians, accomplished in all the gay, riotous ramifications of seductive syncopation'.[190]

Jazz could have been just a passing fad; nevertheless, the jazz players intimidated some traditional musicians. Black makeup removed, the Tom Katz band appeared at an after-show function at Dunedin's Orphans Club whose acclaimed orchestra included one saxophonist. After hearing the Tom Katz band play, he placed his instrument on the stage with a notice: 'For Sale Cheap'.[191]

DANCE FLOOR FLAPS

It was the novelty dances that defined the age and captured the headlines. In late 1925, a new, energetic dance arrived from the United States, shortly after sweeping through the dance halls of Britain. To novices who felt that dancing was all elbows and knees, this dance *was* all elbows and knees.

At the time, a 'natural movement technique' was beginning that distinguished modern from old-time dancing. Then a gatecrasher shocked the dance floors: the ungainly, if spirited, Charleston. 'Here was a dance which violated every rule of the newly established technique', recalled prominent Wellington dance teacher Phyllis Bates. 'Many will remember the twisting and flying feet, the tapping heels and bending knees to the rhythm of "I'm Gonna Charleston Back to Charleston".'[192]

The bright young things in knee-length skirts were labelled 'flappers' for their dizzy manner and the way their arms flapped like wings. What some saw as decadent showing off, dance teachers saw as an opportunity, and they offered lessons to curb the excesses perpetrated by the unschooled on the dance floor.

The initial, American version of the Charleston was 'decidedly eccentric and quite unsuited for the ballroom', said Bates. Exhibitions were given by overseas experts and local pros such as Eddie Hegan; one of the most prominent was in the Auckland Town Hall's concert chamber in July 1926, during a concert by the Ritz Dance Orchestra, 'direct from New York'. Double tickets were 7/6; for those who just liked to watch, single balcony seats were only a shilling. The Majestic cinema on Queen Street screened *How to Dance the Charleston*, a short, silent film by Arthur Murray, the American who taught the dance to the Prince of Wales. A Queen Street shoe shop even marketed the Dixie Charleston: 'the shoe the modern maid is wearing . . . for street, for dance, for sport and holiday wear'.[193]

Recorded by Sydney's Will Quintrell and his Tivolians especially for the New Zealand market in 1928, 'Breeze (Blow My Baby Back to Me)' accompanied the Yale Blues dance and was a massive hit. J. Albert & Son, Sydney, 1928

In October 1927, Bates took advantage of 2YA's powerful transmitter to give New Zealand's dancing public on-air lessons in the Charleston. The dance had kept evolving: English instructors simplified it 'to tame the wild exhibitionism' the dance seemed to encourage.[194]

But the Charleston was soon eclipsed in New Zealand in 1927 when the quickstep arrived, an adaptation of the foxtrot that suited the increasing tempos of the dance bands. The song 'Valencia' was ubiquitous, wrote Wellington historian Brian Salkeld, becoming 'the most hated in a dance band's repertoire, but there were a considerable number of people who thought it "divine" and continued to request it'.[195]

New Zealand's biggest dance phenomenon yet arrived in 1928: the Yale Blues. The success of this dance can be seen as a pioneering moment in the country's music industry, for it used a song that was especially recorded for the New Zealand market.[196]

'Breeze (Blow My Baby Back to Me)' became a hit in New Zealand due to the combined efforts of Bates and an astute Wellington record distributor, Sid Vause. Reports had come from Britain in late 1927 that the Yale was the new dance in London's fashionable *palais-de-danse*, to the delight of everyone: it was more graceful and practical than the Charleston, and the 'most desirable innovation since the foxtrot saved us from the monotony of the one-step'. It was also easy to master, its steps 'reminiscent of the pre-war tango' and its slower tempo of 48 to 50 bars per minute was 'just right for the British temperament'.[197]

Bates came across a sample of an American recording of 'Breeze' that seemed suitable for the Yale Blues. When Vause, the New Zealand rep for the British company Columbia, visited Bates in his studio with an 'official' tune for the Yale, they both agreed that 'Breeze' was better. However, it was on the Brunswick label out of the US – Vause's competition. So he found some sheet music of the 1919 song and sent it – with the record – over to Columbia in Sydney and asked them to copy it. Will Quintrell, the Sydney conductor who had formed the Tom Katz Saxophone Band, arranged the charts and recorded it with his Tivolians for Columbia. By April 1928, just nine months after the Yale Blues was unveiled in London, 'Breeze' was advertised for sale in Wellington, on disc (5/-), sheet music (2/-) or piano roll (7/6).[198]

Although 'Breeze' was a ten-year-old song, the Quintrell version was an immediate hit, selling 21,000 records in Wellington, Taranaki and Hawke's Bay alone.

'The record sold in thousands, far surpassing the sales of any other record before or since', said Bates in 1935. Vause's marketing campaign worked: at the chic Adelphi Cabaret in Wellington, 'Breeze' was played repeatedly by the Australian band Dave Meredith and His Melody Five. The craze for the dance spread; among those who gave exhibitions was New Zealand's doyenne of dance teachers, Margaret O'Connor. Bates wrote a column in *Truth* giving step-by-step instructions, saying the Yale Blues combined 'a lilt and a contrary body sway'.[199] A local sheet-music edition of 'Breeze' was published, with Meredith's band on the cover and advertisements for the record by Quintrell.[200]

While the Yale Blues was a favourite dance of 1928, its popularity soon faded. 'The original steps altered, and it became known simply as *the blues*', said Bates. A host of new dances appeared, all hoping to emulate the success of the Charleston and the Yale Blues. By July, the next dance trend was predicted on the B-side of another Yale Blues disc whose A-side was 'Shine On, Harvest Moon'. Dancers were encouraged to flip the disc and 'Do That Heebie-Jeebie Dance'.

The release of 'Shine On, Harvest Moon' saw a 'sensational rush' on record stores. At home, the rise in popularity of the gramophone record seemed unstoppable. On 30 June 1928, the government abolished the duty on records, enabling HMV and other firms to lower their prices. Newspapers started publishing weekly record review columns, at first of the light classics and then deigning to mention ballads, hillbilly and dance records. Display advertisements more accurately reflected the wide variety and topicality of releases: the haunting waltz 'Ramona' and Gershwin's *Rhapsody in Blue* arrived quickly. If a customer brought 50 packets of Chess – 'the perfect cork-tipped cigarette' – into a record store, they would be rewarded with a free, double-sided 10-inch Zonophone disc. Local hits included expatriate New Zealander Ernest McKinlay's ballads and Maori songs, recorded at Homebush, and comedy discs by the Black Crows. This black-faced US duo was so popular – in New Zealand and around the world – that their dubious catch-phrases became part of everyday dialogue. But most music advertising emphasised the desirability of dancing, to the latest music, almost in perpetual motion. Companies such as Albert's published portfolios of sheet music of popular dances for home and dance-band use, to songs such as 'Me and My Shadow', 'The Alabama Stomp', 'Blue Skies' and 'Bye Bye, Blackbird'.[201]

Looking back at the late 1920s, Phyllis Bates recalled the Black Bottom, Heebie Jeebies, Baltimore, Tile Trot, Varsity Drag, Skater's Waltz, Six-Eight, Viennese Waltz, Moochie, Blues Waltz, the Charleston Blues and the Croon. 'Some of these dances had the advantage of a distinctive musical rhythm, but none of them was taken up by the public', she said. They were more useful as display dances when professionals put on a show, and their steps were incorporated into the standard dances. But the Black Bottom had great popular appeal, with its provocative buttock-slapping move causing it to be banned in some clubs. The *Evening Post* described the dance as vulgar and 'too close to the antics of the jungle'.[202]

By the late 1920s, all the main centres had venues favouring modern styles of dancing. In Auckland, the two Dixieland cabarets had plenty of competition. Other leading venues included the Click-Clack in Newmarket and the Orange Hall in Newton. Attracting dancers from the eastern suburbs was Nixon's cabaret in Mission Bay, which began as an outdoor cabaret in 1926 at the tearooms of Richard Nixon. When it opened, recalled his daughter Elsie, the road from downtown Auckland was still unsealed, so Nixon chartered a bus to make the 45-minute journey from the central post office. He recruited a Maori dance band from nearby Orakei marae: 'They arrived immaculately turned out, with white trousers, leis around the neck – they really were something. Dad had advertised them as the Hawaiian Band. The bus arrived with people hanging off the sides, it was packed.'[203]

In the 1930s, the tearooms became a very popular venue called the Pig and Whistle. By then, the harbour-side road was sealed and musicians would arrive after their gigs were over in the city. 'We didn't get going really till 12 o'clock and then go till three in the morning', said Elsie Nixon. 'There were no residents to worry about then.'[204]

On the North Shore, a major entertainment venue was purpose-built beside the Milford beach. Following the success of the Picturedrome, a group of businessmen paid Fletcher Construction to build Ye Olde Pirate Shippe. It opened in January 1929, to 'a flourish of trumpets – or more precisely saxophones – prophetically in the middle of a howling north-easterly gale.'[205] Built to resemble a pirate ship, with several decks, three masts, a bowsprit and rigging, the venue contained dance floors, a sweet shop, tearooms and a penny arcade. The walls were 'festooned with ships' lanterns, cutlasses and pirate hats. Glass-covered hatches were opened to let the sea breezes waft inside the ballroom and a series of small cubicles around the edge of the dance area were formed from the "ribs" of the ship's hull', wrote Jacqueline Ottaway. Her mother would wistfully recall, 'It was a wonderful place for romance to blossom.'[206] The Pirate Shippe launched many before its demolition in 1957.

DANCE CARDS

By the late 1920s, there were weekly previews and reports of the prominent balls held in the main centres, many under the auspices of firms, societies or dance clubs. The musicians would occasionally be mentioned: 'The band, under Mr Clyde Howley's direction, played the latest and most popular dance music with its customary vigour . . . . Howley again gave an exhibition of the Black Bottom and the Argentine Tango.' The scene on the dance floor was of more interest to readers: every woman present at, for example, the Click-Clack had her outfit described. 'Miss Scantlebury, black satin and lace; Miss Ashton-Warner, cameo pink taffeta; Mrs Battle, apricot taffeta trimmed with gold lace . . .'.[207]

In the social pages of the *Weekly News*, Katherine Carr compared dances of the past with the contemporary craze. Then, the pace at balls had been stately, possibly in gavotte time, 'with deep, graceful curtseys and slow, mincing steps'. Now, in 1928, life itself was faster and 'young folk demanded something brisker and sprightlier; they invented the polka and the waltz, and couples danced joyously round, clasped in each other's arms, while the elder folk looked and whispered, "Oh, fie! What is the world coming to?"' The dancing youths, Carr wrote, would laugh and answer, 'Who knows and who cares?'

Carr dated the changes to the demise of the chaperone. Before the First World War, frocks were pale to be girlish and dainty, hair was elaborately styled and skirts swirled around ankles. The chaperones were 'plump and kindly in their black or lavender gowns', and 'smiled benignly and indulgently upon us' – unless a girl happened to be with the same escort for three or four dances. 'Those days are gone', Carr wrote.

> The war obliterated them completely and with them went chaperones and coil of hair and long skirts and lancers. Out of the war came jazz and, cheated of four years of our youth, we whirled into it. Still we dance on. We learn new steps with new, fascinating names, and we have forgotten the old dances and all the pomp and the ceremony that attended them. Today

girls do what they like in the ballroom. Emancipated from chaperones and gloves and long skirts, they dart, unescorted, across the floor . . .[208]

In rural New Zealand, however, the old dances still called the tune in 1928. 'The foxtrot may change, the Charleston and the Black Bottom may come and go, but the waltz, the schottische and the one-step still hold sway in the back-blocks. The back country has not yet tasted "jazz".' On New Year's Eve, the *Weekly News* predicted, Auckland cabarets would have been carnivalesque. But 'while city people are responding light-heartedly to "So Blue" and "Moonbeam, Kiss Her for Me", country folk will be gliding and twirling through the old waltz tunes.'

The *Weekly News* visited a typical dance in the backblocks of Taranaki. During the day, volunteers had decorated the wooden hall with greenery; at night, it was filled with dancers and – still – admiring matrons. The orchestra was just a piano on which 'a Maori youth, rising 20 years, strummed out the music'. He was wedded to the instrument and hardly left it during the evening, which lasted until about 3.00 am. Vamping was his specialty and this the dancers really enjoyed. He scorned the modern pieces, giving what seemed to be an endless repetition of 'Doodle, De Doo' and 'Show Me the Way to Go Home'.

There was no jazz on the programme; instead, the sixteen dances included waltzes, valetas, la rinkas, d'alberts, schottisches and one-steps. Besides the dancing, there were different rituals for drinking and getting home. A country dance involved an illicit keg of beer rather than hip flasks, and often an early morning horseback ride over rugged tracks.[209]

The urban dance scene hoped to convey an air of cosmopolitan sophistication, and in this it was assisted by the social pages of newspapers and magazines. By 1928 regular items on dancing were featured in the *Auckland Sun*, the *New Zealand Herald* and the *Observer*. Even *Truth* came to the party, exploiting the fad by publishing dancing instructions while at the same time stoking the perennial moral panic with headlines such as 'She Went to Cabaret at Thirteen' and 'She Met Him at a Dance'.[210]

The Wellington City Council was petitioned by dozens of inner-city residents to close regular dances held at the Early Settlers' Hall in Abel Smith Street. The patrons were said to be a rough crowd, many of them seamen. When police and city inspectors investigated, they found the

In February 1924, Begg's encouraged Wellingtonians to foxtrot to 'Swanee Smiles'. *NZ Theatre and Motion Picture.*

problem was not the behaviour inside the dance hall but outside: patrons going to and from their cars during the evening, making noise when leaving the dance, fighting, drinking, swearing, and especially 'the starting of cars and the blaring of motor horns'. The police wanted to cancel the hall's licence, while the council pondered a bylaw limiting parking near the hall, and its hours of operation.[211]

In Christchurch, the city council acted decisively, prohibiting dancing in public dance halls after 11.30 pm on Saturday nights. This brought indignation, not just from dance-hall proprietors, but also from the dancers themselves. 'It has even been suggested that a public indignation meeting should be held', reported the *Press.* One dancer declared: 'Imagine what the effect must be on overseas visitors who, going to a cabaret for a night's entertainment, find themselves sent home at 11.30. Sent home, mind you!' Another dancer recalled that dances used to carry on until daylight. Then 2.00 am finishes became the norm, and now it was 1.00 am. 'Perhaps the residents would not complain if those who attended the dances drove away in gigs drawn by horses. If they do not like to be disturbed, let them shift to some other locality.'

As with the Abel Smith Street dance hall, when residents were consulted about the issue, their responses ranged from outrage at being kept awake to denial that there was a problem. '"They have a most enjoyable time and don't create any nuisance at all", said one middle-aged householder. Asked if there was any noise when the dancers were leaving, he replied, "Good heavens no! Not at all."'[212]

FADE TO BLACK

It was not just a new, provocative form of music that gave the 1920s its nickname, the Jazz Age. Life was noisier. The population was becoming increasingly urban, sprouting new suburbs that could be reached by trams and cars. The architectural signature of this housing boom was the bungalow, an import from California. They came with electricity to power new gadgets such as vacuum cleaners and refrigerators. The changes in technology, entertainment, fashions and social mores had been giddying. Hemlines had risen, nightlife was less sedate, radios and gramophones were in most homes.

The popularity of the cinema, and its rapid response to change, exemplified how popular music was a beneficiary of developments in fashion and technology, and was also at their mercy. The high-profile, lucrative life of the silent film musician came and went in a fifteen-year period, recalled pianist Henry Shirley. 'A whole new branch of music-making was born, reached a splendid maturity and suddenly died. Thousands of musicians were needed in a hurry, so much teaching flourished. Everything connected with the production of music – composing, arranging, publishing and retailing – enjoyed a boom.'[213]

The bust occurred in 1929, when feature films with sound arrived in New Zealand. Already, some major theatre owners had cut costs by installing a Wurlitzer organ rather than hiring an orchestra.[214] April 18 was the pivotal day. Two years after Al Jolson starred in the first successful talkie, *The Jazz Singer*, Auckland's Regent unveiled the courtroom drama *The Bellamy Trial*, which had a brief talking scene. Two weeks later, the first 'all-talkie' opened at the Princess: *The Singing Fool*, another Al Jolson vehicle. It ran for weeks.

Musicians felt the impact of the talkies almost immediately. For veteran violinist Harry Engel, it was especially bad timing. He had played at the opening of His Majesty's in 1902, and was always in demand for the best theatre and cinema jobs in Auckland. In 1926 he was wooed to the Majestic by the manager Phil Hayward, who offered him a twenty-year contract. But Engel said he didn't want a 'life sentence': a two-year contract would do. On the very last day of the contract the whole 26-piece orchestra was sacked: the talkies had arrived.[215]

1930-1939

When the silents turned to sound in 1929, it was just in time for the redundant musicians to participate in the next development in popular music. The jazz-influenced music of the 1920s' 'dance craze' would become even more popular in the 1930s. The cinema boom enabled lavish nightclubs to be built on the premises, such as Auckland's Civic Wintergarden and Wellington's Majestic. These gave the elite and influential a venue, and the best contemporary musicians regular work. As the Depression deepened, however, their fees plummeted and the 'wild' dance fashions of the 1920s jazz age calmed down.

Concurrent with the Depression, increased radio ownership provided cheap instant access to the latest music styles. Through live broadcasts, radio airplay exposed the talents of top jazz musicians to people who would never be able to visit the metropolitan clubs. Arthur Pearce's long-running programme *Rhythm on Record* was essential listening for jazz aficionados and musicians, and hugely influential. Also significant were several overseas bands that visited for lengthy periods, eventually employing many New Zealand musicians and passing on authentic performance styles. Local band leaders became stars, through residencies and broadcasts.

Musicians turned their focus towards America for their inspiration, not just in the dance field but also in country music. Tex Morton emerged as New Zealand's first international country star. In the more conservative – and British influenced – genre of light music, band leaders and performers such as Ossie Cheesman, Gil Dech and Henry Rudolph became widely popular. Swing was in, but not for all.

Theo Walters' Personality Band – with guest singer from the US, Bob Parrish – at the opening of the Christchurch station 3ZB in September 1938. From left are: Bob Parrish, Theo Walters, Jim Watters, Roy Lester, Phil Campbell and George Campbell. (A second trumpeter is obscured.) Photo News Agency/RNZ Sound Archives

From Douglas Lilburn to Johnny Devlin, with the Ratana brass bands and many others in between, musicians in Wanganui have made a strong contribution to New Zealand music. This musical group from Wanganui was photographed by Frank James Denton of Tesla Studios c. 1930. F-17321-1/1, Alexander Turnbull Library, Wellington

TWO | Mood Swings

the 1930s

Ten days out from 1930, a fanfare of trumpets heralded the gala opening of the Civic Theatre on Queen Street, Auckland. Built in less than a year, the fantasy Moorish architecture of the Civic was immediately appreciated by its inaugural, packed house on 20 December 1929. 'All the glamour of the Orient is spread before the audience and vice-like holds its attention', reported the next morning's paper, declaring the celebration 'one of the outstanding events in the theatrical history of Auckland'.

But the band playing the overture was nowhere to be seen. In a few moments, the overture became louder as a large, ornate gondola appeared on the stage. The 'barge' had risen from the depths of the theatre on a hydraulic lift, and on it was a 30-piece orchestra led by Ted Henkel, an American based in Australia. They played Ponchielli's *Dance of the Hours*, exhibiting 'vitality and fire', and Henkel also received a bouquet: 'He is a musician for whom Auckland should be grateful.' The orchestra then accompanied a silent film that had been especially shot to illustrate the music, the lush scenery providing a backdrop to items from Mendelssohn and Liszt.

Henkel's 'much heralded' stage band then emerged, arrayed on a staircase, and playing 'I'll Always Be in Love With You'. A painted backdrop showed the sun rising upon a brave new world of entertainment. An acrobatic trio and ballet display prepared the audience for the finale before intermission: a virtuoso exhibition by Fred Scholl on the theatre's Wurlitzer organ.

Then the real show stopper could begin, the debut screening of a feature film with the latest novelty: sound. A comedy set in London, *Three Live Ghosts* was quickly forgotten, especially with *Gold Diggers of Broadway* doing great business at the St James, and Alfred Hitchcock's first talkie *Blackmail* on at the Strand. Advertisements for the Civic's rivals testify to the almost complete takeover of talkies or 'synchronised sound' films among Auckland's cinemas, only a few months after they had arrived in New Zealand.[1]

Technological developments had already impacted upon musicians in the 1920s: the popularity of records and the emergence of radio. As the 1930s began, they suffered another double blow with the Depression and the introduction of films with sound. The public now had less disposable income for entertainment, and the talkies could provide music without the need for actual musicians. But the hydraulic barge on which the Civic's orchestra had ascended hinted at the theatre's exotic underworld: the Wintergarden, a glamorous Auckland dance venue for the next 25 years.

The jazz-age buoyancy of the late 1920s that had inspired an expansion in the entertainment industry was now peaking at just the wrong time. Two months after the Civic opened, after fifteen years of discussion, Dunedin's new Town Hall opened on 15 February 1930. The £85,525 building was partly paid for by the proceeds of the 1925–26 Exhibition, with the town's pipe organ costing an additional £17,000. Elsewhere in Dunedin, though, the conversion of theatres into cinemas capable of screening talkies was an indication that an era had ended. Vaudeville entrepreneur John Fuller announced that the venerable Princess would be refurbished as a 'talkie theatre' in just a few weeks. Risking sacrilege, Fuller said that in many respects the cinema would offer better entertainment than live theatre. The music was by the great orchestras of the world and acts were a lot closer on the screen.[2]

Within a year, the Depression's effect on theatrical entertainment was apparent. Many months could now pass between visits by overseas acts. Ticket prices at the cinema fell to as little as threepence per session, and the lavish musical productions featured on the screen also lifted expectations on the stage. 'All this posed increasing economic problems for the live promoters, many of whom were driven off the circuit', recalled Walter Sinton.[3]

Assisted by radio, theatres and halls were packed in the early years of the Depression: but not for entertainment that made box-office music for promoters.

Radio Record – Tuesday, 1 January 1929
2YA schedule
10.01 pm: Community sing
Artists, Staff, and Listeners, 'Love's Old Sweet Song' (John Molloy) (soloist: Mrs Albert Russell). (Listeners are asked to join in this number with the artists and staff. This will be the first time a 'Community Sing' has been broadcast.)
10.05 pm: Dance programme

A form of popular music at its most populist was the Community Sing movement that swept through the country, especially in the 1930s. The Sings were a weekly event in many centres, in a town hall or theatre, during winter and spring. Often they were midweek during a lunch hour, with live broadcasts on the YA or ZB stations taking them nationwide and even across to Australia, gleaning more participants and donors. Their heyday was during the Depression, but this phase was really a revival rather than an innovation: the Sings had actually begun in Wellington in 1922, led by a committee of stalwarts that included vaudevillian Ella Shields and local musical

éminence grise H. Temple White. Soon, 3000 people would pack the Town Hall, a contemporary account reasoning that 'there is psychologically a cheer germ in community singing'. The Sings were informal, encouraging people to come and go, bring their lunch or even some knitting. The audience would heckle the performers, and often celebrities would be invited to sustain their interest: Harry Lauder, Dame Sybil Thorndike, an All Black team, visiting sailors and politicians all took part. An MC would auction off their talents: 'What do you think he's worth? Come on now! At least a fiver, surely!'[4]

In Dunedin, where the Sings continued long after other centres had lost interest, they were dominated by three men called Demmy, Himmy and Alfie. Herbert Desmoulins and Jimmy Himberg were front men, a comic double-act, while Alf Pettitt was their foil – a shy pianist who could play any song, by sightreading or by ear. Like circus barkers, their role was to keep the crowds actively involved, and to keep the donations rolling in for relief funds during the Depression. The Sings were broadcast each week, and listeners would take part by donating 'cheerios': cash or items to be auctioned. These could be anything from a case of apples or 10 pounds of potatoes to silk stockings or a baby's bonnet. From 1931 to 1950, Dunedin's Sings were estimated to have raised £45,000 for charity. During the war, the Sings became patriotic events, the funds going to the war effort or welfare.[5]

Musicologist Michael Brown suggests that the repertoire of the Sings fell in three categories. There was a core repertoire of songs that everybody knew, such as parlour songs, patriotic songs, sea shanties and hymns. There were popular songs, whether current or from before the First World War, such as 'K-K-K-Katy', 'You're In Style When You're Wearing a Smile', 'Happy Days Are Here Again' and 'Bye Bye, Blackbird'. And there were novelty items such as parodies, Kiwiana, local and 'cheerio' songs. The latter group featured snippets of well-known tunes that had been adapted to convey the hyper-optimism peculiar to popular song in this era. Among them were 'The Joy Germ Song', 'The Happy Song' and 'Keep On Smiling'.[6] Other ideas to keep the crowds smiling were limerick competitions, rounds, 'song battles' and sitting-and-standing contests.

The Sings became like spontaneous variety shows, with local performers of all kinds making a contribution, especially in the grand finales at the end of each season: singers, dance bands, soloists, harmonica bands, 'even precocious five-year-olds making their public debuts'.[7] They were predominantly good fun, but with a serious agenda: to bond struggling communities and to help the needy. 'Workers, shoppers, students, school pupils (if they could get in and out incognito) and country visitors all flocked to the theatre', wrote Irene Gurr. 'They had fun, they made great music . . . they had a sense of belonging.'[8]

Concurrent with the Depression, the 'new miracle' of radio became commonplace in homes, just as the silent film era came to an end, taking with it hundreds of musicians' jobs. Heavily dependent on music in its early years, radio brought the latest songs and styles into more homes, more quickly. In the long term, this stimulated the dance-band environment so that a live scene featuring accomplished, jazz-aware bands was in place when swing emerged later in the 1930s. The milieu of the silent film pit band directly influenced the players of the swing era. Small combos of disparate instrumentation required flexibility and agility to leap from 'cowboy music' to 'custard-pie music', accompanying chase scenes, love scenes and death-bed scenes.

There was plenty of scope for improvising: 'the variety . . . sent shivers down the back of any competent musician who was unlucky enough to be in the audience', said visiting Australian broadcaster and musician Dr Keith Barry. 'In due time the music of the silent films improved . . . and just before the talkies came, city cinemas of the world had begun to build up first-class symphony orchestras. Then [came] the talkies . . . and existing ideas and ideals crashed overnight. The industry became panic-stricken and the first thing to be sacrificed was the orchestra.'[9]

As a boy, Jules Regal had spent the First World War serving his musical apprenticeship on trombone in Auckland's Fifth Battalion Band. He then trained as a pit piano player, to accompany silent movies. 'Unfortunately the Depression came and the talkies came and my career vanished, liked thousands of other musicians in New Zealand', he recalled. 'That's how I got into the Columbian Dance Band and from there on I had to learn chords.'[10]

Many paying gigs evaporated with the Depression. For a while, the Auckland musicians organised Sunday concerts that also included a 'talkie', but a strong faction on the city council disapproved of entertainment on Sundays and put an end to the musicians' 'innocent means of raising funds to assist a body of men and their families'.

The council also required that every item in the concerts be submitted to the town clerk, who was 'entrusted by the City Council with the important duties of censor'. To add insult to injury, the town clerk – Mr J. S. Brigham, a man often called 'czar of the town hall' – was also the president of the Auckland Municipal Officers' Guild, whose members did not want to work on Sundays.[11]

On 9 April 1930, the Internal Affairs Minister, the Hon. P. A. de la Perrelle, received a deputation that expressed the 'serious plight of the professional musicians who had been displaced from employment by the introduction of the "talkies", and the increased use of the gramophone in restaurants and other places of assembly'. The Minister sympathised and appealed to those who had previously employed musicians to now reconsider. The popularity of 'mechanical music' meant there was a 'grave danger of the art of music being lost to the community'. His sympathies were with one style of music, however: 'I know of instances where sons and daughters of musicians, attracted by the modern form of music, are neglecting the opportunity to take up the serious study of natural music.'[12]

On 10 March 1931, the secretary of the New Zealand Musicians' Association, Frank Egerton, said that conditions for musicians were steadily getting worse. The importing of Australian musicians compounded the threats of the talkies and recorded music; an example was the Adelphi Cabaret in Wellington. 'Seven musicians will be displaced. Owing to the state of the music profession throughout the world, it is almost impossible for a musician to obtain employment, except in his own country.'[13]

Overseas, foreign musicians needed work permits or a union card before they could perform. The Australian Musicians' Union entrance fee was substantial – £21 – and six months residency was also obligatory. But Australians coming to New Zealand could immediately become members of the musicians' union after paying the five shillings entrance fee.[14]

Professional dance bands also found themselves being undercut by amateurs, and so were forced to lower their fees well below the union rate of fifteen shillings per musician. 'The low prices caused a number of really good men to disgustedly give the game [away]; others have left the country', wrote Wellington *Music Maker* correspondent Jack McEwen.[15]

Bass player Spike Donovan recalled, 'All the musicians were out of work, full stop. No one had any money to come to the places . . . . Doing a job from 8.00 pm until

Kings of swing: Auckland's branch executive of the New Zealand Musicians' Union, 1939. Back row, from left: Epi Shalfoon, Johnny Madden, P. J. Lye, Ian 'Nin' Pitcaithly, C. Alldritt. Front row: Bert Peterson, P. D. Buffett (president), Frank Egerton (secretary).
Dennis Huggard Archive, PAColl-9492-11, Alexander Turnbull Library, Wellington

midnight, 2/6 to five shillings was top money. At one time the Pirate Shippe, which was over the other side of the harbour, was charging 3/6 a double, and that included a free bus trip from Devonport out to the ship and back again, and a light supper.' A single ticket at the door got as low as sixpence.[16]

Also, conservatism returned to the dance floor, where the waltz challenged its usurper the foxtrot: worldwide, the decadent jazz age appeared to be over. The public

wanted music that suggested 'domestic stability', wrote Australian jazz historian Bruce Johnson, songs such 'My Blue Heaven', 'Goodnight Sweetheart', 'When Day is Done' and 'I'll See You in My Dreams'. In straitened times, the professional musician needed to keep an eye on the market. 'The dance band industry was generally at some pains to distance itself from the jazz fashion of the '20s, now so inappropriately indecorous and so embarrassingly dated.'[17]

A New Zealand fashion columnist predicted that winter 1930 would see a revival of 'the quaint old dances of bygone days, so different from the modern hectic whirl of "heebie-jeebies", "Charleston" and saxophone. There is fashion in dancing as in all things, and its recent phase has been inevitable, because it is in dancing that man expresses his mood of the moment . . . . We have not succumbed completely to the wiles of jazz; in fact some of us are rather tired of it, and are anticipating new things this winter.'[18]

Looking back three years later, McEwen confirmed this was the case: 'The Depression has caused the public to request simple melody tunes, and a heavy swing back to old-time dancing has characterized 1933. This is probably only a passing phase, as was the "jazz" era of 1918.'[19] The Realm in Hataitai held a 'funeral of jazz' before switching to old-time, only to get a full house.

However, Arthur Pearce, already regarded as an authority on jazz in New Zealand, observed that although in America fashion had swung towards the sweet and pleasant, in New Zealand the majority of dance bands still favoured the 'snappy and stimulating' to the soft, crooning fare. The top bands in New Zealand in 1933, said Pearce, were those led by Mervyn Bree (Peter Pan, Auckland), Tommy Stratton (Majestic, Wellington), the High-hatters (Mayfair, Wellington) and the Bailey-Marston band (the Winter Garden Cabaret, Christchurch). 'These bands could not hope to remain popular in the Dominion if they featured the Paul Whiteman type of jazz to the exclusion of the "gingery" music that New Zealanders seemed to prefer.' By March 1934, McEwen noticed that old-time was once again waning; the return of modern dancing would bring jazz-oriented players more work.[20]

Like Pearce, some of the bands were able to keep up with the latest overseas hits through personal contacts or even their own travel. Musicians playing on board the *Niagara* and *Aorangi* were particularly influential, as the steamers had a circuit that included Vancouver, San Francisco, Honolulu, Suva, Sydney and Auckland. Bill Egerton, a drummer in ships' bands, said that he learnt a modern style of drumming from going to nightclubs and dance halls while on leave in the States, to listen to the rhythm sections.[21]

Whenever the *Niagara* pulled away from Queen's Wharf in Auckland, an American trumpet player in the ship's band would get up on the bow of the ship and play 'Now is the Hour':

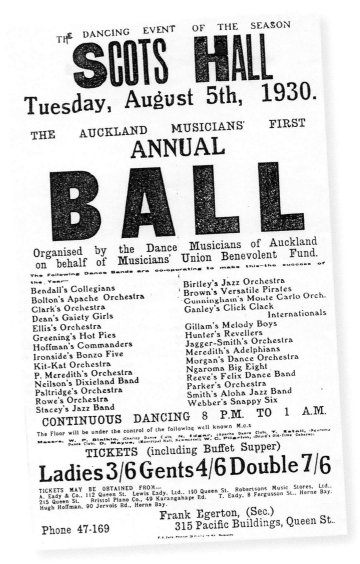

As the only night that musicians could hear their peers, there was no shortage of talent at the annual ball organised by the Auckland Musicians' Union. This flyer is from the first ball, in 1930. Dennis Huggard collection

This man would bring the latest music back for us, at the Dixieland or Peter Pan. We'd hear [the music] on records – he'd bring us the latest, the Victor records, and Maurie Gilman would copy the arrangements. You'd hear a good tune and sing it to him, and it'd be orchestrated that night. In later years, we would get music sent over, and arrangements done. We would pick out maybe three we liked. But these tunes had already been proved popular.[22]

Also on the *Niagara* was Ted 'Chips' Healy, a steward and saxophonist playing dinner and dance music. When the steamer arrived in Auckland, he would provide Vern Wilson at the Dixieland Cabaret with new arrangements acquired in the States. 'Chips brought back a lot of good pieces', said Wilson. 'They'd go to dances over there and come back and tell us what they were doing.'

Healy would become one of Auckland's most prominent musicians. A member of Ted Henkel's orchestra for the opening of the Civic, he would soon lead the band there, a role he held for nearly twenty years. The son of a trombonist in the Artillery Brass Band, Healy was teaching himself the clarinet when he saw his first saxophone and became an instant convert. A regular dance-band performer before joining the *Niagara*, in 1923 Healy played in Auckland's first experiment broadcast from Scots Hall on Symonds Street. A technician asked him to blow his saxophone into a massive horn. 'I had to practically climb right inside', said Healy, who played the latest hit 'Yes! We Have No Bananas'. He was doubtful about the technology but to his surprise, 'Some people fiddling with their crystal sets actually heard us.'[23]

With his band from the Pirate Shippe, Healy appeared in the early Rudall Hayward talkie *A Daughter of Auckland*, miming the song 'That Certain Party' to a gramophone record. After time spent in a Fuller's vaudeville pit band, he settled into the first saxophonist's seat at the Civic Wintergarden. It was a busy night: the band played an overture in the main theatre then backed the ballet show. While the main feature was on, the musicians would linger backstage, yarning and smoking cigarettes; one of them would keep an eye on the action to give the band its cue. Spike Donovan recalled the routine: 'We would sneak onto the bandstand five minutes before the end of the picture, while everything was in darkness. We'd have our instruments tuned and already be on the barge. Then we would come up as the picture finished, blowing lustily popular tunes of the day or perhaps an extract from that particular picture. The crowd always stopped for about five minutes to hear the band play, and enjoy it. That was something they got for nothing.' Then, the band would descend in the barge, having wooed couples to the cabaret, and the dancing would begin, to tunes such as 'Top Hat', 'Sugar Plum' and 'I'm in the Mood for Love'; at 1.00 am supper would be served.[24]

Fastidious about presentation, Healy wore white tie and tails as he led the band, dressed in dinner suits. Although he was billed as 'Ted Healy' he was always referred to as Chips: the affectionate nickname came from his wily way of doing deals. 'He was good-tempered, and a very good boss', said Spike Donovan. 'He was paying professional wages and he expected professional conduct

and ability. I think every good musician in Auckland at one time or another played for Chips.'[25]

Vern Wilson was always amused by Healy's secretive nature. 'We used to call him the Mystery Man. We never knew who his girlfriends were, where he went or what he did. Matter of fact, I never met his wife. He used to leave each night and you never knew which direction he went in. Being the leader, he had no music to put away or instrument, and he would be off while we were packing. One time we tried to trail him.' Nevertheless, Healy 'was a remarkable man. He became a leader because of his personality, and his knowledge of music. He was never an arranger, but he had a good ear. He could detect when anything was wrong.'[26]

To Healy, being a musician at the time was like being part of an amiable brotherhood. The musicians enjoyed playing together, the audiences felt that too, and they enjoyed listening and dancing to them. 'Musicians were good drinkers, too', he said just before he died in 1982. 'We'd meet in the pub in the afternoons. That's where you found people you were looking for . . . where the word of jobs got passed around.'[27]

In 1935 Healy heard that New Zealander Maurie Gilman's band was about to leave its residency at the Ginger Jar in Sydney. Although some regarded it as a dubious venue – 'there were some good fights there and occasionally pistols were drawn' – the Ginger Jar was a place where musicians were appreciated by the varied clientele, and jam sessions were encouraged. The woman who owned the cabaret was on holiday in Auckland. Impressed by Healy's band, she offered them the job.[28]

En masse, the band quit the Civic, and bought new suits and boat tickets to Sydney; among them were Ossie Cheesman, Vern Wilson and drummer Alan Brown. They were broke when they arrived, but their Ginger Jar residency was assured. What happened next was a pivotal event in trans-Tasman relations between musicians. Recalled Healy, 'The unions were very strong over there and they were waiting for us. They wouldn't let us play.' The New Zealanders were left high and dry. They could either return to Auckland, jobless, or split up and try and find work individually. 'They said, "If you like you can join the union" – it was about £20 whereas here it was 7/6', said Wilson. 'Ossie, Alan Brown and I stayed. I eventually got a trumpet job out at Coogee. They said, "You're good. Where are you from?" *New Zealand*. "You one of that mob that came over?" *Yes*. They never talked to me again that night.'

Chips Healy with 'a swell outfit', the dance band he formed at the RNZAF base at Hobsonville, 1941. From left: Jim Warren, Nolan Rafferty, Bruce Craighead, Gerry Horsup, Baden Brown, Chips Healy and Dick Morris. Jim Warren collection

Wilson auditioned for another job at the Palais Royale in Sydney. The band leader hired him immediately, then asked where he had been playing. 'New Zealand', said Wilson. 'He said, "I'm sorry." The union had put the screws on him. That's how tough it was.' Wilson, with a wife and child to support, eventually got a job in Brisbane; Cheesman joined a band on a cruise ship visiting the Pacific Islands. Healy and others headed home, having sailed for Australia 'under a misapprehension', reported the *Australian Music Maker and Dance Band News*, 'and the band is now a thing of the past'.[29]

Soon, Healy was back at the Civic, though under straitened circumstances. By November 1936, a reduced band struggled to fill the spacious Wintergarden with music. 'A drop from 12 instruments to six is certainly a wallop and it doesn't give the band a fair go.' Even through the Depression, though, the venue was popular. 'People wanted entertainment in hard times', Healy recalled.[30]

When the war began, Healy joined the RNZAF and formed a stellar band at the Hobsonville air force base. First to be recruited to this 'swell outfit' was his close friend Baden Brown, the second saxophonist in the Civic band

(and later Healy's partner for nearly 30 years in a musical instrument repair business). Another was trumpeter Jim Warren: 'They had to try and find guys within the personnel of the air force to make the band up. It was pretty hard going because there were not many musical people about. So Chips approached Nolan Rafferty and me to join up.' Musicians had to take up an air force trade, while playing in the band after hours. The bass player Charlie Fuller came from a folk music background, and used a three-string bass. Albert Hansard, another bass player, occasionally doubled on the sousaphone, giving the arrangements the sound of an American society band.[31]

After the war, Healy was again hired to lead the band at the Civic. For another ten years, he donned his white tie and tails to appear at the Wintergarden, sometimes whipping across to the 1ZB radio theatre for a quick live broadcast while the film was on. He wheeled and dealed, and led bands at the top balls in the city: 'His band could swing into ragtime, Dixieland, boogie-woogie, rhythm and blues at the twitch of their leader's coat-tails.' When the Civic Wintergarden cabaret suddenly closed in June 1955, Chips Healy's famous big band was a sextet.[32]

Cinema was the essence of democratic entertainment, akin to the community and rural dance halls. Films offered a window to an alluring world, and their popularity the financial means to emulate it. Opened in 1929, the same year as the Civic Wintergarden and the Crystal Palace, Wellington's Majestic Cabaret was another by-product of the late 1920s cinema boom. When the Fuller-Haywards theatre chain opened the 2500-seat Majestic picture theatre at 100 Willis Street in May 1929, space for a cabaret was allocated downstairs. For the next 55 years, it was Wellington's most prestigious ballroom, where the smartest people danced to the finest bands.[33]

For most of that time the proprietor was Fred Carr, always impeccably dressed, and finicky about his club's presentation and decorum: fresh flowers daily, spotless crockery. Irascible but generous, he was 'very artistic and ruled the place with an iron fist', said Jim Gower. 'He didn't like raucous, loud music, even jazz had to be easy to listen to.' In the early 1930s, Carr also ran the Ritz restaurant in Manners Street, a large, lavishly decorated room – oak-lined walls, linen tablecloths and silver cutlery – where a combo from the Majestic band performed music acceptable to ladies who lunched or took afternoon tea during the week. Concerts were scheduled for place on Sunday nights. The venture failed – the building later became the Manners Street Post Office – and Carr is said to have walked out with just a gold cage containing a bird.[34]

The atmosphere and standards to which Carr aspired meant that the Majestic quickly became Wellington's premiere dance destination. It was the hub of a small music precinct: across the road was the Nimmo's building, which contained a music instrument shop and a concert hall, and hosted early radio broadcasts by jazz bands in the 1930s and, post-war, meetings and jam sessions of the Wellington Swing Club. A commercial photographer in the building took photos of the well-dressed couples at the Majestic and would have the prints ready for sale as they left.

Lauri Paddi (centre) with his band, backstage at the Majestic Cabaret, Wellington, in the late 1930s. Beside him, in the spotted tie, is Majestic owner Fred Carr. Others in the picture include (front, from left) Bob Girvan and Jack Roberts; and at the back, from left, Pete McMurray, Art Rosoman, Ted Hall, Norm D'Ath and Bill Sinclair. The cigarette smoker and the woman are unknown. E. M. Alderdice Collection, PA1-q-182-10, Alexander Turnbull Library, Wellington

BLUE SMOKE

Cheer up at the Peter Pan: a 1936 marketing campaign floats down Customs Street, Auckland.
Dennis Huggard Archive, F-90428-35mm-10, Alexander Turnbull Library, Wellington

Around the corner on Manners Street were other music and record stores, such as Begg's, and Jack McEwen's, where musicians could buy a new reed or record, pick up a gig or just shoot the breeze.

The Majestic Cabaret stage was outlined with neon lights, and the dance floor was originally made of glass bricks, lit from below. Ruined during the war by the heavy boots of dancing American marines, it was replaced by a sprung wooden floor. Windows at the top of the room opened onto the grand staircase of the Majestic Theatre; Carr ensured that the curtains were left open as the films came out, with the band playing, so that departing film-goers could be tantalised by glimpses of the dancers in the cabaret. During the week, the functions were mostly private: the annual balls of businesses, organisations and debutantes, booked up to three years in advance. On other nights members of the public – such as the more elegant film-goers – could attend the cabaret if they could afford the entrance fee and were suitably dressed; eventually lounge suits were acceptable.

Alcohol was illegal but the Majestic was never dry. Patrons brought their own inside women's fur coats or handbags, then hid the bottles beneath the overhanging tablecloths or inside the cabaret's false chimneys, which had concealed shelves. If the police or, more enthusiastically, city council officers made an inspection, immediately the spirits bottles would evaporate, leaving only ginger ale or tonic mixers on the tables.

The Auckland venue most similar to the Majestic was the Peter Pan Cabaret on Lorne Street, which also paid top rates for long residencies and so attracted the best musicians. There, recalled Jim Warren, the prized seats were beside the windows overlooking Rutland Street:

Sometimes there would be a guy with a strong fishing line or rope. He would throw it out through the window, down to the street, perhaps 20 feet below. A mate would be down there and he would have the grog. He would attach it to the line to be hauled up . . . avoiding the bouncers on the door. In the middle of the ball in would come the police, usually two or three of them. They would go around and the grog would all go under the tables, or even under the women's long skirts. That was all part of the thrill of it.[35]

Like the Majestic, the Peter Pan hosted many live broadcasts and had a musician-friendly manager, Neil Edgar. It also experienced a boom during the war, and with its regular balls and weekend dances stayed in business through changes in fashion; in 1952 the Peter Pan relocated to Queen Street and took over the Metropole's lease. Some of its liveliest nights took place from the late 1940s when the Musicians' Union hosted its annual ball, and half a dozen of the city's top bands would be chosen to perform for their peers. These balls were a rare opportunity to hear rival bands; inevitably they became cutting contests. Union secretary Tom Skinner would MC and, from 1954, the Epi Shalfoon Memorial Cup was awarded to the best dancers among band leaders and their partners ('Perhaps musicians can dance, after all', reported Jim Warren). Spike Donovan recalled the night an Australian band leader turned up late to an important night at the Peter Pan. 'He strolls in, as drunk as a lord, eating a meat pie with the gravy running down the front of his shirt. He said to the manager, "I've been listening to the band – I've got a bloody good band, haven't I?" The manager said, "You did have. You're fired!"'[36]

The Peter Pan's competition in central Auckland was the Metropole, which opened on 16 July 1938 at the top of Queen Street. No expense was spared preparing this 6000-square-foot ballroom. Multi-coloured neons highlighted the shell-like proscenium arch in the largest of two ballrooms. Vaudeville veteran Ernie Beacham led a new big band from the piano; the band's formation poached several players from Art Larkins, who ran what was regarded as the best swing group in town. Larkins' band was often featured at the Peter Pan, or at Romano's on Karangahape Road, a venue known for being less-than-selective about its clientele ('a lot of chaps off the boats and their lady friends', said Spike Donovan).[37]

Frederick Rayner's second Dixieland Cabaret – 'by the sea' at Point Chevalier – was a large, airy building overlooking the water. It was hailed as the finest and most modern dance venue in Australasia. The 3600-square-foot dance floor could accommodate 600 people, with lighting concealed inside the scarlet walls, and spotlights illuminating the tables and cubicles along the sides. Underneath the cabaret were bathing sheds to enable night-time, flood-lit swimming. The Point Chevalier Dixieland hosted celebrities such as Australian aviator Charles Kingsford Smith, American heiress Barbara Hutton and the departing 1935 All Black team. The venue flourished until 10 September 1935, when the manager woke up in his flat at 3.30 am to find the building ablaze. It was gutted before the fire brigade arrived, and never rebuilt.

Just over a year later, another Auckland waterfront cabaret came to a dramatic, suspicious end. A schooner was transformed into a cabaret called the Showboat and moored off a wharf at Mechanic's Bay. Led by Trevor Eady, the band was highly regarded, but business was slow. After a dance one night in late 1936, the cabaret was the victim

Opened in 1925, the second Dixieland Cabaret was a lavish venue 'by the sea' at Point Chevalier, Auckland, until it was gutted by fire in 1935. Neg. 7-A11118, Auckland City Libraries

Formed in the mid-1920s, for over ten years the Bailey-Marston Orchestra was the leading dance band
in Christchurch. By 1930 it had started to be heard nationwide due to a radio relay from the Winter Garden Cabaret.
Bailey is the sousaphone player at the back; Marston is the saxophonist second from the right. *Radio Record*, 7 June 1935

of industrial sabotage when vandals bored holes in the hull
beneath the water line. Soon the entire lower dance floor
was submerged in four feet of water. The Showboat was
refloated, towed away and briefly reopened before being
scuttled near Rangitoto.[38]

Dancing was clearly a danger as well as a moral
threat, especially in Christchurch where the city council
continually discussed the issue, and decided in 1929 to ban
dancing after 11.30 pm on Saturday nights.[39] A feature of
the city's nightlife was the number of men who arrived at
dances on their bicycles, balancing on the bar a girlfriend
in full-length gown; musicians had the added complication
of carrying their instruments as well as their girlfriends.

Christchurch had many dance halls and cabarets, the
most famous being the Winter Garden on Armagh Street.
On one wall, beneath the ornate plaster ceiling, was a
mural: 'a sylphan scene with females dancing'. Originally,
the painted dancers were nude, but the city council did
not approve and an artist was commissioned to dress
them in gossamer-thin red frocks. The Winter Garden
opened in 1927 as a ballroom and function venue, and
was still operating, almost preserved, well into the 1960s.
For nearly twenty years, the Bailey-Marston Orchestra
was in residence: a ten-piece band formed in 1928 by
amalgamating the bands of bass player Harold Bailey and
pianist Les Marston. Bailey's Jazz Band had formed in the
early 1920s. With the extra players the band could split
into two groups, to perform continuously through the
evening, including the supper break.

'As the best band in town it always gave a polished
performance and players were well groomed and
immaculately dressed', recalled Bill Gamble. 'For a big
hunt club ball one year, every member of the band was
fitted with a specially tailored uniform from Ballantynes.
They wore vivid red jackets.'[40] Occasionally the ballroom
was so packed that its sprung dance floor seemed about to
collapse, so the band would stop playing.

Another Christchurch big band in demand during
the 1930s was the Dawson-Winfield Orchestra, which
played at society dances. A freelance ten-piece, including
two violinists, it secured all the 'big jobs' in Christchurch
even though it emphasised modern dance styles rather
than old-time. Each year they played the biggest function
in Christchurch, the combined Army, Navy and Airforce
Ball, at which up to 700 guests – the men in different
dress uniforms – packed Beath's tearooms. The Dawson-
Winfield Orchestra was also commissioned to accompany
vaudeville revues.

Christchurch had its own Dixieland Cabaret, at the
corner of Chancery Lane and Cathedral Square from the
1920s. Here, Les Marston and Bob Bradford cut their teeth
as band leaders. Other leading venues included Frascati's

Johnny Madden, the 'crooning drummer', gets his driver's licence from Lauri Paddi in the late 1930s. He was still playing in the early 1980s. E. M. Alderdice Collection, PA1-q-182-29-1, Alexander Turnbull Library, Wellington

restaurant and, from 1938, the Mayfair Lounge. But the city's biggest dance hall was at Ferry Road, in an old bus factory. In the early 1930s, the large building served as a dance hall and roller-skating rink, operated by the colourful promoter Reg Stillwell. At a time when the Depression forced him to lower his door prices to as little as threepence, he still had to work at attracting a clientele by holding theme nights such as A Hard-Up Kitchen, Gipsy Night or A Night on the Farm. Stillwell also had difficulty preventing dancers from falling into the fountain he installed in the middle of the dance floor.[41]

In 1959 Ron Williams, an amiable all-rounder whose entertainment career stretched from vaudeville to rock'n'roll, looked back at the dances of the late 1920s and early 1930s without nostalgia. They were usually poorly organised, he said, and often bands seemed interested only in their pay. And if a tune was popular, 'it was nothing to hear it six or seven times during the evening'.

A typical lineup would be a piano, violin, trumpet and drums. The drummer also had an arsenal of novelty noise-makers on hand: a swanee whistle, triangle, various hooters and a set of temple blocks fastened to the bass drum. 'No waltz was complete without a run on the blocks', said Williams. Vocalists usually sang using a megaphone, and while dance floors were full by 8.00 pm, dancers mostly stuck to 'orthodox' rhythms: the waltz, the foxtrot and the quickstep. 'There were always a few couples who would stake out their claim to small pieces of floor and get in the rut (sorry, groove) with what was called the dixie stomp.'

When microphones appeared, 'almost overnight vocalists came into their own, also MCs. Instead of shouting and yelling they found that things were made much easier. Music was more rhythmic and a definite beat was making an impression.' By the time the war arrived, violins and banjos were old-hat, while string

Based in Wellington in the mid-1930s, Parkes Maori Band ventured as far as Westport and Napier for engagements. Their accordion player Harry Unwin (pictured below, and above at far left) later became a bass player and violinist for the Kiwi Concert Party. Peter Downes collection

bass and guitars 'made the combinations more solid and rhythmic'.

The most professional dance band in Wellington in the early 1930s was that run by the pianist Basil Bird, said Williams. At the Pharmacy Hall on Cambridge Terrace, Bird employed many of New Zealand's best players, including banjo and guitar player Charlie Lees and saxophonist Syd French. They played songs made popular by records, such as 'Stampede' and 'Boiling Point'. Soon, they would leave for Australia and acclaim.

There were more than twenty Saturday night dances to choose from in Wellington, among them the Adelphi Cabaret on Cuba Street (that became the Mayfair in 1933), and Taia Hall in Kilbirnie. Pharmacy Hall became the Peter Pan and then the Palm Grove. One of the most popular acts there was Parkes Maori Band, whose accordion player Harry Unwin later played bass with the Kiwi Concert Party. Future radio star Jack Maybury held court at The Realm, Hataitai, where a local hit was 'I'll Be Glad When You're Dead, You Rascal You'. And at all the venues, patrons continued to do variations on the dixie stomp until the jive arrived: 'a soft-shoe form of stomp', said Williams.[42]

Women musicians – usually pianists – were often the backbone of silent film pit orchestras. In dance bands, women players were common in rural areas, where dances maintained traditional styles for longer, as well as chaperoning rituals. Accomplished musicians were at a premium, and rural women more likely to have had lessons. In North Canterbury, 'all of the bands have lady pianists', a 1935 report noted, with most of them also leading their bands.[43] Despite the Depression, and years before the Second World War broke down gender roles, in the 1930s there were many pioneers challenging the boys' club of the urban dance band.

In Auckland, Elsie Nixon's Gala Girls Dance Band featured the experienced musicians Dinah Greening, Alice Clark and Eva Hewitt. 'We got a lot of work', recalled Nixon. 'We were a showband, with red and white satin uniforms. We used [stock] orchestrations and improvised a little.' Their music stands matched their uniforms: red satin covers with silver fringes. Dinah Greening, Walter Smith's niece, played banjo and sang. 'She knew how to be a showgirl with her instrument, and Eve was the same with her violin: you never saw a frown on her face. I'd learnt about showmanship and decided I was going to stand up when I played the saxophone.'

The Gala Girls' repertoire included contemporary hits such as 'Always', 'Crazy Words and Crazy Tunes' and 'Dinah' (sung by Greening), performed mostly as waltzes and foxtrots. Clark, a pianist, was the most talented, said Nixon: 'Men accepted me because I was accepted by Al. She was a band leader, and boys loved to play with her . . . . But there were lots of women around, they were jolly good, too.'[44]

McLoughlin's Ladies' Band – a Wellington quintet that emerged in 1936 – also contained dedicated professionals. It was led by Wyn McLoughlin, a violinist and saxophonist who had studied at the Sydney Conservatorium, and could be heard playing old-time and modern styles at local dances several times a week. Prominent local pianist Basil Bird was surprised by their 'good rhythm, tempo and musicianship': it wasn't just their uniform evening dress and matching music stands.[45] Pember's Popular Players, led by Thelma Pember, were in demand for Wellington old-time dances, while Wanganui's all-women band was the Tempo Teasers.

'Sax Appeal' read the caption to this 1931 image of Elsie Nixon, leader of the Gala Girls Dance Band which performed at Auckland dances in the early 1930s. *NZ Observer*, 19 February 1931

Perhaps the most influential female musician in the 1930s emerged just prior to the war. Vora Kissin was a pianist and singer who quickly became active in Auckland jazz circles. In 1937, aged 22, she was elected the secretary of the newly formed Auckland Rhythm Club, where she gave illustrated talks on jazz and her experiences in the Sydney music scene, and even made a recording of 'I Can't You Give Anything But Love'. A proselytiser of swing, for years she organised jam sessions, which were an outlet for her energy and enthusiasm. In May 1938, she gave a talk on 'the drug "Marihuana" and its use, particularly by American musicians'. Her discussion 'showed evidence of extensive study of the weed, and its effect on jammers in the States'.[46]

ROTORUA RHYTHM

Epi Shalfoon's Melody Boys, 'disguised as Arawa Braves'
for their promotional film shoot at Whakarewarewa,
Rotorua, December 1930. Reo Sheirtcliff collection

The setting is Rotorua's replica pa at Whakarewarewa.
Epi Shalfoon and his Melody Boys wait beside an imposing
Maori carving.

Shalfoon steps forward earnestly and says, 'I wish to
introduce to you Rotorua's famous jazz band . . .'. He
then picks up a saxophone and joins in as the band starts
playing 'E Puritai Tama E'.

The sound is primitive, but the jaunty style is instantly
recognisable as dixie. The banjo scratches out chords
and occasional responses to the saxophones, while the
sousaphone's 2/4 rhythm dominates the large bass drum.
After 60 high-spirited seconds, it is all over. Shalfoon
steps towards the camera again and calls out, 'Watch the
newspapers! This band will be playing *real!* dance music in
your town soon.'

The short film clip from December 1930 is New
Zealand's first jazz recording. Sadly, when the footage
came back from the processors in Miramar, it was so
indistinct that the local cinema managers declined to
screen it. The film was useless for promotion so when the
bill for £28 arrived, Shalfoon refused to pay. He was taken
to court, and *NZ Truth* enjoyed reporting the case:

ALL TALKIE AND NO PICTURE
Epi Shalfoon Wasn't Shook On It
*Saxophones Sobbed Out Jazz, but Rotorua
Syncopaters Were a Blur*

After hearing the evidence from both sides, the magi-
strate watched the film at a private screening. He agreed
with Shalfoon, saying the 'squeakings and gruntings far
from did justice to the band'.[47]

A 1930s envelope reads simply, *Epi Shalfoon Esq, Jazz
King, Rotorua, North Island.* There was no question it
would reach its destination, for the hard-working, affable
Epi Shalfoon was already on his way to becoming the
country's most popular dance-band leader.[48]

He was born Gareeb Stephen Shalfoon in Opotiki in
1904, the son of George Shalfoon, a prominent Syrian

Epi Shalfoon, 1946. His rhythm-oriented band reigned at Auckland's Crystal Palace from 1935 to 1953. Lesnie/Reo Sheirtcliff collection

in 1925. 'It went like a bomb', recalled professional dancer Ted Priestley. 'The Shalfoon recipe of soft melody and perfect dance rhythm over bash and noise was a hit.'[50] The band received offers to play at dances around the Bay of Plenty. The lineups of the Melody Boys were never static; the instruments included saxophones, piano, violin, drums, trumpet, banjo and sousaphone.

The Melody Boys moved to Rotorua in late 1928, and quickly made an impact thanks to Shalfoon's entrepreneurial skills. On the main street he opened Melody House, a small music shop with the latest products: gramophones and, eventually, records by Maori.

Shalfoon converted the King's Theatre into the spacious Majestic Ballroom, where the Melody Boys had a residency of many years. The band was also venturing further afield, travelling in a car with the band's name emblazoned on the side, to perform at dances from Waikato to the East Cape. Their first Auckland appearance was in 1929, at a lavish charity ball attended by the governor-general Lord Bledisloe and 3000 guests.[51]

The appeal of the Melody Boys was a mix of personality and rhythm, both generated by Shalfoon. His early nickname was 'Chuckles', and he always insisted that a clear, consistent rhythm was the most important attribute of a dance band. On-stage 'Shalfoonery' also helped, a 1930 review saying, 'It seems impossible for them to sit still and their beaming faces helped the dancers to enjoy themselves for each time they whirled past the stand some new prank was being perpetrated.'[52]

While in Rotorua the famous Australian aviator Charles Kingsford Smith invited Shalfoon to play at a private party at Brent's Hotel. Kingsford Smith brought out his banjo and jammed with Shalfoon till the early hours. He then invited the Melody Boys to perform for a party in Auckland.[53]

As the Depression deepened, fewer tourists visited Rotorua, so there was less work for musicians, at lower rates of pay. Competition was fierce, and admission charges went down to sixpence each, which included supper. Young people had little spending money, so the dance halls relied on an older crowd; this meant strict tempo dances came back in vogue. For a hip band like the Melody Boys, that was bad for business. Their last dance they played as a quartet, at Ngaruawahia: after shaking hands with his band Shalfoon left immediately for Auckland, and the Melody Boys returned to Rotorua.[54]

Shalfoon began working for the Auckland music instrument store Atwaters; he also set up his own

retailer, and his Maori wife Raria Hopa. Among the customers at the family's general store, which existed for over a century in Opotiki, were the prophet Rua Kenana and the politician Sir Apirana Ngata; George Shalfoon was the translator when Rua was arrested in 1916.[49]

The name Epi was an abbreviation of Karepi, the Maori transliteration of Gareeb. He began learning the piano with 'Professor' Anderson, an Opotiki music teacher, and taught himself clarinet and saxophone. By his teens he was performing at parties, and in the late 1920s was listening to jazz on shortwave radio beaming from the west coast of the United States.

In 1924 Shalfoon formed his own dance band, and within a few months they made a nervous debut as the Melody Boys at the Lyric Hall, Opotiki. Their first out-of-town gig was at the prestigious Tauranga Hunt Club Ball

Epi Shalfoon (with banjo) and his Melody Boys relax in Rotorua, early 1930s; the flyer below is from 1932. Reo Sheirtcliff collection

dance-band agency, eventually having 'eight orchestras available'. In July 1935, Shalfoon began the residency for which he is most famous: Saturday night dances at the Crystal Palace, beneath the picture theatre on Mt Eden Road. It was known as one of the hottest venues in the city, in both senses. Some nights were so steamy that water would drip down the walls in the basement venue. Shalfoon and his band played weekly at the Crystal Palace for eighteen years, while clocking up hundreds of miles during the week playing at out-of-town dances. By 1938 the *Music Maker* said he was 'to be found in all the gig jobs worth while', from vice-regal balls to Rod Talbot's *Diggers' Session* on 1ZB. On radio, exception was taken to Shalfoon's foot-stomping, which he did to keep the band in time. The radio technician insisted Shalfoon remove his shoes and laid a quilt over his foot. These Sunday broadcasts were for ex-servicemen, and unpaid, for which Shalfoon was reprimanded by the union. 'What the heck?', recalled Frank Gibson Sr. 'Are you just going to sit around and do nothing for these people?'[55]

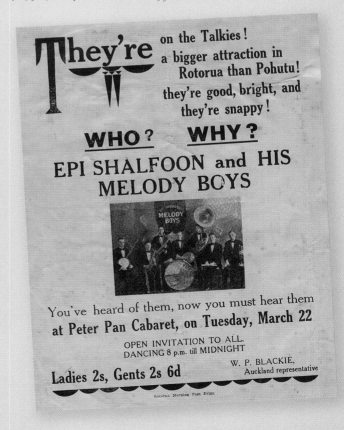

They're on the Talkies! a bigger attraction in Rotorua than Pohutu! they're good, bright, and they're snappy!

WHO? WHY?

EPI SHALFOON and HIS MELODY BOYS

You've heard of them, now you must hear them at **Peter Pan Cabaret, on Tuesday, March 22**

OPEN INVITATION TO ALL. DANCING 8 p.m. till MIDNIGHT

Ladies 2s, Gents 2s 6d

W. P. BLACKIE, Auckland representative

Rotorua Morning Post Print.

Epi Shalfoon at the piano, jamming with his band at the Auckland Swing Club, 1947. From left are Bob Griffith, Nolan Rafferty, Dale Alderton, Frank Gibson and Albie Parkinson. Reo Sheirtcliff collection

To Gibson, Shalfoon's Crystal Palace combo 'was an exciting little band and a training ground for just about every musician of note in Auckland'.[56] Shalfoon had an ear for promising young talent and was willing to give them a chance. The musicians who served an apprenticeship with Shalfoon is a roll-call of New Zealand's leading jazz players. Besides Gibson – Auckland's premier drummer in the 1940s – the band included Dale Alderton, George Campbell, Lew Campbell, Spike Donovan, Bill Egerton, Bob Ewing, Eric Foley, Bobby Griffith, Derek Heine, Tommy Kahi, Julian Lee, John MacKenzie, Albie Parkinson, Nolan Rafferty, Niel Randrup, Lloyd Sly, Jim Warren, Thomson Yandall and many others.

The professional dancer Ted Priestley commented: 'The strange thing was that though most of Epi's boys played "hot jazz", Epi himself was strictly "straight".'[57] On

Sunday afternoons he would invite musicians around to his Ponsonby home, set a metronome going on top of the piano and make sure they played in time. He explained, 'They're dancing: they pay your wages, that crowd out there.'[58]

Rhythm was Shalfoon's priority, and always a strength of his bands. He would adjust the tempos so that even those who had never had a dancing lesson could take part. 'You couldn't resist dancing to the Shalfoon sound', said bassist Spike Donovan. 'It guided your feet like some kind of musical hypnotism.'[59]

Many erroneously thought that Shalfoon couldn't read music, due to his insistence that no sheet music was visible on stage. They were what musicians called a 'lug band', explained Donovan: they played by ear. 'His band didn't use written arrangements like most other outfits because Epi thought that playing by ear and memory meant a more

Reo Shalfoon, on tour with the Melody Boys,
Bay of Plenty, 1947. Reo Sheirtcliff collection

she started school. For two years in a row she was voted 'top jazz singer' by the Auckland Jazz Club. A jazz reporter described her as 'rather shy, and takes her work very seriously . . . . she models her style of singing after Billie Holiday.'[62]

On the piano, Shalfoon could play classical, honky tonk and blues. During the war, he often played saxophone and clarinet as pianists were easier to find. 'He was a better musician than people gave him credit for', said Reo, '[but] he always played dixie, and people didn't associate good musicianship with dixie music. He was always particular about counting tunes in. He would sit in the front when he was playing the sax and go *1, 2, 3, 4*, stamping with his foot, and away they'd go.'

Shalfoon went for an earthy, driving sound, in the riff-based, dixie-influenced style of Fletcher Henderson rather than the sweet, big bands of swing. (At a 'three-bit job' one night, when asked to play Glenn Miller's arrangement of 'American Patrol', Shalfoon gave the stock response: 'It has three flats, and we don't play in three flats.')[63] But he encouraged his musicians to improvise while he concentrated on the melody, said Reo:

> Especially at the Crystal, because the kids loved it. He'd say to them 'The next number is not going to be a dance, you can come around the band stand. Frank's going to play a solo and Bobby Griffith is going to play a solo.' And we'd do 'Hawaiian War Chant' or something like that. You'd have the

relaxed type of musical sound and also gave the boys more room for showmanship. He had a wonderful gift for playing numbers at exactly the right tempo to make them danceable.'[60]

During summer in the stifling Crystal Palace, he would slow down the tempos to make an evening more comfortable. In the breaks, regular customers – who regarded him as a close friend – would surround him. A couple of times during the night, he would take to the dance floor with one of them. According to Donovan, Shalfoon had 'a smile that was warmer than Bombay on a summer's day and a disposition to match'.[61]

In the war years, depending on which musicians were on leave, the Melody Boys would fluctuate in size and lineups. By then the star attraction was Shalfoon's daughter Reo, who had wanted to be a singer even before

Dennis Huggard Archive, MSD12-0142,
Alexander Turnbull Library, Wellington

The Melody Boys go formal at the Metropole, Auckland, 1947. From left are Jack Clague, Albie Parkinson, Bobby Griffith, Nolan Rafferty, Frank Gibson, Jack McDonald, Epi Shalfoon and Reo Shalfoon. Reo Sheirtcliff collection

bass player soloing on it, you'd have Frank Gibson soloing on it, and then if he wanted to, he would highlight me, because he knew there were a lot of numbers that I couldn't sing with the dance band. 'Embraceable You', things like that, he said were no good for dancing to. They were too slow.[64]

Apart from the primitive 1930 film soundtracks, acetates and tapes of rehearsal sessions at his home on Islington Street, Ponsonby, Shalfoon's music survives on one 78 for Tanza. Recorded in Auckland in 1951, 'Come On-A My House' and 'All Dressed Up to Smile' features Reo singing with Epi Shalfoon and His Orchestra. Actually it was a sextet, but the backing has all the rhythmic force for which Shalfoon's bands were famous. 'Come On-A My House' could be jump blues, with a swinging, sassy vocal from Reo. The B-side 'All Dressed Up to Smile' is early 1950s American pop, with a sweet vocal chorus and a solo from Epi himself on alto. With slippery metre and the warm tone of a village wedding band, it captures his unhurried, amiable personality.[65]

Sadly, Shalfoon's health began to deteriorate early. In 1952 he was in and out of hospital, and the *Music Maker* followed his progress: 'His smiling face will be seen around again shortly . . . look after yourself, Ep.'[66]

On 23 May 1953, Shalfoon asked Reo if she would like to make a visit to the Crystal Palace, home of his longest residency. That night, during a dance with Reo, he collapsed and died. Forty years later, she wrote, 'Epi had always said if he couldn't die in his own home, he would hope it would be on a dance floor. The Crystal Palace, of all the dance halls he had played in, was the most fitting place.'[67]

The Auckland music community was shocked. Epi Shalfoon was only 48, and was much loved. He was modest but amusing, a showman but not a show-off. 'My band is not the *best* band in town by a long way, but it's the most *popular* band', he said. His greatest satisfaction was seeing dancers enjoy themselves. 'I make my music easy to dance to and easy to listen to. If the dancers like dancing to me and listening to me they will always come back.'[68]

RADIO DAYS

The number of households with radio licences leapt enormously in the 1930s. In 1925 just 4702 licences were held; when the Broadcasting Board took control on 1 January 1932, there were 71,680 licences. By 1935 the figure had grown to 152,808 licences, and by 1940 it had leapt again, to 345,682.[69]

The decade would see the structure of New Zealand's radio service change several times due to government policies towards the influential medium. The Radio Broadcasting Company (RBC) of the 1920s evolved into the government-controlled New Zealand Broadcasting Board (NZBB) in 1932. At the time, there was a great variety of private radio stations spread throughout the country: the YA stations in the four main centres, operated by the RBC, and more than 30 local 'B' stations that operated under severe restrictions about accepting advertising and sponsorship. When the Labour government came to power in 1935, it nationalised the radio industry. The National Broadcasting Service (NBS) was set up in 1936, with James Shelley as director; the National Commercial Broadcasting Service (NCBS) was launched in 1937, directed by Colin Scrimgeour. In 1943 the two were amalgamated as the National Broadcasting Service, with one director, James Shelley.[70]

The audience was excited by the new opportunities that radio provided, a world of riches including comedy, sport, talks and music. Small, isolated communities worked together to build aerials that would bring signals to their districts. Ships at sea were no longer limited to Morse code for news from the mainland. Off the coast of Greymouth in 1932, the crew of the *Kaponga* eagerly awaited a song they had requested to be broadcast on 3YZ, 'He Played His Ukulele as the Ship Went Down'. After playing it, the host Mick Speirs heard the wail of the ship's siren. Thinking it was the crew expressing its gratitude, he spun the song again. But the enthralled crew had let the *Kaponga* run aground on the Grey River bar; the ship was wrecked, though no lives were lost.[71]

By 1932 there were seven stations in Auckland alone, with 1YA belonging to the NZBB. The other six were private, including 1ZB (owned by La Gloria Gramophone Company) and 1ZR. The latter was owned by the long-established music retailer Lewis Eady, a pioneer in music technology even before its foray into broadcasting began in 1930. From 1928 the firm offered a recording service, which enabled customers to record their voices onto aluminium discs using the Speak-a-Phone system. The firm also sold radio sets and parts, as well as instruments and concert tickets.[72] 1ZR was the most popular station, broadcasting every day for a total of 53 hours a week.[73] Several key figures emerged from 1ZR: Uncle Tom (Garland), whose Friendly Road choir made its debut on the station; Uncle Scrim (Colin Scrimgeour); Aunt Daisy (Maud Ruby Basham); and actor/broadcasters Dudley Wrathall and John Gordon. New Zealand's oldest music instrument chain, Charles Begg, found that by the mid-1930s selling radios was the biggest part of their business.[74]

In 1933 – when the government had announced that B-stations were to be phased out – 1ZB was sold to the religious group Fellowship of the Friendly Road for a song or, according to legend, a piano. Tom Garland of the Friendly Road religious society is said to have paid £50 for the station, on £5 deposit; Scrimgeour claimed that he paid £100 for the station, selling his wife's piano to raise the cash.[75]

By 1934 the four main centres were receiving seventeen hours a day of broadcasting in the evenings, including five hours from the private stations. Music comprised 70.13 percent of the content, of which 17.26 percent was serious music, 42.88 percent light music, 9 percent modern dance music and 0.99 old-time dance music.[76]

One of the initiatives of the NZBB was to bring overseas artists to New Zealand, mostly in the classical field. Among them were violinist Joseph Szigeti, composer Percy Grainger, pianist Eileen Joyce and conductor Malcolm Sargent, but Australian operetta star Gladys Moncrieff also visited under their auspices. In the main centres, however, the backbone of live music broadcasts was performances from a panel of local artists, again mostly in the light classics. Their standards were sufficiently reliable for them to make regular appearances and become household names to the listeners.[77]

With radio in its infancy, the airwaves were uncluttered enough for New Zealand listeners regularly to receive stations from Australia and the west coast of the United States at night. Taranaki saxophonist Len Barton often tuned in to the dance orchestra of KGO Oakland, California. When he sat in to perform with Auckland bands he found he was more up to date with the latest songs.[78] In 1931 other stations that were easily picked up included 2FC Sydney, KFI Los Angeles and KGU Honolulu.[79]

Radio listeners quickly became passionate about the medium, making them vociferous about how this alien in their living rooms should and should not behave.

The letters columns of the Radio Record reflected how jazz polarised listeners, but the New Zealand Broadcasting Board stations advertised their hipness. *N.Z. Radio Record*, 15 September 1933

Complaints that became perennial quickly emerged: according to their own tastes, listeners wanted more classical, less high-brow music, more dance music, less jazz, some old-time, please. An Oamaru 'Lover of Crooning and Jazz' sympathised with the NZBB's inability to 'satisfy all the grumblers'. Nevertheless, he wrote, was there any chance of hearing more yodelling records from Harry Torrani and Jimmie Rodgers?[80]

Americanisation was one of many crimes against civilisation of which the fledgling New Zealand radio industry was accused. 'How much of every weekday programme from 3YA is devoted to that ghastly croon-jazz-blare-baby-doll American rubbish', a reader called 'British' asked in the Christchurch *Press* in 1936. 'I fully realise that the wireless stations have to fall back a great deal on records, but surely there is more variety to be obtained.'[81]

The over-exposure of certain songs caused 'illness', Young Pro told the *N.Z. Radio Record*. Among them were 'The Channel Swimmer', 'Almost a Film Star', 'Daft Sandy', and songs by Clapham and Dwyer, or Layton and Johnstone. Another correspondent, Atlanta, decried the 'uncivilised din of Negro bands': American tunes were much more acceptable when played by British bands.[82]

A survey by the *N.Z. Radio Record* in 1934 to gauge the popularity of different styles of music attracted more than 33,000 entries. Light opera was an easy winner, with

7322 votes. Following it were old-time melodies (6755), dance music (5824), classical (5194) and grand opera (4650). Crooning was the straggler, with 3518 votes.

The emergence of crooning – singing quietly into an electric microphone, Bing Crosby style – brought many in the audience almost to apoplexy, especially those fond of the light classics and clearly articulated lyrics ('Degrading, immoral piffle', spluttered a typical letter).[83] Although crooning appeared first in the late 1920s – with New Zealand having its own popular exponent, Billy Hart – the style continued to polarise listeners. In early 1937, the Wellington jazz enthusiast Arthur Pearce was invited to debate the style on air with Stanley Oliver, the head of the city's Harmonic Society. Oliver – in good humour but also with relish – described crooning as a 'menace to the real art of singing'. It had no vocal value, and its cramped nasality caused the performer – he refused to use the word singer – 'to emit distorted and often unlovely vowel sounds'. Pearce responded with a well-researched explanation of the developments in popular music and technology that had enabled crooning to flourish.

Oliver concluded by expressing admiration for Pearce: he was clearly 'as much a purist in his line as I am in mine . . . . If guidance in the dissemination of popular music expression is desirable, it can best come from the enthusiastic discriminating devotees of the calibre of

In the mid-1930s, the Radio Rhythmic Symphonists were the biggest band to broadcast on 2YA. Photographed in 1935, they are (back row, from left): Norm Hull-Brown (drums); George Love, Ralph Owens and Bill Matson (trombones); Ron Cudby (guitar); John Robertson, Stan Crisp and Ernie Ormond (trumpets); Frank Bourke (double bass). Front row, from left: Jack Harfell, Dennis Collinson and Mert Stace (violins); Maurice Hayrice (alto); Percy Watson (tenor); Cecil Day (alto); Jack Maybury (baritone); Claude Bennett (piano). The conductor is unidentified. S. P. Andrew, F-18528-1/1, Alexander Turnbull Library, Wellington

Mr Pearce.'[84] Within weeks 2YA would invite Pearce to host a weekly dance programme, and over the next 40 years – as 'Turntable', hosting *Rhythm on Record* – he would become New Zealand's most influential jazz broadcaster.[85]

The impact of radio upon music in New Zealand cannot be overestimated. For a few musicians, it provided regular work, although record companies and concert producers were suspicious of the medium's effect on their prosperity. But to those in the radio audience who loved music, it could change their lives. Les Andrews was twelve when his family acquired its first radio for their Timaru home. Besides the serials and wrestling commentaries, it was the light classical singers who captivated Andrews: 'I wondered, could I ever make a recording, a career as a singer? Dreams are made of such stuff and I sang more loudly in the bath in case some passing entrepreneur would hear and say, "What a voice – just what we're looking for!"' Over a decade later, in a dark cellar in Italy, that was virtually what happened when Andrews was in a spontaneous singalong. Among those listening was a soldier who asked if Andrews would like to join the Kiwi Concert Party. 'Bloody oath!', he replied, before noticing the red braid on General Freyberg's cap.[86]

In the Manawatu during the Depression, Bill Hamer's father occasionally sold radios during long periods of unemployment. This meant that new stock often came home for testing. 'Ear-splitting sounds of static and hiss – relieved occasionally by real radio programmes – would pervade our house', recalled Hamer, who would eventually become a broadcasting technician and jazz aficionado. Among the offerings for the Depression audience were 'mostly dull talks on how to cook potatoes', with music favouring middle-of-the road performers such as John Charles Thomas and the Palm Court Orchestra. Hamer found more interesting fare on Australian commercial stations until, in 1937, he found Turntable on 2YA. Aged just thirteen, Hamer's tastes soon shifted from the Boswell Sisters to Artie Shaw: 'It could have been "Traffic Jam" or "Lady Be Good". Whatever, to my youthful ears these were angelic sounds from heaven.' At the Foxton cinema, among the short films before the main feature were 'soundies': clips of the leading swing bands and small combos. 'These were usually Negro entertainers, made no doubt on the cheap. Such artists as Slim Gaillard ("Flat Foot Floogie") and Jimmie Lunceford ("Taint What You Do") come to mind.'[87]

THE EVANGELIST

Arthur Pearce called himself Turntable, but he was more of a radar. He beamed in on unfamiliar sounds coming from offshore, deciphered what he captured, then broadcast his discoveries to an eager audience. New Zealand's taste-making broadcaster of popular music for 40 years, Pearce was first with the best, in many genres. For his audience, his programmes were essential listening; for musicians, they were like church.

Born in Wellington in 1903, Pearce came from a well-to-do family that helped found Levin & Co, a prominent import company. As a child he listened to music hall and operetta, when few families owned phonographs. At fourteen, after winning a three-year scholarship of £5 per year, he devoted the money to buying records and sheet music of post-war songs. But it was in the early 1920s that Pearce heard a new type of music: the disc was by the Original Dixieland Jazz Band, the first group to record jazz, and he was immediately captivated.

At the time, jazz was becoming popular in some dance halls, but to upstanding citizens and especially the musical establishment, it was a four-letter word. Pearce spent his life determined to have the genre regarded with respect. With his enthusiasm and fastidious nature, he quickly became a jazz scholar. Because of his work at Levin & Co as a shipping clerk, he had connections in the United States who would send – or bring in personally – the latest discs and catalogues. His tastes quickly changed from the white dance bands who imitated and popularised the music, to the black originators of jazz. Duke Ellington became especially important to him.[88]

In Wellington, Pearce became renowned as a jazz aficionado, and he was invited to give a talk on radio about Ellington in 1935. This programme polarised listeners but won many over to the music. Two years later, with 2YA needing to respond to the new ZBs, he was asked to host a weekly programme of acceptable dance music. Pearce began to slip his own selections among the light orchestral dance music chosen by the station, and the programme soon became dedicated to jazz. With the heyday of swing just beginning, Pearce's encyclopaedic knowledge – and

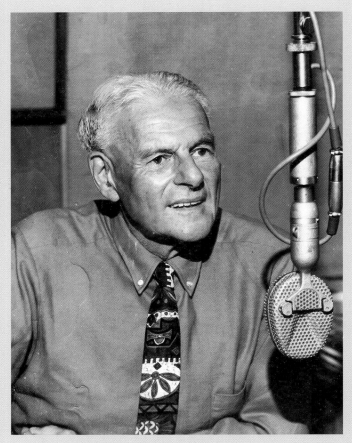

Arthur Pearce at the microphone, Wellington, 11 September 1970. Pearce family collection

access to the most recent releases from the US – gave the programme the edge against any rivals. His jazz programme *Rhythm on Record* ran from 1937 until 1977. Each programme opened with a theme – Bob Crosby's 'Woman on My Weary Mind' – and a catchphrase suggesting the sales cry of a hip Cockney barrow-boy: 'Any rags, any jazz, any boppers today?'

Pearce's great strength was his musical broadmindedness: he had an uncanny ear for the best in any style, and astutely followed jazz as it changed from dixieland to fusion. In 1948 he launched *Cowboy Jamboree* to cater for the neglected audience for hillbilly records; it aired on 2YD and the shortwave band, with a script of Pearce's outrageous puns. As popular music kept changing, so did the programme's title – to *Western Song Parade* and finally *Big Beat Ball* – and the playlist was typically eclectic. Folk and classical were his only blindspots, only because he did not have the time.[89]

Besides jazz, Pearce was equally at home proselytising about honky tonk, R&B and the beginnings of rock'n'roll,

Arthur Pearce shows Duke Ellington the manuscript of 'Black Butterfly', for which he
wrote the lyrics to Ellington's melody, 1972. Pearce family collection

or surf music, grandiose pop and funk. *Big Beat Ball* broadcast until 1975, when the programme was judged 'out of character' with the station (now called 2ZM and Top-40 oriented). But the lack of a format was the strength of Pearce's programmes. A final *Big Beat Ball* placed schmaltzy Wayne Newton alongside avant-garde bluesman Captain Beefheart and the pop-funk of Earth Wind & Fire; at the time Pearce was 72. The last *Rhythm on Record* aired on 4 July 1977: it featured, naturally, Duke Ellington. The piece chosen was 'Maori: A Samoan Dance'.[90]

Pearce was a guru to other broadcasters, musicians, the record trade and his listeners. In person he was modest and reserved, except when it came to pursuing or enthusing about music, be it a rare record from a distributor, or a fact-chasing conversation with any visiting musicians. Artie Shaw, Louis Armstrong, Dave Brubeck, the Beatles and the Rolling Stones were all bemused by this quietly spoken man who knew more about their oeuvre than they did. Among the artists he met, he formed two special friendships. Duke Ellington appreciated Pearce's understanding of his music, published the lyrics Pearce wrote to an instrumental, 'Black Butterfly' – and, at Pearce's request, performed it during his 1970 concert in Auckland. Pop singer Gene Pitney affectionately called Pearce 'the oldest teenager in the world' with 'the weirdest show I have ever heard'.[91]

In 1936 the Labour government nationalised radio, buying the stations it did not yet own and closing down the B stations or letting them disappear as their licence fees expired. But throughout the 1930s, a feature of New Zealand broadcasting – no matter which incarnation was currently running the medium – was the number of local artists who performed live-to-air. 1ZB in particular promoted local talent, especially after recruiting an expatriate opera singer, Barend Harris, as its studio manager. (Harris is credited with discovering Inia Te Wiata.)[92] An early star was an expatriate English drummer called Ed Silver, who had played in jazz bands on both sides of the Atlantic. After touring New Zealand with Gladys Moncrieff, in 1937 he conducted the Rhythm Symphonists for 2YA: the largest dance band yet heard on radio. He found wider fame at 1ZB as the children's host 'Neddo'.[93]

Dance music was regularly scheduled on the leading stations late in the evening, in *Music, Mirth and Melody* sessions of recorded music (in 1936, the leading requests included 'Cheek to Cheek', 'Top Hat', 'Roll Along, Prairie Moon' and 'Red Sails in the Sunset'). In another 1936 survey, 38 percent of the audience stated they enjoyed dancing to broadcast music; the same survey revealed 'an overwhelming majority in favour of the reduction of classical, symphonic and chamber music'. This did not mean, however, that those who didn't like serious music wanted more jazz. 'Evidently New Zealand is tiring of crooners.'[94]

MR DANCE

At the National Broadcasting Service the sign on Bob Bothamley's door read 'Head Office Dance'. For almost 30 years he was Mr Dance of radio, and the musician's friend. Within the walls of his small but powerful mini-empire, purchasing and programming decisions were made that gave New Zealand radio its swing. Defining the genre, the *New Zealand Listener* once said: 'Swing is what Bob Bothamley has in his little room at the NBS head office in Wellington.'[95]

Born in 1903, Bothamley played saxophone and fiddle in Wellington dance bands from the mid-1920s. He was a member of the elite Wellington Symphonic Dance Orchestra – '20 of the keenest from the best bands' – who would be introduced in rhyming couplets by conductor Jack Maybury. Bothamley was also leader of the Star

Mr Head Office Dance, 1941: within Broadcasting, former saxophone player Bob Bothamley was the best friend of jazz. Photo by Spencer Digby. Bob Bothamley collection/Peter Downes

Orchestra, a ragtime band that played at the Star Boating Club on Wellington's waterfront and around the district. When Bothamley retired from performing in 1932, friends noted that he 'cannot keep away from the dance halls as he has been seen on quite a number of occasions tripping the light fantastic'.[96]

The Star Orchestra evolved into the first sponsored radio dance band in New Zealand. The Plume Melody Makers broadcast a three-hour show every Tuesday night on Wellington's 2ZW, a B-station owned by the piano and radio dealers Hamilton Nimmo & Sons, and operated from the top floor of their building on Willis Street.[97]

The programme was sponsored by the Plume Motor Oil Company. The privately owned B-stations earned their income through listener subscriptions and the sponsoring of programmes, although there were severe restrictions on what could be said on air. The United/Reform coalition government was keen to develop a national broadcasting service modelled on the BBC, with no advertising, and the popular B-stations disappeared through attrition as

Bob Bothamley, third from right, was musical director of the Plume Melody Makers before he joined the National Broadcasting Service. Sponsored by the Plume Motor Oil Company, in the early 1930s they broadcast live from the Nimmo's building on Willis Street, Wellington. Photo by Spencer Digby. Bob Bothamley collection/Peter Downes

sponsoring regulations changed and their licences were purchased or not renewed. In 1933 both 2ZW and Eady's 1ZR – the two most powerful B-stations – were bought by the government and they ceased broadcasting on 4 December.[98]

Bothamley continued to move in Wellington music circles, and cut some of the legendary aluminium discs that were Tex Morton's first recordings.[99] Joining the NBS in 1937 to manage its dance music and jazz broadcasts, Bothamley increased the broadcasting of dance bands from the main centres, often via relays from venues such as the Show Boat at the Auckland waterfront or the Pirate Shippe on the North Shore. NBS memos reveal the system: Auckland radio staff would audition a band, perhaps recommended by a member of the public, then report back to head office in Wellington asking for approval to broadcast – and for the band's fee. In September 1937, a Huntly listener wrote to 1YA that 'the best dance band playing in Auckland is under the conductorship of Art Larkins'. Within a few weeks, a memo went south

reporting that the Larkins band gave 'a highly satisfactory performance'. The band was performing at a dance to farewell the Springboks on 30 September, so 1YA would take 'a relay of the music in lieu of the recorded dance session previously scheduled'.[100]

Back and forth went the memos: the Pirate Shippe's band was suitable for an old-time dance programme, using the Shippe's telephone circuit for the relay (fee: £7/7/-). Bert Peterson's band wasn't up to standard. Johnny Madden's Swing Kings were booked for broadcast although head office complained: 'Our authority has not been given.' Where is the paperwork?

At NBS, Bothamley worked closely with Arthur Pearce, who was beginning to make regular jazz broadcasts on 2YA. The pair had originally met in the early 1930s at a musical instrument shop at 69a Manners Street, run by saxophonist and *Music Maker* columnist Jack McEwen. Each Friday night about a dozen Wellington dance musicians would gather around a gramophone to analyse the latest jazz 78s from the US. These after-hours sessions

From 1929 to 1957, Ye Olde Pirate Shippe cabaret was berthed on Milford Beach, Auckland, decked with nautical accoutrements inside and out. This 1950 incarnation of the Pirate Shippe Orchestra featured, from left, Stan Hills, Allan Hills, Jack Pepper, Joe Sims (drums), Jimmy Johnson and John Dewar. Folio Portraits, neg. A12099, Auckland City Libraries

were more for jamming than listening, the musicians playing along to records by acts such as Duke Ellington, Cab Calloway and Louis Armstrong.

Like Pearce, Bothamley was the black sheep 'of a society family which did not appreciate the boy's interest in being a musician, however successful'. At the NBS, his new position was 'programme director for dance music and jazz broadcasts', although true jazz was yet to be regularly heard on radio. 'It is quite conceivable that Arthur Pearce and Bob Bothamley may have been the only people associated with 2YA in 1937 who had any real conception of the difference between the two music styles.'[101]

The NBS director of broadcasting Professor James Shelley was a domineering evangelist of high culture who regarded light music with disdain. When appointed in 1936 he declared, 'If the New Zealand public really wants vaudeville, it is not the slightest use appointing me director of broadcasting.' A week later he clarified his attitude. 'Those who want vaudeville will get vaudeville', he conceded. 'Broadcasting is a medium that should be used

not only for vaudeville, but for more important things as well . . . . whatever listeners wanted, vaudeville or anything else, it must be the best.'[102]

Opinionated, argumentative, elitist, Shelley's ultimate nightmare must have been the evening that Prime Minister Peter Fraser – his leading patron – was trying to broadcast to the country. 'A crossed connection gave him a dance-band accompaniment. Shelley screamed into the studio, threatening to fire everybody involved with this *lèse-majesté*, however remotely. But he soon calmed down; he did not bear grudges.'[103]

Tastes were changing as quickly as radio itself. Listeners reacted favourably to the commercial stations of the new National Commercial Broadcasting Service, where Scrimgeour's innovations such as imported radio serials were proving a strong drawcard. But on 2YA at NBS, Pearce's new Friday night dance and jazz-oriented programme was already proving successful. The working relationship of Bothamley and Pearce would have a great impact on music and musicians in New Zealand for 30 years.

BLUE SMOKE

A LITTLE LIGHT MUSIC

The light music genre is described by UK historian James Nott as 'more populist than "serious" classical music yet more conservative than modern dance and jazz music'. Like most popular music, it was a fusion of many styles, but had pretensions beyond the dance floor. Touching upon light classics, Viennese waltzes and the occasional popular song, it needed to be well played and well behaved, to suit cautious talent bookers for Broadcasting or tearooms with tablecloths. Light music was, says Nott, 'A vague and peculiarly British category which included orchestral music, operetta, musical comedy, ballads, and café, restaurant, or cinema organ music and ranged from solo performance and palm court trios to small orchestral ensembles.'[104]

The pianist in Chips Healy's band who made the ill-fated journey to Sydney went on to become a household name in New Zealand light music. Ossie Cheesman was born in Hamilton in 1913 and began on the cornet in his school band, before showing precocious ability at the piano. While still at school he formed the Rhythm Boys, which played at country dances in the Waikato and at Hamilton's Regent Ballroom. By 1931 he was a member of Auckland's prestigious Civic band, but of no fixed abode. Meanwhile he bunked on a boat in the harbour with Les Stewart, a drummer nicknamed 'the Hangman'. When the Sydney gig evaporated, Cheesman survived by playing piano in a non-union club from midnight until 4.00 am, earning £3 a week. At a day's notice for an audition, he taught himself the piano accordion and was soon working in the orchestras of Pacific cruise liners such as the *Aorangi*, *Monowai* and *Niagara*.[105]

Back in New Zealand, he was in demand for radio broadcasts, arranging and composing. He opened a school of music and established a reputation as an accompanist. (Eventually, he would back visiting artists including Larry Adler and Stanley Holloway. A national tour with the Soviet tenor Senia Chostiakoff lasted six months, travelling from Kaeo to Nightcaps. The worst part of it, Cheesman recalled, was that he had to dress as a Cossack.) In 1941 he conducted a ten-piece dance band for the weekly 1YA

Ossie Cheesman plays accordion for Continental Rendezvous with Helen Hopkins (violin) and singer Ellen Vann. Hill-Thomas/RNZ Sound Archives

programme *Fashions in Melody*, which opened with a signature tune he had written, 'Improvisations'. He joined the army, hoping his knowledge of German would get him a post in Intelligence (in time, he would learn French, Spanish and Japanese). Instead he began by digging ditches. Before long, his musical talents were put to use in the Third Division, where he formed a brass band and became the director of the Pacific Kiwi Concert Party. After the war, he led an entertainment troupe to Korea and Japan, and was a foundation member of the National Orchestra – with which he often performed as guest pianist or conductor. Not until 1950 did he undergo advanced musical training.

With perfect pitch, instant recall and a photographic memory, Cheesman was the epitome of the proficient all-rounder, 'as much at home in front of a symphony orchestra as he was on the back of a truck at a street festival'. Musical snobbery was unknown to him. 'His only concession to formality was the use of his given name, Oswald, when performing the classics.'[106]

Another who became highly regarded for his versatility, especially in light music, was Henry Rudolph. Although best known for his work as a vocal arranger, Rudolph was a pioneer in Wellington dance music and live broadcasts.

Besides conducting all-women singing groups and his own large dance orchestras, Henry Rudolph made
a very elegant one-man band during a professional career of over 50 years. Peter Downes collection

The Londoner's musical breadth was apparent before he
emigrated to New Zealand in 1920, aged eighteen. He
played violin and piano, and just prior to the First World
War was taught pump organ by a German priest, with
whom he also played flugelhorn in a brass band. Settling
in Wellington, Rudolph formed a band in 1924 and began
a long residency at the St Francis Hall. Among the dances
were the 'Poor Joneses' and the 'Excuse Me Waltz'; his
band insisted on playing tunes such as 'Bugle Call Rag',
while Rudolph knew the audiences wanted 'The Donkey
Serenade'. ('Things the average person liked', he recalled.
'That was part of my success.')

Hearing a visiting American on the saxophone inspired
him to take up the instrument; he also learnt the clarinet,
piano accordion and xylophone, mainly because the
pianos in dance halls were usually sub-standard. By the
1930s, Rudolph was playing regularly on 2ZB with his
women's trio the Swing Time Harmonists. During the
Second World War, he was asked to be the musical director
of the 2YA Camp Entertainers. 'This gave me my biggest
lift', he recalled. 'I had the best musicians, and the best
singers, and I used to experiment with arranging.' The
troupe would visit army camps and make live broadcasts

– 'from somewhere in New Zealand' – with an orchestra
that included violinist Vincent Aspey and a chorus of
women called the Melody Maids. Broadcasting supplied
him with acetates so he could write arrangements of
the latest pop songs, which were unavailable in record
stores. In 1944 he led a troupe to New Caledonia, and his

Henry Rudolph and the Melody Maids, for the late 1940s radio programme
Is This Your Favourite Melody? Photo News/RNZ Sound Archives

BLUE SMOKE

Gil Dech with Te Mauri Meihana of the Rotorua Maori Choir, c. 1930. Peter Downes collection

arrangement of 'Wing and a Prayer' caused an audience of 10,000 American soldiers to throw their hats in the air. 'Old Shep' had the WAAFs and nurses crying. 'Variety was the secret, also building to a climax', said Rudolph: 'Chattanooga Choo Choo' followed by community singing.

Rudolph's name became forever linked to all-women pop vocal groups such as the Harmony Serenaders and the Henry Rudolph Singers, but he did not rate himself as a singer: 'I heard myself sing on a record and I thought, that's the finish.' From then on, he only performed novelty songs such as 'Knees Up Mother Brown' and 'The Laughing Policeman'. A working musician for nearly 60 years, Rudolph never gave up his day job as a watchmaker.[107]

The 1930s' most lasting piece of light music was nostalgic even when it was new. Shortly after Gil Dech produced the historic Rotorua Maori Choir recordings at Ohinemutu in 1930, the pianist returned to Sydney and recorded the piece of music with which he will always be associated. Carl Reber's romantic 'Remembrance' became a perennial radio request, and a rite of passage for thousands of young piano students. Dech recorded 'Remembrance' several times, but his contribution to New Zealand music went beyond its lush arpeggios.

Gil Dech was his third and final name. He was born Gilbert Thomas Pinfield, near Birmingham, in 1897. After studying piano at the Royal Academy of Music in London, he began a concert career using the name Gilbert Dechelette. A tour on the Tivoli Circuit in Australia and New Zealand led to his being appointed director of music for the Columbia Graphophone Company in Sydney, hence his involvement in the Rotorua sessions. Besides

'Remembrance' and its popular B-side, 'The Robin's Return', Dech made more than 80 piano recordings of his own, accompanied soloists such as the soprano Gladys Moncrieff, and produced sessions with studio orchestras and dance bands.[108]

For a career in popular music, a more popular name was required, so Gilbert Dechelette became Gil Dech. After an eight-month tour of New Zealand with Moncrieff in 1936, he joined the NBS, becoming the musical supervisor and conductor of the 4YA Orchestra in Dunedin. 'The slim, immaculate figure of Gil Dech was part of the Dunedin scene for many years', wrote the *Evening Post*. He led many 'community sings' with local identity Alf Pettitt, and performed and taught music, while working as a music producer at 4YA. He lived in a flat behind 'Ma' Blaney's famous Tattersall's Hotel, but 'seldom went into the bar, and was never known to play its piano. He drank his gin in the seclusion of his flat, from where in quiet moments the music from his nimble fingers reached from his Bechstein grand into all corners of the hotel.'[109]

There was an element of self-invention to Dech; his father was not French as he claimed, but William Pinfield, a 'journeyman bricklayer' in Birmingham. But his influence on light music in New Zealand was widespread, his professionalism and dedication being credited with helping to 'raise performing standards to levels not previously attained'. For 'Remembrance' Dech was never forgotten: when he died in 1974, he was still receiving mail from school children learning the piece and feedback from elderly radio listeners who kept requesting it. Television

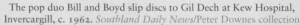
The pop duo Bill and Boyd slip discs to Gil Dech at Kew Hospital, Invercargill, c. 1962. *Southland Daily News*/Peter Downes collection

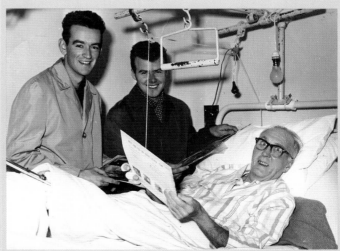

host Pete Sinclair even featured the piece on the early 1970s pop show, *Happen Inn*.[110]

The most prominent exponent of light music left not a musical legacy but a scandal. Eric Mareo's arrival from Britain in 1933 had made headlines: he was here to launch a symphony orchestra in Auckland. Within a week he had hired 45 players and started rehearsals.

His curriculum vitae was impeccable, his ambitions were grand: years of study at London's Guildhall and conservatories in Berlin and Paris, years as a conductor of grand opera, pantomime and everything in between. He had written music for several West End shows, and over 700 works. They were published under seven different pseudonyms because 'in England, they won't allow you to be versatile. They think a man who can write a symphony ought not to be able to write light stuff.' He had even written a series of piano studies for the left hand (these were also published in Braille, so a pianist could read the music with the right hand, while performing the piece with the left). The *New Zealand Observer* reported all this faithfully and anticipated the new orchestra's debut, just three weeks after its formation: 'Lovers of music will have something to look forward to.'[111]

Mareo rapidly became a man about town, often promenading down Queen Street wearing white gloves, a long white cigarette holder jutting out of his mouth, and swinging a cane. A tobacconist displayed his portrait with the boast, 'We stock the Mareo cigarette holder.'

Just two years later, the *Observer*'s headline would read: 'Mareo the Enigma: Sublime Optimist Whose Dreams Have Ended in Dust and Tragedy'. By this time, he was in prison for murdering his wife and sentenced to death. Arguments between the couple had escalated after his wife Thelma had left the Dixieland Cabaret at Point Chevalier with her friend, the dancer Freda Stark. When a drunk Mareo arrived home, he found them in bed together.[112]

Mareo had made few friends: many regarded his theatrical, cosmopolitan manner as arrogance. He was, said one music critic, a 'musical poltergeist' that had invaded the city. Nevertheless, he achieved a lot during his short time on Auckland's podium, including several symphony concerts and early performances of Gershwin's *Rhapsody in Blue* and Ravel's *Boléro*. Many musicians greeted him as a godsend in grim times, when the industry 'had been hit hard by the combined influences of radio, talking pictures and the slump', although he quickly

Eric Mareo, pictured shortly after his 1933 arrival in Auckland: dapper but doomed. *Independent News*

found himself in debt.[113] Others were disdainful of his showmanship – on stage, his name was emblazoned in flowers, and he used a tinselled baton – and they even suggested that performing Gershwin's classic was 'lowering the prestige of his orchestra'. Envy was behind much of the animosity towards Mareo, it has been suggested, including from the jury that convicted him to an applauding nation: a flamboyant figure in a depressed climate.[114]

Mareo would eventually serve twelve years, leaving Mt Eden gaol with £500 in his pocket from royalties earned while he was incarcerated. 'He was a genius, from start to finish', said one member of his orchestra. Spike Donovan heard another musician – who had written arrangements for which Mareo had taken the credit and the cash – saying, 'I hope they hang him.'[115]

DOYENS OF DANCE

Cole Porter walked into the lounge of Wellington's Hotel St George just as 'Night and Day' was playing on the radio. Music had no borders, and his was more well-travelled than most. The songwriter visited New Zealand in 1935, with his wife and the playwright Moss Hart, as part of a cruise on the *Franconia*. 'I've got a song that is even better than "Night and Day"', Porter said, though he was cautious of 'swanking' about his own work. 'It's called "You're the Top", and it's having a wonderful run in New York in my latest musical comedy, *Anything Goes*.'

The *Radio Record*'s reporter was awestruck by Porter and his casual dropping of names such as Fred Astaire, Gertrude Lawrence, Noël Coward: all 'old friends'. A-list celebrities didn't often walk the streets of Wellington, and Porter brought with him glad tidings from abroad. In the theatre, the Depression was over: 'New York is bright at the moment, but London – London's the gayest spot on the face of the earth. Everyone's got their money back, and they're spending it!'

Posters saying 'Go to New Zealand' were spread all over the Continent, England and America, he said. 'I took the hint – and here I am!' The cosmopolitan bon vivant was impressed by the variety available on radio, for such a small population. 'There's only one complaint I have to make', he said. 'The number of restrictions that are imposed. If your Government wants to attract people to this country they've got to make things as pleasant as possible for them.'[116]

For Porter, that meant being able to get a late breakfast in a hotel, or a late drink legally. He was perhaps unaware of restrictions aimed at keeping the influence of American

Theo Walters hypnotises his band, Peter Pan Cabaret, Auckland, 1937. From left: Baden Brown, Vern Wilson, Phil Campbell, Bernie Duggan, Jim Watters, George Cambell, Lal Martin and Walters. L'Atelier/Dennis Huggard Collection, F-90427-35mm-6, Alexander Turnbull Library, Wellington

culture at bay. The main threat was through the film industry. A large number of picture theatres in New Zealand had names celebrating the Empire and the monarchy, such as the Regent, the Majestic, the King's, the Royal, the Rex and the Britannia. But the overwhelming number of films being screened in them came from America. In 1945 the *Listener* film critic Gordon Mirams wrote: 'If there is any such thing as a "New Zealand culture" it is to a large extent the creation of Hollywood.'[117]

Yet from 1928 a quota system required cinemas to screen a growing percentage of British films; by 1940 the quota had reached 20 percent. British films also attracted less customs duty than films from elsewhere, and a reduced fee for a censor's classification. Only during the Second World War were British films more popular with the New Zealand public than American films.[118] In the 1930s, the same American influence was being felt in music, on the records that were sold and broadcast, in performances in films such as *Hollywood Hotel* (with Benny Goodman) and *St Louis Blues* (Maxine Sullivan), and increasingly in the music played by New Zealand dance bands. Visits by actual Americans would be rare until the late 1930s.

Considering Chips Healy's experience, it is ironic that lengthy tours by Australian bands were an inspiration to New Zealand musicians and dancers as swing took hold through the 1930s. One of the earliest to visit – and stay long enough to make an impression on the local music scene – was Tut Coltman, a trumpet player from Sydney. At Easter 1931, Coltman began an eighteen-month residency with his band at the Adelphi Cabaret on Wellington's Cuba Street. They then embarked on a six-week tour that ventured as far as New Plymouth before Coltman went back to Australia.[119]

Returning in 1936, he found there was competition from another top Australian act that had just arrived: Theo Walters and his Personality Band. Originally from England, Walters was 'an unusual combination – a showman combined with a musician', whose looks resembled actor David Niven. Always immaculately dressed in white tie and tails, Walters would remain in New Zealand until the early 1940s. His Personality Band was a quintet renowned for its versatility; all the band members could play several instruments, with the trumpet player George Dobson also being adept on 'the mellaphone, the fiddle, and the only "goophos-horn" south of the line'.[119]

The US musician who Walters most admired was Benny Goodman; Duke Ellington was too futuristic, Cab Calloway too raucous. Swing was Walters' thing, 'modern music which causes listeners to feel a definite urge to dance'. He found that New Zealand dancers divided into two categories: those who danced seriously, and those who danced merely for pleasure. New Zealanders were less demonstrative than Australians, he said. A few people would approach the band and say how much they enjoyed the music, or tell the dance-hall manager. 'But no one will think of clapping.'

Walters' band was soon filling the Majestic most nights of the week, and began regular broadcasts on 2YA, its rhythm and 'pep' being a revelation to Wellington dancers. After six months, and briefly changing their name to the Velvet Rhythm Band, they moved to Auckland with similar success at the Peter Pan and on 1ZB. In both cities, they made strenuous efforts to socialise with local musicians and enjoy the scenery. The band kept changing as Australian players returned home: in Auckland, the saxophonists Jimmy Watters and Baden Brown, and two trumpeters, the veteran Vern Wilson, and the Paeroa prodigy Phil Campbell.

Wilson had just returned from Australia after the Musicians' Union debacle, and was promised the position of first trumpet. When he arrived for an audition at the Peter Pan, he found a young Maori man waiting outside with a trumpet case. 'You're Vern Wilson, aren't you?' he said. 'I'm the other trumpet player. Theo says you'll be playing first.' It was Phil Campbell, who was ready to move aside. But once Wilson heard him play, he told Walters he couldn't push the young player out, and played rank-and-file trumpet instead.

During the Peter Pan shows, Walters parodied Cab Calloway, and musicians took part in comedy skits, playing characters such as 'Olga Pulovski, the beautiful spy' while the audience clustered around the stage. Walters 'taught us a lot as regards showmanship', reported J. R. Allanson, and 'proved to be a big money booster'. Walters took a pay cut coming to New Zealand, but his fees were soon breaking records, making 'our employers big-money conscious'.[120]

By late 1939, Walters' band at the Peter Pan had evolved into an all-New Zealand outfit, in high demand. Each night they would perform a curtain-raiser before the film at the State Theatre on Symonds Street, then quickly pack up and head down to the Peter Pan on Lorne Street to begin at 8.30 pm.[121] The addition of 'petite vocaliste' Winsome Walsh – 'endowed with plenty of personality' – proved an instant drawcard.

GAIETY THEATRES (AUST.)—IN CONJUNCTION WITH MARTIN, DOOHAN & CARROLL PROUDLY PRESENT

TEX MORTON

"THE GREATEST AND MOST VERSATILE ENTERTAINER OF OUR TIME"

On Stage in Person

3 COMPLETE SHOWS IN ONE!
SINGING! SHOOTING! HYPNOTISM!

...RS OF RADIO,
...ECORDS, STAGE
AND SCREEN

2½ HOURS OF
MUSIC, AMAZING
SHARP-SHOOTING,
FUN, SINGING,
YODELLING, AND
ENTERTAINMENT!!

FINAL, BRIEF
NEW ZEALAND
TOUR, BEFORE
LEAVING FOR
HOLLYWOOD
DIRECT FROM
ALL TOP-LINE
AUSTRALIAN
THEATRES AND
KERRIDGE-ODEON
(N.Z.) THEATRES

with SISTER DORRIE

New Songs and Old Favourites

BE WISE
BOOK NOW

WATCH YOUR
NEWSPAPERS AND
LISTEN-IN FOR
FURTHER DETAILS

AND !!
THE BOMB-SHELL OF 1949!!!

This amazing man, TEX MORTON, famous all over Australia as COMIC STRIP, RADIO SERIAL HERO, ACTOR, COMPOSER, AUTHOR, POET, ACE SHARPSHOOTER, SINGER, LECTURER, ROUGH RIDER, CIRCUS RODEO PROPRIETOR, and ENTREPRENEUR, now shows for the first time in New Zealand how as ROBERT LANE (Master Hypnotist), he intrigued and enthralled Australian audiences for years, whilst at the same time becoming famous on Radio and Records as TEX MORTON!!

TEX MORTON

(Acclaimed by Australian Press "Surely the Greatest and Most Versatile Entertainer of Our Time!".)

HE DEMONSTRATES:—
PSYOCHOMETRY—
MIND-READING—
MESMERISM—
HYPNOTISM

HE'S MYSTIC!!
HE'S AMAZING!!
HE'S DIFFERENT!!

GUARANTEED
ABSOLUTELY
GENUINE, SCIENTIFIC,
AND EDUCATIONAL!!

Hailed by Press, Experts
and Critics Alike,
as one of
the Finest Professional
Hypnotists Ever!!

Unusual, Entertaining and Amazing
HYPNOTIST

ENTIRELY DIFFERENT! IF YOU LIKE HYPNOTISTS, DON'T BE TURNED AWAY!
SOMETHING NEW! YOU'LL ENJOY THIS LEARNED BOOK NOW!
MAN with the "MASTER MIND"
NOTE: Tex had originally intended to bring to New Zealand his famous Rodeo and Circus, which has toured all States of Australia for about 10 years. However, on looking around he found there are several excellent shows of that type at present touring N.Z, also several other very good Theatrical Shows . . . He therefore decided, on hearing how interested New Zealanders are in Hypnosis, to present, on this final tour, before commencing work in Hollywood, his really top-line, amazing and scientific demonstration of Hypnosis which gained him the reputation of being one of the finest Hypnotists in the world to-day, long before he was known world-wide as "Tex Morton." He has been a student of Psychology, Hypnosis, and Mesmerism for many years, and his experiences in all walks of life have given him a vast knowledge and insight of the human mind. We have seen some amazing Hypnotists, but feel sure that you will be more than pleasantly surprised when Tex demonstrates his remarkable—and at times, uncanny powers.—THE MANAGEMENT. Hoping to meet you when we visit your town. Yours—
P.S.—Mr Morton will explain the "mystery" of Hypnotism, reveal the so-called "secrets," and show how any intelligent, normal person can become a Hypnotist.

Tex Morton displayed his versatility on this 1950 tour of New Zealand with Sister Dorrie, 1950. Eph-E-Cabot-Variety-1950-01, Alexander Turnbull Library, Wellington

SINGING! SHOOTING! HYPNOTISM!

Tex Morton wore many hats, and they were all on display when he returned to New Zealand for a series of shows in 1960. It had been a dozen years since he had performed in Dunedin, so the Town Hall was packed on 1 September to witness The Great Morton in his various guises. After an opening set by the Big Beat 5, the star of the show was introduced by Jamie Beal, his Australian drummer.[122]

To generous applause Morton took the stage carrying his guitar. He was dressed formally – dark suit, white shirt, black tie – though wearing a stockman's hat. The audience was in for a fast-moving variety show of the old school. The first act was Tex Morton the singer, running through his many hits in a medley, segueing between them after a verse and a chorus. He gave a lively rendition of 'Waltzing Matilda', and earned a rousing ovation for his hit 'Drover's Song'. He closed the set with a novelty 'The Cat Came Back'.

Placed beside his microphone was a large brown-paper bag. Morton dipped into it as the evening progressed to change his hat and his persona. In a top hat he became The Great Morton, sharpshooter. His first target was a playing card, with its edge facing towards him. No problem: his bullet seemed to split it in two.

A member of the audience then held up four pieces of chalk between his fingers. The first three exploded into dust as the bullets struck them just millimetres from the fingers. Aiming at the last piece of chalk . . . Morton missed twice, to his obvious disgust. He shocked the audience by covering the sights of his rifle with a piece of cardboard, growling, 'As the damn sights on this thing are not accurate anyway, I might as well shoot without them altogether!'

His rifle blindfolded, he shot the final chalk. Another bullet snuffed out a burning candle. Then he turned his gun on his assistant, who was smoking a cigarette but not looking at all relaxed. A crack of the rifle saved any need for an ashtray, then Morton swivelled to take out his last target: a piece of chalk swinging on a string like a pendulum. End of Act One.

After an interval Dr Robert Morton took the stage to display his expertise in extra-sensory perception and hypnotherapy. He made wisecracks while, behind his

Tex Morton (left) with friends in Papatoetoe, 1933. Gordon Spittle collection

back, ten members of the audience placed personal objects such as watches and rings into blank envelopes. After they shuffled the envelopes Morton 'by puzzling methods' gave each one back to its rightful owner. He finished by hypnotising the same ten people, who then had the audience 'convulsed in laughter at their antics' while under his spell.

In his various guises Morton's visit was much appreciated. It was rare that a western performer visited Dunedin, and he donated half of his proceeds to intellectually handicapped children.

Any eye-witness account of an appearance by Tex Morton is valuable, as even the facts about him take on the quality of myth. But this much we know: he was New Zealand's first international popular music star, and Australasia's most influential performer in country music. Hypnotism and Hollywood are all part of the legend.

This colourful character was born Robert William Lane in Nelson on 30 August 1916. He was taught some guitar chords by local friends, among them a young Maori called Benny Morgan. 'I used to get round the camp fires with the Maori boys every apple-picking season', said Morton in 1939. 'Whilst I could get plenty of noise from

a guitar, I don't suppose there was a mistake in technique of which I wasn't guilty. Then when I was just 16, I met a Spaniard, the handsomest man I have ever seen, and a perfect wizard with a guitar. From him I learned to play properly, and anything I can produce out of a guitar I owe to his tuition.'[123]

Morton spent time on the Nelson wharves, listening to merchant seamen's songs and stories. If a circus came to town, he would busk the waiting crowds until the proprietors chased him away.[124] He said that he used to 'whistle and sing and yodel all the time – you know how boys are. The story is that I learnt to yodel up in the Maitai Valley, but it was just one of the things I did in vaudeville. I used to sing a comic song and a straight song and a ballad, and then put in a yodel occasionally for variety.'[125]

Morton started running away from home at age fourteen. As the Depression intensified, he began singing with local dance bands. His repertoire included pop, ballads and jazz, but he found his niche with the country songs of Vernon Dalhart ('The Prisoner's Song') and Jimmie Rodgers ('Waiting For a Train').

Just sixteen, he hit the road, travelling from Gore to Waihi, busking for his keep where he could (the city fathers of Hamilton asked him to leave).[126] He worked as a fruit-picker, electrician, buying gold, selling radios and canvassing for dry-cleaning. In 1932 he was in Napier, where he sang with the touring dance band of Tut Coltman. He took up with a travelling boxing troupe that was part of a vaudeville show run by the Foster family of Australia. He sang, erected tents, fought a round or two if required, and drove a truck.

In that year, he made his first recordings, in Wellington. About twenty songs were recorded, direct to aluminium disc using the Speak-a-Phone system; among the songs were 'The Insult', 'The End of the Hobo's Trail', 'Mexican Yodel' and 'Last Round Up'. Although not commercially released – Morton himself scratched the titles on the discs – they are some of the earliest recordings of country music outside of the US.[127]

With a group of other young entertainers, in 1933 he decided to try his luck in Australia. By this stage, he had a new surname: Morton. He claimed to have plucked it from a sign on a garage in Waihi when he was questioned by the police and asked if he was the runaway Bobby Lane. The nickname 'Tex' was bestowed on him by singer and broadcaster Jack Davey, who emigrated from New Zealand to Australia at about the same time.

In Sydney, Morton busked for a couple of months, then hitch-hiked to Queensland. He hoped to find work as a singer with a travelling show; instead he became known as the tent-hand who would try anything. He boxed, rode motorcycles on the Wall of Death, tamed wild animals, and even 'subdued and kissed lady wrestlers as a come-on stooge'.[128] He jumped aboard trains and busked his way to Darwin, where he was collared by a railroad detective and sent packing by a judge.

Back in Sydney, while trying to break into show business, there are reports of him labouring at Luna Park, on the Sydney Harbour Bridge, for Claude Neon Signs and at sea as an electrician and stoker. He won first prize in a talent quest for radio station 2KY, and this led to him recording four songs for Regal Zonophone that influenced the future of country music in Australia and New Zealand.

The sessions took place on 25 February 1936 at Homebush, the Sydney studios of the Columbia Graphophone Company. Two of the songs were his own, 'Swiss Sweetheart' and 'Happy Yodeller', and two were American, 'Texas in the Spring' and 'Going Back to Texas'. Australian country music historian Eric Watson was impressed by the lack of nervousness shown by the young man as he explored new territory. 'The vocal style that always seems original rather than derivative is already set. The guitar is recognisably Tex Morton . . . . the yodelling clearly shows its debt to Goebel Reeves, but even there the imprint of Tex's own individual personality is firmly stamped.'[129] Australian musicologist Peter Doyle also remarks on the assured yodelling: 'Quite unlike that of other country singers, Morton's trilling, freely melismatic yodel displays a high degree of unselfconscious virtuosity.'[130]

A week later he recorded two songs that stayed among his best-sellers: 'Wyoming Willie' and 'You're Going to Leave the Old Home Jim'. He was paid a flat fee, with no future royalties, and went back to scrambling for a living. He decided to go home and visit his parents, and once in New Zealand busked his way south so he arrived with some money in his pocket. While walking down the street in Nelson he saw, in the window of Cull's music store, a large cardboard cut-out of a singing cowboy. In big letters, a sign read: *Tex Morton, the Singing Cowboy Sensation*. 'The records were selling like hot cakes', recounted Watson, 'and he was already famous in New Zealand.'

Returning to Australia, he toured with Gladys Moncrieff, was greeted by crowds and courted by

Tex Morton and Sister Dorrie (Dorothy Carroll) in the 1940s, when stage names served many purposes. Gordon Spittle collection

celebrities. At his first appearance in Brisbane, 50,000 people turned out to see him. Between 1936 and 1943, he recorded 93 songs at Columbia, which were released on the company's Regal Zonophone label with the credit 'The Yodelling Boundary Rider: Tex Morton'. According to a 1939 promotional poster, at his peak he was selling 10,000 records a month, more than any international artist in Australia and New Zealand, and more than all Australian artists combined.

Watson attributed much of Morton's early success to the following he had built up as a busker and circus performer, because the business establishment of show business – the agents, managers, radio DJs – regarded country music with disdain. 'The "hillbilly" stigma was already growing, and radio more often played his records on sufferance because of the demand . . . . usually the announcers took care to make it clear that they considered that kind of thing to be beneath them.'[131]

Much of the material Morton recorded was cowboy songs, but from his earliest recordings he included songs with an Australian flavour or setting that he picked up on his travels or wrote himself. According to Graeme Smith, Morton's most important innovation was his localising of hillbilly themes to Australian places and events. His song 'The Yodelling Bagman' is an example: a swagman is looking for work, 'jumping rattlers in NSW and cane trains up in Cairns, cutting sugar in the sunny north, and riding way out west'.[132]

Other songs made use of his circus, vaudeville and rodeo experiences. He added music to poems by bush bards such as Henry Lawson and Banjo Paterson, and 'fused turn-of-the-century Australian poetry with American country music, and helped create the modern legacy of Australian country music'.[133]

In 1941 Morton introduced two other innovations to his recordings: Australia's first with a country band, the Roughriders, and the first recordings with a female country singer, Dorothy Carroll. The pair recorded five duets together; for their tours, Carroll was called Sister Dorrie, because the very idea of a woman joining a travelling show was considered risqué.[134]

Morton's fame seemed to know no bounds in Australia: he was mobbed in the street, sold thousands of 'Tex Morton' mail-order guitars, published his own songbook, and even had his own monthly comic series, *Tex Morton's Wild West Comic*. In 1940 he formed his own travelling show, the Tex Morton Wild West Rodeo: an eye-catching caravan of vehicles touring Australia.

He returned to New Zealand in 1949 to record 24 songs at Astor Studios in Auckland. Wally Ransom organised the band: Johnny Bradfield on rhythm, George Campbell on bass and Tommy Kahi on steel guitar, later replaced by Bill Sevesi. (Kahi said Morton arrived late and drunk for the sessions, so he asked to be paid for the work done thus far, and left. Sevesi remembered being called in when another player couldn't make it, and that Morton was easy to play with.) Three of the songs were Morton originals: 'The Stockman's Prayer', 'A Soldier's Sweetheart' and 'A Rollin' Stone'. Morton explained to Sevesi that he always wore his cowboy hat when recording, as it bounced the sound back towards his ears, just as it would when singing in a concert.[135]

Although Morton continued to record, Watson suggests that all his important recordings were done before 1941. 'Almost his entire reputation as a country singer rests on the 87 tracks he produced in the five years and eight months till then.'

Morton was always seeking another challenge, so his ability to wear several hats enabled him to diversify. In early 1950, he toured New Zealand with 'three complete shows in one! Singing! Shooting! Hypnotism!' and it was this style of variety act that he took to the United States that year.[136]

Watson wrote that, by orthodox musical standards, Morton was never a good singer:

He had nothing of a voice in the accepted sense, he broke almost every law of voice production, his own melodies were very elementary, his guitar playing about fifth-lesson stuff. But remember that this scanty equipment was sufficient, in a few years of his early life, to sweep through a nation that is notorious for deriding its own artists, and to make his name a household word . . . .

We know how he did it. The sheer drive and vitality that he could breathe into a number, the superb control of voice, the intensity of feeling for his subject, the effect and sympathy he could achieve with half-a-dozen first-position chords and three or four elementary runs.[137]

Morton's North American sojourn lasted nearly a decade; it is *Crocodile Dundee* rewritten as a musical. He was met at the airport by Gene Autry, and befriended Oscar Davis, the man who discovered Elvis Presley. After six months of performing, acting in films, and mingling with the high-spending Autry gang and Hollywood friends who included Roy Rogers and Errol Flynn, Morton was given 24 hours to leave the country by the immigration department. Canada then became his base, and while in North America he toured as Hank Williams' support act – holding Hank up was part of the job – and studied hypnotherapy.[138]

As The Great Morton, he became a big box-office draw, especially in Canada. This one-man show featured music, monologues, rope tricks, whip-cracking, sharpshooting, memory displays, hypnotism and extra-sensory perception exhibitions. He held a Carnegie Hall audience spellbound with his monologue about the background to 'Waltzing Matilda'.[139]

When Morton returned to Australia in 1959, he brought a 'Grand Ole Opry' touring show with him. Also

Lou Clauson (left) and Simon Meihana (right) ask Tex Morton for advice about the Lou and Simon hat-changing routine, Australia, early 1960s. Lou Clauson Collection, PA1-f-192-36-05, Alexander Turnbull Library, Wellington

on the bill was US country star Roy Acuff, who meant little to Australian audiences, and Morton was suffering from laryngitis. The show closed very quickly: the market had changed since his late 1930s heyday. Rural districts could now receive television, and there was a surfeit of roadshows.

Morton's response was to go bush. He took his station-wagon, a two-way radio, his hunting and fishing tackle, a terrier, a tame magpie and his beloved yellow cat, and headed into the outback of Australia. For five years he visited his old haunts before a call from home – his real home – brought him back into the limelight. In 1967 the New Zealand Broadcasting Corporation asked him to host a television variety show, *Country Touch*. The programme was hugely successful and ran for three years.

Variety could have been Morton's middle name: his own publicity described him as 'the most versatile talent since Leonardo da Vinci'.[140] His flair for publicity,

showmanship and extravagant claims led to suggestions that Tex and the truth were not closely acquainted. But in 1976 Watson wrote, 'I wonder no longer, for lately I've had the privilege of looking through Tex's huge collection of cuttings and souvenirs . . . . there is no story that he cannot back up with evidence.'

Morton died on 23 July 1983. His legacy is the interest he stimulated in country music in Australia and New Zealand, a body of quality work that has had lasting appeal, and his role in establishing a style of country music that was unique to his location. In the 1940s, said Watson, he inspired thousands of performers who 'seized on his style and made it a national one', and then created an Australian country music that would always reflect the imprint of his personality. During his 1949 trip to New Zealand, Morton said, 'What I've been trying to get into the skulls of people over in Australia is that they've got a folk music of their own.'[141]

Wellington had never seen anything like the parade that promenaded noisily down Willis Street in August 1938. Tut Coltman and his band were saying farewell with a bang before embarking on a North Island tour. Leading the convoy in a car was the Majestic's proprietor Fred Carr, a publicity conscious showman of the old school. Besides giving the Coltman band a lively send-off after its year-long residency, Carr wanted to promote the next over-seas act appearing at the Majestic: Sammy Lee and his Americanadians.

'To the accompaniment of blaring trumpets', the Coltman parade made its way towards Lambton Quay in

Tut Coltman, Australian band leader, spent long periods in New Zealand during the 1930s. *Jim Gower collection*

two cars and a six-ton truck. The Americanadians' brass section provided the salute although, while rehearsing 'Pagan Love Song' the day before, Carr had run from the kitchen to the dance floor, waving his arms and saying 'I don't want that noise in here!'[142] On board Coltman's truck were his band's instruments, golf clubs and equipment; among the musicians were a signwriter and a carpenter, handy skills on a tour that would last months. An advance man had gone ahead of the band, arranging dance gigs in the central North Island and plastering lamp-posts with posters saying that Tut and his Swingstars were on their way. The band based itself at a hotel in Palmerston North, paying for its accommodation with a gig each Saturday night, while venturing around the district for dances: Woodville, Dannevirke, Pahiatua, Marton, Bulls, Wanganui. After two months, they moved on, taking their slick dance music to Hawke's Bay, Taranaki, the King Country. 'We travelled right up the island, as far as Kaikohe', Coltman's bass player Jim Gower recalled:

> These little country dance halls would be absolutely packed. We never had a contract among the band, we just said, right, we'll run the dances and split the take. The first night we played Palmerston, we earned eight or nine pounds each for four hours' work. When this started going on, three or four nights a week around the country, we were probably the rich-est musicians, the only ones really making money because all the others were just on part-time jobs. There was really no money to be made as a musician before the war.[143]

Coltman's band was now mostly New Zealanders.[144] They played stock arrangements or new scores written – after listening sessions with the latest discs at 2YD – by local pianist Emil Kew or Coltman's reed man Bob Girvan. Taking a song such as 'Marie', Girvan's arrangement would emulate Tommy Dorsey, with a vocal trio taking the lead, or Benny Goodman's version of 'Stardust', with Girvan himself on clarinet.

On the road, the Coltman band entertained with novelty items such as 'Slap That Bass' and 'Mama Don't Allow It' that showcased each instrument while the audience gathered around to watch. The hot novelty dance of the season would get them back on the floor: the Lambeth Walk. A group dance, like the earlier Palais Glide, the Lambeth was designed to help the less confident feel comfortable on the floor. As much a walk as a dance, the Lambeth – like most group dances – encouraged more

August 1938, outside the Majestic cinema on Willis Street, Wellington: Fred Carr, manager of the Majestic Cabaret, farewells Tut Coltman and his band on a six-month tour of the North Island. Among the band are Bob Girvan (third left) and bass player Jim Gower (second from right). Jim Gower collection

spontaneous participation than the intimidating rituals of couple dancing. Originally a song from the 1937 musical *Me And My Girl* – until Adele England, a London dance instructor, invented the steps – the Lambeth Walk became the most popular new dance since the Charleston. Sid Colin described it as 'a piece of bogus cockneyana' in which dancers, emulating Pearly Kings, perform a 'sedate knees-up suitable for the ballroom: *Any time you're Lambeth way, any ev'ning, any day – you'll find them all, doing the Lambeth walk. Oi!!*'

With heavy promotion and demonstrations by England, the Lambeth spread from London's chic Mayfair ballrooms to dance halls in the suburbs, then the provinces

and soon the world. By November 1938, Dunedin dance promoter Joe Brown had introduced it at his Town Hall dances. Every night, lessons were given at the Empire theatre, with the local commercial radio station involved so people could join in at home.[145]

Joe Brown's dances at the Dunedin Town Hall were such a social success they became known as his 'matrimonial agency'. For 30 years, the Town Hall dance was the place to meet and mingle with the opposite sex. Brown, a born entrepreneur, capitalised on his success as a match-maker by starting spin-off businesses. Couples who had met at a Saturday dance needed 'somewhere decent' to nurture their friendship, so Brown opened a tearoom for Sunday afternoons, the Highcliff Café. He launched Caledonian Catering to handle weddings and developed property in Mosgiel so that newlyweds could buy their first homes, which they could furnish by shopping at Brown's Furniture Mart. He also hired out prams and cots.[146]

Brown began early as a dance promoter. At the age of nine, he was the captain of a rugby team that needed a bus to get to a tournament, but their headmaster refused to pay for it. So Brown organised a 'grand dance' featuring a well-known dance band and cut up shoeboxes for tickets. The band was actually just a pianist and violinist, but the tickets sold out, the evening made money, the team got to the tournament and did well – and Brown was hooked.

Rugby also led to the first of the Saturday night dances. In 1936 a Ranfurly Shield game between Otago and Southland was to take place in Dunedin. Brown reasoned that the crowd needed somewhere to go after the game, so decided to run a dance at the Town Hall. There was a slight problem: to hire the hall cost £30 and Brown was broke. So he borrowed a pound off his brother, bought some rabbiting gear and got busy. A few days later, he had his £30 and the hall was booked.

Saturday 1 August 1936 was a red-letter day in Dunedin: Joe Brown's first dance, at the Town Hall's concert chamber, was a great success. His profit was £65. Within a couple of months, Brown was running the event every Saturday night; by November, the dances had moved to the larger main hall, with Brown guaranteeing his patrons a 'thrill for every tick of the clock'.[147] Eventually Brown booked both halls, so that for their two shilling entrance fee, dancers could move between them. In the concert chamber were the old-time, strict tempo dances such as the maxina, the Alberts, the Canadian three-step and gypsy tap, while the main hall featured modern dances such as the foxtrot, quickstep and Latin American. The patrons could also enjoy a sandwich, a piece of cake and a cup of tea in the sit-down supper room. To add to the atmosphere Brown introduced gimmicks such as quizzes,

Seen here in 1938, the Dick Colvin Orchestra was popular in Dunedin for many years, performing at Joe Brown's Town Hall dances and on 4YA. From left: Monty Howard, Dick Colvin, Malcolm Chisholm, Frank Robb, Jim Burbery, Fred Gedson, Keith Harris, Jack Priestley and Frank Reader. *Bob Bothamley collection/Peter Downes*

BLUE SMOKE

competitions, scavenger hunts and talent quests. A 'masked mystery singer' competition was a 'horrible flop'. And at the end of the evening, after the all-important last dance before men escorted their partners to their front gates, came 'God Save the King'. The *Evening Star*'s musical martinet L. D. Austin insisted that: 'Any musician worth his salt should be able to play "God Save the King" in every key.'[148]

From 1937, the Joe Brown dances were broadcast on 4ZB, which meant the music was heard nationwide from 10.30 pm each Saturday night, opening with the strains of the theme song, 'All Ashore'. Among the bands that regularly played at them were Bob Shannon's Slavonia Dance Band, Dick Colvin's Orchestra, Alex Swan's Orchestra, Harry Strang's Excelsior Dance Band and Jock McCaw's Commodores. The live broadcasts caused some resentment among the musicians, who didn't have time for a rehearsal or sound check. 'Their reluctance only intensified when random scathing comments by musically minded critics appeared in the local papers.'[149] Angered by the slapdash broadcasts, one night the three bands booked to play went on strike. Harry Strang was among those who 'cornered Joe and told him we weren't happy . . . . we finally got an extra half-crown a player for the ones that played over the air.' However, as the bands changed, the pay rates reverted to what they had been. 'So it was a bit of a hollow victory, but at least it was a victory.'[150]

Calder Prescott, band leader and pianist, said that Brown did not mistreat the musicians, but they were not pampered either; the standing joke among local players was 'How many times have you been sacked by Joe Brown?' As a businessman and promoter, 'he knew exactly what was happening, but musically he didn't have much idea'. Perhaps the entertainer in Brown enjoyed playing the role of a musical ingénue: as a regionalist, he always referred to 'Alexandra's Ragtime Band'. Prestcott remembered him watching a brass section sitting through a pause of a few bars and complaining, 'They're not even playing! And I'm paying them the same money as the pianist.' On that point, Prescott could only agree.[151]

Brown's dances were not the only game in town: in the late 1930s, his competition included dances at the Early Settlers' Hall, the New Century at Milburn, Cargill's Castle Cabaret, and smaller dances such as the Regal, the Sunshine and the Piccadilly.[152] Dick Colvin launched the Peter Pan Cabaret in 1938 and, post-war, Strang started his own dances at the St John Ambulance Hall in South Dunedin. But Brown's dances were the epitome of

egalitarian entertainment: thousands of Dunedinites glided across his dance floors, hundreds met their spouses, and he employed many of the best musicians in the city, among them Dick Colvin, Keith Harris and Julian Lee.

Describing New Zealand's leading dance-band musicians in 1941, the *Listener* turned to Gilbert and Sullivan. 'The modern oompy-doo experts are wandering minstrels, without the rags and patches of that restless musician in *The Mikado*.'[153] The most prominent, and peripatetic, local musician was band leader and saxophonist Lauri Paddi. During the 1930s, his second home was a sleeping berth on the Limited, when not on the road in a truck full of instruments marked *Lauri Paddi Band on Tour*. Originally from Christchurch, Paddi had become a professional musician in 1926, flitting between bands such as the Rhythm Kings and Orpheans in Auckland, and residencies in Wellington with bands at the San Toy Cabaret, the Adelphi and the Ritz. His travel on the main trunk line intensified once he became band leader at the two top venues in the country, spending usually six months at the Majestic in Wellington, then another long contract at the Peter Pan in Auckland, before returning to Wellington to start again. In the summer, outside of the ball season, he would decamp with his Peter Pan band to Mt Maunganui where, after their gigs, they would hold jam sessions in the large country house they rented, then sleep till past noon.[154]

Paddi's dances at the top cabarets were often broadcast live-to-air, giving him a national profile that came in handy when he took his bands on lengthy tours. In 1938 and 1939, they toured extensively around the country, reaching the deep South. One night they might play in Winton or Balclutha, and the next they could be the much-hyped guest attraction at Joe Brown's Dunedin Town Hall dances. 'Devoid of blatancy', a Dunedin fan wrote to the paper, 'the northern players are well worth hearing, and should prove a source of musical education to the many good instrumentalists in this city.'[155] Among the band-members were the star trumpeter Phil Campbell and his eighteen-year-old bass-playing brother George.

Paddi bought a small bus to transport the musicians and their instruments, with adventures typical of touring in an era when sealed roads were rare. 'You know the kind: raining like the devil and a puncture; somebody crawls under the car in his dinner suit to fit the jack and gets his

Lauri Paddi and his band alternated between the Majestic in Wellington and the Peter Pan in Auckland. In this 1937 lineup are, from left: Johnny Madden, Jack Thompson, Ken McDonald, Lauri Paddi, Nin Pitcaithly, Hugh Tatton and Bill Pritchard. E. M. Alderdice Collection, PA1-q-182-04, Alexander Turnbull Library, Wellington

hand trodden on as he emerges, upon which everyone laughs except the victim.'[156]

The roll call of players who spent time in Paddi's bands reflects the privileged status of the Peter Pan and Majestic cabarets. Most famous among them was expatriate Canadian saxophonist Art Rosoman, who would come to lead his own bands there. Crooning drummer Johnny Madden had been a drawcard in Auckland bands since the 1920s, while reed man Bob Girvan was later a foundation member of the National Orchestra. Others who shared stages with Paddi include the pianists Jack Roberts and Jack Thompson, Fred Gore, Monty Howard, Pete McMurray, Wally Ransom, Jimmy Watters, vocalist Jimmie MacFarlane, and arranger Ken McDonald. He also recruited the best women vocalists, among them Jean McPherson and Marion Waite. A gig with the Paddi band was a coup for any musician, recalled bass player Jim Gower. 'You were really

getting shoved from pillar to post, there was nothing permanent for dance musicians except the Peter Pan Cabaret in Auckland and the Majestic in Wellington.'[157]

A special night at the Majestic could be 21 shillings a double, which included an item by the Majestic Ballet, demonstrations of the rumba and tango by Jimmy James and Estelle 'Lolita' Katene, as well as Paddi's 'sweet music and good tempo, in an atmosphere of good taste'.[158] By comparison, a Saturday 'dress night' at Wellington's Roseland cabaret was 12/6 for two, and a regular night only seven shillings.

Paddi's heyday was in the late 1930s and early 1940s, although he continued to lead bands after the war. His band was usually an eight-piece, but its significance outweighed its size, thanks to his ability to choose – and pay for – the best players available, and his national profile through tours, long residencies and regular broadcasts.

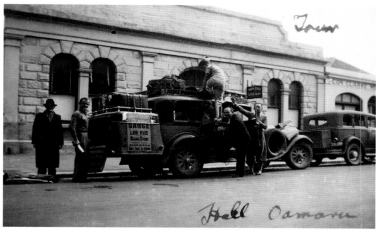

The Lauri Paddi band on the road during its 1938 South Island tour. In the Timaru photo, Paddi is in the togs, Phil Campbell in the dark shirt and Art Rosoman in the sports coat. E. M. Alderdice Collection, PAColl-0089-1-29 (top) and PA1-q-182-17-4 (bottom), Alexander Turnbull Library, Wellington. Poster: Eph-C-DANCE-Social-1940-01, Alexander Turnbull Library, Wellington

In 1937 his band performed at the Majestic for a record ten months, broadcasting three or four times a week.

A teenage Jim Warren first saw Paddi on stage at the Peter Pan in 1936, and he was an inspirational figure, dressed in a dinner jacket with cuffs braided in a musical motif. 'The guys were all playing, having a great time and a laugh, playing music and I loved the sound of it.' To Don Richardson, who was briefly in the band after the war, Paddi's strength was his reliability: always reading scores the same way, not taking risks, playing 'trustworthy' sax and violin. Jim Gower remembered him as 'very quiet, probably more sober than the rest of us'. 'Dr Paddi' was also known as an amateur physician, with a stash of patent medicines for any musician's malady. He was regarded as a gentleman and a gentle leader: 'If you were a bit late, he'd say, *Try and be on time . . .*', recalled Richardson. 'It was a happy band.' Besides hiring the top musicians, Paddi's

greatest skill was reading the crowd, wrote the *Music Maker*: 'He knows his public and he knows his swing fans and pleases us all.'[159]

One visiting band was especially influential in bringing swing to New Zealand's dance floors, and inspiring local musicians: Sammy Lee and his Americanadians. Lee was a flamboyant Canadian who had been in show business since the age of thirteen; he was a large man and loud dresser with a glamorous singing girlfriend. The Americanadians arrived in late 1938 and for the next eighteen months held down lengthy residencies at the Majestic in Wellington and the Metropole in Auckland. Their dances were broadcast regularly on 2YA and 1YA. As the name suggests, the Americanadians were a mix of musicians from North America, plus English pianist Len

Hawkins; some Australians and New Zealanders replaced members of the band who left during the tour.

'They were a big influence', recalled Auckland trumpeter Jim Warren, who heard them often in 1939. 'We'd never heard anything like it. The brass could *blow*. They could just play so loud with a marvellous, lovely shimmering sound. They played dance music of course but they also had some good jazz players within the group.' Bob Reid was the arranger and trumpeter, and most of the musicians could double on other instruments. Among them was trumpeter Pete McMurray, who stayed in New Zealand to play with the Lauri Paddi band. But New Zealand musicians also contributed, such as Bob Girvan, Roy Lester and Norm D'Ath. Lee himself was 'a powerful drummer, a bit loud at times', and his girlfriend Joy Rovelle would often join members of the band performing as a vocal quartet that emulated the Merry Macs.[160]

Audiences were impressed by the freshness and vitality of the Americanadians, who mid-set could provide their own floor show, mixing comedy, variety and glee-club.

'These boys certainly know how to dress up a number', wrote Bert Peterson. 'Sammy Lee has a unique method of band leading. He gives all the limelight to the members of his band, and sits in the background himself, constantly devising new means of putting the boys over.' In early 1940, Lee and his band recorded several tracks at Auckland's Beacon Recording Studios, including 'Smiles' sung by Joy Rovelle and 'Jeepers Creepers' sung by Roy Lester.[161]

The Americanadians made many friends among New Zealand musicians, and when a farewell dance was held in their honour at the Dixieland Cabaret in July 1940, it became a cutting contest between the bands of Johnny Madden, Ted Croad and the visitors. Soon Lee was back in Sydney, running his own King's Cross nightclub, the Roosevelt; he later opened the famous Sydney clubs Les Girls and the Latin Quarter.

Described as 'generous, excitable and as hard as nails', Lee was known for high standards in a nightlife scene quickly being taken over by lowlife. He died of a heart attack in 1975, remembered as 'a likeable scoundrel'

Sammy Lee at the drum kit with, from left, Auckland musicians Jim Warren, Roy Lester and John MacKenzie, at the Masonic Hall, Queen Street, Auckland, early 1940. *Jim Warren collection*

Sammy Lee and his Americanadians arriving in Wellington in 1938, to begin a long, influential stay in New Zealand. In the back row are, from left: Bob Reid, Del Davies, Sammy Lee, Joy Rovelle, Majestic Cabaret manager Fred Carr, Len Hawkins and Stan Grant. In front, Bill Arstad, Neil Thurgate and Pete McMurray. Jim Warren collection

whose band brought sophistication and energy to the music scenes of Australia and New Zealand. 'They were brilliant musicians', remembered Jim Warren. 'They played classy, swinging dance music of the day.'[162]

A decade earlier, a sophisticated Wellington magazine called *Tit-Bits* could still run a column called 'News from Home', write editorials decrying Americanisation of New Zealand culture, and hyperbolically describe jazz rhythms as 'the tom-toms of natives who still feature missionary on the Sunday menu'.[163] But the cultural influence of 'home', with its decorous light orchestras and formal dance rituals, had dramatically declined during the 1930s. Now, the swift changes in music and dance came via the US, on record and radio, in films, and the succession of imported band leaders. The need to keep up with cultural fashions had become increasingly urgent, but there were few doubts as to their source.

A black American dancer passed through Auckland in October 1938 on his way to work the Tivoli circuit in Australia. The hoofer, Peter Ray, described his skill as 'terpsichorean art. Rhythmic toe dancing you might call it.' While in Australia, he hoped to introduce a dance that was the latest New York craze, 'a hotted-up version of the lindy hop'. In his cabin on the *Aorangi*, Ray gave details of the dance, using terms like 'trucking' and 'pecking'. And he gave an enthusiastic demonstration, 'with quaint cries of *Yeah, man* and *How'm I doin'*.' The new dance was called the jitterbug.

Based in Harlem, and a brother-in-law of band leader Cab Calloway, Ray explained that jitter-bugging was another trend in folk-dancing. Like the now-fading dance 'the big apple', it was an amalgam of what had come before, but more suitable for the ballroom. Ray offered to come back and teach New Zealand the dance. A delightful idea, responded the *Radio Record*. 'Perhaps, beautiful thought, we may even become jitter-bug minded.'[164]

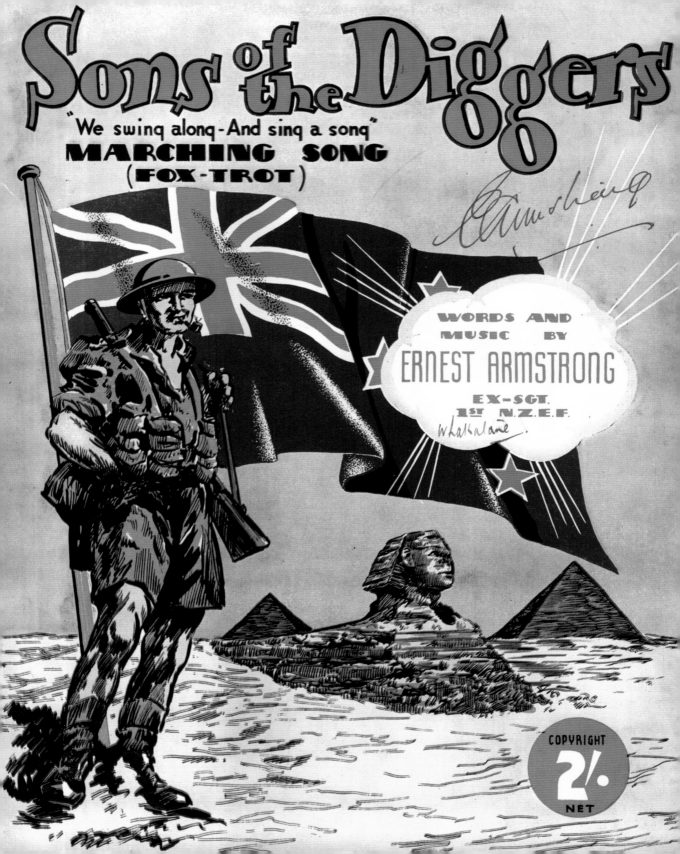

1939-1945

The Second World War had a lasting impact on New Zealand's musical life: on the careers of key musicians, on songwriting and dance styles, on radio broadcasting and the infrastructure of the popular music industry. As elsewhere, the conflict began with the 'phoney war', in which the nation worked out how to respond. Musically, there was a search for a popular song that would capture the mood of patriotism and hope. The closest song to achieve this was the Maori Battalion march, written to an American melody. As its rallying cry faded, another song – locally written – epitomised the sadness of separation and inevitable losses to come.

Dance bands lost musicians as they enlisted, and women lost their dancing partners. The arrival of the US Marines escalated the influence the Americans had on music-making and consumption. Shortages also had an effect: a lack of instruments, the scarcity of new recordings. But women musicians became more prominent, not just in the smart cabarets but also in amateur dance groups throughout the country. Everywhere, musicians raised morale and hard cash for the war effort.

New Zealand musicians in uniform entertained – and developed their skills – in outlets such as the Kiwi Concert Parties and the RNZAF band. Their highest-common-denominator approach mirrored the worthy, paternalistic style of the National Broadcasting Service, and similarly mixed genres. Away from this hearty and healthy entertainment, however, another musical subculture existed in the songs the soldiers sang amongst themselves. All these elements would have a lasting effect: the Italian songs' influence on Maori popular music, the performance skills of the Concert Party musicians, the loosening of social mores and rituals in dance halls, the increasing contribution of women musicians.

When peace arrived, music's central role in the war effort was revealed, like a cacophonous catharsis. And when the Maori Battalion returned, their leadership and their music influenced a generation. The song written during their departure, 'Blue Smoke', helped establish the New Zealand recording industry, and a song written to welcome them home, 'Tomo Mai', would become one of the most beloved in the New Zealand repertoire.

Opposite: Ernest Armstrong of Whakatane, formerly with the 1st NZEF, responded to the need for homegrown patriotic songs in 1941 with 'Sons of the Diggers'. Archives New Zealand, WAII/2/60

Theo Walters with the RNZAF showband on Bougainville, 1944. Standing, from left, Jim Warren, Cliff Inns, Doug Kelly, Roy Miller, Tia Bennett, Bill Egerton, Peter Glen, Theo Walters, Bob Girvan, Nip Spring, Jack McCaw, Keith Harris, Pat Watters, Frank Robb. In front, from left: Des Lavin, Alf Ramsay, Fred Coleman and Bill Shardlow. Jim Warren collection

THREE | Music Declares War 1939-1945

FOR GOD, FOR KING AND FOR COUNTRY

In New Zealand, the Second World War began to the sound of jazz. At 9.00 am Berlin time on Friday, 1 September 1939, Germany invaded Poland. As the air raid sirens began in Warsaw, Hitler gave a typically passionate and self-justifying speech to the Reichstag.

Two hours later, at 10.00 pm New Zealand time, in the control room of 2YA Wellington, technician Ken Collins needed more hands. He was putting *Rhythm on Record* to air, juggling and cueing up 78s while Arthur 'Turntable' Pearce read his links live. Standing over Collins was his imposing boss, Professor James Shelley, who tolerated rather than enjoyed jazz: he was there to listen to a feed coming from the Voice of America. The shortwave station was broadcasting a recording of Hitler's speech, in which the dramatic ranting was overlaid with an American announcer translating the words into English.

Collins could cope with listening to two things at once, but this night he was getting rattled dealing with the incompatible quintet of Pearce, Shelley, Hitler *and* an American, accompanied by the latest jazz. He said to Shelley, 'Professor, I just can't continue with this damn jazz, and I don't think we should. Can I cut it and broadcast the recording we are taking from Voice of America and Hitler's speech?'

Shelley didn't need any persuading, so Collins brought *Rhythm on Record* to an early conclusion with its theme tune 'Woman on My Weary Mind'. Later, he recalled that 'Not one phone call of protest was received as a result of our action.'[1]

When war with Germany was officially declared two days later, it took radio by surprise. The 'phoney war' was well named. Partly due to production deadlines, for several weeks after the war began the *New Zealand Listener* and the *New Zealand Radio Record* continued to publish programme details for German shortwave radio. Deutschland's daily broadcasts began with German folksongs at 4.35 pm, followed by lengthy excerpts from the 1939 Reich Party Rally at Nuremberg.[2]

Although the *Listener* prepared its readers for another long, arduous conflict, an additional pressing issue was musical: a new war needed a new marching song. The magazine noted that in London, Jack Hylton's hit 'Boomps-a-Daisy!' appeared to be the successor to 'Tipperary', even though the new dance craze was in waltz time: 'Troops couldn't even goose step to it . . . . tradition would surely not stand for the spectacle of soldiers waltzing into battle.'

In Britain, the song's publishers had given it the biggest publicity push since 'The Lambeth Walk', with

Morale boosters: 'Freedom's Army', by Wellington choral conductor H. Temple White, with J. Finlay Campbell; in 1944 J.H. Fell anticipated the end with 'After Victory is Won Dear'. Tireless songwriter J. J. Stroud encouraged others with his short-lived NZ *Writers and Composers Magazine*. National Library of NZ/Chris Bourke collection

corresponding success. 'Boomps-a-Daisy' was quickly taken up by New Zealand musicians – although the august Turntable declared the song 'trash' – and the *Listener* helped the campaign by printing lyrics, melody and dancing instructions.[3]

Two weeks later, 1ZB personalities displayed the 'Boomps-a-Daisy' dance at the Auckland Town Hall farewell to Dorothy of the station's Happiness Club. At an Auckland musicians' party, with 'a galaxy of talent present', accomplished jamming took place and 'dancing was resorted to'. The highlight of the evening was 'an exhibition of eccentric "Boomps-a-Daisying"'. Plus there was news from France: the British troops were marching to 'Boomps-a-Daisy' as well as 'Tipperary'. At Auckland's Peter Pan, Johnny Madden's Swing Kings were sceptical: the song was still a waltz, although their patrons took to it with gusto.[4]

But another song, 'Beer Barrel Polka' – in common time – looked likely to be 'one of the outstanding War Songs of the year', predicted the *Listener*, perhaps unaware that the song, of Czech origin, had already been a hit in a German-language version. 'The words have a strong appeal to the soldier: "Roll out the barrel/We'll have a barrel of fun".' For added musical balance, the magazine also published the origins, melody line and lyrics of the Horst Wessel song: 'Soon Hitler's flag shall wave o'er every street unchallenged/ And Serfdom's days are doomed to pass away'.[5]

As the war began, there was almost a national campaign to come up with a song that reflected the Dominion's patriotism. New Zealand already had its own new marching song. 'March of the Men of New Zealand' was receiving 'innumerable requests' to be played on the ZB stations, after its first broadcast by Colin Scrimgeour in his Sunday night *Man in the Street* programme.[6]

But this choral march was not the only New Zealand song getting regular airplay on 1ZB in October 1939. Another original, 'King Tawhiao', was being heard on

In the image: *The N.Z. WRITERS & COMPOSERS Magazine* / IN THIS ISSUE / SONGS, Words & Music / SKETCHES / POEMS / INTERESTING / ARTICLES / NO. 1 PRICE 1/6 / "THE FIRES OF INSPIRATION BURN BRIGHT WITHIN THESE PAGES"

which lasted for twelve issues. Although an aspirant poet himself, Stroud used a variety of lyricists; melodies flowed from his pen and became songs such as 'The New Zealand Lads Are Marching' and 'When You Are Over the Sea'.

By October 1941, band leader, Musicians' Union executive and *Music Maker* correspondent Bert Peterson had had enough: 'Of all the corny pops I have ever heard, these patriotic songs that are flooding the market take the biscuit. It beats me why composers go out of their way to rob the nursery to dish up music just because it's patriotic.'[8] (Such a plethora of creativity was seen as significant by the chief war archivist Eric McCormick. In 1946 he recruited former Kiwi Concert Party leader T. J. Kirk-Burnnand to compile an Official War Music Collection.)[9]

A song that became ubiquitous had only a tangential connection with the war. The difficulty of exporting caused a glut of apples: over one million extra cases needed to be eaten within New Zealand. With 'The Apple Song', written by expatriate film and theatre composer Ivan Perrin, the Apple and Pear Board hoped to increase consumption. Recorded by the choir of the Lyall Bay School, Wellington, for weeks the song was broadcast every morning at 8.15 am on the commercial stations, preceded by the ringing of a school bell that told children to be 'on their way'.

> Any time is apple time
> Whether you're nine or 99
> Here's a healthy, golden rule;
> Take an apple each day to school.[10]

The public was yet to be convinced: romance and novelty were still in more demand than a jingoistic call-to-arms. The most popular song in 1ZB's Sunday request session in late 1939 was Miliza Korjus singing 'One Day When We Were Young' – especially with teenage girls, followed closely by Gracie Fields with 'Trek Song', then Nelson Eddy and Deanna Durbin. A gimmick at the station was to devote each weekly programme to requests from a particular sector of the audience. Selections by members of the police would be followed by nurses, cashiers, high school boys, then girls, then their teachers. From more than 700 letters each week, the choices varied considerably, with the greatest difference being between high school boys and their teachers.

'The boys came out hot and strong for swing music and hot rhythm numbers. The school teachers in the main followed a more classical trend, although one university

the station's Maori programme. Like 'Beneath the Maori Moon' before it, 'King Tawhiao' – about the chief on the £10 note – was written by Auckland music teacher Walter Smith. It was recorded by one of 1ZB's most admired announcers, Lou Paul (Uramo Paora). Backed by Ted Croad's band and recorded at Beacon Studios, its limited run of 78s was pressed in the US. 'It really is a swell disc', wrote Bert Peterson, 'and Vern Wilson's trumpet chorus is a gem.'[7]

New Zealand's songwriters got to work. Songs came from professionals such as H. Temple White ('Freedom's Army'); Lew Jones ('The Mine-Sweeper'); Will Keen ('Anzacs on Parade'); Bert Pizzey ('When the Home Guard's on Parade'); and T. J. Kirk-Burnnand, using the pseudonym Russell Murray ('The Kiwis on Parade'). Most of the songs were set to the words of others.

Even more songs came from amateurs, especially the indefatigable James Jesse Stroud of Rotorua. So keen was Stroud on indigenous songwriting – especially his own – that he launched the *N.Z. Writers & Composers Magazine*,

professor wrote in asking for Fats Waller.' The song most in demand by the boys was Bing Crosby singing 'Little Sir Echo' ('. . . How do you do? Hello, hello, hello, hello/ Little Sir Echo, I'm very blue'), which led the host Doug Laurenson to announce, 'No fewer than 47 misguided boys have asked for this.'[11]

In Wellington as a schoolboy, future jazz critic Ray Harris remembered that the Andrews Sisters' 'Down in the Valley' seemed to have a permanent hold on 2ZB's number one position in 1944. So he went around his friends and collected signatures for Tommy Dorsey's 'Well, Git It'. 'We never got it to number one, but we did get it to number two.'[12]

Just after the war began, a man of intrigue visited Auckland. He called himself Manuel Raymond and his task was to interview musicians for the 'biggest job in the country': he was recruiting for a dance orchestra to perform a six-month residency at the Centennial Exhibition cabaret in Wellington. The specially built cabaret would have the largest dance floor in the country, with room for 400 dancing couples as well as a gallery for 200 onlookers. The musicians would be paid £10 a week and live in a Wellington hotel.[13]

Raymond, a violinist and band leader, was already known to New Zealand dancers. He led the imported dance band that held the residency at Dunedin's South Seas Exhibition in 1925, when he was billed as 'Manuel Hyman, late of the Ritz, London'.[14] His band was among the first to play at Wellington's Adelphi ballroom when it opened in 1928. He returned to London, changed his name and led the band at Frascati's restaurant. For his new role back in New Zealand – which he accepted after 'long negotiations and the promise of a princely salary' – he had already hired two noted London players.[15] Raymond wanted his Centennial dance orchestra to be 'an all-star combination, with representatives from each centre'.[16]

The six-month Centennial Exhibition marked a hundred years since the signing of the Treaty of Waitangi. It was intended to display a sense of national pride and maturity, while also being a showcase for the Labour government. Although the outbreak of war trimmed the planned grandeur of the Centennial, after five years of preparation, the lavish buildings were already in place for its opening in November 1939. The Exhibition was on a 22-hectare site at Rongotai, on which a 50-metre art deco tower stood above six hectares of modernist show buildings. Despite a £25,000 investment and 2.6 million

Manuel Raymond with his hand-picked Centennial Cabaret Band, Wellington, 1940. From left, Jack Roberts, Ken McDonald, Ken Waldridge, Manuel Raymond, Lauri Paddi, George Campbell, Phil Campbell, Alan Brown, George Taylor and Doug Lawrie. E. M. Alderdice Collection, PA1-q-182-23, Alexander Turnbull Library, Wellington

Private Anania Amohau wrote new words to a US football song and created the 'Maori Battalion Marching Song' in time for the Centennial Exhibition's opening in November 1939. National Library

Lee Swing', written in the United States in 1906 by Mark Sheaf. By the 1920s, it had become widely popular in the US. But with Amohau's lyrics, the song became a New Zealand anthem.

> Maori Battalion march to victory
> Maori Battalion staunch and true
> Maori Battalion march to glory
> Take the honour of the people with you
> We will march, march, march to the enemy
> And we'll fight right to the end
> For God! For King! And for Country!
> Au-E! Ake, kia kaha e!

Once the 'Maori Battalion Marching Song' was given an arrangement by the Trentham camp's bandmaster Lieutenant Pike, it was quickly adopted by troops of the Battalion as their own. Even before the Maori Battalion had left New Zealand, the chief of general staff Jack Duigan wrote to Freyberg in Egypt:

> Going back to the Maoris. They have quite a good Marching Song. It might be a good thing if you could put them through the streets of Cairo; they would create a great impression. They are very smart at their drill, and take a good deal of pride in themselves, which is all to the good.[18]

When published by Begg's, the song became widely heard throughout New Zealand. 'Over the next five years it was to be sung in countless bars, music halls and wherever Maori gathered together. As well as being a stirring marching song it also served as a nostalgic reminder of home to all soldiers of the New Zealand Division.'[19]

Maori cultural groups had a high profile at the Exhibition, whether through a sense of obligation or by ministerial command; to many visitors, it was as close as they had ever got to Maoritanga. Four times a day, a group from Wellington's Ngati Poneke Young Maori Club performed in the Maori Court. Groups from other tribes travelled to Wellington to take part, among them a contingent from Te Arawa that included Ana Hato, Deane Waretini and Guide Rangi. But the burden fell upon Ngati Poneke, all volunteers, who kept visitors to the Exhibition – about 10,000 a day – entertained for six months, with any proceeds going to the government.[20] Meri Mataira recalled: 'A lot of people had asked for authentic Maori stuff at the exhibition

people visiting when the country's population was less than two million, a deficit of £36,000 was recorded. But the Exhibition's cultural legacy was long-reaching, especially in music and historical scholarship.[17]

A music festival was included, and the thirteen-piece NBS String Orchestra formed by Dundee-born violinist Maurice Clare evolved into the 34-strong National Centennial Symphony Orchestra in April 1940. Plans for it to become the country's first national orchestra were stymied by the war, but it did tour New Zealand.

At the Exhibition's Maori Court, singing and action songs were a regular feature. Sir Apirana Ngata also wanted a military guard of honour for the opening of the Court, so a hundred men were assembled and quickly trained at the Trentham military camp from the raw volunteers who would soon form the Maori Battalion. Among them was Private Anania Amohau, who led the haka party. Amohau was from Rotorua, where he had been working on a song that would be part of Te Arawa's local contribution for the Centennial. The melody was from a university football song, 'The Washington and

and Apirana [Ngata] had told them, "You will not like authentic Maori music." Sure enough, when it was dished up to them they didn't like it one little bit, so the concerts were running at a loss.'[21]

The Centennial Orchestra's difficult birth and brief life may have revealed 'how limited were New Zealand's musical resources'.[22] Perhaps, but the official history of the home front considers only the country's classical musicians. By contrast the dance orchestra formed by Manuel Raymond for the Centennial's cabaret revealed the breadth of talent among the country's popular musicians. Raymond's group, wrote Arthur Pearce, 'quickly settled down into a first-rate ensemble unit, with a commendable lack of stiffness'. Attracting as much attention as the London ring-ins were the local musicians recruited by Raymond: saxophonists Lauri Paddi and Ken McDonald, pianist Jackie Roberts and the drummer Alan Brown. Two Maori brothers, originally from Paeroa, garnered special praise from Pearce: Phil and George Campbell.[23]

INTO THE DEEP BLUE SKY

It was time for the 28 Maori Battalion to go to war. On 1 May 1940, Palmerston North said farewell to its adopted battalion as it marched to the train; friends and relatives lined the streets to the station and then, in a convoy of cars, followed the train south to Wellington.

The troop train bypassed Wellington railway station and went straight onto the wharf, with its windows shuttered. Families were cordoned off at Aotea Quay, and so were unable to watch or speak to the soldiers as they moved from the train onto the *Aquitania* during the night. Before dawn, women from Ngati Poneke were taken by bus onto the wharf; some in the crowd booed, but their turn would come. 'The Maori Battalion's last contact with its own people was the sight of the crowd allowed on the wharf at the last moment, and the sound of the Ngati Poneke girls singing farewell songs as the distance widened between ship and shore.'[24] Mihi Edwards, a member of Ngati Poneke, remembered:

The Number Two Contingent orchestra was in great demand for ship concerts during the voyage to the UK', 1939. War History Collection, F-980-35mm-DA, Alexander Turnbull Library, Wellington

'Blue Smoke' composer Ruru Karaitiana,
late 1940s. Karaitiana family collection

While the *Aquitania* waited in the middle of the harbour for two other ships to cast off, the governor-general circled in a launch. To repay the gesture, the Battalion again sang its farewell song, 'Po Atarau'. Then, with the *Empress of Britain*, the *Empress of Japan* and the *Aquitania* lined up, the convoy passed through the Wellington heads and out of sight.

On board the *Aquitania*, work – and seasickness – began immediately. A routine developed: training in the morning and afternoon, and evening mess at 5.30 pm. Afterwards, there were card games, concerts and singalongs. An enthusiastic participant in all these activities was Private Ruru Karaitiana, a dance-band pianist from Dannevirke. He recalled that one day, 'halfway across the Indian Ocean', he was sunbathing on the deck when a sergeant came along, stopped beside him, and looked up. '"Look at that b— smoke", he observed, pointing to the smoke trailing from the funnels. "It's going the right way – back to New Zealand – and we're steaming farther from Home!"'[26]

'These things are simply a matter of luck', Karaitiana said later. 'He put the song in my lap. It was a natural.' The image of the blue smoke drifting back to their loved ones was sad and evocative. Within half an hour he had written lyrics 'in his head' to a melody he had already composed, and two days later he sang it in a shipboard concert.[27]

Six weeks after leaving New Zealand, on 16 June, the *Aquitania* berthed in a port near Glasgow. With the rest of New Zealand's Second Echelon, the Battalion stayed in Britain for nearly seven months, training and being available to help repel the expected German invasion.

During this time, Karaitiana approached Chappell's of London, offering them the publishing rights to his new song, but without success.[28] Meanwhile the 2NZEF band, led by Lt C. C. E. Miller, recorded eight songs in Britain, three of which – 'Maori Battalion', 'Haere Ra' ('Now is the Hour') and 'Gallant Hearts' – became steady sellers on Regal Zonophone over the next ten years.[29] Then, in January 1941, the Second Echelon got its marching orders: in Liverpool the Maori Battalion embarked on the *Athlone Castle* and departed for Egypt. On board was Private Karaitiana, looking into the deep blue sea, contemplating home, while working on his melody.[30]

As the Aquitania, a huge ship, was starting to pull out, the girls and some of the men (Maori girls and men, that is) sang songs of farewell. We were all crying, tears streaming down our faces . . .

E heke ana nga roimata, the tears are falling, for sweethearts, and brothers; mothers as well, seeing their sons going away. Sadder still when the Battalion boys, heads poking out of portholes, sang songs back to the home people left on the wharf.

Po atarau	Now is the hour
E moea iho nei	When we must say goodbye
E haere ana	Soon I'll be sailing
Koe ki pamamao	Far across the sea
Haere ra, ka hoki mai ana	While I'm away, Oh please remember me
Ki te tau, e tangi atu nei	When I return, I'll find you waiting here.[25]

BAND OF BROTHERS

From very early in their careers, the Campbell brothers – Phil, George and Lew – made a lasting impression on New Zealand jazz and popular music. Their musical peers all regarded the Campbell trio with awe and affection. And later sadness, because Phil, the oldest of the three – and, his siblings said, the most gifted musically – would be denied his potential.

In 1934, Jack, Max and Tiki Roberts – three musical brothers from Auckland – were on holiday when they came across three young brothers performing in the small town of Paeroa. They couldn't get home quick enough to tell their professional musician friends what they had heard.[31] Spike Donovan was one of the first: 'They came back raving about some Maori musicians they'd met there and how terrific they were.' Auckland musicians were sceptical, recalled Donovan. 'If they were all that hot what were they doing in Paeroa? Soon

after this they came to Auckland and they just laid the town on its ear.'[32]

Phil Campbell got his start playing country dances in small halls around the Bay of Plenty; with his Blue Boys Band he was soon venturing further afield, to Thames Valley and the Waikato. Seeing Campbell perform in Hamilton in 1936, the *Music Maker* commented, 'Phil, who leads on trumpet, is a neat, stylish player, and should do well if he ever hits town.'[33]

Jim Gower, who first encountered Campbell playing with his Blue Boys Band at a Waikato dance in 1936, described him as 'the most brilliant trumpet jazz player New Zealand has ever produced. At times he was Armstrong . . . . a very artistic trumpet player as well as being a real out-and-out jazz player.'[34] Within a year, Campbell would hold the first trumpet position in Theo Walters' stylish band at the Peter Pan.[35]

Phil and George Campbell in 1943, just prior to their departure with the Kiwi Concert Party; younger brother Lew Campbell at the piano, late 1940s. Bob Bothamley collection/Peter Downes; Jim Warren collection

A jam session on Karangahape Road, Auckland, c. 1940. From left, Neil Thurgate, Jim Foley, Al Smith, Jim Warren, Red Logie (a visitor, holding Warren's trombone), Phil Campbell and Tiki Roberts. Jim Warren collection

Campbell toured the South Island with Walters, taking a star role at the opening broadcasts of 3ZB and 4ZB, then he took up a twelve-month season with his own band at Hamilton's Regent, with forays around Waikato and the Bay of Plenty. 'Breaking all box records for box office receipts, fan mail and what-have-you', he quickly became regarded as the top band leader in the region, and one of New Zealand's best trumpet players. 'This band certainly knows how to swing the crotchets', reported the *Music Maker*, 'and it is a shame to see them wasted in the bush playing for a crowd of locals.'[36] Later that year, Bob Allanson wrote that on trumpet Campbell was 'the nearest thing to [Nat] Gonella that I've heard'. The rhythm section was drummer Wally Ransom – a recent émigré from London, with excellent dance-band credentials – and George Campbell, 'Phil's little brother of 18 tender years, [who] plays the bass better than all'.[37]

Phil Campbell, said the Auckland pianist Jim Foley, was 'one of the most thrilling trumpet players New Zealand

has ever produced'. He was the lynchpin of the late 1930s jam sessions that used to take place in Newton Gully, in a large room above a shop called The Outlet. Mrs Smith, the proprietor, 'was a very jovial woman and she had a great love for jazz. She used to encourage us greatly with our music.' On tenor was the veteran Jimmy Watters, while the trombonist Des Blundell used to change out of his short pants before playing. The rhythm section was usually the three 'brilliant' Roberts brothers. 'One night Des brought along a fluffy-faced youth up from Rotorua for a brass band contest to play some clarinet solos for us. We all thought he sounded like Artie Shaw. His name was Derek Heine.'[38]

Phil and George Campbell began 1939 on a South Island tour with Lauri Paddi, who – after years of driving through storms and slips and over gravel roads, and fixing punctures in his dinner suit – had bought a bus to transport his New Radio Band. In Dunedin, Phil was part of a small combo from Paddi's band that recorded acetates

Top: At the Cocoanut Grove, Palmerston North, 1938 (L-R): Art Rosoman, George Campbell, Phil Campbell, unknown and Lauri Paddi. E.M. Alderdice Collection, PA1-q182-24-1, Alexander Turnbull Library, Wellington

Bottom: George Campbell with some Wellington fans, 1938. Thérèse Gore collection

of 'Who', 'Tea for Two' and 'Runnin' Wild'. The brothers also jammed with prominent locals Dick Colvin and Keith Harris. 'Did these boys swing?', wrote John Spedding. 'A purely rhetorical question, my alligators.'[39]

As the oldest boy, Phil was the musical motivator of the Campbell brothers. In their Paeroa home was a trumpet and an upright piano. Somehow, said Lew, the youngest, 'We all seemed to have this music bug.'[40]

Phil got his grounding on trumpet in a local brass band before forming his own dance group. He always encouraged his younger brothers, inviting George to join his bands and paying for Lew's piano lessons.

Phil's Blue Boys Band did not have a bass player, so one night when the quartet was playing across the road from the Campbells' house, Phil asked George to sit in with the band. By nine o'clock, George conquered his shyness and struggled over, a small boy in short pants with a big double bass. The crowd cheered, and for the first time he heard jokes he would get for the rest of his career: 'Where did you get that over-grown violin?', 'How do you stick it under your chin?'

But once George started playing he was right at home. The band played 'Wahoo' and 'Goody Goody' – both in C, the only key George could play on the double bass – and by demand they kept repeating them through the night.

When George was fifteen he went to sea as a deckhand on the *Niagara*. While up on deck late one night he heard a band rehearsing: it was musicians travelling from the US to Australia. He spent the rest of that voyage staying up as late as he could, listening to this band play contemporary dance music. The band was Sammy Lee and his Americanadians, who had yet to visit New Zealand. George found the experience so moving that he quit the *Niagara* to become a musician.[41]

He returned to Paeroa, picked up his double bass and headed for Hamilton to join Phil's band. Within a year the pair was in Auckland, playing the best rooms with their peers.[42] Band leader Ted Croad said the Campbell brothers were some of the finest musicians ever to play in his band. 'They were accomplished musicians and real gentlemen. Never got into trouble, never any arguments. The only thing they didn't like was playing with musicians who weren't up to their standard.'[43]

MUSIC ON THE HOME FRONT

New Zealand dance halls and cabarets felt the impact of war through the musicians who, in a flurry of enlisting when the war began, disappeared from their stages. At Auckland's New Dixieland, Art Larkins' Sweet Swing Band lost several key players when they joined the Air Force, which was about to form an orchestra.[44] An Air Force band for dances and social functions was also planned, with Roy Lester recruiting players.

The lineups in the clubs soon stabilised for a period; within a year conscription had been introduced, so voluntary recruitments tapered off. 'Most of the bands have settled down to steady work, and changes of personnel are rare.' But, at first, the engagements decreased. During 1940 the Peter Pan found that many businesses cancelled their annual ball: 40 fewer functions were booked than a year earlier. 'It seems a pity that the leading cabaret and the best band should only be on view twice a week.'[45]

In Dunedin in 1941, Joe Brown's weekly show at the Town Hall – which promised two bands and non-stop dancing – could still be enjoyed; and there were dozens of other bands at venues around the city. There was no

'Lolita' – Esther Katene – was one of Lauri Paddi's regular wartime vocalists in Wellington. Bob Bothamley collection/Peter Downes

dearth of gigs, but by 1942 the shortage of men due to the call-up led Brown to start a competition to encourage women to dance together at his Dunedin Town Hall dances. He offered £25 prize money, and women reacted enthusiastically, with many couples entering. They danced in a variety of styles to the Georgians' Strict Tempo Band while, in the concert chamber, old-time dancing continued to Freddie Hinds and His Royal Hawaiians, among them the 'girl drummer' Miss Rosalie Plank.[46]

On radio, dance music was receiving more airplay following the Labour government's establishment of a commercial service, beginning with 1ZB in 1936. By contrast the NBS had 'let the popular side of its programmes languish', wrote the *Music Maker* in 1940. 'Lengthy concertos and symphonies have occupied far too much valuable air space, considering their listener appeal. With Mr C. G. Scrimgeour more or less at the head of all broadcasting activity now, things have started to brighten up.'[47]

Although some were critical that the radio stations would not 'let a dance band broadcast to be put over in a snappy style, instead of the stilted formal announcements method', there was plenty of radio support for light music. In 1940 Ted Croad's band was heard on 1ZB in a weekly relay from the Orange Coronation Ballroom. *Every Friday Night at Eight* was a lively dance programme on 2YA driven by the Rhythm-makers: players from 'Wellington's best combines', with bright patter in between songs and a 'vocaliste' called Lolita (Esther Katene).[48]

The opening of 1ZB's new, purpose-built art deco radio studio in Auckland in 1941 called for a celebration. The station commissioned three months of musical shows by New Zealand artists with, as its centrepiece, Theo Walters' dance band. The popular Australian band leader was offered New Zealand's most lucrative contract. His Personality Band was to play every night, including Sundays, and the high fee they negotiated shocked local musicians who knew of 1ZB's 'parsimony': the gig had 'usually been a love job in the past'.[49]

By 1941 resident dance bands had been hired by the commercial and non-commercial services. Twice a week on 1YA, *Fashions in Melody* showcased Ossie Cheesman's ten-piece band: 'from sweet to swing, opera to musical comedy is included in their repertoire, and no trouble at all'.[50]

In Dunedin, Joe Brown's Town Hall dances were broadcast live on 4ZB; even enemy propagandist Tokyo Rose was said to be a listener, allegedly saying on air that when the Japanese invaded New Zealand, one of the first things they would do was take over the Dunedin Town Hall dance.[51] On 4YA Dick Colvin's band was busy, after resigning from the two biggest residencies in the city. Both the Town Hall and Savoy restaurant had decreed that 'only ancient "pops" and old-time tunes should be played – hot music, although extremely popular with Joe Public, being taboo for some peculiar reason'.[52]

An army marches to a beat, so early in the war Gladstone Hill, presenter of 2ZB's *Band Session*, put the word out on the troops' behalf. A mention that the army was forming an orchestra and needed a piano accordion brought a call from a woman offering £30 so that they could buy a new one. A request for spare records elicited an overwhelming response: Hill drove around Wellington picking up 78s from listeners, and weighty parcels were shipped from around the country to the railway station. Very soon the haul included ten gramophones – including three very sought-after portables – six radios, 3000 records, orchestral dance music and one violin.[53]

For those hoping to buy new records during the war, Friday night was the busiest night of the week. In Wellington, the best music store was HMV on Cuba Street, where Mrs Bird looked after the aficionados. Early in the evening the store would close its doors for a dinner break, while a queue formed outside. When it reopened at 7.00 pm, two small piles of new 78s would be on the counter: the latest jazz and swing records. The queue would rush in, and the lucky two at the front would get the first pick. Those in the know could buy a budget Decca or Regal Zonophone disc featuring an uncredited star performer like Artie Shaw. But for a hit like 'Chattanooga Choo Choo' the wait might be a year or more.[54]

In Auckland, Murray Marbeck recalls that new shipments were very infrequent. So rare were new records that his father Alfred Marbeck obtained a second-hand dealer's licence, and each Saturday Murray would use the firm's petrol allocation – two gallons per month – on a well-planned buying trip through the inner suburbs. For a slightly worn record, they would pay a shilling; two shillings if it was pristine. If they bought in bulk, the dross and the worn rejects would go in the bin. On rubbish night, scavengers would rustle through the bin for whatever 78s they could find.[55]

If new records were scarce, steel needles to play them with became almost impossible to get. People improvised,

polishing old needles, or trying out alternatives and sharing their ideas. Marbeck: 'We had customers coming in saying, "Oh I found pyracantha thorns, pickled them in Gum Arabic, dried them in the oven and I got five plays out of a point!"'

To most record fans, though, supplies of fresh discs were almost impossible to find, which was one reason Arthur Pearce's *Rhythm on Record* was essential listening for working musicians and their audiences. His programme premiered any innovative swing, jazz or 'experimental' records received by the NBS.

In 1941 the NBS could still boast that within three weeks of release in Hollywood or New York, it could have the latest hit tunes on the air. The first thing Bob Bothamley did when receiving a new swing record was pull out a stopwatch, time the song and mark down its dance tempo. He sent out any commercial jazz to radio stations around the country, where the records circulated for months until returning to Wellington for 'a well-earned rest'.

Bothamley enjoyed seeing how long it took for a tune to become a hit in New Zealand. In the US, where new songs were plugged on radio and in films, the life of the average popular song was three weeks. 'In New Zealand, on the other hand, it may take nine months to a year before a number has caught on sufficiently for it to be asked for regularly by dancers here.' Among the songs popular among New Zealand dancers in late 1941 was 'With the Wind and the Rain in Your Hair', written ten years earlier but recently revived. 'Ferryboat Serenade' was nine months old but was likely to be played several times 'during an evening's dancing'.[56]

Rhythm on Record's competitor on the commercial service 1ZB was *Rhythm Review*, which presented 45 minutes of swing every Wednesday night. The programme – which former stalwarts of the defunct Auckland Rhythm Club helped produce – was aimed at a mainstream audience rather than swing elitists. The *Review* compère explained:

> It is the intention of the session to hold as many of the station's listeners as possible, and raucous and 'killer diller' swing is kept for the end of the programme. The commentary is quiet and dignified, with no 'jitterbug' atmosphere – the sincere students of jazz look with disfavour on the jitterbug development of recent years. The older type of swing, 'righteous jazz', is also kept to a minimum as it is not appreciated by the average listener.[57]

In 1943 the NBS and NCBS were combined after the dismissal of Scrimgeour as director of the commercial service (the government didn't appreciate his on-air criticisms of its policies). James Shelley became director of both: the great champion of the fine arts now had the ZBs as part of his remit, with their diet of popular music. Journalists wanted to know how such a domineering cultural snob would deal with this dilemma:

> He gave his answer so often he must have been tempted to record it. His policy would be to broadcast all kinds of music; but in so doing he would ensure that only the best of any kind reached the air.
>
> Exercising this discrimination, he instituted his own form of censorship. Generally tolerant over the kinds of music which could be broadcast, James Shelley found himself unable to abide Gershwin's music, ensuring that it never went to air. Fats Waller also was excluded, but readmitted on appeal.[58]

Music ranked high on Shelley's cultural scale, just beneath art and drama. Although he had 'an intense personal dislike of the more extreme forms of vocal and instrumental swing or jazz',[59] mostly, he did not let his personal prejudices affect programming. A listener wrote in, asking for a station devoted to classical music: 'God! I would love to see crooners hanged – like Hamlet good and high.' Shelley replied: 'I need hardly tell you that I sympathise very much with your point of view, but there are ramifications involved.'[60]

But a few acts – and songs – were beyond the pale. 'For some reason he used to go nearly berserk on hearing Vera Lynn', recalled 2YA technician Ken Collins. 'Once I saw him lift a disc of hers off the spinning turntable as it was awaiting broadcast, and smash it across his knee.' Another who witnessed Shelley's wrath was Arthur Pearce, who in 1941 received a call from Shelley asking him to visit, and to bring with him the current hit by Woody Herman, 'Golden Wedding'. With a melody based on a popular light classical piece called 'La Cinquantaine', the success of 'Golden Wedding', suggests Laurie Lewis, was probably due to its long drum solo, over which Herman slowly enters with an ascending clarinet line. It culminated 'in a long-held-penultimate high note before sliding to the high tonic, a chord from the band and a cymbal clash to close proceedings'. The song was receiving a great deal of airplay on NBS, especially in request sessions.

Pearce walked over to 2YA, collecting on the way a copy of the record from the station's library. 'Ah, Arthur, thank you', said Shelley. 'You have the record?' Pearce handed over the 78, and Shelley checked the label to see that 'he was actually holding the offensive article'. Then to Arthur's astonishment, he smashed the shellac disc over his knee, saying, 'I'm not going to have that emasculated music on my programmes.' After 'an embarrassed pause and a short exchange of pleasantries, Arthur left the office . . . .'

The pair actually got on well: after presenting *Rhythm on Record*, Pearce would often give the workaholic, micro-managing Shelley a lift home. But music was never discussed between the godfather of jazz in New Zealand and the driving force behind the country's symphony orchestra.[61]

To listeners who wanted their pet hates removed from the airwaves, Shelley would reply, 'I refuse to be a *dictator* of broadcasting. We are at war fighting dictatorship. My job is to see that listeners get the best available music, the best artists, be it classical music, opera, or *jazz*.'

NBS employees learnt to work around the Professor's foibles. Marked on the records to be played on the breakfast sessions would be the codes BPWU or APWU: 'Before Prof Wakes Up' and 'After Prof Wakes Up'. After about 6.30 am the music calmed down; each morning at 7.00 am Shelley would ring the 2YA control room to tell the staff he was awake and listening.[62]

To Ray Harris, then a schoolboy, before 7.00 am was indeed the time to hear some swing gems on 2ZB. 'I used to get up and tune in from six o'clock onwards, to the test programme. Depending on who the guy was running the test programme you could get a whole hour of good swing band music. We got good music. Then they'd start off at seven o'clock and we'd have Bing Crosby and Connie Boswell. "Start the Day Right", a wonderful number. The music of the swing bands wasn't jazz, it was popular music.'[63]

All around the country, musicians contributed to the war effort, professionals and amateurs. The consummate professional was Henry Rudolph, music director of the 2YA Camp Entertainers. 'I had the best musicians, and the best singers, and experimented with arrangements', he recalled. In the chorus were nine young women – the Melody Maids – and four men. The lead violinist was Vincent Aspey. They performed at camps in the Wellington region and at Waiouru, with a monthly broadcast from the Trentham army camp. When broadcasting from a military

The 2YA Camp Entertainers, at Waiouru military camp, 1942. Front row, from left: Sylvia Devenie, Dorothy Kemp, Doreen Harvey, Yvonne Andrews, Merle Gamble, Sylvia Petrie, Margot Dallison, Alice Graham, Laurie Jones, Jean McPherson. Back row, from left: Len Hopkins, Malcolm Rickard, William Yates, Henry Rudolph, Ken Macaulay, Wally Marshall, Ken Strong and technician Cyril Brown. Bob Bothamley collection/Peter Downes

camp, the location was described only as 'Somewhere in New Zealand'. The shows would include mini-dramas, and Tom Morrison singing 'Old Shep', the maudlin favourite of dog-lovers. 'The nurses and WAAFs in the front row would cry as he sang it. Then we'd move on to a comedy number.' The evenings would end up with a community singalong, occasionally led by broadcaster Winston McCarthy. 'Knees Up Mother Brown' and 'The Fly' were inevitable, though cautious NBS producer Malcolm Rickard never allowed them to go to air.[64]

No aspect of musical life remained unchanged. More people of all ages began learning to play music, even though instruments were already scarce, including accessories such as strings, reeds and sheet music.[65] 'Queer thing', a music teacher told the Listener, 'the only ones who've got no grouse are the teachers.'[66] The De Luxe cinema in Wellington lost its flamboyant Wurlitzer organist to army service in the Middle East. Reg Maddams

was described as having 'the physique of a footballer and the features of an ascetic'. His farewell performance 'reflected the celebrity status he enjoyed': the De Luxe was decked out with bunting and his name was in lights above the entrance. Queues started forming in Kent Terrace hours before the doors opened. When Maddams returned to New Zealand, he became the musical director at Auckland's Civic, 'quickly building up the same sort of movie star-like following he had in the Capital'.[67]

Like an undercover agent for culture, energetic Christchurch music identity Elaine Moody – a founder of Begg's Musical Army there – travelled 'in wartime blackout conditions' with her group to Wellington and Dunedin to start similar armies.[68]

Perhaps the unluckiest professional musician was Austrian émigré Paul Schramm, pianist and composer. In exile from the Nazis, he and his wife Diny enjoyed mixing classical with light music, and playing 'in jazzy

The Melody Maids of Okato, Taranaki, created several sets of elaborate costumes for their wartime performances. Swainson's Studios, New Plymouth

styles'. By 1939 they were settled in Wellington, hosting parties in their central city home with two grand pianos. 'The convivial Paul loved to smoke, drink and play cards, and had a penchant for large automobiles. He and his beautiful and talented wife were an attraction at social gatherings.' However, when the war started, Schramm lost his sources of income: concerts for school children, radio broadcasts and advertising jingles. As an alien he was forbidden to broadcast in case he sent coded messages through his playing. He drove a taxi until his licence was revoked, and ended up working in a factory making hair combs. After the war, his application for naturalisation was refused: by failing to buy war bonds, he had not shown enough support for his adopted country. In 1948 he left New Zealand – and his wife – never to return.[69]

In provincial and rural dance halls, there were hundreds of local stalwarts who kept parties going, introduced new songs and gave young players a start.

All over Northland, pianist Dorothy McLennan led her own dance orchestra, which played patriotic concerts and dances; in west Auckland, Jack Faulder's Dixieboys added troop concerts to the gigs they had played in the region since the 1920s, until petrol shortages immobilised the group; the Pukekohe/Franklin area was kept entertained by pianist Mrs Ivy Midgely, her blind husband Mr T. H. Midgley, also a pianist, and her three daughters, the Moore sisters.[70]

Among the most colourful were the Melody Maids of Okato, seven young Taranaki women who began performing in 1936. Resplendent in elaborate homemade costumes as cowgirls, sailors or Arabian Princesses, they sang at concert parties at venues such as the New Plymouth Opera House, the airport, the army camp and dances. With practices twice a week, 'we were very busy', said one member. They 'disbanded in 1947 when the girls married their returning boyfriends'.[71]

BETWEEN WAIOURU AND THE DEEP BLUE SEA

One night in June 1940, a bedraggled figure staggered into the Peter Pan cabaret. It was the saxophonist Pat Watters, whose brother Jim was on stage playing tenor. Trumpeter Jim Warren was there: 'The significance of it didn't strike me till later. Pat was blown up on the *Niagara* – what he must have gone through – he had come to see his brother, probably to get a bed for the night and some clothes.'[72]

The *Niagara* had hit a German mine in the Hauraki Gulf. No lives were lost among the 136 passengers, but £2.5 million of gold bullion and half of New Zealand's small arms ammunition went to the sea floor. The crew lost everything; the band, all its instruments. The call went out for replacements, which were scarce and expensive.

Within a year, Watters was at the Waiouru army camp, training in the tank corps, making a 'blind rush' back to Auckland to sit in with his musician friends. He formed a small swing band, the Waiouru Wildcats, to play for camp functions.

It was not long before Watters was transferred – or poached – to the Air Force, where an all-star dance band was emerging from the larger RNZAF band. Many players later featured in the fledgling National Orchestra after the war, but this was as close as New Zealand would get to the national dance band that was often discussed but never realised.

To the Defence Department, recruiting musicians into the services to play music was an essential part of the war effort. They were needed to entertain troops at the front; at home, they would not only raise morale, but also a substantial amount of money for the Patriotic Fund. A few citizens did not see it that way. In 1940 'Play Fair' wrote to the Minister of Defence, Fred Jones:

Why is it that the NZAF Band men [are] not called upon to do military training, when they have been called up in the ballot. They are doing no training at all, only for the Band. What good is that if they are wanted to defend our own country. The Band will not be wanted, will it. They are only shirking their duties and they seem to get away with it too . . . . those men have only joined the Band to shirk

their duties, so what can one look upon the Band, only as a Shirkers' Band.[73]

The grumblings continued, so RNZAF's personnel branch briefed the Minister of Defence with a response:

Whatever the expense involved may be, the Band by its assistance in raising funds for patriotic purposes, and in the recent drive 'Bonds for Bomber Week', has more than offset the cost. Moreover, the Bandsmen are not exclusively employed as musicians. For your information, but this, of course, could not be released to the Press, the personnel of the Central Band are engaged on Aerodrome Defence duties, apart from their normal duties as Musicians, and have received extensive training in the use of machine guns and small arms, on which they have reached a high standard of proficiency.[74]

Perhaps the RNZAF band attracted more flak because it worked so hard and was highly visible, spending much of the war touring New Zealand, when not training at – and defending – their art deco base at Rongotai on the recently vacated Centennial Exhibition site. By April 1944, in less than four years, the band had raised more than £150,000 for the Patriotic Fund. 'There are no fair-sized towns anywhere in New Zealand that have not enjoyed three or four visits from the band', said their director, Flight-Lieutenant H. Gladstone Hill.

If he sounded beleaguered by 1944, it had been a musical but bureaucratic war. Hill had to justify the RNZAF band's existence, especially with two Kiwi Concert Party troupes in the Mediterranean and Pacific theatres. He had to find instruments and musicians, and try to retain both. Men kept getting transferred into the regular forces when they reached 21, or manpowered into essential industries. Many of the older musicians had difficulty standing the pace.

Playing a wind instrument calls for physical fitness as any medical man will confirm, yet we have one man in the band with only one lung! The Bb bass instruments weigh from 25

The dance band of the RNZAF, 1943. At back, from left: Bill Crawford, drums; Toby Tobeck, bass. Middle row, from left: Nip Spring, Tia Bennett, Jim Warren, Jim Loper, Doug Kelly. In front, from left: Pat Watters, Bob Girvan, Jack McCaw, Frank Gurr (all four of whom were foundation members of the National Orchestra). At far right, Speed Hughes with an unknown woman singer. Jim Warren collection

to 40 pounds and to carry those for one, two, or three miles on a march, playing all the time, even with a break for a few yards, calls for physical fitness equal to that of any branch of the service . . . . there is no such thing as a bandsman marching at ease and playing at the same time. Physical exertion and mental concentration are his lot.[75]

With 60 band members at its full complement, the RNZAF Central Band was actually three bands in one: the big Central band for ceremonial duties, playing light classics and Sousa-style marches; the Symphonic Swing Orchestra, complete with strings; and its smallest combo, the Swing Wing.

Like the Kiwi Concert Party, the RNZAF band recruited some of the best dance-band and jazz musicians in the country, and in turn demobbed them just as the National Orchestra was being formed after the war. The Central band included star band leader Corporal Theo Walters, saxophonists Bob Girvan and Pat Watters, and trumpeter Doug Kelly. Station bands included players such as Chips Healy, Nolan Rafferty, and George and Phil Campbell, based at Hobsonville, and Brian Marston at Wigram. Among those who went on to classical careers were Girvan, Peter Glen and Frank Robb. Even when in a war zone, saxophonist Jack McCaw practised Mozart on his clarinet every spare moment, in training for the classical career he later achieved in Britain.

Jim Warren, an Auckland dance-band trumpeter who joined the Air Force for two years of regular duties before being transferred to the Central band, ruefully agreed it was a privileged way to spend a war: '*We* were the lucky musicians.' They were there to perform, not to fight. That did not mean the living was easy, but it was less dangerous.[76]

In 1944 the band toured the islands of the Pacific, entertaining New Zealand and American troops. The cramped US troopship *Rochambeau* took them to New Caledonia, and over the next fourteen weeks they visited Tulagi, the Russell Islands, Bougainville, Espiritu Santo and Fiji. The heat fatigued the instruments as well as

The Hill-Billy Hot Shots, absent without leave from the RNZAF show band, Wellington, 1944.
From left, Eric 'Chook' Sundberg, Bob Girvan, Theo Walters, Jim Warren and Toby Tobeck. Jim Warren collection

the musicians, but they gave 180 performances over 75 working days. A typical day was in Fiji, where trucks jolted them over 150 miles of dusty roads, so the band could give three or four concerts en route. Some days there would be afternoon parades as well.

The band was often battling the elements. On one occasion, GIs sat for hours in a tropical downpour waiting for a concert that finally took place under oilskins to protect the instruments and players. On Bougainville, an electric power failure meant the band 'faultlessly played Suppé's *Morning Noon and Night* overture in complete darkness'.[77]

The concerts would begin with the curtain down; once the audience had gone quiet, a rifle shot would ring out. 'The audience would jump, and Theo Walters would come out and say, "It's all right, ladies and gentlemen, we just wanted to ensure everyone was awake before we started." And away the pit band would go.'

Through the evening, the band would build in size, from the small 'Swing Wing' to the full 65-piece military band. There would be solo items – Eric Sundberg on the xylophone, pianist Keeble Thurkettle with *Warsaw Concerto* – sketches, impersonations, mock ballet, mini-dramas, swing, chamber music, and the Hill-Billy Hot Shots 'sowing instrumental corn' such as 'Deep in the Heart of Texas' or 'Pistol Packin' Mama'.[78]

Before its Pacific tour, the RNZAF band presented a week-long season of its *Flying High Revue* at the Wellington Opera House. The shows opened with a chorus of 'Smile' and closed with 'God Save the King'; the repertoire ranged from the 'Maori Battalion Marching Song' to Beethoven's Fifth Symphony. In the revue, a white-jacketed Corporal Walters was the wise-cracking MC, and he also led the swing band and, wrote the *Evening Post*'s reviewer, 'crooned with that tonal uncertainty so common to this class of singer'.[79]

In Dunedin, the 4ZB announcers satirise the Munich incident during their weekly Community Sing early in 1940. From left: Spud Murphy, Ted Heaney, George Thorne, Jimmie MacFarlane, Lionel Sceats and Jack Bremner. RNZ Sound Archives

At the amateur level, the community singing movement also helped the war effort, raising hard cash. In some centres, the popularity of the singing evenings had faded since their height during the Depression, but not in Auckland, where Mrs Barrington Snow was a stalwart at the piano for several decades, 'one of those rare people who could read music like lightning, play by ear or improvise an accompaniment at a moment's notice'.[80]

The Auckland 'sings' moved from the Town Hall to theatres around the city, with the emphasis on fundraising. Community singing evenings began to include advertisements during the broadcasts. This was due to copyright issues: fees were required for the public performance and for reprinting the lyrics of any songs whose writer had been dead for less than 50 years.

In Dunedin, community singing thrived for decades longer than in other centres. The Red Cross wanted to generate £250,000 nationwide from community singing, of which Dunedin's share was £25,000. A tenth of that was raised at one Sunday evening variety show at the Town Hall, with the live broadcast encouraging phone calls to come in from around the country offering donations. Walter Sinton recalled:

Every single person in the audience and the thousands listening in, had sons or daughters, brothers, sisters, sweethearts, relatives or friends at 'the front', or due to go and when one recalls that at that moment the war was not going well for the Allies, the emotion created that night by that contralto voice was quite beyond description.

When several radio stars from 4ZB travelled to Gore to lead a community sing, the 'house full' signs went up at the Princess Theatre. The broadcasters also auctioned items ranging from tea, eggs and fruit cake to budgerigars, babies' outfits, Angora rabbits and a wrinkle remover, raising over £1000 for the patriotic fund.[81]

Called back on stage to repeat her songs was Mary Pratt who, looking as imperious as Britannia in crown and ermine cloak, sang 'Land of Hope and Glory' and 'There'll Always Be an England'.

In Wellington, the Ngati Poneke Young Maori Club were morale-boosting stalwarts. Based a stone's throw from Parliament, they were constantly called upon to perform at official functions, farewells, tangi, concerts and charity events. Led by Kingi Tahiwi, a Ngati Poneke group entertained a packed Wellington Town Hall concert on

A TALENT TO AMUSE

Right up to the outbreak of war, New Zealand received regular visits by touring variety shows. With a downturn in theatre work in Britain, early in 1939 there was a flurry of visitors. The magician Nicola brought with him a mind-reader, eccentric dancers and Dobsky, 'the man who made awkwardness an art'. Stanley McKay's *Gaieties* came over from Australia for its annual six-month tour of cities and small towns. The most extravagant revue show was Frank Neill's *Why Be Serious*, with almost 60 international acts; among them – on his first visit home as a legitimate performer – was Tex Morton.[82] Another visitor early in the war was the Te Awamutu-born bass Oscar Natzke. He was, declared the *Dominion*, 'blessed with a super organ and brains to give it interest'.[83]

And then the vacuum: 'Overseas stage and concert performances ceased abruptly . . . and did not recommence on a significant scale until peace returned.'[84]

One overseas visitor who did get to New Zealand during the war rarely failed to amuse: songwriter and playwright Noël Coward. During a three-week fundraising tour in January 1941, Coward praised New Zealand's devotion and loyalty to 'home'. At a Wellington civic reception, he was responding to the welcome of the mayor Tom Hislop, who told Coward that an especially 'Empire-minded' crowd had been assembled for the soirée. Then the mayor's wife put her foot in it, Coward later recalled:

> She said to me in ringing tones that I was never to dare to sing 'The Stately Homes of England' again as it was an insult to the homeland and that neither she nor anybody else liked it. I replied coldly that for many years it had been one of my greatest successes, whereupon she announced triumphantly to everyone in earshot: 'You see – he can't take criticism.' Irritated beyond endurance I replied that I was perfectly prepared to take intelligent criticism at any time, but I was not prepared to tolerate bad manners. With this I bowed austerely and left the party.[85]

The NBS producers also offended Coward when they asked him not to include a risqué song in a concert that would be broadcast live; they considered it 'if not "objectionable" then certainly unsuitable' for a mixed audience. Coward responded by refusing to do the broadcast, but the NBS would not budge: 'no broadcast, no fee'. A stand-off took place. Twenty minutes before show time, Coward backed down.[86]

As stage manager for Coward's show at the Wigram air force base, variety performer Eddie Hegan saw another side: 'When I asked him if there was anything he would particularly like on stage he replied, "Just any old thing, dear boy." Then, with raised finger, "So long as the piano's in tune".'[87]

Wellington aside, Coward's busy tour glided efficiently through the country from the moment he strode down the gangplank of the *Mariposa* in Auckland. He described his hectic tour as a mix between the serious (broadcast talks) and 'gay' (entertainment). He attended a chic soirée at the Queen Street apartment of expatriate Australian photographer Robert Steele. Those present pleaded with Coward to play something on Steele's beloved white baby grand piano.

> After a few bars, Coward stopped, his fingers on the keyboard. Then disdainfully he turned around and admonished Steele: 'That piano is terrible. You should get rid of it.' Watched by his astonished guests, Steele dashed from the room, snatched the fire axe from the corridor and smashed his beloved piano to pieces.[88]

In concert, his accompanist was Christchurch-born Sefton Daly, who had passed Coward's audition in Australia. Daly, a composer as well as pianist, had departed New Zealand two years earlier after he had been branded a musical crank by a Christchurch department store. He began working in the store as an interior decorator, and moved on to become its restaurant pianist.

Coward complimented Daly on his pieces 'Serenade to a Snake' and 'Automatons' Dance', which the pianist performed in a Wellington concert while the star was recovering from a dizzy spell. Daly was 'the most interesting and intelligent young composer on this side of the world', said Coward.[89]

After enjoying a Maori concert in Rotorua, Coward urged Maori to 'concentrate on their own songs, which were both beautiful and unique'. He hoped that the younger generation of Maori 'would not spend its time learning "snappy, modern American tunes" merely to please tourists'.[90]

Canadian tenor saxophonist Art Rosoman arrived in New Zealand just before the war, played with all the leading bands, then returned home in 1949.
Bob Bothamley collection/Peter Downes

21 April 1941. There were action songs, the haka 'Ka Mate, Ka Mate' and, reported the *Dominion*, some 'melodious old part songs, adapted from the earlier hymns of the missionaries, ingeniously invested with the idiom of the Maori, which lends such enchantment to such adaptations'. Henare Tahiwi 'lifted a serviceable tenor' for Maori ballads and songs by Alfred Hill including 'Waiata Poi'.[91] It was the poi dances that the audience most enjoyed, as well as 'Aue Mama, Aue Papa', which was so well received it had to be repeated.

Aue Mama! Aue Papa!	O Mama! O Papa!
Homai te aroha	Give me love
Ki haere ahau e	For I'm on my way
Ki runga Tiamana	To Germany
Ki te whawhai i a Hitler	To fight Hitler
Mo te Kingi mo Niu Tireni	For King and New Zealand[92]

'It was a hectic time for the club', recalled Mihipeka Edwards. 'Ngati Poneke was on active service entertaining non-stop on board ships, at the Majestic Cabaret, the Opera House, Town Hall, army, navy and air force camps, and for any important visitors to the country. I would

get a bit hoha sometimes. I felt like a performing monkey or a puppet . . . . it is beautiful if you're performing spontaneously, like at a party or hui. But the other – I felt like a jack-in-the-box.'[93]

AMERICAN PATROL

The American invasion of New Zealand did not arrive unaccompanied. On 12 June 1942, five US troop ships – protected by a cruiser and a destroyer – surprised Aucklanders when they steamed into Waitemata Harbour. During a mayoral reception the next day, the harbour ferries blew their horns and four military bands set the tone with 'Stars and Stripes Forever' and 'Colonel Bogey'. On board ship, wide-mouthed sousaphones responded with 'Roll Out the Barrel'. A similar scene took place in Wellington the following day.[94]

It had been only six months since the Japanese attack on Pearl Harbour, and four since the fall of Singapore, but the US was pouring vast resources into the Pacific to repulse the enemy. Over the next three years, approximately 150,000 American servicemen would pass through New Zealand, with up to 50,000 GIs camped in the country at a time, not including the thousands of sailors on ships berthed in Auckland and Wellington harbours.[95]

They brought music with them – in the form of military and dance bands – and they heard music when they got here. They left behind dance steps, memories and music. The musical environment had been altered: local musicians' style of performance, broadcasters' approach to radio presentation and programming, and the audience's tastes in popular music. This was a cultural as well as military invasion, with little resistance offered.

In Petone, Mihi Edwards had the choice of two dance halls on a Saturday night: the Rowing Club and the Labour Club. The Americans – 'charming, polished, reckless' – were staying at Hutt Park Raceway, so often went to both. Edwards and her friends learnt to jive, and found they were good at it, almost as good as their well-groomed consorts:

> The Yanks are beautiful dancers, and a lot of new hits are played by the bands: such songs as 'In the Mood', that was really 'hep', as the Yanks used to say; the very catchy 'Chattanooga Choo-Choo'; and 'The Boogie-Woogie Bugle Boy from Company B'. We jive to 'Johnny Doughboy Found a Rose in Ireland' and many others coming on the scene.

July, 1943: US Marines loiter outside the Manners Street Post Office, in the heart of Wellington's wartime music precinct. Pascoe collection, F 1/2 82275, Alexander Turnbull Library, Wellington

Oh, I have never ever had such fun in all my life. Sometimes we just sit and watch the boys dance – they are spectacular to watch and they know they are good.[96]

From around the walls of dance floors, some New Zealand males glared at the uniformed interlopers. From the bandstand, the musicians enjoyed the spectacle. To drummer Johnny Madden, the jitterbuggers at the Peter Pan were a revelation: 'You should have seen those girls dancing with the navy guys. They'd throw them between their legs, and over the heads, gosh they were clever, they were acrobats. Terrific.'[97]

Even those who stayed at home felt the cultural impact of the American invasion. New Zealand radio had already made many changes to its programming since the war began: weather forecasts were dropped, because they could benefit the enemy, as could any references to the location of troops, in New Zealand or overseas. In Christchurch, 3ZB broadcaster Happi Hill was investigated by military police in case he was cryptically communicating with enemy submarines. An advertisement he had read out was suspicious: Hill had referred to women's coats in battleship grey.[98]

Many programmes requiring listener contributions, such as request sessions or birthday calls, were suspended, as they might contain secret messages. For the same reason, scripts were altered or censored before broadcast, and programmes were pre-recorded so the timing of broadcast could not contain coded topical intelligence. Henry Rudolph, running an old-time dance band for live broadcast on 2YA, received requests from Australia; if there was a specific date mentioned, it was ignored.[99]

A commission of inquiry held to decide upon wartime broadcasting practices reported, 'As to musical numbers we are satisfied that the programmes are built round an advertising unit so far ahead that it is impossible for any announcer to put on a record, such, for instance, as one which could indicate the presence of warships in any of our harbours without prior notification.'[100]

The NBS incorporated the NCBS as its 'commercial division' in June 1943 (on 1 April 1946, a new title would encompass both: the New Zealand Broadcasting Service). With the banning of ad lib material – impossible for sports commentaries, and difficult for the more informal style of the commercial stations – the gradual infiltration of American programming on New Zealand airwaves understandably made its impression. This was aimed at the American troops who were passing through, but keenly listened to by the local audience. The first programme was *American Hour*, weekly on NCBS from mid-1942, in which the host – a marine – played the latest records from the States. Complete programmes were recorded on 12-inch and 16-inch discs by the American Armed Forces Radio Service and broadcast on the ZBs.

The most significant change took place in Auckland on 12 April 1944, when the American forces were given control of 1ZM by the NBS. It was programmed in the American style by Sgt Larry Dysart, with standalone series such as *American College Song*, *Turn-Tune-Time*, *Music America Loves Best*, *Classical Corner* and even 30-minute dramas. A typical day's schedule was:

BLUE SMOKE

6.00 am–8.00 am	News and *Music Time*
11.00 am–1.00 pm	Theatre, Music, News and *Yarns for Yanks*
4.00 pm–5.15 pm	Music, Sports, *GI Jive*
5.45 pm–6.00 pm	Harry James
6.00 pm–7.00 pm	*Carnival of Music*, Bob Hope
7.00 pm–9.15 pm	*Comedy Caravan*, *Spotlight Bands*, News
9.15 pm–10.15 pm	Boston Symphony
10.15 pm–11.00 pm	*Make-Believe Ballroom Time*[101]

Broadcasting from the basement of the 1YA building in Shortland Street, the 1ZM signal could be heard clearly in Wellington, and was relayed to the Pacific. Whereas the NBS had policies that prevented individuals displaying too much personality, the casual broadcasting style of the forces' radio was enjoyed by the local audience. 'The large amount of fan mail we received confirms this', said Dysart, who took home a New Zealand war bride. 'The American accents of the announcers distinguished the station on the dial, and made us easily identifiable . . . . New Zealanders were searching for good entertainment, and I think we were able to give it to them. What pleased the forces, pleased Aucklanders.' Pianist Lyall Laurent credits Dysart with introducing the first US hit parade onto New Zealand airwaves, featuring singers such as Frank Sinatra and Joan Edwards.[102]

Denys Bevan suggests that local reaction was mixed, 'but despite the American-style humour, the freewheeling method of announcing and the different types of programmes, it was soon the most popular station, especially among the younger generation'. The station made outside broadcasts and played requests for New Zealand listeners.[103]

By December 1944, most of the Americans had left New Zealand for the Pacific and the station was handed back to the NBS. A broadcasting official recalled, 'There were no such things as listener polls, and we had absolutely no knowledge whether 1ZM was stealing our audience or we were stealing theirs. I know this; they had all the privileges and fewer responsibilities. They ignored copyright and we did it at our peril . . . . I regarded them as pirates in a way, "fly-by-the-nighters".'[104]

Despite a shortage of musicians, by 1943 Auckland's musical nightlife was booming. Ted Croad would shut the doors of an overflowing Orange Coronation Hall at 9.00 pm; Hugh Tatton was drawing consistently good houses

at the Peter Pan; at the new Trocadero, drummer/vocalist Johnny Madden held court; Billy Elder and Wally Holmes shared band-leader duties at the Cabaret Metropole; and Bert Peterson was at the Civic Wintergarden with his Radio Swing Orchestra.

The Wintergarden found that restricting one night to officers and their partners attracted the largest crowd of the week. There were special evenings when films such as *This is the Army* or *Blues in the Night* premiered, the 3000 theatre tickets selling out in an hour; and on Independence Day and Thanksgiving, when turkey was on the menu at the cabaret. Another attraction at the Civic was the nightly floor show put on by a chorus line of ballet dancers, the Lucky Lovelies. Afterwards, the dancers would quickly change their costumes then slip in the back door to the Wintergarden downstairs and become the Pony Dancers. Freda Stark was famous for her solo dance wearing little else but gold paint, and also the Balloon Dance, in which 'great bunches of balloons were attached to her scanty attire and burst by American servicemen's cigarettes, to shouts of laughter, as she danced alongside their tables'.[105]

Saturday matinee dances became popular because wartime regulations closed the pubs for two hours in the afternoons, which meant many servicemen on leave were at a loose end. With the Americans in Auckland, every day seemed like Christmas, recalled Johnny Madden. 'The city was flowing with money. They were big tippers, the Americans; $10 was nothing to them. And the florists did a roaring trade. Every time they took a woman out they bought her a corsage. Women were treated like princesses, something they weren't used to from the locals. They laid it on with a trowel.'[106]

While there always seemed to be new ways to smuggle alcohol into these supposedly unlicensed venues, clubs outside of the central city could push the licensing laws a little more. On the southern edge of Auckland, in the then remote suburb of Hillsborough, was the El Rey: a nightclub for US officers. The large room featured a bay window giving expansive views of Manukau Harbour, while Del Crook's five-piece band entertained an exclusive audience consisting mostly of US Army officers and their partners. Some of Crook's band members – Nolan Rafferty, Gerry Horsup – would go AWOL from the Hobsonville air force base if they could not get leave. They would use a car parked outside the grounds of the base, and be back in time for parade the next morning.

THE PENGUIN

Ted Croad relished leading Auckland's most popular big band for over twenty years. He dressed for the part, usually in white tails, and wielded a long conductor's baton. As a band leader, he was a stickler for dress standards and punctuality. While his own musical standards may have been lacking – causing his musicians to play pranks, such as striking up in common time when Croad called for a waltz – he knew enough to hire the best musicians in town, and kept them by paying higher wages. They laughed at his pretensions and nicknamed him the Penguin. But he was loyal to the big-band concept, long after others had reduced to combos due to fashion or economics.

Croad's home base from 1934 until 1955 was the Orange Coronation Ballroom on Newton Road. It was built in 1923 by the Orange Lodge, whose deed of trust stated that its duty was to 'promulgate the principles and further the practice of the Protestant Religion and to afford its members the means of Social intercourse, spiritual

involvement and rational recreation'.[107] The trustees of the Orange were as particular about their hall as Croad was with his presentation. They gave him only a weekly lease; constantly harassed him about overcrowding; and imposed bans on liquor, chewing gum, pass-out chits and jitterbugging.[108]

Born in 1898, Croad made his musical debut aged eight, in an Invercargill drum and fife band. After travelling the world as a merchant seaman, he began his musical career dressed as a gypsy, playing violin and flute.[109] He was told to smarten himself up for the stage, a warning he often gave to musicians in his own bands. With Ted Croad and the Chevaliers, he ran dances at Point Chevalier, and at Scots Hall in Symonds Street before settling in at the Orange.

The heyday of the Orange under Croad's baton was the Second World War, when his band performed three nights a week before a stylish art nouveau backdrop. 'He must have made a fortune because the Americans were lined up outside the door', recalled Jim Warren. The Orange was licensed to hold 400 people, but on Saturday nights 700 would often pack the dance floor. The 'house full' sign would go up outside, and couples formed a queue down Newton Road. 'Although he was making a lot of money, Ted spent it on the band. He could have got

Ted Croad, with the violin, far left, at the Orange Coronation Ballroom, Auckland, 1938. In the rhythm section are his son Eddie on drums, and Bill Earwaker on sousaphone and bass. The other musicians are unknown. Dennis Huggard Archive, PAColl-9492-05, Alexander Turnbull Library, Wellington

BLUE SMOKE

Ted Croad with his band at the Orange Ballroom, Auckland, c. 1948. At the piano beside Croad is Crombie Murdoch. Back row, from left: George Campbell, Ed Croad, Bob Davis, Bob Leach and Jim Warren. Front row, from left: Jim Watters, Charlie Welch, Tug Wilson, Gordon Lanigan, Tommy Simpson. Jim Warren collection

away with an eight-piece band, but he liked the sound of a 12-piece.'[110]

Croad said in 1980, 'I had brilliant musicians. All my fellows were well trained, they could read music, had a good ear, and could play a tune. We played what the public wanted – not what the band wanted.' By the time of the war, the band had moved on from its 'old-time' emphasis to a repertoire featuring the standards of 'sweet' swing: 'One O'Clock Jump', 'In the Mood', 'I'll Be Seeing You', 'String of Pearls'. On the bandstand over the years was a 'who's who' of New Zealand's jazz players: Ossie Cheesman, Gordon Lanigan, Julian Lee, 'Tiny' McMahon, Crombie Murdoch, Nolan Rafferty, Jim Warren, Jimmy Watters, and the three Campbell brothers, Phil, George and Lew. On drums from the earliest days at the Orange, aged only thirteen, was Croad's son Eddie.[111]

A prominent female vocalist was always featured, sitting demurely on stage between numbers as they were strictly forbidden to mingle or dance with the crowd. During the war, the vocalists included Jimmy FitzPatrick,

Pat McMinn, Hazel Peel and Flo White. McMinn stayed with Croad for nearly ten years, marrying Eddie (and observing how her father-in-law took his frustrations out upon his son, rather than his mischievous band).

In 1955 the Orange Hall trustees ended Croad's lease, deciding to run the dances themselves. So he moved to the Trades Hall on Hobson Street, calling the venue Roseland. But Croad's stint at the Trades Hall proved to be brief: dance fashions changed, but Croad stayed still. 'People were starting to jive and rock'n'roll and he wouldn't let them', said Warren. 'He would stop it if he saw it, because he played music for ballroom dancing. But this was what people wanted: there was a change of attitude.' The Trades Hall room would soon become Auckland's first venue for rock'n'roll.

Croad had seen good times come and go. When he started his first big band he was a mobile saw-doctor, using a motorbike and sidecar; soon he was driving a Packard. 'He became a very wealthy man but he lost it all in the finish', said Vern Wilson. In his retirement, Croad worked as a groomer of poodles; he died in 1984.[112]

Hillsborough Road was unsealed, and the suburb itself was dry, but no one went thirsty at the El Rey. 'There used to be loads of grog there, it was very blatant', recalled trumpeter Nolan Rafferty. 'But there was never any trouble; I never saw a fight of any sort. There was a good class of person.' The customers would insist on shouting the band, which had its own stash in the laundry. After midnight, musicians who had been playing in central city clubs would arrive with their wives. Their ticket in was a promise to get on stage for a blow.[113]

The Australian saxophonist Reg Cranham was not shy about taking advantage of the Americans' generosity, recalled drummer Gerry Horsup.

A Yank would come up and he would want us to play a request. Reg would say, 'It'll cost yer – 10 quid', and the Yank would pull out a roll of dollar notes – they didn't know the value of a dollar, they were hillbillies some of 'em, didn't know what to do with the money, just rolling in money.

Reg would help himself and when we had finished our bracket we would share it out. Another time there was a woman there, no names, no pack drill. She knew one or two of the boys. This night she was with a Yankee major, helluva nice chap. She said, 'This major of mine is from Texas, would you play "Deep in the Heart of Texas"?'

Reg said, 'It'll cost him a whisky' – they used to bring whisky in by the carton in those days. We played 'Deep in the Heart', they were smiling up at us . . . . from then on, whenever he was in there with a woman we played 'Deep in the Heart of Texas' and the bottle of whisky was always there for us.

One night the administration officer from the Hobsonville base arrived with a WAAF; in their uniforms the couple took to the dance floor while Rafferty and Horsup ducked their heads. 'The officer came right up to the bandstand and said, "It's all right boys, I've seen you." He never said anything else.' Later, when they were playing at the base, the officer came over and said, 'You boys look better than you do in dinner suits.' And that was the end of it.[114]

Musicians loved playing the El Rey, because of the generosity of the manager, Cecil 'Peter' Peterson, who provided T-bone steaks and kept everyone guessing as to whether he was American or Canadian or just pretending. Pianist and band leader Del Crook emphasised the almost refined atmosphere of the venue, attracting

Auckland socialites as well as American officers. 'It was a most interesting night club. I never heard anyone's voice raised in anger. If they got full, they got full in a gentlemanly way.'

Auckland's Methodists were shocked by the depravity taking place in the parish. An inspection committee spent a night on the town, and found that many clubs were dens of iniquity:

Beneath very subdued lighting, a band of three or four instruments blared forth loud music, while on a restricted space men and women followed the cult of the American 'jitterbug'. Their dancing space, which was so limited as to make one believe that dancing was not the main attraction, was railed off.

Among the dancers were many whose wayward feet told of an over-indulgence in alcohol. The majority of the servicemen's partners displayed this tendency, and many of them were girls not yet out of their teens. In spite of their youth, their lined faces were evidence of their fast and furious living. They performed their dance with the fixed faces of people who were doing a set task on which a living depended.[115]

Originally published in the *Methodist Times*, this article was widely read when it was reprinted in the *Auckland Star*, but it amused and annoyed the music and entertainment community. Bert Peterson described its author as 'a young and enthusiastic moralist', and the story as 'full of righteous horror at the sights to be seen if you look hard enough'. 'Anyone who knows Auckland is only too painfully aware of the staidness of the city, and it might even come as a relief to many to learn that it has suddenly been declared a wild, wild city of evil!'[116]

Alfred Fenn, director of Cabaret Metropole, responded with a letter that ridiculed the sensationalised article. Perhaps the young man had seen too many jitterbuggers and deduced that they were drunk. Fenn himself was no fan of jitterbugging, and was grateful it didn't happen in his club. ('That's what he thinks', a Metropole patron was heard to say.) Peterson, the Musicians' Union president, thought the article was part of a steady propaganda campaign. 'To appease the present agitators, it would probably be necessary to close all hotels, dance halls, and night clubs, and throw out of work every musician in New Zealand.'[117]

To many GIs, from farms or small towns in the Midwest or the Deep South, cities such as Auckland or Wellington

The original caption for this photo from the Majestic Cabaret, Wellington, reads: '"Tony" McKenna and Carol Sanders of 2ZB give out hot rhythm for the doubtful enjoyment of the US Marines Dance Band'. Hall Raine/RNZ Sound Archives

seemed cosmopolitan. Others tried it on with the locals, who quickly progressed from gullible to sceptical. Band leaders such as Lauri Paddi at the Majestic or Hugh Tatton at the Peter Pan got used to being approached during a gig by someone in a uniform insisting, 'My buddy is a swell crooner from Artie Shaw's band' . . . 'Do you mind if George here plays the drums, he was in Bob Crosby's band . . .'.[118] Once invited on stage, recalled Del Crook, 'You'd sit them up there with a trumpet or a sax and they were hopeless. But some of them were really great players, they had it.'[119]

Every night but Sunday, there was live music and dancing in clubs and halls: at the elegant Peter Pan and Wintergarden cabarets in Auckland, or the Empress and Majestic in Wellington. The Navy League and the American Red Cross could organise 'respectable' girls as partners. Auckland's Shortland Club was extremely popular, offering the combination of 'wine, dine and dance' with Ian 'Nin' Picaithly's band, and the club led to many imitators, such as the National and the Rio. For those of a more staid persuasion, dancing and games were offered at the YWCA's Down Town Club in Auckland.

US soldiers and their dancing partners at the Majestic Cabaret, Wellington, c. November 1942.
E. M. Alderdice Collection, PAColl-0089-1-16, Alexander Turnbull Library, Wellington

On the seventh day, those wanting a nightclub were told the joke about the parachutist who foolishly took a jump, then bitterly complained when his 'chute failed: didn't he know that nothing dared open in Auckland on a Sunday? But city bylaws were changed so that selected cinemas could open on Sundays 'for the entertainment of members of the Allied Forces and the Merchant Navy, each of whom may bring two civilian friends'. To Bert Peterson, this was a welcome development that came about only through the arrival of the 'vigorous newcomers' from overseas, and he looked forward to 'an attempt to emulate lighter-hearted people in other parts of the world, who are prepared to allow dancing on Sundays'.[120]

There was one place to dance on a Sunday, however, and although no alcohol was allowed, it did feature the only iced water machine in Auckland. The Down Town Club had originally been set up so that uniformed women – WAACs and WAAFs – could mingle with men without

having to go to bars. The club, on Customs Street, was used by 1000 people each day; it had a lounge, library, sun room, games room and dancing room. By March 1943, there were 5000 members, of whom only 477 were in the armed forces.

At the Down Town Club, there was dancing every night to a gramophone, a piano or, twice a week, a band; even during the day, couples danced to the radio. The club had a more sober reputation than others, but that was part of its success, recalled volunteer club hostess Cath Lylian. 'Because it was the YWCA, it was not a place where wild young men came. It brought in the quieter more respectable servicemen . . . the kind who wanted to be introduced to a girl.'

As well as dances, the club offered dance classes: strict tempo as well as the racier modern styles. 'There were foxtrots, one-steps and jitterbugging', recalled Lylian. In the cinderella dance, women would put one shoe in the centre of the dance floor, then men would rush to grab one and look for the partner whose foot fitted the shoe.[121]

The sedate foxtrots gave way to the 'razzle-dazzle' of the jitterbug. Taboos were evaporating but not without a backlash: on the wall of the Peter Pan Cabaret was a sign that read, 'No full skirts while jitterbugging'. The dance took up too much room and disturbed others on the floor.[122]

But the jitterbug was the hot dance of 1943, and when New Zealanders saw it done properly, they never forgot. Late in the evening of 10 August, several black American GIs were brought in to the Civic Wintergarden cabaret. On the stage was the Artie Shaw Navy Band. Aspirant entrepreneur Pat Quinn – who later had an international career as the hypnotist, Franquin – had managed to secure the band for an appearance at the Wintergarden during its visit. But it was the black dancers giving a jitterbugging display – flying about with abandon – who stole the show.[123]

Black American GIs were occasionally seen, but their music was never heard, during the American forces' stay in New Zealand. Some have disputed that they were present here at all, writes historian Harry Bioletti, but there are photographs that settle the matter.[124] Their profile was certainly low: US authorities were worried about trouble if they were allowed to socialise in town, so interaction was rare.[125]

Paekakariki woman Jean Matekitewhawhai Andrews attended dances at local camps with her husband and friends:

> Oh boy did we used to dance! . . . We had to have these flared skirts, and I always made sure to go once a week in there because they had all this jiving music.
>
> Oh gosh . . . dance! . . . . Maoris, although I say it myself, Maoris got this thing about them eh? Timing. Music. Dancing. And it didn't matter what dance.
>
> We used to chase the Negroes in particular – oh, we used to chase after them because they could dance, *really dance*. They were really good.[126]

There was a policy of segregation, said Eldred Stebbing, so the black Americans socialised together in their own venue, the American Negro Club. He remembered it being on the ground floor of the Hampton Court flats on Wellesley Street, near St Matthew's church. 'You never saw many of the Negroes at the Town Hall', he said. 'They'd be in their own club. They used to have jazz groups, it was

a fairly seedy sort of situation. The Military Police used to go in there and have a tidy up every now and then and they didn't ask twice.'[127]

Music and conviviality did not always revolve around alcohol. In Wellington, the Spinsters Club talked Majestic Cabaret proprietor Fred Carr into letting them use his venue, free of charge, for Sunday afternoon gatherings.[128] Besides clubs and cabarets, milkbars proliferated with the arrival of the Americans. The Red Cross clubs were oases of American culture: hamburgers, Coca-Cola and ice cream sodas. Wellington's was at the Hotel Cecil, near the railway station. In 1943 it hosted a week-long festival of entertainment, with one act being a variety show by the Cheer-Oh Girls' concert party, visiting from Christchurch. A Marine band played for 'wholesome' dances, although there were group lessons in dancing the jitterbug, conga and rumba.[129]

Within the American forces were several swing bands that performed concerts and on 1ZM, the most prominent being the 290th Army Band, which had been a peacetime band in Boston, and regularly provided the music at Auckland Town Hall dances. New Zealand musicians were thrilled to hear swing played with an energy and flair they could not capture from the stock arrangements they had imported. To Bobby Griffith, a young Auckland naval rating and trumpeter, even the US military bands were inspiring, 'Because they *blew*. Those guys used to blow their heads off. New Zealand was very mickey mouse, very Charlie Kunz-type music. The Americans really got me . . . . Jazz in those days was still a dirty word. My, we were in a corny state.'[130]

From within the 43rd Division came three bands – the Commandos of Swing, the Rhythmaires and the Tropicats – that performed at venues such as the Peter Pan, Civic Wintergarden and Catholic Social Centre. 'The Tropicats were perhaps the most popular of the three', writes Denys Bevan. 'It was a rare evening that their talents were not being made use of.'[131]

The Tropicats had an alien within their midst, though: pianist Jim Foley was a New Zealander who had been injured during army night manoeuvres on Rangitoto, and was on indefinite sick leave. With no commitments, he started playing for the 290th – who couldn't rely on their drunk pianist – and the Tropicats. Just after the war, Foley recalled:

Auckland pianist Jim Foley occasionally performed with the Tropicats – a band from the US 43rd Division – when the band's pianist was worse for wear. With Foley (far left) and the Tropicats on the stage of the Civic, Auckland, is the Australian singer June Mendoza. Bernie Allen collection

The standard of music was wonderful. I learned over 500 jam tunes, and enjoyed the company of musicians so keen on their musical product that they would never dream of talking when one of their members was taking a solo. A habit that New Zealand musicians would do well to imitate. Playing with this band was the biggest thrill I have ever had. My spine used to tingle every night.[132]

During this time Foley – who played in the manner of Teddy Wilson – recorded several discs with the visiting musicians, which made their way back to the States. An American clarinettist called Danny Polo heard them and this led to some engagements in the US for Foley after the war.[133] Other Auckland musicians who impressed the visiting Americans were saxophonist Jimmy Watters and the pianist Jack Thompson. Reg Maddams, maestro of the Wurlitzer organ, estimated he played for 40,000 US troops while they were in New Zealand; a romantic rendition of 'Stardust' became essential at his Sunday concerts at the Civic. He performed on the same bill as Artie Shaw and comedian Joe E. Brown, and before 3000 women at a reception for US first lady Eleanor Roosevelt.

Musical groups – be they amateur or professional, from the US or New Zealand – travelled around the military camps to perform. Arriving on the back of an army truck, they set up makeshift stages at halls and hospitals, often performing to casualties in the wards. Groups included the Ozark Mountaineers and, under the baton of L. C. M. Saunders, the schoolboy choir of King's College Chapel. The Arcadian Revellers Revue entertained troops at Papakura military camp; among them was the blind accordionist and ventriloquist Toni Savage who had been performing since the late 1930s. With Pat McMinn she was in the floor show at the opening of the Trocadero in August 1943 (attended by some of Shaw's band); also on the bill was the female impersonator and teenage window-dresser John Hunter, later in the Kiwis Revue. After the war, Savage was the only entertainer among seven supportive Aucklanders awarded a certificate of merit by the US Navy.[134]

Because many older New Zealand musicians were in the military, blind pianist Lyall Laurent was one of many who got his break playing at the American bases, hospitals and clubs. The Americans preferred jazz, which Laurent was happy to provide, and was paid 30 shillings a night for his efforts. He also received tips: $US5 one night, and at other times chocolate, peanuts and other scarce treats.[135]

In Wellington – doing a Shirley Temple act – seven-year-old Leigh Brewer charmed many Marines, and also popular was the Kinky Campboy Club, with the dancer-contortionist Heather May. Especially in demand were Jean McPherson, New Zealand's Vera Lynn, and, in Auckland, Pat McMinn.[136]

Besides Artie Shaw, several other American celebrities passed through New Zealand as enlisted men or to entertain the troops. Among them was the singer Harry Mills, of the Mills Brothers, who gave a few solo performances at the Hotel Cecil in Wellington in late 1944. But it was two years before another act arrived with similar mana to Shaw's band. At the end of the war, between VE and VJ days, the Claude Thornhill Show visited Auckland and Christchurch. The musicians included men who had performed with Benny Goodman, Jack Benny and Rudy Vallee. Among them was the former child actor – now a serious drummer – Jackie Cooper. They attended a party at the Metropole cabaret, where the bands of Epi Shalfoon and Bert Peterson were performing, and took over the instruments for a jam session. Local jazz fan Peter Sellers, attending the first concert, wrote that the eight-piece band was 'all powerful':

> 'Bugle Call Rag' was truly the most sensational number ever rendered in a hall in Auckland. 'Smokey' Stover and Jackie Cooper were on two sets of drums, going flat out for two and a half minutes with perfect synchronisation. They were then joined by the whole unit, driving it along like the late Glenn Miller's arrangement to a shattering conclusion . . .[137]

Not all interaction between the visiting Americans and their New Zealand hosts was convivial, of course, but the so-called 'battles' in streets such as Manners and Cuba in Wellington, and Queen in Auckland have become exaggerated over time. 'Each occasion was only a barroom-type brawl on a rather larger scale that spread to the streets', writes Denys Bevan. 'Prompt action by civilian and military police, shore patrols and calmer heads actually stopped these brawls from becoming anything more serious.'[138]

The scuffles with a music connection had the potential to become more serious. At a dance in Avondale in January 1944, some American servicemen were found to have concealed blackjacks, or coshes, within bouquets of flowers.[139] The Cuba Street fracas on 12 May 1944 started at the Mayfair Cabaret, its root cause being the tension between the attitude of some US servicemen to Maori. According to one army report, after a Maori accused a US sailor of stealing his hat, a disturbance began which moved onto the street. The Maori were outnumbered, so a message was sent to the Ngati Poneke Club for help; meanwhile, civilians came to their aid and a 'free for all' quickly developed. Americans inside the cabaret threw chairs out the windows onto the street, which became used as batons. By this stage, the Maori reinforcements arrived, along with civil and military police. In the end, the main casualties were a jeep that had been overturned and a few cuts and bruises on both sides.[140]

Antagonism between Maori in the Waikato and American servicemen – over the way the visitors treated Maori women – became worse when Princess Te Puea visited the US commanding officer to discuss the issue. While waiting, she overheard a racial insult by his aide-de-camp and walked out. Incidents between Maori and American soldiers then increased, which Te Puea defused by inviting American officers to the Ngaruawahia marae for music and hospitality. The US commanding officer did not front up, but the entertainment from Te Puea's performance troupe Te Pou o Mangatawhiri – and the lavish welcome his officers received – calmed tensions, and no more incidents were reported in the region.[141]

The only music-related casualty of the Americans' sojourn in New Zealand appears to be Walter Lee, a US sailor. While stopping over in Dunedin, the nineteen-year-old attended a dance at Cargill's Castle cabaret. Between brackets he took seventeen-year-old waitress Joyce Lawrence out for a walk along the cliff edge, slipped and fell 350 feet. Lawrence scrambled down to help him but found he had been killed, then climbed back up the cliff to contact the police.[142]

The experience of another US sailor was probably more typical. As his ship got closer to New Zealand, Thomas N. Parlon was monitoring the radio and picked up a local station. 'They had a male quartet on, and they were singing "On the Banks of the Wabash"', he said. 'That told me something. They were as ignorant as we were, I guess.' While based in Wellington, he socialised with Maori in local bars and at parties. He remembered that when it was time to go, the Maori would sing together. 'It was a beautiful tune, and they were good musically. The song was local, and it was new to everybody down there. After the war, some enterprising Yank came back with that tune. You've probably heard it: "Now is the Hour".'[143]

SWING KING

Rumours of an impending visit to New Zealand by one of the world's leading swing bands spread among Auckland musicians in June 1943. The band would be big, its name even bigger, the *Music Maker* teased: 'We hesitate to publish the name at this early stage.'[144]

The nineteen-piece group was officially called Navy Band # 501, but to the rumour-mongers' delight it was actually the band of Artie Shaw, clarinettist and swing star. Shaw's biggest worldwide hit was with Cole Porter's 'Begin the Beguine' in 1938, and this would be the first time a major figure in jazz had toured New Zealand close to the peak of his career. He had assembled his band from the cream of musicians who had joined up, players from the big bands of Benny Goodman, Tommy Dorsey and Glenn Miller.

Shaw and his band were exhausted when they arrived in Auckland aboard the troop ship *Mormacport* on 30 July. For seven months they had toured the Pacific war zone in an ad hoc fashion, hitch-hiking from island to island. 'Each time they moved, Shaw had to scrounge a trip to the next atoll, then scrounge food and digs, and also take care of their instruments in the heat.' Over the airwaves, Japanese propagandist Tokyo Rose could be heard playing Artie Shaw records and taunting the troops: 'Hi GIs – if your government really cared about you, you'd

An exhausted Artie Shaw escapes the Pacific war zone for New Zealand, July 1943, but not for rest and recreation. Redmer Yska collection

be seeing Artie Shaw in San Francisco instead of being in that dirty foxhole.'[145]

Shaw recalled the experience later: 'The whole band, including myself, began to come apart at the seams. By then our instruments were being held together by rubber bands and sheer will, having survived any number of air raids and damp spells in fox-holes, and the men themselves were for the most part in similarly varying states of dilapidation.'[146]

Their first Auckland concert was at the St James Theatre on Sunday 1 August, before a combined audience of servicemen from New Zealand and the US. During rehearsals on the morning of the concert, it was decided that nineteen-year-old Auckland singer Esme Stephens would perform with the band.

'It all happened through Jack Chignell of 1ZB, who was in charge of the Shaw band while they were in New Zealand', said Dale Alderton. 'Jack knew her ability and suggested to Shaw that they should have a local singer for a couple of numbers. Shaw didn't care: "Yeah, okay, whatever".'

Ticket for an Auckland dance featuring Artie Shaw's Navy Band, 1943. Dennis Huggard collection

An acetate of Auckland singer Esme Stephens's performance of 'White Christmas' with the Artie Shaw Navy Band. Dennis Huggard Archive, MSD 10-0705, Alexander Turnbull Library, Wellington

Stephens suggested 'White Christmas' and 'This Love of Mine', and Shaw instructed David Rose and Dick Jones to write arrangements quickly for that night. Noel Peach of Astor Studios was hurriedly recruited to record Stephens' performance backstage on a portable recorder. Over a landline to the Spackman and Howarth studio in Albert Street, Eldred Stebbing copied the song onto an acetate. Beside him was trombonist Dale Alderton, who later married Stephens.

While she sang with the band, Shaw took a break from the stage. 'I guess Esme was nervous, but it didn't affect her – she sang well', recalled Alderton.[147]

Three days later, the *New Zealand Observer* reported:

Judging by the reception they had from a large and enthusiastic audience on Sunday evening, theirs should be a popular tour. Their programme was a varied one, including such old favourites as 'Begin the Beguine', 'Stardust' and 'St Louis Blues', and new hits such as 'White Christmas', 'This Love of Mine', 'You'd Be Nice to Come Home To' and 'Dearly Beloved'.

The band has no vocalists of its own, so the vocal items were left in the capable hands of Miss Esme Stephens, of 1ZB, and two American sailors from camps in the Auckland district . . . .

Students of human nature were amused at one of the sights presented by the audience . . . . Looking down the

aisles between the seats, long rows of single feet could be seen. The feet were all tap-tap-tapping in perfect time with the music. Swing, they say, has that effect.[148]

Over the next ten days, Shaw's band performed at many venues around Auckland, including the Civic Wintergarden, Papakura Military Camp, Westhaven marina and in the middle of the harbour on board two US warships that were lashed together. The musicians also split into small combos to visit military hospitals.

Saxophonist Mark Pierce accompanied Shaw to play for the wounded at one of the military hospitals: 'After we finished playing in one of the wards everything was quiet. The musicians didn't know what was wrong. Artie said to me, "What did we do wrong?" An orderly told Artie that it was an amputees' ward. Artie started to cry, saying, "It's a bitch, it's a bitch".'[149]

The audiences at the dances and concerts were mostly American and New Zealand servicemen and their dancing partners, with very few civilians getting tickets. But the visit by Shaw's band galvanised New Zealand's jazz community, who knew the pedigree of these players. At some of the concerts, local musicians were able to get in if they presented their union membership cards.[150]

Younger musicians used many ruses to get tickets, while Auckland clarinettist Derek Heine even got the chance to sit in with the band. Murray Tanner spent the evening avoiding a caretaker who had spotted him sneaking in with some friends; he hid high in the balcony, in heaven. 'We had such a thrill listening to names that I remembered for years afterwards.'[151] Lew Campbell befriended trumpeter Conrad Gozzo. Frank Gibson couldn't get in so listened by the stage door. In Wellington, Don Richardson met a GI who said, 'Give me another 10 minutes – if I can't find some nice young lady who wants to come back with me, you're it.' He was struck by the clean sound and regimented playing from careful orchestrations, 'which made it straightforward when you were trying to learn to play them yourself'.

Singer Pat McMinn and some of her band at the Trocadero slipped across Queen Street to check out the Shaw band at the Town Hall: 'We were knocked out by it', she said. 'The sound was just unbelievable.' Some of the Shaw musicians sat in at the Trocadero afterwards.[152] Veteran local trumpeter Vern Wilson also couldn't believe the volume the band played at, even in Greenlane Hospital, in a concert for the nurses: 'Flat out, full bore all the way, the brass players had to be the fittest.'[153]

The band travelled by train to Wellington and stayed in the barracks of the US Navy Boat Repair Unit, built above the boatsheds in Oriental Bay. Shaw took the chance to find something more comfortable and moved into the modern Spanish-style Midland Hotel on Lambton Quay. Word of the Shaw's visit had filtered down from Auckland, so his reception in Wellington was even more exuberant. A crowd of female fans assembled outside the hotel but Shaw 'made it known that he is of a retiring disposition'. When the *Listener* sought an interview, its reporter was told Shaw 'had neither the inclination nor the permission'.[154]

One man who broke through the barrier around Shaw was Arthur Pearce, who had received a telegram from Auckland:

ARRIVING WITH ARTIE FRIDAY MORNING
WILL CONTACT YOU DURING DAY + JACK +

Pearce's 1ZB colleague Jack Chignell came through with an invitation for New Zealand's leading jazz broadcaster to meet Shaw and some of his band. Pearce invited Dave Tough and Max Kaminsky to his home in Karori. 'No sooner had the men entered the flat than they realised that this fellow knew what he was talking about, and that he personally was largely responsible for the local fans' acceptance of the sidemen in the band, who were virtually overlooked in their own country.' Pearce surprised them with detailed questions about their recording history, and produced a rare bottle of imported whisky. Asked what they would like with it, Tough replied: 'Glasses.'[155]

Shaw was given the keys to the city. In Manners Street, the Opera House featured short films of his civilian band performing 'Begin the Beguine' and other hits before the main feature, *Four Mothers*. On Willis Street an audience of 2400 packed the Majestic Theatre for the real thing, 'on the stage at the theatre in which he and his ex-wife, Lana Turner, have appeared so often on the screen'. The band also performed at various bases around Wellington – at Hutt Park and Camp McKay near Paekakariki – and at the Majestic Cabaret and a ball at the RNZAF hall, Rongotai.

At the Majestic, reported the *Dominion*, 'St Louis Blues' was 'played as it has never been heard in Wellington before'. The crowd – mostly US servicemen – 'roared their approval of every one of the band's numbers . . . . The "hot" music was too much for one sailor, who rolled down the dress circle stairs and was quickly removed by the patrols.'[156] Backstage, saxophonist Sam Donahue reacquainted himself with Canadian expatriate Art Rosoman, thirteen years after they played together in Sunburst, Montana. He then took part in a jam session at the Hope Gibbons mansion at Lyall Bay, attended by Freddie Gore and jazz fan Peter Sellers.[157]

Summing up the visit in the *Music Maker*, Bert Peterson described the impact on Auckland musicians:

That music went right to the hearts of dance musicians, who applauded vociferously and cheered the players to the echo . . . . the arrangements the band played put new life into every musician present. I guarantee all hands tore home to put in a few hours' practice on the strength of it. Long-forgotten tutors, textbooks and studies were rescued from the attic and thumbed anew.[158]

The feeling was mutual. Shaw's pianist Rocky Coluccio recalled: 'The people in Auckland were unusually warm and friendly. The ladies were wonderful. Despite the concerts and dances played, it was more like a rest and rehabilitation situation for the band. After the New Hebrides, Solomons and New Caledonia, the food seemed like manna from heaven.'[159] And trumpeter Max Kaminsky never forgot walking up Queen Street and hearing a sound coming from a shop, stopping him in his tracks: Billie Holiday singing 'I Cried for You'. He bounded in and asked the young Chinese shopkeeper, 'How in hell did you ever hear of Billie Holiday in this nowhere place?' The proprietor explained that 'he had friends in England who shipped him jazz records, and it turned out he even had some of mine'. For the rest of his stay in Auckland, Kaminsky spent most of his spare time in the store, listening to records and enjoying the Chinese cooking.[160]

Another New Zealander to perform with the band was 'Maori girl singer' Molly Te Meihana, who sang the 'Maori farewell song' at an Auckland concert for furloughed 2NZEF men at the Town Hall.[161] After 35 days in New Zealand, the Shaw band said haere ra, flying out on 2 September aboard a cargo plane bound for Brisbane.

SWEETHEARTS OF RHYTHM

Community singing cultivated community spirit, but in times of sacrifice glamour also plays its part. The big-band female vocalist needed to look fabulous, with a wardrobe of full-length ball gowns, even if many were sewn by friends and paid for by the singers themselves out of their meagre performance fees.

Apart from the occasional pianist such as the ground-breaking Vora Kissin and the 'swinging' Marie Darby, both from Auckland, women musicians were severely under-represented in dance bands except as singers. But the prominence of the vocalist role meant that each city soon developed its stars. Early in the war, two women singers often featured on Auckland bandstands were Betty Spiro and Winsome Walsh, both with Theo Walters' band. Spiro, 'an exceedingly charming girl', was the daughter of Lou Spiro, bass player and vice-president of the Musicians' Union. Visiting tenor Peter Dawson was enthusiastic about Spiro's singing of 'more serious' music: 'I strongly advise her to go over to the other side as soon as the war is over.'[162] The petite Walsh was 'a most attractive and accomplished vocalist', said Bert Peterson of the *Music Maker*. 'This little girl is full of life and literally radiates personality.'[163]

Singing with Ted Croad's band in Auckland were Flo White and 'little' Hazel Peel. White had been a member of the original Metropole band, while Peel was so called because she was 'a child prodigy', said Peterson, 'with a wonderful range and amazing clarity, and perfectly true pitch, which I find unusual in child singers'.[164]

But as the war dragged on, the true professionals emerged. In Auckland, Pat McMinn began her singing career while still a teenager. Wellington's stars were Jean McPherson and, from 1945, US war bride Marion Waite. In Christchurch, there was Anita (Ann) Osborn and Coral Cummins; according to Peterson, Cummins was 'probably the most stylish jive singer of them all'.[165]

At the Dixieland on Auckland's Queen Street, Swing Kings band leader Johnny Madden was called 'the most popular vocalist the New Zealand dance world has ever produced', but as he was also the band's drummer, another focal point was needed.[166] So Madden organised a 'ladies' vocalist competition', with a contract for the winner. By May 1942, after four heats, no one impressive had emerged.

Enter Patty McMinn, a fifteen-year-old from nearby Freemans Bay, who had some experience singing 'Alexander's Ragtime Band' on 1ZB in the children's radio

While still a teenager, Pat McMinn was a leading Auckland vocalist during the war. Pat McMinn collection

show *Neddo's Jolly Pirates*. Growing up in Taumarunui, all of the McMinn family were musical: Patty's parents played at dances around the King Country, father on piano, mother on violin. Her brothers – who were sixteen and seventeen when she was born – already had their own dance band. After touring New Zealand as a nine-year-old dancer in J. C. Williamson's *White Horse Inn* company, McMinn continued dancing and singing lessons in Auckland.[167]

McMinn's grandmother put her name down for the Dixieland vocalist competition. 'It was done unbeknownst to me, so I was annoyed by this', said McMinn.[168] But she went along to the audition, where she was the youngest entrant; she sang in the empty cabaret for Madden and pianist Jack Thompson and won the competition. Afterwards, the Dixieland manager Norton Hammond wrote to her: 'I am able to offer you an engagement for two

Pat McMinn with the Trocadero band, c. 1943. From left are: Len Hawkins, Ernie Butters, Bill Egerton, unknown, Pat McMinn, Thomson Yandall and Jimmy Johnson. Pat McMinn collection

nights a week at 10/6 per night . . . . I hope to see you in a tap dance or two and if suitable I'd offer you an extra fee for this.'[169]

Twice a week McMinn walked with her mother from their home in Wellington Street to the cabaret. McMinn would sing several items during the evening and, in the breaks, knit and embroider in the dressing room with her mother. 'I wasn't supposed to mix with the customers.' Soon, McMinn was performing six nights a week with Madden's band at the Trocadero, a block north on Queen Street. Among the songs she sang were 'Paper Doll', 'Moonlight Becomes You' and 'I'll Walk Alone'.[170]

By day McMinn had been manpowered to work in a Freemans Bay sack factory, after which she taught dancing; then 'I'd get myself all dolled up in my long frock and sing. That was my life.' The Trocadero gigs included a floor show in which McMinn sang and danced, accompanied by the piano-accordionist Toni Savage.

To a teenager, the wartime audience was an eye-opener: 'I used to get a little put out the way some of these women used to drink. They'd come in dressed all beautifully with

their hair all done and towards the end of the evening they'd be all tousled and staggering around.' Although the audience was there primarily to dance, they would send requests for songs up to the stage. It was when the Americans arrived that the music received even more appreciation: not that they were sober, either, and the atmosphere put McMinn off alcohol.

> An American captain invited me to go down to the table: 'Come down and have a drink, honey.' So I went down and it was, 'What would you like to drink?' I said, 'I'm sorry, I don't drink.' Have a cigarette, then. 'I'm sorry, I don't smoke.' He said, 'You don't drink and you don't smoke?' I said, no.
> 'Well, you must be hell on men.'[171]

An American saxophonist called Bob Kingsbury became a friend, and when he heard how difficult it was to get sheet music, he asked his mother to send a regular package out from the US. 'I never met her, and we used to write to one another and she'd send me the six top hit parade songs, in sheet music. So I was able to sing them before they came out here.' Expanding the sheet music into band arrangements was Len Hawkins, a London-born pianist who had arrived in 1938 with Sammy Lee's Americanadians and stayed. Hawkins' style emulated the bands of Glenn Miller and Ray Anthony: 'sweet-sounding harmony with a little pep in reserve'.[172]

After the thrilling experience of seeing Artie Shaw's Navy Band at the Town Hall, McMinn was invited to perform at a Sunday night concert with an American band in a cinema on Karangahape Road. With Hawkins she went to the US camp at the Domain to rehearse his arrangement with the band.

> They handed out the parts of this big band arrangement, and the guys were sitting there looking at them. The leader said, 'What tempo?' Len gave him the tempo, so they counted, 1,2,3 – and off, they started.
>
> Well, I thought Len was going to faint. It sounded so good hearing these top American musicians playing his arrangement. He was knocked out by it. Being a Pom, he had a peaches-and-cream complexion and he went bright red. It was a wonderful sound.

Then it was my turn to rehearse with the band. I was very young – and not very sophisticated – and I was singing, 'I'm getting tired, so I can sleep/I want to sleep, so I can dream' – I gave a slow bow and then, 'Weary, but not too young or too old/They're either too young or too grassy green . . .'

And the leader who was conducting said, 'Come on, honey: get that bedroom look in your eye.' Ohh, I was all shy. They were used to saying that to the American girls, but I was too young, you know. Just seventeen.[173]

In Wellington, Jean McPherson quickly became the star vocalist, after performing on 2YA with the Melody Makers dance band. Born in Scotland, but raised in Lower Hutt, McPherson came up through a church choir background, before converting to 'modern music'. She played in small dance bands before being invited to join Wellington's slickest outfit, Art Rosoman's Rainbow Rhythm.

Rosoman had a weekly show on 2YA that was heard nationally, and McPherson's reassuring, intimate voice was a big part of the attraction: 'She had Betty Grable's clear diction, Vera Lynn's sincerity, and a natural style all her own.'[174] The *Music Maker* declared, 'Her vocals are in

Jean McPherson with the Lauri Paddi band at the Majestic Cabaret, Wellington, 1941. From left: Jack Roberts, Bill Sinclair, Harry Unwin, Lauri Paddi, Art Rosoman, Pete McMurray, Bob Girvan, Norm D'Ath and Jean McPherson. E. M. Alderdice Collection, PA1-q-182-06, Alexander Turnbull Library, Wellington

Henry Rudolph with Jean McPherson, members of the wartime 2YA Camp Entertainers, Wellington. Hall Raine/RNZ Sound Archives

McPherson found the routine of being a peerless performer hard going though she disguised it well. Singing to men about to sail off to war was emotionally taxing. She knew many of them would never return, and that added to the significance of finale favourites 'We'll Meet Again' and 'When the Lights Go On Again'.[176]

In 1944 the 2YA Camp Entertainers gave a variety show in the more elegant environs of the Wellington Opera House. Thanks to their concerts and broadcasts, wrote the *Dominion*, the group's fame 'has spread across the Pacific . . . . though amateur in status, [they] cannot be classed as such in performances.' Henry Rudolph led a troupe through light opera, romantic duets and barber shop quartets and presented classical soloists, while McPherson 'made her customary impression in "Boy in Khaki", "I Love a Lassie" and "Coo-ee".'[177]

As a young adult in Christchurch during the war, Anita Osborn went to the weekly dances at the Addington Workshops with her sisters. They would spend most of Saturday preparing: getting their nails and hair done, pressing their dresses and shining their shoes. 'It was part of the excitement, and not knowing what it was going to be like, or whether you were going to meet the man of your dreams. You just loved the dancing, and were hoping you'd be invited for each dance.'[178]

After an exhausting evening on the dance floor, Osborn and her sisters would walk back to their central-city home carrying their shoes in their hands. She also enjoyed going to Tipson's in St Asaph Street where, one night in 1943, Martin Winiata's band was playing. Osborn's boyfriend whispered to Winiata that she could sing, 'much to my embarrassment. Martin must have said yes, so rather than make a fool of myself I went up and did sing'.

Instantly, Osborn was in demand. While Winiata was asking her if she was singing regularly anywhere, Tommy Aspell, drummer with the prestigious Mayfair Lounge band, came up to ask if she was in a band. Although Osborn had never performed professionally, she had been singing in small concerts for the troops with other family members and was taking classical singing lessons. Aspell invited Osborn to the Mayfair for an audition, which she passed singing 'When Day is Done', with pianist Johnny Thompson transposing to her key. Osborn would be replacing Coral Cummins, who had left to join Martin Winiata's band at its Union Rowing Club residency overlooking the Avon River.

the best recording style, and she hasn't a "corny" bone in her body, Allah be praised!'[175]

McPherson was hired by Lauri Paddi as vocalist for his band's residency at the Majestic Cabaret. With thousands of men and women on leave from the services, plus the arrival of the US Marines in 1942, the Majestic was the premier venue. McPherson also gave recitals at the De Luxe, accompanied by Findlay Robb on the cinema's Wurlitzer organ.

She performed in fundraisers and variety shows around the country, and travelled out to Trentham camp on the back of an army lorry to give radio concerts for the troops and for wounded servicemen at Silverstream Hospital. With McPherson also recording many songs for broadcast to the troops in the Middle East and the Pacific, she became New Zealand's 'Sweetheart of the forces'.

It was a whirlwind period for the entertainer. Rehearsals and engagements were a daily package for five years . . . .

Anita Osborn at the Mayfair Lounge cabaret, Christchurch, 1943. In the band are, from left, Gerald Gebbie, bass; Lou Warren, trumpet; Wally Ransom, drums; Brian Marston, trombone and leader; Vic Boatwood, piano; Ron McKay, saxophone. Ann Marston collection

On Fridays, Osborn would get her hair set and bleached blonde – 'for a singer, it *had* to be blonde' – and on Saturdays, she would be back to the hairdressers to get her hair combed up again. Wartime clothing shortages meant it was difficult to get the material needed for a selection of especially made gowns, so her sisters helped by pooling their coupons.

Earlier in the war, the music played by the Mayfair Lounge Orchestra had been dixieland, reminisced L. Robinson in *Jukebox*: 'Scores of "Singing the Blues", "Clarinet Marmalade", "All Of Me", and many others – whilst not commercially melodic – became popular with Christchurch dancers, who, it must be admitted, possess more than conservative tastes in regard to music!'[179]

During 1943, the Mayfair's Friday Night Swing Show became the 'Mecca of Allied servicemen on leave', Robinson recalled:

To boys who had been accustomed to generous helpings of rug-cutting on the menu back home, here was a haven indeed. With popularity soaring, the Orks library increased in leaps and bounds, and included some Art Rosoman specials.

Up to the time it left the Mayfair Lounge in March, 1946, the band was the last stronghold of really modern music in the country – Auckland and Wellington having succumbed to the strict tempo style.[180]

When Osborn joined, the leader of the Mayfair orchestra was trombonist Brian Marston, who was then based at Wigram with the airforce. Marston was in the Services Band, and did not go overseas because of deafness in one ear. Whenever he could get leave from Wigram, he would come into Christchurch and perform with the Mayfair band, and he continued writing arrangements for them. Keeping the band intact was difficult, with men

LEND-LEASE CROONETTE

Marion Waite was a war bride who went against the tide. When the war began, she was a nightclub singer in her home town: Detroit. In its last months, she was in Wellington, on stage at the Majestic Cabaret and rapidly building a following as the leading swing vocalist in town.[181]

Lauri Paddi's new singer was 25, a willowy brunette who sang with a languid, fluid style some compared to Dinah Shore. The *Listener* sent a reporter to investigate this curiosity: a genuine 'crooner' in Wellington. 'I don't go in for this "jive" business, which is too rough and noisy for me', said Waite. 'I am known at home as a "sweet swing"

Marion Waite with pianist John Parkin, drummer Wally Ransom and bassist George Campbell, just prior to a national tour, c. 1946. Sparrow/RNZ Sound Archives

MY HAPPINESS

Words by BETTY PETERSON Music by BORNEY BERGANTINE

Photo by SPENCER DIGBY, Wellington.

FEATURED & BROADCAST BY

MARION WAITE

2/- NET

CHAPPELL & CO., LTD. 50, New Bond Street, London, W.I.

BLASCO MUSIC INC. U.S.A.

Authorised for Sale only in New Zealand.

and Guam. To Waite, the mail was a revelation. 'I didn't think New Zealanders would write letters like that.'[184] Waite would often appear at the Sunday night meetings of the Wellington Swing Club, performing with the ever-changing lineups of the club big band, the Swingmen.[185]

In November 1949, Waite had to return quickly to the US with her daughter to renew their passports. During her five years in New Zealand, she had noticed that appreciation of local popular music had increased. The proof was in the number of people now composing their own songs. 'Blue Smoke' and 'Paekakariki' had become hits, but there were many others being written: 'Hardly a week goes by without someone sending me a song.'[186]

It would be another six years before Waite returned to New Zealand. In August 1957, she provided the swing at a Rock'n'Roll Jamboree on a bill headlined by Johnny Devlin. The era of the croonette had passed.

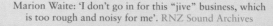

Marion Waite: 'I don't go in for this "jive" business, which is too rough and noisy for me'. RNZ Sound Archives

and "blues" singer. My music must be kept right up to the minute . . . the public demands the latest.'[182]

Waite quickly found herself in demand, appearing with the 2YA Camp Entertainers in charity variety shows at the Wellington Town Hall and Trentham army camp. She toured the main commercial radio stations in live-to-air broadcasts accompanied by the popular pianist John Parkin (well known for his live request show *If You Please, Mr Parkin*).

In June 1945, she began a three-year association with Freddie Gore's 2YA Orchestra, broadcasting every Monday evening. 'Embraceable You' became her theme tune. In just a few months, she was the talk of the town. 'Picture a slender, dark-haired young woman with blue eyes and an Irish colleen look about her and you have a picture of New Zealand's leading radio singer of popular songs', wrote *Maestro*. Although 'keeping up her vocal career and being a housewife can be a little trying at times', Waite had become 'our leading croonette'.[183]

Her broadcasts were hugely popular, attracting fan mail from all age groups, and from as far afield as Fiji

persistently being called up, so some unusual combinations of players meant new arrangements were constantly required.

Osborn described her singing style as more straight pop than jazz. When performing at the camp concerts, her repertoire was weighted towards English material that the troops knew, but at the Mayfair Lounge, American swing favourites were in demand.

After three years in the band, Osborn and Marston married. The Mayfair Lounge briefly closed, and by late 1946 Marston's band was performing 'all around town, and the boys defrost the Winter Garden frequently on Saturday nights'.[187] Marston also led a radio band for broadcasts on 3YA, with Osborn making occasional appearances, but children were now her priority.

> When the war ended the bottom fell out of the ballroom dancing scene. People took up families; there was a shortage of all sorts of things that you had to have coupons for, clothes as well as food. People starting building their homes and their families and they just didn't go dancing. Quite a number of firms had their own ball, and people would go to those, but by and large the dancing fell away.[188]

GUYS AND DOLLS: MUSIC IN THE WAR ZONE

The Kiwi Concert Party was New Zealand's oldest established, permanent, floating entertainment troupe of the Second World War. What began in October 1940 as a hastily organised concert at Maadi Camp, near Cairo, finished nearly fourteen years later at His Majesty's Theatre, Auckland, to rapturous and deafening applause.

The concert in the Maadi 'Tent' was produced by Sgt-Major Tom Kirk-Burnnand, a choirmaster and organist who had spent the previous decade in radio in New Zealand. He had quickly assembled a small group for the hour-long concert, and rumours rapidly spread about the attractions. In the audience was Major-General Freyberg, commander of the 2NZEF, but few of his troops; before New Zealanders could get there, 500 British soldiers had packed the venue, having heard that a 'smashing' English soprano would be headlining. They were generous in their applause, recalled the tenor Tony Rex, 'but one felt they were only awaiting the return of the soprano'.

At the end of the show, when the last notes of 'Indian Love Call' faded, the soprano bowed, wig in hand. The audience was shocked into silence: she was in fact a he. 'It had never occurred to the British boys that this stunning singer was not a girl', said Rex. When Freyberg rose from his seat and started to applaud, the audience joined in. 'The Tommies kept whistling and cheering until the performers came back for encores.'

Wally Prictor was a baritone who became famous as a soprano, dressed in a blonde wig and glamorous ballgown. In the desert, it was Prictor who could take the audiences 'away from it all', said Rex. As a choirboy, when the time came for his voice to break, Prictor had resisted and began singing in falsetto; a high palate helped. To his fellow performers in 'the Kiwis' he was a natural soprano: a crucial talent they appreciated, along with his quick wit. Towards the end of the war, Freyberg spoke about the Kiwis' impact upon morale during the North African campaign: 'In those days I regarded Prictor as worth a company of infantrymen.'[189]

Freyberg asked Kirk-Burnnand to recruit men from the Division for an entertainment unit, so he quickly arranged auditions and head-hunted those he already knew were

Tom Kirk-Burnnand, founder of the Kiwi Concert Party and collector and writer of patriotic war songs. War History Collection, DA1447, Alexander Turnbull Library, Wellington

lurking within its ranks. By March 1941, he had assembled the Kiwi Concert Party, from a motley crew. They ranged from the pianist, Terry Vaughan, with years studying music at London's Royal Academy, to the impish child impersonator Tim Bonner. 'Thirty of 'em', Rex recalled. 'Every variety of shape and height, from all walks of army life.' Gunners, sappers and hospital orderlies became singers, comedians and orchestral musicians; drivers doubled as carpenters, cooks as lighting crew. Much of the equipment and costumes came about through scrounging and ingenuity, though public fundraising at home contributed to their costs.[190]

A king and a queen: Tony Rex and Wally Prictor of the Kiwi Concert Party perform songs from *Rose Marie* in the Middle East. War History Collection, DA1442, Alexander Turnbull Library, Wellington

The Kiwis differed from other wartime concert parties: the troupe was assembled in the field, from fighting troops. Other countries' entertainers were usually professionals and civilians, sent on package tours of army bases. The Kiwi Concert Party was created to entertain troops as close to the frontline as possible, and to be self-contained, with its own transport and support crew. Yet they needed to be thoroughly – well, occasionally – trained as infantrymen while taking their revues to the troops.

In just two months, they were 'a fully rehearsed company, complete with lighting set, curtains, wardrobes and staging, able to travel at the shortest notice'. They blended 'We Are the Boys from Way Down Under' with 'Waiata Poi', and Vaughan wrote an opening theme song, 'Whistle as You Go': 'Here's a song to start the show, it's just a tune to whistle as you go/If you don't like it, then hike it . . .'.[191]

Kirk-Burnnand wanted a quick-fire variety show, with songs and musical comedy items, plus formal renditions of popular songs and light classics; then a big finale to showcase all their talents. 'No army songs, gags or sketches, no military clothing and above all no crude humour.' The Kiwis' revues emphasised ensemble pieces rather than soloists taking all the limelight, from ever-changing combinations of players, in a wide variety of styles. In the programme, Tchaikovsky, Schubert and Ravel stood alongside 'In the Mood' and 'Bye, Bye, Blues'.[192]

In May 1941, the Kiwis' tenacity was tested when the troupe arrived in Crete just before the airborne invasion by the Germans. They performed for four days, sometimes under bombardment, before joining the fighting. Then they had to flee, abandoning their instruments. An arduous forced march took the Division to Sfakia, and evacuation; hundreds of exhausted men dropped out to become prisoners, including four Kiwis. The rest of the Kiwis made the last boat to leave the island.[193]

After two weeks' rest, they began a routine that did not change for four years: constant packing and travelling on three-ton trucks, building and breaking down sets, rehearsing new material written by Vaughan. Then, show time: sometimes several in a day, even at 9.00 am. Between January 1941 and August 1942, they performed for up to 140,000 people. Days before the battle for El Alamein, they performed a season in the sand, guarded by machine guns. One show was attended by Freyberg with

Terry Vaughan conducts an outdoor dress rehearsal of the Kiwi Concert Party orchestra, somewhere
in the Middle East. War History Collection, DA1446, Alexander Turnbull Library, Wellington

General Montgomery, and an estimated 4000 men; it was, said Monty, 'the finest army show I have seen, this war or the last'.[194]

In November 1941, Kirk-Burnnand was invalided back to New Zealand with a hearing condition, leaving behind his creation and a chorus song he had written, 'The Kiwis On Parade'.[195] Vaughan took his place as musical director, producer, unit leader – and tap dancer and comedian. He arranged popular classics such as 'Ave Maria' for male soprano (dressed as a nun) and chorus, *Liebestraum*, selections from *Rio Rita* and *Showboat*, recent films and old shanties – even 'Whistling Rufus' for three clarinets.[196]

Occasionally, a package of music would arrive from New Zealand, 'a mixed bag – old sheet music, stock danceband arrangements . . . piano albums of "Famous Overtures" and, luckily, vocal scores of old musicals. Potential had to be sought in everything.' Vaughan found a middle ground between classical and popular music,

knowing it was wrong 'to underestimate one's audience, even one of seemingly tough soldiers. On the other hand, I was well aware that music should suit the occasion and the surroundings.' 'The Flight of the Bumble Bee' was a fiddle solo for Cyril Pasco, Verdi's aria 'M'Appari' a showcase for Tony Rex, and Vaughan himself parodied Stokowski playing a crazed conductor Leopold Popoffsky demolishing the *William Tell* overture.[197]

There were no women in the Kiwi Concert Party, due to the arduous conditions, the constant travelling, the shows' proximity to the front and the fact that the entertainers were still expected to be fighting soldiers if required. The female impersonators were essential, said Vaughan. 'Otherwise, how would you get the female interest? But we did it straight. We weren't a drag show. I was lucky in the men I had doing it – it was off with the makeup and into the battledress and "Yes, I'll have a beer, thanks".'[198] Besides Prictor, the company's wartime 'femmes' were Phil Jay, Bill Bain and Ralph Dyer.

Kiwi Concert Party 'femmes' Wally Prictor, centre, and Phil Jay, far right. Peter Downes collection

In June 1943, the troupe was included in the three-month furlough back to New Zealand with the men who had been serving overseas the longest. It was no holiday: they performed almost daily on the voyage home then, after a break of two months, embarked on a whistle-stop tour through the country. From Invercargill to Whangarei, they played 22 shows in 25 days; every theatre was booked out before rehearsals had started. Tens of thousands of New Zealanders saw them, and the tour raised £6600 for the Patriotic Fund.

The Kiwis needed to re-group. Some men were eligible to stay in New Zealand, and there was a protest that able-bodied men who had not served overseas should go to the front before the veterans were sent back. Vaughan enlisted fresh talent, such as the magician Ces Morris and impressionist Red Moore. He recruited several top jazz musicians, among them the three Campbell brothers from Paeroa. Phil Campbell was New Zealand's star trumpeter before

the war, George a leading bass player. But Vaughan was especially impressed by nineteen-year-old Lew, a trumpeter, who he found after hours on the piano, transforming Debussy's *Clair De Lune* into a fluid boogie woogie.

The Kiwis returned to Italy to join the weary soldiers of 2NZEF, and the gruelling, inch-by-inch advance north. For the campaign, Vaughan wrote a new finale, *Soused, the Truth About Grand Opera*. It offered a medley of well-known opera melodies, sung in nonsense-Italian by a lavishly costumed cast. The loss of some of the original Kiwis 'was offset by the brilliant musicianship of the modern band', said Rex. 'They really did "wow" the boys particularly the Yanks to whom we played many shows.' He watched the orchestral musicians 'grow in stature when the three Campbell brothers got into gear'. In particular, the song 'In the Mood' was 'Lady Luck's gift to the band', said Rex, its dramatic structure being perfect for showmanship.

During its furlough home to New Zealand in 1943, the Kiwi Concert Party toured nationwide with *Kiwi Revue No. 8*; the programme had an Egyptian theme. Peter Downes collection

By late December 1944, the Allied advance had come to a standstill. The Germans were on one side of the Senio river, the New Zealand Division on the other. The winter was bitterly cold; the Kiwis were to perform in a former Fascist Youth Centre, 'an island in a frozen sea of mud, slush and ice'. In anticipation of the war coming to an end, and many Kiwi originals going home, some new performers had come on board: among them was tenor Les Andrews.[199]

On 20 January 1945, a request came through for a jazz combo to play at a celebration the Maori Battalion was having at nearby Faenza. Vaughan sent the Campbell brothers over in a truck, with three others. That night, the Germans began shelling from across the river. One shell struck the building where the party was to take place, collapsing the roof and killing nine men. One of them was Phil Campbell, crushed by a beam, another was Mete Kingi, an Auckland friend. George was hit

by shrapnel, and his double bass destroyed; Lew was unharmed but in deep shock. So too was the Concert Party. 'They were all stunned, and found it hard to believe', recalled Lew. The Kiwis had gone so far, with no casualties except those taken prisoner on Crete. And now, after so long and at a time when it seemed the war must end, their jazz virtuoso had been killed.[200]

Through 1945 the longest serving members began to be repatriated, Vaughan among them. On his arrival home, he was asked if he thought the Kiwis would become a permanent troupe on Civvy Street. 'No', he said. 'It was simply a product of the war and meant solely for the troops.'[201] The last full-scale show took place in Sienna on 6 November 1945, four-and-a-half years after the first revue. The Kiwi Concert Party's war was finally over in January 1946, if not their work: they continued to entertain the troops on the ship home.

In fact, some former Kiwis were already performing in New Zealand as a Kiwis Revue, causing resentment among those still in the war zone. Several in the civilian production had been with the Pacific Kiwi Concert Party, featuring men from the 3rd Division. Led by Ossie Cheesman, this had operated in the Pacific theatre since 1943, travelling by boat, barges, aircraft and jeeps. The Pacific Kiwis' musical fare was broader than that heard in the desert, from serious classical pieces to 'the wildest of burlesque': songs from the 'shadier side' of Tin Pan Alley, harmony songs, comic items on the banjolele, originals by Cheesman, solo instrumentals and swing. Other cast members who had lengthy careers were pianist John MacKenzie and tenor Maurice Tansley; the 'femme' Ralph Dyer showed remarkable diversity in his roles: playing Hitler one moment, a hula dancer the next.[202]

When the independent Kiwis Revue went on a New Zealand tour, approaches were made to the government to prevent the use of the word 'Kiwi' in relation to concert parties, just as the term 'Anzac' was protected. But the War Cabinet decided this was unworkable; besides, when the Kiwi Concert Party returned from Europe, they would be accredited as the 'pukka' revue company.[203] The situation resolved itself when Vaughan was hired as musical director upon his return, and recruited men from the Mediterranean and Pacific Kiwi Concert Parties. The journey home from the war was just an interval: the second half would be even longer.

KCP Entertainments Ltd was formed in partnership with J.C. Williamson Theatres Ltd, with the performers

Terry Vaughan conducts the post-war Kiwi Concert Party orchestra in Sydney. Peter Downes collection

being equal shareholders. Appointing Terry Vaughan producer and musical director, the Kiwis became professional entertainers, beginning with a two-week season at Auckland's His Majesty's in March 1946. New members were recruited, such as the elegant femme John Hunter, and a teenage saxophonist Don Richardson. Their first foray into Australia went badly – Queensland had had enough of soldiers, after the wartime American invasion – but the Kiwis quickly established a bridgehead in Adelaide. The post-war career of the Kiwis is one of the great success stories of New Zealand entertainment: seasons in Sydney and Melbourne that kept getting extended for years, and sold-out return tours to New Zealand. Performers such as the comedians Stan Wineera and Red Moore became stars alongside the veterans Wally Prictor, Ralph Dyer and Taffy Owen.

After eight years, they brought down the curtain at His Majesty's on 16 January 1954: over three million people

had seen them since the war. Besides Terry Vaughan, who remained mostly in Australia, two of the orchestra players would go on to make significant contributions to New Zealand popular music. Lew Campbell became a radio dance-band leader and arranger, a jazz pianist, a trumpeter for the NZSO and eventually a teacher at the Sydney Conservatorium. Don Richardson became a high-profile figure in Wellington music, as a band leader and promoter; in the latter role, the showmanship he learnt with the Kiwis would be pivotal in popularising rock'n'roll.

Looking back at his Kiwi Concert Party revues, Terry Vaughan was proud that he did not have to cheapen music to make it acceptable to the soldiers, and that he never included 'those pseudo-patriotic marching songs that people seem to think soldiers like'. Also excluded were references to army life and its inconveniences. 'We had no

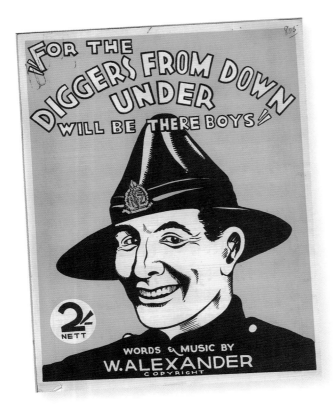

'For the Diggers From Down Under Will Be There Boys' was Christchurch songwriter W. A. Alexander's contribution to the war effort in 1940. Andrews, Baty/WAII/2/61 Archives New Zealand

"longing for home" sentiment . . . no nonsense about "New Zealand, the little Pacific Paradise".'[204]

Nevertheless, there were subversives in the ranks who found the Kiwi Concert Party's offerings alien. 'Not everyone thought men dressed up as women in a smoke concert travesty of 1930s Kiwi male humour was amusing or entertaining', wrote Les Cleveland who – while 'plodding around in a rifle company' through Italy with the 2NZEF – took note of the songs the soldiers were actually singing.[205]

Between battles and drills, they were not chatting in an army mess, drinking cups of tea, and gathering round a piano to sing light opera and sentimental selections from the hit parade. 'You can't imagine a bunch of Kiwis sitting around in dugouts waiting to go into an attack singing "There'll be blue birds over the white cliffs of Dover"', said Cleveland.[206]

When not at the front, he recalled, soldiers spent as much time as possible getting drunk, chasing girls, playing two-up or crown and anchor, joy-riding in trucks, and scheming to get more rations or booze. When they succeeded at the latter, they sang. 'But not "We're Gonna Hang Out the Washing on the Seigfried Line", "There'll

Always Be an England" . . . patriotic ditties. That stuff was just establishment propaganda.'[207]

> A torrent of musical slop of the 'White Cliffs of Dover', 'In the Mood', 'White Christmas', Glenn Miller, Vera Lynn, 'Now is the Hour', 'Maori Battalion', 'Blue Smoke' variety was certainly pumped over the broadcasting services, and a similar claptrap was assiduously cultivated by the Kiwi Concert Party and its imitators, but the common soldiery in frontline units – though pathetically grateful for any distractions at all – were generally inclined to more ribald, vulgar tastes.[208]

What they sang, Cleveland argued, was true folk music: uninhibited, learnt without written sources and known by thousands. Some songs were carried over from the First World War and even further back – with adjustments – or sung to the melodies of hymns. Several of the folk 'hits' in the 2NZEF were originals, written by Arthur Wallis and Earl Taylor from Wellington, two soldiers and members of the Maadi Melodymakers that played around Cairo during the war.[209] Among them were 'Saida Bint', 'General Freyberg's Stew' and 'Aiwa Saida'. Also known as 'Middle East Swing', the latter became widely known during the North African campaign:

> Now you've heard the music of Benny Goodman
> Tommy Dorsey and stars like these
> But have you heard of the Kings of Rhythm
> Who put the pep in the Eastern shows.
> (Chorus) Aiwa, saeeda, Aiwa, anna muskeen
> Aiwa, shufty gharry, if you've ever
> Been to Cairo you know what I mean.[210]

Contrary to the claims of the Kiwi Concert Party leaders and official histories that New Zealand soldiers appreciated that their revues were not saucy like those of the British, when amongst themselves the soldiers' repertoire gravitated to the obscene, because 'this is the only way the intolerable and the monstrous can be mentioned'. Some were standards at male-only gatherings ('The Good Ship *Venus*', 'The Old Red Flannel Drawers that Maggie Wore'), and others were topical ('Abdul Abulbul Emir', 'The Ball at Kissiemus').[211]

Bawdiness and irreverence were one thing; what the authorities did not tolerate was rebellion: 'Won't You Take Us Home' – an adaptation of 'Lili Marlene' – was banned for its politics. In the 2NZEF version, the troops pleaded

Private J. W. Black of Te Kuiti leads members of his company in a song on Stirling Island, c. 1944.
War History Collection, WH-0612, Alexander Turnbull Library, Wellington

with the New Zealand Prime Minister to repatriate them from Italy, feeling they had been used 'as a battering ram' against the Germans:

> Oh Mr Fraser, won't you take us home
> We've had enough, we want no more to roam
> We've had all the bints both young and old
> And signorinas leave us cold
> Oh won't you take us home.

In the song's conclusion, the soldiers warn of their power as a voting lobby: they can keep Fraser in office, or 'run your gang right out of town. You'd better take us home.' Written when Fraser was in Italy visiting the troops, the commanders of 2NZEF tried to suppress the

song – and even the singing of 'Lili Marlene' – without success. Although, wrote Cleveland, 'It would be naïve to think it had any direct force in the strategic councils of the New Zealand command, it nevertheless was evidence of a declining morale.' The soldiers' songs were the 'muted sound of protest . . . . They indicate pretty closely how people felt. Much more so than the Tin Pan Alley material that we got squirted at us.'[212]

An atypical but widely performed song was 'Castel Frentano', which movingly conveyed a soldier's inner thoughts about the campaign. It was composed by an unknown member of the Maori Battalion, about the Sangro River clash, in which they suffered heavy casualties. The bells of the Castel Frentano monastery ask the soldier where he is going: he is heading north, to more fighting, to

After the war, song collector and singer Les Cleveland and the D Day Dodgers recorded two albums of songs New Zealand troops enjoyed among themselves after hours: some were Italian, many were ribald. The cover artist, Eric Heath, served in the Pacific before a long career as the *Dominion*'s cartoonist. Kiwi Records, LA6, 1960

Cassino. His thoughts keep returning to Sangro and its torrid battles, but he would rather be there than in Milan where the Nazis and Fascists still hold power.[213] The song encapsulated the impact that Italian opera had on the Maori Battalion, which would leave a lasting impression on New Zealand popular music.

THE LAST DANCE

During the war, music had provided a release, a diversion and a conduit to companionship. In January 1945, the German U-boat U-862 spent twelve days on the east coast of New Zealand after sinking a US ship in the Tasman Sea.

Cruising above the surface one night they skirted Napier harbour, and looked towards the shoreline. In his diary, the German officer on watch noted there was: 'No blackout. You can see the promenade café lit up with bright red lights. The band is playing old tunes with couples dancing . . . . In New Zealand everyone seems to feel very safe.'[214]

Music made a more tangible contribution to the war effort as well. While Berlin was falling, the DSIR's industrial psychology division released a study on improvements to productivity if music was played. New Zealand's young women, it seemed, did like to whistle while they worked. By playing records in a small munitions factory, the DSIR found that the women's output increased by up to 10 percent when music was played for two and a half hours in a normal day.

The women's preferences were for the current hits by

> . . . singers like Bing Crosby, Kate Smith and Vera Lynn; light music such as waltzes, musical comedy and dance music; Schubert songs and popular classical pieces; swing music of the Duke Ellington and Artie Shaw type. Different groups of workers had various preferences: young girls usually wanted popular tunes; older women favoured light music; only Strauss waltzes had universal appeal. It was the beginning of a new era in work-place sound.[215]

One month later, the ultimate release came, and music played a central role.

The news arrived just after midnight, early on Tuesday, 8 May 1945. The Germans had surrendered: the war had ended in Europe. But the official announcement had to wait a few hours, until an aide-de-camp at Government House, Wellington, could tell the governor-general when he woke at 7.00 am. Then the nation could be informed.

But the news was already in that morning's *Dominion*. Wellingtonians arrived at work wearing rosettes, and from the top storeys of buildings along Lambton Quay thousands of pieces of paper were launched into the air. After a cautious start, the serious business of revelry got underway.

That night, cabarets and churches quickly filled to beyond their capacity. 'Churches ran out of hymn-books, and preachers must have wished their normal congregations were even half as large. "All People That On Earth Do Dwell" was sung by thousands.'

At the Basin Reserve the following day, an official celebration featured a choir singing 'God Save the King', 'God Defend New Zealand' and 'The Star-Spangled Banner', with the governor-general's wife knowing every word. But the 'Maori Battalion Marching Song' and 'Waltzing Matilda' were what the crowds chose to sing. 'Old-timers of the 1890s vied with "Roll Out the Barrel" – and usually won . . . . Bands everywhere proved irresistible magnets.'[216]

The partying continued. At 1.00 pm in Auckland on the Wednesday, Queen Street was oddly quiet, the shops had closed, 'no music, no bands, not even radios blaring from open windows'. Soon, throngs of people materialised, waiting for something to happen. By 3.00 pm, spontaneous parties had broken out; the hotels were packed to the last

inch. In the evening, a conga line wove its way down Queen Street, stopped to do the 'Hokey Tokey' and moved on. 'Gay young parties, servicemen and girls, singing patriotic songs, aye, even "Tipperary".'[217]

In Christchurch, VE Day opened with sirens, church bells and thanksgiving services before the streets became packed. 'One or two brass bands were out and these found instant favour when they led impromptu parades and community in the streets.' The next day, bands led a procession to Cathedral Square, for music and singing by choirs. And again on the Sunday, a victory music festival with a grand parade, singing by massed choirs and brass bands.[218]

> DUNEDIN GOES GAY: Students wore gay carnival dress. The streets were thronged with cheering crowds all day long and till well into the night . . . . Hitler's body danced from the post office . . . . at noon the bells rang and the Mayor, Mr D. C. Cameron, declared a half holiday, followed by enthusiastic cheering and the singing of 'For he's a jolly good fellow'.[219]

Crowds gathered in the Octagon to be entertained by the Dunedin Ladies' Band, and pipe bands and brass bands that had marched in from the suburbs. The carnival spirit took control, with 'impromptu bands, concert parties, and crowds of happy school children all taking part'. At the Stock Exchange several hundred dancers responded to a 'scratch, but quite competent orchestra'.

Well-known Dunedin entertainers gave a victory concert in the Town Hall the following night; an hour of community singing warmed the crowd up before it began. The massed choirs of the city took part, along with soloists such as Mary Pratt and Gil Dech; Arthur Macdonald sang 'Sons of New Zealand' and 'Legion of the Lost'. Dr V. E. Galway played Elgar's 'Pomp and Circumstance' on the city organ, before the choirs, soloists and audience combined to close the concert with 'Land of Hope and Glory'.

Joe Brown hosted two big fancy dress Victory dances at the Town Hall, donating the box office takings to the war effort: admission was 2/6, but free to all men and women wearing RSA badges or New Zealand flashes. In the concert chamber, there was old-time dancing to popular songs from the Great War – 'Tipperary' and 'Pack Up Your Troubles'. In the main hall, 'all modern dancing' to tunes from the present: 'There'll Always be an England', 'White Cliffs of Dover' and 'Roll Out the Barrel'.[220]

Back in Auckland, a crowd of sailors sang its way up Queen Street 'with more heartiness than tune'. They spied a hotel and rushed for it. Ten minutes later one of the sailors reappeared, rolling before him a beer barrel. He was quickly joined by 20 or 30 other revellers. They joined arms, spread out almost across the street, and strode along, rolling the barrel as they went, jumping over and around it. They were singing 'Roll Out the Barrel'.[221]

The war had two endings: victory in Japan was announced at 11.00 am on 15 August 1945. The government took measures to avoid a repetition of the public drunkenness that accompanied celebrations of the victory in Europe. Hotel opening hours would be restricted, and official announcements and celebrations carefully coordinated.

But the measures were a failure. Minutes after speeches by the British and New Zealand prime ministers were broadcast, the streets filled with excited crowds. In Oamaru, people 'downed tools and gave themselves over to three days of rejoicing'. Outside the Town Hall, they 'gave expression to their feelings by singing patriotic songs, shouting and cheering'. A continuous din was heard in the streets for hours until the official celebrations: community singing in the Town Hall, a victory concert in the Opera House.

In the Scottish Hall, an unforgettable victory ball took place. The Chinese community provided free food for everybody. So packed was the hall that people on the dance floor could barely move. The band was the Revellers, and in the middle of the chaos a member of the Scottish Society announced that the hall was too full, closed the lid on the piano and sat on it. The piano was out of bounds, he declared, until some people left the hall. So a piano accordionist grabbed his instrument and led many of the revellers down the road to the Lyric Hall. It overflowed as well, so dancers took to the street.[222]

In Auckland, because of the 'great chorus of noise that rose out of the city none but the deaf could fail to realise great tidings had arrived. Sirens screamed, whistles shrilled, bells pealed and all sorts of instruments trumpeted and blared to create a cacophony of noise that the city has not known in years'.[223] The city then 'forgot itself and unashamedly went out and enjoyed itself. It spent its most thrilling day in years'. Bands took up positions at vantage points along Queen Street 'and began playing popular airs'.

The density of the crowds meant only a few hundred could dance in the street.

Rain did not dampen the spirits of Wellingtonians: two bands played from the balcony of a Willis Street hotel to a crowd that 'opened their mouths and sang from their hearts'.[224]

Prime Minister Peter Fraser decreed that the following day, bars would close for three hours from 10.30 am. But restrictions were lifting in other ways. Press censorship regulations would cease immediately, the government announced, and the manufacture of radios in New Zealand could begin again in two weeks, bringing to an end years of skilled technicians building equipment only for the military.

In Dunedin, few wanted a repetition of VE Day when 'officialdom had complicated the business of rejoicing', so the citizens needed no cue: 'He was his own cheer leader, his own master of ceremonies'. Nothing official had been organised; looking out at the Octagon from his office, the mayor said, 'Do they need it? Just look at them.'[225]

STAUNCH AND TRUE

The war in Europe had been over for eight months; in the Pacific, for five. The Maori Battalion was finally coming home. One in six of the 3600 men who had served in the Battalion had given his life; almost half had been wounded.[226]

When the *Dominion Monarch* reached New Zealand on 23 January 1946, the sea was too rough to enter Wellington Harbour. To the frustration of the soldiers, the ship steamed outside the heads for several hours before it was finally able to make its entrance. It berthed at Pipitea Wharf, very close to where the Battalion had left on the *Aquitania* nearly six years earlier. A march to an official reception at Parliament was cancelled; instead, the acting Prime Minister, Walter Nash, came on board for the welcome home.

On Aotea Quay the returning warriors were greeted by a wero, a challenge, given by Anania Amohau; the writer of the 'Maori Battalion Marching Song' lyrics was now a corporal. 'Then followed the women raising the mourning chant, the tangi, for the men of the race who would never return; they were garlanded with greenery and beat their breasts with green twigs.' After a tapu-lifting ceremony, the Ngati Poneke Maori Club performed a haka and action songs. There were speeches, and replies, by chiefs and

Tomo mai: Amiria and Henare Waitoa. Waitoa family collection

Henare Waitoa had been working on Maori lyrics to the melody of an old US cowboy song, 'Gold Mine in the Sky'.[228] He asked his brother-in-law Maru Karaka how he would describe somebody making an entrance. 'Tomo mai', said Karaka. 'Come in.' That night, Waitoa didn't sleep; by daybreak, he was sitting in the kitchen singing 'Tomo Mai'.

At short notice Sir Apirana Ngata asked Waitoa for a song to greet C Company upon its return to Ruatoria. Waitoa quickly completed the words of 'Tomo Mai' so it became a welcome home as well as a lament for those who were killed in battle. That same evening in Ruatoria, the Ngati Putanga haka party learnt and rehearsed 'Tomo Mai' then performed it as an action song for the return of Lt-Col Peta Awatere and men from Ngati Porou in C Company.

> Tomo mai e tama ma ki roto, ki roto
> I nga ringa e tuwhera atu nei
> Ki nga morehu o te Kiwi
> Ki nga Tama Toa o tenei riri nui.
>
> Hoki mai, hoki mai ki te wa kainga,
> Kua tutuki te tumanako,
> Kei te kapakapa mai te Haki, te Haki
> O Ingarangi i runga o Tiamana e.
>
> Enter boys into
> These arms outstretched;
> To the survivors of the New Zealand Army,
> To the brave sons of this great war.
>
> Welcome, welcome home
> Our wish has been fulfilled,
> As fluttering over there is the flag
> Of England over Germany.[229]

Battalion commanding officers. 'Then the troops moved into the quay shed and sat down to a real Maori meal. Trains throughout the afternoon carried the Maori soldiers to a hundred welcoming marae. The 28 (Maori) Battalion had ceased to exist.'[227]

Many emotional ceremonies followed, but it is the return of C Company to Ruatoria that has its place in music history. While chopping wood, East Cape songwriter

In little more than a decade, 'Tomo Mai' would find a life beyond Ruatoria and outside of the marae. Renamed 'Hoki Mai' and given an exuberant tempo, it became a staple at New Zealand parties and singalongs.

Visitors watch artists broadcasting from a studio at 1ZB, Durham Street, Auckland, November 1947.

1946-1949

New Zealand was very late to establish its own recording industry. Although recording facilities existed here before the war, they were for recording jingles or one-off discs, not to create records for commercial release. Before 1948 artists wanting to record travelled to Australia, which had professional recording studios, a pressing plant and record companies wanting to release local music. The New Zealand market was dominated by HMV, which initially had no interest in local artists; in fact, the company tried to prevent others getting into the field. The actions of HMV were a textbook case of cultural imperialism.

Released on an independent label, 'Blue Smoke' was the opening salvo in a boom in New Zealand recording that began in the late 1940s. The best players available were jazz musicians, who became adept at backing novelty songs and country and western as well as the mainstream 1950s popular song styles.

Public radio and the best local musicians worked together to present live music programmes. But apart from specialist programmes, the musical fare on radio continued to be conservative. The New Zealand Broadcasting Service studiously avoided risk. This was partly due to politics: the senior executives had experienced the government's battles with maverick broadcaster Colin Scrimgeour, and were conscious of being civil servants with parliamentary paymasters. It was also the social context: the broadcasters and much of their audience had lived through a Depression and two world wars. Any material that went to air was required to conform to concepts of good taste and decency.

In 1946 a new weekly programme on the powerful ZB stations changed radio's relationship with pop music. The commercial ZB stations – aimed at the broadest of audiences – began broadcasting the latest pop hits in the Lever-sponsored *Hit Parade*. This 30-minute weekly dose of pop music was hugely influential, but as its playlist was generated by overseas hit parades, at first it acted as a barrier rather than a showcase for local artists. Nevertheless, much local music did go to air through regular live broadcasts, making stars out of musicians such as Julian Lee, Crombie Murdoch and Mavis Rivers. The radio band musicians also dominated the fledgling recording industry, emulating American pop styles. Several of their colleagues in jazz and dance bands had been recruited for the new national orchestra, led by a series of imported British conductors. The immediate post-war years were crucial for New Zealand's musical development. Douglas Lilburn wrote in 1946 of a search for tradition; the search for language could come later.

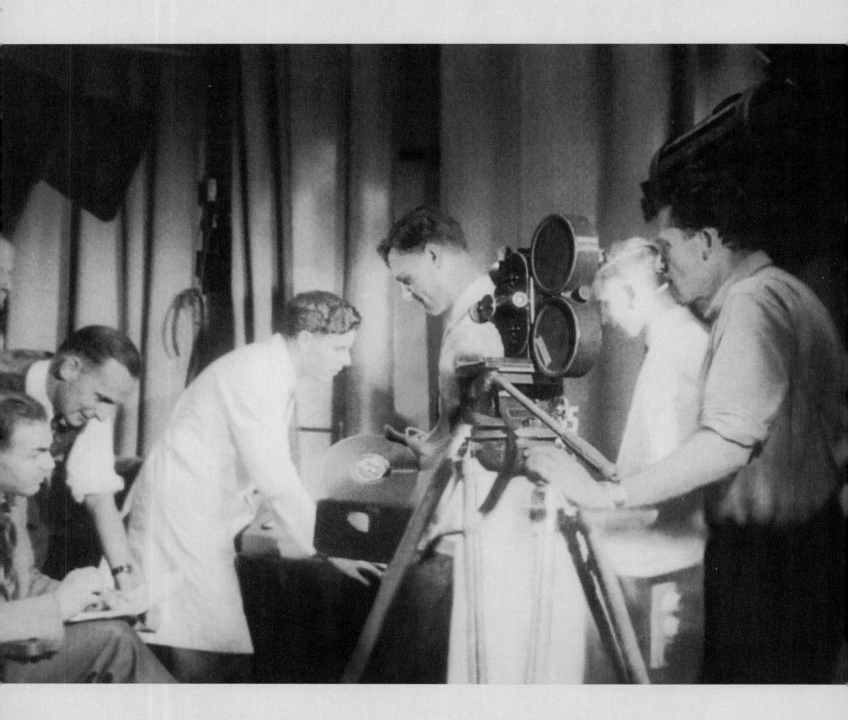

Months after the recording of 'Blue Smoke', the National Film Unit recreates the occasion for a newsreel to screen in the week the disc was to be released in June 1949. The trio of white-coated Tanza staff in this shot are, from left, John Shears, Tony Hall and Stan Dallas. Leaning over at left, in shirtsleeves, is Bart Fortune. John Shears collection

The Birth of a Recording Industry

the late 1940s

WINNING THE PEACE

When the *Aquitania* left Wellington in May 1940, among the Maori Battalion soldiers on board was Te Moananui-a-Kiwa Ngarimu. During a fierce battle in Tunisia on 27 March 1943, Ngarimu was 'killed on his feet defiantly facing the enemy with his tommy-gun at his hip'. For this he was awarded a posthumous Victoria Cross.[1]

Found in the pocket of Ngarimu's uniform was a slip of paper with the words to a song or poem. It read:

> Smoke is drifting away, into a blue sky
> When I think of you, I heave a sigh
> I can see her standing, there with tears in her eyes
> Mother – dear old Mother, please don't cry.
> We are off to our pals
> To give them a hand,
> The greatest little band
> From our Maori land.[2]

Four days after Ngarimu earned his VC in the desert, Ruru Karaitiana disembarked in Wellington. His war was over, and he had come full circle, back to where he had departed with the Maori Battalion on the *Aquitania* three years earlier, his mother among the hundreds wailing their farewells.

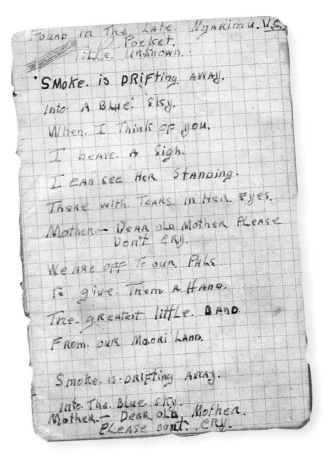

Song lyrics found in the pocket of Ngarimu VC, March 1943.
A/Ref 145/1/4, Upper Hutt City Council Archive

153

Ruru Karaitiana, a decade after the success of
'Blue Smoke'. *Karaitiana family collection*

Karaitiana's experiences during active service in the Middle East were varied. He was wounded in battle and hospitalised, but he also spent time confined to barracks or on detention for minor offences such as disorderly behaviour and gambling. There are reports of him leading a seventeen-piece 'concert orchestra' of the Maori Battalion, of whom all but three were killed, many of them on Crete. For years after the war he suffered nightmares about what he had witnessed.[3] His return home came when he received a 'non-medical discharge' from the army, being 'unfit for service'.[4]

Rangi Ruru Wananga Karaitiana was born on 4 March 1909 at the Tahoraiti marae near Dannevirke, where he was brought up by his maternal grandparents. After a sporting youth – the nephew of All Black Lou Paewai, he was an accomplished rugby player and speed skater – Karaitiana turned to the music he had enjoyed

at St Joseph's Convent in Dannevirke. He taught himself the piano, guitar, trombone and ukulele, playing by ear. Before the war began he was leading his own dance band in Dannevirke, eventually performing in the Wellington area. He enjoyed playing classical as well as dance music, and began composing songs, 'prolifically, but haphazardly'. He often forgot to add words to a new melody, or a tune to the lyrics he jotted on bits of paper; he learnt what worked with the public by trying out his new songs at dances.[5]

'Blue Smoke' was sufficiently completed on the *Aquitania* for Karaitiana to perform it during a ship's concert and for it to become a regular item at singalongs; in the Middle East it was performed by informal groups of singers and musicians from the Maori Battalion. Years after the war, his ex-wife Joan Kennett (née Chittleburgh) was contacted by an Australian nurse who had been on board. Kath Gray told Kennett she remembered Karaitiana 'composed it while he was travelling over. She said he was a very mournful, sad boy, and that he played it on a ukulele and sung it, and the soldiers picked it up very quickly.'

Although extremely shy, 'Danny' Karaitiana was popular and enjoyed socialising, especially if there was gambling involved. But '[w]hen he got on the stage, he got another personality: confident', said Kennett. 'Because he wasn't confident after the war, it affected him very badly.'

By winter 1946, reported *Maestro*, the 'cheery little Maori pianist' Daddy [*sic*] Karaitiana was back in Dannevirke, 'and gradually his smile has come back to him. Now he has organised a dance band, put his name on a dance hall in the centre of town, and set out to provide a popular weekly rendezvous for dances, featuring all sorts of novelties and trimmings. He should get away with it, too, as he is popular with everyone.'[6]

He had been home for three years, performing in bands and working as an itinerant shearer from Hawke's Bay to Taranaki. During this time, he continued to play – and keep tinkering with – 'Blue Smoke'. Wellington pianist Bob Barcham worked in Begg's and recalled Karaitiana coming into the music shop 'almost on an hourly basis' to use a piano to work on the song. He carried a satchel with *Ruru* embossed on the flap in gold letters; occasionally he would be in his army uniform. 'We regarded him as a bit of a nuisance at the time, as the piano was in demand for demonstrating sheet music.'[7]

Since its frequent wartime performances by the Maori Battalion dance band, 'Blue Smoke' seemed to take on a life of its own after the soldiers returned home. In 1945 it was played by a sextette at a student capping revue in Dunedin; the RNZAF band and many dance bands also featured it in their repertoires.[8] By October 1946, 'Blue Smoke' had been widely enough heard for seventeen-year-old Taranaki soprano Jean Ngeru to perform it when the New Zealand Broadcasting Service (NZBS) Mobile Unit visited Hawera to record local musicians. She had often sung it for soldiers home on leave, for whom 'it was a favourite'; the Mobile Unit catalogue notes that the song was 'composed by a member of the Maori Battalion'.

Taken at a brisk waltz, accompanied only by a guitar simply strumming on the beat, Ngeru's stately recording of 'Blue Smoke' uses lyrics similar to those found in Ngarimu's pocket. The song is a maternal farewell; those departing are a 'merry band' of soldiers, off to join the lads.

Eighteen months after the Mobile Unit's visit to Hawera, in May 1948, Ngeru wrote to the NZBS to say she had been advised that the recording had been broadcast, and inquired whether she could buy a copy. If there was a response from the NZBS it has never been found, but within a year of her letter another version of 'Blue Smoke' would be recorded. It was commercially released on a 78 and became a hit.[9]

For a humble song, 'Blue Smoke' carries a lot of weight. Unlike 'Now is the Hour', with its Australian melody – and a 1948 hit for both Gracie Fields and Bing Crosby – 'Blue Smoke' was the first complete New Zealand pop song. It was written, recorded and manufactured locally, then commercially released on a new label dedicated to New Zealand artists. Most importantly for a pop song, it was a hit, a massive hit. Estimates suggest local sales topped the 50,000 mark, and Dean Martin and other overseas artists recorded cover versions. In 2001, after New Zealand songwriters and music experts voted it among the top twenty songs ever written by their compatriots, 'Blue Smoke' re-entered 100,000 New Zealand homes on the *Nature's Best* compilation.

The song's significance is that it marked the real birth of New Zealand's indigenous recording industry. Before 1935, musicians wanting to record had to perform in a radio or advertising studio, with a mobile unit or go to Australia. But there was no one locally to manufacture and release the recordings. The British-owned company HMV (NZ) Ltd dominated the record industry but had

little interest in local artists. HMV also vigorously guarded its monopoly.

Columbus was an appropriately named pioneer of the New Zealand music business. It was the brand given to valve radios and radiograms that were built by the Radio Corporation of New Zealand Ltd, a publicly owned manufacturing company based in Wellington. With their bakelite tuning knobs, walnut laminated cabinets and etched-glass panels with the call-signs of local radio stations, Columbus radios were a feature in thousands of living rooms throughout New Zealand. By the mid-1940s, Columbus Radio Centres – owned by Radio Corp – were prominently situated stores on the main streets of 27 cities and towns.

But to sell machines that play records, one needs records to play on them, preferably bought at the same store. That marketing logic is how New Zealand's indigenous record industry got under way.

At the time, HMV's monopoly over the record business in New Zealand was almost complete: the company had distribution rights to all the main labels out of Britain and the US. So confident was HMV of its local dominance that in 1947 the firm boasted: 'Every record you hear announced over the air, whatever its name, is now made in one of the worldwide chain of HMV factories. Indeed HMV records make possible the record libraries of the Broadcasting Service.'[10]

Radio Corp wanted to offer records at their Columbus shops, but as HMV had distributorships in most New Zealand towns, it refused to supply the Columbus stores with stock. So the Columbus chain had to make do selling records from very minor labels, with the exception of two stores: in Dannevirke and New Plymouth, where HMV did not have a distributor.

Once a week from 1947 a young Radio Corp employee called John Shears would walk along Wakefield Street to HMV near the Wellington Town Hall. His task was to collect a box of 78 rpm discs from HMV to supply the record shops in Dannevirke and New Plymouth; the new releases were shipped from the pressing plant at Homebush, Sydney.

In winter 1948, on his Wednesday visit to HMV, Shears was told that 'the boss' wanted a word. This was the formidable Alfred Wyness, managing director since 1931. 'I went in to see Mr Wyness and he said, "There are no records." I said, "Oh, is the boat late?"'

'No', said Wyness. 'There are no records.' Shears replied that he didn't understand.

'There are no records', Wyness declared again, 'and there won't be any more.'

Shears returned to Radio Corp and told his manager, Bart Fortune, who also oversaw the firm's fledgling recording arm, which made direct-to-disc recordings of advertisements, weddings and race meetings. Fortune called in other Radio Corp executives Fred Green, Ernest Ketko and Alex Marks, whose father William had founded the company. 'Tell them what's happened', Fortune said to Shears. Then: 'Tell us again.'

'This was the gauntlet being thrown down', recalled Shears. 'I suspect that's when the decision was being made that we would press records, not just be a recording studio.'[11]

Bart Fortune had an unusual background for a sales and marketing manager of a radio manufacturing company: during the 1930s he had been an active left-wing intellectual in Wellington. In 1933, aged only nineteen, he briefly managed the struggling, Marxist-oriented International Bookshop; two years later he joined the Communist Party. With W. B. Sutch and J. C. Beaglehole he was a founding member of the Wellington Cooperative Book Society that started Modern Books, a shop managed by Roy Parsons. In 1940, when Sutch and Fortune resigned from the society's management committee, Colin Scrimgeour – controller of the National Commercial Broadcasting Service – was elected president.

During – and after – his International Bookshop experience, Fortune had lived on money given to him for university studies by his brother Reo (an anthropologist then married to Margaret Mead). Needing more income, he joined the production line at Radio Corporation in 1935 at 5/6s per hour, becoming assistant manager. While serving in the army during the war, Fortune was recalled to Radio Corp, which had switched production to defence needs, manufacturing military transceivers; his involvement in politics ended at this time.[12]

Radio Corp had been founded by William Markoff, a Russian émigré who was penniless when he arrived in New Zealand in 1926. Changing his name to Marks, he began manufacturing various brands of radios, and formed Radio Corporation (NZ) Ltd in 1932. Once through the Depression, growth was rapid for the company, enabling it to form Radio Centres Ltd as a retail subsidiary in 1937.[13]

Marks wanted the shops to sell only radios, radiograms and their accessories. After his death in 1946, several key executives could see 'the potential of the power of the company, the energy and ability it had', recalled Shears. Among them were Marks's son Alex and the production manager and board member W. H. (Fred) Green. In 1946 Green spent many months in Britain, hiring technical staff and building contacts for raw materials. On his return, the directors began to discuss plans to get involved in recording.

It had been a good year for Radio Corp, with 2606 radio sets sold by June (the previous summer was the coldest and wettest for 82 years). Staff levels would soon return to pre-war levels, peaking at 300. The only setback was the company's short-lived foray into car-radio production. Its solitary model, the MC7, made 'every mistake possible in the design of a car radio', but in general Radio Corp was known for its quality control.[14]

Perhaps this rare slip was because of the absence of Green, who had stringent standards. He was also a visionary, and a pivotal figure in the birth of New Zealand's recording industry. He pushed for Radio Corp to start a recording service, and for a studio chose an old brass foundry at 262 Wakefield Street, a block away from Radio Corp's head office at 80 Courtenay Place.

In 1947 Green invited a twenty-year-old radio technician with 2ZB, Stan Dallas, to join Radio Corp and establish its recording studio. While at the NZBS, Dallas had been sound engineer for many live-to-air concerts, from its studios, the Majestic Cabaret and Trentham army camp. For his first six months at Radio Corp, he held on to his job at 2ZB while moonlighting to build Radio Corp's recording equipment from scratch. Months went by as they removed 50 years of fine metal dust from the brass foundry, and built a recording studio at the Wakefield Street end of the building and a pressing plant at the back. 'We had magnificent facilities there, it was a huge firm', Dallas recalled in 1994. 'It had all the workshops and good technical people, although no recording information.' He designed the equipment, copied the layout of the 2ZB control room, and built his own microphones and, later, recording heads for a tape machine.[15]

At first Radio Corp recorded using a lathe cutting directly onto an acetate. These discs could only be used a few times before they became unplayable. They were adequate for the earliest recordings of Radio Corp, such as advertisements, but not for commercial releases or even the

Recording Service

Vocal — Pianoforte — Intrumental
Meetings—Functions—Greetings—Talks

Our Recording Studios, equipped and constructed in accordance with modern recording technique, are available to the public for the production of disc recordings suitable for use on any electric gramophone.

Moderate charges provide for instruction in microphone technique and for ample rehearsal and preparatory work in the studios.

Portable equipment is available for covering meetings, functions, etc.

Office: 80 Courtenay Place.
Studios: 262 Wakefield Street,
Telephone: 55-020.

COLUMBUS
RECORDING STUDIOS
WELLINGTON

FURTHER DETAILS FROM ANY COLUMBUS RADIO CENTRE

An advertisement in the *Listener* of 8 October 1948 announces that Radio Corp was ready to make records. RNZ Infofind

next phase of the company's fledgling enterprise: weddings and race meetings.

Radio Corp needed to learn how to press gramophone records in high volumes, so it encouraged its staff to experiment with the complicated process. An acetate master needed to be converted into a stamper or matrix, which would then go into a press to manufacture the actual disc from heated shellac. 'A number of us worked on this project, with total failure day after day', recalled Shears. 'There were nine stages for each side, and it involved chemistry, electroplating and toolmaking skills. The basic concepts were understood but the devil was in the detail.'

For several months they worked after hours, four nights a week, until they solved the problems. 'We would go down to the Bakelite department and use their press after they had quit work. By 9.00 pm it was cool enough for us to press usually *one* record.' Shears would take notes of the settings used each night, which would be discussed the next evening then adjusted for another attempt.

By early October 1948, Radio Corp was ready to advertise that its Columbus Recording Studios at Wakefield Street – 'constructed in accordance with modern recording techniques' – were ready to record singers, pianists, instrumentalists and the spoken word. This was

not strictly accurate: to record the visiting Australian piano trio Musica Viva, arrangements were made to use the Wellington NZBS radio studios at Waring Taylor Street, as Radio Corp did not yet have a suitable piano. On 15 October, Fortune wrote to Green reporting on their recording experiments: the company was getting closer to a usable result. Some trial recordings had been made with the Wellington country singer Jack Christie, and the Musica Viva session was imminent. 'Since you left, we have not gone any further with messing in the studio. Stan has been pretty busy and anyway, I have the feeling that he is out of his depth and doesn't want to go ahead without you.'[16]

Fortune also mentioned a newspaper report that week announcing that HMV was installing two record presses at Kilbirnie, Wellington: this would enable the commercial manufacture of records in New Zealand for the first time. In the article, HMV claimed that the two presses could produce up to 200,000 discs a year. Asked about the prospect of recording New Zealand artists, HMV's Mr A. J. Wyness said that depended on whether there was sufficient demand to justify installing expensive equipment to make master discs.

> 'There are various studios in New Zealand at present making acetate discs, which can be played only once or twice', said Mr Wyness. Permanent records must be sent to Australia for processing. The [Kilbirnie] presses will operate from 'stampers' or imprints of master discs, brought from Australia or England.
>
> 'While we are naturally interested in recording such groups as the National Orchestra', Mr Wyness continued, 'it is doubtful if such recordings could compete commercially with imported records of the best overseas artists. Nevertheless we hope a demand for the work of local artists will develop so as to warrant the marketing of permanent recordings. We are keeping our eyes on such future possibilities.'[17]

The race was on to produce the first commercial discs in New Zealand. Fortune regarded HMV's claims as bluster, or at least premature. He wrote to Green:

> Our friends are pretty pathetic sort of people rushing into print with such a poor story. They certainly are providing a splendid opportunity for us to create a tremendous impression when we get going. I can just see the *Southern Cross* in a few weeks time (all going well with a streamer headline NZ ARTISTS <u>ARE</u> BEING RECORDED). By God, Fred, we will really build our prestige![18]

Green was in Sydney to buy second-hand presses from the Australian Record Company, a competitor with HMV that had suspended pressing during the war. Fortune's letter continued: 'I hope from the bottom of my heart that the doors are open for you over there, and that you are really getting everything you need.' Close to ARC's executives was Colin Scrimgeour, an acquaintance of Fortune's through the Wellington Cooperative Book Society, in exile since the Fraser government 'assisted' his departure from New Zealand in 1944.

Green returned on the flying boat, and the presses followed him by ship. Soon the corridors of Radio Corp were stacked with boxes of 'biscuit': pieces of shellac to turn into records. Months of experimentation followed, in which Stan Dallas completed building the studio and equipment, and Radio Corp staff practised every aspect of record making, including creating the masters. 'We had a lot of problems', recalled Dallas, 'because nobody in New Zealand knew how to make a stamper. You could make an acetate, but nobody had any experience in making it from there on.'[19]

'Blue Smoke' was not the first commercial recording to emerge from Radio Corp's Wakefield Street presses. 'What came before it?', Dallas said to Gordon Spittle in 1992. 'You'll never know. As far as you and I are concerned there wasn't one because otherwise it would ruin the whole of what we told people for the last 50 years.' Dallas was being coy: the first disc was 'I'm Looking for a Sweetheart', featuring the American pop organist Ken Griffin, one of a series of overseas artists Radio Corp released on the Tempo label. The masters came over from Australia, before Dallas and his team had conquered that part of the manufacturing process.[20]

Radio Corp needed a name for its record label for local musicians. Bart Fortune found the answer: 'I woke up in the middle of the night and said, "I've got the name for it – Tanza".' He said it might have come from an Italian song popular in 1948, 'La Danza', by Joseph Schmidt. But to Fortune, Tanza was an acronym that declared his cultural agenda: To Assist New Zealand Artists.[21]

Although test recordings had been made with country singer Jack Christie using just his voice and guitar, the song chosen for Tanza's first completely indigenous release was the local composition that had been building in popularity since the Maori Battalion returned from the war, in singalongs, at parties, in woolsheds and on marae.

'Blue Smoke' by Ruru Karaitiana, in the arrangement by George Winchester published by Begg's in 1947.

By late 1947, Karaitiana's 'Blue Smoke' had gained enough attention to be published as sheet music by Begg's, in a piano and vocal arrangement by George Winchester, with lyrics in English and Maori ('Kohu-Auwahi'). Winchester, an Englishman, was the manager of the music department at Begg's Wellington branch.

How the song came to be selected by Tanza is unknown. Shears thought that Karaitiana just kept 'hammering away' at Tanza staff until they thought, 'Well, let's try this guy – we liked the song right from the word go.' Karaitiana's girlfriend at the time, Joan Chittleburgh (later his wife), recalled that he paid for the recording, using borrowed money. 'He took a bit of persuading to do it, too, because he was very unsure of himself.' Also lacking confidence was Pixie Williams, a nineteen-year-old Maori woman from Mohaka, Hawke's Bay, who Karaitiana approached to sing on the recording. Williams and Chittleburgh shared a room at the YWCA hostel on Oriental Parade, becoming close friends. When Karaitiana mentioned he needed a singer, Chittleburgh suggested Williams, who was always singing in the shower and at sessions around the hostel piano. Among the regular items the young women sang was 'Blue Smoke'.[22]

Pixie Williams (below) and the Ruru Karaitiana Quintette in 1949, the year 'Blue Smoke' was released. From left: Jim Carter, Noel Robertson, Gerry Hall, George Attridge and Ruru Karaitiana. Karaitiana family collection; Jim Carter collection

At first, Williams refused Karaitiana's request. 'I said, *No*. Get somebody else! He came back again about two months later . . . he couldn't find anybody, so I said, Okay, I'll do it.'[23]

Although Karaitiana was an accomplished dance pianist, he wanted 'Blue Smoke' to have a Hawaiian feel. So a pianist wasn't needed in the group he assembled for the sessions: the Karaitiana Quintette. To play lap-steel guitar he approached Jimmy Carter, a Wellington guitarist regularly featured by Bob Bothamley in the 2YA Orchestra. Carter's connections provided the rest of the Quintette: George Attridge on ukulele, Johnny McNeely on bass, Gerry Hall – usually a drummer – on rhythm guitar. The fifth member of the Quintette was singer Pixie Williams.[24]

To the reluctant Williams, the sessions seemed to take a month of Sundays; Dallas remembered there being up to five, often at weekends. One Saturday morning Williams didn't turn up, and Dallas sent John Shears to find her. 'Off I go', he recalled. 'Pixie's going to play hockey. "Oh John, I forgot all about it." On the way there she says, "Oh, my throat –." Remember she wasn't a professional singer, she'd been conned into it by Ruru. "John, I was out with the girls last night, my throat's not very good." "Okay, I'll

Left: John Shears watches over the 'swarf', the inflammable shavings produced during record cutting, June 1949. John Shears collection

Below: an early pressing of 'Blue Smoke' sent to radio stations.

Opposite: the actual release, Tanza 1. Sound and Vision Centre, National Library of NZ

make you a cup of coffee. Keep practising you guys . . . ." And I can still see Pixie in her hockey gear, the striped socks, singing away. And Ruru looking very serious. He always looked serious.'[25]

Inevitably, there were technical problems with Tanza's first commercial recording, so many takes were made, and many masters ruined. Magnetic tape was a year or two away, so they couldn't play back a take without slightly degrading the acetate. Williams recalled takes being abandoned because of noises leaking into the studio, but Shears demurred. The delays were in getting a performance the musicians were happy with, in getting a good balance with the microphones, or high enough levels so that the 78 rpm disc would be at a suitable volume. Dallas improvised new techniques on the spot such as plugging Carter's homemade amplifier directly into a mixer rather than recording it through a microphone. Then there were processing difficulties turning the acetate into a 'stamper', or master, to press the actual discs. The slightest glitch at any stage meant they had to begin again: wearying for the musicians and especially Williams. 'It came to the stage when I thought, Oh *heck* – I wish it would disappear', she recalled.[26]

Dallas was a hard taskmaster, but it was a task that needed completing. 'Sometimes, if it was near enough,

you had to let it go, because after an hour or so you can't expect the artist to keep singing', he said. 'But people were very cooperative, there was no problem getting them to make a record. We didn't actually say it, but I think everybody realised we were making history. I don't think any money changed hands. People would just do it.'[27]

BLUE SMOKE

It was not until late June that Tanza was ready to release its first discs. By then the studio had also recorded Ken Avery's bucolic 'Paekakariki', performed by Bill Crowe's Orchestra with Avery singing. 'Blue Smoke' and 'Paekakariki' were released on 26 June 1949, and Bart Fortune rolled out his marketing campaign. On the actual label of 'Blue Smoke' he emphasised its cultural significance:

SOUVENIR NOTE
of first record
wholly processed
in New Zealand
Recorded 3/10/48
Processed 23/2/49

Throughout New Zealand, window displays advertised the discs in Columbus Radio Centres. In cinemas, the National Film Unit's *Weekly Film Review* showed the Karaitiana Quintette recreating a recording session for 'Blue Smoke' (Pixie Williams had already left Wellington, however, so she was absent for the filming).[28]

The *Southern Cross* declared the release of 'Blue Smoke' to be 'an outstanding New Zealand industrial achievement'. The only musical comment was about 'Senorita', the B-side: 'a gay, inconsequential trifle written by the same composer in Latin American rhythm'. Fortune ensured the newspaper mentioned that Radio

Corp's releases on Tempo on February 25 had been 'the first New Zealand-made gramophone records to reach the market'.[29]

With overseas and local music, Radio Corp had beaten its arch-rival HMV, whose Kilbirnie pressing factory was opened by politician Bob Semple in March. Their first local pressing was Dinah Shore's 'Button and Bows', and – apart from early forays with discs by Wally Ransom, the Knaves and Les Wilson – it would be nearly four years before HMV regularly released New Zealand artists.[30]

Early copies of 'Blue Smoke' had been sent to radio, and advertisements were broadcast and placed in newspapers. Initial reaction was 'ho-hum', remembered Shears. 'You hoped for more.' But radio play escalated quickly, especially on Sunday request shows. In 1994 Williams said that she kept the recording sessions secret from her friends and family but they could not avoid hearing the song on radio. On its first release, the disc sold 20,000 copies, and another 30,000 after a second pressing a year later. The first all-New Zealand pop record was massively popular.[31]

Some were sceptical that Karaitiana had written the song. The local representative of Sydney publishing firm J. Alberts confronted Shears whenever he visited her office on Willis Street. Miss Fanning was a veteran in publishing, working in an office with an upright piano for demonstrating sheet music. One of Shears's tasks for Tanza was to buy sheets of royalty stamps to stick on record labels, so that five percent of the sale price went to the song's publisher. He recalled that Fanning would take the cheque while saying, 'By the way Mr Shears, I have been thinking about [alleged similarities in] "Blue Smoke" and "Carolina Moon".' 'The banter went on forever. She was never nasty about it, never threatened legal action.'[32]

Dallas had no doubts that Karaitiana wrote the song. 'I worked quite closely with him in that period and I'm absolutely convinced that Ruru wrote it, no problem about that at all. All the stories that it was somebody else were absolute nonsense.'[33] After 'Blue Smoke', Karaitiana produced a flurry of songs, many of them released by Tanza. He said later that 'Blue Smoke' was 'a poor first effort' at songwriting; he was prouder of its more sophisticated follow-up, 'Let's Talk It Over'. Recorded with the same musicians, 'Let's Talk It Over' is another sad, slow waltz: the melody takes more risks but Williams handles it with confidence; it sold over 10,000 copies.[34] She also recorded discs with the Allan Shand Orchestra ('Maoriland') and Jimmy Carter's Hawaiians ('Bellbird Serenade'), but her days as Tanza's leading pop vocalist were quickly over when she followed her heart to Motueka.

In Wellington, Karaitiana enjoyed the early spoils of 'Blue Smoke'. There were parties when the record came out, and he soon married Joan Chittleburgh. 'We rented a posh place at Oriental Bay, and were there about nine months, and then he'd spent all his money', she recalled. 'He was a very generous kind person, he'd give anyone money. If they were hard up, he was sorry for them – and he forgot that we needed to eat too.'

In late 1949, the couple moved to Dannevirke and then Dunedin, to be close to their families. Karaitiana was keen to avoid the attention that came after the success of 'Blue Smoke', suggested Kennett. 'He didn't mind the attention on stage but he didn't like people coming home to talk to him, it seemed to embarrass him.'

Soon, the attention spread around the world. While visiting Britain, Gisborne-born twins Greta Heeney and Winnie Thompson – the wives of New Zealand boxing identities Jack Heeney and Snowy Thompson – sang 'Blue Smoke' on a BBC variety programme. 'Compliments were lavished on its composer', wrote one report. 'The opinion was expressed that "Blue Smoke" would soon surpass "Now is the Hour" in popularity . . . . frequent calls were received at the studio asking how the song could be purchased.'[35]

Big things were being predicted for 'Blue Smoke' when the Sam Fox Publishing Company started plugging the song in the United States in December 1951. Helping it was 'a quartet of hit records now making their presence felt by jukeboxes and disc jockeys', reported the New York music press. Versions had already been 'waxed' by Leslie Howard, Dean Martin, Al Morgan and Teddy Phillips. Martin telephoned Karaitiana from Los Angeles, asking if he had any more songs. In Britain, Webster Booth and Anne Ziegler released 'Blue Smoke' as a duet in July 1949, having met Karaitiana a year earlier when visiting Wellington. 'Very snobbish', recalled Kennett. 'They didn't want to meet me, I was married to a Maori. I liked him, but she was snooty.'[36]

Early in the 1950s, Karaitiana travelled to the US to follow up opportunities that proved elusive. For Kennett, supporting their son Ruma and several foster children back in Dannevirke, this year-long trip was 'a bone of contention'. Ruma recalled, 'He certainly enjoyed the fame and the fast-moving fortune that passed through his hands, and he found it quite hard to settle down again when he returned.'[37]

Settling down was not in Karaitiana's repertoire, but music and other activities always were. In 1951 he reunited with Pixie Williams for concerts at Dunedin's His Majesty's Theatre. 'Although the show lacked polish and quick tempo', wrote a local reviewer, 'one thing it did have was variety.' The bill of Tune Parade also featured a 'rather shaky' roller-skating act and kapa haka exhibitions, but it was the music that received 'unstinting applause'. Williams sang many of Karaitiana's songs, including the debut of his tribute to Dunedin, 'Saddle Hill', and 'It's Just Because', written in honour of the troops of K-Force departing for the Korean War. The songwriter himself closed the show with a solo piano medley of his songs.[38]

He would often call in at Tanza's office, seeking royalties, and in 1952 received a £25 award from APRA to mark the success of 'Blue Smoke' and 'Let's Talk It Over'. In the mid-1950s, the Karaitianas separated; after this, 'Ru drifted', said Kennett. In a Pahiatua courtroom in 1955 – for breaking a prohibition order and for his debts – he claimed that he had been hounded by the press; he was sentenced to fourteen days' jail.[39]

By that stage, recalled his son, 'Blue Smoke' was 'old news, and to some extent Dad was old news as well. He spent the rest of his life doing all sorts of odd jobs, but always drifting in and out of the music world.' Karaitiana played in dance bands, or solo piano in clubs of dubious legality, and took seasonal work as a shearer and in freezing works. His circuit was Hawke's Bay, Manawatu, Wellington and Taranaki (where he befriended Ronald Hugh Morrieson).[40]

Ruma remembered being taken as a child to establishments where 'powdered ladies' looked after him, while his father performed in tails, or local halls where he ran a floating casino and a liquor still. '"Blue Smoke" was always around. Because of that, people would know who he was, and at the drop of a hat, Ru would find himself at the piano. People were usually inebriated – we are talking six o'clock swill days here – and I would sit on the bar with my legs dangling over with a raspberry drink while Dad attended the piano.'[41]

Karaitiana was widely read – 'psychology, poetry, very intellectual things' – and was always taking notes of song ideas. Although he never read music, Karaitiana spoke of musical aspirations beyond the sentimental waltzes for which he became known. 'I hope to write popular dance

Ruru Karaitiana with his son Ruma, Woodville,
c. 1954. Karaitiana family collection

music till it's brought me enough money to devote my time to composing music which might add to the Maori culture', he said in 1950. 'I want to write a Maori symphony, but it may be many years before I am free to start.'[42]

When Karaitiana died on 15 December 1970, the editor of the *Dominion* Jack Kelleher wrote: 'I don't know whether Ruru ever felt free to start. He continued to drift about Wellington, always it seemed on his own, a short, stocky, hesitant figure, an island in a community with musical tastes which had no room either for his vintage of pop or for a Maori symphony. He worked as a hospital gardener but was often in hospital himself . . . . For Maori Battalion mates, and some others, the blue smoke will linger.'[43]

Tanza was first with an all-New Zealand record, but only just. As well as beating HMV, the release of 'Blue Smoke' eclipsed the initiative of a recording engineer who would soon be Tanza's greatest ally. Noel Peach came to be regarded as 'Mr Tanza' by Auckland musicians: at his Astor

Studios on Shortland Street he recorded the label's northern acts, sending the results down to Wellington for pressing. Peach was soon making most of Tanza's recordings.

In 1949, while Tanza was working towards releasing its landmark recording, Peach was trying to do the same thing in Auckland. He had already been recording dance bands for one-off vanity discs at 30 shillings a side when he decided to attempt a commercial release. He recorded Esme Stephens with Wally Ransom's Rhumba Band performing 'You Can in Yucatan', a song that had been a US hit for Desi Arnaz. Peach hoped that HMV would press it and three other songs at the new Kilbirnie plant, from stampers made in Sydney. However, a coal-mining strike in Australia meant that HMV's Sydney plant was out of action, so Peach's masters could not be converted to stampers. Meanwhile, Tanza released 'Blue Smoke', making the first commercial disc to be produced wholly in New Zealand an all-indigenous event rather than an Auckland take on Latin-American pop. 'You Can in Yucatan' was released in December 1949 as HMV LA-1, with 'Clarinet Samba' as its B-side.

During the war, Peach had recorded Stephens singing with the Artie Shaw band, and since then had been working towards his goal of getting New Zealand musicians onto disc. Shortly after recording 'Yucatan', he explained what drove him: 'We've got our own orchestras, jive bands and choirs, yet the music most of us hear most of the time comes from New York and London. Aren't we good enough to make our own records?'

While managing a cinema in Kingsland, Peach began buying recording equipment to set up his own studio. 'Much of it looked like junk . . . . But gradually, the dials, coils, tubes and wire cobwebs took shape.' Peach and his wife Vida took a lease on a 'grimy, sunless basement' in Shortland Street, set about 'redecorating their dungeon in sunny, modern colours' and turned it into a recording studio. 'Musicians began to trickle in. Callers were received at all hours of the day and night. Music began to pour out; catchy tuneful songs – the kind New Zealanders are asking radio stations to play.'[44]

Some of Auckland's leading jazz players of the late 1940s became part of Peach's stable of backing musicians. They would use Astor as a rehearsal room before radio broadcasts, as well as being available for recording sessions. Several of the regulars became known as the Astor Dixie Boys although, depending on the style of music required, they could evolve into spin-off configurations such as the Astor Barnyard Boys, Astor Trio, Astor Rhythm, the Astorians and the Sunny City Seven.[45] Peach became especially adept at recording Auckland's leading female vocalists, such as Dorothy Brannigan, Mary Feeney, Pat McMinn and Mavis Rivers.

Stan Dallas regarded the recordings produced in Auckland by Peach as 'the turning point'. They showed that 'carefully recorded New Zealand artists could sound like overseas artists. Considering the conditions he worked under at the time, the results were amazing. He produced one top-line vocalist after another.'[46]

Peach was a perfectionist, but 'very patient and very innovative', recalled Jim Warren. 'He had a very good ear. He wasn't a musician but he was very capable at picking up things. We would sometimes think we had done a good cut and he'd say, "Not good enough, you have to do that again." He could hear things. He was very important in the recording business. He *was* Tanza in Auckland, on his own virtually.' Eventually, more than 300 recordings by Peach were released.[47]

Before Peach's association with Tanza he had approached HMV, trying to find a way to get his recordings manufactured and into stores. At first they were dismissive, but their attitude changed when they heard his samples, and his other idea: to record cover versions of songs on the American hit parade. He told HMV, 'Our musicians, all of them popular radio professionals, can record [the songs] and your discs can be available weeks before your New York and London pressings reach the record shops.'[48] But once Tanza in Wellington stole a march on local record releases – with Peach quickly coming on board – HMV seemed to lose interest. They concentrated on pressing overseas artists at the Kilbirnie plant, starting with Dinah Shore's 'Buttons and Bows', which sold 15,000 copies.[49]

Even for overseas releases, their break-even point was high: at this stage, HMV stipulated that 2000 sales would be needed to make it worthwhile pressing at Kilbirnie. But the new manufacturing industry was worthwhile for other reasons: the precious overseas funds that were saved could be spent on importing better music, i.e., classical. 'Local pressing of popular numbers means also that more sterling is available for records of more lasting value.'[50]

The monopoly enjoyed by HMV (NZ) Ltd in the early 1950s would have been complete, 'were it not for one or two New Zealand manufacturers whose activities are becoming rather irksome to it'.[51] Besides Tanza, the other firm to annoy HMV by offering a hint of competition was the Stebbing Recording and Sound Co. Ltd. In 1950 Stebbing's started to expand from its small recording and sound system operation in Avondale to a studio in the Pacific Buildings on Queen Street. In Grey Lynn, they built their own pressing plant for 78 rpm discs, situated in the Auckland Laundry building, drawing water from Western Springs and steam from the laundry's boilers to run the hydraulic presses. The company could now launch its own record labels, Zodiac and Stebbing.

But HMV was not shy of using its weight against any fledgling opposition, especially after it merged with Columbia and became part of the EMI group. The New Zealand public was likely unaware that any artist on a major overseas label – Decca, Parlophone, RCA Victor, Columbia – was actually distributed by HMV. But the company's dominance was revealed when the success of Tanza and Stebbing with local recordings meant that HMV began to flex its weight. The company told retailers that if they wished to sell records by companies other than HMV – be they local or minor overseas labels – then they would pay a higher wholesale rate for their HMV releases; they might even face a complete ban from selling any HMV products.

To a retailer such as Marbeck's in Auckland, that sold only records, this might mean their status with HMV would change from being an 'A' retailer (who bought records for three shillings) to a 'C' retailer (whose wholesale rate was four shillings). With the retail price at 6/3, that was a significant disincentive.[52] But the pressure from HMV could be even more severe, Stebbing recalled:

> If we sold product into any store, the store would lose its franchise, and their franchise in most cases consisted of refrigerators, washing machines, vacuum cleaners: all HMV. That was a real ban, what they did, to stop the distribution of our records. At that stage we were producing Mercury and Nixa records as well, and as far as they were concerned it was getting into their territory. They wanted a monopoly and that was that.[53]

The pressure brought to bear by HMV upon retailers was such that, in 1951, although Tanza and Stebbing were recording many New Zealand artists, it was impossible to buy any of their discs on Auckland's Queen Street.[54] When customers queried retailers, they were told the discs were out of stock. The Musicians' Union began receiving complaints from its members, and the resulting publicity caused a flurry of indignant articles in the press. 'Public opinion rallied to the union's cause, but the company quickly denied that they had attempted to dictate in the manner claimed', wrote Bert Peterson, *Australian Music Maker and Dance Band News* columnist and unionist. Three months later, the controversy flared up again when – despite its earlier denial – HMV defended its marketing methods. The company said it was 'quite entitled to insist on dealers, music shops, etc, stocking their records only, as they look upon said shops as sole agencies'. According to HMV, retailers that stocked other makes of recordings – including those made by New Zealanders – infringed their agreements with the record company.

Peterson didn't agree. 'One-brand stations may be all right for petrol, but not for what we call art. Music stores are usually anxious to help local musicians, as a lot of them are their customers, but the recording company's edict has prevented said stores from helping in this particular direction, despite their earnest wish.' He suggested that HMV's early denial, followed by its admission, had bewildered the musicians and the public, who now didn't know who to believe.[55]

Martin Finlay wrote in *Here & Now* that the union found 'pressure was being put on dealers by overseas manufacturers and that anyone handling local records would not be supplied with their products. This included, of course, not only popular records but the whole output of the EMI group.'[56] (EMI in Britain was the parent company of HMV [NZ] Ltd.)

Although retailers were reluctant to speak out, Finlay published a letter that one had written to an independent New Zealand record company: 'We do wish to carry stocks of "Zodiac" etc, only we are placed in rather an awkward position . . . . HMV dislike the idea of us handling other recordings, and threatened to cut supplies when we started handling your records some time ago, hence the delay in future orders.'

HMV defended itself by saying that every supplier of goods could make his own retailing arrangements. 'This is disingenuous', said Finlay, '. . . the very monopoly has given it absolute control of the field. To forbid the local producers access to all shops now normally dealing in records is to strike them a death blow, and it is no answer to say there are other shops not so far handling records.'[57]

New Zealand recordings were here to stay, said Peterson, 'whatever the outcome of the present argument,

and discs recently released are up to the usual high standard we have come to expect from them'.[58]

One advantage the independent New Zealand record companies had over HMV was flexibility; another was speed. When a song was a hit overseas, the local labels could record and release a cover version weeks before the original went on sale in New Zealand. In 1951 the Duplicats' rendition of 'Mockin' Bird Hill' sold 6000 copies, most of them before any of the overseas versions arrived. Finlay commented: 'Not all of the local productions reach such a level of supply and demand (though the general level would have been higher had it not been for the "squeeze"), but obviously a few weeks' start in the short life of a "hit" tune is a great asset and goes far to meet our limited market.'[59]

It was all about beating HMV, said Stan Dallas. 'Were we trying for a New Zealand sound? I don't think so, we were just copying America, using local talent – trying to fill a gap in the market and record New Zealand music if it was worth doing.'[60]

Competition was also intense between the independents. Up against the Duplicats' 'Mockin' Bird Hill' on Zodiac in 1951 was a version by Mavis Rivers on Tanza. Auckland vocalists such as Dorothy Brannigan, Pat McMinn, Mavis Rivers and Esme Stephens competed against the imported discs of Rosemary Clooney, Doris Day, Dinah Shore and Jo Stafford. Any inkling of an

Dennis Huggard Archive, MSD10-0224, Alexander Turnbull Library, Wellington

A LONG PLAYER

Eldred Stebbing had tinkered with music from a very early age. He began learning the violin aged five, built a radio transmitter aged eleven – broadcasting records from his bedroom to a friend in the next suburb – and left school at fourteen for a radio factory job. Stebbing's mother Claudia played the violin in Auckland orchestras, at silent films and on 1YA: the family home in Avondale was often a rehearsal venue for fifteen to twenty musicians playing Strauss waltzes. A key influence was his brother Philip, an accomplished pianist and radio hobbyist who taught Eldred to make his first transmitter. Stebbing followed him into his first job, assembling Ultimate valve radios on the production line at Radio Ltd. Before the Second World War, the brothers began supplying the sound systems at the Town Hall and Western Springs, and at A&P shows and cinemas.

When Phil Stebbing entered the army, Eldred took over the business. He was soon providing the PAs for dances at Mechanic's Bay, the Point Erin kiosk and those run by the American Red Cross. He also supplied the sound equipment for concerts, such as Gracie Fields' performance in the reception room at the Farmers department store. Stebbing was in the emergency fire service: if an air raid had occurred, his task was to drive up Queen Street in a van with a speaker mounted on the roof, urging people to go to shelters beneath Albert Park.

During the 1943 visits of Artie Shaw's band and the US first lady Eleanor Roosevelt, the American Red Cross asked Stebbing to record their concerts and speeches onto 16-inch glass acetates, for broadcast to US troops in the Pacific. Stebbing used a landline from the Town Hall to Spackman and Howarth's studio on Albert Street, which had been requisitioned by the government during the war. (Auckland's first proper recording studio, Spackman's pre-recorded programmes such as Uncle Tom's Friendly Road Choir for 1ZB.)

The experience encouraged Stebbing to enter the recording business, and in 1945 he established Stebbing's Sound Systems. Using the latest Presto portable machine, the firm recorded weddings, parties, anything – from race

Dennis Huggard Archive, MSD10-0346, Alexander Turnbull Library, Wellington

meetings to board meetings – direct to disc. They could give newlyweds a copy of their service as they left the church. Stebbing had recently married Margaret, and they converted a bedroom in their Avondale house into a studio. 'Most recordings were people who wanted to make a lacquer disc of their singing, or send a message, or weddings and functions.' Soon this evolved into recording jingles for advertisements. The company was on its way to becoming a fully fledged recording studio that over the next 60 years would outlast many competitors.[61]

It also launched two record labels. Originally, Zodiac was to be for pop, and Stebbing for jazz and other genres, but many artists appeared on both. Zodiac's first release was the Big City Six with 'Harbour Lights' in 1951, while Stebbing's debut was the Duplicats' 'Beautiful Brown Eyes' the following year. Soon a stable of local musicians had formed around the two labels, among them Crombie Murdoch, Esme Stephens and star multi-instrumentalist Julian Lee. In 1952 Lee became the musical director for the labels, arranging and producing records by Stephens, Mavis Rivers, Ellen Vann and many others. Zodiac also tried country, with Johnny Granger and Jack Riggir; and Hawaiian-style pop with Bill Wolfgramm, the Zodiac Paradise Islanders and the Hulawaiians.

overseas hit could lead to a race to record a local version and get it into the stores first. After hearing it on shortwave radio, a phone call to the US could have a copy of the sheet music on the next plane. Or Stebbing would monitor the American Top 40 on shortwave radio, using an early tape-recorder to make copies of promising songs for his musicians to transcribe. 'We would make a cover version and could probably get it out six to eight weeks before HMV got theirs out. That's how we worked.' It was a system that helped create a local industry, getting musicians involved in recording and an audience interested in local artists. (A similar reliance on cover versions also occurred in Australia, where HMV/EMI 'had a stranglehold on the recording industry and were determined to maximise their profit by releasing only one hit from overseas per month, and blocked the release of others for up to six months'. So when local artists' versions of hits by acts such as Nat King Cole and Frankie Laine were successful, they broke the company's grip and forced it to release their hits.)[62]

One of Stebbing's biggest successes was Esme Stephens' recording of 'Between Two Trees' in 1951; it was the firm's first release using a tape-recorder. A minor hit for the Andrews Sisters in the US, Stephens' version sold 23,000 copies in New Zealand and about 2500 overseas.[63]

In 1953 Stebbing's sold its pressing plant to Fred Green and Tony Hall, formerly with Tanza, whose new company Green and Hall would become HMV's leading competitor in record manufacturing. Stebbing's faced many obstacles in its pressing division: LPs and 45 rpm discs were becoming the dominant formats, but their presses only made 78s. The Labour government restricted the use of overseas funds and import licences, and refused the company a licence to acquire new presses. Plus, there was the on-going battle of distribution, despite the assistance of Radio Ltd, the company with which a fourteen-year-old Eldred Stebbing had started his career back in 1935. Wherever Ultimate radios were for sale, Stebbing discs were also able to be displayed, as well as in stationery stores and petrol stations. Radio Ltd's competitor Radio Corp led the way with its Columbus stores, 'stimulating the market so people realised they could buy records in places other than just record stores'. By the mid-1950s, as companies such as Tanza, Philips, G. A. Wooller and Philip Warren Ltd secured the franchises to release more significant overseas labels, cracks began to appear in the HMV monopoly.[64]

RED-LIGHT RADIO

Just before 7.00 pm on Saturday nights in the 1950s, the 1ZB Radio Theatre in Auckland is packed with people, 'the air heavy with the scent of Palmolive hair oil and Three Flowers perfume'. The crowd is there to witness the weekly live broadcast on 1YD by a radio dance band: a free show starring the cream of Auckland's dance and jazz musicians.[65]

On the stage, the band members are watching the clock; they are professionals, and look the part in their dinner suits. But inside, many are shaking with nerves. An MC walks to the podium and addresses the audience in the room and at home: 'Ladies and gentlemen . . .'. At the last moment the veteran band leader Chips Healy whispers: 'Alright fellas, here we go. If anything goes wrong, somebody stays in G . . .'. The band falls about laughing; it becomes a musicians' catchphrase around town. At that moment the second hand hits the top of the hour. On a cue word from the MC and the wave of a baton, the musicians hit the downbeat: the nerves become energy and focus.[66]

There was plenty of work for New Zealand musicians in 1949, if you were one of 'the lucky few'. That was the word recent immigrant George Wood sent back to the *Melody Maker* in London.

The music profession in New Zealand was small and its scope was limited, he wrote. Few dance venues operated full time through the year; mostly they were open four nights a week during the ball season (June to September). The rest of the year, even the leading venues only ran one or two nights a week. During the quiet months, the best musicians found it hard to earn a living and could do so only with the help of radio, 'which gives a small amount of comparatively poorly paid work to just a few musicians'.[67]

Wood described the radio dance-band system, which Bob Bothamley set up and ran like a well-oiled machine in 1948. Every four months – in each of the four main centres – a new radio band began a contract to play a live broadcast each week. For these broadcasts and a rehearsal, the musicians were paid £3/7/6. When it was time to offer another band a contract, there would be a shuffling of musical chairs, with the band leaders and arrangers taking a seat among the rank-and-file when their stint was over. Auditions took place according to strict broadcasting policies, with Bothamley 'scrupulously honest', but in effect it was a closed shop. 'The personnel very often remains much the same, such is the shortage of

Martin Winiata (standing, with saxophone) and his 3YA Radio Band, featuring vocalist Coral Cummins. Bob Bothamley collection/Peter Downes

top-line musicians', wrote Wood. 'The outstanding few are constantly re-engaged by the incoming leaders.'[68]

Among the British immigrants whom Wood found to be prominent in the Auckland jazz and dance-band scene was Wally Ransom, who would soon record 'You Can in Yucatan'. The London drummer had made an immediate impact upon his arrival in New Zealand in 1938. Earlier in the 1930s, 'a busy drummer back home', Ransom was now one of the busiest men in music in Auckland, as a jovial radio compère, band leader, drummer and rumba expert.

While serving in the RNZAF at Wigram, Ransom gave a few lessons in swing to a former pipe-band drummer called Harry Voice. In post-war Wellington, Voice was in demand for radio dance-band broadcasts and the best cabaret gigs. He remembered a virtual hierarchy existing at the time: 'There were musicians that played the dance-band gigs, and others who did places like the Majestic. Once you got into the recording scene and Broadcasting, you'd made it: you were in the top echelon.'[69]

While it meant that the same people – in different configurations – got much of the work, it also gave valuable arranging experience to a host of young band leaders. Musicians such as Doug Caldwell, Lew Campbell, Freddie

Gore, Julian Lee, Brian Marston, Crombie Murdoch, Calder Prescott and Don Richardson seized the opportunity to find their own musical voice with their chosen lineups. Vocalists included Coral Cummins, Mavis Rivers, Esme Stephens and Marion Waite. As well as providing an outlet – and income – to the best young musicians and arrangers, the post-war radio bands became familiar in the studio, which proved valuable when the recording industry got under way in the 1950s. Whether the singer was performing mainstream pop, country and western, rumbas or rock'n'roll, the backing musicians had usually passed through the public-radio-funded Bothamley school.

Prestcott – then boarding at Waitaki Boys' High – remembered being in heaven after hours. The teenage jazz pianist could listen to 'Auckland on a Tuesday and a Saturday night, Christchurch on a Thursday night, Wellington on a Wednesday night and Dunedin on a Friday night, all 20-minute to half-hour programmes'.[70]

The radio bands' golden age was from the late 1940s through to the end of the 1950s, when they were broadcast live-to-air, in front of a studio audience. The broadcasts helped silence critics such as the *Tempo* columnist who harrumphed in 1948: 'Dance music in

Ted Andrews and the Revellers, taking it gently at 4YA, Dunedin, 1948. Campbell Photography/Peter Downes collection

New Zealand is more or less the *unwanted child* of radio. Not that the public do not want it – they most certainly do. But because certain executives on the Broadcasting Panel do not like it.'[71]

Bothamley's radio-band initiative came at no small cost. But the system ameliorated the effects of an even costlier musical initiative: the formation of the National Orchestra in 1946 (known as the New Zealand Symphony Orchestra from 1975). This had plucked many top musicians from dance bands, and Bothamley's radio bands in the four main centres helped pacify Musicians' Union lobbyists. 'Bobby Girvan has gone legit and joined the national symphony orchestra on bassoon', reported union president Bert Peterson, '. . . they are doing wonderful work. Nevertheless, Bob Girvan's loss is serious for 2YA maestro Freddie Gore.'[72]

Peterson and others championed the idea that a national dance band should be formed. For support they turned to expatriate trumpeter Jim Gussey, who had left New Zealand for Australia in 1927 with £3 in his pocket. By the time Gussey made a return visit in 1951, he was director of the prestigious ABC Dance Band in Sydney. Auckland musicians threw a smoke concert in his honour, with the

requisite jam session. The standard of the playing convinced him that 'No time should be lost in establishing a National Dance Band. We have the talent, and we have it here.'[73]

Although a national dance band never eventuated, the radio bands were an effective alternative. The broadcasts on the YA, YD, ZB and – from acetates – regional stations also gave the urban players a wider congregation than the studios and elite dance venues' small capacities would suggest. The free 30-minute concerts from Auckland's Radio Theatre became hot ticket events, with fans standing in the aisles and a system introduced to ease the queues outside the deco building in Durham Lane. On opening nights in each main centre, Bothamley would be on hand, arranging the microphones and supervising the sound mix.

During this period, the man whose job title was Head Office Dance – 'that covered a multitude of sins, I'm sure', said Calder Prestcott – seemed rarely to be in his office. His work spanned the country, fuelled by his perfectionism and love of dance music and jazz. Within the NZBS, Bothamley was tolerated by his superiors, who may not have liked his music but respected the fact that he knew what he was doing, and did it to a very high standard. 'He was a remarkable friend to musicians', said Doug Caldwell.'[74]

recording sessions for Tanza and Stebbing's from the late 1940s, 'Most people hated jazz', said Crombie Murdoch. 'Only musicians and a few members of the public liked it. To others it was wicked, criminal, decadent.'[75]

Two radio band stalwarts and their mentor. From left, Ray Gunter, Bob Bothamley and Bob Ewing. Dennis Huggard Archive, MS-Papers-9018-05-001, Alexander Turnbull Library, Wellington

The music ranged from the popular 'sweet' style of swing, exemplified by Dale Alderton's arrangements accompanying his vocalist wife, Esme Stephens, to contemporary jazz arranged by Lew Campbell, Derek Heine or Bart Stokes. The live local music content on NZBS stations went beyond dance bands, with regular YA broadcasts by vocal groups such as the Knaves and the Duplicats, swing combos such as Campbell's Four Aces and Julian Lee's Symphonettes, or showcases by Mavis Rivers, Esme Stephens, Dutch cabaret singer Ellen Vann and others. Easy-listening 'salon orchestras' led by Henry Rudolph and Ossie Cheesman were also very popular. For although jazz musicians provided the backing to hundreds of pop

'Those bloody lights are on.' Peter Young's words were an inauspicious start to a moment in posterity. The event that took place on 7 August 1950 was billed as 'Auckland's first jazz concert', meaning an all-New Zealand cast playing for sitting listeners rather than dancers. Recording it was engineer Noel Peach, using a 'landline' – the copper telephone line – from the packed Town Hall concert chamber to his Astor Studios on Shortland Street.

Peter Young, the compère, was discombobulated by the late start: the audience was much bigger than expected. Hundreds were turned away, with tickets costing 3/8 being scalped for up to fifteen shillings. The organiser was Epsom drummer Bruce MacDonald, who wanted to expose the audience to something more cutting edge than the music heard in the dance halls. On stage were the finest popular musicians in the city. Backing local headliners Mavis Rivers, Julian Lee and Crombie Murdoch was – to the cognoscenti – a band of all-stars: trombonist Dale Alderton, guitarist Mark Kahi, tenor saxophonist Colin Martin and trumpeter Murray Tanner. In the rhythm section were guitarist Dick Hobday, bassist George Campbell and drummer Denny O'Brien.

Inside the room, wrote the *Auckland Star*'s reviewer DFT, 'the air was heavy and tense with concentration. The audience was fairly young, mostly in pairs paying no particular attention to each other.' The repertoire was mostly standards – 'September Song', 'I Can't Get Started', 'How High the Moon', 'Perdido', 'Caravan' – with the combinations of players changing through the evening. The audience was especially struck by the evening's novelty, dazzling tin-whistler Hugh Gordon.[76] He was 'nothing short of a virtuoso on an instrument which looks as if it might have come out of a lucky dip, and actually cost 3/6', wrote DFT, who throughout affected a naiveté:

At intermission I spoke to a foreign expert from the country where they know about these things. He told me that this was the best jazz I would hear in New Zealand, and that it was very creditable.

'They seem extremely flexible', I said.

'They are relaxed. That is the great thing. They are relaxed.'

Esme Stephens sings with the radio band at the 1ZB Radio Theatre, Auckland. Her future husband Dale Alderton is the taller trombone player; also identifiable are George Campbell, double bass; Crombie Murdoch, piano; Frank Gibson, drums; Julian Lee, third saxophonist from the left; and Jim Watters, second from the right. Bob Bothamley collection/Peter Downes

The arrangements were formal, the musicians' dress casual; 'future concerts might reverse these trends'. Despite being unable to dance, the audience's response was 'remarkably keen'.

> Being unused to jazz except as a background, I found it hard to tell one tune from another, capricious or otherwise. It didn't matter, because the variations were the interesting part . . . . The programme did not say who wrote the main tunes. Everybody seemed to know that.[77]

Although programmed, 'sit-down' jazz concerts became a regular event in the 1950s, the music was still risqué to many in the community, a factor reflected in the gleeful demeanour of the compère at the Auckland event, and confirmed by on-going bureaucratic battles with city councils about the use of their grand pianos for jazz concerts. In 1952 the Auckland City Council decided that jazz musicians could use the Town Hall's Chappell, but the new Steinway was out of bounds. A similar furore in Whangarei inspired satirical journalism from A. J. McCarthy: 'A new committee, to be known as the Committee for the Preventation of Piano-Thumping, may shortly be set up by the Whangarei Borough Council to carry out its ban of bebop on the Bechstein.' Committee members would have to attend all concerts, and if a majority of them decided the pianist was 'drifting into a jazz tempo, it will be the committee's duty to rush to the stage and stop the pianist immediately'.[78]

THE G MAN

Freddie Gore was Wellington's hepcat. He was gregarious, flamboyant and handsome. Being Lebanese, he had a permanent tan; coming from a family of drapers, he always dressed in the latest styles. He wore the first zoot suit that many New Zealanders ever saw and greeted everybody with a big grin and an American accent. 'Crazy, baby!'

Born in 1913, Gore started playing drums on the family fire-screen before teaching himself the trombone, piano, string bass and guitar. He was passionate about jazz from an early age, and by 1937 he was performing in Wellington with the Campbell brothers George and Phil, and the husky singer Lolita.[79] In the late 1930s, Gore travelled to

Mavis Edmonds and her Rhythm-makers, 1939. From left: Ron Cudby, Ross Floyd, Fred Gore, Ted Hall, Mavis Edmonds, M. Hayvue, H. Harrop. Spencer Digby – Bob Bothamley collection/Peter Downes

Freddie Gore shows his passion for jazz in the late 1930s, just prior to visiting the US. Thérèse Gore collection

the US, Britain and France to experience his heroes first hand. In Britain, he heard the bands of Jack Hylton and Bert Ambrose, but his time in the US remains a mystery. He was away long enough to acquire American musical techniques, an obsession with Duke Ellington and a fashionable drawl.[80]

Returning to New Zealand, Gore was one of the original members of the band at the 1940 Centennial Exhibition in Wellington and became a key player in bands led by Lauri Paddi and Art Rosoman. After-hours jam sessions became a regular feature of Wellington's nightlife for any musicians who happened to be in town. Many were held at the grand home of wealthy local hipsters Barney and Don Hope Gibbons in Lyall Bay. Breathless accounts of these evenings were reported in *Swing!*, the capital's short-lived 'modern music lovers' magazine'. Gore appeared alongside a 'who's who' of jazz musicians from throughout the country, but with his ebullient character he seemed to dominate proceedings, on 'tailgate' trombone or piano.

> They played 'St Louis Blues', and Freddy lifted up his voice and bewailed the infidelity of his girl friend and his lack of success in affairs of the heart. However Freddy's is apparently a very volatile temperament, for two numbers later he was vocally declaiming 'It's a Wonderful World'. He also produced some very creditable animal imitations with his trombone during the playing of 'Tiger Rag'.[81]

By 1944 Gore was making forays to Auckland, leading his own band at the Metropole. In a 'sensational upheaval' in March, Gore and his band jumped ship

A flyer for Freddie Gore's national tour with the Civic Wintergarden Orchestra, February 1945. Eph-C-CABOT-Music-1945-01, Alexander Turnbull Library, Wellington

to the Civic Wintergarden after the sudden resignation of Bert Peterson and his band (who then took over the vacancy at the Metropole).[82]

It was at the Civic with a fourteen-piece dance orchestra that Gore – and many of his musicians – really established their reputations. In May, with Esme Stephens and Reg Munro as vocalists, they performed at a patriotic premiere hosted by the Civic for the Irving Berlin film *This is the Army*.[83] Twice a week the Gore band filled the Civic Wintergarden, receiving wide acclaim. By the end of the year, they were hired by Warner Brothers to go on 'the biggest national tour ever attempted by a big band in New Zealand'.[84]

This tour, which opened in Te Awamutu on 29 January 1945, was the highlight of Freddie Gore's career. Travelling everywhere by train, it took Auckland's most prestigious dance orchestra to the small town halls of the nation. Newspaper advertisements stressed the glamour and above all the scale of what they were about to experience: 'modern dance rhythm stylists that 149,500 paid to hear in their sensational cabaret season in the palatial Civic Wintergarden, Auckland – 14 Star Players – 32 Instruments – The Top Tunes of the Hit Parade, with the singing sensation, Reg Munro, at the microphone.' All for five shillings.[85]

In each town, Gore announced that young women were invited to audition to sing with the band. An early gig was at the Theatre Royal in Taumarunui, where the town's

'swing enthusiasts and dancing addicts' crowded the venue. The evening was a 'bright moment in Taumarunui's dancing life which is generally so devoid of variety'. Gore sang, played the trombone and piano, and 'proved his versatility by penning all the band's arrangements'. During the evening, a small combo stepped forward from the orchestra to play 'inspired improvisations of "The Blues" that were well worth hearing'. But the big moment of the evening was 'the presentation of the four local girls to sing, accompanied by the orchestra'. Afterwards, Gore said that many local girls had answered his advertisement and the Taumarunui applicants were the best he had seen and heard since he had left Auckland.[86]

The tour was only four days old, and they had already played Otorohanga, back-tracked to Te Kuiti and were now on their way to Stratford. It was a charity tour, raising funds for the sick, the needy and the Patriotic Fund. The Civic dance stylists headed south, with a gruelling itinerary of mostly one-night stands: the Woodville Women's Institute Hall on a Monday, the Pahiatua Drill Hall on a Tuesday . . . all the way to Invercargill, practising in the guard's van of the trains. On tour, Gore learnt that he liked to find his own sound by moulding younger players rather than asking mature musicians to change their styles. Consequently he nurtured several younger players in the touring band.[87]

After the tour finished on 24 April, the band split up. Gore had been tempted home by the offer of a regular programme on Wellington's 2YA, and he took several of his key musicians with him. The powerful transmitter of 2YA ensured that, over the next three years, Gore's profile expanded nationwide. An added attraction was the sweet, swinging voice of the American war bride Marion Waite.

The 2YA band used original arrangements almost exclusively, written by Gore or his pianist Bill Hoffmeister. The instrumental star of Gore's 1946 band was clarinettist/saxophonist Bob Girvan, who had played with Gore in Lauri Paddi's band before joining the RNZAF band. *Music Maker* noted Girvan's penchant for 'very futuristic and sophisticated arrangements', which suited Gore's aspirations to be more than a dance band.[88] Jazz was moving towards a symphonic stage, Gore told the *New Zealand Listener*, with 40-piece bands overseas that featured large string sections.[89]

His desire to lead an innovative jazz concert orchestra – Freddie Slack aspiring to Stan Kenton – did not always suit radio's need to be entertaining. But the radio band

The Freddie Gore big band look on nervously as their leader (in white glasses) and vocalists skylark, late 1940s. Standing at left is Bill Hoffmeister, pianist; Vern Clare is on drums; and Jim Carter the guitarist. Jim Carter collection

was usually well received, despite his adventurous arrangements.

Gore was a man-about-town who liked to lead fashions in dress, language, harmonies and even food. Influenced by the American invasion of Wellington, in Upper Cuba Street he opened a waffle shop that became a musicians' daytime meeting-spot. Gore greeted everybody with a 'Hey, darlin'' and accompanied the fare – waffles, hot dogs and ice cream sundaes – with his adopted American slang.[90]

The Wellington Swing Club held its first public meeting on 1 August 1946, and its weekly sessions at Nimmo's Hall on Willis Street provided a place for swing aficionados to meet.[91] They could listen to Gore's fifteen-piece big band the Swingmen without the distraction of dancing, and to talks by experts such as its president, Arthur Pearce. 'It builds into a real jam session', reported the NZ Free Lance. 'Dancing is taboo: the people who attend go to listen, analyse, criticise and appreciate.'[92]

In early 1951, Gore set up his own Wednesday night gigs at the Savage Club Hall, near Courtenay Place. The Modernists included promising up-and-comers such as Laurie Lewis and Bart Stokes, plus Gore's sister Marguerite on vocals, but the weekly sessions faded after a year. Gore was in demand: with Mavis Rivers from Auckland, he was the star attraction at the New Plymouth Press Ball in late 1951. He and Stokes travelled up from Wellington for the gig, and were joined on stage by Metronome, a local combo that included Ronald Hugh Morrieson on Spanish guitar and bass. Metronome and New Plymouth's Modernaires opened the evening with old-time dances then, stated the invitation, 'the programme really begins. Maestro Freddie Gore said he ignored instructions after 10 o'clock. No one should leave the hall without striking up a nodding acquaintance with the punchbowl.'[93]

By now, Gore was shifting his focus beyond Wellington. In October 1952, *Music Maker* lamented that 'The old meeting place of most of the swing fans in Wellington, who went to talk and eat waffles, has closed down. Freddie Gore is at this moment taking a well-earned rest.'[94] His next goal was to build a family home – a log cabin – at Brown Owl, north of Upper Hutt. On weekends he invited musicians there to enjoy outdoor, Lebanese-style family lunches then to jam in the backyard shed. These gatherings at Brown Owl made an impression on many, including the teenage Mike Nock, then an aspiring saxophonist not long out of Nelson. 'He had a farm, a beautiful wife, a lot of kids and animals. He used to have these jam sessions out there and big parties, it was all music orientated. I thought, *Wow* – this is living life.'[95]

Gore was admired for his arranging skills, his dedication to progressive jazz and his willingness to train beginners into a well-oiled ensemble.[96] These attributes may have stalled his career, however: modern jazz was not what audiences or radio required. Laurie Lewis: 'He'd get enthusiastic kids like me and Bart Stokes and all the youngsters, get us together to rehearse, and then we would go and audition.' After the successful three-year stint on radio with Marion Waite as the singer, Gore found his 1950s bands being turned down by Bob Bothamley. Disillusionment started to set in, suggested Lewis. 'I think he just got to the stage where he thought, it's passing me by, forget it, I'll make waffles and play a bit occasionally.'

'Pappy G' inspires the musical youth of Upper Hutt during the 1950s. Thérèse Gore collection

Gore's life became centred in Upper Hutt, where he continued to nurture aspiring young big-band players, using American methods. Gore did not talk about his time in America, but that – combined with his energy – gave him mana among young musicians, said Lewis. 'Freddie was a wonderful enthusiast but because of this unruly thing musically, the technicians of the town, and the teachers, just wrote him off. [But] to us he was some kind of guru.'[97]

By 1958 the man young musicians nicknamed 'Pappy G' saw the gap widening between his musical goals and the audience's needs. 'He'd had enough of the music scene, the late nights, the gigs, the whole thing', recalled his daughter Thérèse. So Gore pursued another goal: to become a farmer, in the warmer climate of the Far North.[98]

The days of zoot suits and conducting big bands with his trombone were in the distant past. Until his death in 1993, though, musicians from his heyday would venture north of Kaitaia to seek him out. 'Crazy, man, crazy.'[99]

The jazz and swing clubs that had been flourishing since the war were for the hardcore aficionados: several hundred people in the main centres who wanted to attend meetings where jam sessions took place, talks were given by experts, and records were played and discussed.[100] By 1951 the Auckland Swing Club had limited its membership to 700, while Wellington had over 200 members, and they both began organising formal concerts. 'Jazz for listening' became a catchphrase: this was not merely dance music.[101]

But the general public did just want to dance. Live music could be experienced at whichever tier suited one's needs. There were countless dance halls in the cities – as well as in the suburbs and the provinces. Town halls such as those in Dunedin and Lower Hutt held weekly dances, as did venues such as the Crystal Palace or Pirate Shippe in Auckland, the Empress and Roseland in Wellington, and the Mayfair and Union Rowing Club in Christchurch. The advantage that these had for the general public was that they were less formal than cabarets such as the Peter Pan or Majestic – a sports coat rather than a dinner suit was all that was required for men – and one could buy a ticket at the door rather than needing to purchase entry to an invitation-only ball. All of these venues featured name players: some on their way up, others who had already peaked. Even the Gaiety in Grey Lynn could boast 'the Julian Lee Orchestra, good prizes and supper' – madeira cake and sandwiches.[102]

Mary Throll, a singer with the Neville Carlsen Revue Company known as 'The Scottish Nightingale', also performed at venues such as the RSA, and the Cosmopolitan and Workingmen's clubs. In the early 1950s, more options became available: 'Nightclubs featuring floor shows were very much in vogue', she recalled. Her 40-minute turn – singing standards and nostalgic items, accompanied only by a pianist – offered variety to the patrons, and a simple solution for venue operators when the band needed a break. Throll's busy engagement book gave her an overview of inner-city musical nightlife in post-war Auckland: the Carlton Cabaret on Karangahape Road (Art Larkins band, with pianist Edgar Bendall), the

A Swing Club jam session at the Ritz, Auckland, c. 1947. From left, Des Blundell, Peter Lishman, Lew Campbell, George Campbell and Jim Foley. Jim Warren collection

Metropole on Upper Queen (Johnny Madden, with the Campbell Brothers), the Trocadero on the corner of Queen and Airedale (Len Hawkins's band, or the George Hatton Quartet), the Polynesian Club on Pitt and Beresford (Lou Mati), the Wintergarden beneath the Civic (Chips Healy), and the Peter Pan Cabaret on Rutland Street (Hugh Tatton and others). Also, Ted Croad held court at Newton Road's Orange on Wednesdays and Saturdays, Epi Shalfoon at the Crystal Palace in Mt Eden, and a young pianist called Benny Levin was settling in with his band at Bayswater, while launching his own agency, the Dancetime band bureau.[103]

The arrival of the Hi Diddle Griddle in 1952 introduced an alternative for cosmopolitan adults: a restaurant with live music. The owner was a man-about-town called Jim Jennings who had an obscure background: some thought he was an American expatriate, a South Pacific beachcomber who had 'washed ashore' after the war. Billy Farnell was certain he was from Tauranga. But he knew how to set up a room with class. Situated at 507 ('food from heaven') Karangahape Road, hospitality pioneer Otto Groen could be seen cooking in the window; chicken-in-a-basket made a change from colonial goose. On the dimly lit walls inside were black velvet murals of Polynesian maidens and a mythical Pacific, painted by Kristen Zambucka.[104]

The Hi Diddle Griddle had no dance floor but it had a tiny stage that showcased small combos led by Lew Campbell, Nancy Harrie and Crombie Murdoch. It would open late, and close even later – sometimes 4.00 am – and visiting musicians such as Nat King Cole might drop in. Late in the 1950s, Paul Lestre – a reed player and violinist from the East End of London – began a residency that led to the album *A Night at the Hi Diddle Griddle*, with Lyall Laurent, Bob Ofsoski and Ray Gunter. The Hi Diddle Griddle inspired many other venues offering food garnished with music: in town, the El Morocco, the Gourmet and the Arabian Theatre; out west, the Dutch Kiwi, the Back of the Moon and the Toby Jug.[105]

Vora Kissin was an early stalwart on piano at restaurants such as the Hi Diddle Griddle, Gourmet and La Bohème: the flexible employment allowed her to make several trips to the United States to explore the music scene. She moved to the US in the early 1960s, performing in New Orleans and Las Vegas during her eleven years there. On her arrival back, the *Auckland Star* hailed the return of 'New Zealand's outstanding jazz bar pianist'.[106]

In the dance halls and the cabarets, top musicians wanting to express themselves were hamstrung by the task for which they had been hired: customers were there to meet the opposite sex and to dance with them. But there were many opportunities for local artists to be heard as the main attraction, although the fare was usually middle-of-the-road. In concerts, on the commercial stations and on YA stations – outside of Bob Bothamley's influence – many cultural gatekeepers, tastemakers and promoters kept it comparatively conservative and wholesome: their standards were usually high and they avoided risk. A Wellington Town Hall variety show produced in 1950 by long-serving NZBS music manager Malcolm Rickard is an example. Rickard, in his private life a choral conductor and church organist, booked musicians who were often featured on radio – and were beginning to appear on the fledgling Tanza label. Backing the performers was a ten-piece 'variety orchestra' assembled by Henry Rudolph featuring local classical and dance-band players. Among them were popular pianist John Parkin, the Harmony Serenaders (a female quartet), the Tawharu Quintet, wartime star Jean McPherson with 'songs of the day' and 'hillbilly entertainer' Jack Christie.

These were among the best mainstream musical entertainers on offer when dancing was not the purpose. Another indication of the talent available, and the music establishment's sporadic encouragement beyond the middle-of-the-road, were the acts chosen to entertain New Zealand and Commonwealth troops serving in Korea. Ossie Cheesman led the first troupe, which left in September 1952 for a six-week tour, featuring music, comedy and variety items such as ventriloquism. Musicians on the tour were Coral Cummins, Martin Winiata (taking his saxophone, clarinet, guitar and ukulele) and comic vocalist Pat Otway. The scheme continued until 1955, the music contingent including singers Pat McMinn and Pauline Ashby (the latter in 'soubrette' style, as well as Maori action songs), Johnny Cooper, plus pianists Jean Kirk-Burnnand and Stewart Gordon (who claimed to be the only blind man to leave New Zealand in an army uniform). McMinn and Cooper went twice. 'We were under very trying circumstances', recalled McMinn, 'No privacy. But I was a tough cookie, brought up having to put up with things, so I was able to cope.' Cooper remembered his first tour stretching to six months, taking in Hong Kong, the Philippines, Australia and New Zealand; and also that McMinn 'went over solid with the troops – femininity of

Khaki-clad and Korea bound, 1955. From left: Johnny Cooper, Ces Morris, Pat McMinn, John Reidy and Jean Kirk-Burnnand. Pat McMinn collection

course'. On his second tour, in September 1955, the antics of Stewart Gordon won over the audiences. During the trip to Korea, the troupe's Qantas Constellation lost power in one engine while flying over the ocean. Gordon 'brought the house down', said Cooper, by glancing out the window and remarking 'I can't see any good place to crash land.'[107]

New Zealand's radio programmes were among the least offensive and most severely censored in the world. This was the proud boast of Fred Jones, the Minister of Broadcasting, in 1949. He was discussing radio serials such as *Dr Paul* and *Portia Faces Life*, which were studiously checked by NZBS officials in advance, with suspect material edited out, but the same went for radio's music programming. Specialist shows such as those run by Arthur Pearce on jazz and country, or Jim Foley on swing, were the exception.[108]

Commercial radio stalwart Ian Mackay later described the stultification of the ZBs from 1943, after the departure of Scrimgeour and the amalgamation of Broadcasting. With Shelley in charge, inevitably the power base was held by the non-commercial (YA) service. But when competition disappeared from the radio scene, said Mackay, the zest disappeared from Broadcasting.[109]

A Christmas variety show produced on 1ZB in 1951 gives an idea of the local acts acceptable to the programmers and the public: Ossie Cheesman's variety orchestra, the Duplicats vocal group, singers Pat McMinn and Stewart Harvey, and piano duo Nancy Harrie and John Thomson.

Broadcasting was required by legislation to present material that conformed to conservative standards of decency and taste. Outside of music, this resulted in an avuncular environment in which the on-air name of a top star was Aunt Daisy, and a long-running programme was run by Uncle Tom. Personality cults had been discouraged even before Scrimgeour fell out with the government, with corresponding upheavals. The Scrim saga had a lasting effect within Broadcasting: many working within the NZBS in the early 1950s had been employed there when the political pressure had come down on Scrim, so caution ruled. This applied to music as well, where several key staff members came from choral, church or classical backgrounds.

But they did see it as their role to encourage local talent. Although much of what was heard on radio in the late 1940s – the majority of the music, and the radio serials – came from overseas, there was 'considerable New Zealand programming as well'. As historian Patrick Day notes, 'there was a growing concern that New Zealanders needed a stronger presence on their nation's radio stations. This surfaced first with regard to music.' No matter what the style of station, music was 'the mainstay of all programmes', most of it from records released by the international record companies.[110]

There have always been demands, Day observes, that New Zealand broadcasting should feature more of the country's singers and musicians. In 1948 Labour MP Martin Finlay pointed out that the Australian government required 2.5 percent of broadcast time to be devoted to Australian compositions. Could New Zealand follow suit? The Broadcasting Minister thought not. 'He stated that the NZBS was always willing to broadcast work of acceptable standard and type by New Zealand authors and composers, and there was no difficulty in finding broadcasting time for the amount of such work available.'[111]

The key word is *acceptable*: the Minister's response reflected the policy that broadcasting was about excellence, 'and that such excellence was not readily available locally . . . . the concern remained in following years that insufficient opportunity to broadcast was given to New Zealand composers, authors and performers.'[112]

Lobbying for the local, wrote Mackay, made for good copy in the newspapers, or worthy gestures from politicians, but it did not guarantee good radio. 'There can only be one rule in broadcasting – the listeners require the highest standard be it in dramatic work or crooning, and they make no allowance for the home-grown product.'[113]

By the 1950s, when William Yates was director-general, the ZBs once again took precedence over the other, non-commercial stations. This left the YAs 'at a great disadvantage' in their programming of popular

Sid Vause, the founder of the *Lifebuoy Hit Parade*: his experience in popular music stretched from Edison cylinders to rock'n'roll. Photo News/RNZ Sound Archives

music, said Peter Downes. 'But we got around it and we played hit parade material. But not in any sort of competition with the ZB.'[114] In 1956 a radio critic said of the YAs: 'Its music falls between two stools, neither popular nor interesting.'[115] But, Downes points out, the YAs 'nonetheless attracted satisfyingly large audiences who preferred advertising-free programmes'.[116]

The godfather of pop radio in New Zealand began his career in the music business when radio meant little more than Morse code. Sid Vause's first job in Wellington was selling Edison cylinders and sheet music in a Lambton Quay store. The year was 1904, and the earliest hit he could recall was J. W. Myer's 'The Shade of the Old Apple Tree'. When he retired from the NZBS in 1953 – to launch Philips recording division in New Zealand – Nat King Cole's 'Too Young' had recently topped the ZB hit parade.

For half a century, Vause had witnessed the pivotal changes in the record business: the shift from cylinders

Opposite: A variety store window for the *Lifebuoy Hit Parade* encourages listeners to wash while they whistle. RNZ Sound Archives. Above: *Parade* pop pickers: Sid Vause, Rex Walden and Selwyn Toogood discuss selections for the *Lifebuoy Hit Parade*, late 1940s. Peter Downes collection

to discs, the accelerated global dissemination of popular songs after the First World War, the leap in quality once electrical recording arrived. All the while, he was developing the encyclopaedic musical memory for which he became renowned. His interests ranged from ragtime to rock'n'roll.

In 1928 it had been Vause's initiative to record 'Breeze (Blow My Baby Back to Me)' in Australia expressly for the New Zealand market, where it became a Yale Blues dance hit. At the time, he was the Wellington representative of the Columbia record company. It was at the urging of Vause – and Bill Bell-Booth, Columbia's man in Auckland – that the company sent over its portable equipment and a team of technicians from Sydney to record the Rotorua Maori Choir in 1930.[117]

But Vause's most influential idea came in 1946 when he instigated New Zealand radio's first hit parade, hosted by 2ZB announcer Rex Walden on the ZB stations. Best known as the *Lifebuoy* and – from January 1955 – the *Lever Hit Parade*, the programme was produced and recorded by its sponsor's advertising agency, Lintas. The *Hit Parade* was based on a simple but novel concept: to play the hit records each week, as chosen by the

programme's producers from the US charts in *Billboard*, the UK charts in the *New Musical Express* and overseas samples of the discs themselves. It would be years before pop music on radio was genuinely driven by popular demand, rather than by institutional approval. So the first steps were, naturally, cautious.

The *Listener*'s radio reporter reluctantly allowed the audience its right to hear the hits. 'Listeners to whom music is at its best only when it induces rhythmical foot-tapping, and tickles the ear with its novelty, may have half an hour of their favourite stimulus from any of the ZB stations by tuning in to the *Hit Parade* session at 8.00 pm every Tuesday.' While Selwyn Toogood became the most public voice of the programme, Vause was its ears. Each week he listened on shortwave to the US *Hit Parade* and took note of the popular songs; he also consulted trade publications that arrived by airmail. 'From what he hears, from his experience of dance music, and from intuition, he selects what he thinks will suit the New Zealand ZB *Hit Parade*.'[118]

By these means, the radio audience occasionally heard songs within 48 hours of their becoming hits in the US or Britain. Being popular overseas, however, did not automatically qualify a song for inclusion on the ZB

Hit Parade. Many were dropped because their content was meaningless to New Zealanders, or 'capable of appreciation only by those who like swing in its most extreme form'. Songs came from stage shows, or were the latest releases of the most popular singers. In 1946 a *Hit Parade* was likely to feature entries by the Andrews Sisters, Bing Crosby, Frank Sinatra, Dinah Shore or Kate Smith; another hit that year, 'Money is the Root of All Evil', was popularised by soldiers returning from the war who had heard Tessie O'Shea sing it in the London show *High Time*.

At first it was difficult to get the disparate elements of a fledgling music industry to play ball; Toogood later recalled: 'Apra often held up the copyright release on pop numbers, the record companies held them up, and publishers held them up because they couldn't get the sheet music out in time. This applied particularly to musicals. The classic example was *Oklahoma!* The records were released by the theatrical agency that held the rights about a week before the live show opened and it was not a howling financial success because people didn't know the tunes. Everybody was feeling their way, and pop music was nothing like the industry it is now.'[119]

Also slowing things down was the NZBS but to the *Lever Hit Parade*'s advantage: 'Broadcasting used to withhold the music for seven or eight weeks, it could not be played except in the *Lever Hit Parade*', said Toogood. 'Then as soon as they started to go down the *Lever Hit Parade* chart, they would be released to the ordinary programming. It was one of those things that made it a little more exclusive.'[120]

When the programme began in 1946, in an atmosphere of post-war austerity, perhaps it seemed appropriate to concentrate the latest pop tunes into 30 minutes of airtime a week (they could also be heard occasionally dotted throughout a day's schedule). But the *Hit Parade* would become a huge hit itself over the next nineteen years. The show was clean and the sponsors sold a lot of soap.

In 1952 the programme was in its sixth year on the ZBs. Its eclecticism could make it eccentric.[121] The selections were almost exclusively from overseas and family friendly: hillbillies need not apply, but could lobby request sessions at local stations, or do-si-do to Cotton-Eyed Joe's *Western Song Parade* on 2YD. Each year the *Hit Parade* ran a contest in which the audience chose their favourite songs broadcast by the programme in the previous year (from a list of sixteen, whittled down in advance by the producers). The eight most popular songs on the *Hit Parade* for 1952 were:

'Mockin' Bird Hill' – Mary Ford and Les Paul
'The Loveliest Night of the Year' – Mario Lanza
'On Top of Old Smoky' – The Weavers
'My Truly, Truly Fair' – Guy Mitchell and Orchestra
'Too Young' – Nat King Cole
'Beautiful Brown Eyes' – Rosemary Clooney
'Sweet Violets' – Dinah Shore
'The Roving Kind' – Guy Mitchell and Chorus[122]

As teenagers became a key market for record companies, increasingly the show included material oriented towards this burgeoning consumer group. For them, it was like church. In the mid-1950s, Justin du Fresne, later a pioneer pop DJ, was a young teenager living in Hastings.

> The house where I boarded had a daughter about my age. We were both into this music, so each week we would get up close to the radio to listen to the *Lever Hit Parade*. We never missed it. 'Cross Over the Bridge', 'Three Coins in a Fountain' . . . it was all there was. In the programme, you might get one piece of music in the half-hour that we'd call a pop record. Apart from that, there was no dedicated showcase for pop.[123]

Actually, there was an alternative in the early 1950s, although teenagers weren't the target audience. In 1952 the *New Zealand Hit Parade* was launched on 2YA, using votes compiled by five regional stations from their local hit parades, which were assembled from voting cards filled in at record stores. In Wellington, 2YA programmer Peter Downes would aggregate the scores and prepare the playlist for the programme, which reflected New Zealanders' reactions to overseas songs, especially those featured in films currently screening. It was not scientific: the voting system was crude and favoured visitors to record stores (ironically, usually teenagers). In addition, the results needed to be songs that could be played on 2YA. But the programme did allow for the occasional local recording to emerge, sometimes with an encouraging nudge from radio programmers.

One example was Esme Stephens' 'Between Two Trees', an American song she recorded for Stebbing's in Auckland. The song was not a hit in the US, but received such regular airplay on New Zealand's non-commercial stations that it almost inevitably became a hit, eventually selling over 7000 copies. 'It was a put-up job, really', recalled Downes, 'because we played it so often people couldn't get away from it.'[124] The affirmative action came from belief in the

GOLDEN EARS

Truth's headline was from the 'believe it or not' file: *Traffic Officer Stared; Driver Was Blind*. The driver was indeed blind, and had been since birth. Nothing seemed insurmountable for multi-instrumentalist Julian Lee. When hired early in his career by Auckland band leader and Musicians' Union president Bert Peterson, it seemed Lee's arrival would put several musicians out of work: 'He only plays alto, tenor, trumpet, trombone, drums, bass, piano and piano-accordion, but he makes up for this by singing the vocals.'[125]

'My ears have been my salvation', Lee once said. Many musicians would say that Lee's ears were their salvation, also. Golden Ears was his nickname: Lee was able to pick up small errors in a performance before anybody else was aware of them, even the musician who made the mistake. Besides his musical abilities, Lee was renowned for his humour and his extraordinary aural memory.[126]

Born in Dunedin in 1923, Lee was four years old when the band from the Jubilee Institute for the Blind visited from Auckland and let him beat the bass drum. 'And I

Julian Lee, 1953: 'I'd like a chat with you', said Sinatra. RNZ Sound Archives

thought I was something', he recalled. Within a year he would be living at the Institute, a 48-hour journey from home by train and boat. 'I was five. Too early. It was kind of scary, but it was a great place.' At six he began lessons with Vivienne Martin, one of the Institute's music teachers: 'A very fine blinded lady. She broke me into music gently.' She taught him the piano and how to read Braille music. He also learnt how to avoid her raps on the knuckles when he was naughty. 'My hands weren't there, and of course she landed on the piano with rather a hefty blow.'[127]

Lee became a member of the Institute's brass band, which had been founded in 1927, and its dance band. For 30 years the bands raised thousands of pounds for the Institute through their concerts and national tours. Its most prominent leader was Captain George Bowes, fondly referred to as the General. Gifted musically – he also led the band of the Auckland Regiment's First Battalion – Bowes transcribed countless scores using a Stainsby Braille writer. His players remembered his smell – Steradent – his gifts of broken biscuits and apples, and his advice when touring: 'Keep your head clear, your feet warm and your bowels open.'[128]

Julian Lee was aged 12 when he toured New Zealand for three months with the Jubilee Institute for the Blind band in 1935. He is pictured here in the front row, at the far right. George 'The General' Bowes, the bandmaster, is third from left in the same row. Royal New Zealand Foundation of the Blind

Julian Lee on saxophone at the Auckland Swing Club, late 1940s, with drummer Neil Dunningham, bassist Thomson Yandall and pianist Crombie Murdoch. Dennis Huggard collection

Lee was touring with the bands when he was eleven, playing cornet. 'I was one of those prodigy, obnoxious little bastards, that knew everything and probably didn't know it. I was fairly thorough in the [music] knowledge I had, so I was usually pretty right. But when you look back on it, you don't think much of kids like that.'

Returning to Dunedin in 1938 he was billed at the Empire cinema as 'Master Julian Lee, at the console of the mighty Christie Organ'. Walter Sinton recalled him playing for a show that required two pianos. His partner Jean Kirk-Burnnand needed a light for her piano, so Lee insisted on one as well.[129] He became part of the 4ZB 'radio family', performing requests in the children's session; as a DJ, operating his own equipment; and reading the scripts he had written in Braille. He starred in

a programme called *Stump Julian Lee*, in which he was given the name of a song and was expected to perform it live-to-air. 'There were 250 tunes and I think I played about 225 of them. Some of them I had never heard of, I think they were made up.'

He played trumpet and tenor sax in Dick Colvin's band, broadcasting live on Friday nights, and playing at Joe Brown's Town Hall dances. By the early 1940s, he was heading north: a year in Wanganui playing dances with Maori musicians from Ratana pa, a stint in Wellington playing trumpet with Fred Gore on 2YA and Lauri Paddi at the Majestic, and piano at Jimmy James's Roseland cabaret. He was wooed back to Auckland in 1945, playing almost every night of the week with the bands of Bert Peterson, Ted Croad and Epi Shalfoon, and with the 1YA

rep.[131] In September 1952, he was appointed the musical director at Stebbing's, arranging and producing countless sessions by artists such as Esme Stephens and Mavis Rivers, as well as his own recordings.

Lee moved to Australia in 1956, playing piano for a hotel chain until he started writing arrangements for ABC radio, contracted by expatriate New Zealander Jim Gussey. Television and radio commercials followed, then he became the staff arranger at Channel 7 for four years. Visiting musicians such as George Shearing and Winifred Atwell, impressed by his talents, tried to woo him overseas without success.

It was at a Sydney cocktail party in 1962 that Frank Sinatra came over and tapped Lee on the shoulder. 'I'd like a chat with you', he said. 'Come backstage this evening before the show, we can talk while the support act is on.' Lee borrowed the lead trumpeter's instrument to get past security and, in his dressing room, Sinatra said, 'I've heard some of your things, I want you to come over to the States. You have to do that, because you're a talent we want to foster.' Lee replied, 'Well, what senor commands, I must do.'[132]

In 1963 Lee left for the States with his Dunedin-born wife, Elaine, who had become his musical amanuensis. Although he never worked for Sinatra, many doors were opened for him by that contact, and sessions with Chet Baker, Harry Edison and Gerry Mulligan and many others followed. Stan Kenton conducted a concert with all the arrangements written by Lee. He became a staff producer at Capitol Records, but in 1974 when the first oil crisis lifted the costs of the record business, those working in the less fashionable areas of music were let go. After four years back in New Zealand, during which he worked at the Blind Institute and was a stalwart in the Neophonic Jazz Orchestra and on radio, Lee returned to Australia.[133] Among his last hit records were two albums he produced for Ricky May in the late 1980s, singing jazz standards.

Lee regarded his blindness as a great advantage: 'I got all the musical training early in my life, which I wouldn't have been able to afford had I been a sighted person.' And with his talents, he was never short of work. 'One door opens, another slams in your face', he joked.

radio band. Within a couple of years, he took his first opportunity to lead the radio band, experimenting with 'semi-sweet' arrangements that featured three violins. By 1950 Lee was adept at bebop, quickly becoming one of Auckland's leading exponents. At the landmark concert at Auckland's Concert Chamber in August that year, he played alto sax throughout the night as part of the core band, plus a virtuoso showcase in 'Messin' Around', soloing on tenor, trombone and trumpet. The *New Zealand Herald*'s reviewer also noted Lee's 'excellent line of sombre waggishness'.[130]

The breadth of Lee's talent seemed limitless. At the jam session to welcome home the Kiwis that winter, he was 'the hero of the hour', playing piano in a dixieland band. His influence was felt by players around the city. He could be heard on air playing popular songs with his group the Electrotones (with vocalist Esme Stephens) or standards with his Quartet (with Mavis Rivers), and alto with Bob Leach's radio band. 'No matter how you like your music – sweet, hot, jive or bop – it's all in a day's work to Julian Lee', wrote Alan Siddall, Auckland drummer and HMV

HMV pop pickers Dave Van Weede (left) and Ray Isaacs, at the company's Wakefield Street factory, Wellington, May 1957. Photographed by Morrie Hill. 1/2-177241, Alexander Turnbull Library, Wellington

song, the quality of the performance, the fact that lush love ballads were in vogue – and that the artist was local.

How true to public taste was the 2YA *New Zealand Hit Parade*? 'It's as authentic as we can make it', said Downes in 1952. 'It's true locally for the districts covered by the five stations who send their results to us, and in that respect it does show something of the trend throughout New Zealand.'[134] To Downes – looking back over 50 years later – it was a relief that the programme ceased before rock'n'roll became popular. 'Otherwise there would have been some very awful decisions to be made, it would not have happened. Up to that point, there was nothing offensive or so-called offensive in any of the pop material. It was Jo Stafford and Guy Mitchell and the rest of them and that was fine.'[135]

But the non-commercial stations had only a small section of the radio audience, and most of it was of an older age group. The regional stations – virtually self-contained before networking – were similarly conservative, if a little

eccentric, with their parish-pump duties and steam-radio facilities. Alwyn Owen, at 1YZ Rotorua in the early 1950s, described a typical music mix: 'Jo Stafford, Bing Crosby, the Ink Spots, Carmen Cavallaro, Rawicz and Landauer, Evelyn Knight, Anne Ziegler and Webster Booth, Patti Page, Mantovani and his orchestra . . . until, destroying the comfortable sleepiness of the pop music scene for ever, Bill Haley and the Comets.'[136]

It was the ZBs that really mattered, with 80 percent of the radio audience of 500,000 people. Airplay on the *Lifebuoy/Lever Hit Parade* became crucial to record companies, especially local independents. At HMV, sales manager Dave Van Weede made his decisions about what to release on the same sources as the *Hit Parade* compilers: overseas music magazines. They would then rush to get the master tapes and press and release a song here so that it coincided with airplay on the ZB *Hit Parade*.

'Radio was under the control of the New Zealand Broadcasting Service', recalled Van Weede, 'and I think they had a rule at one stage that no record could be played more than once in any one day. So the chance of developing a hit by having it repeated was virtually nil. We used to try and get our records played on the *Lever Hit Parade* . . . . there were ten discs played, so if you could get your record on that hit parade, then you were made.'[137]

As more record distributors entered the market, the pressure increased on the sales reps to secure some scarce airplay. With Broadcasting's stringent policies to avoid commercial influence – all records had to be ordered, and paid for – opportunities for lobbying were limited. But lobby they did, said Van Weede: 'You could socialise, and of course a lot of the radio announcers I knew. I'd certainly go and have a beer with them, and privately we would play records and they would enjoy it. But then they had a job too and were acting under very strict rules.'

HMV had the best catalogue in the world from which to choose new releases, but it could only cope with a limited number, either as imports or made at their own pressing plant. Like their Australian colleagues, they wanted to maximise their profits on fewer releases. There were many records that were hits overseas that were never released in New Zealand, and the two months it took records to arrive by boat gave the independent labels an opportunity to make covers of some of them. With so few pop songwriters in New Zealand, and programmers in Broadcasting monitoring what was successful overseas, cover versions were more likely to receive airplay, and consequently dominated New Zealand recording for many years.

At Tanza, John Shears developed a canny way of generating sales. Through his contacts who managed cinemas, he would find out which hit songs featured in forthcoming films that had not received any radio play. He would then recommend titles to Noel Peach for possible recordings. Before they could go ahead, Shears had to get permission from local publishing representatives such as Alberts, Chappell and Southern. 'I used to punt and print labels sometimes before we had that, it was a bit of a dangerous game. But that's the way it was, you used to have to go like stink. A few labels down the gurgler didn't really matter that much, it didn't happen very often.'

At this stage, films were not released nationwide simultaneously but were staggered through the country. This gave Shears time to get his recordings done and marketing plans in order. 'It was pretty easy: get the music, get the guys in, and do it. Put a cover version on the back

we may have had sitting around for a while, do a silkscreen and some posters for the windows, have something to go in the lobby in the theatre . . . . that's how we did it, time and time again.'[138]

Murdoch Riley experienced both sides of the fence. As purchasing officer for the NZBS after Sid Vause left, Riley supplied Toogood with material for the *Hit Parade*. 'Sometimes there would be disputes over what would be provided. Then I might say, "Well I don't think we should be using that version, this is the one that's popular overseas. And there you were getting into politics a little bit. I did my best to promote local versions if I could, but of course when HMV had the top version, what we did was, you'd play the overseas one and then slip in the local one for the odd week, so it got a place. But you couldn't really deny the top version entirely, the whole time.'

It was a balancing act. As part of the public service, the NZBS was determined to be above board, and to avoid being used by private companies for commercial promotions. Among the staff there was also the desire to be fair to local releases, but not to the extent of damaging the programme through playing inferior cover versions. 'You did feel a sense of power', recalled Riley, 'that you had control over what happened to somebody's product. I don't believe I abused it. I wasn't told not to promote product but I used my common sense. I didn't want a rocket from above, either. I did turn things down on technical grounds. Musically if I could possibly promote local artists, I'd do so.'[139]

In 1954, when Riley left NZBS to go to 'private enterprise', *New Zealand Truth* gave a salute: 'He has brought the local *Hit Parade* as far up to date with those in America and Britain as possible, in view of the delay in getting the discs here.' He joined Tanza, and later launched Viking Records, and so found himself lobbying Broadcasting from the outside. He achieved success in 1957 with his first release for Viking, the Q-Tees' smooth cover of 'Little Darlin''; like the Keil Isles' version of 'The Twist', it was a rare case of a local version eclipsing an R&B original (before Pat Boone had a go). 'The R&B version was not as attractive to a New Zealand audience', said Riley.

By the late 1950s, the programme's success led to a proliferation of similar hit parades on regional stations, which listeners in other centres could receive. The amount of contemporary pop on New Zealand radio was slowly inching ahead.[140]

1950-1959

The early local pop recording industry was dominated by three American genres. Female singers and male vocal groups performed mainstream pop, a wave of recording in a faux-Hawaiian style occurred, and a posse of country and western artists arrived. On the live scene, big bands still featured in cabarets and ballrooms, while in Auckland the Maori Community Centre was a Mecca for aspiring talent.

Hawaiian music's long popularity in New Zealand had begun in 1911, and a key part of the attraction of 'Blue Smoke' in 1949 was its use of the steel guitar. In Auckland, the style was led by two Tongan steel-guitar players who became stalwarts of the live and recording scenes: Bill Sevesi and Bill Wolfgramm. Daphne Walker, a Maori from Great Barrier Island, was the most prominent singer, and it was Sam Freedman – a Russian Jewish songwriter based in Wellington – who wrote the biggest local hits.

Country and western has a history in New Zealand that is almost as long, and evolved from recordings and film. Country recordings by US acts were available in New Zealand in the late 1920s, and western films also inspired those wanting to emulate the cowboy sound (and look). New Zealand's earliest prominent country artist, Tex Morton, remains the most influential. Radio also spread the popularity of country music, through request shows, live broadcasts from regional stations, and specialist shows hosted by Happi Hill and Cotton-Eye Joe (Arthur Pearce). Also important was a square-dancing fad in the early 1950s. The new independent labels jumped onto the country bandwagon immediately, with Tanza finding wide acceptance for the Tumbleweeds, who toured nationally. Otherwise, solo singers dominated the early country scene, so there was little of the interaction seen in jazz and dance bands. It was as if they heard a lonesome whistle while mustering on distant paddocks and practised their yodelling in isolation.

Maori pop music was nurtured at the Maori Community Centre in Auckland's Freemans Bay. Here, the families of the urban migration of the 1940s and 1950s met, mingled and made music. Its stage was an on-going talent quest and proving ground for a diverse array of acts, such the Howard Morrison Quartet, Lou and Simon, and the young Kiri Te Kanawa. It also helped establish many of the Maori showbands that later flourished overseas. For many careers in pop music, the road leads back to the Maori Community Centre.

Opposite: In 1962 Auckland's Maori Community Centre was peaking as a gathering place for Maori – young and old – who had moved to the city in the previous 15 years. *Te Ao Hou* magazine commissioned photographer Ans Westra to capture the Centre's rich musical life. Friday nights would attract 500 dancers, and on Sunday nights, 1000 people enjoyed talent quests that featured many future stars. Ans Westra

Cowboy's dream: the Tumbleweeds perform for a Dunedin audience, and for 4ZB listeners, from a temporary exhibition studio, c. 1949. Campbell Photography/RNZ Sound Archives

Canaries and Cowboys 1950s Pop Scenes

By the early 1950s, local singers were competing in record stores against overseas performers like Rosemary Clooney, Patti Page and Dinah Shore. In Auckland, vocalists such as Dorothy Brannigan, Pat McMinn, Mavis Rivers and Esme Stephens were starting to make headway with their releases on Tanza and Stebbing. One Auckland retailer reported to *New Zealand Truth* in 1953 that sales of local records had more than doubled, and were now running neck-and-neck with their overseas rivals.[1]

For those who followed local pop music, there even seemed to be a small-scale star system developing. Thanks to radio play – much of it live broadcasts with dance bands, or recorded jingles, rather than 78s – some young women singers were almost becoming household names. To fans, wrote a *New Zealand Listener* reporter, they were known as 'chicks' or 'canaries', although for those who did not venture to the cabarets, it was difficult to put a face to the voice. Mavis Rivers was the most polished of the class of 1952, said the reporter: always at ease with a song or a band, she was 'hep to the beat and does a fast bounce tune as well'. Her 78s could be heard on Auckland jukeboxes, and sold to 'collectors and kids'. Even Mavis's sisters – Natalie, Sally and Mitzi – became a recording act, releasing five 78s on Tanza as the Rivers Sisters.

DANCING IN MY SOCKS

In each main centre, a female singer was prominent, on the wireless and on cabaret stages. Usually this led to recording work as well, even for those outside Auckland. With Marion Waite temporarily back in the US, she missed out on the early 1950s boom in recording. After the initial burst by Pixie Williams, Wellington's main contribution came from Jean McPherson, who recorded for Tanza and HMV in the twilight of her career. The two Tanza discs are charming if contradictory: the follow-up to 1951's 'I Don't Wanna Be Kissed' was 'Kisses and Affection'.

In Christchurch, Coral Cummins was a household name, especially through her work with Martin Winiata. 'She sings with a cozy, intimate jauntiness', said the *Listener*, her voice coming out of the radio 'as personal and intimate as a kiss from your fiancée'.[2] Cummins was always elegant, whether in rehearsal – all in black, with a string of pearls – or in flowing satin ballgowns on stage. She began singing in her teens and during the war was appearing with the bands of Brian Marston and Winiata. The residency with Winiata – at the Union Rowing Club on the banks of the Avon – made them a drawcard right into the 1950s. Cummins was also regularly featured on 3YA with the studio bands, and ventured up to Auckland for a year to appear at the Peter Pan and Metropole with Art

Coral Cummins broadcasts over 3ZB, Christchurch, with band leader Brian Marston on trombone.
E. M. Alderdice Collection, PA1-q-182-28, Alexander Turnbull Library, Wellington

Rosoman. 'Coral's hip style is just what is needed to do full justice to [the] fine Rosoman arrangements', said *Jukebox* in 1946.[3]

In Dunedin, Leone Maharey began as a child singing in the competitions and on radio, before becoming the featured vocalist in Dick Colvin's band on 4YA. The band regularly played Joe Brown's Town Hall dances, where her future husband and singing partner, Dave Maharey, was a 'crooner'. The ZBs took Leone on a national tour, and after the war she sang with clarinettist Keith Harris's group the Rhythmaires. In 1951 the Mahareys recorded a duet for Tanza, 'Perimpo Perampo' backed with (b/w) 'Don't Sing Aloha'. The *Listener* commented, 'With Leone the tune always comes first and the feeling that puts the tune across; after that the frills. In a word she's a torch singer.'[4]

But Auckland had the stars whose names resonated for years: Mavis Rivers and Esme Stephens, ostensibly rivals at Tanza and Stebbing, and Pat McMinn, dedicated to pop. Stephens was the first to become prominent, when she sang with Artie Shaw's band during its visit in 1943. She had been singing pop songs since childhood, accompanying herself on the piano when she should have been practising her scales. 'In fact, she liked to sing all the time, at home, at school, and at her first job in an Auckland store.' A part-time musician working at the store suggested she audition for Theo Walters, who needed a vocalist for his Friday night *Band Wagon* show on 1ZB. When his contract ran out, there was no shortage of work: Stephens sang with the bands of Len Hawkins, Fred Gore, Art Rosoman and her future husband, Dale Alderton. She described herself as 'strictly a commercial singer', and 'a nervous one at that'. Perhaps because of her modesty, said the *Listener*, 'her warm love of singing comes through very satisfactorily and makes the customers feel warm, too'.

Stephens was the vocalist on HMV's first release by New Zealanders, the Latin-flavoured 'You Can in Yucatan'. Her biggest solo hit came in 1951, 'Between Two Trees', which sold over 7000 copies and was often featured on 2YA's *Hit Parade*; her best seller was a collaboration with the Duplicats, 'Mockin' Bird Hill', which had already sold 6000 copies before the original version by Les Paul and Mary Ford had arrived from overseas.[5] Besides Stephens, this vocal group featured Alderton, Ena Allen and pianist John Thomson, modernising pre-war popular songs such as 'If You Knew Susie'. The group was soon in demand for its 'old songs in new dresses', some in the style of Spike Jones.[6]

Alderton described Stephens as 'a romantic singer, who liked Rosemary Clooney and Ella Fitzgerald, of course, all those marvellous singers: it was part of her in-built repertoire'. She died suddenly in 1992, aged 68, within a week of her 1950s contemporary, Mavis Rivers. Forty years earlier, the pair had released a duet for Stebbing's Zodiac label: 'Ya Got the Makin's of Love' b/w 'Promises'.[7]

Of the top three female vocalists, Rivers and Stephens concentrated on sophisticated pop, aimed at adults, while the other member of the triumvirate became best known for her novelty songs. Pat McMinn, an accomplished singer during the war while still in her teens, was probably New Zealand's busiest vocalist in the early 1950s. In fact, she had never stopped singing professionally since winning the Dixieland's talent quest in 1943, aged fifteen. After five years at the Trocadero came another six singing for Ted Croad's big band at the Orange, where she met her first husband, drummer Eddie Croad. During an evening at the Orange, a trio of McMinn's Astor collaborators would support her singing a bracket of her latest Tanza hits. 'We would make a feature of doing them while they were on the hit parade', said McMinn. The audience would stop dancing and stand in front of the stage, watching.[8]

McMinn released more than 25 sides for Tanza, including several of the label's biggest hits. Her first recording was on 'Choo'n Gum', as vocalist for John MacKenzie and the Astor Dixie Boys.[9] Besides her biggest hit, 1956's 'Opo the Crazy Dolphin', her other successes included 'Bimbo' (on which she duetted with herself, thanks to Peach's over-dubbing), 'Dancing in My

A few days after the Tangiwai disaster, Pat McMinn performs at Whangamata, late December 1953; Colin Martin on saxophone. Pat McMinn collection

Socks' and 'Just Another Polka'. 'Mr Tap Toe' was also a hit in Australia: McMinn's version was on the market there before Doris Day's. She learnt it from sheet music, parcels of which were still arriving from the US, sent by the mother of the GI she befriended during the war.

Stan Dallas regarded McMinn as the finest vocalist Noel Peach recorded in Auckland: she was always in tune, and brought drive to every song.[10] All her recordings are sprightly, even 'Bell Bottom Blues'. McMinn's success at novelty songs meant she rarely got the opportunity to record adult material, like torch ballads. Instead, she was given 'I Want a Hippopotamus for Christmas' (b/w 'Too Fat for the Chimney').

MAVIS, SING!

Her voice took her from Apia to Las Vegas, but the six years during which Mavis Rivers was Auckland's leading singer were crucial to her career – and the fledgling New Zealand pop industry. Rivers, whose pure voice managed to combine subtlety and confidence, would record with Frank Sinatra, stand in for Ella Fitzgerald at her request, and perform regularly with the bands of Benny Goodman and Red Norvo. Before that, however, came a busy apprenticeship of which her international fans were largely unaware.

Mavis Rivers in Hollywood, 1959. Fairfax Media Sundays Archive

From 1947 until she left for the United States in 1953, Rivers was the queen of Auckland's pop vocalists, flitting between gigs at the Peter Pan and Orange ballrooms to recording sessions for Tanza and Stebbing's. By day she was a stenographer at Farmers Trading Company, often falling asleep over her typewriter after getting home at two in the morning. As a shy nineteen-year-old she impressed her co-workers when she picked up the sheet music of a song she hadn't heard, 'Mona Lisa', and started singing.[11]

Mavis was one of thirteen musical children born to Moody and Louisa Rivers in Apia, Western Samoa, in 1929. Moody was an alto sax player in a dance band with his brothers. Once a week he organised Family Night, at which every child was expected to perform an item, culminating in a finale featuring all fifteen members of the Rivers family. As a girl, Mavis went everywhere with a ukulele, and her grandmother encouraged her to perform for women's clubs. 'Mavis, sing! [But] I was singing before they asked. I was destined to sing.'[12]

When she was twelve the Rivers family moved to Pago Pago, American Samoa, and soon the harbour was full of US warships; hundreds of tents were pitched near her home, sheltering the troops. She began singing with her father's band – 'I loved big bands with a passion' – and became a favourite of the Americans. Still in her early teens, she was almost a mascot, travelling from camp to camp singing several shows a week. For the marines based in outlying areas, a special hookup was arranged using the telephone system linked to camp intercoms.[13]

The family moved to Auckland in 1947, settling in Grey Lynn. It was guitarist Tommy Kahi who first spotted her talent when she sang with a Mormon choir in Auckland. 'She had this one bar and I thought, Gee, what a voice. I went back and said, "Was that you? Look love, I'm having a jazz show tonight, would you sing?" . . . "Yes, I'd love to."' At the rehearsal Kahi introduced her to George Campbell, Frank Gibson and Derek Heine. 'I said, "Look, you guys, I'd like you to back this young lady" . . . . She sang about eight numbers, and once she sang "How High the Moon", the boys were rapt.'[14]

Mavis Rivers with Crombie Murdoch, Auckland, c. 1950: 'I was destined to sing'. Dennis Huggard collection

After meeting Noel Peach at Astor Studios, work quickly followed: jingles, nightclubs, radio bands, record releases. At the Auckland Swing Club she met Crombie Murdoch and soon she was singing 'The Coffee Song' at the Peter Pan with his group. 'We were all very impressed . . . . Like all good vocalists she almost invariably got her lyrics wrong but the thing that always struck us about her was her natural musical ability and perfect diction.'

At Astor in 1949, Rivers was commissioned by Warner Brothers to record four songs from the film *My Dream is Yours* – 'I'll String Along with You', 'Canadian Capers', 'Someone Like You' and the theme song. These became Peach's first productions for Tanza. 'Mavis was a wonderful little trouper', Peach said later, 'and she could accept direction when necessary – not that she needed teaching, for she was a born singer.'[15]

Rivers became Tanza's leading vocalist, recording over 40 sides for the label. Among them were pop novelties ('Choc'late Ice Cream Cone', 'Candy and Cake'), lush ballads ('Too Young', 'At the End of the Day'), jazz standards (a delicate version of 'How High the Moon' with guitarist Mark Kahi), and the requisite Polynesian romances ('Farewell Samoa', 'Fijian Holiday' and even 'The Maori Way'). She broadcast on 1YA and 1YD with the radio dance bands and with Nancy Harrie's Quartet on the show *Around the Town*. Harrie later said, 'I was completely captivated by Mavis's voice and her strong sense of rhythm.' Together they recorded the novelty 'Aba Daba Honeymoon', in which a chimpanzee falls in love with a monkey.

A more celebrated session took place on 1 February 1950, when Duke Ellington's former trumpeter Rex

TANZA
Z98

FAREWELL SAMOA
(Nelson)
MAVIS RIVERS
with Bill Wolfgramm and His Rhythm
Recorded by Astor Recording
Studios, Auckland.

RECORDING CORPORATION OF NEW ZEALAND

Dennis Huggard Archive, MSD10-0538, Alexander
Turnbull Library, Wellington

Stewart was in Auckland for a brief stopover. He was persuaded to enter the Astor Studios to back Rivers recording 'I'm in the Mood for Love'. Harrie, also on the session, said, 'Rex prophesied quite a future for Mavis, but even he never realised how far she'd go.' Stewart's endorsement did not come cheaply: after the session, when asked if he wanted a fee, instead of just suggesting a standard union rate, he replied, 'You can give me £50 if you like.' Peach and the Tanza musicians, stunned by the massive amount, could only respond by having a whip around.[16]

In August, Rivers had the starring role with Auckland's top players at the city's 'first' jazz concert; she had been singing professionally for little over a year. But there was always a plan: to get experience, then go to the States. When Rivers moved there in 1953 – to a secretarial scholarship at the Brigham Young University at Provo, Utah – the Auckland papers said she was destined for the Mormon Tabernacle Choir. She took part in Salt Lake City's limited entertainment scene, including television appearances, but had to leave the US when her student visa ran out.

After six months back in Samoa – where she worked as 'girl Friday' and disc jockey on the island's only radio station – she returned to the States in January 1955 as an immigrant, determined to have a singing career. In Los Angeles, as a singer and guitarist, she joined a Hawaiian band named the Johnny Ukulele Quartet. Rivers did not share the musical tastes of its virtuoso leader, but met her future husband, the bass player David Catingub.

Rivers put her singing on hold while she had two sons until, in 1958, some friends encouraged her to make a demo tape and found her an agent. Two weeks after approaching Capitol Records, Rivers had a deal: the company's A&R man made his decision after hearing only eight bars of her voice. 'I was such a *greenhorn*, so overwhelmed by this', Rivers said in 1990. 'And they asked what I wanted to do, and I said I'd give my right arm to record with Nelson Riddle. "Let's ask!", they said.'

A legend for his productions earlier in the 1950s for Frank Sinatra, Riddle agreed. At the first recording session at the Capitol Tower studios in Hollywood, when Rivers heard the orchestra strike up, she started to sing, then sat down and wept. 'All of a sudden I was thinking of my dad. Look at me! I'm big time, recording with Nelson Riddle! We did one number and then the string players applauded with their bows. So I started crying again.'[17]

A glittering US career followed for Rivers: three albums with Capitol; several more with Sinatra's label, Reprise; and a residency at his hotel at Lake Tahoe. Riddle described her as having 'the authority of a poised nightclub singer, the beat of a jazz vocalist, and the expressiveness of a girl who really feels what she sings. What's more, she combines these qualities in a professional style that comes to very few. I think she's just great.'[18]

From the late 1970s Rivers returned several times to perform in New Zealand, often in a band led by her son, saxophonist Matt Catingub. She died in 1992, aged 63, shortly after a performance in Los Angeles. Frank Sinatra allegedly described her as having the 'purest voice' in jazz, comparing her to Ella Fitzgerald.[19] Rivers once acknowledged, 'I guess I'm up there with the Sarahs, Ellas and Carmens. At least, that's what they tell me.' But, she said, the best thing to happen to a singer is when people stop saying you sound like someone else. 'After a while you want them to say, "D'you know that singer? I think she's been listening to you."'[20]

But McMinn always sang with a smile, and had the last laugh when a frippery she recorded in just one hour was broadcast every day for nearly 40 years on Auckland radio stations. It was a jingle about false teeth, which became as familiar as a playground chant to several generations of Auckland school children:

> Broke my denture, broke my denture
> Woe is me, what can I do?
> Take it in to Mr Geddes
> And he'll fix it, just like new.
>
> What's the address, what's the address?
> Hurry please and tell me do.
> Top of Queen Street, on the corner
> And the number's 492.

Geddes Dental Renovation clinic was in the same block as the Metropole, just 100 yards away from the original Dixieland (which had been built on the profits of Frederick Rayner's denture empire). Written to the tune of 'Clementine', the jingle has lyrics attributed to Mrs Geddes.[21] It featured Astor Studio's top session musicians of the day – George Campbell, Nancy Harrie, Lee Humphreys and character actor Athol Coates, plus McMinn – all on their way to the annual Musicians' Union ball. Forever more, McMinn fielded requests to sing it, especially at parties.[22]

Usually, McMinn's sunny pop songs were accompanied by the honky-tonk piano of Crombie Murdoch. But the person tickling the ivories on 'Broke My Dentures' was the most successful female session musician in New Zealand: pianist Nancy Harrie.

With Noel Peach energetically recording at Astor, many other Auckland women made it to disc. Dorothy Brannigan began as a violinist, in a family that contained its own chamber group, giving camp concerts during the war as the Diggle String Quartette. Church choir and light opera performances led to radio work on 1ZB, as a vocalist with John MacKenzie and Maurice Tansley, and as a violinist with the station's orchestra and dance band. She released more than twenty sides with Tanza, many of them smooth, country–pop duets with Buster Keene (the pseudonym of the Knaves' Doug Mowbray).

John MacKenzie with vocalist Maurice Tansley, 1ZB studio, Auckland, early 1950s. RNZ Sound Archives

Ellen Vann, born in the Netherlands, was a cabaret singer in Europe before emigrating to New Zealand in 1951. RNZ Sound Archives

Brannigan had a warm, confident voice with clear enunciation that, in her duets, conveyed farm-girl wholesomeness rather than a knowing sassyness. While the trained exactness of her tone keeps her solo ballads earnest, the duets benefit from a subtle humour. In 'Free Home Demonstration' she invites Keene to 'take advantage of this opportunity', which he does in their combined chorus: 'It's a little bit of hug, and a little bit of squeeze, a little bit of kiss and a little bit of tease – guaranteed to make you fall in love.' The pair's biggest hit was a cover of 'Seven Lonely Days', a juxtaposition of pathos and parody, in which a forlorn woman is comforted by her former lover in the chorus: 'Oh my darling you're crying, boo hoo hoo hoo . . .'. But she was perhaps best known for her cover version of the song that epitomised the sanitised novelty pop of the early 1950s: 'Doggie in the Window'.

A local hit in 1953, the barking 'Doggie' was another duet, in which Brannigan was joined by young Tanza singer Mary Feeney. Discovered by Noel Peach at a talent quest, Feeney was just seventeen and working as a machinist when she made her recording debut, 'Half as Much'. She also came from a church choir background, and her light,

pure soprano always conveyed this, especially on the Coronation-oriented double, 'In a Golden Coach' b/w 'The Windsor Waltz'. *Truth* commented that Feeney 'still seems slightly overawed with the whole recording business . . . small and dainty and completely unsophisticated'.[23]

Ellen Vann's formal training was revealed on her local debut, 'Love's Roundabout' b/w 'Longing for You' – despite Julian Lee's heavy-handed production, which featured a ghostly choir and Wurlitzer organ. But the Dutch immigrant, who came to New Zealand in 1951, had solid credentials as a cabaret singer in Europe, performing on US bases in Germany just after the war and recording discs in several languages. For 1YA she hosted *Café Continental*, backed by the mysterious Rinaldo and his Gypsy Quartet ('the players prefer to be somewhat incognito').[24] Her half-dozen releases for Stebbing and Tanza show she was especially at home with sophisticated pop that took advantage of background, such as the Latin-styled version of 'Perfidia' (recorded with Santos Romero, i.e., Wally Ransom), the samba standard 'Anna' (with Crombie Murdoch), and the trés continental 'Si Tu Voulais'.

IVORY QUEEN

'Jazz is for fun', said Nancy Harrie. 'You earn your bread and butter in the commercial field.'[25] Harrie's brilliance at the keyboard was matched by a pragmatism and musical open-mindedness, which meant she was always sought after for recordings, live radio broadcasts and television shows. For her, the Astor Studios became 'like a second home', she said. 'I was a professional – and I hope I behaved like one.'[26]

Born in Ngaruawahia in 1919, Harrie grew up in Greymouth where she learnt music at the Mercy convent. Harrie collected her letters – ATCL, LTCL – but was especially lucky to find a teacher who did not mind her playing jazz. Sister Mary Anthony was 'a splendid teacher who took no nonsense', remembered Harrie. 'There was no mercy on my bones. [But] I consider her responsible for my career.'[27] At sixteen she was performing both classical and jazz in Christchurch, demonstrating sheet music at Begg's, and playing at the Mayfair Lounge on Worcester Street and the Winter Garden on Armagh Street. 'Nancy's piano style is her own', said *Music Maker*, although early influences were US pianist Teddy Wilson, as well as Carmen Cavallaro, Johnny Guarnieri and Nat King Cole.[28]

By 1946 Harrie had moved to Auckland, and for 30 years she was in demand for recording and broadcasting sessions. She was a rarity, a female musician in a male world, who survived through her talent and sense of humour. There wasn't a radio band she didn't perform with, as well as small combos and duets, and accompanying singers such as Mavis Rivers, Marion Waite and Mary Feeney. In 1950 she married Lee Humphreys, leader of the Knaves vocal quartet, and they often collaborated on disc and broadcasts.

Harrie said, 'I was never a jazz pianist, much as I would like to have been.'[29] Her style could be romantic or rhythmic, in whatever genre was required, and she credited her ability to sightread as the reason she was offered such diverse work. She remained the quintessential mainstream all-rounder, recording a light piano album of standards *The Colourful Piano of Nancy Harrie*,

Easy to remember: Nancy Harrie, right, with vocalist Marion Waite, perform standards on 2YC, June 1950. Spencer Digby/Peter Downes collection

and backing singers on TV's *Have a Shot* programme. She was also involved in two radio programmes, *Fashions in Melody* and *The Keysters*. Wally Ransom recalled, 'Faced with "Pagliacci" on a nose flute, or "I Want to Hold Your Hand" on an uncertain violin, her "simpatico" accompaniment has immeasurably helped both artists and listeners.' Harrie just said the programme was 'ghastly'.[30]

As a soloist, Harrie made use of her virtuosic technique, which could be florid ('The World Outside') or finger-busting ('Jim-Jams'). Whatever was popular in the shows or on radio, she could transform into something suitable for the parlour: a medley from *South Pacific*, or Winifred

Nancy Harrie at the Novachord, and pianist John Thomson, *Keyboard Capers*, 1ZB Radio Theatre, Auckland, 1952. RNZ Sound Archives

Atwell's hit 'Black and White Rag'. With Lloyd Sly she recorded a double-sided disc for the crowning of a young Queen, 'Coronation Medley' b/w 'Queen Elizabeth Waltz'. As an accompanist Harrie was just as happy providing the rhythm for a big swing band or a Latin combo, as she was sliding grace notes behind a country and western tune.

Harrie, who died in 2000, was involved in many firsts, such as recording 'You Can in Yucatan' with Wally Ransom in 1949, and being the first pianist on television,

in a 1951 experimental broadcast. Although she was in demand as a light pianist providing dinner music at prestigious nightspots such as the Hi Diddle Griddle and the Hotel Intercontinental, of the latter she said, 'All it had was money.'

She loved performing, but chose to stay out of the spotlight. 'I'm very nervous', she explained. 'I prefer to settle down, shake my shoes off and keep a cigarette close to hand. I just like playing the piano.'[31]

CROONERS AND CHARMERS

In the pop vocalist field, recordings by solo women far outnumbered those by men. 'We have plenty of talent amongst girl singers', said Bert Peterson in 1953, '. . . but male vocalists of merit are seldom discovered.' It was a unique area of the music industry in which women were predominant – and ironic in the wake of the Kiwi Concert Party's use of female impersonators – but some male singers did challenge the record companies' preference for women. The follow-up to 'Blue Smoke', Tanza # 2, was another New Zealand original, 'Paekakariki', sung by its composer Ken Avery in a style that suggests Noël Coward in the shade of a pohutukawa.[32]

The next male vocalist recorded by Stan Dallas was plucked from Henry Rudolph's Harmony Serenaders. John Hoskins was a Wellington shop assistant with a voice that could out-croon Bing Crosby. On a series of recordings Hoskins was given sumptuous backing – a string section led by Alex Lindsay, an angelic choir of sopranos – to songs that would have met the approval of Uncle Tom's Friendly Road Choir. Among them were 'Auld Lang Syne', 'Oh, What a Beautiful Morning', 'Ave Maria' and 'Our Lady of Fatima'.[33]

It is a curiosity that on the flipside of Hoskins's first release, 'A, You're Adorable', were Rudolph's young sopranos singing 'More Beer'. He also provided the vocal to 'Misty Moon', a Tanza 78 written by Wellington's aspirant musical spy, George Fraser. (A mole for Special Branch within communist circles, Fraser was told by his minder to stop playing music: 'It's too petit-bourgeois for the role you're playing . . . . Folk songs are okay because they are into that, but not that sentimental American stuff.')[34]

Most Tanza pop would soon be recorded in Auckland by Peach, and one group dominated the male vocalists. The Knaves began as a trio whose core members were Phil Maguire, Lee Humphreys and Doug 'Buster' Mowbray. Their debut was HMV's second release by New Zealand artists, recorded in 1949 by Noel Peach before his association with Tanza began. On 'He Holds the Lantern

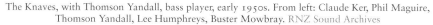

The Knaves, with Thomson Yandall, bass player, early 1950s. From left: Claude Ker, Phil Maguire, Thomson Yandall, Lee Humphreys, Buster Mowbray. RNZ Sound Archives

(While His Mother Chops Wood)' b/w 'Powder Your Face With Sunshine', the Knaves were backed by Wally Ransom's band; a follow-up, 'Riders in the Sky', became the first record by New Zealanders to top the *Lifebuoy Hit Parade*.[35]

The Knaves' trademark was their velvet-voiced harmonies, and they were fond of updating well-worn songs, usually as novelties. They would rearrange them with Spike Jones effects bordering on corn, carrying with them 'box loads of sound effects, including cowbells, tins of nails, whistles and hammers'. Eventually they became just vocal effects, the singers emulating gunshots, bird noises, train and boat whistles. 'An empty beer bottle often comes in handy.'[36] So did local references, such as: 'I'm goin' to ride the TAB trail/Because they've locked up my bookie in Mount Eden Jail . . .'.

After their brief association with HMV in 1949, they became one of Tanza's most prolific groups. Their earliest recordings were in a mock-Irish style – 'Molly Malone's Wedding', 'Bridget O'Flynn', 'Who Threw the Overalls in Mrs Murphy's Chowder' – but they were soon mocking other genres. Early in 1950, they were featured in a weekly fifteen-minute session on the YA stations. A reviewer approved of the group's 'lilting style which is far, far ahead of some of its American counterparts. This is definitely not for high-brows, but most middle brows could listen without squirming.'[37]

To the disappointment of many, the Knaves disbanded in 1953, after seven years: their success was interfering with earning a living, so they thought it best to quit while at a peak, said Mowbray. 'We are signing off before there is any tendency to go down hill.' The *Music Maker* described it as a 'bombshell', but with vaudeville now history, their performing options were limited (even if 'On one occasion, it is said, they topped the hit parade in Pakistan').[38] Two of the original Knaves also recorded as soloists. Lee Humphreys made the disc 'Goodnight Irene' and 'On Top of Old Smokey', but died in April 1959 from illnesses related to time spent as a POW. His wife, Nancy Harrie, survived him: she was just 39, a widow and mother of two.

Doug Mowbray had the most extended career, using his alter ego, Buster Keene. Mowbray began singing on Milford Beach, practising his harmonies with a ukulele (when the Knaves made their first appearance on 1ZB, their guitarist was so nervous he couldn't perform, so Mowbray removed two strings and played it like a ukulele).[39] As Keene, he cut around 40 sides for Tanza in a variety of

styles: campfire country ballads, novelties, standards, spirituals and duets. Most of the latter were with Dorothy Brannigan, including a double-sided gender debate, 'Woman (Uh Huh)' b/w 'Man (Uh Huh)'. After the demise of the Knaves he joined the Three Lads, who recorded novelties for Tanza and Zodiac such as 'Robin Hood', 'Drunken Sailor', 'A Pub With No Beer' and 'Eating Goober Peas'. An early experiment in 1954 was the doo-wop classic 'Sh-Boom', performed barbershop-quartet style: it was a genre that Mowbray enjoyed as a hobby prior his death in 2003.

In the mid-1950s, the Stardusters became the most prominent male vocal group, famous for joining Pat McMinn on 'Opo the Crazy Dolphin' in 1956. Two years earlier, their recording debut 'They Were Doing the Mambo' became a hit on request sessions: it was a camp, spirited, time-signature-shifting fusion of Latin and doo-wop. Lawrie North and the Langford brothers – Bill and Jack – honed their style at suburban parties to become a professional musical act. The trio was billed at jazz concerts at the Auckland Town Hall, and performed regularly with Crombie Murdoch's trio on 1YA and in the nationally broadcast *Radio Roadhouse* comedy show. Influenced by the Four Aces, with their close harmonies they would try anything on the jukebox – country novelties, ballads, light R&B, Dean Martin-style crooning – in a manner appropriate for the ZBs. Among their releases were 'I Love Paris', 'Sixteen Tons', the Coasters' 'Black Denim Trousers and Motorcycle Boots' and, with Graham Godber, 'Memories Are Made of This'.[40]

At Tanza in Wellington, Stan Dallas nurtured the Tawharu Quintet. Often featured on 2ZB, the Otaki group recorded a dozen sides, recalling the Mills Brothers – or anticipating the Howard Morrison Quartet – with their soothing harmonies, whether on standards such as 'Chattanooga Shoeshine Boy' or the bucolic serenade 'Land of the Long White Cloud':

> You will find skies are blue/folks are kind, friends are true
> In the land of long white cloud
> Every one welcome there/there is none can compare
> To the land of long white cloud
> Just wait till you see/the magic charm of Rotorua
> Just wait till you hear a Maori haka and song.

In Auckland, Peach tried several male soloists in the pop field. Mel Scott and Jeff Lee were tenors in a tradition

that went back to John McCormack. Fraser Daly was more
reflective of the 1940s, his confident, resonant voice being
in the Bing Crosby/Guy Mitchell mould on songs such as
'My Truly, Truly Fair' and 'Belle, Belle, My Liberty Belle'.
Daly's lush vibrato on 'Ever True, Ever More' is contrasted
by an understated, lyrical guitar solo by Mark Kahi.

Daly was taught violin as a child by Sister Mary Leo,
and as a teenager began performing – and occasionally
sitting in on drums – with the bands of Epi Shalfoon, Chips
Healy and Bill Sevesi. One night, while playing violin in a
band at the Catholic Social Centre, Daly was press-ganged
into singing. During Frank Sinatra's 'Pistol Packin' Mama',
the drummer handed Daly the microphone and told him:
'Take a chorus.' 'Apparently it went down well', Daly
recalled. 'I had to sing it three or four times that night.'

In April 1945, Daly won a talent quest at the Auckland
Town Hall; the prize was 30 guineas and a two-week
contract singing jingles for Colgate-Palmolive in Sydney.
Unfortunately, no one told Colgate he had won, so when
he arrived a local singer had already filled the contract.
Only fifteen, Daly was stranded in Sydney. He got a job as
a theatre usher and after a year returned to New Zealand
and started singing at the Peter Pan and for Tanza.

He recorded for Noel Peach at his home studio, before
Astor Studios was opened. Peach was running the Astor
Theatre in Dominion Road at the time. 'He invited me and

my wife along one night, and played the number in the
interval. It was the first time I heard my voice.'[41]

In the early 1950s, romantic balladeer Barney Erickson
was another vocalist to try Australia. He recorded only
one 78 for Tanza, accompanied by an other-worldly organ
and Nancy Harrie's florid arpeggios: 'Because of You' b/w
'Cold Cold Heart' (shortly after the Hank Williams song
had been a hit for Tony Bennett). But Erickson did not lack
for ambition, performing with Martin Winiata and the
Kahi brothers in Christchurch, and with Epi Shalfoon and
Chips Healy in Auckland, then setting his sights overseas.
Courting a girl from Australia, he moved to Sydney in
the 1950s, sang with the ABC Band, won several talent
quests run by Sammy Lee and joined Prince Tui Teka in the
original Maori Troubadours. In the 1960s, he toured the
world with the Maori Hi-Liners.[42]

Edwin Duff came the other way: born in Scotland,
raised in Melbourne, he was in Auckland long enough
to record several sides for Stebbing. Although billed as

Edwin Duff could sing Sinatra, bebop and Danny Kaye, though his stage
clothes needed a volume control. Bothamley collection/Peter Downes

a Sinatra copy in Australia, and capable of a capella bop choruses, Duff was 'as much a pint-sized Danny Kaye', famous for wearing stage clothes that needed a volume control: red trousers, green tuxedo, pink socks. Renowned for his showmanship, he already had a fan club in Australia before his sojourn in Auckland, and quickly established a following singing with Crombie Murdoch's band. The mainstream pop he recorded at Stebbing was no challenge for his singing skills. He left for North America in 1954, intending to join the Australian Jazz Quintet, but they had already become established there as an instrumental group. Returning home, he enjoyed a long career as a leading jazz singer on Australian television.[43]

SAMBAS, BANJOS AND BOP

Apart from middle-of-the-road pop, Tanza and Stebbing experimented with an array of genres in their recordings of the early 1950s: country, Maori, novelties and, with increasing regularity, faux-Hawaiian. Also popular in the early 1950s was dixieland jazz – which enjoyed several revivals – and, to a modest degree, Latin-American pop. Among the influential Latin lovers were drummer Wally Ransom – who championed the exotic, busy rhythms among musicians – and Murdoch Riley, NZBS record purchasing officer and programme producer.

Ransom was a musical jack-of-all-trades: by day he was New Zealand representative for Southern music

Wally Ransom's Rhumba Band rehearse without vocalist Esme Stephens, Astor Studios, Auckland, 1949. From left: Lee Humphreys, Charlie Welch, Jim Warren, Wally Ransom, Phil Maguire, Nancy Harrie, George Campbell. Jim Warren collection

publishers, working in the Pacific Buildings alongside Stebbing's studio. At night, he was a working drummer, and what he played often reflected his love of Latin. Soon after recording 'You Can in Yucatan' in 1949 with his own rumba band, Ransom's alter ego Santos Romero released 'Because of You' b/w 'Choo Choo Samba' for Stebbing.

Ransom arrived in New Zealand in 1938, after a stopover in South America. An experienced London drummer, he was endeavouring to take an English dance band to Tahiti, but when that fell through he decided to stay in New Zealand and become involved in the local music scene. He spent much of the war in the RNZAF based at Wigram, stripping aeroplane engines by day, and performing in a dance band and in revues and bond drives after hours. By the end of the war, he had played with many of the top musicians in the country, among them Phil Campbell, Tut Coltman, Brian Marston, Lauri Paddi, Art Rosoman and Martin Winiata. With his genial nature and exceptional talents, Ransom was never short of work

and he would try anything. Besides drumming, he played cornet and vibraphone, performing music on advertising jingles and in radio bands. He worked as a song publisher, scripted and hosted radio shows, and eventually become one of New Zealand's first television compères.[44]

Many other musicians dabbled in Latin American while it was in vogue during the 1950s: 'cummerbunds and swarthy complexions' were not required, announced the *Listener*. Broadcasting from 2YA in 1950 was Johnny Williams and his Latin-Americans, a well-drilled combo of Wellington's radio band players, including guitarist Jimmy Carter. Williams, usually a saxophonist, was a percussionist in his Latin incarnation; at local cabarets, dancers enjoyed the *chicka-boom-chick* rhythms of 'Johnny's Samba'. In Auckland, George Campbell and his Cubanaires broadcast regularly on 1YA in 1953, with pianist Crombie Murdoch arranging and Frank Gibson playing claves, bongos, timbali and whatever else he could hit. Later, Doug Caldwell and Ernie Wilson led Latin radio

Johnny Williams and his Latin-Americans, 2YA studio, Wellington, 1950. From left: Allen Wellbrock, piano; Johnny Williams, claves, saxophone, flute; Bob Barcham, piano-accordion; Stan 'Slim' Dorward, bass; Harry Voice, drums; Stan Crisp, trumpet; Jim Carter, guitar; Geoff Mechaelis, clarinet; Vern Clare, timbales; Jimmy Golding, vocals. Jim Carter collection

bands in the South Island; in Auckland, Ricky Camden introduced Afro-Cuban rhythms with his band the Featurettes. A young Billy Farnell handled the piano while Camden played percussion.[45]

For radio producer Murdoch Riley, a love of Latin-American dancing was part of the genre's attraction. After hours he taught dance classes in the style at the Wellington studio of Margaret O'Connor, and learnt Spanish at Victoria University. At Broadcasting in Wellington in the early 1950s, besides being record-purchasing officer for the ZBs, he scripted *Come to the Fiesta*, a weekly programme of Latin music for 2YD. *Joy* magazine approved of Riley's musical detective work: 'He was always on the lookout for a newly arrived diplomat who might have had some unusual records collected during a Latin-American term of office.'[46]

When Riley launched the Viking label in the late 1950s, he released some 'genuine' Latin-American records and found the fad had passed: on average they sold less than 150 copies each.[47] Nevertheless, the genre had its adherents. Dance bands became wary of exhibitionist couples who came up and said, 'There have been a lot of requests for a Latin-American bracket', recalled Ken Avery:

> Always willing to oblige, the band would then strike up a Latin-American medley – rumba, tango, samba – and find that only one or two couples (who really could dance these things and appreciated an almost empty floor to show off their prowess) took the floor, smiling with dancing-competition confidence to imaginary judges at every corner of the dance floor. We soon found out that these requests had to be taken with a grain of salt in the interest of the bulk of paying customers.[48]

Dixie is that anomaly among music genres: rarely fashionable, always popular. There have been several dixie revivals, in New Zealand and overseas, each an evolution of its predecessor: the strongest local reincarnation took place in the mid-1950s. Perhaps, as in the US and Britain, it was an accessible, entertaining form of jazz when bebop was sorting out the modernists from the 'mouldy old figs'. Its musical trademarks are unmistakeable: fluid improvisation played by small combos, often dominated by clarinet and banjo, two instruments that became pigeonholed by the genre.

Dixie's first prominent revivalist in New Zealand was trumpeter Nolan Rafferty, who played with Epi Shalfoon for nearly fifteen years. Rafferty's band the Dixielanders caused a sensation in 1952 when it played at the first jazz concert in Auckland's Town Hall, a much bigger room than the concert chamber. 'The group was an immediate success and popular, unassuming Nolan Rafferty awoke to find himself the star of the concert. Since then the sextette has gone from success to success.'[49]

Over the next two years, Rafferty's group was a big drawcard at concerts and dances in Auckland and the Waikato. Usually, the 'house full' signs went up early, and the band played encore after encore while the crowd stomped, clapped and even danced in the aisles. The band could fill Auckland's Town Hall, while also appearing twice a week at the Holy Sepulchre hall in Newton (better known to the dancing public as St Sep's). Apart from Rafferty, the key players were Neil Dunningham, trombone and vocals; Pem Sheppard, clarinet and tenor; Johnny Corban, piano; Don Branch, drums; and Alby Parkinson on bass (later replaced by Bob Ofsoski).

The group said farewell at a concert in Wellington in 1954. Rafferty's plane to Paraparaumu was late, so an hour into the show he made a dramatic entrance at the Town Hall. 'By the time he dashed up the aisle shedding overcoat, scarf and bonhomie, we were all agog', wrote the *Evening Post*'s Owen Jensen:

> As soon as Nolan Rafferty and his boys struck up on the 'March of the Bobcats' we were back in the days of Model Ts, hot clarinets, and razz-mah-jazz.
>
> It was Dixie, not quite the original perhaps, but with a genuine flavour of New Orleans. Corny they called it in the twenties, but it's on the band wagon again. The jazz boys, it seems, are likely to be as conservative as the longhairs.[50]

Among the enthusiastic crowd, the *Post*'s photographer snapped a man dancing alone in the aisle, dressed in black polo neck jumper, loose safari jacket and suede shoes: he has a beard, and he is in ecstasy. A bohemian, far gone. Many in the audience – in gaberdine overcoats and ties – turn towards him, bemused.

But Rafferty didn't rule the roost: in 1953, another Shalfoon veteran, trumpeter Bobby Griffith, was touring the country with his All Star Dixielanders. They played 'concerts galore' and fed themselves on free pub lunches until they got to Invercargill, where they celebrated with oysters. 'A shilling for a dozen beauties', recalled Griffith. By then, they deserved a treat. Somehow, the lengthy tour lost money: 'We started off in cars, then we bought a bus and when we went broke and couldn't afford places to stay, we ended up sleeping in the bus.'[51]

In Wellington, Dorsey Cameron was also diverted by dixie, leading two groups in during the mid-1950s, the Dixielanders and the New Orleans Stompers; and whenever Ken Avery turned to clarinet rather than sax, the results were perceived as dixie rather than swing, especially in his band the Darktown Strutters.

By the late 1950s, another generation of local musicians took up the mantle: some student jazz club combos dared to dabble in dixie, to the scorn of more 'progressive' members. The Mahon brothers, Denny and John, were the 'trad' leaders in Wellington, while in the 1960s Ernie Rouse

of Hawke's Bay became well known for his bands playing in the style.[52]

Auckland's most enduring dixie act offered an acceptable alternative when dance halls were infiltrated by rock'n'roll, along with teenage hordes. In 1958 Merv Thomas and His Dixielanders were offered a residency at the Crystal Palace in Mt Eden: the venue had struggled after Epi Shalfoon's death. Phil Warren pulled out all his marketing tricks, promoting the Crystal Palace as Auckland's leading *adult* dance spot, where ladies were welcome even without escorts. Among his gimmicks were floor shows, toasted sandwiches, and giveaways ranging from chocolates and cigarettes to à la carte restaurant meals at Fagel's. His advertisements emphasised his

Wellington, 1950s: band leader Don Richardson discusses arrangements with trombonist Dorsey Cameron. John McIvor at left. Don Richardson collection

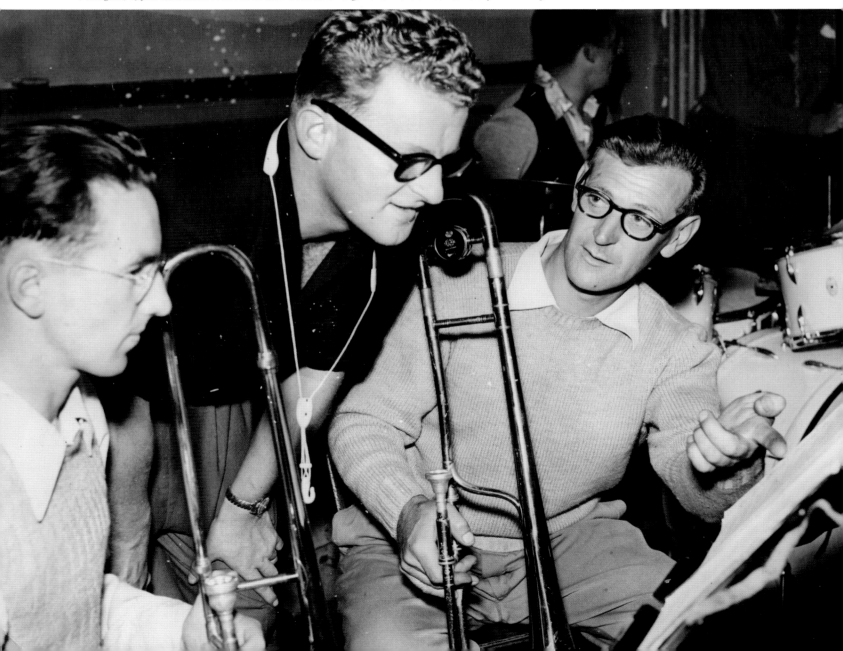

Merv Thomas, centre, with two of his Dixielanders: Clive Laurent, left, and Tony Ashby, right; Crystal Palace, Auckland, late 1950s. Rykenberg Photography/Merv Thomas collection

latest ideas: Coke, cookies and especially perked coffee, served 'by one who knows' for the patrons' 'comfort and stimulation'. This was code for saying the coffee contained alcohol. 'Direct from the United States . . . you've tasted nothing like this around Auckland.'

'Oh!' exclaimed the Crystal Palace ads each week. 'If Epi Could See It Now!'[53]

The main attraction, though, was Merv Thomas, who quickly established a reputation for his musicianship and for being a great entertainer. 'With his big smile, his obvious pleasure in performing, and his shining trombone, he made me forget all the things I've said about rock'n'roll', wrote Jim Warren.[54]

Thomas's Dixielanders were a drawcard at the Crystal Palace for nearly five years, evolving from a dixie act – with Thomas on vocals and trombone – to more of a comic cabaret turn. Leading the humour was multi-instrumentalist and showman Clive Laurent, who was happy to dress up as an Arab (for 'Sheik of Araby') or an ape (playing bebop). Newly engaged couples were often serenaded on

a two-stringed, out-of-tune gypsy fiddle, played by bassist Bob Ofsoski while wearing a knotted handkerchief on his head. Stan Freberg parodies were also popular. By 1961, limited by their band name, the Dixielanders became Merv Thomas, Marlene Tong and the Prophets.

Thomas would try any style of music, although some of his colleagues looked askance at his variety. In 1957 he was part of the elite Auckland radio band led by Bart Stokes, who was fond of bebop and experimenting with 'progressive' arrangements. When musicians made mistakes, Stokes would tell them their next gig would be at the Crystal Palace. 'Certain things were very uncool if you were a jazz musician', said Thomas. 'One of them was dixieland and another was singing. Bart was very serious about the music and I very quickly learned it's about entertainment.' Ironically, Stokes had played in dixie bands himself in the mid-1950s; in 1960 he left for London and remained overseas for many years. 'For a long time Bart has been too advanced for the Auckland scene', commented the *Music Maker*.[55]

THE QUIET MAN

Most musicians want a hit record, but actually getting one can be a curse for the serious jazz player. If it is a novelty hit, even worse. 'Opo the Crazy Dolphin' was an immediate and much-loved hit, but one that Crombie Murdoch regretted writing. New Zealand's most acclaimed jazz pianist of the 1950s, Murdoch earned £200 from the song, but 'It was hack work', he said. 'I sold my soul to the devil to make a living.'[56] Like most of his music contemporaries, for much of his career he also had a day job, reading gas meters. Looking back at his heyday, he wryly said, 'If you were prepared to work day and night, seven days a week, you could make quite a good living.'[57]

Murdoch's versatility disrupted his jazz aspirations but helped keep him in the forefront of music-making for 30 years. His experiments at the piano had to wait while his other skills were in demand: arranging for big bands, leading a trio, accompanying a variety of pop singers and writing radio jingles.

Born in Winton, Southland, in 1926, Crombie Murdoch knew his destiny when he witnessed a pianist and drummer play 'pulse music' in a country hall. His mother was against a music career, so he went to teachers' training college in Dunedin instead. While living in the YMCA he met Julian Lee, who encouraged him and shared his stash of 78s. The result was inevitable. Murdoch moved to Auckland in 1945 for his teaching probation, his recently widowed mother in tow. She was realistic – 'Music is something Crombie just can't do without', she later said – and he swapped classrooms for dance halls. Within weeks of his arrival, Murdoch was reunited with Julian Lee, a member of the Swing Club, and sitting in with the city's leading bands.[58]

Music was a cerebral business, which Murdoch conveyed with an aloofness while at the keyboard, and a quiet disposition away from it. But he was also capable of arguing that jazz should be experimental and progressive. 'When he sits down at the piano one expects Chopin rather than bop to come from under the lid, but Murdoch is as serious about his jazz as any concert player is about his sonatas . . . . anyone who likes his music thoughtful and

imaginative, and yet still have a beat, will concentrate on the Quiet Man at the piano.'[59]

Despite his solemn approach and sophisticated piano technique, it was through throwaway music that most of New Zealand heard Murdoch's playing: pop novelties such as the bouncy 'Bimbo' ('Bimbo, bimbo, where ya gonna go-ee-o . . .'), 'Opo' and radio jingles such as the country-style 'Keans for Jeans'. These recordings called upon his skills at honky-tonk piano, a world away from the jazz he was playing in nightclubs.

Tanza's Noel Peach had the idea for a song to celebrate the dolphin Opo, which was captivating holidaymakers in Opononi during the summer of 1955–56. Murdoch wrote the words and music 'overnight,' getting his science and Opo's sex wrong: he was a she, and a mammal rather than a fish. Written to be topical, it certainly succeeded: Opo was found dead just as radio airplay began, so the song became the dolphin's 'upbeat obituary'. Manager of Tanza

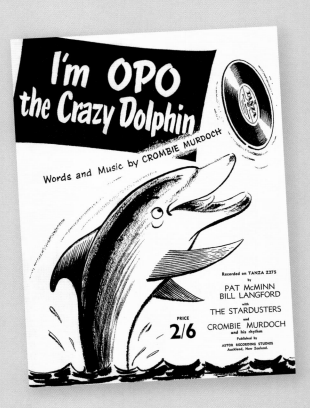

at the time was Murdoch Riley, fresh from his Broadcasting record-purchasing role where discretion came before valour. 'The damn thing died, just as we were about to release it', he recalled. 'I rang Noel and said, "What do we now?" He said, "We've spent the money recording it, now let's put it out and hope for the best." And it was a great seller.'[60] 'Opo the Crazy Dolphin' sold 10,000 copies in its first week, recalled Stan Dallas: 'If Opo had lived for another bloody week, we would have sold 20,000.'[61]

The arrangement is as infectious as the melody and the sentiment ('there never was a fish that looked so cute'). A bassoon bobs as if beneath the waves, Bill Langford's vocal portrays Opo as a cheeky cockney, while Pat McMinn and the Stardusters' cheer-leading chorus speak for the nation. Beneath it all, Murdoch tickles the ivories.

When McMinn arrived for the session at the Astor Studios in the early evening, Murdoch had just finished composing the song. The ink was still wet on the manuscript paper, and got even wetter as they experimented

with ways to achieve the bubbling water effect (eventually achieved by blowing into a jug of water through a straw). As the score became saturated and almost illegible, McMinn kept breaking into giggles. 'It was about one o'clock in the morning before we finished it.'[62]

'Opo the Crazy Dolphin' was a rarity: a New Zealand-composed song that became a runaway hit. Apart from the Hawaiian-styled songs of Sam Freedman, the bulk of the songs recorded in the 1950s were local interpretations of overseas hits: cover versions. 'We were mostly copying the top American music', recalled Stan Dallas. 'Whatever America put out on HMV, we would beat them to it. We would copy them as quickly as we could, using local talent. Were we looking for a New Zealand sound? I don't think so, we were just copying America . . . . trying to fill a gap in the market and record New Zealand music if it was worth doing.'[63]

Whether this was what the audience wanted – and the success of the few locally produced songs suggests

Crombie Murdoch at the piano with (from left) Frank Gurr, Jim Warren and Doug Kelly; Auckland, 1946. Jim Warren collection

Crombie Murdoch, an 'incurable romantic', c. 1959. Dennis Huggard collection

otherwise – this is what they got, from a fledgling, cautious recording industry. With airtime for popular music so scarce on radio, playlists mostly stayed safely in the middle of the road, apart from specialist shows such as those presented by Arthur Pearce and Jim Foley.

Crombie Murdoch's debut as a big-band leader came in 1951 with his *Symphony in Swing* shows, broadcast live on 1YD from Auckland's Radio Theatre. He felt that arranging for a big band in the style of his influences (Tommy Dorsey, Glenn Miller) was his true metier, but described this dream as an 'unhealthy occupation', fraught with difficulties such as deadlines, budgets and the musicians themselves. For much of the 1950s, his main outlet was a trio, usually featuring Don Branch on drums and George Campbell on bass, often backing Pat McMinn or Esme Stephens on vocals. Even for such a leading player, variety was necessary to stay afloat: within a short space of time he could be playing with Julian Lee's Electrotones, George Campbell's Cubanaires or Dale Alderton's Latin-American group.

Besides his many recording sessions, Murdoch was a pioneer in providing live music in restaurants once the restrictive laws allowed 'dine and dance' venues.

'Auckland', he recalled, 'was opening up and getting with the style of the rest of the world. It was new and it was exciting.'[64]

A career highlight came in 1960 when the Crombie Murdoch Octet opened for the first New Zealand tour of the Dave Brubeck Quartet, and was complimented by Brubeck when performing at the party afterwards. Another was in 1972 when Murdoch had to substitute for an exhausted Earl Hines. In 1955 Murdoch played behind Nat King Cole, who was so impressed he invited him to the US. The closest he ever got was a two-year working holiday in Australia in 1965, after gigs began evaporating following the arrival of rock'n'roll. Thirty years later he admitted, 'I never got over it; it was a terrible shock.'[65]

Often lugubrious about the music scene and self-deprecating about his achievements, Murdoch's modest opinion of himself was not shared by his peers. 'Playing with Crombie Murdoch', wrote drummer Bruce Morley, 'is like having another entire rhythm section on board in the shape of one man . . . . Crombie may affect a certain well-earned cynicism these days, but he's actually an incurable romantic, a trait that spills out in his wonderful piano playing.'[66] Murdoch died in 2003, aged 77.

While bebop and dixie bands were often featured together on the same bills at the many formal jazz concerts of the 1950s – sometimes using the same musicians – bebop was not a style that found a wide audience. Many musicians were themselves bemused by the emergence of bebop, and it became a regular talking point immediately after the war. A debate kept the excitable pages of *Jukebox* lively in 1946. This new form of 'musical banality' was unlikely to last as long as dixieland jazz, predicted Glen Menzies. All the musicians seemed to be individuals striving for effect, he said: an unhealthy sign, but bebop was 'a musical child born of an unhealthy mind'.[67]

Expat Canadian band leader Art Rosoman was also sceptical. 'It is a style only for very hep musicians', he said in 1947, 'and I haven't got any time to think about it.' Rosoman was then at his post-war peak, having moved from Wellington to lead bands at the Metropole and Peter Pan in Auckland, while also introducing a small-combo 'jump' style in both cities. Freddie Gore was one of the few older band leaders who expressed respect for bebop.

'It takes terrific phrasing. Joe Public wouldn't go for a lot of it. It's too far advanced.'[68]

The hep musicians did indeed follow the overseas vogue for bebop, with Julian Lee being regarded as the leading local exponent, and the pop-oriented Esme Stephens being early to 'bravely tackle' the style, in the vocal trio the Bopcats. 'We were all intrigued with it', Dale Alderton recalled, 'but there weren't many ways we could use it. Not in dance bands. You could insert little phrases and that sort of thing which we did, but bands were all still playing stock arrangements right through the 50s.'[69]

Bart Stokes, a saxophonist prodigy, soon mastered the style, and at a 1952 Wellington Town Hall concert Laurie Lewis's quartet – all wearing Dizzy Gillespie berets and dark glasses – performed 'newer bebop with all its ramifications, slickly wrapped up in familiar tunes'.[70] Jim Warren recalled two Englishmen being among the best beboppers in Auckland: saxophonist Derek Neville, who enjoyed soloing for chorus after chorus, and a Cockney pianist, Don Turner. By day Turner was a piano tuner for

Saxophone prodigy Bart Stokes, right, with Fred Gore, early 1950s. Bennie Gunn collection

Atwaters, where Warren once heard him playing in the basement. He sounded like Art Tatum, and when Warren complimented him, Turner replied, 'Oh, you liked that? Not many people like that. They don't like what I play.' (Turner was regarded as brilliant but eccentric: he could play any song, but never knew their names, so needed a quick whistle of the melody beforehand. He was also known for taking his tuning spanner to gigs; if the piano was out, he would quickly tighten it up – then detune it again afterwards.)[71]

The doyen of New Zealand jazz broadcasters, ArthurPearce, remained unconvinced by bebop. He saw it as a cult. 'It's intellectually brilliant, but you can't dance to it', he said in 1950. Don Richardson found that playing at the Majestic kept him grounded. 'I was never extreme. Bop I didn't mind but there was a lot of jazz I didn't like. There was a block of years there where everybody thought it clever if every chord had at least seven voices. They were ugly years – it wasn't smart at all. Nobody liked it, and I think that's when country and western came in.'[72]

If jazz was to remain popular music in the 1950s, it had to reach out to its audience: it had to embrace pop. Overseas, some astute artists realised the possibilities, and an example visited New Zealand in January 1955: Nat King Cole. Thousands of young Aucklanders, most of them young women, flocked to Whenuapai aerodrome west of the city to witness his arrival. An Auckland Swing Club band kept the crowd entertained while it waited; some couples even jitterbugged. Once the TEAL aircraft landed, police and airport staff struggled to keep the crowd back as Cole tried to make his way from the plane to the terminal. Women shouted 'We want Nat' and 'Man, he sends me'. Cole, who was accompanied by his family – including young daughter Natalie – was taken aback by the commotion but had enjoyed it. 'I didn't know American pop music had got this far', he said.[73]

Cole's 48-hour visit had an impact on New Zealand music that went beyond the rapturous reception to his concert in the Auckland Town Hall. At the airport he was met by two arch-rivals from the local record industry. To Bart Fortune of Tanza, Cole apologised for 'being the bearer of bad tidings'. As a director of Capitol Records in Hollywood, Cole was delivering in person the company's decision that Tanza would no longer handle its New Zealand distribution. Standing alongside Fortune,

Crombie Murdoch with Nat King Cole, Auckland, 1955. 'I didn't know American pop music had got this far', said Cole. Dave Ross collection

receiving happier news, was HMV (NZ) Ltd's Jack Wyness, finally running the company since the retirement of his father. Tanza may have released the first all-New Zealand record – though if it was a race, Wyness hadn't entered – but HMV now had another lucrative overseas label to distribute.[74]

In Auckland, Cole's trio rehearsed through the night with a dance orchestra led by Crombie Murdoch. The local musicians were hired to provide the lush accompaniment required by the more pop-oriented hits in Cole's catalogue: 'Mona Lisa', 'Unforgettable' and 'Too Young' (the latter had already sold 15,000 copies for Tanza). The audience listened attentively – with the occasional swoon – before breaking into 'almost threatening' applause between songs. Among them was a fourteen-year-old Mike Nock, changed by the experience. So were the Auckland musicians on stage: it was their first opportunity to 'prove themselves' against Americans, using the visitors' arrangements. 'That threw new light on it', said bassist Bob Ewing. '. . . that's when it showed up just how good the Auckland musicians were.'[75]

SOUTH SEAS RHYTHM

It was a moment of great satisfaction when Sam Freedman realised he had sold a hula to Hawaii. In the 1980s, the Wellington songwriter was on his way to visit a sister in Los Angeles. Over the speakers in a transit lounge at Honolulu airport he heard a familiar melody, then the vocal welcomed him:

> Haere mai, everything is kapai
> You're here at last, you're really here at last.

Freedman was in his 70s. Travelling alone, it was a tremendous boost to hear in that context a song he had written over 30 years earlier to emulate the sound of Hawaii.[76] In 1954 'Haere Mai' had been a hit for Bill Wolfgramm and His Islanders, an Auckland group that recorded it for Tanza with singer Daphne Walker. Nearly 50 years later, it was revived in a hugely popular airline advertisement.[77]

In 2000 the song's hypnotic reverie seduced a new generation of listeners just as it had in 1954, when it was one of the first New Zealand songs on a local hit parade. Nostalgic even for those who had not been born when it was first written, its aural and lyrical images evoke a Pacific paradise, tapping into an alluring fantasy that had endured for over a century.

Hawaiian-influenced music dominated the first boom in New Zealand's local recording industry, starting in 1948 with the gentle weep of Jim Carter's steel guitar in 'Blue Smoke' and reaching its zenith of popularity in the 1950s. But the phenomenon had been building for decades. Just as some early New Zealand recording artists embraced the image of cowboys riding the range, others dreamt of watching languid sunsets to South Seas rhythms. Both imaginary lifestyles were accompanied by a guitar that sat in the player's lap, with a metal bar stroking haunting melodies from its strings.

Ernest Kaai's Hawaiian Troubadours present *A Night in Honolulu* at the Town Hall, Greytown, 22 November 1927. Eph-A-VARIETY-1927-02, Alexander Turnbull Library, Wellington

A romanticised concept of Hawaiian music had been fashionable in Western popular culture since before the First World War. According to the music historian George Kanahele, the Hawaiian Islands were always quick to assimilate any styles of music that drifted ashore. Traditional forms of Hawaiian music such as the *mele* (chant) had been suppressed from the early nineteenth century, after the arrival of missionaries and other visitors. They brought with them hymns and secular tunes, and the guitar became the instrument of the 'common folk', with vocal harmonies taken from hymns. Between 1900 and 1915, ragtime infiltrated Hawaiian music, and musicians began to write songs with English words, creating the *hapa haole* style: *half white*.

Tin Pan Alley then commercialised *hapa haole* music, making it more palatable for a mainstream audience, and the genre gained a beach-head on the continental United States. Films and travelling Hawaiian revues reinforced the invasion, and the sliding steel guitar became irrevocably linked with notions of Hawaiian music.[78]

New Zealand first witnessed the style in 1911, when the Royal Hawaiians musical troupe made a national tour. The Honolulu-based group brought with it more than twenty instruments of 'native and European origin'. Standing out from the guitars and mandolins was a stringed instrument that the group's leader Ernest Kaai claimed to have invented: 'a little baby guitar in appearance, but any musician can strike every known chord in music upon it'.[79] Wellington audiences were enchanted by the 'mothering' music, reported an enthusiastic *Evening Post* reviewer, especially the 'lilting

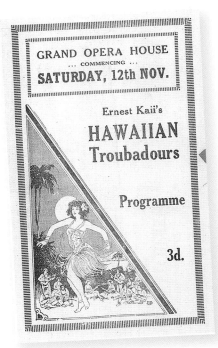

Ernest Kaai's Hawaiian Troubadours, prior to their 1925 visit; Wellington programme, 1927. *NZ Theatre and Motion Picture*, October 1925; Eph-A-Variety-1927-03-cover, Alexander Turnbull Library, Wellington

guitar accompaniment, the mandolin and the "brhm-a-brhm" "brhm-a-brhm" of the Hawaiian strings'.[80]

This tour preceded two events that are credited with spreading the taste for Hawaiian music around the world. In 1912 the musical *Bird of Paradise* opened to great acclaim on Broadway, with an ensemble of guitar, acoustic steel guitar, ukulele and *ipu* (gourd drum).[81] Hawaiian music was a sensation at the 1915 exposition in San Francisco to celebrate the opening of the Panama Canal that made the Pacific accessible to the old world. This attracted over 17 million people, with many of them visiting the Hawaiian pavilion to hear songs that would become standards: 'Waikiki Mermaid', 'On the Beach at Waikiki', 'Tomi Tomi' and 'Song of the Islands'.

J. C. Williamson staged a production of *Bird of Paradise* in Australia and New Zealand from 1917 to 1919. The manager was a musician and singer called Henry A. Peelua Bishaw, who had visited New Zealand in 1911 as a member of Kaai's group (and would do so again in 1924 with his own trio).[82] After the *Bird of Paradise* tour, he settled in Sydney and put out his slate as Australia's 'only genuine' ukulele and Hawaiian steel-guitar teacher. Like Kaai, Bishaw soon published tutors on the instruments, emphasising that their size and extreme lightness made them perfectly suited to

the outdoor lifestyle of Australians.[83] Bishaw's books used his own chord-numbering system for the ukulele accompaniment that many New Zealand musicians learnt, including Auckland bass-player Spike Donovan. This prevailed locally until the more conventional approach of May Singhi Breen – known as 'the ukulele lady' in the US – was preferred on mass-market sheet music in the 1920s.[84]

While the Royal Hawaiians were visiting New Zealand in 1911, expatriate musician Walter Smith was in the United States touring with the Royal Hawaiian Quintette and forming his own 'Hawaii-Maorian Quintette'. By 1924, when Smith was well established as Auckland's leading teacher of popular stringed instruments, he could claim to be New Zealand's 'pioneer of the ukulele and Hawaiian guitar'.[85]

Music in the Hawaiian style had become commonplace in New Zealand. Princess Te Puea's concert troupe Te Pou o Mangatawhiri was formed in late 1922, and its string band featuring a lap-steel guitar, mandolins, banjos and 'the popular Hawaiian ukuleles'. Their extensive 1923 tour to the far north raised morale and encouraged a revival in Maori music and kapa haka, the concerts including –

... men's haka parties, women's pois and Hawaiian hula dances, and a dozen little Maori maids, whose charming dancing was one of the most popular features of the show .... Braves, wahines and piccaninnies, the whole party sing and dance with that naturalness that gives a good Maori display its unique charm .... Born to be musical, they all kept perfect time in their movements and in their singing, while many a choir of Europeans might envy the skilful blending of their voices and instruments.[86]

In 1924 among the advertised new record releases were 'Moe Uhane Waltz' and 'Hawaii I'm Lonesome For You', performed by American duo the Hawaiian Guitars. The following year the Auckland department store Farmers offered Hawaiian instruments for sale in its mail-order catalogue (ukuleles from 19/11, steel guitars from £3/3).[87] On summer evenings, banjoist Jim Higgot played in bands on ferries plying Waitemata Harbour, 'mainly Hawaiian music, but sometimes we would blast out something else, like jazz'.

New Zealand radio also reflected the fashion, with many live broadcasts on the YA stations in the late 1920s by local acts such as the Waikihi Hawaiian Orchestra (also known as Barry Ingall and His Hawaiian Orchestra), Elaine Moody's Trio and the Tui Hawaiian Orchestra.

In 1925 and 1927 Ernest Kaai returned with his Hawaiian Troubadours for national tours, with the latter visit featuring several New Zealanders among its musical combinations, among them Maori saxophonist Sid David Kamau, Walter Smith's 'favourite nephew'.[88] The Hilo Duo – Wehi and Keoki (George) Greig – performed 'past and present favourites'. (A decade later the Greigs would return as a cowboy and Indian duo in Stanley McKay's Gaieties revue.)[89]

In Rarotonga, when atmospheric conditions cooperated, 1YA could be picked up from Auckland. On Saturday evenings, 'numbers of native chiefs' would gather to listen through the static to *Island Nights' Entertainments*, especially enjoying the Hawaiian music on guitars and ukuleles. Their interest encouraged the station to broadcast a special programme to them in 1929.[90]

A taste for Hawaiian music was also well established in Australia. From the early 1920s, *hapa haole* records are listed in the advertisements for new releases which were also distributed in New Zealand. In 1921 the touring American singer Louis London performed the pseudo-Hawaiian novelty hit 'Yaaka Hula Hickey Dula' (originally

sung by Al Jolson).[91] Three years later this song made an impression on New Zealand jazz musicians during a tour by Bert Ralton's Savoy Havana Band. Having visited Hawaii on the way to New Zealand, Ralton claimed he heard similarities between Hawaiian and Maori melodies. When the band returned to London in 1926, Ralton arranged and recorded 'Yaaka Hula', segueing it into his 'Maori–Hula Medley'. On this, he combined 'Pokarekare' and other Maori melodies, singing the vocals himself in English and his version of Maori. 'While Mr Ralton's discernment could be the subject of conjecture, at least it provided [one of] the first recording[s] of "Pokarekare"', writes music historian Brian Salkeld.[92]

A curiosity about the popularity of Hawaiian music in Australia in the late 1920s is that many of the leading players were Maori who had emigrated from New Zealand before making a name for themselves at home. Among them were Mayo Hunter, Billy 'Kalua' Bishop, and two who also taught: Tui Hamilton and Arthur Thompson. The latter had first heard Pacific-style guitar playing while visiting Fiji in the mid-1920s, joining in with locals at a 'kava joint'. In Australia, he performed and broadcast with his Maori wife Grace Thompson using the stage names of Buddy Wikara and Ruahine Wikara, aka Lani Kalua. In studies of Hawaiian music in Australia, no locally based Polynesian musicians are mentioned as playing there, whereas they became a key element of the New Zealand scene from the 1940s, having been active in the islands for at least a decade.[93]

Supporting the international fashion for Hawaiian music were the developing cultural industries: film, radio, tourism. Around the world the smart hotels opened Hawaiian reception rooms, and recordings by Hawaiian guitarists such as King Benny Nawahi, Sol Hoopii and the pioneer Joseph Kekuku were among the biggest sellers during the recording industry boom in the 1920s.

A languorous, idyllic Pacific was portrayed in the widely syndicated radio programme *Hawaii Calls*, which came 'live from the courtyard of the Moana Hotel' in Honolulu from 1935 to 1975. Local purists complained that *Hawaii Calls* bastardised Hawaiian music, and descriptions of the programme do suggest *Grand Ole Opry* as broadcast from under a banyan tree.[94] But, like *South Pacific*'s Bloody Mary, the programme was seductive, tempting its audience not just to listen to the music, but also to visit the islands in person. Other key disseminators of Hawaiian romanticism were the Matson cruise ships that from the early 1930s steamed between San Francisco, Sydney and Auckland, with a stopover in Hawaii. Disembarking passengers were greeted by a Hawaiian band and garlanded with frangipani leis by hula dancers, and hotels such as the Royal Hawaiian offered hula and ukulele lessons.[95]

Whatever the attitude of Hawaiians themselves, their culture was successfully marketed as utopian, with music as a key element. In the 1930s, Bing Crosby recorded 'Sweet Leilani', and Louis Armstrong performed with his 'Polynesians'; in the 1940s, a popular British act was Felix Mendelssohn and his Hawaiian Serenaders; and the hit musical of 1949 was the ostensibly idyllic *South Pacific*.

The stage was set for New Zealand's own South Sea island paradise recording boom in the 1950s. Yet to some, the Hawaiian style seemed to have been ubiquitous since the 1930s. Robin Hyde was thankful, when visiting Jerusalem on the Wanganui River in 1935, that a Maori group singing waiata by Alfred Hill did so unaccompanied by ukuleles: 'the South Seas melody is so sticky'.[96] That J. H. Hutton's Hawaiian band was spotted doing its 'grass-skirting' in Dunedin during winter 1938 gives an idea

of how much the style was in vogue. In the same year, visiting American Tex Rose – a former pupil of Sol Hoopii – entertained the Auckland Rhythm Club with a display of electric steel-guitar playing with his Kalua Boys. Responding on ukulele, Rod Ingall 'astounded the meeting with a couple of solos on that usually despised instrument'.[97]

Although jazz players such as Jim Higgot, Bob Ewing and Bill Hoffmeister dabbled in Hawaiian music in the 1930s, it was during the war that the dedicated Maori and Polynesian players first emerged who would create the New Zealand–Hawaiian genre during the 1950s.

In 1944 a Palmerston North firm saw enough of a market to copyright *The Learn-Quick Method for the Hawaiian Steel Guitar*, while in Auckland a sheet-metal worker Bunny Milne began manufacturing electric steel guitars. At first he used kauri for the bodies, which produced a lovely soft tone but little volume. He shifted to rimu and, using the brand names Royal, Milton and Commodore, kept the same design for ten years.[98]

In Auckland, Ray Walker was pulling crowds under the name of Tupu Waka and His Islanders. 'This is a Hawaiian-style band similar to that of Gus Lindsay,

Pixie Williams (far right) with, from left, musicians Doug Brewer, Bill Hoffmeister, Jim Carter, Keith Willet and Russ Laurence. The women from the audience are unknown. Wellington, late 1940s. Jim Carter collection

Bunny Milne, who manufactured Commodore steel guitars, amplifiers and accessories, Auckland. Mac McKenzie collection

Pin Point (Spike) McKenzie on lap steel with the Wicky Wacky Wooers, Kawau Island, c. 1951. Mac McKenzie collection
Tommy Kahi, guitar teacher, entrepreneur and mentor, Christchurch, 1962. Mac McKenzie collection

Tony Lindsay, Bill Sevesi, etc', reported the *Music Maker*. 'Auckland has quite a few bands of this style, and they have a good following.'[99]

Post-war, the epicentre was the inner-city suburb of Newton where the pioneers were Gus Lindsay and Tupu Waka at the Orange Ballroom and Lou Mati at the Polynesian Club; Tommy Kahi would also play in the style when required.[100] By the 1950s, musician Mac McKenzie recalled, 'if it had a steel guitar in it, it was a Hawaiian band, and they were everywhere in Auckland'. Every region had its steel-guitar stars: in Wellington, Mati Hita and Jim Carter were at Ngati Poneke; Fred Radich roamed the Hauraki Plains; while Tawhao 'Bronco' Tioke ruled Rotorua. After moving to Christchurch, Tommy Kahi held court at North Beach Memorial Hall, while Dunedin swayed to Colin McCrorie's Kalua Islanders (also his Hawaiians, who were the Tumbleweeds with grass skirts); and in Invercargill, Bill Wakefield performed weekly on 4YZ using a twin-neck guitar.

BLUE SMOKE

Colin McCrorie's Kalua Islanders present *Songs of the Islands*, 1956; in hats and chaps they were the Tumbleweeds. From left, Doug Reeve, Myra Hewitt, Cole Wilson, Nola Hewitt and Colin McCrorie. Campbell Photography/Colin McCrorie collection

Steel guitar virtuoso Mati Hita, late 1940s. Mac McKenzie collection

Gus Lindsay was born in Tahiti in 1903, and is said to have played ukulele in his cousin Lou Mati's Hawaiian band when it toured the United States in the 1920s. A decade later, he started an all-accordion band at the original Point Chevalier Sailing Club, and performed often with his brother Tony, his son Mason and Lou Mati. Lindsay was a hard taskmaster, his son recalled, telling musicians to take a solo with just 'a glance, a nod or even an ear movement'.[101]

The first New Zealand steel-guitar virtuoso was Mati Hita, who never recorded commercially but was the star attraction at venues such as the Maori Community Centre in Auckland, former wrestler Lofty Blomfield's Holiday Inn dance hall/restaurant on Waiheke Island and the Ngati Poneke Club in Wellington.

Born in Taranaki in 1914, Eruera Hita adopted the name Mati when he moved to Auckland. By this stage, he was a 'fully fledged, self-taught musician' and a natural showman, so he was quickly in demand in dance halls. Some patrons would stop dancing to watch as he played complicated licks while conversing; another of his stunts was to play the guitar behind his back. Years later, McKenzie was still awestruck: 'Mati was

exceptionally fast and had perfect pitch [and] a magic thumb. At speed, he would mix multiple single notes, third and fifth harmonies, chords, octaves, harmonics – and at the end of the number you would not be able to remember where he had put what.' One special evening Hita played '12th Street Rag' with his lap steel behind his back, accompanied by Royal Maka and Mark Kahi. In a gimmick often used later by the Maori showbands, Maka fingered Kahi's ukulele while strumming his own guitar, and Kahi did the opposite.

Hita never looked at his instrument unless a mistake happened, and then he would frown at it, as if the guitar had erred. McKenzie said that Hita didn't use picks but his harmonics were crystal clear; his chord voicings seemed unique and his vibrato on the steel 'was that of the Maori voice'.[102] The Sunday afternoon dances at Blomfield's were exhausting for the dancers, if not for Mati:

He would play any sort of music: pops, evergreens, tricky ones from shows, jazz numbers. But when he played Hawaiian, it was pure Hawaiian. He used his thumb as a plectrum to play '12th Street Rag' at a speed no one else could even hope for. The big afternoon event was

Mati Hita, second from left, with the pianist Nicky Smith and June and Jim Carter; Ngati Poneke Club, Wellington, early 1950s. Jim Carter collection

the marathon challenge between the band and the crowd. The three-step polonaise would start: the couple that fell out was not allowed back in, the band could rest one player at a time. When Mati thought the thing had gone on long enough he would up the tempo again and again until the drummer could only manage every second beat. The band always won with Mati.[103]

For all his virtuosity, Hita was let down by his disorganisation. 'Mati was a bit of a gypsy on it, really. You never quite knew whether he would turn up', said Jim Carter, who played with him at Ngati Poneke in Wellington for seven years. 'Because if someone offered him a better dance job he'd go with them, and you'd find yourself short of Mati one night.' Carter struggled to keep the band together after Hita left. 'We couldn't get anybody to replace Mati, he was far too good.' He tried bringing in seasoned players such as Lauri Paddi and Dorsey Cameron, but 'crowds weren't so interested. The steel was what brought them in the first place.'[104]

WOLFGRAMM AND SEVESI: THE NAVIGATORS

In Auckland, the Hawaiian style was dominated by two consummate professionals, both originally from Tonga. Bill Wolfgramm found his niche in the recording studio, while in the dance halls Bill Sevesi became a much-loved band leader, motivator and entrepreneur. It was two Mormons who brought the steel guitar to Tonga in the 1930s. The first, a missionary from Utah, left behind an 'exceptional silvery beauty, a National tricone steel guitar' after serving in the islands. Meanwhile, a Tongan named Charlie Sanft left to study in Utah; on his way home, he became sidetracked in Hollywood, acting in minor roles and learning the steel guitar from the US star Dick McIntire and others. Returning to Tonga he became a prominent player and teacher.[105]

Wolfgramm was born on Vava'u, Tonga, in 1925. While at school he sang with the Tongan Free Church Choir, learning music from his brother-in-law, the choirmaster. He formed a popular three-piece dance band, playing rhythm guitar and ukulele; on lead guitar was Dick Sanft,

Charlie's nephew. Wolfgramm picked up the steel guitar aged nineteen, after seeing a musician named Matairi play the instrument.[106]

Emigrating to New Zealand in 1948, Wolfgramm settled in Ponsonby, and bought a black-and-chrome Commodore eight-string steel guitar made by Bunny Milne. His first gigs were at Lofty Blomfield's with Royal Maka and he quickly became a regular at Auckland's leading venues, among them the Catholic Social Centre in Newton, where Pacific Islanders mingled 'under the watchful eye of Father Schwere'.[107] By the early 1950s, Bill Wolfgramm's Hawaiians were broadcasting regularly on 1YA, with Daphne Walker as the vocalist.[108]

In 1952 Wolfgramm went to Wellington, and spent about two years performing rhythm guitar with Phil Paku's Hawaiians, which also included Mati Hita on steel and Daphne Walker as vocalist. Radio broadcasts on 2YA led to frequent radio and recording work on his return to Auckland. His first recording was 'Fijian Holiday', to accompany a promotional film for TEAL's flying-boat service around the Pacific. Written by

Crombie Murdoch, and credited as Mavis Rivers with Bill Wolfgramm and His Rhythm, it was released on Tanza in 1951.[109]

Wolfgramm is best known for the 78s he recorded on Tanza with Daphne Walker, in particular 'Haere Mai'. The timing was perfect, wrote Mac McKenzie. 'It was sung everywhere by everyone, all trying to copy Daphne's soft yet clear voice with the perfect vibrato for hula or poi.'[110]

Wolfgramm was writing his own arrangements and, he explained in 1955, 'Sometimes we do some Island music – Samoan and Tongan – and some Maori music, but mostly we stick to Hawaiian.'[111] On a couple of occasions, Wolfgramm performed for Queen Salote of Tonga at Government House in Auckland, and after 'Haere Mai' he increasingly emphasised the local, whether it was Polynesia or Ponsonby. He changed the name of his band from the Hawaiians to the Islanders, a popular move as his band included Tongans, Samoans, Maori and Europeans – but no Hawaiians. Ironically, their first release as Bill Wolfgramm and His Islanders was 'Honolulu March'.

Tongan guitar masters Bill Wolfgramm (left) and Bill Sevesi, at the Papatoetoe RSA, Auckland, 1990. Chris Williams/*Metro*

On 21 November 1955, Tanza released the first 'all-New Zealand' album: *South Sea Rhythm*, a 10-inch disc by
Bill Wolfgramm and His Islanders, with Daphne Walker, recorded by Noel Peach. RNZ Music Library, Wellington

This group was responsible for a major milestone in local recording: the first 'all-New Zealand' album.[112] *South Sea Rhythm* was a 10-inch disc on Tanza, and the initiative of engineer Noel Peach and Tanza's new in-house producer Murdoch Riley. One side features Bill Wolfgramm and His Islanders performing instrumentals; on the other, Walker sings, accompanied by Wolfgramm's band and the Hager Sisters. Although it still included several songs that referenced Hawaii or were actual standards, it was quickly followed up by *Melodies of Maoriland*. Many of these songs had already been released on 78s, but all celebrated their local content, among them Sam Freedman's 'Haere Mae', 'When My Wahine Does the Poi', 'New Zealand's Christmas Tree' and 'Pania of the Reef'.

After the arrival of rock'n'roll, live gigs in the Hawaiian style dropped off, and although Wolfgramm was still in demand for private functions, 'the young ones when they married wanted their music, not the music of their parents', wrote McKenzie.[113]

But when Wolfgramm died on 25 September 2003, his music was being heard by a new audience. He had left behind a substantial catalogue of New Zealand recordings in the Hawaiian style; although few New Zealanders knew his name, most could sing along to 'Haere Mai'.

EVERYTHING IS KAPAI

Daphne Walker's voice conjured up South Sea island magic, although she grew up in the Hauraki Gulf rather than Bali Ha'i. On Great Barrier Island as a child she would get together with her friends, light a fire on the beach and have a singalong. She moved to Auckland to attend secondary school, and in 1949, after appearing in a talent quest, she received a call from guitarist Johnny Bradfield who was putting together a band with Bill Wolfgramm.

Dennis Huggard Archive, MSD10-0577,
Alexander Turnbull Library, Wellington

legs start to buckle because she was out of air. But it was a beautiful recording.'[117]

Despite the diversity of songs – a mix of Maori, Hawaiian and novelty songs – Walker would record a batch in one session. 'You had to do the lot, it was strenuous and tiring, but you weren't allowed to get tired.'[118] She would learn the Tahitian words from older recordings, and found the language very similar to Maori.

Walker's smiling, creamy voice belongs to a lost era of Hollywood musicals, a Dorothy Lamour foil to Bing Crosby's croon. Her singing is feminine and charming, but she never tries to sound sultry or even coy.

Walker shifted to Viking Records in 1960, where Murdoch Riley wanted to move away from Hawaiian material, but record in that style using original New Zealand songs. Riley: 'I was getting fed up with "The Lovely Hula Hands", "On the Beach at Waikiki" and that type of song. I felt we had songwriters in New Zealand

They broadcast on 1YA in Shortland Street, and recorded down the hill at Noel Peach's Astor Studios for Tanza.

Walker's first release under her own name was 'Maori Brown Eyes' in 1954. She recorded more than 30 sides for Tanza, and her 78s quickly found an appreciative audience; the country song 'Hootchy Kootchy Henry' was a hit in Samoa after being transformed 'into the palm-hip-swaying idiom' by Wolfgramm.[114] Two songs in particular have been lasting favourites, both written by Freedman: 'When My Wahine Does the Poi' and 'Haere Mai'. 'Haere Mai' originally sold over 40,000 copies, while 'Wahine' – on the same 78 as 'Aroha' – was New Zealand's first double-sided local hit, holding the first and third spots on the 1YD *Hit Parade* in the same week in 1955.[115] Others also became perennials: 'Aroha' and 'An Okey Dokey Hut ('Neath the Co-Co-Coconut Palms)'.

Walker's prolific recording career was in stark contrast to her reluctance to perform before an audience. For a brief period she appeared twice a week at the Orange Hall with Bill Sevesi's band. 'I couldn't face singing in public', she said. 'I've always been like that – I just freeze.'[116]

In the studio, she was in her element, said Sevesi. 'She has the best breath control I know of. She usually marks down on her music when to take a breath. There was an instance where she went past that spot, and didn't take a breath. I could see Daphne go blue in the face and her

Daphne Walker in 1954, at the time of 'Haere Mai': 'You weren't allowed to get tired'. *Gordon Spittle collection*

to write material in the same vein, so why didn't we use them?'[119]

A reporter from *Record Monthly* visited 'Miss Walker (or Mrs Clarke, as she is at home)' and found himself captivated. She was a 'modest, quietly spoken girl with a ready smile and no high-flown ideas about the artist's life. "I don't think a girl needs to work too hard to become a singer", she said. "In fact, I don't think anyone should work hard."'[120]

It was Wolfgramm's friend, collaborator and rival who became the godfather, motivator and patron of New Zealand's steel-guitar players and Polynesian music. Late in his career, Bill Sevesi enjoyed a respect and high profile greater than he had received in his heyday, although among the cognoscenti, it seemed overdue.

Sevesi was born in Nuku'alofa, Tonga, in 1923, to a Tongan mother and a Liverpudlian father. He was named Wilfred Jeffs after his father; Sevesi is a Tongan transliteration of Jeffs, and became his preferred stage name.

It was while attending school in Papatoetoe, Auckland, in the late 1930s that Sevesi first heard Hawaiian music.

It was broadcast by 1ZM, and listening on his crystal radio set Sevesi was fascinated by the sound, especially the way notes on electric steel hung in the air.

He began an apprenticeship at an Auckland radio factory, and after work technicians helped him build a steel guitar and amplifier based on photographs of performers such as the McIntires and Felix Mendelssohn. Sevesi's first homemade guitar, however, 'was terrible. You never heard a cat meowing so badly in your life.' His second attempt – from a heavy slab of kahikatea – produced a twin-necked guitar that lasted him for decades.[121]

By playing along with records and jamming with other musicians, he taught himself to play. Epi Shalfoon was intrigued by the teenager: he was a regular patron who never danced, only watched. 'I learnt a lot from him just by watching his playing and the way he walked around the floor – he was a great musician.'[122]

A 1940 performance at a Mt Eden fundraising dance led to a local residency that lasted until 1944. The organiser said the band's name – Wilfred Jeffs and His Islanders – didn't sound Polynesian, so Will Jeffs adopted the name Bill Sevesi. When he returned from the war in 1946, the Islanders were still active and there was plenty

Regatta day at Ngaruawahia, 1947. Foreground, from left: Bill Sevesi, Joe Marvin and Don Stacy. Mac McKenzie collection

BLUE SMOKE

'You have to give the public what they want': Bill Sevesi and His Islanders, 1958. From left: Trevor Edmondson, Bobby Wynyard, Malu Natapu, Richard Santos, Bill Sevesi. Gordon Spittle collection

of work about: the Masonic Hall in Upper Queen Street, St Sep's in Khyber Pass, Railway Hall in Newmarket and the Te Papapa Football Club.

Sevesi's first session in a recording studio was backing the expatriate singer Tex Morton in 1949. 'They couldn't get another steel player and I was the one at the time', recalled Sevesi, who felt uncomfortable playing country and western. Although he enjoyed the music, he was 'a stranger to that style. I felt I didn't belong there.'[123] Still, he later played on other country sessions, notably backing expatriate Canadian singer Luke Simmons as a New Zealand version of his Blue Mountain Boys.[124]

Near the corner of Newton Road and Symonds Street is the Orange Coronation Hall, also known as the Orange Ballroom. Many of Auckland's leading bands established residencies there on different nights of the week, among

them Ted Croad, Epi Shalfoon and Ernie Butters. When the manager, George Searle, approached Sevesi in 1954 and offered him two nights a week, replacing Gus Lindsay's Hawaiians, Sevesi didn't think twice.

For the next sixteen years, Bill Sevesi and His Islanders became a regular fixture at the Orange. As the years went by and fashions changed, the configuration of the band changed too: a trumpet, a piano accordion, a saxophone . . . 'When we first started we played some very peculiar music', said Sevesi. '"Hands, Knees and Boomps-a-Daisy", the statue waltz, the maxina, valetas, the gypsy tap and all that old-fashioned stuff. Then the pop music came, and the rock'n'roll. It was no good playing the wrong music at the wrong time. You have to give the public what they want.'[125]

With regular work and good crowds, Sevesi was quickly paying double union rates, attracting the best musicians to join his bands and even bigger crowds. 'All the roads seemed to lead to the Orange Hall. After about a year there we were so popular that when we got to the hall people were already sitting on the steps at seven o'clock waiting to get in. At half past eight it was shut, they couldn't take anymore.'[126]

The longevity of Sevesi's popularity was due to his willingness to try different styles, to nurture new talent, and to see opportunities and to seize them. As rock'n'roll arrived, the Islanders included it in their repertoire, often learning the tunes from Australian shortwave radio stations and performing them weeks before their release. The steel guitar retreated in the band's sound, making way for an electric lead guitar. There were recording sessions for Tanza and Viking: Polynesian and Maori music, rock'n'roll and pop. And there were gigs backing overseas acts such as the Everly Brothers, Gene Pitney and Clarence 'Frogman' Henry.[127]

In 1958 Phil Warren hired Sevesi and his band to back English immigrant Vince Callaher recording two songs at Bruce Barton's Mascot studio on Wellesley Street. Sevesi suggested a song for the B-side, Col Joye's 'Bye Bye Baby Goodbye'. It became No. 1 on the *Lever Hit Parade* for seven weeks, whereas the A-side, 'Moo Cow Boogie Blues' – written by local musician Gene O'Leary – only reached No. 4. For these sessions, Warren thought that the name Bill Sevesi and His Islanders was inappropriate, so they became Will Jess and his Jesters.

More pop followed after Callaher's return to Britain, when Sevesi recruited sixteen-year-old Aucklander Ronnie Sundin, trained him to sing and backed him at concerts and on several hit records.

Sevesi's most significant recording with the Islanders is probably *Sea Breeze*, a Viking album from 1960 credited to the singers Daphne Walker and George Tumahai. Besides Sevesi's own song 'Meama Chimes' – played on a ten-string guitar – and 'Waihi Moon', the album mostly featured Polynesian and Hawaiian songs. It harked back to the Hawaiian-influenced sound of Sevesi's youth, and was a big seller for many years, even getting released in Canada and Tahiti.

Sevesi has kept the Hawaiian influence prominent in New Zealand pop, but his real lasting legacy is as a mentor: talent-spotting the Yandall Sisters and Annie Crummer and making their first recordings, encouraging innumerable Polynesian musicians and bands, and teaching children the ukulele. For this, his energy has seemed tireless.[128]

WILL YOU BE LONESOME TOO? PIONEERS OF NEW ZEALAND COUNTRY MUSIC

'The Cowboys Are Coming!' The breathless advertisements in the Auckland newspapers of August 1928 hoped to build excitement about Fred Mayfield's Cowboy Band, which was about to arrive on the MS *Aorangi*. Advance photos showed the nine-piece band lined up on deck, wearing grins as extravagant as their woolly chaps.

Mayfield's Cowboys attracted full houses to Auckland's Majestic, and their music ranged from classical to jazz and dance music. They appeared on stage in front of a backdrop showing a western scene of rolling, grassy hills, dressed in cowboy hats, 'flaming neckerchiefs' and their outsized chaps. Their musicianship on constantly changing instruments dazzled the audience, especially the imitation of a train on the steel guitar. Mayfield's cheerful demeanour and leadership were an inspiration to all. His posse promised 'Symphonies! Melodies! Jazz!' – but delivered one of New Zealand's earliest encounters with something that resembled country music.[129]

In the same period, the first country records began to arrive in New Zealand via Australia. From 1926, the discs were manufactured in Sydney, and most of the early country artists were released on the HMV and Regal Zonophone labels. The latter was especially important: its discs were a shilling cheaper than HMV's, and its catalogue contained many US labels releasing 'hillbilly' music. Among them was RCA Victor's Bluebird, with the cream of early country acts: Jimmie Rodgers, the Carter Family, Gene Autry, Johnny Barfield and many others.[130]

Records, radio, films and visitors were the ways that country music was disseminated. Early in the century, Zane Grey's western novels had brought the cowboy to New Zealand popular culture before Hollywood (and before Grey's celebrated 1926 fishing trip to the Bay of Islands). But films would become crucial in exposing the image, mythology and sound of the cowboy singer to New Zealanders, especially those starring Gene Autry and Roy Rogers; without dirt on their boots, they were the house-trained salesmen of country music. From the get-go, the country music genre relied on performers who were playing roles that described and romanticised rural life. Both artist and audience required imagination and identification with those roles. Ronald Hugh Morrieson's Te Kauwhata Kid – the character later played by Billy T. James in the 1985 film *Came a Hot Friday* – satirised

Above: Pete Kloss, 'New Zealand's yodelling cowboy'.
Merry Go Round, March 1939

Left: Gene Autry greets his New Zealand fans,
Radio Record, 1 April 1938. RNZ Infofind

genuine local identities that related to the myths a little too closely. But the connection was real, on Australian ranches and in New Zealand's backblocks.

'In the Depression years', recalled singer Jack Riggir, 'men would mix together, light a fire, sit on tins or boxes, and have a guitar or mandolin, a mouth organ or a comb with tissue paper around it, and make music. That is the start of country and western music in New Zealand. Around the camp fire.'[131] By 1940 the music's popularity – and the market's recovery – was such that Marbeck's record store in Auckland produced a mail-order catalogue of country discs.[132]

Another touring musician arrived in 1932: the Kansas-born hillbilly singer Carson Robison. With his band the Buckaroos, Robison's New Zealand visit was part of a tour to Australia, Canada and Britain (where he sang for King George V). Robison, who could simultaneously whistle two tones in harmony, recorded for Victor as early as 1924, as a soloist and also accompanying Vernon Dalhart.[133]

Tex Morton was the first major figure in country music in New Zealand and Australia, and Dalhart was one of his key influences, along with Jimmie Rodgers, Goebel Reeves, the Carter Family and Robison. All had discs

available in Australia from the late 1920s, and as imports in New Zealand. Morton left for Australia in 1933, and his first professional recordings in 1936 were seminal on both sides of the Tasman. He inspired Australians such as Buddy Williams and yodelling queen Shirley Thoms, who themselves inspired New Zealanders. Morton and his acolytes conveyed the message that country music was for enjoyment *and* involvement.

The music was accessible and achievable, apart from one element, with which the performer could display virtuosity yet polarise the audience: the yodel. Jimmie Rodgers popularised the yodel in recorded country music, but musicologist Graeme Smith points out that the phenomenon had been experienced in Britain and the US since the 1840s, when the touring Tyrolese singing group the Rainer family unveiled their bravura yodelling while performing Swiss melodies. In the early 1850s, a minstrel troupe called Rainer's Original Ethiopian Serenaders brought the technique to Oceania. The skill required contrasted with the often unsophisticated elements of country music, and prowess at yodelling made a performer stand out. It could also make the audience switch off, which Tex Morton satirised in one of his wartime radio shows. Claiming a listener had sent him something for his vocal cords – a cut-throat razor – Morton broke into 'a most extravagant yodel, complete with trills and gargles, clearly using this to signal his right to occupy the role of performer'. The godfather of New Zealand country knew that showmanship required more than just looking the part.[134]

A blizzard in August 1939 caused chaos at Dunedin's biggest dance of the year, the Charity Ball. All public transport was cut in the city, and many private cars were stranded. Still, 400 people turned up, including one dancer who arrived on skis. Dick Colvin had a ten-piece band ready to broadcast live-to-air, although his drummer and xylophonist Fred Gedson was missing. He was walking through knee-deep snow to a hospital with his wife, who had gone into labour. The live broadcast had to be cancelled as the landlines to the 4YA and 4ZB transmitters were cut off by the snow. So New Zealand missed out on hearing the radio debut of a young country singer who went on to have a lengthy career.

Billed as the '14-year-old yodelling cowboy', Les Wilson had recently been impressing crowds at the Dunedin Town Hall.[135] His older brother was Cole Wilson, later of Tumbleweeds fame, although Les was first to perform. Growing up, they shared their love of the genre, then achieved similar success with different approaches. Les Wilson was influenced by Wilf Carter, a Canadian who was performing country before there were record companies, and yodelling before Jimmie Rodgers.

Wilson's career began well: he first appeared on stage at the age of nine, playing a harmonica. He graduated to violin, banjo and guitar, and found that 'western'-style songs received the best response, so that became his style. By the age of twelve, he was performing at shows around Dunedin, and while still in his mid-teens was signed to appear at Joe Brown's weekly dances at the Town Hall, which were broadcast over 4ZB. His name quickly became well known in Otago and Southland and beyond. 'The fan mail he received during this period would be the envy of any movie star', wrote country reporter Garth Gibson.[136]

A month after the snowstorm, Wilson's promising career was interrupted when the Second World War broke out. He was still just fourteen, but had a six-month contract with 4ZB and was about to make a tour of New Zealand's radio stations; as soon as he was old enough, Wilson joined up. While the war stalled the momentum

No fool: Happi Hill, expatriate Canadian proselytiser of country music for 23 years on 3ZB. RNZ Sound Archives

of country music in New Zealand, live performances still took place on radio and at A&P shows, by the likes of Jack Brown in Canterbury; in Auckland, accordionist Toni Savage formed a very popular comic hillbilly act, the Kentucky Korn Kobs.[137]

Beaming out of Christchurch, though, was a radio show that was pivotal to increasing country music's popularity in the South Island. It was run by Happi Hill, an expatriate Canadian born in Lost Lake, Alberta, who became a popular hillbilly broadcaster on 3ZB. Every weekday morning during *Breakfast Club*, he presented *Keeping Up with the World*, a fifteen-minute sponsored feature; on Saturdays he hosted a country and western show, *Haywire Hookup*.

Hill had arrived in New Zealand in 1937, after growing up in one of Canada's more remote regions. With a fondness for wearing Stetsons, white tuxedos and cowboy accessories – and working in the advertising business – he quickly became one of the most flamboyant characters in Christchurch, 'a larger-than-life individualist with a wicked sense of humour'.[138]

Born Petersen Happe Hill – his parents were happy he wasn't a twin – he had got his start in Calgary taking part in a 'cowboy yell', a contest in which cowboys see who can yell the loudest. This led to a role with a group of vaudeville players who toured rural Canada.[139] Hill tried 'cowpunching' but was becoming disillusioned when the tough winter of '36 wiped out a year's work. So when a New Zealand tourist described his country in utopian terms, Hill decided to come south.

Hill's broadcasts had a strong western flavour – with appropriate music and tales from the Wild West – and lasted for 23 years. He became notorious for publicity stunts, such as bringing a horse into the 3ZB studio to get some authentic sound effects. Hill was a man about town, running talent quests and concerts, appearing at A&P shows and calling square dancing. In 1951, during the square dance boom, he recorded several 78s with the Tanza Square Dance Band. He also recorded two novelty discs for Zodiac in the early 1960s: 'The Full Pack of Cards'/'Pine Trees to Toothpicks', and 'Rugby Solitaire'/'Big Deal'.[140]

To many performers growing up in the South Island in the 1940s and 1950s, Hill's programme was a formative experience. 'He presented himself as a western guy, he had a style that was very natural and catchy', said singer Rocky Don Hall. 'He would mainly play western music, but also had the unusual things, the novelty items. He stood out for his unusual antics. He had something that captivated you each day.'[141]

Among the regular performers on Hill's show during the war were the Canadian Sisters. Irene and Violet Tomblin were actually born in Christchurch, but spent their childhood in Saskatchewan: visiting an uncle on their way to Britain, the family had been stranded by the Depression. They lived in a log cabin, and while singing in school concerts discovered their talent for harmony. Returning to Christchurch just before the war began, within two weeks they were performing on the 3ZB children's session. The 3ZB accompanist Maisie McNair suggested they call themselves the Canadian Sisters, and the whole Tomblin family also appeared as the Maple Leaf Quartet, with Irene on steel guitar, Violet on Spanish, their mother on ukulele and father on concertina.

Born in Christchurch, raised in a log cabin in Saskatchewan, Violet and Irene Tomblin became known as the Canadian Sisters. Rocky Don Hall collection

They performed current hillbilly songs with the Ada Jones Concert Party at military camps and hospitals. The sisters made private recordings at a Christchurch studio operated by Strath McKnight, but their only professional release was on Tanza in 1950: 'Goodbye Little Darlin''/'When the Cactus is in Bloom'. The other highlight of their career came in 1955 when they toured New Zealand with the British crooner Donald Peers. After marriage, Irene moved to Wellington; it would be eighteen years before the Canadian Sisters performed again.[142]

Although country and western was keenly listened to in New Zealand, with Tex Morton based in Australia, it was not until just after the Second World War that the style became a significant force in the local music scene.

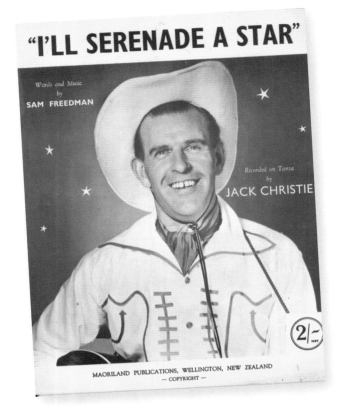

"I'LL SERENADE A STAR"

Words and Music
by
SAM FREEDMAN

Recorded on Tanza
by
JACK CHRISTIE

2/-
NET

MAORILAND PUBLICATIONS, WELLINGTON, NEW ZEALAND
— COPYRIGHT —

Jack Christie, worked at Tanza by day and yodelled at night. 'I'll Serenade a Star' by Sam Freedman was one of many successful recordings for the company. Sound and Vision Centre, National Library

Several developments occurred simultaneously, in different parts of the country, which helped bring performers into the public eye. While Happi Hill continued his regular broadcasts in Christchurch, at Wellington's 2YD on 1 April 1948 Arthur 'Turntable' Pearce launched another alter ego. As 'Cotton-Eye Joe', he began hosting *Cowboy Jamboree*, devoted to new releases from the hillbilly genre. From its first disc – Eddy Arnold's 'I'll Hold You in My Heart' – the programme offered the same approach as *Rhythm on Record* did to jazz. Through various incarnations, the programme lasted until 1975, anticipating developments in country, R&B and pop. Pearce's tortured puns were a key element in the programme's early years, when it concentrated on hillbilly and western swing, and it rapidly became a cult among country fans.[143]

Tanza was quick to exploit the popularity of country music, even before it began releasing discs. Jack Christie was already on the premises helping prepare the company's record division, and recorded several sample acetates while Stan Dallas was building the studio. A Broadcasting employee before the war, he performed with the 2YA Camp Entertainers once it began, then served – and

sang – in the Pacific with the RNZAF. His 1949 recording of 'Overlander Trail' b/w 'She Came Rolling Down the Mountain' became Tanza's third release, after 'Blue Smoke' and 'Paekakariki'. Tanza produced over ten discs by Christie, with 'The Freight Train Yodel' being a recording breakthrough for Stan Dallas in 1950. Beneath Christie's vocal and yodelling, the demanding guitar part emulating a steam train was achieved by multiple dubbing. Dallas had recently acquired an early tape-recorder – a PT6 Magnacorder – from a staff member at the US Embassy who was returning home. Many aspiring country guitarists broke strings trying to emulate the sound. Christie, a singer and yodeller in the Tex Morton mould, was a good earner for Tanza, said Dallas: being on the premises and accompanying himself on guitar, he was cheap to record. 'Jack had everything', said Dallas, 'good voice, good vocal, good stage and off-stage personality, and sales of his "Rolling Down the Mountain" rolled into thousands.'[144]

In the five years he was with Tanza, Christie made many cover versions, including novelties such as 'Nittie, the Nitwit of the Network' and 'Where the Roly Poly Grass Rolls O'er the Plains'. But he also recorded some significant originals. 'The New Zealand Cowboy' was his own composition and a request-show perennial after its release in 1951. 'I'll Serenade a Star' was an early effort by Sam Freedman, in which the singer wants to flee the bustle of city life for clean country air:

> I'll find a soft haystack
> 'Way off the beaten track
> And with my old guitar
> I'll serenade a star.[145]

With Tex Morton spending almost all of his career overseas, it left the way clear for the Tumbleweeds to become New Zealand's most important domestic country act. The group is significant in many ways: it was the first country band to record on Tanza, and a song from those sessions, 'Maple on the Hill', became a huge success and was extremely influential in country circles for decades. The Tumbleweeds were the first local country act to turn regular radio play into a successful recording career, and introduced many people to their first country band on two national tours. And the band's music reflected a combination of influences that made theirs a distinctively New Zealand form of country music: a mix of Hawaiian, cowboy and hillbilly styles.

FAMILY STYLE, COUNTRY STYLE

The Tumbleweeds' origins exemplified country music traditions. The band emerged from music-making in the home, and at its core was a family band: two husbands and their two wives, who happened to be sisters.

Musically, Dunedin in the 1930s was remarkably buoyant. Community singing and variety shows were drawing big crowds, and reflected the British heritage of the citizens. But the influence of music from the United States, heard on radio and records, was also making in-roads. The household in which Myra and Nola Hewitt grew up was very social and very musical: their mother played banjo-mandolin, their father steel guitar, and together they harmonised to cowboy, Hawaiian and Maori melodies. Nola quickly picked up the mandolin, then the guitar and ukulele; Myra briefly learnt the steel guitar with the Begg's Musical Army (a group-teaching method).

On 4ZD's *Smile Family* session, the sisters began singing their favourite style of music: cowboy. *Pinto Pete and His Ranch-hands* was essential listening on Friday nights: fifteen minutes of cowboy music, straight from the US.[146]

In 1944, tuned in to a broadcast of a local talent quest, the sisters were spellbound by a steel guitarist. It was Colin McCrorie, performing 'Sing Me a Song of the Islands' on an electric instrument made by his brother. They voted for his trio, which came second to a classical singer. The performance also attracted the attention of Bill Ditchfield, a bass player who had learnt banjo and mandolin from Louis Bloy, and played with Dunedin dance bands. He approached McCrorie and suggested they form a band: the Hawaiian Serenaders.

It was the Begg's Musical Army, run by Bill Coulter, that brought the various Tumbleweeds together. While

The Tumbleweeds of Dunedin, 1950. From left: Bill Ditchfield, Cole Wilson, Nola Hewitt, Colin McCrorie. Campbell Photography/Viking Records collection

Myra and Nola were performing with the large group of Begg's students, they were very impressed by a guest guitarist, Cole Wilson. Self-taught – apart from a few lessons in reading by Sol Stokes – Wilson had discovered country and western as a boy through discs by the Carter Family and Jimmie Rodgers. Besides country and Hawaiian, he enjoyed playing jazz and was a fan of Django Reinhardt and Slim Gaillard. He began visiting the Hewitt home to play at their many parties, singing harmony with the sisters.

Nola Hewitt had been learning the hula from a Dunedin-based Tahitian chef who went by the name Charlie Murray. The pair performed the hula at a Musical Army concert at which the Hawaiian Serenaders were guests, and Ditchfield asked them if they would dance for the band when they needed a floor show. At about the same time, Wilson and the Hewitt sisters sang 'Maple on the Hill' on 4YA. This gave Ditchfield the idea that together they should form a country and western band, with McCrorie on steel. 'At this stage there were not many groups – if any – doing cowboy music, but rather one person singing with a Spanish guitar accompaniment', recalled Nola.

Intrigued by the idea, the original quartet had its first get-together in March 1949: Nola Hewitt, Ditchfield, McCrorie and Wilson. After a few practice sessions, they were accepted to perform on 4YA. Wilson came up with the Tumbleweeds name, and within weeks they were regulars on the station for fifteen-minute live broadcasts, using 'Cowboy's Dream' as a theme ('Tumblin' Tumbleweeds' was already taken).

Just six months after their first rehearsals, Tanza Records invited the group to Wellington. With Stan Dallas engineering, over a weekend they recorded six numbers, including the song that brought the band its greatest success. Against strenuous objections from the others, Wilson insisted they record 'Maple on the Hill', a hillbilly hit for Zeke and Wade. 'Myra and I thought it was too monotonous', said Nola. 'However he was adamant, and we did it. Following the enormous popularity of "Maple", Cole said he was taking no notice of us two in the future.'[147]

'Maple on the Hill' was an immediate hit when it was released early in 1950 as Tanza # 10. The tale of a man who hopes to be remembered after his death, especially by the lover whom he courted beneath a maple, the song is deeply melancholic. Wilson's plaintive voice is complemented by ethereal steel lines from McCrorie, and Nola Hewitt's subtle harmony; Ditchfield's upbeat bass makes the song a gentle dance rather than a dirge.

Wilson's vocals would always reflect the influences of his idols, at first Tex Morton and later Hank Williams. His guitar playing revealed his jazz interests and the informal tuition received from Americans he met serving in the air force in the Pacific. McCrorie's steel-guitar playing was unique. In the Serenaders, he had experimented with tunings, finding that E7 and C#m7 were more suitable for Hawaiian music, and that influence remained with the Tumbleweeds, giving their country music its own Pacific flavour.[148]

The Tumbleweeds returned to Wellington in 1950 to record more than a dozen titles. Among them were four written by Cole Wilson: 'I've Wandered Too Long', 'The Outlaw', 'Violets Blue' and 'On the Plains Away Out There'. Although it was finished just moments before the recording session, 'The Outlaw' shows how quickly Wilson had become an accomplished songwriter, and how well he had absorbed his influences. A narrative ballad taken at a gallop, 'The Outlaw' tells of a boastful fugitive hiding out in the badlands, while a lawman – 'a man who knew no fear' – is on his tail. The outlaw's beloved pony falters, then can run no more. By the time the lawman catches up with them, both lie dead on the ground; the outlaw's gun is still smoking.

After these sessions, Stan Dallas threw a party for the Dunedin visitors, inviting other Tanza musicians such as guitarist Jim Carter, and a jam took place. McCrorie unveiled some of his repertoire from the Hawaiian Serenaders. 'I can still see Stan Dallas', said McCrorie nearly 60 years later. 'He had a faraway stare most of the time, but he just said, "We've got to get some of that on record before you go home!"' Next day, in a rush to beat an 11.00 am power-cut and to catch their afternoon ferry south, the musicians gathered to record six titles as Colin McCrorie and His Kalua Islanders, all released by Tanza in 1951.[149]

Myra Hewitt joined the group in November 1951, as a second vocalist. She had already been working with the group as their stylist. A clever seamstress, Myra had created their outfits from watching Gene Autry and Roy Rogers films, making fringed cowboy shirts by shredding silver braid. Because cowboy boots were virtually impossible to buy, Myra had a cobbler build up the heels of gumboots, cut the uppers into shape, braid them with rubber and then paint the boots white. 'They looked good on stage, but weren't for close inspection', said Nola.[150]

Although radio airplay made the Tumbleweeds well known in New Zealand and Australia, they rarely

Country jam: Tex Morton and the Tumbleweeds, 1950. From left: Bill Ditchfield, Tex Morton, Cole Wilson, Sister Dorrie, Nola Hewitt and Colin McCrorie. Colin McCrorie collection

ventured from their southern base. Unlike Cole's brother Les, they never visited Australia, and they made just two New Zealand tours. Garth Gibson credits the first of these, in the summer of 1951–52, as introducing many New Zealanders in the provinces to their first country band (as opposed to solo artists, such as Tex Morton). Eight performers went on the tour, travelling by – and sleeping in – a truck and caravan. Between them they could offer a complete variety show, with country, Hawaiian, hillbilly and Latin-American music, as well as comedy, magic and hula dancing. Others in the troupe were the magician Escilante (Ewen Blackley), risqué comedienne and makeup artist Kaye Hewitt (aunt of Nola and Myra), and Stewie Whip as a compère/comedian. Understandably, the Tumbleweeds regarded this eight-month tour as the highlight of their lives: in the fifth month a double wedding took place, with Cole Wilson marrying Myra Hewitt and Colin McCrorie marrying Nola Hewitt.[151]

'Maple on the Hill' became a standard for aspiring country acts to master, but Wilson was also respected for his song writing (although he was uneasy about making New Zealand references). As the front man, his guitar skills, yodelling, emotional delivery and commanding stage presence took prominence, but the Tumbleweeds were all gifted musicians and a true ensemble. The group recorded prolifically, with Tanza releasing fifteen discs before the group moved to the fledgling Viking Records in 1957. Launched by ex-Tanza employee Murdoch Riley, Viking released many more singles and albums by the group, which continued performing for 40 years. The Viking discs included many original songs, as well as re-recordings of their popular but out-of-print Tanza tracks. Most of these were recorded in Dunedin by the resourceful Leao Padman, who built his own equipment; the McCrorie's living room on Signal Hill Road was often the venue for the sessions. The Tumbleweeds didn't need to leave town to find the country.

New Zealanders Best Hill-Billy Buyers

Recording companies and publishers report that New Zealanders buy more hill-billy numbers, per head, than any country in the world – including the United States. There are two main classes of customer, Maoris and men in Ministry of Works and other camps. Both types favour them, because they can be easily played on a guitar.[152]

In the wake of the Tumbleweeds' success, the popularity of country and western grew quickly in New Zealand. Among those who recorded 78s in the early 1950s were Fay Doell ('Daddy Was a Yodelling Cowboy'), Buster Keene, Lee Smith, Reg Stuart and Glory Thorburn. Radio was supportive, especially in the regions such as Wanganui and Palmerston North, and on specialist shows run by aficionados such as Terry Riley on 4XD in Dunedin and Percy Stevens at 2ZM Gisborne. Fifteen-minute live spots on regional radio were common, from the likes of Johnny Cooper, Ron Hayward and Rex Franklin in New Plymouth and Wanganui, while Jimmy Long and the Longshots sang of the Canterbury Plains on 3ZB.[153]

Local record companies recorded numerous country acts, among them Rex and Noelene Franklin, Rusty Greaves, Jack Riggir, Garner Wayne and many singers named Johnny. In Auckland, a citified genre of country–pop evolved, with singers such as Dorothy Brannigan and Pat McMinn being backed on disc by groups such as the Astor Barnyard Boys (the Astor Dixie Boys adding a twang to their jazz chops).

The Otago Rambler

HMV's first country signing was Cole Wilson's brother Les. Ten years after being a child star in Dunedin, he finally got his career back on track with a recording session in a country hall, a long way from home. Once demobbed,

Country style: in 1954 '3ZB's picturesque hillbilly' Jimmy Long (left) sang of the Canterbury Plains, while Ron Hayward performed his 'King Country Waltz' on Palmerston North's 2ZA. *Green & Hahn Photography/RNZ Sound Archives; Desgranges Studio, Te Kuiti/Ron Hayward collection*

Jean Calder and her husband, Les Wilson, the 'Otago Rambler'. Ron Hayward collection

Wilson chose music over a possible career in engineering. He did not return to Dunedin, where his brother Cole was becoming prominent as a musician. Instead, he moved to Gisborne, pursuing Jean Calder, a local girl who worked in a home cookery shop and occasionally performed on the local private radio station 2ZM. She sang popular songs such as 'Little Old Lady Passing By' and 'The Holy City' in a 'clear, true soprano voice'.[154]

Wilson began performing on 2ZM when Stevens, its owner/operator, suggested they make some recordings using his newly acquired disc cutter. Inspired by Wilf Carter, Wilson had become a dedicated yodeller, and on the recordings he and Stevens wanted to capture an authentic 'western' echo. So the pair transported the heavy disc-cutting machine across winding gravel roads to a reverberant hall at Nuhaka, 60 miles away. They used a single microphone, and achieved the desired echo by having Wilson sing directly into the microphone until the yodels. Then Wilson would turn his back and sing at the walls.[155] These recordings led to Wilson becoming one of the earliest local artists to be signed by HMV, and his first discs were released in 1953 ('Shadows On the Trail'/ 'Old Faithful and I', 'Yodelling Cowboy'/'Prairie Rose').[156]

Wilson and Calder married in 1952 and began performing as a duet. Unusually for the time, Calder's 'western' influences were not male performers such as Tex Morton and Jimmie Rodgers, but Australian 'yodelling cowgirls' Shirley Thoms and June Holms.[157] Apart from having a female singing partner, Wilson's other points of difference were his yodelling and his accomplished songwriting on New Zealand themes, such as 'The Wahine Song' and 'Rolling Wagons'. Wilson quickly established himself as one of New Zealand's most prolific songwriters to be recorded; by the mid-1950s his leading rival was the pop writer Sam Freedman.[158]

Garth Gibson's first awareness of Wilson's popularity came when he was an army cadet. 'In our off-duty moments some of us used to gather round a guitar for a sing-song. As soon as anyone started singing one of Les's songs there would be a crowd appear . . . to listen and request more of the same. Everybody seemed to know his numbers.'[159] Gibson thought that a big part of Wilson's success was that his songs were original and written for a wide audience. 'His style of presentation is very simple – he just accompanies himself on the guitar, with no fancy playing . . . . even I would consider it a crime to hear a band with Les.'[160]

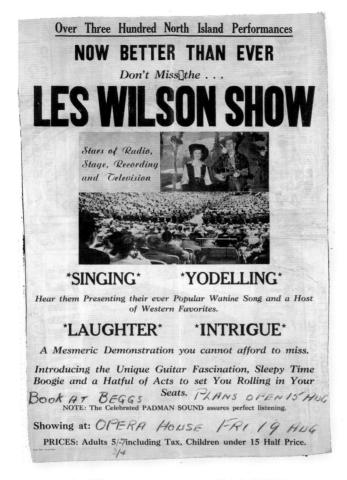

Les Wilson on tour, August 1960. Eph-D-CABOT-Music-1960-01, Alexander Turnbull Library, Wellington

In 1955 Wilson returned to Dunedin to perform for the first time since his teens. Although Gibson rated Wilson as 'undoubtedly New Zealand's best-known and best-liked western singer', the *Evening Star* was sniffy: 'Most of the audience were quite prepared to sit back and lap up the lush sentimentality and spurious nasal accents which are a "sine qua non" of this brand of sound effect – accompanied, of course, by the usual drab strumming of a guitar.'[161]

Wilson and Calder toured widely throughout New Zealand in the early 1950s, with full houses the norm. In winter they would 'hole up' due to power-cuts and other inconveniences. Gibson reviewed another show in 1956 that featured just Wilson and Calder, but offered 'enough variety to keep any audience happy for over two hours . . . . I particularly liked the complete absence of any doubtful humour throughout the show.' The songs were all of a 'western' flavour and none had been popularised by other singers. 'This always rates high with me.'[162]

This was a farewell tour before Wilson and Calder's first visit to Australia. A 10-inch album on HMV was imminent (*A Cowboy and His Guitar*) and another appeared in 1958 (*Rambling with Les and Jean*), but Australia became home base for the rest of their performing career. They set themselves up first in Sydney and made forays into rural New South Wales and Victoria, and broadcast on the syndicated *Harmony Trail* programme.

Wilson and Calder returned to New Zealand often to perform. A 1960 poster promised the ever-popular 'Wahine' song, as well as 'singing, yodelling, laughter, intrigue: a mesmeric demonstration you cannot afford to miss'. After over 300 North Island performances, and using the 'celebrated Padman sound', the Les Wilson Show claimed to be better than ever. For five shillings, audiences were guaranteed 'a hatful of acts to set you rolling in your seats'.[163]

The Cowgirl's Father

As a teenager on the family farm in the 1930s, Jack Riggir sought refuge with his guitar and enjoyed leading singalongs. His father didn't approve – there was work to be done – and Riggir and his brothers would escape to their hideaway, an island in the middle of their farm. Like Huck Finn and Tom Sawyer, they would sneak out in the middle of the night and make their way by moonlight to their island. To deter the mosquitos, they would coat themselves with kerosene. Then the boys would 'really go to town on those guitars'.[164]

Riggir was born in 1918 and grew up near Te Kuiti. During the Depression, with wool at sixpence a pound, he and his brothers made clothes and moccasins out of sacks. Swagmen were regular visitors to the farm. They came with songs from the road, many of them in the country style.[165]

The family had a wind-up gramophone, and among their 78s were a few by US country pioneer Jimmie Rodgers, which arrived on the Regal Zonophone label from Australia. Records by other artists occasionally appeared: Wilf Carter, Vernon Dalhart, Red Foley and Ernest Tubb. 'Gene Autry came in on films – he was the number one cowboy on film – and after the Depression started to lift, we were a bit more financial, and we decided we were all going to buy Jimmie Rodgers. Every trail leads back to Jimmie Rodgers.'

Just before the war, in a Hamilton street he saw a big crowd of people. Nudging his way to the front, he saw a

Betty and Jack Riggir, parents of 1980s country star Patsy. Ron Hayward collection

man sitting on the pavement with a guitar, yodelling: it was Tex Morton, then known as Robert Lane. Riggir watched as he was arrested: later a local music shop owner and justice of the peace put up £8 so that Morton could leave the country and try his luck in Sydney. During the war, said Riggir, 'We all wanted to be Tex Morton. Slim Dusty started off copying Tex Morton, I started copying Jimmie Rodgers, Tex, Ernest Tubb.'

In 1949 Riggir took part in a talent show run by 1XH, which had just opened in Hamilton. Also that year, he met Tex Morton during his tour, and after Morton's show in the Civic Hall, Te Kuiti, performed several songs for him in the dressing room. 'You have an excellent voice, which could take you a long way', Morton told him. A year later, at 1XH's live-to-air Christmas party, compère Haydn Sherley announced: 'We've got a visitor from Te Kuiti who's just blown into town all the way on horseback. I'm glad he's left his horse outside, it's getting a little crowded in here. Well, welcome stranger! What am I saying, you're no stranger, yes folks, it's Jack Riggir!'

Good evening friends, it's nice to be here to wish you a very happy Christmas, I haven't been doing much singing lately. Being a sheep farmer – I've also got a few cows to sing to – I haven't had time to do much singing. However, I'm planning to do a lot more in the coming year. Here's a song that I hope will make your Christmas happier: 'Once my soul was in sin and my heart was in shame, I didn't know Jesus, not even his name . . .'[166]

In 1951 Riggir signed with Eldred Stebbing, who had expectations of high sales. 'One shop alone would take 5000', Stebbing wrote to Riggir in 1951 prior to recording his debut 'Mother, Queen of My Heart' b/w 'The Little Old White House'.[167] The following year 'The Cowboy's Heaven'/'The Cowboy's Mother' came out, also on Zodiac. But Riggir's lack of ambition, or confidence, saw him turn down several opportunities that may have taken his career further. When Stebbing suggested he record with Pat McMinn, he was too shy. 'I said to Eldred, "No way! I'm a backwoods, country man. I couldn't sing a duet with her, I'd get all trembly, all shaky in the knees. You'll have to get someone else."' Stebbing recruited Johnny Granger for the duets with McMinn. Then, Riggir was invited to try his luck in the US by Ralph Peer, a legendary Nashville music publisher who was visiting New Zealand to see Wally Ransom of Southern Music. Not wanting to leave his family and farm for up to a year, Riggir turned him down.

Patsy Riggir performs with her father, Jack, in the King Country, early 1950s. Ron Hayward collection

Instead, he farmed and – with his wife, Betty – performed regularly at A&P shows, charity concerts and in halls throughout the King Country, Waikato and Taranaki, often sharing the bill with Stratford's Ron Hayward and Hamilton's Rusty Greaves.[168]

It was several years before Riggir's next recordings, and they proved to be his last. In 1959 Tanza released 'Pretty Baby (I Love You So)' b/w 'Gone But Not Forgotten', in a honky-tonk, almost rockabilly style. Although others were more prolific, Riggir was a key figure in country music in New Zealand, a stalwart of country clubs and supporter of young talent. His most famous protégé was his daughter Patsy, who was performing in public by the age of five. Standing on a chair in cowboy boots, accompanied by her parents, Patsy won a Buddy Williams Talent Quest, then a nationwide radio talent quest, singing live-to-air on 1XH. When her career was starting to blossom in the mid-1970s, she encouraged her father to pick up his guitar again, after a sixteen-year break.

No Wallflowers

In July 1951, a man who looked like Errol Flynn in a ten-gallon hat arrived in Auckland by flying boat from Sydney. His name was Billy Blinkhorn, and he was in New Zealand to make hay out of the current fad for square-dancing. He had given himself three months to make it even more popular. While here he recorded a few discs such as 'Cheat'n Swing' for Tanza, and toured the country giving demonstrations of dances with the Collegiate Circle, a group of enthusiasts from Auckland. At the Auckland Town Hall, 700 people took part, and the Do-Si-Do Club in Wellington was attracting crowds of 500.

One of the benefits of square dancing was that there were no wallflowers: instead of dancing with just one partner, you danced with seven, while the caller sang the changes. The *New Zealand Woman's Weekly* explained the folk ritual like an anthropologist: 'The calls are linked by phrases of patter, which serve to tie the call into a unified whole.'[169]

Billy Blinkhorn arrives in Wellington to share the joy of square dancing, 1951. *Evening Post* Collection, 114/335/07, Alexander Turnbull Library, Wellington

Everybody swing, and allemande
Right to your partner, a right and left grand
Pass old Sal and pass old Sue
Meet the girl that came with you.

A Canadian who had grown up singing along to hillbilly singers performing live on radio, Blinkhorn had formed his own band for dances and broadcasts in British Columbia. In 1938 his radio-show sponsor Dad's Cookies suggested Blinkhorn move to Australia for them. He started recording, performing and broadcasting there, and made a name for himself as a square-dance caller. In Australia, where the square-dancing boom coincided with the arrival of the hit musical *Oklahoma!* in 1949, the dances were promoted by department stores as a way of advertising western clothing styles.

Square dancing was an amalgam of folk dances that immigrants had brought to the US from Europe and turned into something fresh. 'Dances tended to take on local

characteristics', said Blinkhorn. Australians had made use of vernacular such as 'jumbuck' and 'billabong', and the same thing could be done with patter calls in New Zealand. 'Such as?', asked the *Weekly*. 'Such as', grinned Billy,

Swing your partner around and around
Like a pukeko hops on the frozen ground.

Square dancing proved so popular that the Physical Welfare Department started to organise classes as part of a national fitness campaign. Professional dancing teachers were outraged that amateurs were cutting in on their territory. 'I thought this was a private enterprise Government', said prominent Wellington teacher, Mr L. McKee. 'Where will it stop?'[170]

Dunedin entrepreneur Joe Brown heavily promoted the impromptu style of square dancing, in which the dancers reacted quickly to the caller's instructions rather than follow set steps; it made the dance more challenging and

Happi Hill (in boots, at left) calls the dance during 3ZB's *Women's Hour*. Green & Hahn Photography/RNZ Sound Archives

competitive. From early 1954, when 1000 people attended the first class on a wet Wednesday night in the Dunedin Town Hall, it quickly took off, with 1200 people joining ten clubs that were formed in the city over the next fifteen months. 'To whoop like Red Indians and perform intricate square dancing steps when requested to do so by callers . . . were taken as a matter of course and impromptu square dancing was an instant success.'[171]

Blinkhorn did not introduce square dancing to New Zealand: it had been popular, without the gingham, since the nineteenth century. He was yet another in a long line of Canadians who had played a disproportionate role in promoting country and western music in New Zealand. Wilf Carter's discs were influential, as were later visits from performers such as Don Reynolds and Hank Snow. Musicologist Graeme Smith refers to the romantic connections between rural life and that of the cowboy, shared by Canadians, Australians and New Zealanders, as 'new world pastorale'.

Luke the Drifter

The Canadian with the strongest connection to New Zealand country music lived in Auckland for three years in the mid-1950s. Luke Simmons came from British Columbia – close enough to Nashville not to matter. He began performing hillbilly music at thirteen years old, and his early adult life was like that of a character from Jack London or John Steinbeck: he jumped freight trains, and worked on ranches and on the railways until the war intervened. When he arrived in New Zealand in 1953, he quickly established himself on the local scene as a surrogate Hank Williams. Talent-spotted by Noel Peach, Simmons was soon in Tanza's studio with a mix of Auckland and expatriate Canadian musicians. Among the locals were Bill Sevesi on steel guitar, Ray Gunter on guitar and Lloyd Sly on piano accordion. After his Tanza debut in 1953, 'Howling at the Moon'/'Just Waiting', he recorded and released over 30 songs for the label, including many songs by Williams. Simmons won a lot of New Zealand

In the mid-1950s, Luke Simmons recorded many discs for Tanza in
Auckland before returning to Canada. Ron Hayward collection

fans and then returned to Canada for health reasons.
Though two 10-inch albums later came out on Viking, they
were from tapes recorded in Canada. His career peaked in
the wrong country.

In 1957 *Country & Western Spotlight* credited
Simmons with diluting the Australian dominance of
country music in New Zealand during the early 1950s.
When Simmons arrived, wrote John Cooke, the Australian
cowboy set the style: '10-gallon hats, high-heeled
boots and cheap guitars – this was country music in the
doldrums'. Record companies were content to stay with
the status quo, 'without enough initiative to promote true
country music fully'. Simmons quickly won the acceptance
of New Zealand country fans – even the tolerance of the
pop audience: 'In one week, Luke Simmons threw such a
jolt into major record companies here – with sales figures
never dreamed of by the label that sponsored him – that
country music rose from obscurity.' Soon afterwards,
releases by Hank Snow, Hank Williams, Slim Whitman

and Jim Reeves all made their New Zealand debuts.
But Simmons set the standard, and 'record companies
either crumbled with the speed Luke had set, or else piled
onto his bandwagon'. The Australian monopoly would
soon fade, so that discs by their artists became hard to
get. The trans-Tasman connection that had existed since
country music first became available – and was once
dominated by Tex Morton – would be replaced by another
over-bearing model, direct from Tennessee.[172]

But first, an Australian star – and disciple of Morton
– would make his own contribution to New Zealand's
country scene. Buddy Williams toured New Zealand for
four months in 1955, running talent quests as part of his
show. The young Patsy Riggir was not the only singer to be
successful at these contests. When Williams visited Kaeo,
just north of Whangarei, he was impressed by an eighteen-
year-old farmer called Johnny Hamblyn singing 'The
Golden Rocket'. Hamblyn not only won the talent quest,
he was invited to join Williams on his tour. Afterwards he

met Noel Peach of Tanza in Auckland, and soon released several smooth country 78s on the label (including a cover of 'One By One', already a hit for Johnny Cooper). Despite his western twang, the recordings are as much in the Polynesian pop genre as country, which is not surprising considering that the sessions at Astor Studios used musicians better known for their jazz and pop work, including guitarists Ray Gunter and Johnny Bradfield, Bill Wolfgramm on lap steel and, occasionally, Crombie Murdoch on piano.[173]

The Yodelling Drover

Johnny Granger was New Zealand's first country crooner: his warm, smooth voice had a smile. In 1951 he became one of the first to record for the Stebbing brothers' Zodiac label, where Julian Lee was often guesting as musical director.[174] This perhaps explains Granger's approachable crossover style, which was closer to the country–pop of Eddy Arnold than the honky tonk that Hank Williams and Lefty Frizzell were recording in Nashville at the time.

That Granger recorded two duets with Pat McMinn indicates that the Stebbings saw a broader audience for him than the 'hillbilly' purists. The arrangements he used were diverse, his backing band the Rhythm Pals featuring at various sessions Spanish acoustic and electric steel guitars, a honky-tonk piano, a string section or just a violin that romanced more than it fiddled.

The pop coating was deceptive: Granger was no costume cowboy, but the real thing. Born at Whitford, south-east of Auckland, in June 1929, Granger worked as a dairy farmer before, during and after his recording career. This made him especially qualified 'to sing about cowboys', wrote Garth Gibson. 'His stage name the Yodelling Drover was particularly apt, as he always felt most at home in the saddle behind a herd of cattle.'[175]

Granger had two ambitions, though: he wanted to travel, and he wanted to be a singing star. 'He entered talent quests in the hope that he'd catch the eye of someone who could help', commented Gibson. 'Strangely enough, it happened.' He was spotted by the agent of an Australian vaudeville company, who offered Granger a contract to tour with Barton's Follies in New Zealand and Australia.

The milking could wait; Granger jumped at the chance, and in 1950 found himself on a bill alongside 'specialty acts, beautiful girls, funny comedians [and] scintillating scenes'. Among them was Nola, 'contortionist extraordinary'; the Brittons, a trio of trick cyclists; Willie Berrigan, 'the perfect fool'; and the Follies' 'lovelies'.[176]

After the tour, Granger returned to dairying. Appropriately, his second release in 1951 was 'You Don't Know What Lonesome Is'. Perry Como also had a hit with the song that year, but Granger probably identified more with its sentiment: 'You don't know what lonesome is/Till you git to herdin' cows . . .'. Granger's original monologue emphasised that the dairy farmer was closer to a lighthouse-keeper than a cowboy: 'No gal, no pal for company – just cows.' His cocky yodel and the band's upbeat two-step rhythm gives the recording a jaunty feel, though the inclusion of actual cows mooing ensures the song was unlikely to be misinterpreted.

Granger's next 78 was similarly cutting edge: 'Cold Cold Heart', recorded just weeks after its release by Hank Williams, who wrote it, and Tony Bennett, who turned it into a pop hit. Gibson said Granger's records met with considerable success and gave a momentum to the fledgling Zodiac label. He performed in the occasional show in his spare time, but decided to concentrate on farming. His fans were disappointed: the recordings he had made in the early 1950s still compared favourably with what was being released five years later.[177]

Within weeks of Gibson's comment appearing, Granger came back with one last recording. On 'I'm Stickin' With You', he was backed by a slick combo called the Rock'a'billys. Despite his band's moniker, Granger had not joined the rockabilly revolution: this was honky-tonk lite.

Granger had already scared the horses five years earlier with the rocked-up western swing of 'Tear Down the Mailbox' (1952), a favourite with his audience. In the bridge he exhorts the band to 'get real gone': 'C'mon Yehudi – let 'er scrape, boy! . . . Okay, Bobby with the big bass fiddle . . . and a little bit of geetar . . .'. With the likes of Ray Gunter tinkling fluidly on electric guitar and Bobby Ewing on bass, Granger was never in danger of becoming a bodgie.

The Ruahine Rambler

With a Tex Morton guitar, a young man could make friends quickly. He would be invited to picnics and outings, and be the centre of attraction wherever he went. So claimed advertisements for the mail-order Morton guitars, which ran widely through the country in the early 1950s. In the illustration, the guitar had on its soundboard an etching of a lassoing cowboy.[178]

One teenager tempted by this offer was Rex Franklin, who was working on a farm in Hawke's Bay. His employer had several country 78s, and Franklin liked to learn the songs then ride into the hills and 'yodel my head off. I used to imagine myself as a real cowboy, and round up the cattle.'[179]

Franklin's interest in country music – or 'hillbilly music, at it was known then' – began early. Tex Morton was his idol; at school in Takapau, he was called Tex's twin brother because he would wear a straw hat and guns slung over his hips.[180] His other favourites included Hank Snow, Wilf Carter, and the Australians Slim Dusty and Buddy Williams. When Morton visited Takapau on a tour, Franklin saw his car parked outside the hotel, with a guitar sitting on the back seat. Franklin was desperate to go inside and say hello to Morton, or even to see him. Attending the concert was out of the question, as he was the oldest of eight children, living in the settlement of Kopua. The closest he had got to cowboys and country music was the films of Hopalong Cassidy and Gene Autry. 'We used to go to dances and the pictures on the back of a pony, park the pony in a paddock close to a hall and put a saddle under a tree. I used to live it to the full.'

At fifteen, flush with his first pay cheque, Franklin ordered a Tex Morton guitar. When the instrument arrived from an Auckland warehouse, included were some sheets of lessons, guitar chords, and tips on how to play it and use a microphone. A friend from his rugby team showed him how to tune the guitar, but for the next couple of years he struggled to make headway.

After 18 months he moved to Norsewood, working in a dairy factory and living in a hut at the back. Here, Franklin had the time and isolation to put the work in. Using the lesson sheets as a guide, and tuning his guitar with a G-chord arpeggio from a Buddy Williams 78, he made 'slow and painful progress'. He felt confident enough to enter a talent quest in Dannevirke on 29 September 1953, singing 'Beautiful Girl of the Prairie' and 'Have You Ever Been Lonely' to his own accompaniment. He didn't get placed, but he met two crucial new friends. Horace and Tui Hartley had their own group, and felt that Franklin would suit their style better than their current vocalist. Horace played steel guitar – emulating the Tumbleweeds' Colin McCrorie – and Tui was a pianist, and they gave Franklin a few pointers about performing.

As the Ruahine Ramblers they made their first performance on 7 January 1954, singing to a crowd waiting for the arrival of a train carrying Queen Elizabeth on

Rex Franklin and Noelene Anderson grew up on either side of the Manawatu Gorge and met at a Palmerston North talent quest in 1954. Ron Hayward collection

her first New Zealand visit. A month later the Ramblers performed live-to-air on 2ZA Palmerston North. From then on, offers to perform flowed in from organisers of dances, concerts and radio shows from Wanganui to Hawke's Bay. At an audition for Tanza on 20 January 1955, they recorded seven tracks, including Jimmie Rodger's 'When the Cactus is in Bloom', but were unsuccessful. Franklin was with the Ruahine Ramblers for about eighteen months, performing in person and live-to-air on 2ZA.[181]

In Feilding, on the western side of the Ruahine ranges, Noelene Anderson was also the oldest of a family of eight, and keen on country music. But there were very few 78s at her grandmother's apart from discs by Ano Hato and Deane Waretini, so in the record booth of the local electrical store, Anderson enjoyed listening to 78s by Wilf Carter and Hank Snow. She occasionally sang with her guitar-playing sister Audrey, and friends persuaded her to enter a talent quest in Palmerston North

The Ruahine Ramblers from Manawatu (from left): Tui Hartley, Rex Franklin, Horace Hartley, 1954. Ron Hayward collection

on 30 May 1954.[182] 'I don't know how I plucked up the courage, and that was the night I met Rex.' She sang Vera Lynn's 'The Homing Waltz' and Nat King Cole's 'Answer My Love', and came fourth. Anderson went back stage to wish Rex Franklin luck and the Ruahine Ramblers came second and got through to the finals.[183]

Franklin and Anderson began 'courting and singing together' in 1955. For their first performance, at Ormondville on 25 November, they called themselves the Sun Valley Trail Singers. They began broadcasting on local stations, and performed around the central North Island, and in Gore, Dunedin and Timaru. In August 1956, Franklin travelled to Wellington for the first time, and made a pitch to Murdoch Riley of Tanza Records. Riley liked what he heard, and asked Ivan Tidswell in Dannevirke to record the duo.

The first of several Tanza sessions took place at Tidswell's home in Swinburn Street, Dannevirke, on 1 September 1956. Four songs were recorded, two made

popular by Hank Snow, and two Franklin originals. 'Oh Why Can't You Say?' was his first effort at songwriting, while the exuberant 'Rocky Mountain Lullaby' remained in their repertoire for years:

> Cowgirls swayin', guitars playin', I could hear those girls a
> sayin'
> Rocky Mountain Lullaby . . .
> They're dancing for the joy of life, if you don't believe me ask
> my wife
> 'bout the Rocky Mountain Lullaby . . .

The duo's style is already intact: Rex's brisk, emphatic low-string picking, Noelene with the penetrating tone of the Carter Family. She ends each line with a hint of vibrato, but never launches into a yodel (her sister was the yodeller of the family).[184] All that separates these debut recordings from their later work is a lift in confidence – in their performance and Tidswell's engineering.

Rex and Noelene Franklin serenade record buyers, c. 1960. Ron Hayward collection

The couple married in Palmerston North on 17 November 1956, then hit the road to promote their first Tanza release.[185] They organised Western Variety Shows around Manawatu, taking their own PA – a crystal microphone and a single speaker – in case the sound systems in the hall were not adequate. There were more live broadcasts and the couple visited the radio stations of the central North Island. 'We camped out at the side of the road between Taupo and Palmerston North, somewhere along the highway by the forest', Franklin recalled. 'We pitched a tent, and when we woke up in the morning we could hardly talk. There was a bit of a chill. So when it came to broadcast that afternoon, we got our voices back just in time.'[186]

After their two Tanza 78s, the Franklins released nine albums through Viking, with Noelene performing an occasional lead vocal; she later took up electric bass to fatten their sound. Costs were kept to a minimum: in the early 1960s, some of the releases would be from their radio broadcasts, which paid £3/7/2.[187] Franklin was working for the Post and Telegraph Department, based mostly in Manawatu and southern Hawke's Bay. A stint as the night clerk at the Takapau telephone exchange led to Franklin writing 'On the Takapau Plains', which described the small farm the family rented. 'It was very quiet, with tuis and night owls, horses and cows, and our own chooks', recalled Franklin. 'A real country atmosphere.'

The Tex Morton guitar Rex Franklin bought as a fifteen-year-old lived up to its promises. In 1999 the esteemed German reissue label Bear Family bestowed upon the Franklins the ultimate accolade. Their early recordings were re-released in their own anthologies, *A Real New Zealand Cowboy Song* and *Upon the Outlaw Trail*, alongside legends such as the Carter Family, Hank Snow and Roy Acuff. 'Right from the word go, I wanted to sing and play my guitar on radio', said Franklin. He demurred about contemporary country music. 'We sing traditional country', he said. 'It's the real thing.'[188]

'I was a cowboy man': Johnny Cooper (centre) with his Range Riders,
early 1950s. Sonic Records/RNZ Music Library, Wellington

The man who became known as the Maori Cowboy was
heavily influenced by another singer playing a role. Born
in 1929, Johnny Cooper grew up on an isolated farm
at Te Reinga, 30 km from Wairoa. During Christmas
holidays, Cooper would stay in town with relatives, go to
the pictures and immerse himself in the images and songs
in Gene Autry's films. 'He was a singing cowboy, and I
was a cowboy man, brought up riding horses.' His Wairoa
uncle, a dance band saxophonist, gave Cooper a spare
ukulele and showed him a few chords. He began playing
along to 78s by Tex Morton and Wilf Carter, and was
soon performing in woolsheds, standing on bales while
entertaining the shearers.

Cooper won a scholarship to go to Te Aute College
in Hawke's Bay for two years, and although he won an
extension, he had had enough. His elders were determined
he stay, but he was just as determined to leave. So he
went through the pretence of returning to school on the
train, but stayed on board and ended up in Wellington.
Knowing no one, he slept the first few nights in a railway

carriage. 'My parents disowned me', he recalled. 'They
said, "You're on your own."'[189]

He took a room in a boarding house and began
working as a gravedigger at Karori cemetery. Wellington
may have seemed the big smoke to Cooper – he had never
seen such tall buildings – but there was little entertainment
for a teenager, especially on weekends. Having bought
himself a cheap guitar, Cooper started entering the charity
talent shows held in cinemas on Sunday nights. 'They had
to start at 8.15pm, after church. They were always packed,
with all ages, family groups.'

Cooper was 'cowboy mad' and soon met up with
musicians who shared his passion. His playing improved
with the help of his flatmate, guitarist Jim Gatfield. As
more musicians joined, they called themselves the
Range Riders, sewed their own outfits, bought hats and
neckerchiefs, and became regulars at the Sunday night
shows.[190]

In 1950 Cooper made his first recording at Alan
Dunnage's studio, behind an electrical shop in Island Bay;
performing solo, he chose the Gene Autry song 'Too Late'.
The Range Riders later joined him for sessions, recording
songs straight to acetate. Among them were Hank Snow's
'The Convict and the Rose', Hank Williams's 'Your
Cheating Heart', Tennessee Ernie Ford's 'Chew Tobacco
Rag', and the song that became their theme, 'Ridin' Along'
('Ridin' along, singing a song/home on the range where I
belong').

The band entered a talent quest at the Paramount
theatre, for which the prizes were £20 and an audition
with HMV. In the finals, they pipped the favourites – a
country comedy act – thanks to the young woman
handling the voting papers being sweet on Cooper. HMV
had no studios at the time, so for the audition the band set
up in the company's tearoom. 'They said, "Away you go."
So we sang two or three numbers, and they said, "Don't
call us, we'll call you . . . ."'

After about a year of badgering phone calls from
Cooper – during which he visited Korea with a concert
party entertaining New Zealand troops – HMV invited

the band to do some recordings. Although 'The Convict and the Rose' was released first – receiving good radio play – the first song HMV recorded was 'Manu Rere', which had been featured in the soundtrack of *The Seekers*, a British film recently shot in New Zealand. Several more followed in the first few months of 1955, including 'Sippin' Soda' (with a chorus from Wellington Girls' High School) and Sam Freedman's 'Haere Mai'.

The breakthrough came with 'One By One', a hit ballad for Kitty Wells that suited Cooper's croon; on the B-side was a Cooper original, 'Look What You Done'. The epitome of minimalism in lyrics, chords and melody, 'Look What You Done' became a singalong favourite and was recorded by many others (Wilf Carter and Slim Dusty were among those who covered it, and the song was included on the *Once Were Warriors* soundtrack). When presented with the song, 'HMV thought I was joking', said Cooper. 'The song was all repetition.' With its simple chorus ('I've got those lonely, lonely, lonely blues'), the hardest part was getting HMV to release the song.[191]

'One By One' was a duet with Margaret Francis, a receptionist at NZBS. A double-sided hit, it eventually sold 80,000 copies. 'Wherever we went, in shearing sheds or anywhere, every party you went to in that period, that's all you heard them play', recalled Cooper. The Range Riders played weddings, parties, anything: in woolsheds after the shearing was cut out, at dances, charity shows as far afield as Waiouru and Wanganui, and on 2ZG's *Radio Trail*.

Surprised by the sales, HMV offered Cooper a five-year contract. Despite their initial reluctance to sign him, the company – in particular, A&R man Dave Van Weede – proved remarkably committed. HMV released five 78s in the first half of 1955, before Van Weede invited Cooper in to his office in August. He wanted to discuss a record in a new genre that had been a huge hit in the States; it was called 'Rock Around the Clock'.[192]

Ridin' along with the Range Riders. From left, Don Aldridge, Jim Gatfield, Johnny Cooper, Will Lloyd-Jones and Ron James. Sonic Records/RNZ Music Library, Wellington

Western Roundup

While Cotton-Eyed Joe took country music to the country via his radio programme *Cowboy Jamboree* – later called *Western Song Parade* – another tireless evangelist for the genre was based on a 900-acre farm in West Otago. Garth Gibson was a guitarist and farmer from Kelso, near Gore, whose interest in country music had started as a twelve-year-old in the mid-1940s when he heard Hank Snow's 'I'm Sending You Red Roses'.

For twenty years, Gibson edited and published his own country music magazine, the *Country & Western Spotlight*, which acted as a network for a dedicated musical community that even then considered itself outside the mainstream of popular music. It offered profiles of local and international performers, expert columnists from around the world, and reviews of the latest releases and concerts. Gibson also commented on relevant music and record industry issues with a feisty style and zealous purism.

When Gibson began *Country & Western Spotlight* in November 1955, he was 21 and already contributing to periodicals such as *Record Monthly* (Christchurch) and *Spurs* (Australia). With his wife, Violet, after working on the farm he would write, type, duplicate and assemble the magazine at night, then post it to subscribers in New Zealand and around the world. Throughout the magazine's life, Gibson championed country music and railed against its enemies: radio programmers, apathetic record importers, rock'n'roll, pop-style orchestrations and sweetening, even pianos.

Gibson's preferred name for the genre was 'western': he was quick to notice sneers. 'Have you ever realised how much those who are against western music use "hillbilly" as a derogatory term? Ever noticed what great ammunition it is for these supercilious radio announcers when they're taking a western session?'[193]

Gibson was sceptical of reports that New Zealanders were the biggest per capita buyers of western records, joking that 'Perhaps the Broadcasting Service is trying to correct this by a process of starvation.'[194]

Even as he started the magazine, Gibson could sense the tide turning. The early 1950s had seen a local boom in the 'authentic' country music he favoured, with many recordings by the Tumbleweeds, Les Wilson, Jack Riggir and others. In December 1955, he noticed the dwindling

In the spotlight: Garth Gibson (left), Kelso-based country music authority. Ron Hayward collection

number of local releases and radio time: 'A couple of years back, you could tune to most any radio station and pick up a programme by a local western artist. Some of these were solo singers, some had bands, some were good, and some could be considered very lucky to get a broadcast. But there were a large proportion who showed real promise.'[195]

Whatever its stance, the magazine was always consistently passionate. The appearance of Johnny Cooper's debut album may have warranted an 'ovation', but six months later he worried that Cooper was becoming monotonous, and his partner Margaret Francis didn't impress, either: 'she prefers singing opera!'[196] Gibson's isolated location did not prevent him from providing detailed information about artists and his opinions of them. He offered to help readers obtain records, pointed them towards Ray Lusk's shop in Gore for mail orders, began a record-exchange service and wrote a column on how to play the guitar.

Eight issues from its launch Gibson declared his opposition to the noisy fad coming out of the US. In June 1956, he was disappointed that Cooper, one of his favourite acts, was releasing a cover of 'See You Later, Alligator': 'I won't comment, except to say that rock'n'roll numbers are unwelcome guests in this magazine.'[197] His demarcation line was strict: 'Columnists seem to love linking rock'n'roll with "hillbilly" music, which I do *not* approve of . . . . Some say rock'n'roll is here to stay, others say it's a passing craze, but whatever the case, we don't like it being associated with country music.' By April 1957, he was quick to report that country music's flirtation with rock'n'roll seemed to be 'dying a natural and overdue death'.[198]

Gibson, who died in 2006, was a guitarist and bass player, and had a vast collection of country music. He became known worldwide as a leading authority on country music in New Zealand and Australia. As a member of the Mountaineers, fronted by Southland singer Max McCauley, he was featured on several EPs and LPs in the 1960s and 1970s. In 1965 McCauley and Dusty Spittle took some space in *Country & Western Spotlight* to pay tribute to its editor: 'Without Garth and *Spotlight*, country music would not have had the chance to become as well known or as popular as it is in Australasia.'[199]

Saddle Pals

By the late 1950s, rock'n'roll had stolen the spotlight. To Gibson's annoyance, Cotton-Eye Joe was moving on from country music in *Western Song Parade*. Pearce's astute

selections of rock'n'roll, pop and R&B now dominated the programme, which would eventually be re-named *Big Beat Ball*. Gibson's colleague in the Mountaineers, yodeller Max McCauley, had no difficulty mixing his music, attending Johnny Devlin's visit to Gore, enjoying Elvis and Bill Haley alongside Ray Price and Carl Smith, and performing with guitarists Wally Scott and Jimmy Hill years before they found fame in Ray Columbus's Invaders.[200]

Despite the flash of rock'n'roll, country music entered another boom phase in the early 1960s. The pattern would become permanent: it remained underground in its pure form, and hugely popular when urbanised. While metropolitan radio occasionally deigned to include country, regional stations embraced it (and request shows were obliged to). The Tumbleweeds experienced a revival recording for Viking, and many other bands enjoyed long careers, such as the Overlanders from Wanganui and two from Timaru: the Plainsmen and the Caroline Ramblers. Solo artists such as Rusty Greaves, Ron Hayward and Johnny Morris remained loyal to authentic country, while successful pop crossover acts included Paul Walden and Des Gibson.

Dunedin entrepreneur Joe Brown became pop–country's biggest supporter through touring ventures

For the cover of Southland singer Max McCauley's 1961 *Yodelling Out West*, photographer George Kohlap used North Island models. Viking Records

such as Search for the Stars, the Joe Brown C&W Stage Show and the musical acts he included in the Miss New Zealand shows. He also launched his own label, Joe Brown, with an emphasis on promoting Otago country music. From a 1963 talent quest run by Brown, a singer emerged who – with the support of television – would lead country music into yet another boom later in the decade: John Hore.

But a singer and songwriter who became ubiquitous in this period had been striving for his moment since Tex Morton first left New Zealand. Garner Wayne was born in 1920 and spent most of his life in Canterbury. His introduction to country music was typical of the 1930s: besides the requisite singing cowboy films, he enjoyed Sunday night variety concerts at the Civic in Christchurch.

I love the land: Garner Wayne sang of love in a fowlhouse and his love of New Zealand. Viking Records collection

Among the performers, about 1935, was a duo from the West Coast called Billy and Buddy. 'They'd come on stage wearing hats and chaps, singing country songs. I came away from there and said, that's what I want to be.' [201]

While still a teenager, Wayne won a talent quest as a one-man band, playing a guitar with only four strings, using ukulele chords. He was given two more strings and some lessons by an American musician while serving in Fiji during the war. He also wrote one of his first songs. 'It went, "I don't like the army, I don't like the pay/I guess I'm just a dude in army clothes". They almost court-martialled me for that.'

Wayne wrote more than 300 songs and recorded over 100. Many had a nationalistic sentiment, such as his first release in 1960, 'I Love the Land'. Others that followed included 'Roaming Round New Zealand', 'The Mainlander', 'New Zealand is My Home' and ' Kiwi Hobo'. All were delivered in his proudly Kiwi vernacular, and most were backed by the Saddle Pals, his group from 1953 until the 1980s. His most successful record was the spirited, Celtic-tinged singalong 'Birthday Wishes': a request-show perennial, and Viking's biggest seller for two years. But another of his songs became part of the soundscape.

I'll be yours and I'll be true
And I'll lay lots of eggs for you
I'll be yours for the rest of my life . . .

'Love in a Fowlhouse' had the naïve charm and kindergarten appeal of 'Old McDonald's Farm' and 'Rock Island Line'. An archetypal novelty song – at first irresistible, made unavoidable by generous radio play – its innocence hides its songwriting craft. Wayne found his inspiration in his chook house, where his young daughter was moping about an early playground romance gone awry. 'There was a real commotion at the time: the roosters were chasing pullets. I said "Don't worry, even fowls have love problems – look at them in there." And I started clucking and crowing and eventually got a grin out of her.' That night over dinner, Wayne kept clucking and thought, 'We've had love in every other way, why not this?'

Wayne's poultry love song proved so popular that it became a series. Emulating Joe Brown's cradle-to-grave business philosophy, Wayne wrote several follow-ups: 'A Fowlhouse Wedding' begat 'Fowlhouse Honeymoon' begat 'Twin Chicks in the Fowlhouse'. And there Wayne

Messing with the Canterbury Kid: John Harper of the Saddle Pals with Garner Wayne, 1950s. Viking Records collection

let it rest; Christmas never arrived in the fowlhouse. 'Of course the record company wanted me to go on with divorce and everything, and I said "No – leave it with a happy ending."'

MAORI MUSICIANS' MECCA

It's another Saturday night in Auckland in the 1950s. Cinema attendance is booming, but musicians playing in the formal nightclubs and cabarets are feeling the pinch as tastes change and the audience evolves. Jiving is banned in some of these venues: the exuberant couples disturb the cautious fox-trotters.

In July 1955, the *Music Maker* reports that the Civic Wintergarden is closing its doors. The original Peter Pan has recently closed, followed by the Trocadero, the Gold Room and the Catholic Social Centre. Still pulling in crowds for balls and casual dances are the new Peter Pan, in upper Queen Street, and the Orange Ballroom.

But for Maori, especially those new to Auckland, there is a thriving venue for conviviality, kai, sport and dancing:

the Maori Community Centre in Freemans Bay. In its heyday, 'It was the jazziest, jumpingest place in the city', wrote Jack Leigh. 'Its talent quests were legend. On a long weekend the festivity and feasting hardly stopped, day and night. Taxis banked up outside.'[202]

The Community Centre was set up as an 'urban marae', but the utilitarian wooden building on the corner of Halsey and Fanshawe streets developed a secondary role as the crucial venue for a generation of Maori musicians. It was their turangawaewae, the home to a musical subculture with links to every genre of popular music – jazz, country, pop, Hawaiian, rock'n'roll.

The inner-city suburbs of Freemans Bay and Ponsonby had a large Maori population, many of whom flocked to the Community Centre on Friday and Saturday nights to dance. Among the first bands to play there were the Huimai Boys, Dave Dockery and His Rhythm Pals, and the master of the Hawaiian steel guitar, Mati Hita. The makeshift stage later welcomed fledgling performers such as the Howard Morrison Quartet, the Quin Tikis and Prince Tui Teka. Kiri Te Kanawa and Hanna Tatana sang

'Tai at the Tama' became Rotorua's leading act in the 1950s. Taiaroa Paul and his Pohutu Boys would draw locals and tourists to weekly dances at the Tamatekapua meeting house on the lakefront at Ohinemutu. Born in Whakatane, Paul was blinded while fighting at Mersa Matruh in Egypt with the 28 Maori Battalion. Already a musician before the war, he learnt to read music at St Dunstan's Institute for the Blind in Auckland. (At this time he recorded an army satire, 'The Kiwis in Solumn', broadcast in the Digger's Session on 1ZB.) 'Forming a dance band was one of my ways of readjusting myself to civilian life,' said Paul. The Pohutu Boys' musical director was English pianist Vic Bartholomew, who in London had worked with Billy Cotton and led his own bands. The vocalist/guitarist Angus Douglas had been a Maori All Black, and the group later featured Nick and Ronnie Smith, who became prominent in the Wellington jazz scene. The Pohutu Boys also launched the career of Tai's son, Rim D. Paul, vocalist with the Quin Tikis in the 1960s; he credited the Pohutu Boys as a key influence on the showband format of quick changes and themed brackets parodying Hawaiian, Latin and other styles of music. Tai Paul, who also worked as a hospital telephonist for 20 years, was performing with his Pohutu Boys up to two months before his death, aged 57, in 1978. National Publicity Studios, AAQT6401-A33689, Archives NZ

light opera there, and Hone Tuwhare was one of many who learnt to jive on its dance floor. Overseas acts visiting Auckland often received a Maori welcome at the centre, among them Paul Robeson, Winifred Atwell, Isadore Goodman and the Platters.[203]

On Sundays, after a church service then rugby or other games on Victoria Park, teenage dances took place in the afternoons, and games of netball or table tennis would spill out onto the street. The evenings were reserved for talent quests, and there was never any shortage of talent. If some courage was needed, flagons could be hidden among the oak trees on Halsey Street; if romance blossomed, the wooden grandstand on Victoria Park offered some privacy.[204]

The building was originally a warehouse for the US army during the Second World War. In 1948 the Labour Prime Minister Peter Fraser offered it to the Maori of Auckland for use as a community centre, rent-free. The centre had already been active for six months before it was officially opened by Fraser on 9 July 1949. A hangi was laid down in Victoria Park to feed guests from all over the North Island. The weekend's musical guest of honour was Ana Hato; the two solos by the first star of Maori popular music acted as a karanga for the generation of musicians that followed.[205]

The Community Centre became a home-away-from-home for Maori who had recently migrated from the provinces to the city. In 1935, 1766 Maori lived in Auckland; by 1945 there were 4903, and by 1951, 7621.[206] Between 1945 and 1966, the percentage of the national Maori population that lived in Auckland rose from 6 percent to 19 percent.[207]

Some Auckland Maori criticised the centre's cleanliness, catering, entertainment and clientele. They regarded it as 'non-Maori' because it did not have the open space of a marae and guests could not sleep there overnight due to fire restrictions. (The Parnell Maori Hostelry offered beds for out-of-town visitors.)[208]

Run by a trust of community groups, the Community Centre also offered health advice and workshops in Maori culture. The kitchen could feed large numbers, reported the *Weekly News*: 'Tubs of potatoes and cabbages and huge saucepans of meat form the backbone of the meal. Young people butter stacks of bread . . . . an oven is handy where 100 pies at a time can be heated . . . .'[209] Maori bread was the most popular item on the menu, which also offered puha, watercress, fish heads, pipi and mussels. The volunteers

Lou Clauson presents the young Maori showband the Sunbeams with a prize, late 1950s.
Lou Clauson Collection, PA1-f-192-17-03, Alexander Turnbull Library, Wellington

in the kitchen – many of them from the Maori Women's Welfare League – seemed to be constantly cooking.

The visit by the Platters in 1959 was typical of the way the Community Centre opened its doors to overseas guests – as long as they sang for their supper. Under the kowhaiwhai panels around the walls, the Platters were greeted by a challenge; they responded with 'My Serenade' and 'Goodnight Sweetheart (It's Time to Go)'. The Howard Morrison Quartet performed an item, then the Platters joined a kapa haka group in two action songs, sending the packed audience into fits of laughter as they tried to follow the hand movements. As the evening came to a close, the Platters slowly made their way to their car, with the crowd singing 'Now is the Hour' in Maori and English.[210]

Gerry Merito of the Howard Morrison Quartet remembered that the centre was also a place for professional performers to come down to earth: 'It didn't matter how many shows you were doing or how many big concerts you did, you were just another one of the team. If Ben Broughton or Mr Kitchen or Aunty Hobie called you up to sing a song, you got off your butt. Otherwise you didn't get any pork bones afterwards. You didn't get the boil-up!'[211]

At first, the dances were relatively formal, with men expected to wear ties, and waltzes the norm. No dungarees or gumboots were allowed and Maori wardens on the door frisked people for bottles of alcohol. Musicians didn't just double on instruments: some, like Dusky Nepia, could be called upon to stop fights if required. To deter them from starting, manager Jack Kitchen made a point of introducing from the stage burly members of the centre's boxing club, and each night several policemen would drop in for a cup of tea. 'Any disorderly behaviour was always defused, I never saw a brawl there', a trustee recalled in 1974.

> You didn't throw your weight around, or you got thrown out. And I mean thrown. I've seen blokes with blood on them. I can see the fellows in their zoot suits with the sweat pouring off them. One joker would dance with two girls at once, and the whole place stopped to watch. There was Big Lydia Kingi, who would sing blues and play the piano, and I remember Dobbie Paikea – later the MP for Northern Maori – six foot four and 20-something stone, playing his trumpet and his glasses misting up.[212]

Audiences started falling away by the early 1960s, with Maori families moving from the centre of the city to the outer suburbs, the arrival of television – and rock'n'roll. Younger audiences were being drawn to the Trades Hall/Jive Centre on nearby Hobson Street where 'the lights were dim, the music was real cool and there were no regulations'.[213]

The Playdates rehearsing at the Maori Community Centre, 1962. From left: Paul Robinson, Colin Clarke and Danny Robinson. Not pictured are the saxophonist/leader Dusky Nepia, pianist Heke Kawene, and drummer Ian McKaye. Ans Westra

The Community Centre management responded by relaxing its policies. Good behaviour was still essential but, said Kitchen, 'We gave the kids the rock'n'roll they wanted and didn't care if they did wear jeans. After this it took us three months to break the other place, and then we were right.'[214]

Simon Meihana came in from Pukekohe with his friend Danny Robinson; their fledgling band evolved into the Hawaiian Swingsters and regularly played the centre, backing singers such as Freda Morrison or Pukekohe's Elvis, Ray Paparoa. The Swingsters wore bright yellow and black shirts, with white trousers, pink socks and black suede shoes. In 1959 their drummer was Doug Young, twelve years old but already a five-year veteran. 'We sounded good and we were snappy', said Meihana, who

credited the Community Centre with providing his start in a long entertainment career. The standard of performance meant musicians had to improve quickly. 'If you weren't good enough, [kuia] Waka Clark would come straight up to the stage and say, "Now you fellas either smarten up your ideas, or you are out!" And that was it, because you could be replaced easily. There were bands busting to get into the Maori Community Centre.'[215]

In 1958 Jack Kitchen told the Hawaiian Swingsters he had booked a 'tall, neat, handsome-looking Pakeha fellow. He's got the flash coat and the flash pants and he drives around in a 1958 two-tone Chevy. He can really sing: he's a tenor.' Lou Clauson took the stage, said 'Kia ora' to the audience and launched into an almost operatic ballad. Simon Meihana was pushed forward from the Swingsters

Lou and Simon – Lou Clauson and Simon Meihana –
perform their enduring hat act. Lou Clauson Collection,
PA1-f-192-01-11, Alexander Turnbull Library, Wellington

group Herbs: Maurice Watene and Charlie Tumahai. Both came from Kitemoana Street, or 'Boot Hill', near Bastion Point, and were members of the children's showband, the Sunbeams. Aged between six and twelve, with two guitarists, they were 'a real knockout', wrote Jim Warren. 'They dress well and sing the latest pops with great style and presentation . . . wonderful entertainment.'[218] Merito remembered them upstaging the Howard Morrison Quartet at the Auckland Town Hall in 1958. 'They blew us away. They did exactly the same as we did but with much more vigour and enthusiasm. We were trying to be flash and neat and do it all right, and these kids just went out there and did it like the Jacksons!'[219]

In the breaks between the amateur acts in the talent quests, professionals who were present were expected to get up for a quick bracket. Meihana remembered 'big musos' such as Toko Pompei, Dusky Nepia, the Hi-Five and Howard Morrison being among them. 'It was the "in thing" at that time to be seen on that stage . . . . the professionals entered, not as contestants, but just to be recognised, and they'd come for miles just to get on that stage. Their thinking was, who cares if it cost me £5, just to get here. That was because the Maori Community Centre had a lot of mana.'[220]

From the stage, the MC Ben Broughton would call, 'Take your partners for a Maori war dance. Any Pakehas on the floor will be eaten!'[221] In fact, Pakeha visitors were welcome, and among the Pakeha performers who played the centre were early rock'n'rollers Johnny Devlin and Red Hewitt, pianist Mike Perjanik, singer Ray Woolf and female impersonator Noel McKay.

But as the 1960s progressed, other venues were a strong temptation for those wanting to socialise away from the familial, chaperoned environment of the Community Centre. Dancers would do the 'rounds' from club to club through the evening. 'There were so many dances on at the time', recalled Ben Tawhiti. 'You just poked your head in and if you didn't like the music, you went to another one.'[222] In a typical evening later in the 1960s, the young Charlie Tumahai would be on stage at the Trades Hall, engrossed in his bass guitar:

. . . oblivious to the attempts of his tane cousins on the dance floor, daring each other to go over and ask the Pakeha sheilas sitting on a form across the room for a dance, because all the wahine cousins insisted on dancing with each other. The tanes would eventually get hoha, leave

to sing with him, and Meihana started acting the goat. The laughter from the audience flustered Clauson at first, but at that moment the folk-comedy duo Lou and Simon was born.[216]

By 1962 a Friday night could see a crowd of 500 people enjoy music in the centre, while the talent quests on Sundays had grown so that an audience of 1000 packed in to witness the final of the £800 Monster Talent Quest that year. Reported *Te Ao Hou*, 'The Centre has become famous as *the* place for aspiring entertainers to make a name for themselves – provided they are good enough, that is. They don't dare stand up at the Centre unless they really are good.'[217]

Many musicians later prominent in showbands got their start at the centre, as did two members of 1980s

and walk down the road to the Picasso where most of the Pacific Islanders used to hang out. I think a lot of stories they told us about the Picasso and their attempts to imitate a scene out of *West Side Story*, were a lot of teka. I think they used to go down to the Picasso, just stand there, Coca-Cola in one hand, one of those old rubbish-tin lids in the other, flex their muscles, yell some abuse, get hungry and go down to Mr Chips for a big feed then go back to the Trades Hall. There would be Charlie and the band, bouncing out

the music, the wahine still dancing with each other, and the Pakeha sheilas dancing with the clever tanes who decided to stay at the Trades.[223]

Maori musicians had been making an impact on Auckland's nightlife for many years, and the Community Centre was only one of many venues at which Maori performed in the 1950s. They could also be heard at St Sep's, the Gandhi Hall, the Crystal Palace, the Jive Centre,

Television and rock'n'roll drew people away from the Maori Community Centre, until the venue started organising dances of its own. Ans Westra

the Manchester, the Orange and Oriental ballrooms, or coffee lounges such as the Picasso and Montmartre, and dine-and-dance restaurants such as the Arabian and Hi Diddle Griddle.[224]

In 1959 *Te Ao Hou* described the scene in the city's 'plushest nightclub'. The atmosphere was lit by candles; the food was exotic. A young Maori at the piano led a chic trio: 'Tourists, wealthy businessmen and sophisticated men-about-town looked up from their shrimp cocktails, their deep-fried chicken or their T-bone steaks as the three Maoris weaved fascinating patterns of sound.'[225]

The pianist was Lew Campbell, joined by his brother George on bass and Mark Kahi on guitar. The Hi Diddle Griddle restaurant on Karangahape Road was only a mile from the Community Centre, but a world away from the young Maori 'in jeans and bright shirts . . . plunking guitars, blowing saxophones and filling the hall with vibrant, happy song'. At the Community Centre, explained *Te Ao Hou*, 'There are raw amateurs with only enthusiasm and the Maori's natural sense of harmony to carry them through; there are good amateurs – mostly self-taught – who are nearing professional standard; and there are the professionals.'[226]

Lew and George Campbell would soon back Dizzy Gillespie in Auckland; Lou would join the national symphony orchestra, while George and Mark Kahi would settle in Christchurch. Kiri Te Kanawa – trained by Sister Mary Leo at St Mary's on College Hill – sang at the Maori Community Centre a few hundred metres away, then entered the elite world of international opera. At every level, Maori musicians are disproportionately represented.

April, 1960. In the Auckland Town Hall, a Maori in a white tuxedo stands at the microphone and holds up his hand. 'Okay folks', he says. 'This is where the natives take over.'

Everyone in the audience laughs; the MC Ben Broughton has them on side. Half the audience is Pakeha, witnessing the array of Maori talent presented by Benny Levin at the Maori Rock Show. 'You Pakeha think this rock'n'roll is something new', he says. 'But we Polynesians have been doing it for years.'

Setting the pace is Ray Paparoa, Pukekohe's exuberant Elvis impersonator, backed by the Hawaiian Rockers. The junior Maori showband the Sunbeams delights the crowd,

Among the many members of the Sunbeams, a children's Maori showband, were Maurice Watene and Charlie Tumahai, future members of 1980s band Herbs. Lou Clauson Collection, PA1-f-192-15-17, Alexander Turnbull Library, Wellington

especially their diminutive six-year-old singer. Imposing female vocalist Rama White is anything but diminutive: this 'big girl with a big voice had the crowd screaming with laughter at her Maori words with pop songs'.

The audience hangs on every note. No one is unimpressed by the depth of pop talent among Maori and Polynesians: the smooth vocal quartet the Silhouettes, amiable pianist Heke Kawene as 'the Maori Fats Domino', Samoa's slick Keil Isles and especially the sensational partially blind soprano Flo Castle.

In the audience, *Music Maker* correspondent and jazz stalwart Jim Warren is struck by the sheer professionalism: the smart, colourful stage outfits, the top-line instruments and their control of the audience. They even inspired the audience to 'clap on the beat when they were carried away'.[227]

The backbeat of rock'n'roll had infiltrated. In only five years, the genre had become dominant in popular music, and Maori and Polynesian musicians were at the forefront.

1954-1964

Out of the country scene came a performer who recorded New Zealand's first rock'n'roll record, Johnny Cooper. This new genre quickly infiltrated the market, spread by film, jukeboxes, and dedicated concerts and showcases. Pop music was now aimed at a specific audience: the teenager. With the sudden success of Johnny Devlin, rock'n'roll had its first star and young musicians a role model.

The old order did not disappear overnight. A lively after-hours club scene emerged featuring small jazz combos, solo singers such as Ricky May and Marlene Tong, and cabaret acts such as Kahu Pineaha. The sun may have been setting on jazz, but aficionados got their reward by the visits of artists such as Nat King Cole, the Dave Brubeck Quartet, Louis Armstrong and Dizzy Gillespie: these tours helped establish a concert tour industry more sophisticated than the variety show approach of the past.

Local songwriting continued, but in the 1950s these songs became hits rather than hobbies, for composers such as Ken Avery, Sam Freedman and Gene O'Leary. The folk club scene of the late 1950s also provided an outlet for determinedly Kiwi songwriters such as Peter Cape and Rod Derrett.

Radio was slow to be convinced by this bolshie development in New Zealand pop. It still had to cater for the widest of audiences, without dedicated pop music stations, but the success of the *Lever Hit Parade* inspired many imitators around the country; in 1962 the first daily pop music programme was launched, *The Sunset Show*. The young rock'n'roll bands that had emerged from youth clubs – among them, the Keil Isles and Max Merritt and the Meteors – made many recordings, and were given some radio support. With energetic young entrepreneurs and promoters, recording labels fired up by the possibilities, and television flickering into living rooms, the local pop scene was making its first steps towards a focused industry.

The act that stimulated New Zealand pop's coming of age was a middle-of-the-road musical comedy team. The Howard Morrison Quartet was a one-stop variety show that incorporated Maori concert parties, the Italian songs heard by the Maori Battalion, the sweet harmonies of doo-wop and the comedy of Stan Freberg. As an entertainment entity, their success helped create the infrastructure of an industry. Their act was not rock'n'roll, but it was popular music at its most popular, and their influence was felt for decades.

Opposite: Johnny Cooper rocks the Wellington Town Hall, December 1956, with
Don Richardson on saxophone and Bill Hoffmeister, Spanish guitar. Don Richardson collection

Overleaf: Mabel Howard MP leads Johnny Devlin to his pink convertible, Christchurch, January 1959.
Green & Hahn Photography/Lou Clauson Collection, PAColl-5679-03, Alexander Turnbull Library, Wellington

Sunsets and Sunrises

SIX | ## Into the 1960s

ROCK AROUND THE ISLAND

Nobody noticed when the first rock'n'roll star visited New Zealand in 1954. He didn't arrive on a Sunday, when it was 'closed'; it was just too soon in his career. Two years before he would become England's Elvis, Tommy Steele – a Cockney steward on the *Rangitane* – was in Wellington long enough to attend a few dances 'and sing for a smile'. Local hairdresser Marie Courten met him during his stay. 'Tommy was very quiet and pleasant', she recalled. 'He could sing more than just rock and roll songs. He said that we would see his name in lights one day, but of course we just laughed at him then.'[1]

In the early 1950s, debates often flared about foreign influences on New Zealand life. Special relationships forged by the recent war no longer seemed to apply. It was hard to know what to fear the most: the Communist infiltration of New Zealand institutions or the insidious Americanisation of its culture. Pseudo-American accents were adopted by a few, even on radio.

'The "American way of life" seems to be creeping like a fungus disease over the English-speaking world', fumed poet and cultural critic A. R. D. Fairburn.

> A very large proportion of the music broadcast in New Zealand is sentimental clap-trap played by American bands. At certain times of the day and night the air is befugged with this sort of stuff . . . .
>
> By all means let people play this sort of thing on their own gramophones, if they like it. But a State-owned broadcasting service is surely allowing itself to become a mere extension of the commercial recording racket when it imports and uses such huge quantities of pulp-music.

If new American terms such as 'teen-ager' weren't bad enough, said Fairburn, there was the fashion among young men 'to wear those appalling ties that are, I imagine, designed in America for English spivs'.[2]

Announcing the launch of 2YA's *New Zealand Hit Parade* in 1952, the *New Zealand Listener* noted the 'strong tendency to let America set the fashion in modern music'. Local voting would help get around that. However, once the programme began another trend emerged: the increasing influence that these teenagers were having on music. *Variety* had recently noticed that 'the major disk companies are frankly pitching their pop releases to buyers in the 12–16 year age bracket'. This was the comic-book reader class, said the *Listener*, and accounted for the sentimental and novelty US hits 'which New Zealand audiences seem willing to accept'. It was a relief, then, that the

At the Star Boating Club, Wellington, visiting British seamen lurk while, at right, local teenager Costa Christie jives with Pauline, 1956. Costa Christie collection

song receiving the most votes in the first six weeks was English: 'Tulips and Heather'.[3]

But vast changes were coming. At the beginning of the 1950s, the family radio was a heavy cabinet that took pride of place in the living room. Portable radios existed but weighed up to 10 pounds. By 1960 transistor radios small enough to fit in a woman's purse had become affordable. With jukeboxes in milkbars, and sound booths in record stores, by the mid-1950s music no longer needed to 'have a middle-aged heart that the whole family could enjoy as it gathered around the wireless on a Saturday night'.[4]

The American influence had been strong before the war, with musical tastes being affected by films, radio, 78 rpm discs, sheet music and arrangements imported by dance-band musicians. After the war, that influence became stronger, with faster links and a new music for a fresh target market: the teenager. But the historical links to Britain had also intensified, with constant visits from cargo and passenger ships bringing goods and immigrants from the 'old country', which itself was susceptible to 'Americanisation'. If New Zealand ever attempted to defend itself from the invasion of foreign popular culture,

it needed to do so on two fronts, against the United States and Britain.

Tommy Adderley first arrived in New Zealand in the mid-1950s as a teenage apprentice steward on the *Dominion Monarch*. He recalled the Auckland wharves being full of passenger ships: the *Rangitoto* and the *Rangitane*, the *Mariposa* from America next to the *Captain Cook* from Glasgow. The voyage out took five to six weeks and, depending on how long it took to unload and then reload the cargo, the ships stayed as long as a fortnight in Auckland and Wellington. Working day-on, day-off, there was plenty of time for the merchant seamen and stewards to get involved with local nightlife, music and women. They could mingle in milkbars and start fights with one another or with local bodgies.[5] Or they could hit town in style, wearing Italian suits and after-shave. 'They got all the birds', recalled David Gapes, later a founder of Radio Hauraki. 'The girls thought they were wonderful. The blokes thought they were terrible.'[6]

Besides giving New Zealand men inferiority complexes, the visits were a nice little earner for the scrubbed-up British seamen. While coming through the Panama

Canal they would stock up on Wrangler jeans, white T-shirts, pea jackets and Old Spice, all rare and desirable commodities in New Zealand. 'We had to smuggle it ashore, I used to bring out sometimes 20 pairs of jeans and get rid of them here', said Adderley. 'There was also a problem getting records here. I made a packet bringing out copies of the *My Fair Lady* album. People couldn't see the show, but they'd heard of it. If you had copies, you could sell them anywhere.'[7]

Some of the seamen were musicians and would find work performing in dance halls while in port. Adderley's first band the Hound Dogs was a skiffle outfit formed on the *Dominion Monarch* that spent many hours practising in the boiler room until they were good enough to play for the 600 passengers. The band got gigs in Auckland, Christchurch and Dunedin; Adderley was offered a job at Wellington's Empress Ballroom. He had a local girlfriend and, after four years at sea, he jumped ship. To a well-travelled musical teenager from Birmingham, 1950s New Zealand seemed a happening place.[8]

'MORAL DELINQUENCY SAID TO BE WIDESPREAD'

New Zealand Truth's July 1954 headline sounded the alarm. A sex scandal among Hutt Valley teenagers saw nearly 60 'youths and girls' taken to court, for charges such as carnal knowledge and indecent assault. Sid Holland's National government – facing an election later in the year – hurriedly established the Special Committee on Moral Delinquency, chaired by an upstanding party stalwart, Dr Oswald Mazengarb.[9]

For six weeks, the committee received over 200 submissions exposing a debauched hormonal demi-monde. They heard tales of milkbars, motorbikes, second-rate picture theatres, riverbank trysts, heavy petting and condoms. The Mazengarb report, as it came to be known, was delivered to Holland at great haste, and three bills following its recommendations on youth morals were passed into law. The government printed 300,000 copies of the report and on 11 November 1954 – two days before the general election – every household in the country receiving a family benefit also received the hefty tome. 'If the Government had hoped to make the morals report into an election issue, it was disappointed', comments Redmer Yska. 'Juvenile delinquency proved a fizzer; the economy dominated the campaign.' Nevertheless, the National government stayed in office, and the report had

been useful. 'By spelling out the conventional values it felt New Zealand was abandoning, it fired a warning shot that echoed for the rest of the decade.'[10]

A key passage of the Mazengarb report addressed Broadcasting and its responsibilities towards the morals of the nation's youth. There was criticism of some of the 'suggestive love songs' heard on radio. The Broadcasting Service needed to avoid giving any public offence, and while it 'aims to reflect the standards of its listeners . . . some may feel that it should try to raise those standards'.[11] In fact, since just after the war the NZBS had an ad hoc system banning records that could have caused offence. Among the early rejects were 'Doin' What Comes Naturally' in 1946, 'Pretty Little Bridesmaids' and 'I Don't Wanna Do It Alone' from 1947, and 'I'm a Big Girl Now' and 'Divorce Me COD' from 1948. Almost as a pre-emptive strike, while the Mazengarb hearings were taking place the NZBS banned obvious offenders such as 'Den of Iniquity'.[12]

Broadcasting's existing standards – as proscribed by legislation – should 'satisfy the morals of the most particular', said the report. Recordings needed to conform to strict codes, and then be scheduled in suitable programmes, or at times when children were not expected to be listening. The NZBS assumed that responsible parents controlled the use of family radio sets, but admitted that this assumption was 'not well founded'. The report recommended that a married woman should be included on the Broadcasting committee that checked serials and records; and also made the point that the frequent repetition of recordings 'capable of misinterpretation' was not desirable, 'particularly in times like the present'.[13]

Formed in the early 1950s, before the Mazengarb report, Broadcasting's Standards Recordings Purchasing Committee met each week to listen to and discuss new records that might prove contentious. Among the committee's early members were two senior Broadcasting staff from opposite ends of the music spectrum, dance and jazz specialist Bob Bothamley, and church organist and classics devotee Malcolm Rickard. Post-Mazengarb, sharing the role of the married woman were Mrs Buckley and Mrs Lloyd.

Aiming to present programming with a 'consistent wholesomeness', the NZBS committee carefully considered songs that contained religious content in a disrespectful or exuberant manner, had overt or covert sexual themes, encouraged socially unacceptable behaviour, indulged in

'Of course, we couldn't let the listeners hear that one!' – Neville Lodge on NZBS's standards committee in the *Listener*, 11 September 1953.

innuendo, and were crude or simply too noisy. Those that did not pass the committee's strict criteria were not bought for distribution among the nation's radio stations. Earlier casualties included 'Easy Does It' by Eartha Kitt, *Kiss Me Kate*'s 'Too Darn Hot', Andy Griffiths' 'Make Yourself Comfortable', Louis Armstrong's 'Don't Fence Me In', and songs containing double entendres (Noël Coward's 'I Like America' and 'I Wonder What Happened to Him', George Formby's 'It's No Use Looking at Me'). Cole Porter's 'Love for Sale' was only acceptable as an instrumental. 'The Orange and Blue' was banned from broadcast on St Patrick's Day. Two hits from *South Pacific*, 'Bloody Mary' and 'There is Nothing Like a Dame', had been banned in 1952 but after reconsideration in 1959 could be broadcast as part of the whole musical.

The brassy, energetic soundtrack to the 1953 Marilyn Monroe film *Gentlemen Prefer Blondes* was especially popular among bodgies, two Lower Hutt housewives told the Mazengarb committee. The disc also had wide appeal among young musicians, and the film influenced the fashions adopted by widgies, but Roseallen Wolfe and Shellah Smith were concerned at the film's role in popularising 'a certain type of song'. The *Hit Parade*, they submitted, was 'a menace. The older people in general

don't like this modern American music. It is filling up space and taking the place of the things the older people want.' Nevertheless, two songs from *Gentlemen Prefer Blondes* ('Little Girl from Little Rock' and 'It's High Time') managed to retain radio play until they were banned by the NZBS in 1957.[14]

In August 1954, as the Mazengarb panel began its hearings, the Marlon Brando biker film *The Wild One* was banned by the chief film censor Gordon Mirams (a restriction not lifted until 1977). That didn't matter; there were other motorbike films. By January 1955, there was anguish in Auckland over the larrikins on motorcycles – 'milkbar cowboys' in peaked caps and leather jackets – who were menacing Queen Street. By parking dozens of motorbikes together outside milkbars, lounging upon them, crowding the footpath and playing daredevil games on their bikes, they were drawing crowds and intimidating them at the same time. Within six months, the fears of the public seemed vindicated after two murders in Queen Street milkbars, for which both killers were hanged.[15]

Several of the Broadcasting committee's decisions in the mid-1950s epitomised the prevailing moral attitudes. 'Black Denim Trousers and Motorcycle Boots' was banned in September 1956, stifling both the US original and a wholesome cover version by Auckland's Stardusters. 'Gonna Cut You With a Razor' and 'Give an Ugly Woman

Dennis Huggard Archive, MSD10-0249, Alexander Turnbull Library, Wellington

Matrimony' were banned the following year. 'Three Juvenile Delinquents' was 'humorous and satirical', but the song 'glamorised delinquency'. Banned. On 5 June 1957, Little Richard's versions of 'Long Tall Sally' and 'Tutti Frutti' were considered: 'Coarse and ugly performance. Words always difficult to hear and often unintelligible.' Banned.[16]

Such caution did not go unnoticed. 'Who is Radio's Ban Man?', asked the *NZ Observer*'s Moliere on 11 August 1954. Records requested by the public were often found to be 'unsuitable' or 'not available', or they received the response 'can't find it in the library, sorry'. No one at NZBS headquarters used the word 'ban', wrote Moliere; no one even knew who the Solomon of taste was within Broadcasting. The radio columnist believed in freedom of expression, as long as he agreed with what was being expressed. That didn't include songs 'masquerading as entertainment' in which 'Heaven is a branch office of Tin Pan Alley and the Deity is an equal . . . . Where good taste is transgressed, there is the place to call a halt. A little bawdiness, on the other hand, is inherent in the makeup of most of us.'[17]

The ZB stations were radio's most important outlet for popular music, programmed to be acceptable to all ages, from children to grandparents, with a special daytime emphasis towards women, busy working in the home. The latest hits were first heard on the *Lifebuoy/Lever Hit Parade*, on Thursday nights. Once released into general programming, these songs were still broadcast only once a week: 'high-rotate' airplay was not allowed. The YD stations broadcast a 'non-commercial light programme' in the evenings only; commercials were not introduced until 1957. With Broadcasting aiming at the broadest audience, while maintaining its standards, the programmers of the mid-1950s faced a dilemma when rock'n'roll arrived. Peter Downes, a member of the NZBS committee during the 1950s, recalled:

> The problem was that 'Rock Around the Clock' and all the Elvis songs and those things arrived here suddenly, more or less in a block. Nobody knew what to do with them, there was no alternative youth station. Whereas we had been going along safely with Perry Como and Andy Williams and all the rest, suddenly we were confronted with this music, which was not on the ZB Hit Parades, at the start. The radio people dealing with it were not teenagers and certainly not rebellious. They had been brought up on the Bing Crosbys and the Dinah Shores. What were we going to do with this new music?

Nobody had the foggiest idea, and there weren't really young people on any of the radio stations to say, 'This is our music and this is the popular music of the future.' Which is what it became. At first, it was a teenage phenomenon and it was teenage music.[18]

To future rock'n'roll star Max Merritt, growing up in Christchurch, early 1950s pop was 'a bit dreamy'. He and his teenage peers felt jazz 'was becoming too cultured with such unjazzy instruments as cellos, French horns, tubas and even strings invading the scene. Then, as if from nowhere, the rock rolled into the scene.'[19]

THE BEAT OF JUNGLE DRUMS

A year after the Mazengarb report, *Truth* warned of the foreign scourge about to infiltrate the country's airwaves and dance halls. A fever was currently spreading through the United States like an epidemic: 'the rock'n'roll craze'. *Truth*, then at the height of its powers, advised its readers to 'Be prepared, for it's bound to strike us sooner or later.' Rock'n'roll had already been banned in some parts of the US, as it was aggravating 'negro-white segregation difficulties' – and stories about the plague sold a lot of newspapers. *Truth* described the music as a combination of blues and 'hot gospel'; among the early best-selling tunes were 'Rock Around the Clock', 'Flip, Flop and Fly' and 'Shake, Rattle and Roll'. Within days, these songs could be experienced in picture theatres throughout New Zealand, in films such as *How to Be Very Popular* and the 'juvenile delinquency-themed' *Blackboard Jungle*.[20] The song titles sounded unthreatening, even daft, but the combination of overseas accounts of rock'n'roll riots, the Mazengarb report and press campaigns had their effect. For months New Zealand had been on high alert for teenage misbehaviour and its noisy soundtrack.

HMV was also on edge, for its internal conservative culture had let it down.

In the US, the season's hottest tune was Bill Haley's 'Rock Around the Clock', on the American Decca label. HMV had first option to release the disc in New Zealand, but artist and repertoire manager Dave Van Weede decided against it. Later, reading in overseas music papers about the song topping the US charts after its inclusion in *Blackboard Jungle*, Van Weede realised that by turning down Haley's disc, he had made 'the biggest mistake of my life'. So he called in HMV's only popular singer, the country performer whose recording of 'One By One' had been so successful: the 'Maori Cowboy', Johnny Cooper.[21]

> Dave said, 'Have a listen to this, Johnny, this is the biggest thing in America and we want you to record it.' So when I listened to it, I couldn't believe it. I said, 'That's not me – I'm country and western.' Van Weede said, 'Well, you better learn it, because we want you to record it. It's going to be big. It's called "rock'n'roll".'
>
> I had never heard those kind of words before. *One two three o'clock, four o'clock rock* . . . . I never sang stuff like 'rock around the clock'. I sang love songs. It was foreign. I said, 'Look, we'll never be able to record that because I don't know what I'm singing about.'[22]

But Van Weede was keen and Cooper was under contract. Van Weede remembers making a first attempt to record the song at the Majestic Cabaret, with engineer Harold Southern using portable equipment. Twenty-six copies were made and sent to radio stations around New Zealand. However, 'the recording was over-modulated and caused problems', recalled Van Weede. Selwyn Toogood played the song on the *Lever Hit Parade* and complained about the over-modulation, 'so it was decided to re-record it'. The Majestic Cabaret was unavailable, so Cooper and the band went to the Island Bay recording studio of Alan Dunnage.[23]

The pressure was on, because Cooper was about to leave for Korea on his second concert party trip. His group the Range Riders were either unsuitable or unwilling – guitarist Don Aldridge wasn't interested in rock'n'roll – so Van Weede asked saxophonist Ken Avery to put together a band from Wellington jazz and dance band players. On Saturday 27 August 1955, they assembled at Alan Dunnage's recording studio at 223 Clyde Street, Island Bay. Avery recalled the session:

> We set the thing in the key of G to suit Johnny and recorded it almost note for note from the Bill Haley disc, except that I asked Vern Clare to put a sustaining drum beat near the end where Haley's band cuts out completely. For the B-side we recorded 'Blackberry Boogie'. It's interesting to note that HMV sent no representative to supervise that recording. It was all left to Alan Dunnage. Late on Saturday night, Alan rang to say that HMV liked the 'Rock Around the Clock' number, but couldn't accept 'Blackberry Boogie' because it had a 'popping' sound in the parts where Johnny sang 'blackberry *pickin'* time'. Could we re-record the 'Boogie' side early on

Alan Dunnage, owner/engineer of Sonic Recording Studios, Wellington. RNZ Music Library, Wellington

> Sunday morning so Johnny could catch the afternoon plane? A bleary-eyed group turned up and remade the 'Blackberry Boogie' side as requested and all was well. We received three guineas each. The record sold really well and there was talk of the band members getting a double fee to compensate for the extra time put in through no fault of our own, but no extra money was forthcoming.[24]

Van Weede's press release announced 'Johnny Cooper – Mr "One By One" – has converted to rock'n'roll', and he pitched the recording to the *Lifebuoy Hit Parade*. The programme had already played Haley's version, but after a preview of Cooper's recording, *Truth* reported that 'for a local production, it really is something, believe me. You'll be hearing it on the *Hit Parade* too.'[25] Cooper returned from Korea in late September, in time to hear Selwyn Toogood introduce the song to the nation: 'He called it "the new sound from America, done by our local boys". They played it a few times and then, not long after that, they released the Bill Haley version [to retailers]. A lot of people couldn't understand what we were singing about anyway, because rock'n'roll wasn't known here in New Zealand.'[26]

One of those listening was a teenager from Wanganui aspiring to be an entertainer. Johnny Devlin was already well aware of Cooper, who often came to Wanganui to perform. 'As kids we all used to sing his songs along with those of Slim Dusty and Tex Morton', Devlin recalled. 'This was before rock'n'roll was even thought of. It was all country and swing until 1956. We used to listen to the *Hit Parade* and they used to play the top 10 and one particular night they played a song called "Rock Around the Clock". We all jumped out of our seats and thought, what *is* this? This is *great* music. That was the start of it all.'[27]

There were few outlets to propagate this new genre of popular music: radio airplay was minimal; the press was usually patronising or scare mongering; music magazines were scarce, foreign and favoured jazz; and television did not exist. But the impact was almost immediate. The most influential media for disseminating rock'n'roll were films and jukeboxes. In the first week in September 1955, advertisements began appearing on the *New Zealand Herald* entertainment page. 'They turned a school into a JUNGLE! What happens in a big city school when teenagers run wild . . .'.[28]

Blackboard Jungle was given a Special A certificate by the New Zealand film censor: general admission, but 'definitely unsuitable for children'. The *Herald*'s reviewer

thought the film was too exaggerated to be credible, 'too loosely knit to be thoroughly compelling', but nevertheless it was 'an effective entertainment of its kind'.[29]

When the curtain went up on *Blackboard Jungle* at Auckland's Century cinema on Queen Street, a young Auckland drummer called Tony Hopkins was ready in the stalls. Again, it was that song, that introduction. 'It started off in the credits, right at the beginning of the film. "*D' dum*. One two three o'clock, four o'clock rock . . .". *Ooh*, this is pretty wild. I went to the theatre on my own, and was knocked out by the band.'[30]

In Christchurch, a fashion-conscious, tap-dancing teenager called Ray Columbus was selling ice creams at the Grand in Cathedral Square: three sessions a day on the weekends. 'It gave me a chance to see movies that were illegal for someone of my age, I was able to see *Rebel Without a Cause*, *East of Eden* and *Blackboard Jungle* long before I should have been allowed to. I saw *Blackboard Jungle* many times – that was where I heard the song. In the context of the movie, it had a violent undertone, which gave it special status.'[31]

With radio airplay of rock'n'roll extremely limited – at this stage, perhaps one or two songs, once a week – jukeboxes were another way to hear the new music. Although the machines had first appeared in New Zealand in the late 1930s, many more arrived with the American GIs during the war. By the 1950s, jukeboxes were in the milkbars on the main streets of most New Zealand towns, a drawcard for teenagers and – with pubs closing at 6.00 pm – young adults.[32] They offered forbidden fruit: songs that had been banned by the NZBS. Sonny Day sought out Little Richard's 'Tutti Frutti' in lieu of the sanctioned version by Pat Boone.

> It sounded so silly and the boys would be chuckling and go down to the jukebox and play the original.
>
> At the milkbar were all sorts. We would get out of school and go and put our jeans on and blue suede shoes and bright socks and go straight down to the milkbar and buy a Coke and sit there playing the jukebox. Little Richard and these guys: Fats Domino, Elvis, Bill Haley. Most of them were American.[33]

One person who was not surprised by the dawn of rock'n'roll was Arthur Pearce. Through his alter egos Turntable and Cotton-Eye Joe, he was in the perfect position to observe the influence that rhythm and blues was having on country music. According to his biographer Laurie Lewis,

Dennis Huggard Archive, MSD10-0369, Alexander Turnbull Library, Wellington

Pearce had taken note as rhythm became more pronounced, more country bands featured drummers and the sexuality in the lyrics became more explicit. Soon, elements of R&B and western swing became the foundation of new style rock'n'roll. Lewis commented: 'It is really quite eerie that Arthur Pearce had foreseen that a white performer or group who could sound "black" could become the catalyst that would certainly take popular music in a new direction.' When Elvis Presley's first discs came through on the Sun label, Pearce 'immediately sensed that this new singer was going to be a megastar. Arthur was utterly convinced that here was the crossover artist, the link between black and white he had been expecting for some time.'[34]

To Pearce, this was as exciting as when he first heard Duke Ellington in 1929. He immediately put an order in to the US for everything Presley had recorded thus far, well before the NZBS had copies. On the 26 January 1956 edition of *Western Song Parade*, after playing discs by Jean Shepherd, Bob Wills and His Texas Playboys, and Speedy West, Pearce introduced his last item:

> Every once in a while the various departments of popular music come up with an artist who is different. The western song world has such a newcomer in Elvis Presley, a handsome 19-year-old Mississippi boy who is a veritable ball of fire when it comes to putting a tune over . . . . Elvis Presley tells the secret of the 'Mystery Train'.[35]

'As had happened so many times before, the 2YD listeners were the first to hear another new arrival on the scene', said Laurie Lewis.[36] For three weeks in a row, and several more times in 1956, Pearce included Presley songs on the programme, which was still oriented towards country music. By this stage his Cotton-Eye Joe scripts no longer featured outrageous puns, just the latest information he could glean from his sources:

> In these days of 'gimmicks' Elvis Presley presents a different style, which owes nothing to tricks and novelties, for it is a musically sound blending of the west and rhythm and blues. His girl Dixie declares that recently Elvis, at one sitting, ate eight De Luxe cheeseburgers, two bacon-lettuce-tomato sandwiches and three chocolate milk shakes. This gives her food for thought as he sings 'Baby, Let's Play House.'[37]

Compared to the nationwide reception of 2YA, which used a powerful transmitter, 2YD's coverage was limited:

on a good night, it stretched from north of Christchurch to south of Taranaki. So Pearce's *Western Song Parade* reached fewer people than his *Rhythm On Record* programme, although its audience was similarly dedicated, with many musicians among them. From 1955 *Western Song Parade* was also re-broadcast on the shortwave band, which enabled overseas listeners to tune in and New Zealanders who were dedicated enough to change radio bands. His influence went beyond the immediate audience, however: a hard core of his listeners were other music aficionados, themselves influential figures as performers, broadcasters or record importers. In its various incarnations, *Western Song Parade* was essential listening, as Pearce shared discs well before they were commercially available in New Zealand. And as a trusted veteran, his programmes were left alone by the Standards committee.[38]

Despite the support of the *Lifebuoy Hit Parade*, Johnny Cooper's version of 'Rock Around the Clock' could not compete against the original, especially once the film *Rock Around the Clock* arrived. HMV's decision proved to be a windfall for Tanza, which had picked up the distribution rights to Haley's version through Festival. Stan Dallas recalled telling the record presser to put 'Rock Around the Clock' into production 'and we will tell you when to stop pressing . . . . they had never had those instructions before.' The most popular Haley discs sold 50,000 to 75,000 copies in New Zealand. Tanza could not record a local version of 'Rock Around the Clock', Dallas said: to do so, they would have lost the rights to the original.[39]

After nearly twenty years of enjoying and performing swing, New Zealand's jazz players were askance at the arrival of rock'n'roll and its swift impact on the local music scene. 'We couldn't believe it was so popular', said drummer Harry Voice, 'yet so *dumb*.' Another respected drummer, Don Branch, said in 1963: 'In former days, bands in Auckland were composed of "13 musicians and a drummer". These days they seem to be "three guitars and a musician".'[40]

To pianist, trumpeter and arranger Lew Campbell, 'It was an anathema. That's the only way I can describe it. There wasn't much in it for someone who was dealing with dominant 13ths and flat 9ths and sharp whatevers. It was like a retrograde step.'[41]

Laurie Lewis was a 25-year-old jazz saxophonist when rock'n'roll appeared. 'We were probably mystified

Don Richardson, front right, with a combo that includes Mike Gibbs on trumpet, Vern Clare on drums and Bob Barcham on piano; Wellington, 1956. Don Richardson collection

Wanganui and Palmerston North. Richardson wrote the big band arrangements, in the style of Billy May and Les Brown; it was the 1955 visit of the Ted Heath band that gave Richardson the varied format, and inspired him to outfit the band in matching pale-blue V-neck jerseys and bow-ties.

The first Festival of Jazz opened with 'Up Town Tempo' by Richardson's Big Band. Former Kiwi Concert Party comedian Stan Wineera did impersonations, and through the night the musicians came and went in a variety of combinations. For five shillings the audience heard dixie, standards, piano and vocal blues, cool jazz, mambo bop and 'old-fashioned' Glenn Miller swing. Many of the performers became regulars: Johnny Williams with his Saxophone Choir; Laurie Lewis playing 'something cool'; earthy Pacific vocalist Ivy Rodan; and virtuoso teenage trumpeter

Mike Gibbs, who joined the National Orchestra aged 17, moonlights playing in a Wellington jazz festival, 1956. Don Richardson collection

more than anything else', he said. 'Certainly we weren't jealous, that never came into it. None of us were making any money, we'd be lucky if we covered the cost of getting to and from gigs. But if someone came out and absolutely wiped out an audience doing a copy of someone else's song – a lousy song to start with – you'd have to say, what the hell are we doing all this stuff for?'[42]

As always in popular music, for the musicians it was a case of adapt or stay home. Shortly after *Blackboard Jungle* opened, smooth vocal combo the Stardusters began including 'Rock Around the Clock' in their repertoire.[43]

A musical go-between during the rise of rock'n'roll, while maintaining his musical integrity, was saxophonist and arranger Don Richardson. After eight years with the Kiwi Concert Party in Australia, he had recently returned to Wellington and had quickly become a major player in the music scene. In early 1955, with his friend Vern Clare, he formed a music promotions company, Modern Enterprises. Emulating other formal jazz concerts that had been produced by musicians since 1950, the pair began organising Festivals of Jazz at Wellington's Town Hall, a popular and lucrative concept that continued until the end of the 1950s, evolving with the musical fashions.

From the first concert on 16 May 1955, the one-night festivals showed a musical eclecticism and willingness to adapt to the demands of the audience, while also satisfying the musicians' aspirations. They regularly packed the venue with audiences of over 2000 people; occasionally they would repeat the concerts afterwards in the Hutt Valley,

Bob Barcham plays boogie-woogie at the Wellington Town Hall, 1956. *Don Richardson collection*

and the top-rating *Lux Money-Go-Round*. In 1955 the biggest hit by a New Zealander was not Johnny Cooper's 'Rock Around the Clock' but his earlier cover version, 'One By One' (eventually selling 80,000 copies, by far New Zealand's biggest single yet). Tanza's biggest seller was Daphne Walker's dreamy 'When My Wahine Does the Poi'. The summer that followed is remembered as the idyllic season in which Opo, the friendly dolphin, entertained holidaymakers in Hokianga harbour.[46]

Mike Gibbs, already a member of the National Orchestra. A novelty at each concert would be leading Wellington 'modern' pianists Bob Barcham and Bill Hoffmeister with their party piece, a four-handed boogie-woogie (in September 1955 it would be 'Rock Around the Clock').[44]

Auckland's musical nightlife in January 1956 offered Benny Levin's nine-piece band at Bayswater, 'dispensing a tonic of tuneful melodies' (vocalist Mary Feeney, last ferry home at 11.45 pm); Ernie Butters' Metropole Orchestra at the Orange (with Kath Amy, 'the girl with the golden voice'); and at the Realm on Upper Queen Street, Bill Sevesi and His Hawaiian Band (vocalist, the popular Morgan Clark). At the Crystal Palace on Mt Eden Road, Bob Griffith's band featured Pat McMinn singing, good prizes and, with delicate dancers in mind, advertised its policy: 'Jiving Prohibited'.[47]

It was the audience's reaction to the festivals that reviewers found remarkable: the physical way in which they expressed their enthusiasm. 'The under-20s, maybe half the audience, shrilled and stamped their feet. The other half clapped and tried to look elderly and tolerant.' But quickly everyone began to react to the strong beat: 'tapping their heels, slapping their hands on their thighs, swaying their whole bodies. Sometimes a row of apparent strangers linked arms and swayed in unison.'

> Upstairs, where they could be seen by everybody in the hall, two Maori girls were jitterbugging uninhibitedly; a Teddy boy and girl – anxious to cash in on the limelight – pushed their way along a row, then, sheepishly had to push their way back again when the aisle proved too narrow for rug-cutting.[45]

Despite some elements of 1950s youth asserting themselves as they came of age, adults – who had lived through two world wars and a depression – were in charge of popular culture. In a radio popularity poll conducted by *Truth* in 1953, Selwyn Toogood hosted four of the top seven programmes. The *Lifebuoy Hit Parade* came in fifth, ahead of *On Stage Tonight* but behind *Quiz Kids* at fourth

Benny Levin emphasises the wholesomeness of his Bayswater dance. *Bennie Gunn collection*

AS FRIENDLY AS A COUNTRY BARN DANCE ! !
AS UP-TO-DATE AS THIS WEEK'S HIT PARADE ! !

THIS SATURDAY ... THIS SATURDAY

Make "YOUR" Dancing Date

★ BAYSWATER
★ BAYSWATER

FOR YOUR GOOD LISTENING AND GOOD DANCING

★

BENNY LEVIN and his 9-piece BAND

PLAYING REQUESTS IN TOE-TAPPING DANCE-TIME.

Vocals by

MARY FEENEY ★ VIC EISENHUT

Sub. 3/6   ::   Excellent Supper

JOE WHEELHOUSE, M.C.

AUCKLAND'S NEW SONG HIT . . .

TANIWHA BLUES

Recorded by
PAT McMINN
'THE STARDUSTERS'
and
The CROMBIE MURDOCH Trio
(Popular TANZA Recording Artists)

THE TANIWHA BLUE SONG
Taniwha Blue, Taniwha Blue
It blues as it washes, blues as it washes,
Blues as it washes whiter than brand new,
It's a brand new powder blue right through
It blues your clothes as it washes too
A perfumed powder, amazing new
Taniwha Blue.

HEAR IT OVER 1ZB

Taniwha BLUE
ALL-PURPOSE POWDER
BLUES AS IT WASHES!

TANIWHA BLUE – – it blues as it washes

Pat McMinn and the Stardusters sing the soap opera 'Taniwha Blues', 1956.
Eph-B-VARIETY-1956-01-back, Alexander Turnbull Library, Wellington

Although not yet 30, McMinn was identified with the generation that had experienced the war and cherished the cosy stability evoked in the pop music recorded at Astor. She was about to enjoy two of her biggest hits: a novelty song and a radio jingle. 'Opo the Crazy Dolphin' was an immediate success, even before Opo's mysterious death in May. 'Taniwha Blues' was recorded with the same backing team, Crombie Murdoch and the Stardusters. About laundry detergent rather than a sea monster, it conveyed the secure domestic aspirations of the era:

Taniwha Blue, Taniwha Blue . . .
It's a brand new powder blue right through
It blues your clothes as it washes too
A perfumed powder, amazing new Taniwha Blue

At Astor, Noel Peach was intrigued enough by the lighter rock'n'roll coming from the US to ask his amenable vocalists to attempt ZB-friendly facsimiles. Recorded in January 1956, the Stardusters' version of 'Black

Denim Trousers and Motorcycle Boots' romps along, a cautionary tale delivered with a wink. Shortly afterwards their harmonies rocked the Pacific with 'Rock Around the Island', by US film songwriter Ken Darby. With Chet Atkins-style picking from Ray Gunter on electric guitar, against accents by Bill Wolfgramm on steel, it simultaneously alluded to several styles: jazz, country, Hawaiian and rock'n'roll.

In this flurry of activity, Peach also recorded the Gedson Sisters performing the unthreatening 'Rock and Roll Waltz', a parody of 'Tennessee Waltz' with pianist Crombie Murdoch providing a hard-driving boogie bass line. The Stardusters' version of Ivory Joe Hunter's ballad 'Since I Met You Baby' sways rather than swings, burdened by an American-accent voiceover and heavy reverb. They backed Pat McMinn on another R&B standard, 'I Hear You Knocking' – both songs feature smoky, after-hours blues piano by Murdoch.

In early 1956, HMV released its first local album, *Rock and Sing With Johnny Cooper*, a 10-inch compilation of his earlier country and pop recordings, plus 'Rock Around the Clock' and 'Blackberry Boogie'. (In November 1955, Tanza had made the first original New Zealand 10-inch album, Bill Wolfgramm's *South Sea Rhythm*.)[48] As a follow up to his rock'n'roll debut, the company chose the most obvious song: Bill Haley's other big hit, 'See You

TANZA

Distributed by
COLUMBUS
RADIO CENTRE
Z272

23181

ROCK AND ROLL WALTZ
(Ware-Shorty Allen)
THE GEDSON SISTERS
with Crombie Murdoch and His Rhythm

Dennis Huggard Archive, MSD10-0268,
Alexander Turnbull Library, Wellington

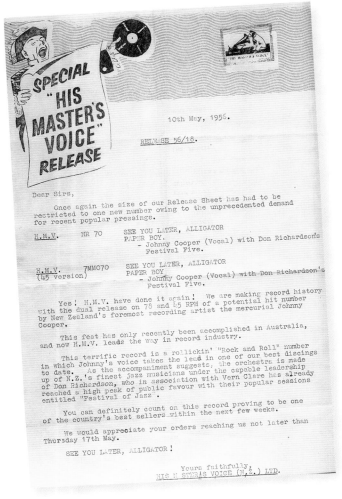

In May 1956, Johnny Cooper's version of 'See You Later, Alligator' is the first record to be simultaneously released on 78 rpm and 45 rpm discs. Don Richardson collection

Later, Alligator'. For the session, Van Weede re-hired the musicians from 'Rock Around the Clock', with Don Richardson replacing Ken Avery on saxophone. Calling themselves Don Richardson's Festival Five, they assembled at the Majestic Cabaret one evening when it was closed and Van Weede laid on some beer to get the musicians in the mood. Roping in several bystanders and the engineer, Van Weede led the chorus shout of *See you later, alligator/ after while, crocodile*.

Cooper's version of 'See You Later, Alligator' was released on 10 May 1956, on 78 rpm and 45 rpm discs. To cope with the demand at the presses, it was HMV's only release that week. Four days later, thanks to his regular radio play and stage work, Cooper had a starring role at Modern Enterprises' sixth Festival of Jazz. Backed by Richardson's big-band arrangements, 'He threw himself into his four numbers with vitality and had the audience behind him

from the first bar', wrote one reviewer. After 'See You Later, Alligator' and 'Seventeen', the audience called out '"Rock Around the Clock", Johnny', and so he sang it; 'everybody sang it, and he was just one of the chorus'.[49]

Clare's showcase was a 'battle of the drums', competing with four other top drummers. He said that Modern Enterprises had 'no fears about rock an' roll': they didn't need to resort to phoney accents or exaggerated dress, just to 'provide the music most of the young people want to hear'. By satisfying that demand, they could stay in business: 'Progressive jazz often has to take a back seat while more hackneyed pieces come to the front; but we play what everybody wants.' He described rock'n'roll as 'glorified Dixie – it's the old two-beat with a strong second and fourth beat. The style is 99 percent vocal, the rest instrumental. Adopting a phrase, instrumentation sticks to it and increases the volume till the rhythm is really ponderous.'[50]

Richardson and Clare learnt to adjust with the times and avoid the mistake of being too elitist in their approach to jazz. They quickly realised that their festival concerts were not the place to experiment with new, inaccessible material. So the set-lists featured hit songs from the swing era by Benny Goodman and Glenn Miller; spirited dixie brackets; musical duels between drummers or trumpeters; alongside vocalists such as Johnny Borg, Ivy Rodan and Johnny Richards performing orchestrated versions of rock'n'roll and R&B.

Disorderly behaviour at concerts existed before rock'n'roll. The wave of formal jazz concerts in the early 1950s, especially those with a dixie component, also saw a sudden change towards informality among elements of the audience. Foot-stomping, clapping along and cheering during the actual music became de rigueur to a hard core; their exuberant reactions brought complaints from music buffs and concerned citizens alike. The Wellington town clerk Mr B. O. Peterson wrote to Clare about patrons dancing in the Town Hall corridors, in the gallery, 'and generally acting in a manner which was entirely uncalled for . . . . when spoken to by the Custodian's staff the persons concerned resorted to abuse and continued with their unseemly behaviour.'

Letters to the *Evening Post* protested about 'the incessant uproar of screaming and stamping by adolescents during items'. The concerts, wrote Jazz Lover, were an opportunity for hundreds to 'throw off civilisation for two or three hours and take on animalish and wild manners – screaming, catcalling, etc, instead of listening to the music'. Inevitably,

Above: Vern Clare, master drummer and showman, Wellington Town Hall, 1956. Don Richardson collection
Below: Got no kick against modern jazz: a varied programme at the Auckland Town Hall, 27 April 1957. Merv Thomas collection

musical grouch L. D. Austin weighed in, closing the
correspondence by saying that jazz 'is a debasing influence,
a social evil of appalling significance, which originated from
a decadent source in Darkest Africa, and the degrading
effects of which are reflected in the misbehaviour of listeners
wherever and whenever it is perpetrated'.[51]

While city councils and moral guardians discussed the
impropriety of rock'n'roll dancing, *Truth* pointed out that
such alarm was typical for any new dances enjoyed by the
young. Be it the polka, the Charleston or the waltz, the
latest enthusiasm brought with it an inevitable backlash.
In ballrooms from the late 1930s, signs often said 'It
is the official policy of the management to discourage
jitterbugging.' Those jitterbugging 'were written off as
degenerate beyond redemption', but now, having gone
through the war, the offenders spent their weekends
'dissolutely mowing the lawn'. Besides, teenagers had been
buying rock'n'roll records for the last fourteen months,
and the ZBs had broadcast 'entire breakfast programmes'
of the offensive music. 'And even this does not raise a riot
among the lethargic masses.'[52]

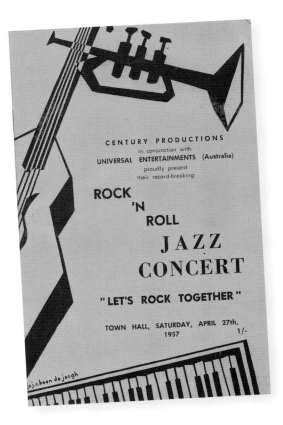

CENTURY PRODUCTIONS
in conjunction with
UNIVERSAL ENTERTAINMENTS (Australia)
proudly present
their record-breaking

ROCK
'N
ROLL

JAZZ
CONCERT

"LET'S ROCK TOGETHER"

TOWN HALL, SATURDAY, APRIL 27th,
1957   1/-

In the year since *Blackboard Jungle*, rock'n'roll had built up a momentum that would be difficult to stop, despite the moral concerns of the public and the efforts of authorities. Regular mentions of the phenomenon appeared in the cable pages of daily newspapers, concentrating on bad behaviour or just expressing bewilderment. These news items tantalised its potential audience and troubled their guardians. In June 1956, the dyspeptic film censor Gordon Mirams cut a newsreel from Sydney that showed the 'exaggerated hip movements' of rock'n'roll dancing, and a reference to 'Elvis, the Double-jointed Pelvis'. Yet in August he passed the feature film *Rock Around the Clock*. And on 6 August, Elvis Presley's 'Heartbreak Hotel' was approved for broadcast by the NZBS. The floodgates were about to open.[53]

The master of hype Graham Dent (right) gives the *Auckland Star*'s entertainment reporter John Berry a hot tip. Lou Clauson Collection, PA1-f-192-31-16, Alexander Turnbull Library, Wellington

The release of *Rock Around the Clock* in New Zealand took place almost on the whim of one man, cinema magnate Robert Kerridge, and his instincts about an ambitious young employee, Graham Dent. The occasion marked a coming-of-age for the unsophisticated entertainment business in Auckland, in which hip entrepreneurs would eclipse staid operators, and the various spokes of the industry – the film exhibitors, the record companies, commercial radio, newspaper reporters, musicians and fans – worked together to hype the latest fashion.

Kerridge was a curious figure to unleash the rock'n'roll craze in New Zealand. An unabashed royalist aspiring for a knighthood, his own tastes were strictly middle-of-the-road: these films sold more tickets. In the early 1950s, Kerridge was the most powerful man in film exhibition in New Zealand. His company owned 130 theatres; his main competitor Amalgamated operated 68, mostly leased. Together, this duopoly prevented independent cinemas from screening new releases. Within Kerridge-Odeon, the word of 'Mr RJ' was law, but he was often let down by the subservience of his management team. Stereo sound was a fad, advised one consultant, so the Kerridge theatres went without; in 1960 KO's general manager was asked what impact television would have on the film business. 'None whatsoever', he replied.[54]

Both Kerridge-Odeon and Amalgamated had rejected *Rock Around the Clock* for release, thinking it would not draw good houses, and because of negative publicity about screenings overseas. At a meeting with his head office executives, Kerridge asked about the film. Dent,

twenty years old, contradicted his superiors by saying they were wrong to turn it down. He knew about the success of Haley's music, and thought anything musical would pull a crowd. Also, the New Zealand manager of Columbia Pictures – who produced the film – had given Dent the soundtrack just days before. 'I thought it was tremendous. Albums in those days were collectors' items anyway.'

Kerridge was intrigued by Dent's outspokenness, though he had already been impressed enough to make him a cinema manager at just nineteen. He asked Dent to prepare a marketing plan and to arrange a screening at KO's preview theatre. The pair watched the film together. 'It was magic to him as well', said Dent. 'There was no way that he could have left that theatre not agreeing with me. Because his feet were tapping, and he was gone.'

Dent threw himself into a two-week promotional campaign, with the conservative KO executives discreetly putting up obstacles along the way. They wanted to screen the film at Auckland's rundown Majestic, used for B-grade westerns. Dent argued that using the firm's showcase Regent theatre would draw a much wider audience than just 'bodgies and widgies'. Kerridge supported him, and Dent was relieved that the dwindling box-office takings of the Regent's current film *Anything Goes* – a Bing Crosby vehicle based on Cole Porter's music – ensured that its season would end. He ran teaser ads saying 'Nippers and nannies all agree, *Rock Around the Clock* is their cup of tea.' And he invited 50 people to a preview: journalists, broadcasters, record company employees. The buzz about rock'n'roll became a crescendo.

Just days before the premiere, KO executive Vern Clouston read about riots during overseas screenings of the film. An *Auckland Star* feature from Canada told of mesmerised youngsters stirred into uncontrollable frenzies, and alarmed parents and schoolteachers worried about the music's encouragement of teen sex, crime and violence. Clouston, a controlling figure within the company – he was national exhibitions manager, although he had sight in only one eye – decided to cancel the release of *Rock Around the Clock*.[55]

Kerridge over-ruled Clouston, though he told Dent his job was on the line: the film's season had to run without any incidents. Dent recalled Kerridge saying 'there were people from the Government and the Police breathing down his neck, real heavy. They were not happy about the film being released at all.' In the build-up to its release, Dent met several times with senior police officers and was 'lectured' about possible problems.[56]

Finally, after many hiccups, an advertisement in the *Auckland Star* on Friday 28 September 1956 announced:

See you later alligator, cause we're all off to the Regent
at 11, 2, 5, 8
To see the first great movie on ROCK'N'ROLL
Bill Haley and his Comets in
ROCK AROUND THE CLOCK
And introducing the Platters singing
the top hit paraders, 'Only You' and
'The Great Pretender'

People camped overnight to buy tickets, entertained by rock'n'roll coming from a speaker hooked up outside the cinema. At the premiere, crowds jammed the intersection of Queen and Wellesley Streets outside the picture theatres. Police were in attendance and, remembered Dent, 'Lo and behold all the directors of KO arrive, all smiling at everyone.' Adding to the melee were the fire engines that rolled up, after an anonymous call for which Dent got 'slapped across the wrist', accused of creating a diversion.

In the weeks that followed, Dent kept up the advertising campaign, emphasising the film's suitability for children aged from six to 96, that it was 'uplifting and wholesome', and showed more life than a Henry Moore exhibit. While critics reviewed it like anthropologists studying a primitive tribe, *Rock Around the Clock* 'broke every record at the Regent theatre', said Dent, eventually surpassing the lengthy run of *The Queen is Crowned*, a documentary about the 1953 coronation. (*Rock Around the Clock*

closed at the Regent on 1 November 1956, replaced by Liberace in *Sincerely Yours*.)[57]

The day after the Auckland premiere, a small advertisement appeared in the *Star*'s classifieds:

Jive for Enjoyment
Correct rhythmic interpretation and simple basic principles make jiving fun to do and pleasant to look at. Auckland Academy of Ballroom Dancing. 10 High St, City.

Entrepreneurs could sense there was a new bandwagon to be jumped upon. Even before the release of *Rock Around the Clock*, there had been rock'n'roll brackets as part of larger jazz and dixie concerts.[58] One person who had been watching the emergence of rock'n'roll with keen interest was Dave Dunningham, a classical music buff and shirt manufacturer. His small factory was in a building on Hobson Street that also housed the Yugoslav Hall. It seemed never to be used for anything but the occasional club social. At around the same time, Dunningham recalled in 1986, he was having a drink with the jazz drummer Frank Gibson. 'We were talking about this new craze, you know, rock'n'roll. *Rock Around the Clock* was about to open at the Regent and Frank said, "It's going to happen here." So we thought we'd get into this. I said, "If I can find a hall, can you find a band?"'

Gibson agreed. Dunningham found that most halls in Auckland were already holding regular dances and then

Dave Dunningham, proprietor of Auckland's Jive Centre, contemplates the next trend, 1961. Viking Records/RNZ Music Library, Wellington

remembered the venue right under his nose: the Yugoslav Hall, on the floor beneath his shirt factory. He got a soft-drink company to provide samples of its new drink, bought blocks of ice from a warehouse on the wharf and offered a novelty: ice-cold Coca-Cola. And in the *Auckland Star* he placed an advertisement:

At Last! At Last!
The only ROCK'N'ROLL
Dance in Town
Every night is rock'n'roll night commencing
8 pm Friday October 5 at Yugoslav Hall.

A week after *Rock Around the Clock* opened on Queen Street, Auckland's first rock'n'roll dance began two blocks away. Frank Gibson assembled his 'All Star Rock'n'Rollers' from among his jazz musician friends: it was a curious combo that was heavy on brass but lacked a guitarist. 'All Frank knew were the jazz musicians', said Merv Thomas. 'You couldn't ring up the likes of Bob Paris, because they didn't exist.'[59]

Dunningham held the first dance on a Friday, 'because we didn't think it could compete with the bigger Saturday night dances. Never has a man been more wrong than I was.' On opening night, he recalled, teenagers came up the stairs to the hall and said, 'Is it true? Can we jive all night? No square dancing?'

'No square dancing', said Dunningham. 'The kids were amazed. They packed the place. I just couldn't stop them coming in.'[60]

The night was unforgettable, wrote teenage reporter Bruce Kaplan. 'It was packed to the seams till the cats were crawling up the walls.'[61] So many people turned up that the dance floor sagged and, with hundreds of dancers pounding their feet to the beat, the plate glass windows at street level started to bulge and pulsate to the rhythm.

Dunningham started to panic. 'I raced up and said to Frank, "You've got to slow the tempo down. Slow something down. There's a great pane of glass which is going to bust downstairs." Frank said, "Righto. We'll look after that. Don't worry."' When Dunningham turned his back, Gibson told his band to crank up the volume: how much could the window take?[62]

The glass didn't shatter – it was elastic enough to take the strain – although, just in case, Gibson got the dancers to move to the stronger end of the hall. But Dunningham

Rock'n'roll arrives at the Auckland Town Hall: Bernie Allen honking sax, spurred on by trumpeter Lyn Christie, left, and Les Still. *Vogue Photography/Bernie Allen collection*

Rock'n'roll arrives in South Auckland: from left, Simon Meihana, Paul Robinson, Danny Robinson, Doug Young and Ray Paparoa. *Lou Clauson Collection, PA1-f-192-08-18, Alexander Turnbull Library, Wellington*

and his business partner Lee Brassey needed a new venue. One week later, they shifted along Hobson Street to the Trades Hall, which Ted Croad's big band had recently vacated, and renamed it the Jive Centre. 'We must have had 2000 customers in the first two nights', recalled Gibson.'[63]

Gibson soon reconfigured the group with younger players, among them dixieland trombonist Merv Thomas and aspiring jazz saxophonist Bernie Allen. 'Rock'n'roll was in', said Allen, 'and most of the older musicians were saying that it was just a passing phase and would go. We were desperate to play, however, though we didn't really hold with the music greatly. But it was the only gig we could get.'[64]

Thomas found 'Rock Around the Clock' exciting – 'the rhythm just leapt out of the speaker' – but a problem for the young jazz players in the first professional rock'n'roll band was that they hadn't heard a lot of rock'n'roll. Precursors such as Louis Jordan were almost unknown, it wasn't played often on radio, recordings were scarce and sheet music non-existent. Allen said that the main sources for hearing it were films such as *Blackboard Jungle*, *Rock Around the Clock* and *The Girl Can't Help*

It. 'So Merv and I used to go along to the movies and Merv would transcribe the lyrics and I'd transcribe all the licks and chord sequences, and that's how we put the Trades Hall band together. But it was a mixture because we didn't have that many rock'n'roll tunes.'

Gibson's second rock'n'roll band – which still lacked a guitarist – made its debut at the Auckland Town Hall on 23 October 1956. Thanks to a teasing ad campaign, this rock'n'roll benefit concert for the Henderson RSA hall was the most prominent showcase for the music yet. All 750 tickets were snapped up, and reporters were impressed by the exuberance of the dancers; one teenage girl even danced in shorts.[65]

Two days earlier, on 21 October 1956, Lou Clauson organised a Labour Day rock'n'roll jamboree at a small country hall south of Auckland. Clauson's band was the Moonlets, and for the occasion he wrote a parochial rock'n'roll song, perhaps the first New Zealand rock'n'roll original to be publicly performed. He remembered,

I beat Auckland by a couple days by putting on a rock'n'roll dance at Karaka hall, just out of Papakura,

Bernie Allen, saxophone, Jack Shanks, piano, and Merv Thomas, trombone and vocals,
in Frank Gibson's rock'n'roll band at the Jive Centre, Auckland, 1957. Bernie Allen collection

and I got a band together with members from Ardmore College. Juke boxes were big news in those days, and I wrote a tune called 'Papakura Boogie' and it was number one on the jukebox in a restaurant I had at the time: *You must go out to Papakura way/where they do the rockin' in the hay . . . do the Papakura boogie*. We had 600 people in the Karaka hall, which was capacity, we did dance segments and had the crowd up and dancing – those who knew what to do.[66]

Over the next year Frank Gibson's band would establish the Jive Centre as New Zealand's leading rock'n'roll dance hall, attracting 600 dancers every Friday and Saturday night. When the band took breaks, Dunningham played the latest American discs, from tapes of US shortwave radio broadcasts.

As a riposte to the established venues, the Jive Centre displayed signs that read: 'Ballroom dancing prohibited'.[67] This excited the musicians almost as much as the dancers, said Merv Thomas: 'A whole huge floor full of people jiving is the most exhilarating thing to play for. I mean you could play "God Save the Queen" in the

right beat and the floor would be literally twirling and it was wonderful. All of a sudden the Jive Centre opens and it's this big huge floor and the girls are being tossed over shoulders.'[68]

Dunningham claimed he 'never once found undesirable elements' or teenagers misbehaving in the style described by sensational overseas reports. As *Rock Around the Clock* continued its way down the country, the press followed the international trend and noted any incident connected with the film. In Wellington, the manager of the Regent said 'Our audiences are enthusiastic, they stamp and clap but that's where it stops . . . . I give the youngsters credit for knowing how to behave themselves.' Days later he was attacked while trying to stop fighting and dancing during the film's session; a glass door panel was also kicked in. In just three weeks, 40,000 Wellingtonians had seen the film, and this was the first negative incident.[69]

In Dunedin after an evening screening, teenagers 'rock'd and roll'd down Princes Street', blocked the road and started to jive and chant, causing the three policemen present to call for reinforcements. The screening itself was a theatrical event for the audience, with many dressed in 'exaggerated

Rock'n'roll at the Auckland Town Hall, 1957. From left: Len Hutchinson, Bernie Allen, Don Branch, Lyn Christie and Bart Stokes. Bernie Allen collection

"teddy boy" fashion', and 30 university students marching in together, wearing white shirts and flannels.[70] But exuberant dancing that turned into 'unsavoury behaviour' had become a ritual at Dunedin concerts. At a dance farewelling Julian Lee a month earlier, the foot-stamping, aisle-rocking crowd headed outside to dance beneath the Town Hall clock tower, 'a much frowned-upon practice'.[71] Yet permission was given in Dunedin later in the month for a Caversham hall to be leased to hold 'strictly rock'n'roll dances'. These would be 'non-stop affairs' from 8.00 pm until midnight, with music provided by the Five Yanks dance band and rock'n'roll records.[72]

In late November, a rock'n'roll concert at Wellington's Town Hall featured several older performers getting real gone: the 'matronly' Margaret Watson, with a husky Louis Armstrong number; Ron Williams – a vaudevillian in the 1920s – with a typically animated 'Shake, Rattle and Roll'; Coral Cummins and Doug Caldwell doing the 'Cow Cow Boogie'; and 'Blue Smoke' rhythm guitarist Gerry Hall performing *Liebestraum* on banjo, 'rock'n'roll style'. Closing the show – and representing the right generation – was Rod Derrett, singing Haley's two big hits.

Said the *Evening Post*, 'The applause and screaming was deafening.'[73]

By the end of the year, the act topping the bill at Modern Enterprises' jazz festivals in Wellington was Johnny Cooper. Laurie Lewis knew something was up when a festival rehearsal took half as long as usual: instead of twenty numbers, the big band only practised ten. 'I thought, this is weird, there is nowhere near a concert here . . .'. On the night, the Wellington Town Hall was packed as usual – 2300 people – but applause for the first few items was merely polite. After the big band and dixie items, a drum kit was placed in front of the jazz musicians.

Don went out the front of the stage, none of us knew what the heck was going on. He said, 'Ladies and gentleman, the special guest, Johnny Cooper.' Johnny Cooper? Never heard of him. And a Maori with a white jacket and carnation comes on, with a guitar around his neck. He sort of looks around and he says, 'One two three o'clock . . .'. That's all we heard. The crowd went mad, they absolutely shrieked.

Johnny Williams was sitting beside me playing lead alto and he started getting like nervous. I said, 'It's all right, it's all right.' And he said, 'Man, there's going to be a riot.' From then on, for the rest of the concert the crowd just didn't want to know anything else.

This all happened in the two months since the last concert, we had no idea what was happening. Rock'n'roll just hit, *whack* – like that – and at half time and the guys were all talking to each other. 'My god, we're finished: what happens now?' That's all they had ever done, and I said, well – going back to an old Americanism – 'If you can't lick em, join em.' They said, 'We can't play that stuff' – which of course we couldn't, it's a whole different thing. But it happened that quickly.[74]

Cooper's promotion reflected the response of the audience – and, by now, the critics. The *Dominion* enthused: 'Cooper was as fine a showman as Wellington has seen in some years, throwing everything into "Razzle Dazzle", "Rock Rock Rock" and "See You Later Alligator". This last was too much . . . they simply had to dance and the gallery walls were soon a fringe of leaping figures.'[75]

Jungle rhythms, frenzied dancing, worried parents and councils conscious of public order: history was repeating itself. There was even a new buzzword that, like 'jazz' 35 years earlier, caught the eye in headlines and advertisements. Looking back at 1956, *Music Maker* columnist Jim Warren could write, a little wearily, 'Due to newspaper publicity, rock'n'roll has become a sort of catchword in Auckland. As a consequence, any entertainment which smacks of modern music in any form is dubbed Rock'n'Roll.'[76]

In the month that *Rock Around the Clock* was drawing record audiences to Auckland's Regent, *Tempo* published a New Zealand Hit Parade, from a survey of sheet music, record sales and radio programmes. It gives an idea of the popular fare just before rock'n'roll penetrated the mass market:

1. 'Hot Diggity'
2. 'Man With the Golden Arm'
3. 'No Other Love'
4. 'Ivory Tower'
5. 'The Happy Whistler'
6. 'Wayward Wind'
7. 'It's Almost Tomorrow'
8. 'I'll Be Home'
9. 'I Almost Lost My Mind'
10. 'My September Love'
Coming up rapidly – 'Be-Bop-a-Lula'[77]

Soporific pop may have dominated radio playlists, but it was of no interest to the young rock'n'roll fans who were flocking to local halls and makeshift venues. They wanted to dance, to their music, and they did not want squares cramping their right to jive. Rock'n'roll dancing was as much a phenomenon as the music; in the main centres and smaller towns, promoters began organising marathon dance competitions.

An overseas expert arrived to spread the jive. Milt Mitchell was a 30-year-old Australian rock'n'roll dance exhibitionist who first visited New Zealand in the cast of *The Boyfriend*. Mitchell had been an original bodgie from inner city, working-class Sydney, 'legendary among the group for his dancing ability'. In 1948 he won a marathon dance contest in Brisbane, jiving non-stop for 24 hours. He turned his skills into a career through demonstrations of rock'n'roll dancing. Mitchell and an eight-strong team of dancers began their demonstrations at the first Auckland Town Hall rock'n'roll gig on 23 October 1956, and they became part of the floor show at the Sorrento.[78] During his trips across the Tasman, comments Australian sociologist Jon Stratton, Mitchell 'is credited, with some degree of hyperbole one would think, with having taught more than 50,000 New Zealanders how to rock'.[79]

When he arrived in Wellington, the *Evening Post* warned of the difficulties of emulating Mitchell's gymnastics. 'Learners! Don't forget this is advanced rock-and-roll incorporating jive and jitterbug steps – better to keep off till you really get the hang of the thing.'[80]

Mitchell was 'a mad character, sort of a ballroom dancer-come-jazzeroo', recalled Don Richardson, who hired him in March 1957.

He was almost uncontrollable. He had a flare for advertising. We took him on a trip to Wanganui when we worked up there and the advertising mucked up. There were hardly any bookings so he walked along one side of the street and I walked along the other side and we were talking across the road in a lunch time crowd – 'Yeah well you'll be at the show tonight won't you?' And this went on and he filled the house. Just some Aussie bullshit. He was an incredible guy but you never knew when he was going to blow up. He got into terrible trouble with the girls . . . . I loved him.[81]

Milt Mitchell, Australian rock'n'roll dance exhibitionist, says hello to Wellington, March 1957. Don Richardson collection

opponent Denis Sharp by 30 minutes, lasting 49 hours to win £72. The pair kept dancing while they shaved and ate, and were given a three-minute break each hour, during which their feet were massaged and blisters treated with methylated spirits. Crowds flocked to the hall to witness the closing stages until 'Slowly, like watches running down, the movements of the men slackened until they were barely shuffling.'[82]

With twenty years' experience running dances at the Dunedin Town Hall, Joe Brown had seen fashions come and go. He prided himself that his events could move with the times, but his aim was always to 'please the majority'. Brown had fostered the fad for square dancing early in the 1950s, and while jiving was forbidden as late as 1955, he eventually roped off a special area for jivers in the main Town Hall, to the relief of conventional dancers. In September 1957, he closed the old-time dance in the concert chamber, and devoted the room to rock'n'roll, with an eight-piece Polynesian band.[83] This dismayed the old-time dancers, and musician Harry Strang saw a gap and launched a regular dance at St Kilda. 'Unlike Joe, who placed the emphasis on entertaining his patrons, Strang maintained the importance of the band, and in his words, "pulled enough of a crowd away from the town ball to make Joe think it wasn't worthwhile." Older dancers objected to the "rubbishy" American music that "crept in and took over" at the town hall.'[84]

Eventually, after an altercation, Brown announced in a newspaper advertisement, 'Teddy Boys, Bodgies, Widgies and other such types are banned from the Town Hall dance.'[85]

Newspapers were quick to sensationalise any incident that could use the words rock'n'roll, dancing and delinquents in the same story. There was no shortage of material: in Hastings a dozen youths held a 'rock'n'roll party' in the city cemetery, dancing, drinking and smashing beer bottles on headstones. In a satanic touch, one topless 23-year-old was found 'praying' while wearing a dog-collar around his neck. 'A gramophone stood on the edge of a grave and rock'n'roll records were scattered round . . . . the party had been jiving among the graves.'[86] In Nelson, 50 'larrikins' disrupted a brass band concert by jiving during the programme. A tragic incident in Queenstown seemed to confirm the worst fears, when a student nurse was killed doing 'a combination of jitterbug and rock'n'roll'. During a party, while dancing on concrete-covered linoleum, she attempted a flip but landed badly, striking her head on the

The marathons became Richardson and Clare's latest stunt to attract crowds, encouraging dancers literally to rock around the clock. The dancing began at the Roseland Cabaret on Harris Street, whittling down the contestants. At 23 hours the finalists were transferred on the back of a truck – still dancing – to the Wellington Town Hall a block away. The dancing continued at the Jamboree, with drummer Vern Clare keeping the beat going as the bands changed over.

The marathon craze spread to Auckland and Dunedin, where promoters Benny Levin and Joe Brown knew how to join a bandwagon. The rules were strict: dancers had to keep moving both feet and keep a specified rhythm. Three reprimands led to disqualification. In Dunedin, two men shuffled for two full days, Pat Rache outdistancing his

floor. Her dancing partner demonstrated the move at the coroner's inquest.[87]

Yet the public did not seem to share the newspapers' concerns. Vox pops taken at the marathon dances found most citizens saw rock'n'roll dancing as healthy, vigorous fun – less shocking, in fact, than the Charleston had been 30 years earlier. Some unlikely establishment figures helped to dampen tabloid hysteria. Rock'n'roll probably didn't contribute to delinquency, said Oswald Mazengarb, four years on from his report. In fact, it could be a positive outlet for excess energy. Even the Labour Prime Minister Walter Nash was benign about the alleged threat to social order: 'I've seen nothing that I would not have done myself at your age if I had been so agile.'[88]

Capitulation came quickly. Early in 1957, the Wellington Festivals of Jazz evolved into Rock'n'Roll Jamborees, with Johnny Cooper closing the shows, overwhelming the preceding jazz acts with the help of the audience singing along to every tune.[89] Eventually the increasingly rowdy response led several of the jazz musicians to launch Jazz for Listening, a new series held in the smaller concert chamber, which discouraged dancing. But first there was money to be made by taking rock'n'roll to the provinces.

In Auckland, Benny Levin had already experimented with jazz variety shows, with mixed success. He quickly learnt how to present more popular fare. In February 1957, his touring show was *Don't Knock the Rock*. The night before leaving Auckland, the eight musicians went to a screening of *Rock Around the Clock* at Point Chevalier. 'We listened and watched and wondered', recalled Merv Thomas.

Their rock'n'roll homework paid off. A Christchurch review said, 'Rock'n'roll is like letting a lion loose in a busy beauty parlour. The result – hysteria.' The combo that stole the show were the Rocket Beaters, in which the Auckland saxophonist was billed as a rock'n'roll honker from Australia, performing Bill Haley's hits 'with jangling knees and contortionist feats'. The New Plymouth bass player Galvin Edser threw himself into the required rock'n'roll antics, riding his double bass like a cowboy, or playing it while on his back. Allen recalled: 'Merv, Galvin and I would always be trying to do some sort of act that was going to be better than the last time, or better than the next guy.'[90]

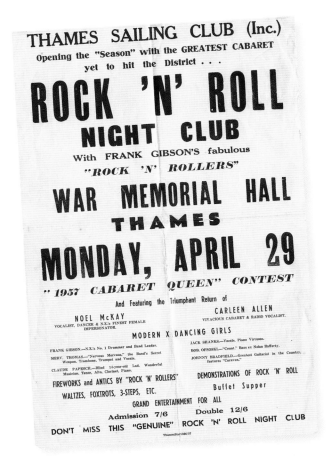

With Frank Gibson's rock'n'roll band, a female impersonator and 'Modern X Dancing Girls', the Thames Sailing Club promises 'grand entertainment for all', 1957. Merv Thomas collection

Johnny Cooper was anointed 'New Zealand's King of Rock'n'Roll' when he topped the bill at the Rock'n'Roll Jazz Concerts in Palmerston North and Wanganui in March 1957. Richardson and Clare's usual jazz collaborators still dominated the lineup, but tucked early into the programme was a singer recently discovered by Cooper in a Palmerston North talent quest. Squeezed between Bob Barcham's 'Keyboard Silhouette' and Johnny Williams' 'Clarinet Styling' was an eighteen-year-old bank clerk from Wanganui billed as 'New Zealand's Elvis Presley'. His name was Johnny Devlin.

The young singer almost brought the house down with his imitations of American idol of millions of teenagers . . . . complete with sideboards, and much 'Elvis-ing of the Pelvis-ing', Johnny Devlin even had his deadpan stooge in the background with a guitar. But this singer was one up on Elvis Prestley [*sic*] – he could play his own guitar.[91]

NERVOUS WRECK

He was the boy from Gonville who got real gone. The meteoric success of Elvis immediately inspired imitators to appear in many countries. New Zealand's Elvis was Johnny Devlin: born in 1938 in the country town of Raetihi but raised in Gonville, Wanganui.

The first pop music Devlin heard was by Guy Mitchell, the Four Preps and Kay Starr, but his first love was country and western: Tex Morton, Slim Dusty, Hank Snow. Much of it was via radio's *Hit Parade* and request sessions, or in cowboy films at the local picture theatre. His mother Bessie had an ATCL in the piano, and his father played the guitar, so there were plenty of singalongs while growing up. Saving money from a paper round, Devlin bought his first guitar aged eleven, and would spend hours perched

Johnny Devlin, teenage country singer, photographed by Dick Hofma at the Majestic Theatre, Wanganui, c. 1952. Lou Clauson Collection, PAColl-5679-04, Alexander Turnbull Library, Wellington

in a tree singing 'Too-Ra-Loo-Ra-Loo-Ral'. Dressed in a cowboy hat, he made his debut in a school production at the Wanganui Opera House, performing 'She Taught Me How to Yodel'. He later organised his own variety show, starring the Devlin family in assorted combinations, among them his mother with a solo whistling routine.

In 1955, a year after he left school, Devlin and his brothers Rodney, Robby and Martin formed the River City Ramblers with their cousin Tony Mercer. They were a skiffle band, he later said, with vocal harmonies, a guitar and a tea-chest bass; beer-bottle kazoos emulated saxophones. Devlin practised singing in an empty water tank on Mercer's family farm, enjoying the reverberations. In a Model-A Ford, Mercer's father drove the Ramblers to the talent quests and charity shows held from Taranaki to Horowhenua.[92]

Devlin didn't lack for determination. He would check out any acts that visited Wanganui. Years later, several of them would remember Devlin coming backstage offering to sing an item with their bands: Benny Levin, guitarist Tommy Kahi and Taranaki dance-band leader Colin King. Devlin's idol at the time was Johnny Cooper, in his Maori Cowboy phase with the Range Riders. He would perform songs from Cooper's early repertoire such as 'The Convict and the Rose' and 'Lonely Blues' and, one night when Devlin was about fifteen, Cooper invited him on stage to sing 'Pretend' by Nat King Cole.

But once Devlin heard Bill Haley's 'Rock Around the Clock' on the *Lever Hit Parade*, he swapped country for rock'n'roll. When Elvis Presley released 'Heartbreak Hotel' Devlin thought, 'This guy has *got it*.' He started reading everything he could about him, buying any Presley discs that came out and copying his style. Not just his singing – Devlin quickly developed a rockified croon complete with hiccups – but his look, which he adopted obsessively. From James Dean's character in *Rebel Without a Cause* he borrowed a haircut and an attitude: 'cool, calm and collected, and we all wanted to be the same way'.

A job as a bank clerk enabled Devlin to buy a hire-purchase motorbike, and on weekends he and Mercer would loiter in Palmerston North. 'They used to call us milkbar cowboys, because we used to hang round the milkbars and play the jukeboxes. With my cousin and a few other people, we'd get round in a motorcycle gang.' Coming home from the movies at night, when the roads were empty, Devlin and Mercer would stand up on their bikes and 'let them go for a burst'.[93]

Devlin's first paying gig was at the Swing and Sway Club in Napier; he cruised over from Wanganui on his motorbike with a guitar slung across his back, earning ten shillings for his trouble. 'I haven't forgotten that. It was a big club, too, and they used to pack them out.'[94] His first appearance as a rock'n'roller was at a Dannevirke talent quest. He had one arm in plaster for a severed tendon but still won the £75 first prize. On his bike he covered the central North Island: to Stratford for a dance run by Colin King (who claimed he was first to bill Devlin as 'New Zealand's Elvis Presley'), to Ohakune (imploring Tommy Kahi for some time on stage), to Foxton (for another talent quest, coming third), back home for a broadcast on 2XA's *Youth Takes the Air*.[95]

For his Wellington debut – a couple of songs, unadvertised, midweek at the Roseland Cabaret – he was backed by local teenage band the Royal Rockers. 'We didn't know who this guy was, or who he was to become', said the Royals' drummer Alan Loney, who recalled that Devlin wore leopard-skin trousers and a green sparkly shirt. 'He did things with a microphone stand that we didn't know were possible.'[96] By August 1957, he was topping the bill at the Wellington Town Hall as 'New Zealand's newest and greatest Elvis' at the 11th Festival of Jazz. Arthur Pearce was impressed, writing that Devlin's 'absorption and application of the Elvis Presley idiom is quite astonishing'.[97]

Despite this high-profile show, Auckland had yet to hear the news of Johnny Devlin. In Wanganui, he was now on the chain gang at a freezing works and spent the summer studying *Jailhouse Rock*; the film showed Elvis in action, rather than loving them tender. 'I wanted to learn the movements and practised in front of a mirror, legs this way, hips this way, got it. I got right into it.'[98] He bought a stage outfit: ming-blue jacket, white stovepipe pants, and – from a Wanganui store – blue suede shoes. 'That's what I wore on stage, before I went professional.'[99]

Devlin's aspirations to perform further afield – Australia, even – led to a breakup with his girlfriend, who wanted to get engaged and settle down. So he headed north for a visit in January 1958. A few days in the big smoke without any contacts or friends disillusioned Devlin and he was on his way to the railway station when he ran into an acquaintance. Dennis Tristram was an accomplished rock'n'roll dancer and pianist whom Devlin had met while performing at a youth club in Palmerston North. Tristram and his wife Dorothy were now the resident dance act at

the Jive Centre, Auckland's leading rock'n'roll venue. He told Devlin he must visit the venue before returning home.

The Jive Centre had earned the right to call itself 'the heartbeat of New Zealand rock'n'roll'. Its visionary proprietor Dave Dunningham remembered Tristram saying to him 'There's a chap up from Wanganui who sings a lot of Presley numbers . . .'.

Dunningham was interested: where is he? 'Right beside me', said Tristram. 'Up you get', said Dunningham. Devlin recalled the moment:

I came out on stage and started shaking around, doing the Elvis thing. All these girls started screaming and I thought I had left my fly undone or something. I quickly turned round and checked that, and found that no, we were right there. I had heard that it happened overseas but I hadn't witnessed anything like it myself. I didn't know why the audience was screaming. I thought they must like the music. I shook my leg and they screamed, then I shook it again and they screamed again. It was the actions, the movements. I don't think it's a sexual thing, I never believed that. I think they're just excited with the music and the whole deal, wrapped up in the song and the singer.[100]

Dunningham told Devlin that he had a job if he wanted one. 'So I had to make some serious decisions because I'd never left home and I had a secure job in Wanganui.'[101] Devlin was soon back on his motorbike, returning to Auckland and taking up a residency at the Jive Centre on Friday and Saturday nights, at £4 per night. The backing band was mostly Merv Thomas's Dixielanders. 'There was no doubt about it, people were coming to the Trades Hall to see him', said Thomas. 'The band was nothing. They came because they could jive and because it was a rock'n'roll venue, not because of the band. It was the Jive Centre and it was just the place to be.'[102] Within a few weeks, Dunningham had the idea of recording Devlin. HMV's Dave Van Weede turned Devlin down, so Dunningham invited fledgling impresario Phil Warren to witness the show. 'I only had to be there one night and see the audience to know we had to make a record', said Warren, who two years earlier had launched his own record label, Prestige, when he was only eighteen.[103]

The song that Devlin chose as his recording debut was 'Lawdy Miss Clawdy', written by Lloyd Price and a minor release for Elvis Presley. On Anzac Day 1958, Thomas assembled the band for the session at the Jive Centre; he also assembled the tape machine. He used one crystal microphone – 'I couldn't afford proper ones' – and the toilet as an echo chamber, and taped Devlin and the band performing the song and its B-side, 'When My Blue Moon Turns to Gold Again', to the empty dance hall.

Much of what happened next – the massive sales, the frenzied six-month national tour – has become legend, helped along by two masters of hype: Phil Warren and Graham Dent. The original 'Lawdy Miss Clawdy' sold very well, allegedly 2000 copies in its first two months, mostly at Devlin's shows and in Auckland stores supplied by Dunningham. Radio play was limited: the NZBS claimed, with justification, that the recording wasn't good enough (and Devlin subsequently agreed). Six months later a second, faster and more popular version of the song was recorded with the Devils at Stebbing's studio. This was done just in time to capitalise on Devlin's biggest success: his national tour of 1958–59.

Graham Dent suggested to Warren and Robert Kerridge that the pair join forces to promote Devlin performing in Kerridge-Odeon theatres. They split the costs, and Coca-Cola came in as sponsors, producing a special Coke-edition EP of Devlin songs and running advertisements: 'Johnny Devlin says "Coke's the most! After a solid session, I dig a Coke."'[104]

A four-week trial tour began in November and kept being extended: it went on for six months. For much of the tour, they travelled by public transport: NZR trains and buses. Devlin would break box-office records throughout the country and sell box-loads of records through in-store appearances. The press joined in the fun, reporting every publicity gimmick devised by the promoters: the lurex stage shirts ripped apart by fans, thanks to Dent unpicking the sleeves; Devlin being whisked away by flamboyant Cabinet Minister Mabel Howard in a pink Cadillac convertible; and Dent and Warren's inflated claims about Devlin's earnings and record sales.

Johnny Devlin conquers Christchurch, January 1959; musician Claude Papesch at left.
Christchurch Star/Lou Clauson Collection, PAColl-5679-33, Alexander Turnbull Library, Wellington

The madness developed its own momentum. In Invercargill fans tried to remove Devlin's trousers, in Greymouth fire-hoses were turned on a mob that broke open the theatre doors, in Dunedin a policeman lost a finger, and in Christchurch the singer had to escape through a toilet's louvre windows, run up the road and take refuge in a Chinese restaurant. Initial slow sales in Christchurch were averted by a summit meeting – and photo opportunity – with local rock'n'roll hero Max Merritt.[105] Right through the country, the lengthy tour was 'greeted by houses full of yelling, uninhibited youngsters who got as much physical exercise out of the show as the cast themselves'.[106]

On stage, Devlin sang a repertoire of rock'n'roll standards and several of his own originals. He also performed a repertoire of gimmicks to keep the audience wound up. He spun them out like a high-energy striptease act: 'All the stuff that Elvis was doing', recalled Devils' drummer Tony Hopkins. 'Lying on the piano, rolling over the stage in his burnt-orange suit with leopard-skin lapels, undoing buttons, taking his coat off and throwing it all over the place. Vibrating and gyrating. All the tricks.'

The touring Devils were young rock'n'roll musicians rather than seasoned professionals, and enjoyed taking part in the theatrics. As the excitement escalated, Hopkins drummed while standing on his seat, and saxophonist Claude Papesch straddled the double-bass player Keith Graham while he played lying on the stage. 'All the antics', said Hopkins, 'and the crowd would go silly. There would be screaming, and big crowds waiting for us when we finished, and in front of the theatres, trying to catch a sight off him. I threw a guy offstage one night in Greymouth. I was playing behind the drums and suddenly this guy appears over the footlights heading for Johnny. I leapt up to push him off the stage. And as he went over, backwards into the front row, he grabbed my shirt front and ripped the front of my shirt out, leaving me with just the arms and back of my shirt. It was all good fun.'[107]

Also on the bill were dance duo Dennis and Dorothy Tristram, comedians Don Lylian and John Daley, magician Clive Weir and, later in the tour, female impersonator Noel McKay. The musical support act was eighteen-year-old Carol Davies, 'New Zealand's Connie Francis'. Although the *Woman's Weekly* wanted to link Davies with Devlin, according to one on-tour report the closest they got was singing together 'at unofficial functions, when they and other members from the cast entertain at hospitals or old people's homes'.[108]

Above: 'To Marise, love Johnny.' Marise McDonald collection

Opposite: Johnny Devlin and the Devils in action, 1959. Lou Clauson Collection, PAColl-5679-14, Alexander Turnbull Library, Wellington

Behind the scenes there were hi-jinks, usually tricks the band played on the blind, sixteen-year-old Papesch, such as a fire-cracker in his breakfast jam or a salad sandwich filled with newspaper. There were constant party invitations to deflect or accept; Weir was the troupe's social secretary. But the headline of a *Press* story declared, during the Mabel Howard encounter, 'Rock'n'Roll Singer a "Nice Young Man"'.[109]

Contrary to his 'Satin Satan' nickname – one of many – and the blasphemy of playing the Devil's music with his band the Devils, Devlin was a practising Catholic. During the tour, he went to church on Sundays when he could. And when it was suggested by a journalist that Devlin meet the visiting US evangelist Billy Graham and attend his public gathering at Athletic Park, the singer sought the advice of a priest as to whether he should go. 'He said yes, that's okay – just don't pray at the crusade.' The meeting with Graham was broadcast so that – authorities hoped – teenagers in milkbars would tune in. Being in the middle of his own tour, Devlin declined Graham's invitation to join the crusade. But he agreed to a photo call with Graham and Labour Prime Minister Walter Nash, and with the Devils later performed to Graham's 20,000 strong congregation at Western Springs.[110]

As the tour came to an end, Warren organised a press conference to present Devlin with a super-sized royalty cheque for £2230, earned by sales of 'Lawdy Miss Clawdy'. Once the photos had been taken, Warren promptly took back the cheque. How many copies were actually sold? In 1998 he preferred to maintain the legend: 'We told everybody we sold 100,000 copies, but I wouldn't have a clue.' After that, he said, the pressing plant lost count.[111]

After the primitive first recording session for 'Lawdy Miss Clawdy', Devlin recorded prolifically. What the recordings lack in fidelity is compensated by their sheer exuberance, Devlin instinctively adopting the rockabilly vocabulary of hiccups, falsetto leaps, uh-huhs and nonsense syllables. His vocal style would eventually borrow as much from Jerry Lee Lewis as from Elvis, though his macho intensity was delivered with a wink more than a leer. His choice of material was hip, beyond the obvious essentials such as Elvis hits, or 'Blue Suede Shoes', '20 Flight Rock', 'Whole Lotta Shakin' and 'Rave On'. Even before the British delinquency film *Violent Playground* was released, he had recorded 'Play Rough' from its soundtrack, and he ventured outside rockabilly for his repertoire, to honky-tonk country and R&B. But Devlin quickly began writing and recording a substantial number of his own songs, among them 'Nervous Wreck', 'How Would Ya Be' and the Latin-American ballad 'Doreen'.

His studio musicians performed with gusto, flair and a witty understanding of rockabilly dynamics. Among them were the eighteen-year-old pianist Mike Nock on 'I Got a Rocket in My Pocket' and 'Straight Skirt' (it was one for the money, just before stowing away to Australia); the Jive Centre's first guitar hero Bob Paris; the Devils' twanging guitarist Peter Bazley; and established jazzers such as drummer Don Branch and saxophonist Bernie Allen. The Devils' Tony Hopkins and teenage sax/piano virtuoso Claude Papesch would have long jazz careers on both sides of the Tasman.

In just over a year since his move to in Auckland in March 1958, Devlin had achieved remarkable success. Music archivist John Baker noted his accomplishments: the

Bob Paris, pioneering rock'n'roll guitarist, 1961. Bruce King collection

release of ten singles, four EPs and an album, and a six-month concert tour that packed theatres throughout the country. Hours after the swish function with the royalty cheque, Devlin was back on stage at the Auckland Town Hall, where 'a mob of screaming teenage girls rushed on the stage and literally mobbed poor, poor Johnny. He rocked them all right, but Johnny was a tired and battered man when the session was over.'[112]

In May 1959, Devlin and most of the Devils left for Australia by boat. A day after arriving, they joined promoter Lee Gordon's Big Show, to share stages with the Everly Brothers, Tab Hunter and Fabian. By December, Devlin was firmly established as a rock'n'roll name in Australia, with weekly earnings ranging from £500 to £700. His New Zealand fan club soon relocated to Sydney. Wanganui's Elvis was in exile.[113]

GUITAR BOOGIE

The hysteria inspired by Johnny Devlin's tour in the summer of 1958–59 was spectacular and short-lived. As it came to an end, Devlin himself was realistic about his future. If he didn't succeed in Australia, he would simply return home, form another band, 'and hope that I still had a good name'. At the height of his fame in New Zealand, he was earning more than £160 per week; a year earlier, his pay cheque as a bank clerk had been £7. How long did he think rock'n'roll would last? Quite a while yet, he said. But if not, he was ready with other styles: ballads, western, calypso, 'as well as rock'n'roll'.[114]

Many were ready to foretell the end of rock'n'roll; some were even willing it to happen. 'Rock'n'roll is past its peak here', wrote *Joy*'s music columnist in April 1959, after enjoying many months of writing provocative copy. 'We'll probably never see a successor to Johnny Devlin, because the demand is dying off.'[115]

Calypso, the cha-cha and folkie hootenannies were all predicted to be the next big thing, usually by hopeful older members of the music establishment. But none found traction. 'It's going to be a long time before we find another musical gimmick that can last the distance that this monster has', acknowledged the band leader and concert promoter Don Richardson. It was public demand that had created the boom, he said, 'and as long as the kids keep buying it you can bet there'll be record companies pressing it. Personally I could stand a change, but I'm not as biased as one of my associates who remarked, "Every time I hear the stuff I feel like washing my radio out with a good old Cole Porter melody."'[116]

The Devlin tour heralded the arrival of a new era in popular music in New Zealand. The fledgling industry now had a target market, the teenager. Before, record buyers were an undefined mass but seemed middle-aged and wholesome; the arrangements were accomplished and acceptable, the listening was easy. HMV's limited interest in recording local acts led to many small independent labels being launched, and some prospered.

Following the success of Richardson and Clare's festivals in Wellington, and Dave Dunningham's Jive Centre in Auckland, a new breed of music entrepreneur emerged, sensing there were ten shillings to be made. Concurrent developments in technology also helped: the arrival of the 45 rpm disc and cheaper record players (many manufactured locally). Soon there would be affordable transistor radios and, eventually, stereo

Four bands for a crown, 1957. Rocky Don Hall collection

recordings. The use of amplifiers meant that big bands were no longer required: the rock'n'roll groups that the teenagers wanted were cheaper to hire, and small jazz combos could play in restaurants.

Despite a shortage of instruments, becoming a rock'n'roll musician seemed achievable and fun. In the working-class suburb of Rongotai in Wellington, eleven-year-old Rod Stone saw photos of Elvis with a guitar around his neck and knew he had to get one. He had never seen him perform: there was no television, and the films were out-of-bounds ('they would doubtlessly corrupt me'). He was thirteen before he could afford his first guitar, an acoustic from Shand-Miller's on Manners Street costing £5/2/6d. 'Looking back, it was a heap of shit with a ridiculously high action, but at the time I was in heaven. I played it until all my fingers were blistered.'[117]

To up-and-coming jazz players, the few remaining big bands such as Arthur Skelton's sweet, 'strictly ballroom' orchestra were of little appeal, beyond paid practice.

To them, rock'n'roll was an annoying diversion, but it could at least offer a start in music. In 1957 Mike Nock was a teenager and aspiring jazz saxophonist when he was invited to join the Fabulous Flamingos, a Maori dance band. Originally from Christchurch, the musicians had been members of Tommy Kahi's much-travelled Royal Hawaiians when they met Nock in Motueka. A spontaneous jam session took place, and several of the musicians decided to go out on their own, intending to play jazz rather than Hawaiian music.

When they called Nock, the Fabulous Flamingos were living in a Palmerston North motor camp, enduring a hand-to-mouth existence while playing dances around the district. Nevertheless Nock, who was working at Begg's in Wellington, jumped at the chance. Born in Ngaruawahia, he had wanted to be a professional musician since the age of eleven. After the sudden death of his father he was encouraged by Bert McNamara, a local dance-band pianist. Joining the Flamingos in Palmerston North, Nock got a rude awakening to the life of a musician. 'I get up there and they've got a little room at the motor camp and no money. They didn't tell me this. The first thing they do is pawn my saxophone. I'm too scared to leave – I'm a little runt of a kid with these big Maori guys.'

The Flamingos' vocalist was Colin Saggus, a teenager able to sing rock'n'roll. 'So we had this very curious band that played a weird mixture of Elvis and Nat King Cole, if you can imagine. "Be Bop a Lula" and hip arrangements of songs like "Sunny Side of the Street". And we're trying to make a living in Palmerston North – you've got to be kidding!'

Enter Johnny Cooper, who had been based in New Plymouth since his success at Wellington's Rock'n'Roll Jamborees. Cooper became the Flamingos' manager, and they became his backing band for gigs in the district. After various Flamingos migrated, it was just Saggus and Nock remaining when Cooper decided to launch a talent quest. Nock was 'the ticket collector in disguise' as well as playing a set of ragtime piano to open the show, supporting Cooper in a few songs and backing the contesting singers.

Cooper's *Give It a Go* talent quests were a phenomenon in the North Island for ten years from 1957, hopping between small towns in one-night stands, drawing huge crowds that – police and thieves both noticed – seemed to empty every home in the district. Besides Johnny Devlin, others who gave it a go included Maria Dallas, Johnny Deep, Marise McDonald, Midge Marsden, John Rowles

Johnny Cooper gives it a go in his home town, 1959.
Eph-C-CABOT-Talent-Quest-1959-01,
Alexander Turnbull Library, Wellington

and the Supersonics. Cooper encouraged hundreds of performers to try their luck for prizes up to £100: rock'n'roll groups, child singers, Elvis impersonators, Johnny Devlin impersonators. However, recalled Nock, 'We used to carry our own winners with us, a trio of Maori girls from Taranaki. We were a totally self-contained unit that would come to town: a talent quest with big prizes, but of course no prizes were awarded.'[118]

While sensationalised headlines might suggest that New Zealand's youth was having a non-stop rock'n'roll party, changes were gradual. In reality, recalled Gordon Campbell, 'For every gone cat there were a hundred squares looking on in fear, loathing and some curiosity.' There were very few concert tours such as Devlin's, and if rock'n'roll was featured in a dance, it was as 'a freak show, a novelty bracket for the "young folk" just before the supper waltz at family dances'.[119]

Nevertheless, in the wake of the Mazengarb report, youth clubs and church halls became venues for dances in the main centres and especially their suburbs. The local dances were often sanctioned by establishment figures, optimistically hoping they were a wholesome diversion from teenage delinquency and pregnancy. In 1958 the *Weekly News* showed the governor-general, Lord Cobham, witnessing rock'n'rolling teenagers at Hutt Valley youth clubs. In a two-hour visit, while petticoats spun on the dance floor, Cobham 'moved about the young people, chatting casually with various groups, encouraging them in community activities and recommending sport as a healthy outlet for leisure time and over-abundant energy'.[120] In Napier, a gardener and handyman called Bill Sykes identified with teenagers who resented being called bodgies and widgies as they roamed the streets. He rallied around for help: the Red Cross loaned a hall, the Ministry of Works social committee a loud-speaker system and the equipment for darts and table tennis. An earlier attempt to set up a Napier club had failed due to the organisers' strict rules, so Sykes left the teenagers in charge. 'These youngsters are confounding the critics', wrote Nell Hartley. 'They are making a grand job of the responsibilities placed upon them.'[121]

Max Merritt said that throughout New Zealand, church and civic leaders who once wanted rock'n'roll banned were now allowing it at youth club dances. In Christchurch, the city's PR office asked Merritt and the Meteors to perform in Hagley Park as part of a dance festival. Also on the bill was a Maori kapa haka group, and Irish, Highland, folk and square dancing. The Meteors were joined on stage by twelve rock'n'roll dancers, and a crowd of up to 15,000 teenagers and their parents watched or took part. Merritt said that police and politicians agreed that 'rock'n'roll is keeping the kids off the street, and without a doubt is helping the delinquency in Christchurch'.[122]

By the late 1950s, an array of inner-city Auckland dance halls catered to different cliques, depending on music tastes and social demographics. To teenagers, the long-established Peter Pan was too formal and aimed at mature adults, and some thought the Orange Ballroom on Newton Road was 'too square' in its music and 'too rough' in its clientele. Judy Hepburn, a teen in the late 1950s, never attended the Jive Centre, which catered to a 'fast crowd' that smoked and drank; she went to St Sep's, where jiving was prohibited. To Lillian Gardner, it was 'the Elvis

Ray Paparoa, Pukekohe's Elvis. Lou Clauson Collection, PA1-f-192-23-03, Alexander Turnbull Library, Wellington

Presley' lot that went to the Orange, whereas she went to the Oriental Dance Hall on Symonds Street, 'home to a variety of musical styles and rock'n'roll, when played, was more Cliff Richard'. Auckland's teens split themselves into tribes, regarding their own as 'with it' and those outside as 'squares'.[123]

Johnny Devlin's dramatic success has almost eclipsed the fact that there were other prominent rock'n'roll groups operating in Auckland before he arrived. Among them were the Bob Paris Combo, the Keil Isles, and Red Hewitt and the Buccaneers, all of which had emerged in the wake of *Rock Around the Clock* to begin long, influential careers.

When the Merv Thomas Band quit the Jive Centre after being refused a raise, Dave Dunningham needed a replacement to back Johnny Devlin. He hired a young, West Auckland group led by guitarist Bob Paris, which had been playing instrumental versions of rock'n'roll hits at the Maori Community Centre. As the Jive Centre Band, the group became as much of a drawcard at the venue as the singers they backed. They dressed in drape jackets with satin lapels, emulating the look, sound and moves of Bill Haley's Comets. The group evolved into the Bob Paris Combo, backed singers such as Eddie Howell and Ricky May, and recorded several rock'n'roll instrumentals – including 'Drag Strip' and 'Rebel Rouser' – in the twang-heavy style of Duane Eddy and Link Wray.[124]

Paris was New Zealand's earliest rock'n'roll guitar hero. He began on the steel guitar, inspired by the virtuoso Hawaiian guitarist Sol Hoopi. Locally, he admired Bill Sevesi and the Dutch immigrant Barry Slot, and he was sent to Walter Smith for steel-guitar lessons. Seeing Bill Haley's band in *Rock Around the Clock* was a pivotal moment. 'It was full of jazz musicians and they played well', said Paris. 'We had the jazz background, country and pop background too.'

As a teenager Paris frequented The Loft, Jim Foley's jazz record store above Vulcan Lane. The pianist introduced him to a wider range of chord voicings, and also to Phil Warren, who offered him a job with his fledgling record company. Bart Stokes taught Paris music theory and took him to Wellington to play steel at a rock'n'roll concert. Paris then abandoned the acoustic steel guitar for an electric, and also took up the vibraphone. The Combo recorded ten singles for Zodiac, La Gloria and Philips before Paris went to Sydney in 1960 and joined Johnny Devlin's Devils. Upon his return he backed Johnnie Ray, Eartha Kitt and Helen Shapiro on their New Zealand tours, then joined the Merseymen, a group formed by Phil Warren to play at his teenage venue the Beatle Inn. Aged just 25, Paris was already a seasoned professional, and he remained in demand for sessions until his untimely death from cancer in 1994 aged 55.[125]

The Keil Isles, 1961. From left: Bill Fairs, Herma Keil, Brian Henderson, Louis Miller, Eliza Keil, Klaus Keil, Olaf Keil. Viking Records/RNZ Music Library, Wellington

The Keil Isles built a large following in Auckland in the late 1950s, through residencies at the Orange Ballroom and the Jive Centre, where they replaced the Bob Paris Combo. The group was formed by guitarist Olaf Keil in 1956, although since their arrival from Samoa in 1951 various members of the family had been performing together at Mormon church functions. Olaf's cousin Freddie asked him to accompany him singing rock'n'roll, so Olaf recruited his siblings to form a band: Herma, Klaus, Rudolph, Eliza and Helga would eventually all be members. Freddie was the lead singer, and there would be many other musicians who were not related.

The Keil Isles were slickly rehearsed and smartly presented, in matching, fringed satin shirts; Mormon connections in the US provided them with stage outfits, good equipment and records to cover. Besides being an accomplished guitarist, Olaf was an electronics whiz who could tweak amplifiers and guitars to emulate the sounds heard on the latest records. Their prolific recording career began in the dying days of Tanza with a 45 rpm single of 'Johnny B Goode' b/w 'Flip, Flop and Fly'. Dozens of singles and several albums followed, for Tanza, Zodiac and Viking; almost all but a few instrumentals were cover versions of overseas hits by an array of 1950s rock'n'roll and pop acts. Always a drawcard wherever they played, the Keil Isles' biggest recording success came in 1962 when their version of 'The Twist' was chosen for radio airplay by the NZBS, whose programmers regarded Chubby Checker's hit to be too raucous.[126]

In 1960 Freddie Keil fell out with his cousin Herma and left to form his own group. As Freddie Keil and the Kavaliers they offered an alternative to the Keil Isles, while having much in common: both groups performed and recorded well-known material with high levels of showmanship and musicianship. The Kavaliers – dressed in shark-skin, Italian-cut suits and with passionate vocals from Freddie – was 'one ballsy, driving band', said writer Roger Watkins, 'a showband inasmuch as they "put on a show." There was fancy footwork from the front line, flash outfits, and they played "Guitar Boogie" with two guitarists on the same guitar.'[127] Besides their contribution to the Maori showband ethos, the constantly changing lineups of both Keil groups meant their influence was greater than their sales or originality.

Red Hewitt also began playing rock'n'roll in 1956. Hewitt – Alan to his parents – had come to the music through country and western. A friend introduced him

to 78s by Hank Snow and Tex Morton, and loaned Red his father's guitar. After singing an Elvis song at a private dance, Hewitt was approached by the guitarist Dick Rogers, and they formed the Buccaneers.

In 1957 Hewitt won an Elvis Presley impersonation contest that ran over several weeks during the intervals of the Presley film *Loving You* at the Regent. With the Buccaneers he played teen dances on Auckland's North Shore, before taking the stage at the Jive Centre with a repertoire of early rock'n'roll standards. During a six-month residency at the El Rancho nightclub in Mission Bay, the Buccaneers' fourteen-year-old pianist Veronica Tierney – wearing heavy makeup to look older – would take time out to give energetic demonstrations of rock'n'roll dancing with Hewitt.[128]

After recording a debut single with Stebbing's Zodiac label, Hewitt and his Buccaneers jumped ship to Audion, a new label launched by three Auckland university students. They presented Hewitt with 'Robbin' the Cradle', a song

Surf's up: Auckland teenagers the Stereotones play Waipu Cove, summer, 1959–60; several went on to lengthy music careers. Main picture: Vince Callaher, vocalist. Top left (L–R): Bruce King, bongos; Mike Dolan and Graham Bartlett, guitars. Bottom left (L–R): Ian Lowe, guitar; Kevin Paul, saxophone; Glyn Tucker, vocals; Fred Gebbie (obscured), manager; Graham Bartlett, guitar; Rick Laird, bass; Bruce King, drums. Bruce King collection

recorded by Jim Bellis, a Canadian. Although Hewitt was initially reluctant to record the song, his version was a smash hit, in the New Zealand charts for sixteen weeks in 1960, four of them at No. 1. (It is said to have sold 125,000 copies.) Hewitt's style of rock'n'roll always stayed close to his country and rockabilly roots, and he recorded several more singles back at Zodiac before breaking up the Buccaneers and heading to Australia to try a solo career. Within a couple of years he returned, and briefly worked as a demonstrator of a new dance craze: the Twist.[129]

Elsewhere in New Zealand, teenagers with guitars had not waited for a visitation from Devlin to get started. Pioneering groups in Wellington included the Royal Rockers from Lower Hutt and the Mana Quintet (later the Supersonics), both of which would back Johnny Devlin during his ascent. The Supersonics' guitarist Barry Walden had served in Japan as a twenty-year-old in 1948, playing piano in the 2NZEF Jayforce Dance Band. When his younger brother, the crooner Paul Walden, needed a backing group on his first recordings in 1958, the Supersonics stepped forward. (Their drummer Jim McNaught became a high-profile pop vocalist in the 1960s.) From Miramar came the Swamp Dwellers: in their plaid jackets they looked like Bill Haley's Scottish cousins, and the band evolved into an instrumental group, the Premiers. Their star guitarist Neil Harrap joined forces with several Supersonics to become the Blockbusters, a backing group regularly used by producer Laurie Lewis at HMV recording sessions. Among discs produced were singles by broadcaster Bas Tubert ('The Hu-Hu Bug', as the Tubes) and Hastings' Elvis, Teddy Bennett. Also from Miramar were the Skyrockets, who replaced the Premiers at the local Rio Grande club and ran their own dances there for a year.[130]

From another of Wellington's eastern suburbs were the Librettos, who formed in 1960 and became the Premiers' rivals. Both had repertoires that favoured the Shadows' formation stepping and guitar-led instrumentals, but the Librettos went on to record several singles and an album with vocalist Lou Parun. By 1965 they were in Australia, playing residencies in King's Cross and downtown Sydney, television shows and supporting the Seekers on a national tour. Guitarist Rod Stone became a sought-after session guitarist in Australia and Britain, and briefly played in a big band led by former Shadows drummer, Bruce Bennett.[131]

In Dunedin, the Typhoons played the 505 Club during the week, and on Saturday nights drew crowds of 1000

people to the Town Hall concert chamber as the rock'n'roll group at Joe Brown's dances (their guitarist Allen Quennell later moved to Auckland to play jazz). During breaks they would watch the New Embassy Dance Band entertain 2000 people in the main hall. From this group emerged the Embassy Six, an HMV recording act whose diverse lineup included the veteran jazz saxophonist Keith Harris and an eleven-year-old singer, Warren Byrnes. Invercargill's Satellites began as a dance band in 1958 and kept evolving – in style and members, most of whom were called Somerville – through changes in fashion until 1973.[132]

But Devlin's greatest rival was in Christchurch, where Max Merritt had an advantage: he ran a Saturday night dance, and on Sunday afternoons he would perform at the Teen Agers Club, launched by his parents and Trevor King at the Railway Hall on Argyle Street in 1957. 'When rock'n'roll happened, there were a lot of kids hanging around the Square in Christchurch getting into trouble and fights', he recalled. 'There was a big riot in Christchurch, so we thought there was something to do on an afternoon.'

Merritt had begun guitar lessons at eleven but gave it up, bored. 'Then all of a sudden rock'n'roll came in and I heard Little Richard . . . . I thought, "Damn, this is so manic. Where *is* this coming from?" You've got to understand that we had gone from "How Much is that Doggie in the Window" to "Awopbopaloobop Alopbamboom." A big jump.'

By the age of sixteen, Merritt and his band the Meteors were playing regularly at the Hibernian Hall.

> I was really innocent and the Hibernian Hall was a bloodbath at times because you'd have the Maori guys in one corner, the Samoan guys in the other, the seamen who used to come into Lyttelton Harbour in one corner, and the Demo Boys were the local ruffians. It was a volatile situation and anything could set it off, but it was exciting because we were playing rock'n'roll and everyone was enjoying it.[133]

Max Merritt and the Meteors became the most prominent of many rock'n'roll bands in Christchurch. Jazz played its part in nurturing these musicians; many were taught guitar by Tommy Kahi, and veteran saxophonist Martin Winiata formed the Moonmen. Playing for an older crowd was jazz guitarist/satirist Rod Derrett, who included rock'n'roll in his repertoire at the 99 Club. At the Top of the House was British immigrant Bobby Davis, performing with his Dazzlers.[134]

Trevor King proudly presents

THE MAX MERRITT STAGE SHOW

Max Merritt, presented noir-style in 1959 by Trevor King. Eph-A-CABOT-Music-1959-02-cover, Alexander Turnbull Library, Wellington

But for the Meteors and other leading groups, the key gigs were the teenage dances held in the Hibernian and Caledonian halls, and the hugely popular Spencer Street hall in Addington. The latter dance was originally set up for Catholic youth, but became a Mecca for teenagers of all denominations. Others appearing at these dances were Ray Columbus and the Invaders, Johnny Heinz and the Revellers, and Phil Garland with the Saints.[135]

Of all the teenagers wanting to emulate Merritt, the most ambitious was Ray Columbus, who had grown up learning tap dancing, his father hoping for another Fred Astaire. When Columbus heard Elvis Presley sing, he found a different vocation: all he needed was the means. His friend Peter Ward drummed with an old-school dance band called the Downbeats, and one night when the vocalist didn't show up, Columbus filled in. In one move, the Downbeats had discovered a new vocalist, and Columbus his vehicle. Soon evolving into Ray Columbus and the Invaders, and concentrating on rock'n'roll, the combo would become a leading drawcard in Christchurch.[136]

The Meteors and the Invaders both enjoyed an advantage over bands further north: the Deep Freeze operation that brought US servicemen through Christchurch on their way to the Antarctic. With them came records by R&B performers, which promptly made their way onto jukeboxes, and the opportunity to buy actual Fender guitars, just like those used by Buddy Holly and Hank Marvin. They could learn the latest songs first, and they could look the part. While rock'n'roll may have kept teenagers off the street, that did not mean their behaviour was restrained. Merritt proudly said that visiting rock stars – among them Johnny O'Keefe, Tommy Sands and the Platters – agreed that Christchurch was one of the 'wildest' towns they had played.[137]

SHOWMEN AND SVENGALIS

The increased American influence on popular music went beyond the musicians to the emerging industry. Dave Dunningham and his Jive Centre epitomised a new breed of entrepreneur/promoter. There were other Auckland agents and promoters in the 1950s, but variety was their currency. Among them were the singer Mary Throll, who launched the prominent Fuller's agency in 1954; Sydney-born Harry Wren, who brought mass-market shows over from Australia; and George Tollerton, a magician, broadcaster and ventriloquist as well as a leading booking agent. Dunningham and his cohorts specialised in pop music and had an element of the 'wide boy' about them. They took risks and their cheek could stray into ruthlessness, but they changed nightlife in the main centres and the lives of the musicians they employed.[138]

After establishing the Jive Centre as Auckland's premier rock'n'roll venue, Dunningham went on to open the Surfside ballroom in a former theatre in Milford, venue to many of the earliest beat bands. He ran it 'with an iron hand and good staff', said his wife Shirley: 'naughty' teenagers were banned for a month. Dunningham also ran two cabarets in Mt Maunganui, and by the 1970s was promoting international tours by cultural groups.[139]

The promoter whose high profile suggested he was his own best client was Harry Miller. An almost reckless risk-taker, while young the flamboyant Miller had played around with the E flat bass trombone and drums. But he quickly discovered that his greatest talent was for salesmanship. Miller cut his teeth in sales and marketing at Silknit, an Auckland fabric manufacturer. Diversification suited Miller's peripatetic style: he dabbled in the hospitality trade with restaurant pioneer Bob Sell, worked as a short-order cook, and as a travelling sales rep and demonstrator of infra-red cookers. This latter role suited Miller, who enjoyed playing the hustler and showman: it was almost inevitable that he would enter the entertainment business. After talking Howard Morrison into letting him act as the Quartet's booking agent, Miller branched out, launching his own record label and promoting tours of overseas acts. Emulating Tanza's relationship with Radio Corporation, he called his record label La Gloria because there was a local radio brand of that name. Appropriately, its first releases were motivational records.

Miller's first forays into promoting overseas acts would have caused anyone less self-confident to be hesitant. A national tour by Australian rock'n'roll star Johnny O'Keefe flopped, and a double-bill starring jazz singer Sarah Vaughan and bebop master Dizzy Gillespie was criticised by many for its disorganisation. But he found a cash-cow in his Showtime Spectaculars: national tours

featuring generous lineups of the top local acts, with sure-fire crowd-pleasers the Howard Morrison Quartet topping the bill. Miller always seemed to rebound from any gambles that misfired; after moving his operation to Australia in 1963, he had great success touring the Rolling Stones, Roy Orbison, and the rock musicals *Hair* and *Jesus Christ Superstar*. Eventually, in 1982, he over-reached himself establishing a computerised ticketing system, which went into receivership and resulted in a jail term for fraudulent misappropriation. But Miller was a pioneer, a New Zealander who approached the music business with an international vision – and had the chutzpah to succeed.[140]

Benny Levin did not have Miller's flashy approach to promotion, but made a much more sustained contribution to New Zealand music. Ironically, the pair had first met as children at Hebrew school, and Miller secured his lucrative management agreement with Levin's discoveries the Howard Morrison Quartet just as Levin, disillusioned, had temporarily decided to quit show business.

Levin had known he would be involved in music since he first laid hands on a piano. In 1943, aged thirteen, he was the youngest member of the Auckland Jazz Club; six years later he formed his first band, Dancetime. For months the swing septet practised in the living room of the Levin family home in Devonport. 'There were either bricks

Far left: Promoter and emoter: Harry M. Miller and US performer Johnnie Ray take time out at the Auckland Showgrounds, 1962. Bernie Allen collection

Left: Benny Levin, dance band pianist, impresario. Bryan Staff collection

BLUE SMOKE

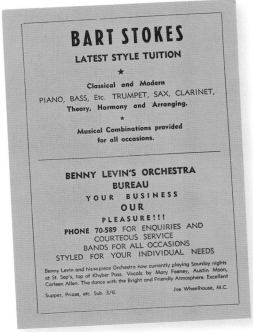

Jazz at Mt Maunganui, and programme advertisement, 1957. From left, Bruce McDonald, Bart Stokes, Greta Greer, Merv Thomas, Benny Levin, Bernie Allen. Bennie Gunn and Merv Thomas collections

being thrown on the roof or people standing out in the street clapping', recalled Levin's brother David. Dancetime secured a weekly residency at the Bayswater Boating Club that lasted seven years, with Joe Wheelhouse as a popular MC. Levin described this period as the best days of his life. 'All the stars came to guest for us', he said. 'Crombie Murdoch, Mavis Rivers, Nancy Harrie, Johnny Bradfield and Kahu Pineaha.' Mary Feeney, the regular vocalist, married the band's trumpeter Terry Armiger. 'We had the knack of timing for the dance brackets and in between I sang the Bill Haley numbers', said Levin.

His first national promotion was an ill-fated venture, suggested to him by progressive jazzer Bart Stokes. 'Can you imagine the South Island in 1952 being terrific for jazz?', Levin later said, incredulous at his naivety. Despite the stellar lineup of musicians, 'We died on our backsides. But it taught me how to do it.'[141] In the mid-1950s, Levin began organising monthly concerts at the Auckland Town Hall, and his flair for presenting a variety of acts on the same bill usually ensured a full house. Among them were Glenn Miller/Benny Goodman tribute shows and all-Maori bills that presented showbands alongside comedians, and introduced the Howard Morrison Quartet to its first big-city audience. In 1958 the *Music Maker* reported Levin's promotion of a 'new type of show . . . a monster dance, a treasure hunt with a car for first prize,

a beauty contest and lots of entertainment with his own band, the Keil Isles, the Scorpions Skiffle Group, the Morrison Quartet and vocalist Austin Moon. This should be a sell-out.'[142]

No matter how successful he became promoting international acts, Levin's commitment to local musicians remained constant. He played a pivotal role in many careers, among them those of Howard Morrison when he went solo, Bunny Walters and Dave Dobbyn. He also won respect for his honesty and his thrift. 'Benny's handshake was his word', said Morrison when Levin died in 1993. 'Whatever happened, if Benny said you were going to get paid, you were going to get paid.' This is where Levin's frugality was to his artists' benefit. His budgets, joked Morrison, were 'so tight he wouldn't let the draught under the door'.[143]

Of all the showmen, it was Phil Warren who earned the title King of Clubland, changing New Zealand's nightlife by establishing dozens of venues, a touring circuit, starting his own record label, and successfully lobbying for changes in liquor licensing laws before running for local office to pour his energy into another, civic-minded career.

New Zealand after hours was not closed for Warren when he was a teenager in the 1950s: it was an opportunity. He got his start in the music business at fourteen, working at Begg's record store. Inspired by his uncle, the jazz trumpeter

Phil Warren, king of clubland, c. 1960. Bryan Staff collection

Jim Warren, he learnt the piano and played the drums, but realised very early on that other people had more talent – and his was for guiding and presenting them. By the age of seventeen he was a businessman with his own record distribution firm, importing R&B and jazz from small US labels run by dodgy characters who nevertheless kept their word. At eighteen he started a Sunday night jazz club at Margaret O'Connor's dance studio off Queen Street, hiring musicians such as Bernie Allen and Mike Nock.

A hit album of the English musical *Salad Days* enabled Warren to launch his own label, Prestige, and start signing local acts. Warren's breakthrough came when he released Johnny Devlin's 'Lawdy Miss Clawdy' and masterminded – with Graham Dent – Devlin's barnstorming national tours. A nationwide chain of coffee lounges and dance halls quickly followed: he revived the Crystal Palace with Merv Thomas's Dixielanders, and launched clubs for teens and adults such as Mojo's, the Beatle Inn, the Montmartre and many others. Their attractions were revolutionary: espresso coffee with 'stimulating' extras, coloured lights, mirror balls. In the 1960s, patrons knocked three times to enter the Crypt, a club that pushed licensing laws to the limit. The profits covered the hefty fines.

He was always quick to see a gap, such as that left by the NZBS when it banned Chubby Checker's 'The Twist': it was Warren's suggestion that the Keil Isles cover the song, giving them a hit. He pioneered the international rock'n'roll tour with a 1959 show starring Johnny Cash, Gene Vincent and Col Joye, and went on to present the Rolling Stones, Ray Charles and hundreds of others.

Warren used his abilities to further his passions – entertainment and the region of Auckland – eventually becoming the city's deputy mayor. He believed show business and politics were natural bedfellows. Both require the gift of the gab, and a natural charisma to encourage people to show their support. He appreciated the old gag – 'politics is show business in drag' – and once put it to use when he booked the female impersonator Diamond Lil for a Labour Party conference.[144]

DISC DEALERS AND DISC MAKERS

Record retailing was another area of the music industry that expanded exponentially. In 1957 New Zealand's 'disc dealers' were 'rubbing their hands with glee at the boom in the record business', said record distributor Fred Noad. All companies found it difficult to keep up with demand. The factor that had contributed the most to the boom, he said, was 'rock and roll, the biggest money spinner the industry has ever known'.[145]

Advertisements show that some rock'n'roll discs were available in 1957, among a wide range of other styles. But of the rock'n'roll on offer, there was little variety outside the biggest hits. In February, among the 78s available through HMV – at 6/3 each – were Chuck Berry's 'Roll Over Beethoven', Lonnie Donegan's 'Rock Island Line', Gene Vincent's 'Be-Bop-A-Lula' and Bill Doggett's 'Honky Tonk'. Other artists prominently featured included Winifred Atwell, Ronnie Ronalde and Perry Como.[146]

The 78 rpm disc was being superseded by the 45 rpm single. In the first six months of 1957, 125,000 singles were sold and 131,000 albums; a year later the first six-month figures had increased to 589,000 singles and 237,000 albums. In the same period, sales of 78s dropped from 881,000 to 412,000. Imports also dropped by two-thirds, from 300,000 units to 103,000 units, reflecting the increased local pressing capacity.[147]

In Wellington, the Lamphouse and HMV stores held massive sales in 1958, placing more than 20,000 brand-new 78s on the market at bargain prices. The stores claimed that these discs included many recordings that would soon be unavailable in New Zealand. This was due to import restrictions, imposed early in 1958. To save overseas funds, only master tapes could be imported, so that the discs had to be manufactured in New Zealand. But for a disc to be worthwhile pressing locally, at least 300 units needed to be sold. In 1959 HMV began phasing out the pressing of 78s at its Lower Hutt factory.[148]

Perhaps the audience for rock'n'roll – teenagers – had helped expand the market, as had the arrival of 45s and LPs, but the genre was yet to dominate record sales. The local release of the *My Fair Lady* album in 1958 was a retail phenomenon not seen again until *The Sound of Music* soundtrack in 1965. For months, it was almost impossible to acquire, as copyright restrictions held up a local release. These delays were not unusual; they could be caused by the sheet music publisher holding back release until their stock was printed, an argument over who owned the copyright, or a theatre company with the rights to a show waiting until they were ready with a production. Or the distributor of the disc had to wait until the firms with the pressing plants – HMV, Radio Corporation and Green & Hall – were able to fulfil the order. Until *My Fair Lady* was finally released, import copies were passed around like Samizdat novels, and gave enterprising TEAL pilots and merchant seamen some extra income.[149]

My Fair Lady was another blow to HMV's monopoly: pressed by Green & Hall – ironically, on HMV's old plant in Kilbirnie – it was released through Philips, which had its own retail chain for its electrical products. Columbus stores were still prominent in most towns, and a plethora of independent record retailers had emerged.[150]

Especially influential to Auckland musicians was Jim Foley's 'swell new discery' The Loft, which opened in mid-1956. Since sitting in with the 290th Army Band during the war, and hosting *Youth Must Have Its Swing* on 1ZB, Foley had been flitting back and forth to the States. Leading musicians such as Bert Peterson, Jim Warren and rock'n'roll guitarist Bob Paris were among the many who found that Foley's enthusiasm and knowledge meant The Loft became a hangout and an education.[151]

In February 1958, the Everly Brothers' 'Wake Up, Little Susie' topped the first hit parade chart to be assessed by retailers rather than estimated by broadcasters. *Truth* complained that 'recent ZB *Hit Parades* have been predominantly racket'n'rhythm', and the paper was relieved that Frank Sinatra's 'All the Way' was soon to be featured.[152] But a survey of record stores on Auckland's Queen Street in May 1958 showed how rock'n'roll had yet to dominate tastes in popular music. The twelve top-selling singles were (in no particular order):

'Sail Along Silvery Moon' – Billy Vaughn
'Moonlight Swim' – Tony Perkins
'Oh Boy' – The Crickets
'Melodie D'Amour' – Ames Brothers
'14 Carat Gold' – Don Cherry
'My Special Angel' – Bobby Helms
'April Love' – Pat Boone
'The Story of My Life' – Marty Robbins
'Witchcraft' – Frank Sinatra
'Great Balls of Fire' – Jerry Lee Lewis
'Sugartime' – McGuire Sisters
'Silhouettes' – The Diamonds[153]

The lack of New Zealand discs in the early charts gives a misleading indication of the recording scene after Johnny Devlin's success. Scores of the early rock'n'roll groups recorded and small independent labels proliferated. HMV's original hesitancy towards local acts left the field wide open for competitors, said Murdoch Riley. 'It was an open invitation. [Managing-director Jack] Wyness couldn't see past his own nose, to be honest. So many things happened where HMV were wrong footed, and they allowed everybody in. It made it a little bit easier: the whole Auckland industry took off.'[154]

Among the independents that set themselves up were Phil Warren's Prestige, journalist John Ewan's Octagon, Alex Jenning's Lexian, Harry Miller's La Gloria and – founded by several Auckland university students – Audion. Christchurch businessman and jazz drummer Jack Urlwin launched Peak, where releases of the rockabilly singer Peter Lewis ('Four City Rock') could stand alongside bebop by pianist Chuck Fowler, and smooth, swinging vocal standards by the ex-All Black captain Pat Vincent.

The precarious existence of the local recording industry that had emerged with Tanza and Stebbing in the early 1950s was at the whim of changes in fashion and technology, or invisible overseas boardroom deals. When Nat King Cole brought the news in January 1955 that Tanza was losing the lucrative Capitol distributorship to HMV, it was a shock to the New Zealand label. Capitol's glamorous catalogue had helped with the cash flow at Radio Corp's recording division, effectively underwriting Tanza. However, the

From Tauranga, the Apaapa Sisters – Cheryl and Lyn – recorded three singles and an EP *Maori Melodies* for Zodiac in the early 1960s. Lou Clauson Collection, PA1-f-192-03-21, Alexander Turnbull Library, Wellington

by Phil Stebbing. Releases soon followed by the Hager Sisters, the Howard Morrison Quartet, Eddie Howell, Bob Paris and the Keil Isles.

Murdoch Riley launched Viking in the same year with two partners, Ron Dalton and Jim Staples. A tape from 2ZA announcer Wally Chamberlain became their first release: the Q-Tees with *Little Darlin'*. They then released an EP of acceptable rock'n'roll hits, sung by Nepia, Rangi and Basil Tawharu, and Arthur McGrath, with backing by the Jazzmen. Sounding like the Manawatu's version of the Mills Brothers, the Q-Tees managed to secure airplay on the *Lever Hit Parade* thanks to Riley's NZBS contacts.

As well as recording local artists, Viking distributed discs for overseas labels such as Roulette and Oriole. A major success was the Canadian group the Beau Marks, whose single 'Clap Your Hands' sold 30,000 copies and topped the Australian charts. Dalton handled most of the musical decisions, and his greatest successes would come in the early 1960s with Dinah Lee and the guitar instrumentalist Peter Posa. Many of the songs that Dalton accessed for artists came from his listening to US radio on shortwave; this method provided Lee with hits such as 'Don't You Know Yockomo' and 'Do the Bluebeat'.[156]

Many of the independents relied on HMV to press their discs, and despite the best efforts of HMV staff such as Dave Van Weede, clients often became frustrated with delays and the obstructiveness of middle management.

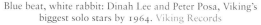

Blue beat, white rabbit: Dinah Lee and Peter Posa, Viking's biggest solo stars by 1964. Viking Records

shock was soon reversed, when HMV lost the rights to the American RCA label, just as Elvis Presley was about to break internationally. At Tanza, Murdoch Riley found himself confronted by a difficult decision: whether to pick up the distribution rights for the respected Columbia label, or RCA. He chose RCA, and the Elvis 78s 'sold like hot cakes'. The windfall briefly kept Tanza buoyant, but changes at Radio Corp meant there was little interest in maintaining its pioneering record division. Frustrated, Riley left to launch his own label, Viking.[155]

Two independent labels, Zodiac and Viking, dominated the pop field in the late 1950s and early 1960s. Five years after closing their Stebbing label due to distribution difficulties, Eldred and Phil Stebbing re-entered the record business with Zodiac in 1957, quickly recording and releasing a vast number of 78s and 45s. Zodiac's first disc was the Hulawaiian's 'Hawaiian Rock'n'Roll', co-written

Ray Woolf, Peter Posa and Eldred Stebbing on Jervois Quay, Wellington, during the Helen Shapiro tour of 1962. Bruce King collection

Naturally, HMV stars such as Cliff Richard had first call on the presses: the independents understood this. A big seller for Viking was Garth Young, who recorded many instrumental versions of pop hits. As the pianist at Wellington's Pines cabaret, Young could record only on a Sunday, so Riley booked the HMV studio and hired a grand piano from Nimmo's. When the session was under way, Jack Wyness entered the studio and demanded they stop: as a religious man, he would not let the studios be used on a Sunday. To Riley's chagrin, the piano had to be returned and the recording session continued at the Pines.

However, a change of attitude did occur at HMV in the 1950s, and the company began to record local artists in earnest. Between 1954 and 1957, the label released 88 New Zealand acts on 78 rpm discs. The company's choices favoured the middle-of-the-road: cautious piano medleys from John Parkin and Jack Thompson, and discs recorded overseas by the National Band of New Zealand and Inia Te Wiata. Johnny Cooper's 'Rock Around the Clock' and Les Wilson's Otago country were exceptions.[157]

Part of HMV's original disinterest in local recording was simply because the company was too busy: the Capitol label alone seemed like a licence to print money and kept the presses rolling. Dave Van Weede recalled:

Sinatra, Dean Martin, Tennessee Ernie Ford, Nat King Cole, it went on and on . . . . Whenever they opened their mouths and recorded something it was a hit, instant hit! And we were absolutely flat out trying to keep pace with the hits and the demand.

I don't think [local acts] were forgotten, the fact was these new releases, in particular Capitol, were so strong it would have been a fool to ignore them. So maybe some artists didn't really get the attention they should have . . . . We weren't going looking for local musicians, it was the other way around: they were coming to us.[158]

HMV's later supportive policy had its beginnings in 1960 when Frank Douglas, studio engineer for Tanza in Wellington during its last days, opened Lotus recording studios with Terry Patterson, his manager at Tanza. Lotus made many pop recordings for HMV, although most sessions were for radio commercials and programmes. Two years later, the studio was sold to a partnership of Green & Hall and HMV; as arch-rivals in the record pressing business, the relationship was probably intended to be short-lived. In 1963 Green & Hall sold its 50 percent share to HMV, which – after recording hits for Dinah Lee and Maria Dallas at the original Victoria Street location

– moved the studio around the corner to be part of HMV's head office on Wakefield Street.[159]

HMV's connection with – and eventually ownership of – these studios gave it the means to record local acts with more commitment than they had managed in the 1950s. With the indefatigable Douglas engineering, the HMV studios soon dominated local pop recording, for a variety of independent clients such as Viking and Joe Brown, and for HMV itself. After the departure of Dave Van Weede, the local musicians' champion at the record label was A&R director Alec Mowat. Douglas recalled, 'He was really keen on local artists and basically if anyone came in who he thought might have a reasonable chance, we went ahead and did an audition tape.'[160]

Between 1959 and 1964, HMV would release just over 100 singles by New Zealand acts. While not a numerical increase, the output showed more focus and commitment to the local market, and almost all were pop and rock'n'roll. By the end of the decade, many of New Zealand's most successful pop acts were on the HMV label.[161]

Max Merritt and the Meteors' fanatical local following came to the attention of HMV and in 1959 they began recording. Their debut 'Get a Haircut' was written by Merritt with Dick Letusier, who sold drinks at the dances. In a year, at the studio of radio station 3YA, they would record *C'mon Let's Go*: New Zealand's first rock'n'roll album that was not a compilation. By 1962 the Meteors had nothing more to prove in Christchurch. Merritt, still only nineteen, was driving a Dodge Kingsland; it was time to head north.

WHERE THE KIWI RHYTHM CALLS

Songs such as 'Get a Haircut' were unusual: conspicuous by their absence in this flurry of local recordings are pop songs written by New Zealanders. Outside of dedicated songwriters such as Ken Avery and Sam Freedman, few original songs made it onto disc. There were many reasons for the prevalence of cover versions. There could be delays before a foreign original was released in New Zealand, due to the song publishers' representatives withholding permission, or the local record distributors deciding against release in the New Zealand market. After listening to overseas hit parades on shortwave radio, New Zealand acts would jump in and record a hit before the original could be released. They hoped this gave them an advantage with the *Lever Hit Parade*. This worked for the duo Bill

and Boyd, who exploited the fact that the Everly Brothers' US label had no distributor in New Zealand, and had a hit with their 'Cathy's Clown'. It also worked for groups like the Keil Isles and Max Merritt's Meteors. Bill Cate recalled:

> While it was rotten having to do cover versions and we weren't creating our own songs and music at that time, in a way it was a good thing because it gave a lot of people a break and a start. Because the hardest thing in this business is getting the ball rolling. Doing those cover versions and getting on to the *Lever Hit Parade* managed to create something for us, which we were able to follow up, and get other songs from other writers and continue to record and have success.[162]

Apart from Wally Ransom as Southern's representative, there was a lack of song publishers plugging New Zealand songwriters: it was easier to collect the royalties on the imported hits rather than nurture local talent. In re-recording hit songs from the US, the early New Zealand rock'n'roll groups were no different to their contemporaries in Britain, such as Lonnie Donegan, Cliff Richard or Marty Wilde. The idea that there was only one, authentic version of a hit song had yet to take hold; to the bands and especially their audience, what mattered was having a familiar repertoire that made dancing possible. Since the 1920s, when record sales took off, song publishers – 'still treating records as a kind of sheet music' – were happy for there to be many versions of a song, and so was the public.[163]

But New Zealand rock'n'roll songs were written and recorded almost from the time the genre became popular, following directly on from the Hawaiian-style originals written by Sam Freedman, Gene O'Leary and others. Adhering to the strict template of a twelve-bar melodic pattern and I-IV-V chord structure, the earliest rock'n'roll originals were not much more than a few words reflecting a local context. Lou Clauson's 'Papakura Boogie' from October 1956 is the earliest known example, though it was only recorded privately. Shortly afterwards, in February 1957, Wellington teenager Sandy Tansley wrote 'Resuscitation Rock' with two friends while watching a life-saving demonstration on Day's Bay beach. By October, a recording was advertised by HMV, but Tansley had been beaten to the stores. Johnny Cooper wrote 'Pie Cart Rock'n'Roll' after one of his band's Sunday-night charity gigs at the Wanganui Opera House, hoping to get a 'free feed' from the owner of a nearby pie cart.[164]

Three other early rock'n'roll songs celebrated their location: in 1957 Stewart Gordon was performing his 'Timaru Rock',[165] and 'Haka Boogie', written by Lee Westbrook, was a Zodiac release by Morgan Clark with Benny's Five (the A-side, 'Hawaiian Boogie', was written by Westbrook with Phil Stebbing). From the Christchurch label Peak in 1959 came 'Four City Rock' by Peter Lewis with the Tri-Sonic Beat. Written by guitarist Pat Neho, it had a restless message and a parochial chorus:

> Yeah they're rockin' in the milkbars
> Rockin' in the halls
> Rockin' on the sidewalks
> Where the Kiwi rhythm calls

Original New Zealand rock'n'roll songs may still have been novelties as the 1960s arrived, but they were no longer uncommon. Johnny Devlin soon began emphasising material he had written, but local references would remain rare: on the flipside of Bas Tubert's 'The Hu-Hu Bug' was 'Waikanae', the Maori Troubadours reminisced about 'Shakin' in the Shaky Isles', while Rim D. Paul did 'The Poi Poi Twist'.

Following trends in the US, the recording boom of the late 1950s and early 1960s saw several solo pop singers being groomed for stardom as teen idols. The most successful was Ronnie Sundin, whose debut release for Viking in September 1959, 'Sea of Love' b/w 'Waltzing Matilda' was a major hit, selling 15,000 copies in four months. Touring him was 'scary', recalled Viking's Murdoch Riley. 'He couldn't survive it. He was a good-looking kid and he was being mobbed. We were doing shows and store appearances . . . . we did not anticipate we were going to get masses of teenagers.' Despite covering songs such as 'Mean Woman Blues', Viking aimed Sundin at the pop rather than rock'n'roll market. 'He had a light voice, but certain numbers suited him well. It was soft rock'n'roll, not heavy.' The record company used Bill Sevesi's group Will Jess and his Jesters. 'If we had put a solid rock band behind him, we would not have heard him.'[166]

Sundin himself was dubious about recording cover versions, even if they were quick earners for record companies. *Playdate* reported on the wisdom of the sixteen-year-old (who defensively stressed he was going on seventeen): 'Imitations never get an artist anywhere, Sundin believes. He likes to give his own interpretation to

Ronnie Sundin, 1959 teen pop idol.
Viking Records/RNZ Music Library, Wellington

a song and looks forward to putting on record some of the originals of Gene O'Leary, a local songwriter.'[167]

Whakatane's Eddie Howell achieved so much in a two-year career that he briefly looked like being a contender for the throne left empty by Johnny Devlin's departure. Although his solo career began with a big statement, a raw, spirited and credible rock'n'roll EP, *Mr Excitement,* aiming to be an all-round entertainer seemed to be the route to a long career. So Benny Levin groomed him for a mainstream audience as well, covering standards such as 'Summertime', 'Just a Closer Walk With Thee' and 'By the Light of the Silvery Moon'. Like Elvis, Howell was polite and respected his elders, name-dropping into interviews old-school stars such as Al Jolson and Rudy Vallee, and taking a mature stand on the rock'n'roll threat: 'Personally I get equal kicks out of singing up-tempo pops, ballads or sizzling rock tunes', he said.[168]

Smooth Wellington pop vocalist Paul Walden impressed journalists at the Pines cabaret, and the publicity he received led to stints at other Wellington 'nightspots', many radio broadcasts and an HMV contract. For his first release, 'Poor Little Fool', HMV took him on a lengthy promotional tour in 1958, hiring a chauffeur-driven Bel Air for his appearances at record stores. A decade later, he was still with HMV though he had moved towards country music in the Jim Reeves mould, and was based in Australia.[169]

Bill Cate grew up in Petone and – aged just four – sang in fundraising variety shows in Wellington's Opera House during the war. At NaeNae College in the mid-1950s he met Bill Boyd Robertson, and the pair spent a year practising their harmonies together before recording a demo to take around record companies. As Bill and Boyd they became regular performers at the Lower Hutt Town Hall dances. At the Majestic Cabaret they impressed musical director Don Richardson, who was soon producing them in recording sessions for Peak. Their early repertoire borrowed heavily from that of the Everly Brothers: when the US duo toured in 1961 Cate booked front row tickets at the Auckland and Wellington shows. But after relocating to Australia in 1964, Bill and Boyd became all-round entertainers. They would perform anything: songs from musicals, pop gospel, 'Hootenany Holiday', a bracket of twist novelties ('Linda's Twist', 'Good Golly Miss Molly Twist', 'Bluebird Twist'), country standards and even Bob Dylan ('I Threw It All Away'). Their career would last nearly 30 years.[170]

Variety was not dead, judging by the release sheets of the local companies, who tried to cater for all tastes in popular music. Before the beat-band era, Viking recorded albums of Second World War favourites played honky-tonk style by Garth Young, solo bagpipe laments by Donald Beaumont, re-recordings by the Tumbleweeds and piano singalongs by Ossie Cheesman. While all were popular, by the late 1950s the genre 'pop music' meant music aimed at teenagers.

JAZZ ALLEY

Self-respecting young jazz musicians went underground. After leaving the Flamingos, Mike Nock arrived in Auckland in 1958 and quickly became immersed in the inner-city jazz scene, occasionally dossing down at 57a Symonds Street, the notorious home to many jazz musicians in the 1950s.

A brick bungalow down a steep path in the gully between Symonds and Queen streets, 57a was home to a moveable feast of musicians, and a crash pad for many who stayed on after impromptu parties, jam sessions or late gigs in the city. The surrounding buildings – doctors' offices, boarding houses and a Masonic lodge – were far enough away from 57a that the music and noise emanating from it did not bother the neighbours. Due to the housing shortage after the war, and limited incomes, it was more common to rent a room than a complete flat. The first musician to live at 57a was reed-player Bob Taggart, whose mother took a five-year lease. Due to attrition or imaginative encouragement, the original residents quickly left and every room was soon occupied by a constantly changing stream of musicians. Early on they included Art Rosoman, Derek Heine, Lyn Christie and the Kahi brothers Tommy and Mark (who later moved to another musicians' pad, The Hall on Carlton Gore Road). Later residents were Neil Dunningham, vocalist Loma Saunders, Pem Sheppard, Lachie Jamieson, Val Leemon, Merv Thomas, Tony Baker, Bernie Allen and Bennie Gunn.

'The only way you got in there was by invitation', recalled Allen, 'so it was equivalent to obtaining a knighthood to be tapped on the shoulder and asked if you would like to move into 57a, because a room was becoming available.'[171] There was no kitchen, refrigerator or living room; residents cooked 'Wattie's survival food' on a gas ring in their rooms. Parties flowed between the bedrooms and hallways; the epicentre was usually the biggest bedroom, where Val Leemon held court. The parties would 'carry on late, with music at all hours', said Gunn.

Jamieson, a drummer and vibes player, was the city's leading jazz bohemian: he painted his room black and had a stash of hip records. At a time when local tastes in jazz leaned towards the George Shearing Quintet and Billy Eckstine, on high rotation at 57a were discs by Miles Davis, the Modern Jazz Quartet, Sonny Rollins, Gerry Mulligan and Max Roach. On Sunday mornings Leemon's bedroom became a rehearsal space, with up to fourteen members of the Bernie Allen Practice Band cramming in to play for hours.[172]

The house was in walking distance to the attractions of the inner city: cheap chop suey at Chinese cafés on Greys Avenue (the Golden Dragon had jukebox selectors in each booth), sly groggers such as Boogie Lane off Nelson Street, or jam sessions at Lou Mati's louche Polynesian club on Beresford Street. By the late 1950s, more nightclubs

Bennie Gunn, jazz pianist, stops on the Desert Road by a plywood car he built, on his way to join the Auckland scene in 1957; saxophonist, band leader and arranger Bernie Allen does the spade work at 57a Symonds Street; al fresco at Mt Maunganui in 1956 are (from left) Merv Thomas, Lyn Christie and Pem Sheppard. Bennie Gunn and Merv Thomas collections

and restaurants began to feature live music, among them the Picasso, the Blue Lagoon and the Arabian; two that welcomed spontaneous, after-hours jam sessions were the Polynesian Club and Phil Warren's Montmartre.

Nock lived in a Parnell garage with Tony Hopkins, the Devils' drummer, and a piano. Each week he would jam with older musicians such as Brian Fagan, Val Leemon, Bart Stokes and Murray Tanner. Jamieson gave Nock his first taste of marijuana, accompanied by a Sonny Stitt album. Nock's payment for playing on Johnny Devlin's 'Rocket in My Pocket' session gave him the whimsical notion of joining two of his friends who were sailing for Australia. With a few possessions inside his primary school suitcase, Nock wandered on board his friends' ship and visited their cabin. When the call came – 'All visitors ashore' – he remained in the cabin, sleeping during the day and living on cups of tea,

until the ship's arrival in Sydney. He then managed to slip ashore with the disembarking crowd, and within a year was being acclaimed for his playing at Sydney clubs. Nock was one of many jazz musicians who left New Zealand in the late 1950s; others included Julian Lee, Bart Stokes and the guitarist Len Hutchinson.

Lachie Jamieson typically went against the tide, returning to New Zealand in 1955 after eight years in the United States. Jamieson was a man of great passions, especially bebop, and a thirst for excitement that he satisfied at great personal cost. Born in Wanganui in 1927, he played his first drumming gig at the age of sixteen, with Pem Sheppard. After the Second World War, he spent two years with Jayforce in Japan, drumming in the Army band and meeting American musicians among the GIs in Japan. He found it difficult to settle back in New Zealand, so made his way to the US, entering illegally through Canada. He lived on the South Side of Chicago just as bebop was at its height, playing almost nightly in clubs and reportedly sitting in with Charlie Parker and Muddy Waters. Best documented is a stint playing thirteen gigs with Sonny Rollins, and he acknowledged the influence of drumming in strip joints with Ira Sullivan.

As the sole white musician in an integrated quintet, Jamieson toured the Southern states and the Midwest, but after a racial incident the US immigration department checked his status; he was jailed and soon deported to New Zealand. He arrived home 'with the real American sound', said Jim Warren in 1955, 'and as far as drumming goes, really has something different. With Lachie, the beat is the thing and his style – after years of assimilating the ideas and styles of the best in the game – is both stimulating and refreshing.' Unfortunately, he also returned with a drug habit, which his 'ox-like constitution' battled for 40 years.[173]

Jamieson's enthusiasm and talent for 'swinging bop' was an inspiration to many musicians in late 1950s Auckland, among them drumming prodigy Frank Gibson Jr and the teenage Nock. He was 'a loose cannon with a lot of energy', said Nock. 'Keen to play but also to give us what we all yearned for: insight into the feel of those US jazz giants.'[174]

He played with a diverse array of groups, such as Len Hawkins' radio band, George Campbell's Cubanaires, and Glenn Miller and Benny Goodman tribute bands, as well as in 'chamber jazz' concerts and with expatriate American saxophonist Bob Gillett. Lew Campbell described him as an extrovert who 'virtually took the place by storm . . . . As a muso he was quite knowledgeable and had taken the trouble to listen to other instruments other than drums. He mentioned names that we hadn't heard of and gave his reasons. He showed a lot of discernment . . . . he seemed to have picked the eyes out of a lot of things when he was over there.'[175]

Lachie Jamieson, left: influential 'swinging bop' drummer with US experience. Wally Ransom seems preoccupied; pianist Jock Nesbit keeps up. Dennis Huggard Archive, MS-Papers-9018-45, Alexander Turnbull Library, Wellington

In the early 1960s, recalled Freddie Wilson, 'many Aussie jazz musicians went to New Zealand . . . to hear what miracle suddenly made the Kiwis swing'.[176]

AUCKLAND AFTER HOURS

For those too old or too urbane to rock'n'roll, there was an alternative to settling quietly in the suburbs. Jazz still thrived but amongst a more select audience. Despite the restrictive liquor licensing laws, by the late 1950s New Zealand's main centres managed to affect a sophisticated nightlife scene outside of the big-band cabarets that now seemed passé. Wellington entrepreneur Harry Booth opened the Mexicali on Harris Street, offering coffee and a variety of music – jazz, the classics and the Maori Hi-Five – to a diverse audience. The room was the first coffee house to feature a rock guitarist on stage.[177]

Auckland boasted over twenty nightclubs by 1960, many of them featuring floor shows. In an all-night exploration,

Playdate's 'after-dark prowler' Des Dubbelt found Vora Kissin at the elegant Sapphire Room, performing Gershwin with husky voice and 'edgy keyboard style'. With original art on the walls, linen tablecloths and a dance floor the size of a grand piano, the Sapphire emulated a New York jazz parlour. The Colony was a 'plushery': over upholstered, with low lighting and music by the Billy Farnell Combo until the main attraction came on at midnight. In tuxedos, the Howard Morrison Quartet worked the tables, followed by spotlights.

Near the Town Hall, the Picasso was 'a coffee shop that kept nightclub hours', where the musicians and hipsters went to congregate, to be cool and be seen. It modelled itself on the espresso bars of London's Soho, which had spawned Tommy Steele and Cliff Richard. Dubbelt found Harry Miller holding court, looking for talent for his fledgling La Gloria record label. At the Arabian at 1.30 am –

> . . . the joint was jumping. Hot jazz licks floated out on to the street, a bunch of people – some of them waving currency in

Sophistication at the Hi Diddle Griddle, Auckland, late 1950s: Paul Lestre's Hot Club de Ponsonbi featuring (from left) Mauri Faiers, Les Still, Paul Lestre (Jim Callan) and Crombie Murdoch. Black velvet mural by Kristen Zambucka. Dennis Huggard collection

Kahu Pineaha, far left, with cabaret pioneer Carmen (in black) and friends, King's Cross, Sydney, 1960 –
the year Pineaha's only album, *I Hear Music*, was released. Adam Gifford collection

the doorman's face – clamoured to be admitted and the dim, smoky light within charged everything with excitement. The attraction at the Arabian was a high-kicking chorus line presenting a lively revue. The scantily dressed Levita danced to exotica music, and MC Alan Fox introduced singers such as Millie Bradfield, the clean-cut Pete Barchard, and Melbourne bombshell Patti Brittain. Watching from tables were other performers winding down from their shows elsewhere: Morrison, Kissin, comedian John Daley. It was 5.00 am, said a patron, shaking his head in wonder. 'And this is *Auckland*.'[178]

The city's king of cabaret in the late 1950s was Kahu Pineaha. Born in Hawke's Bay, he was an accomplished singer but aspired to be an all-round entertainer in the mould of Sammy Davis Jr. Pineaha first came to prominence in the Clive Trio with the Whatarau sisters; when he left to go solo, Howard Morrison took his place. Pineaha could sing; dance; play piano, guitar and other instruments; and had a vocal versatility suitable for heartfelt interpretations or sidesplitting impersonations. One of his more provocative routines was pretending a fly had infiltrated his underwear while he was singing, causing him to writhe, squeal and shriek.

Although a leading draw at Auckland nightclubs in the late 1950s, and fond of risqué material, Pineaha was a strict Mormon who never drank tea or coffee. 'The Mormon elders are not narrowed-minded', he said in 1959.

When a couple of elders came to witness his act, Pineaha told them 'to be prepared for dynamite. I kept glancing over to them as I sang. And when I saw them chuckle I knew everything was alright.'[179]

Just five foot three inches tall, with a roguish gleam in his eye, Pineaha seemed adept at any style: standards, calypso, Hawaiian, country and comic songs. He would only sing Maori songs if especially requested by tourists: 'Nightclubs are not the right place to sing them.' At the Church College of the Latter Day Saints in Hamilton, he trained young Maori in kapa haka; it was as a Mormon missionary that he first moved to Auckland, but he was soon drawn into the entertainment scene. He recorded an EP of popular Maori songs for Viking, and several pop songs for the Top Rank label.

In 1960 Pineaha topped the bill at a packed Auckland Town Hall, backed by Millie and Johnny Bradfield, with Crombie Murdoch on the piano. 'I've never seen anyone like Kahu', Millie Bradfield recalled. 'He was so talented. Just one guy and he filled the Town Hall up. He sang like Belafonte and he was amazing.'[180]

After releasing an accomplished jazz vocal album, arranged by emerging pianist Judy Bailey, Pineaha left hoping to further his career in Las Vegas. He got as far as Sydney, and became an entertainer in King's Cross and at rugby league clubs. The casinos in the clubs were booming and crying out for performers; Pineaha was soon working

BLUE SMOKE

Exotica with the New Zealand Jazz Trio: Les Still, Tony Thiel and Mauri Faiers, 1960; at the Embers, a new wave of jazz musicians: Mike Walker, Les Still and Roger Sellers. Merv Thomas and Dave Ross collections

seven nights a week. Mahora Peters of the Maori Volcanics was in awe of his talent, but watched sadly as Pineaha was torn between his Mormon faith and his homosexuality. 'He tried everything he could to remain "macho" . . . but it was obvious it was a losing battle.'[181]

After meeting on stage at the Maori Community Centre in 1958, Lou Clauson and Simon Meihana decided to turn their chemistry into a career that lasted twelve years. As the music comedy duo Lou and Simon, they became a sought-after act in cabaret, variety shows and on television. They formed a strong bond with the Howard Morrison Quartet, often working as their warm-up act. From one or two gigs a week, Lou and Simon's bookings soon snowballed. At their peak, they worked three shows on a Friday, four on a Saturday and two on Sunday; they performed at corporate conferences, and on one occasion were paid just to turn up and mingle at a swish Remuera party. As recording artists, they specialised in broad, bawdy satires, which often parodied contemporary hits. 'Maori Car' used the melody of Leonard Bernstein's 'America', the Beatles' 'Yellow Submarine' became 'Purple Maori Pa'. Besides being regulars on high-profile tours such as the Showtime Spectaculars and the Miss New Zealand shows, Lou and Simon performed in Australia, round the Pacific and in the US.

Rod Derrett emerged in the mid-1950s as a skilful jazz guitarist with Martin Winiata's band in Christchurch,

before launching his own cabaret, the 99 Club, offering dance music and comedy routines. Shifting to Auckland in 1963, Derrett went on to write songs that coyly satirised Kiwiana rather than evoked it: 'Rugby Racing and Beer', 'Puha and Pakeha', 'Kiwi Train', 'Six O'Clock Swill' and many others. Although often compared to Danny Kaye, Derrett's arch, rhyming, spoken verse was like poet Allen Curnow's Whim Wham alter ego, set to music.[182]

SINGERS AND SCENESTERS

Millie Bradfield sang with the fluid confidence of Ella Fitzgerald or Sarah Vaughan. Her talent emerged while she was in the choir at St John's convent school in Parnell. 'I was the holiest child in Parnell', she told Suzanne Ormsby. 'I used to go to church four times a day – just for the singing.' The choir proved a good training ground for Bradfield, as well as her dedicated listening to records by Fitzgerald and Frank Sinatra.

At the Maori Community Centre a cousin suggested that Bradfield audition for a variety show with a Pacific Island theme. She already enjoyed dancing the hula with her Rarotongan friends and was given a part in Rodney Farry's Hawaiian Show, which toured around the South Island. Also on the show was a guitarist who would become her husband and lifelong musical partner, Johnny Bradfield. Singing along while he practised, Millie's talent

SWING'N'SWAY WITH RICKY MAY

The biggest star to emerge from the Picasso was only fifteen years old when he first stepped on its stage in 1959. Wandering through downtown Auckland, Ricky May spotted a sign on the footpath near Cook Street. 'Free admission', it offered, 'if you can sing.' May went down the stairs into the coffee lounge/nightclub, asked for the microphone and burst into 'Mack the Knife', which was banned from radio at the time.[183]

May had worked his last proper 'day gig'. It was almost a foregone conclusion that music would be his career. His Maori mother was a pianist, but died when he was eleven. His Pakeha father was the saxophonist and leader of a dance band that billed itself Swing'n'Sway with Kotcy May

and the Rhythm Rascals. 'The drummer was a real nice crooner but he was a hard case', recalled May. 'His drums were always in and out of the hock shop and he always used to be quite a ladies' man. I used to play the drums so that he could get into the drink and a couple of ladies.'[184]

With his six brothers and sisters May would sing along to the *Lever Hit Parade*, and they began entering talent quests, in which he played drums and guitar. By the time May walked down the stairs of the Picasso, his musical apprenticeship was well under way. Thanks to his father, he had grown up listening to the big bands as well as the rock'n'roll of his own age group. His idol incorporated both musical worlds: Bobby Darin.

Ricky May, flanked by broadcaster Pete Sinclair (left) and singer/journalist Lew Pryme, c. 1965.
Lou Clauson Collection, PAColl-5679-06, Alexander Turnbull Library, Wellington

May became the Picasso's odd-job man, sweeping floors, serving coffee and toasted sandwiches, taking tickets and issuing pass-outs, for the privilege of a bed out the back and the chance to sing a few songs.[185] The proprietors of the Picasso, Pat McSweeney and Tony Hyde-Harris, believed in May's potential, even buying him a suit so that he could sing at the ritzy Arabian on the corner of Federal and Wellesley streets.[186]

It was Millie Bradfield to whom Ricky May often turned when the aspiring singer wanted some advice or just to shoot the breeze between sets at the Picasso. 'Hey sis', he would say, 'got any tips?' 'Only one, Ricky – don't ever drink!', Bradfield would answer. 'You've got to know your stuff inside out before you have a drink.'[187] It was eating, not alcohol, that was his weakness.

The Picasso was a sophisticated room – gentlemen, a collar and tie, please – and an education for the ingénue singer. 'Everyone was pretty out of it in that era', he recalled. 'I used to say "What's that strange smell?", and they'd say, "That's incense."' For a long time, he believed them.

Word started to spread about the dazzling new singer in town, recalled Bruce Kaplan, who covered entertainment for *Truth*. 'Get along to the Picasso, they would say, there's this guy there, Ricky May. He arrived fully formed and he had talent that stood head and shoulders above everyone else. When Ricky sang, people listened.'[188]

May became renowned for his frenetic performances, his scatting and improvising that took risks but seemed effortless, his exuberant self-confidence. At the Picasso he was often backed by the Radars, the club's resident band. Strong instrumentalists and harmony singers, all the members of the Radars were Maori and blind. The group had formed at the Blind Institute in Parnell, after meeting in the school's brass band.[189]

More sophisticated rooms soon beckoned, such as the Montmartre on Lorne Street, where he threw himself into Louis Prima routines – solo or in duets with Marlene Tong – accompanied by Mike Walker on piano. In 1961 he held a residency at Wellington's bohemian den the Sorrento. Leading the band was Ronnie Smith, a highly regarded jazz

pianist, with his brother Nicky playing vibes and Bruno Lawrence on drums.

It wasn't long before the young entrepreneur Harry M. Miller decided to record May on his new label, La Gloria. The emphasis then was on imitating overseas acts, said May. 'Toni Williams was sort of Sam Cooke, everybody was Duane Eddy and I was New Zealand's Chubby Checker. I thought it was an honour – nobody was looking for anything original then. [I just thought] great, I've eaten myself into a part.'[190]

In 1962 May left for Australia, where he became a major star on the cabaret circuit and on television. He secured residencies at the notorious Latin Quarter nightclub in King's Cross, a venue frequented by gangsters but friendly to musicians thanks to its proprietor Sammy Lee, former leader of the Americanadians. Eventually, after stints in Las Vegas, Europe and South-East Asia, May became an Australian citizen, calling himself 'a Mozzie: a Maori Aussie'. Chronically over-weight for much of his adult life, May suffered a fatal heart attack in 1988 after coming off stage at Sydney's Regent Hotel to a standing ovation. He was just 44.

for jazz emerged. She was soon invited to sing with him at the Arabian club in central Auckland.

For Tanza in 1956 Bradfield made her first recording, 'Keep Your Eyes on the Hands', which played on her background in hula dancing. To the seesaw sway of Julian Lee's organ, and teasing licks from Bill Wolfgramm's Hawaiian steel, in the languid South Pacific pop style she advised that by watching a hula girl dance, one risked being seduced into a romance. It was best to avoid temptation by keeping one's eyes on the dancer's hands, not her alluring hips.

In 1958 Bradfield was singing at clubs such as the Hi Diddle Griddle, the Crystal Palace and Orange Hall. For many years music took a back-seat role to her family, but on special occasions she would emerge to dazzle audiences. She appeared in some of the first scheduled television broadcasts, and at a post-show party in 1964 thrown by the Auckland Musicians' Club she swapped choruses with US blues shouter Jimmy Rushing.[191]

By the early 1960s, Auckland's leading jazz 'chanteuse' was Marlene Tong, a glamorous Eurasian from Epsom. Discovered performing in Rotorua by pianist Ron Smith, Tong began appearing with Lew Campbell's band at the Picasso and the short-lived Asian Club. Although influenced by Ella Fitzgerald, she made her mark playing Keely Smith to Merv Thomas's Louis Prima at his Crystal Palace residency. Jim Warren enthused about their polished, world-class act: Tong had great control over her voice and timing, and although they performed together just once a week, the band quickly progressed from its dixie origins using head arrangements. Eventually called the Prophets, they became accomplished readers, with scores by Bernie Allen. 'The group moves so easily and yet so surprisingly from the Prima style to the Temperance Seven to Martin Denny and even Ray Conniff. All this with seven men and a girl! And no television yet!'[192]

Tong said her biggest break was performing at the Auckland concert chamber with visiting US duo Pete Jolly and Ralph Pena in September 1960. The *New Zealand Herald* later anointed her 'the best jazz singer to be heard in Auckland since Mavis Rivers went away'.[193]

In 1964, however, Tong was in the newspaper after being arrested for using marijuana. To headline writers, jazz and drugs went together like a horse and carriage, and the vice squad had been focusing on the 'beatnik set' in recent years. Lachie Jamieson was fined £50 for possession of marijuana in 1963, and a charge of trafficking was thrown out when the judge accepted that

Marlene Tong and Merv Thomas, in action with the Prophets at the Crystal Palace, early 1960s. Merv Thomas collection

BLUE SMOKE

he was addicted to the drug. According to Roger Watkins, Auckland's Heaven and Hell beat club – in the shadow of St Patrick's Cathedral on Wyndham Street – became 'notorious for reefer peddling and for the loud music that poured out after midnight'.[194] In Wellington, former Devils' saxophonist Claude Papesch and his wife were referred to in court as 'Mr and Mrs X of the Terrace', found among those present while marijuana was being consumed.[195]

An early connection came in 1960 when Ron Polson, a singer at Wellington's Pines, was mentioned in court reports about a Thorndon 'house of jazz' frequented by vagrant females. With noise from jazz records and taxis arriving through the night, the evidence recalled the 'mirth, motors and maledictions' at Theo Trezise's boisterous Thorndon cabaret in the 1920s. A more sinister edge was added by *Truth*'s description of the crime scene inside: ashtrays full of butts, a paper bag of chicken bones, modern paintings, and the thick smell of smoke and opium. Poulson, who also played bass in a quartet featuring Tommy Adderley, Garth Young and Bruno Lawrence, was later acquitted of possession in Melbourne when a judge accepted that marijuana found in his suitcase backstage had been planted by a 'bitter rival'.[196]

Tommy Adderley settled in Wellington in 1959, jumping ship after four years visiting New Zealand as a merchant seaman. All his singing in clubs during his shore leave had led to plenty of work offers. He now had more friends in New Zealand than back in Birmingham, and was in love with a local girl. Adderley began a three-year residency at the Pines, a cabaret he described later as a mix between the Copacabana, the Sands and Ronnie Scott's. Situated overlooking Cook Strait, the Pines was highly exposed to the elements but isolated enough to be relaxed about liquor laws. Adderley worked as a cleaner/singer and stayed for 'three gloriously happy years' performing with a band led by versatile pianist Garth Young. 'He was the first person to introduce me to arrangements', recalled Adderley. 'We were right up with the pop tunes of the time – Neil Sedaka, Bobby Darin, Gene McDaniels . . .'.[197]

After performing in venues such as the Majestic, the Central Park Cabaret, the Empress, the Downtown Club or the Mexicali, Wellington's jazz players mingled at locations such as the Musicians' Club on Wigan Street, the Pines or the infamous Forester's Arms off Ghuznee Street. While its public bar was a haunt for criminals, on Friday evenings the back bar became an informal rendezvous for

Marlene Tong, Auckland's finest jazz singer of the 1960s. Merv Thomas collection

jazzers. The proprietor was fond of the music and willing to extend drinking beyond 6.00 pm. Here, too, the visiting US bluesman Jimmy Rushing and the Eddie Condon band enjoyed a reception, with steaks cooked by Vern Clare and 'New Zealand-type liquid sustenance'.[198]

Soon, the jazz baton was being passed between generations. Many 1950s Wellington musicians – among them Ken Avery, Mike Gibbs, Ray Harris, Bill Hoffmeister and Verdi Mattar– were featured on the albums *Jazz (for Listening) Wellington* and *Private Party – Guests Only*.[199] By the early 1960s, they occasionally shared stages with a younger gaggle of jazz musicians and devotees who emerged from the Victoria University jazz club, such as trumpeter Geoff Murphy, pianist John Charles and poet/bass player Mark Young.

Most prominent among this set was the drummer David 'Bruno' Lawrence, a junior reporter on *Truth* and occasional contributor to *Joy*. He played and mingled with other musicians at the Sorrento, an after-hours

Jazz at Wellington's Sorrento club, c. 1960s, an after-hours joint that was stylish or squalid, depending on one's predilections.
From left: drummer Billy Brown, pianist Dean Wilkins and bassist Jim Wilson. Redmer Yska collection

jazz club on Ghuznee Street owned by John Koolman. Neil Harrap performed there with Lawrence and former Invader bassist Puni Solomon, calling themselves the Measles. 'The Sorrento was a dive', he recalled. 'It was frequented by no-hopers, hookers and the like. After about six months I looked around and decided that I had better things to do with my life than associate with this crowd.'[200] In its heyday, the Nick Smith Combo was a drawcard for other musicians, playing what Ian Hull-Brown called 'far-out jazz'.[201] A visiting Auckland artist's description of the scene is perhaps more accurate than that of the music:

The hipsters wore Italian bum-freezer suits with very slim cuff-less trousers, winkle-picker shoes, and very thin ties. It was very, very stylish, and very slick. The women had bouffant hairdos. The musicians would be doing sessions round the various clubs and afterward they would come down to the Sorrento for jam sessions. It was almost cocktail-type music.[202]

While teenagers in Christchurch flocked to dance halls in the early 1960s, jazz in the city continued to flourish. The Union Rowing Club residency run by charismatic dance-band veteran Martin Winiata had come to an end – the 99 Club took over the premises – but his presence continued to be felt. He had mentored many key jazz musicians – Doug Caldwell, Stu Buchanan, Coral Cummins – and even tried rock'n'roll. As Martin Winiata and His Moonmen, he backed local rockabilly singer Peter Lewis recording 'Teenage Baby' for Peak. With a sharp ear, Winiata was deft at transcribing the latest pop hits from US shortwave radio to add to his band's repertoire. He was renowned not just as a multi-instrumentalist, but for being able to play two saxophones simultaneously. And he was superstitious, never being the first musician to enter the rowing club. When Caldwell asked why, Winiata replied, 'The ghosts of people who have danced to my band could still be in there.' In 1964 Winiata settled in Taupo, but not to retire: he continued to teach hundreds of children in the Bay of Plenty until his death in 1982 aged 75.[203]

The Kahi brothers Tommy and Mark moved to Christchurch in the 1950s and ran very popular dances at the North Beach Surf Club. While Mark was acknowledged as the star guitarist, Tommy's energy meant his influence was wide; among the pupils at his guitar studio were future rock stars Billy Kristian (Karaitiana) and Kevin Bayley. Nick Nicholson's Neketini Brass performed Latin standards, Tijuana-style, as well as arrangements of Maori melodies. Another influential guitarist was Pat Neho, a stalwart at Peak Records. Described as 'the Les Paul of Christchurch', Neho was touring in a Maori concert party when Arthur Smith's 'Guitar Boogie' attracted him to rock'n'roll; he also played Dixieland, Hawaiian and progressive jazz. At small venues and coffee lounges such as the Jazz Inn, the Attic and Pink Elephant, jazz musicians were in demand, and in the 1960s up-and-comers such as Paul Dyne and Malcolm McNeill served their apprenticeships.[204]

Doug Caldwell – a stalwart of Christchurch music for over 65 years – enjoyed a long residency at the Malando on Colombo Street. The restaurant became an after-hours rendezvous for visiting performers such as Jacques Loussier and Zubin Mehta with members of his orchestra. Some of Mehta's musicians jammed with Caldwell, and the conductor left a £50 tip. The night Oscar Peterson walked in with his trio after their concert, Caldwell was still working at the piano although the room was all but empty. 'I didn't know he was there, then I looked up . . . . I didn't play much after that.' Before the Malando became one of the first licensed restaurants in the country, its most popular beverage was a coffee royale; two Americans held

Even Christchurch jazz veteran Martin Winiata tried rock'n'roll. Famous for playing two saxophones at once, he backed rockabilly singer Peter Lewis with his band the Moonmen. Dennis Huggard Archive, MS-Papers-9018-50, Alexander Turnbull Library

the record, consuming 50 laced cups in one night. If the local constabulary visited, Caldwell's trio would segue to 'Policeman's Holiday'.[205]

COFFEE-BAR FOLK

Reflecting trends overseas, some young adults were alienated by anachronistic big bands in fading ballrooms, commercial cabaret, intellectual bop and brash, youth-orientated rock'n'roll clubs. They gathered in small rooms lit by candles stuck in Chianti bottles, the ceilings

Hawke's Bay singer Marise McDonald – later a regular act at Wellington's Majestic Cabaret – performs on a Pacific cruise, early 1960s. Dance-band veteran Alan Shand is the pianist. Marise McDonald collection

painted black and lowered by grids of fishing line. Drawn by the humble acoustic guitar and driven by a seriousness of purpose, New Zealand's folkies mobilised. International hits by the Weavers and Burl Ives helped lay the groundwork for folk as pop music in the late 1940s. The beginnings of a New Zealand folk scene – and local song collecting – can be attributed to left-wing protest singing at this time, says musicologist Michael Brown. In 1951 the student organisation the Progressive Youth League published *Kiwi Youth Sings*, which collected 'folk, patriotic, student and trade union songs, including several local pieces'.[206]

Before folk became fashionable in the early 1960s, the *Kiwi Youth Sings* songbook was an early milestone in a local song-collecting movement, which emulated the

work of Cecil Sharp and Alan Lomax. In 1941 the writer Alan Mulgan had asked, 'Could New Zealand produce a "Waltzing Matilda"?' Commenting on the death of Australian folk-laureate Banjo Paterson, Mulgan said that in New Zealand, while nationalistic poets such as Eileen Duggan were productive, somehow the country had not inspired popular songs with similar sentiments. Maybe, said Mulgan, New Zealand 'awaits its writers with the necessary flair or genius'.[207]

In the mid-1950s, several initiatives gave momentum to the search for the authentic New Zealand song. Inspired by a radio talk by Arnold Wall (junior), Wellington activist Rona Bailey embarked on a quest to find traditional songs. Beginning in 1956, she went on several song-collecting trips into the provinces in search of early indigenous ballads. A popular NZBS radio series on folk music by the expatriate Americans Augusta Ford and Henry Walters revealed to aspirant performers 'how much folk music was part of the living'. The Auckland group Unity Singers performed topical parodies such as 'Everything's Up-to-date in Auckland', as well as American ballads.[208]

Almost in chorus, others shared Bailey's interests: a Levin folk singer, Neil Colquhoun; a Wellington-based librarian, Herbert Roth; rugged renaissance man Les Cleveland, interested in bush ballads and war songs. Auckland odd-job man Lew Williams was determined to refute the idea that there were no authentic New Zealand folk songs, and hitch-hiked around the country with a bulky tape-recorder in his pack.[209]

By May 1957, Bailey, Colquhoun and Wellington singer Jim Delahunty were presenting *New Zealand Folk Songs and Ballads* at the ninth Auckland Festival. Also that year, the Swedish-American folk singer William Clauson made a high-profile national tour. Born in Ohio, Clauson was something of an educated musical gypsy: he could speak twelve languages and travelled the world learning and performing folk material from the countries he visited. During several visits to New Zealand, the ebullient Clauson performed material that became increasingly Kiwi. On the first tour, organised with the NZBS, he also made broadcasts of traditional folk songs arranged by Henry Rudolph. By 1960 his EP *Be Japers! Manawatu* showcased material by Auckland composer Willow Macky, and he finished with the 1965 album *Packing My Tea: Songs of New Zealand*.[210]

Colquhoun began broadcasting and recording EPs with his group the Songspinners in 1959, about pioneering

Auckland's Convairs, clean-cut and in demand. From left: Phil Seth, Johnny Bond and Mike Dolan. RNZ Music Library, Wellington

whalers, and gum and gold diggers. Songs by 'Cazna Gyp' received a Songspinners' EP of their own, *Songs of the Backblocks*. Cazna Gyp was the pseudonym of the restless Lew Williams, his wife Eddie and Bob Edwards.[211] The passion for song collecting continued into the 1960s, culminating in the publication of song anthologies by Bailey and Colquhoun, and the establishment of the New Zealand Folklore Society by Frank Fyfe in 1966.

The popular arm of the folk revival began to 'Wimoweh' after hours in the late 1950s. Wellington's coffee-house scene paralleled contemporary folk revivals in Britain and the US, while also offering a bohemian chic. In Auckland, folk music would occasionally be featured at venues such as the Rafters, and the Artist, a coffee bar/gallery in Airedale Street near the Town Hall. The latter was opened by English immigrant Colin Scattergood, who said: 'It seems, with the growing Continental influence, that New Zealanders are having to realise there is such a thing as night life.'[212] Until the establishment in 1967 of Auckland's own folk-oriented club, the Poles Apart, the city's most prominent folk acts often appeared in cabarets: button-down, Kingston Trio-influenced groups such as the Yeomen, the Coachmen and the Convairs.

The venue that epitomised the folk revival was Wellington's Monde Marie, on the corner of Majoribanks and Roxburgh streets, a stone's throw from the Embassy theatre. It was opened in 1958 by Mary Seddon, the granddaughter of premier 'King Dick' Seddon. She had travelled through Europe alone after the Second World

War and was determined to bring some of the relaxed, intellectual culture she had experienced to the capital's nightlife. With impeccable timing she established the café just as the consumption of folk music and coffee converged. A decade before pub opening hours were extended beyond six o'clock, the cerebral demi-monde needed somewhere to gather.

In Seddon's den, waitresses in black stockings and short skirts served kona coffee in handmade New Zealand pottery, the menu offered pasta, salad and cake, while in the corner the best of Wellington's folkies accompanied themselves on acoustic guitar. Among the earliest was Graeme Allwright, former actor, who specialised in French chansons and went on to have a musical career in France; the journalist Vernon Wright; the artist Dinah Priestley; the song collector, *Truth* reporter and photographer Les Cleveland; songwriters Peter Cape and Willow Macky; and local folk stalwarts Jim Delahunty, Arthur Toms and Max Winnie. 'Rock'n'roll, praise the Gods, is finished now', said

Mary Seddon, den mother to Wellington's folkies at the Monde Marie. Jane Burke collection

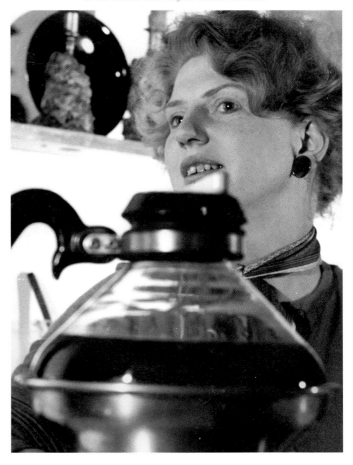

Carrot cake, kona coffee, acoustic guitars: bohemian chic at Wellington's Monde Marie, c. 1960. Jane Burke collection

Wright in 1960, 'and folk ballads look to be the next fad.'[213] Cape's song 'Monde Marie' paid tribute to the venue:

In the flat down below there's a 'cello
Above there's a whole symphonie
So I'm off for a night
Of the music I like
Down at the Monde Marie.[214]

Imitators quickly followed. Seddon was miffed when the most successful of many rivals opened across the street in the Embassy building. 'Woe betide any of Seddon's resident performers who were tempted to betray her by singing at the Chez Paree', recalled Karl du Fresne. 'The Chez catered for a younger, less bohemian crowd, and Seddon despised the place. The Chez was Donovan, the Seekers and Simon and Garfunkel; the Monde was Dylan, Joan Baez and the Clancy Brothers.' As with the folk revival worldwide, the battlelines were drawn between the purists and the merely commercial. Until it closed in 1970, the Monde Marie's reputation was such that visiting performers such as Theodore Bikel, Judy Collins, Paul Stookey of Peter, Paul and Mary, and Josh White visited after their concerts.[215]

Max Winnie, second from left, was a leading figure in Wellington folk circles in the 1960s. Jane Burke collection

Just as the beat boom was getting under way, a Christchurch singer went in the other direction. Phil Garland spent several years singing with the Saints and the Playboys, prominent on the local dance-hall scene (the Playboys' other vocalist, Diane Jacobs, later became famous as Dinah Lee). In 1964 he bought a twelve-string Gibson acoustic guitar and became captivated by its sound. He began practising five hours each day, and performing folk standards at the Plainsman club on Lichfield Street. Garland became hooked on folk, but a lengthy trip to Britain in 1965 convinced him that he only felt comfortable singing New Zealand material. From that moment, he became a dedicated collector and performer of New Zealand's indigenous folk songs.[216]

Willow Macky's songs were often performed, with few people knowing who had written them. Her 1957 song 'Te Harinui – A Christmas Carol' became a school assembly perennial for several decades, and in 1960 her 'Ballad of Captain Cook' appeared in a widely distributed school song book. She wrote over 100 others, and her songs were recorded by artists such as Inia Te Wiata ('The Maori Flute')[217] and When the Cat's Been Spayed ('Tamaki Moonlight').[218]

Born in Auckland in 1921, Macky learnt guitar from Walter Smith, and began writing in the early 1950s. After years of collecting songs from other countries to perform, she realised that few songs were being written about New Zealand. When she first sang 'Tamaki Moonlight' to an Auckland audience, they laughed at the unfamiliar mention of a New Zealand place name in a song. 'Te Harinui' was published by Chappell's in London in 1957, two years before its debut in New Zealand (by an Australian choir). She made many broadcasts and recorded two discs for Kiwi, performing her own songs: *The Four Cities and Two Gold Towns* and *I Remember Summer*. But through Clauson's EP *Be Japers! Manawatu* her songs reached a wider audience.

Macky was a dedicated songwriter – she also completed a three-act opera, *The Maori Flute* – despite feeling discouraged by some institutional music gatekeepers. 'Most intellectuals and academics are inclined to look down their noses a bit at folk-style music', she said, 'especially the songs, for some reason.' However, she did receive encouragement from Alfred Hill, who maintained an interest in folk and vernacular music. Macky, said Te Wiata, was 'the only New Zealand composer besides Alfred Hill who can capture the authentic Maori atmosphere'. In later years, Macky updated her 'Waitangi Anthem' better to reflect the viewpoint of Maori, and she dropped a charming but dated children's ballad 'Hori and His Spanish Guitar' from her repertoire.[219]

Be Japers! Manawatu, a 1960 EP by Swedish-American musical gypsy William Clauson, took Willow Macky's songs to a wider audience. RNZ Music Library, Wellington

KIWI VERNACULAR

Wellington jazz musician Ken Avery was a serious songwriter who specialised in novelty songs. Among his successes were 'Tea at Te Kuiti', 'The Gumboot Tango' and 'By the Dog-Dosing Strip at Dunsandel'. Dennis Huggard collection

Sam Freedman was the only popular songwriter present at the first New Zealand composers' convention in 1957. Though his musicianship was limited, his work had reached more ears than that of anybody else in the room, including Douglas Lilburn and Ashley Heenan. 'I'm really sorry for you classical boys', he said. 'The way's tough enough for us. It must be hopeless for you.'[220]

Even the veteran Wellington music teacher Allan Shand, a mentor to Ruru Karaitiana, was pessimistic about the chances local songwriters had overseas. The lack of a true publishing industry was the main reason; although multinational publishers had representatives in New Zealand, their priority was to plug the songs they owned rather than acquire more. Also, said Shand, 'Songs with New Zealand themes are limited in their appeal by population.'[221]

International hits had emerged from New Zealand in the previous decade, however. Besides 'Blue Smoke' and 'Now is the Hour', there was 'Apple Blossom Time', a 1951 British hit with a melody written by Wynn Smith of Auckland. As with 'Now is the Hour' and Alfred Hill of 'Waiata Poi' fame, there was an Australian connection: Smith was born there, but grew up in New Zealand. He planned to leave his factory job as a polisher and head to the northern hemisphere to try his luck as a songwriter.

Songwriting still seemed to be a hobby in the 1950s, with the exception of three writers whose successes took the craft to another level. Their hit songs determinedly celebrated the vernacular.

Ken Avery was a serious songwriter who did not take himself seriously. A stalwart of the post-war jazz scene in Wellington, playing saxophone and clarinet in many bands, as a songwriter he preferred writing novelties. 'I feel songs should be light and entertaining', he said, 'so I don't write "Why Don't You Come Back to Me?" numbers.'[222] His two biggest hits could fill any local content quota. 'Paekakariki' was his first song, written in 1948 at a time when place-name songs such as 'Managua Nicaragua' were doing well. Avery got the idea from a railway sign while commuting from the Kapiti Coast, and intended to

write a slow foxtrot. At the time he was studying harmony and composition classes at Victoria University, where the lecturer was Douglas Lilburn:

> One day he said to us students, 'I want you all to write a melody line with or without harmony and bring it to the next lecture.' I was a bit ashamed to submit anything as plebian as a foxtrot called 'Paekakariki' so I changed the rhythm to waltz time and took it along. He liked it and suggested it would go better in 4/4 time.[223]

Avery sang and played the clarinet solo on 'Paekakariki', which he recorded with his dance band, the Bill Crowe Orchestra. As Tanza's second release it sold 6000 copies, and Avery's self-published sheet music sold 5000 copies. With characteristic modesty, he said: 'Most people think this is the best song I have ever written; certainly it is the only one that ever sold in any quantity. Maybe this is because there was a Musicians' Union strike on in America at the time.' Hoping to catch another wave, fifteen years later the song was revised as 'Surfin' Paekakariki' and recorded by Bas Tubert.[224]

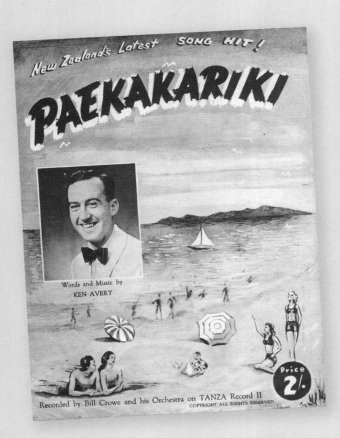

Ken Avery's 'Paekakariki' began as an exercise for Douglas Lilburn's composition class, and became Tanza's second hit. National Library of New Zealand

He loved smooth singers such as Bing Crosby and Fred Astaire, and wrote with them in mind. Their day had passed by the time Freedman started to write in the 1940s, so he concentrated on what the market wanted: Hawaiian-style pop. His first two songs, 'Best Wishes' and 'Maoriland', were recorded by Pixie Williams with Allan Shand's orchestra, and released by Tanza shortly after their success with 'Blue Smoke'.[226]

In the early 1950s, Freedman hit paydirt when several of his songs were recorded by Daphne Walker with Bill Wolfgramm, among them 'Haere Mai', 'When My Wahine Does the Poi' and 'Okey Dokey Hut'. He was very methodical and focused about his writing; he saw Polynesian pop selling, so that's what he wrote. Freedman worked at manual occupations because they left him with the mental energy to work conscientiously at his craft.

His homespun aphorisms offer a primer to pop songwriting. The words come first, he said, then the first eight bars of music. Commercially, those first eight bars are crucial: they can make or break a song. Start from a low position and go up gently. Melodies must ascend at first, but not by too big a leap (the general public can

Avery's 'Tea at Te Kuiti' was a rapid-fire musical travelogue, written as an answer song to an Australian version of the US country hit 'I've Been Everywhere, Man'. Sung in pure, colloquial Kiwi by Ash Burton – newspaperman Alex Veysey – dripping with puns and 1950s Pakeha pronunciation, it remains endearing:

I'm having tea at Te Kuiti with my sweetie
And a row at Rotorua on the waves.
Do a tour of Turangi when the Maoris have a hangi
Then I'll wind up in the old Waitomo caves . . .[225]

Sam Freedman wrote songs while making shoes. At the factory where he worked in his heyday, Freedman composed melodies in his head then went home at lunchtime to play through his ideas on a guitar. Born in 1911, he became New Zealand's most successful songwriter in the 1950s, after a childhood listening to slow waltzes by Irving Berlin. 'I said to myself, if that's songwriting, then I want to be a songwriter.' Like Berlin, Freedman was the son of Russian-Jewish immigrants, with a taste for the sentimental and a knack for simplicity.

Sam Freedman, writer of 1950s hits such as 'Haere Mai' ['everything is kapai'] and 'When My Wahine Does the Poi'. Fay Burns collection

'Far better than quiet to me is a diet of song, à la Monde Marie' – singer/songwriter Peter Cape, right, at his favourite venue; his EP *She'll Be Right* was released in 1961. Jane Burke collection; Kiwi Records EA54/RNZ Music Library, Wellington.

sing an interval of a third easily, but not a fifth; if you write a fifth, throw your song away). Finally, ask yourself these questions: Is it likely to sell? Can it be played by the typical small combinations of musicians? Is it easy to remember? Is it topical? Will it pass the Broadcasting censor?[227]

Freedman would take his lyrics and the guitar chords to professionals such as Shand, sing the melody and get his songs transcribed onto sheet music. 'Haere Mai' he always thought was his 'biggest piece of rubbish', but it was also his biggest hit, selling 40,000 copies. 'Maoriland' remained special to him: 'It was a beautiful slow waltz, it flows beautifully and I can't compare it to any other. But nothing is my favourite: if it sells, it is good.'[228]

In the 1940s and 1950s, the songs came easily to Freedman, sometimes in an hour, and he published more than 300. Murdoch Riley, A&R man at Tanza in the mid-1950s, encouraged Freedman to include more Maori content, so he collaborated with translators such as Alby Bennett and Timoti Karetu to put his lyrics into te reo. Besides his originals such as 'Haere Mai' and 'Best Wishes', he also wrote English lyrics for existing songs, and his arrangements became so popular that they almost

became regarded as traditional. But Freedman's romantic reveries such as 'Haere Mai' epitomise the genre known as 'Kiwiana music'.[229]

Peter Cape's approach was more literary than Avery or Freedman; with his acute eye for social detail his songs worked like documentaries from the heartland. Born in rural King Country to itinerant parents, and always mixing in diverse circles, Cape experienced New Zealand from backcountry stations to suburban church pulpits. So when he wrote 'Down the Hall on Saturday Night' and 'Taumarunui', the 1950s audience recognised itself. Anticipating Barry Crump, Cape wrote of the ordinary joker at the Orange Ballroom, in his new brown sports coat, grey strides and Kiwi haircut, shy with sheilas and secretly pining for Taumarunui on the Main Trunk Line. The public responded, but Cape was more sensitive New Age guy than good keen man. Also a filmmaker, radio and television producer, author and Anglican minister, Cape's varied talents and mercurial nature meant he didn't stay with music for long. 'Taumarunui' and 'She'll Be Right' became an essential part of the canon, yet were more respected than sung: rather than being timeless melodies, they perceptively capture their time.[230]

POP GOES THE RADIO

Folk was radio-friendly in the paternalistic fading days of the New Zealand Broadcasting Service, which even sponsored tours by Clauson, and broadcast balladeers like Cleveland. But how did public radio react to the post-rock'n'roll era of pop? To the executives in the upper echelons of the NZBS, the new pop music was abhorrent. Several of them had begun their careers in the 1930s, and had lived through the broadcasting battles between James Shelley's cultural elitism and Scrim's populism. More recently, the Mazengarb committee's searing comments about the effect of pop music on teenagers had been absorbed. Future radio director-general James Hartstonge joined Broadcasting in 1932 and, by the mid-1950s, was Wellington district manager. Rock music was not music, he once declared: the 'orgiastic writhings' of pop singers made him 'turn away with a sickened stomach'.[231] Even Bob Bothamley was dismissive of – and bemused by – rock'n'roll. He thought it wasn't real music, and saw its appeal as a reaction to cool jazz.[232]

These views were not uncommon, as many Broadcasting executives who had musical rather than administrative backgrounds came from the worlds of classical and church music, choirs and brass bands. There were exceptions among hosts, such as Bas Tubert, whose *Jazz With Bas* was keenly followed on 2ZB. 'Let me say that the music of rock'n'roll is good', he declared in 1958. 'It has an infectious beat with plenty of drive that has made people dance again. It's the music of the times capturing the uninhibited spirit of the rocket age.'[233]

Within the NZBS the executive most notoriously antagonistic towards popular music after the arrival of rock'n'roll was 1ZB's programme manager, Dudley Wrathall. He had a distinguished broadcasting career that began in 1927, when he gave a racing commentary from Alexandra Park while standing on a ladder that overlooked the track. In the 1930s, he commissioned local musical talent to perform on air and, during the war, became known for his role in the popular radio programme *Chuckles With Jerry*, in which he played the straight man for ventriloquist George Tollerton.[234]

By the late 1950s, Wrathall was fighting an idiosyncratic battle against the new pop, especially Elvis Presley and local releases. His method was simply to hide any records that did not meet his approval. For Elvis fans, this meant they had to tune in between 5.00 pm and 6.00 pm, when Wrathall was on the bus home and hipper ZB

Broadcaster and ventriloquist's straight man Dudley Wrathall had idiosyncratic methods of keeping the public safe from rock'n'roll at 1ZB. RNZ Sound Archives

employees would play discs they had stashed. But for Eldred Stebbing, the tactic had more serious consequences: it meant his Zodiac recordings rarely received airtime. He recalled that in Wrathall's office after his retirement 'when they pulled the carpet up they found that the floor was completely covered with local 45s. He used to take them from different record companies and say, "Yes, yes, we'll get right behind that" and never do anything about it. He'd just put them under the carpet so they disappeared entirely. They had the attitude of "Why should we play local records when we can play the top overseas artists?"' ZB historian Bill Francis concurred: 'Dudley had the lumpiest carpet at 1ZB.'[235]

Jazz was now usually confined to specialist programmes such as Arthur Pearce's *Rhythm on Record* and others hosted by stalwarts such as Ray Harris, Dennis Huggard, John Joyce, Cav Nicholl and Peter Sellers. The NZBS radio dance-band system continued, and the man whose job title was Head Office Dance – 'that covered a multitude of sins, I'm sure', said Calder Prestcott – seemed rarely to be in his office. For two decades Bob Bothamley had travelled constantly up and down the country, hiring musicians, discussing arrangements, producing broadcasts. His approach was always hands-on, be it at the mixing desk or finding the material, recalled Don Richardson: 'He virtually wanted to pick the numbers, and he'd give us a record and say "Make it something like that." So we would just take them off. It all helped, it was an education.'[236]

'He was a cunning man in many ways', recalled Doug Caldwell. 'When visiting each centre, he would slip the arrangers acetates. He'd say, "Listen to this, that's what the boys in Wellington are doing." And he would do the same with us, taking our work to Auckland. He created and raised the standards. It was Bob's way of getting things cracking.'[237]

The radio dance bands out-lived the heyday of the big bands, though as technology changed so did the character of the broadcasts: the bands were pre-recorded, then post-produced. In 1962 trumpeter Jim Warren looked back 'wistfully' at the nights the Radio Theatre was the best free show in town, 'when the good sound of a big band and the good-humoured style of compère Wally Ransom really projected. It sounded as if everyone was having a ball, really "live" and at times hilarious.'[238]

On 28 June 1966, Bob Bothamley collapsed and died of a heart attack in a Wellington store. He was only 63, and Bothamley's death shocked his radio colleagues, especially Arthur Pearce, his associate of 30 years. 'Jazz on radio had lost its staunchest supporter', wrote Laurie Lewis.[239]

Pearce would keep broadcasting for another eleven years, but Bothamley's death spelled the end of Head Office Dance. His colleague Peter Downes guarded 'Bob's little room' to stall eager administrators wanting to clean out his power base (and to keep souvenir hunters at bay). For years, Bothamley's 'Whaddaya want? The answer's No' and constant cigarette smoking had acted as a barrier, leading to many legends about his personal record collection. Closing the door on Dance also gave Downes time to work out how Bothamley's idiosyncratic systems

worked. His world was subsumed into a new, Light Entertainment Department, with a brief beyond jazz.

Broadcaster Ray Harris had grown up a jazz-obsessed teenager in Wellington, hearing Bothamley mentioned about town 'almost reverently'. In an obituary, he described the musical values Bothamley sought from jazz: 'The thrill of the big band sound; the well-executed section work; the driving rhythm section; the excitement of infectious swing on the one hand, and on the other, the melodic approach of the small jazz group; the easy beat, so engaging to the ear; and the masterful technique of the talented soloist.'[240]

Radio's approach to pop music was 'terribly conservative', said Johnny Douglas, who began working as a programming cadet at Broadcasting's head office in Wellington in 1956, aged seventeen. 'I was very conscious that overseas, Elvis had arrived, and rock'n'roll and pop. There were very good pop artists around – Connie Francis, Ricky Nelson, Cliff Richard – who were not terribly noisy. But in New Zealand, we were very much sheltered from all those things.' On the YAs, recalled Douglas, a breakfast session in the mid-1950s would feature light orchestral music, instrumentals and middle-of-the-road vocalists.

On the commercial stations, the music seemed random; it was selected by the programme department but occasionally 'de-selected' by the announcer. Playing a hit record several times a week, let alone a day, was out of the question. 'Hits are hits and the public wants to hear them', said Douglas. 'In three months' time, they're sick of them. So the theory of commercial radio is that you play a hit when it's a hit – and we weren't allowed to do that. The most we could play a record was once a week.'[241]

Avoiding personality cults was still a policy, with hosts being moved around the schedule – and the country – and mostly remaining anonymous. 'We weren't allowed to deviate from the set format written down in front of us', recalled 2ZB's Bas Tubert. 'But of course we did. Can you imagine us just sitting there playing it dead straight – and boring? People didn't want that. So we tried to give them what they did want: some fun.'[242]

A radio revolution was inevitable, albeit within the confines of the NZBS. It began in Hawke's Bay, with the emergence of the country's first true pop DJs, Keith Richardson, Neville Chamberlain and Des Britten. The radio history *Voices in the Air* records:

Established rules were cast aside and 'personality projection' took over. Rapid-fire Austral-American accents frenziedly scattered the latest 'hip talk' jargon in between and over the top of the supercharged but infectious beat of the records. Cautious managers tended to regard the breed with suspicion and there is no doubt that some of the deejays abused their new-found freedoms. Older listeners considered them incomprehensible, young people thought they were the saviour of radio.[243]

The mischievous trio of the Hawke's Bay airwaves would soon make a nationwide impact on radio, with fast-moving shows, slick patter, and wacky sound effects and humour. In Napier, said Tubert, Chamberlain 'had things humming along, in many ways achieving more than we were in Wellington, where we were overshadowed by head office and couldn't move without someone breathing down our necks. Neville didn't have that problem then and had more freedom to branch out, running programmes completely different from anything ever heard in New Zealand before.'[244]

Chamberlain had spent four years as a teenage axeman in the bush when he decided to follow his brother Wally into a radio career in 1953. His first stints on air at 2XA Wanganui and 3ZB Christchurch followed the restrictive formats of the era: 'First you'd play a male vocalist, then a female, and that would be followed by an instrumental: Charlie Kunz, Victor Sylvester, someone like that. And you weren't supposed to make any comment, but I did. I was breaking new ground and I used to get marched down to the programme officer every bloody day.'[245]

After helping launch Invercargill's first commercial radio in 1956, Chamberlain was sent to do the same at 2ZC in Napier. There, he found technicians with a similar taste for taking risks, and a tolerant manager, Ken 'Pop' Collins. The regional commercial station, launched in October 1957, established a connection with local pop musicians – the Cool Four was one of several rock'n'roll bands that played live-to-air on Saturday nights – and a reputation for innovation. The staff can claim to have illicitly made the first steps towards stereo broadcasting in New Zealand in the early 1960s. Technicians altered the wiring of a stereo turntable, so that its signal split into two. With 2YZ operating from the same building, they then broadcast the separate channels of a stereo album from the two stations early in

Des Britten, part of the new wave of pop radio DJs in the early 1960s. Merv Thomas collection

the morning, before they officially went on air. At home, two radio sets were needed to receive the stereo broadcast successfully. The surreptitious experiment attracted the wrath of head office.[246]

The technicians dropped in sound effects such as short novelty clips, or reverberation using the time-honoured method of putting a microphone in a bathroom. On his late night show *Anything Goes*, Chamberlain took more risks and began developing his disc-jockey patter. He also challenged the protected status of the *Lever Hit Parade*. 'It seemed to have a first mortgage on most of the new discs arriving from overseas.'[247] The regional stations used to receive a tape of the *Lever Hit Parade* a week in advance, and Chamberlain began dubbing off some of the hit songs and putting them to air first. Also, he found many of the discs circulated by head office stipulated that the B-side was to be played, even though the A-sides were current hits; this was to protect the *Lever Hit Parade*'s exclusivity. Recalled musician Lou Parun, 'It dawned on Cham if he could copy the A-sides before the records were shipped on to the next station, it may form the nucleus of a show he had in mind, which became *The Top Forty*.'[248]

Soon, each Saturday night young listeners from throughout the country were tuning in to Chamberlain's *Top Forty* show from Hawke's Bay. By now called 'Cham the Man', he was promoted to 2ZB, where he met producer Johnny Douglas who was determined to modernise commercial radio. With sound engineer Rocky Douche, Douglas and Chamberlain developed a lively breakfast show hugely popular in the Wellington region. From Scott Newman, another early DJ, Chamberlain took over two shows, *Saturday Night at Nine* and *Gather Round*. Sponsored by Reckitt and Colman, these programmes took a more overtly commercial approach; crucially they were broadcast over 26 stations using the newly established national network. Dedicated to pop music, *Gather Round* was the *Lever Hit Parade*'s first real competitor.

Listening to Chamberlain in Hawke's Bay was a young man in Otane, south of Hastings. Des Britten studied his style, practised at home and would soon follow in his footsteps; a trip to Australia also gave him fresh ideas about broadcasting. By early 1961, he too was a pioneering pop DJ with his own show broadcasting nationwide. *The Hi-Fi Club* had 10,000 signed-up members, drawn by the audio gimmicks and the catchphrases that Britten rattled off in a fast-moving half-hour: 'Hi there you there, this is the daddyo of your radio, spinning around with the modern sound . . . . Stacks of wax and plenty of platter chatter. Let's swing every little thing on the centre aisle of your radio dial . . . . Bye bye for now now – see you round, like a record.'[249]

Douglas had visited Australia in 1958 and was very impressed by Bob Rogers, a DJ on station 2UE:

He ran the most lively evening show from four until seven, called *The Sunset Show*. They played this non-stop hit music, interspersed with lively presentation, competitions, prizes, all sorts of smart, gimmicky phrases. I was just completely overwhelmed by it. They didn't just refer to Sydney, it was 'Greater Sydney-land'. All this hype. It was

just captivating to a teenager like myself. Of course they had got the idea from the States, where Top 40 radio had been introduced by Alan Freed.

During Douglas's visit, on 2 March 1958, 2UE launched Australia's first Top 40 format, in which only the latest hits were broadcast through the day.[250]

Returning to NZBS and a job programming 2YA's music on the breakfast session, Douglas found there was 'rebellion in the ranks' to some of the staid offerings. It wasn't unknown for a technician to quietly damage a disc of an artist such as Mantovani to prevent it being played again. Douglas lobbied to produce a weekly programme of the new, quality pop the station was neglecting. He was reluctantly given two slots for *Tunes from the Charts*: Tuesday nights at 10.30 pm and a repeat at 10.30 am each Saturday morning. The latter was peak listening time, but the announcer Robin Gurnsey did not want to be associated with pop music so insisted on using a pseudonym. Although Douglas had to avoid records that had been banned, such as Bobby Darin's 'Mack the Knife', he found there was plenty of music to choose from: 'There were good records coming out every week, such as "Petite Fleur" by Chris Barber's Jazz Band, or "Wheels" by the Stringalongs. It wasn't all rock'n'roll by any means, it was quite acceptable music. If it had all been rock'n'roll it would have been taken off, for sure.'

By 1962 Douglas was at 2ZB working alongside Justin du Fresne, a young announcer who had grown up in Hawke's Bay, a dedicated listener to Neville Chamberlain. Douglas still had a craving to get a 2UE-style programme up and running alongside 2ZB's other popular offerings, such as Bas Tubert and the housewife's helper, Doreen. He thought a contemporary drive-time show, hosted by du Fresne, would perfect the schedule.

So we went to see our manager, Jim Hartstonge, who fortunately was a progressive and empathetic sort of guy, and said we wanted to put forward this quite radical idea. I said it would feature all the new releases, the nice music that was around, from country and western to pop hits, with a little spiel on the artists. He said, how many nights a week would you do this? When I said Monday to Friday he replied, 'My goodness.' Well, he thought a few minutes then said, 'I like the cut of you two chaps. You are two good young chaps. By god, we'll give it a go.'

It was a punt for Hartstonge: his reputation was on the line as much as that of his protégés. Former NZBS and NZBC employee Godfrey Gray suggested that it was the introduction of television that made radio take tentative steps towards modern pop: 'Although television was still a novelty, it was soon apparent that this medium would dominate the Kiwi "evening at home". It was also apparent that the advertising agencies would be switching their clients' budgets away from newspapers, and from radio in particular, to the new medium. Already radio was feeling the effects of television.'[251]

On 29 April 1963, New Zealand's first daily pop programme began: *The Sunset Show*. The first disc it aired was Cliff Richard's 'Living Doll'. 'It was just the right programme in the right place at the right time', recalled Douglas. 'Listeners wrote in from all over the country – from Gisborne to the Bluff – to say, "Heard your *Sunset Show*: fantastic music." There was no backlash, we didn't present it in an over-hyped, noisy way, just good music and personality content from Justin. And at the end of the year, he went overseas for his OE and Pete Sinclair took over.'

Although on 2ZB only, *The Sunset Show* format was soon copied by community stations around the country. The programme was significant for several reasons. It was the first pop show at the peak listening time of early evening; the first pop show over 30 minutes duration; it supported local and visiting talent through live interviews and airplay; and had the first music rotate, repeating hit songs methodically. Among the local acts that were featured were Tommy Adderley, Pauline Bramley, the Librettos, Jim McNaught, Rochelle Vinson and Paul Walden. 'The interviews were very heavily weighted for the local people', explained du Fresne, though the Beatles, Gene Pitney, the Rolling Stones and others were all featured (usually after their event, to avoid accusations of free promotion). The burgeoning stars of pop radio – Chamberlain, Britten, du Fresne and Sinclair – were invited to MC at gigs by local bands at dance halls within the large reception area. There were many youth clubs in the Hutt Valley, and du Fresne remembers donning his black, mohair suit and thin tie, then travelling out on the train in bright sunlight, 'feeling an absolute prat. You're supposed to arrive in a great big American car, or a taxi. Not take the train and walk.'[252]

Douglas's intention may have been to support local music as much as possible – after all, these performances were accessible and could be used for all sorts of programming ideas – but it was not straightforward. His paramount concern was for 'quality radio' and there was strong competition from sophisticated pop by the likes of Burt Bacharach and Henry Mancini. Local recordings often didn't make the grade, he found. 'There were a lot of poor recordings – most labels had a few tragedies along the way', he said. 'It was tricky, because record producers would come to you and say, "Johnny, I've got the hottest record you've ever heard, it's just fantastic." I'd say, leave it with me, I'm listening to all my records tomorrow. It was up to me to decide whether it was such a great record, and deserved playing. And if you didn't play it they'd be on the phone next week saying, "Hey, what happened?" You'd have to have some reasonable reasons for saying why you didn't like it.'

With the emergence of regional hit parades, *The Sunset Show* and its imitators, the *Lever Hit Parade* looked increasingly staid. After Selwyn Toogood left to front other programmes, it was hosted by Sandy Triggs and, from 1961, Ted Thorpe (who was later lost at sea in a yachting mishap).

In December 1965, as the programme came to the end of its nineteen-year run, Toogood and Thorpe looked back on the changes. When the *Hit Parade* began, most hits came from musicals and lasted many weeks on the charts. Now, there was a rapid turnover of hits often by what these veterans considered were manufactured, short-lived pop stars. Whereas in 1946 most discs were bought by 'the householder: the mother or father', teenagers – a specific demographic with disposable incomes – now dominated the decisions made by the record industry. Originally, said Toogood, 'record companies couldn't have cared less about the *Hit Parade*. Now they come on bended knees saying, "Play our record."'

In the mid-1950s, there had been a sudden shift in the *Hit Parade*'s selections, from swing and adult pop to rock'n'roll. In that time, said Toogood, the policy for selection never changed: a song had to have appeared on the US or British hit parades to be considered. Thorpe demurred: there had been 'a slight broadening to include and encourage local talent', he said. 'But this has always been when time permits – say, most of the pops have been around two-minutes long.'[253] When the programme began, there was no New Zealand pop being recorded; now the local industry was well established and its releases increasingly prolific.

Rock'n'roll got the publicity, and pop the teenage fans, but it would be a music comedy group from Rotorua that would show record companies and radio that New Zealanders could support local artists with a fervour that rivalled any offerings from overseas. The Howard Morrison Quartet amalgamated many cultural influences into a quintessentially New Zealand act. They can be seen as the most polished and popular exponents of a genre that was developing simultaneously.

HI-FIVE HAKA: MAORI SHOWBANDS EMERGE

In 1953 a British film crew visited Whakatane to shoot *The Seekers*, 'an epic tale of Empire building in New Zealand, with hundreds of Maori providing authentic background'. In the lead role was Jack Hawkins but, according to the Hollywood show business paper *Variety*, the 'native players [provided] better value than the stars'.[254]

Some of the film's 'native players' were themselves pioneers. Bringing 'great dignity' to the role of a Maori chief – and acting as the film's cultural advisor – was Inia Te Wiata. Further down the cast list were Henare Gilbert, Mac Hata, Patrick Rawiri and Te Waari (Joe) Ward-Holmes, who took part in scenes of singing and dancing that, while accomplished, sat awkwardly in the narrative.[255]

Forty years after Makeriti Papakura's concert party travelled to England, Gilbert and his colleagues began a new wave of Maori troubadours. They ventured to the other side of the world to entertain – and introduce foreign audiences to a little Maoritanga. All from rural backgrounds, they met in Wellington in 1950 and combined their talents as the Maori Quartet. The following year they left for Australia as the Brown Bombers, then made their way to England.

The Brown Bombers performed in clubs, theatres and on television; they accompanied Gracie Fields on a six-week UK tour, and joined the musicians' circuit of American military bases in Europe. In Italy, they were banned from appearing in their Maori costumes on television, so they had to perform the haka in their dress suits. By 1955, when Jack Leigh witnessed a show in Newcastle-upon-Tyne, they were again called the Maori Quartet: 'They did their guitar-strumming, bare-breasted, flax-skirted routine in the numbing northern cold, with a hula dancer named Vola. Only the applause was warm.'[256]

In 1956 the quartet broke up and two of the former Brown Bombers landed in Germany. Gilbert married an

East German actress, and they settled in East Berlin; he continued to perform, singing Maori and contemporary songs on television and radio.[257] When he returned to New Zealand, after eleven years away, the Berlin Wall had just been built and Gilbert had to get special permission for his family to leave.[258] Ward-Holmes became a booking agent based in West Germany and, in the early 1960s, organised engagements in Europe for the vanguard of the showband era: the Maori Hi-Five.[259]

The eclectic approach of the showbands can be traced back to Princess Te Puea's band and concert party of the 1920s, Te Pou o Mangatawhiri. TPM mixed traditional kapa haka and poi routines, with Hawaiian dancing, comedy, and popular instruments such as the guitar and ukulele.[260] The concert parties wanted to educate and entertain their audiences; so did the showbands but they were even more influenced by the traditions of music hall and cabaret. The showbands were unashamedly in show business, with their Maori culture being a main point of difference from their competitors.

'They were show groups', said Phil Warren. 'They not only played, they entertained. They did steps like the Shadows, they'd play guitars behind their heads and two instruments in their mouths at once – a lot of comedy things and [they] were really, really entertaining.'[261]

Howard Morrison explained that the groups conformed to a template, and the musical influences mixed early R&B and Las Vegas:

> You'll notice every Maori showband had a saxophone player and a good strong girl singer. Two people influenced them. Louis Prima the saxophone player, and Keely Smith. Then you'd have the choreography of the Platters. The Maoris were quick to adapt one style to the other and it became uniquely their own.
>
> Because Prima and Smith were *mestizo*, half Spanish, they were the closest to us. The sound was identifiable, whereas we [didn't do] the Negro sound unless we did a complete ape of it.
>
> In the showbands the impressions were all of the Brook Bentons, the Nat King Coles and the Johnnie Rays; but the basis of the show was the Louis Prima, Keely Smith thing. It's the sound; the *tizo* and Maori thing; the intonation, the dropping of beats and the catching up, the loose meandering through bridges, the sense of adventure.[262]

At a party in the Wairarapa in the late 1940s, eight-year-old Rob Hemi had his palm read. In his future, Hemi was

The Hi-Five Mambo, fledgling Maori showband, Wanganui 1958. From left: Ike Metekinga,
Costa Christie, Jimmy Rivers, Rob Hemi, 'Fro the Pro' and Solly Pohatu. Costa Christie collection

told, he would play music, 'in a very strange way'. At the
time 'rock'n'roll was unheard of', he recalled to Suzanne
Ormsby. 'They were still singing tunes like "Bless 'Em
All", and Gracie Fields was still on the hit parade. George
Formby was the gun instrumentalist.'[263]

Hemi bought his first guitar in 1955 and got lessons
from Max Davis, a shearer and Tex Morton fan. He then
moved to a Mangakino farm, where a guitarist called
Barlow Karaitiana led all the parties on his guitar. 'He was
a teetotaller, and just sat there and picked up every next
song the second anyone opened their mouth to sing it.'[264]
At Te Aute College he played rhythm guitar for a kapa
haka group, and his music confidence was boosted by
Canon Wi Huata. At a hui in Ruatoki in 1957, Hemi met
Ike Metekingi and Kawana Pohe, two Wanganui teenagers
who had their own dance band, the Planets. They played
music together and discussed forming a band.

Hemi moved to Wellington, took some guitar lessons
from Len Doran and was performing Latin-American
music at a coffee bar in Dixon Street when he ran into
Metekingi. This time they got serious about forming a
band. Hemi suggested a singer he had heard at the Ngati
Poneke Club, Solomon Pohatu, who also played piano,
bass and saxophone. With Rarotongan percussionist Fred
Tira and drummer Tuki Witika they began working on
their act. As the Hi-Five Mambo, they secured gigs around
Wellington.

A show at the Club Cubana determined their future:
they were talent-spotted by two men who became the
svengalis behind the showbands. Charles Mather and
Jim Anderson were British immigrants who arrived
in Wellington in the mid-1950s: watching the Hi-Five
Mambo they could see the potential for a touring Maori
cabaret group.[265]

At that stage, the band was an 'out-and-out rock'n'roll combo'.[266] Vocalist 'King' Solomon Pohatu was a natural mimic, famed for his Little Richard impersonations and his rendition of 'Speedy Gonzales', complete with on-stage mule. With percussionist Costa Christie, he would sing duets and lip-synch to Stan Freberg records. Another early member with a penchant for comedy was Jimmy 'Junior' Tuatara, who later had a long career in Britain as 'the Mad Maori'.

As the band evolved from the Hi-Five Mambo into the Maori Hi-Five, they recruited the multi-instrumentalist Kawana Pohe, who brought sophisticated arrangements

'King' Solomon Pohatu – 'New Zealand's Little Richard' – at the Club Cubana, Wellington, 1958. He was later a member of the Maori Hi-Five. Costa Christie collection

*Solomon Puhatu
Hi-Five Mambo
Cubana 1958*

to the group. Severely sight-impaired due to a kick from a horse as a child, Pohe was studying music at the Blind Institute in Auckland. He learnt to read music in Braille, and his saxophone playing 'made the hair stand on the back of your neck'.[267]

Mather and Anderson managed the Hi-Five, and formed the Maori Hi-Five Company to manage many spin-off groups. They developed the showband formula: skilled musicianship, multi-instrumental abilities, a broad range of pop tunes, parodies, impersonations, nutty comedy routines, a dash of kapa haka, and slick choreography and stage craft. They drilled the musicians until their presentation was polished; if they were late or their stage manner was wanting (i.e., they didn't smile enough), they were fined.[268]

As the Maori Hi-Five, the group soon secured a residency at Wellington's Trades Hall dance club, and in January 1960 – after a few lineup changes – they headed for Australia.[269] Their planned visit of three months was so successful the Queensland Musicians' Union tried to have them banned; they stayed for fourteen months then moved on to London. Within two days, the Hi-Five had secured an engagement at the Embassy club, and tours of Europe, television appearances and a part in the Disney film *In Search of the Castaways* quickly followed.[270]

After three years overseas, the Hi-Five returned home to New Zealand in 1963. Their tour was to raise funds so that Pohe, whose vision had deteriorated, could undergo eye surgery (ultimately successful). In Europe they had been earning up to £1400 a week, and toured in their own Rolls-Royce. The opening night of the ten-week homecoming tour was in the Auckland Town Hall, and it introduced the public to the Hi-Five's new members: singer Mary Nimmo, drummer Peter Wolland and impressionist Wes Epae. The *NZ Herald* reported that touring in Europe had turned the Hi-Five into 'a well-balanced and versatile entertainment group . . . . From the opening drum roll to the final wistful strains of "Now is the Hour" the band carried the audience along on a wave of expectancy.'[271]

Within a year, they were supporting the Beatles at their Hong Kong concert on 9 June 1964. Meanwhile, their influence continued, in New Zealand and around the world. When the Hi-Five first left for Australia, Mather and Anderson brought in the Hi-Quins to replace them, and by the time the Quins were ready to tour overseas, another group was waiting. In this way they built up a troupe of experienced musicians and entertainers who

The Maori Hi-Five at the Bankstown RSA, Sydney, 1963, rehearsing for the Johnny O'Keefe TV show. Clockwise from top: Rob Hemi, guitar; Solomon Pohatu, singer/pianist; Tuki Witika, drums; Paddy Te Tai, guitar; Kawana Pohe, saxophone; Wes Epae, singer. Centre: Harata (Charlotte) Pohe. Fairfax Media Sundays Archive

became as intertwined as a family tree when replacement players were needed. The lineups of the bands became almost as interchangeable as their names. Off-stage, they wore a familiar uniform: black blazers, often with a silver fern on the breast pocket.

After the Hi-Five came the deluge. Or rather, went the deluge: a curiosity about the Maori showband phenomenon is that their success – and much of their fame – was mostly overseas. By the mid-1960s, the showbands seemed ubiquitous in Australia, Asia and the Pacific. When the Auckland-based drummer Bruce Morley moved to Sydney in 1964, he was stunned by their high profile:

There were more Maori performers than I had ever seen at home, working as solo performers or in groups of all shapes

and sizes . . . . There were groups with names like the Maori Hi-Five, the Maori Troubadours, the Maori Hi-Liners, the Quin Tikis, the Maori Volcanics, the Sheratons, the Maori Premiers, Te Pois, Te Kiwis, the Maori Minors, Maori Hakas, the Milford Sounds and many more . . . . When I returned to New Zealand some years later, I discovered that very few of the general public knew much about the performers I've just mentioned, apart from the most prominent ones. It was as if it had happened somewhere else, in a dream.[272]

TAHI RUA TANIWHA: QUARTET FEVER

Gerry Merito always remembered the day a convoy of buses brought the Maori Battalion back to the Ureweras after the Second World War. His father let him help dig the massive pit for the hangi, something children weren't normally allowed to do. 'No – you've got to start learning, boy.' When the bus arrived in the small village of Taneatua, all the soldiers got off to say goodbye to the seven men for whom this was the last stop. They stood to attention and saluted each other.

The seven soldiers from Taneatua – all of them relatives of Merito – walked over to a cowshed and washed themselves in a trough. Then one of them said, 'Where's the keg?'

An eighteen-gallon keg of beer was eased out of the creek where several were chilling, as the village had no fridges. They banged it open with an axe – beer went everywhere – 'and they were just into it, from then on'.

The party carried on through the night, with the seven soldiers singing at the tops of their voices, oblivious to the mosquitos. 'They had no guitar, they just sang', said Merito. 'They were all singing Italian songs; it was something you never forget.' Next morning, when Merito got up to milk 40 cows, the keg was in the way. 'Don't touch that – leave it', said his father. When the soldiers emerged, they poured wine into the keg 'to kick the beer along'.

The celebration lasted for three days, and then the soldiers got on a bus and disappeared for a week. They joined their friends down the road and the party and singing continued.[273]

In Rotorua, Howard Morrison – ten years old when the war ended – listened to his father talk with friends about the desert campaign, and saw neighbourhood women clutching photographs of men in the 28 Maori Battalion, weeping. Those who returned home safely brought with

CROWN PRINCE

Tumanako 'Tui' Teka, troubadour, 1972. National Publicity Studios, AAQT6401-A99609, Archives New Zealand

Two showband veterans did eventually make an impact in their home country: Prince Tui Teka and, in the 1970s, Billy T. James. At different times, both were in the Maori Volcanics, who formed in Australia in 1965 and became one of the longest lasting and most travelled of the showbands.

The artist who became known as Prince was born Tumanako Teka. He was a 'child of the mist', born in Ruatahuna in the Urewera Ranges in 1937. It was a musical household: Teka's mother Hinemauriri played a mouth organ and clarinet, and his father Te Waakainga the saxophone, banjo and guitar. He joined a family dance band at the age of eight, the Baby Tawharangi Orchestra, to play the saxophone.

At fifteen, already a year out of school and working on the roads in Kaingaroa forest, Teka took the romantic route of a flamboyant adventurer wanting to leave home: he joined a circus. Teka's charisma and cheek meant he quickly became one of the acts. 'Tui was street smart, content to play along with the roles given to the lone Polynesian in mostly Pakeha acts, while soaking up the atmosphere and the whys and wherefores of the entertainment industry', wrote Mahora Peters of the Maori Volcanics. 'He talked his way into a series of acts, harnessing his natural gifts as a showman. He had a voice that was at the same time husky and warm, and he oozed an easy affability and humour that was to become his trademark for the rest of his too-short life.'[274]

Soon, the Australian company Wirth's had him billed as Prince Tui Latui with the Royal Polynesians. Their job was to be dancing, singing 'noble savages' for the entertainment-hungry Australians of the 1950s. 'What the audiences didn't know was that the Prince had a couple of other jobs for the circus: driving one of the trucks and cleaning up elephant dung. Still, he looked the part. Big, brown and regal.'[275]

Barney Erickson, in Australia since the early 1950s to perform with the ABC Dance Band, encountered Teka in his circus period. 'I went to a party at the showgrounds in Sydney, put on by some of the people from Wirth's Circus, and in this humongous caravan where the smoke was streaming out and the liquor was flowing freely, I met for the first time Prince Tui Teka . . . . He was like a king surrounded by all the circus crowd and he wasn't even involved in music at that stage.'[276]

Erickson and Teka formed the Maori Troubadours together, with Matt Te Nana and Johnny Nichol. In the late 1950s, they began playing the showgrounds circuit across Australia, with Teka eventually leading a convoy of cars, trucks and caravans. 'We were never out of work', said Erickson. 'Tui's band was the first show group of its type, with Robbie Ratana and Tui's brothers and any other musicians that were available.'[277]

In 1963 four performers recently over from Auckland joined the Troubadours. Nuki Waaka, his wife Mahora (née Rewiti) and brother Gugi were working as the Polynesian Trio. They retained this persona in their act. It involved the fusing of cultures: as a 'Polynesian princess' a grass-skirted Mahora would shake her hips while her 'Maori princess' sister Lynda twirled pois. Nuki and Gugi – the 'Maori twins' – performed a haka. Then the music began, with Hec Epae singing until the grand entrance of Prince Tui Latui.

Performing on the showground circuit, they went through this routine many times a day. In tents nearby was the competition: Australian rock'n'roll pioneers Johnny O'Keefe, Col Joye and His Joy Boys. 'Although it wasn't the most glamorous life', recalled Mahora, 'we loved it.'[278] They criss-crossed Australia, up to northern Queensland, through the centre to Perth, and then back across the unsealed Nullabor Plain to the east coast. At night, they would camp at the side of the road and get their guitars out.[279]

In 1965 Mahora, Nuki and Gugi Waaka formed the Maori Volcanics, with Matti Kemp, Hec Epae and John 'Gimmick' Cameron; a year later they were joined by Teka. They became globe-trotting entertainers, including a stint in Vietnam during the war. A reviewer in Thailand described his reaction as the Volcanics opened a show dressed in native costumes:

'Uh-oh', thinks the knowledgeable night-towner. 'Just some more lousy tribal dances.'

But then comes the switch. The dance turns wild and funny, the boys change into business suits, and from that erupts an insane, frenetic, polished comedy instrumental

routine which floors any audience and leaves them screaming for more.

They play a one-handed 'Guitar Boogie', where each fellow fingers the other's guitar, running around the stage. Another then launches into a series of imitations: Yma Sumac (singing, as they say, 'eight octaves'), Louis Armstrong, Elvis Presley, Dean Martin and Johnny Mathis.

After that, they begin some phenomenal instrumental numbers (each of the boys play at least three instruments), and all the time the comedy and slapstick and improvisation is kept under unbelievable control.[280]

After a ten-week farewell tour of New Zealand in 1972, Teka and the Volcanics went their separate ways. Both continued to tour the world, but Teka also became the doyen of the small New Zealand country pub gig. His repertoire was as international as his travels: Italian ballads, country and western, rock'n'roll, novelty songs and Maori popular standards such as 'Hoki Mai' and 'Pokarekare'. No song was too sacred to be interrupted for a joke: 'As the Spaniard said to the Maori girl in the grass skirt, "gracias, gracias" . . . . I'm Nat King Cole's half-brother, Charcoal . . .'.[281]

In 1981, he had the biggest hit of his career when, persuaded and produced by Dalvanius Prime, he performed a new Maori language song written by Ngoi Pewhairangi. 'E Ipo' reached No. 1 in the New Zealand sales charts, and brought Teka another level of fame. When he died of a heart attack on 23 January 1985, he was aged just 48. Weight had always been an issue, as he was typically 20 stone; he joked that when he dieted he lost his sense of humour. 'I had no stomach to wiggle. I was just a singer.'

Three days after attending Teka's tangi at Tokomaru Bay, Pewhairangi also died. A descendant of Tuini Ngawai, she had recently co-written a second No. 1 hit, 'Poi E', for the Patea Maori Club. Twenty years after the heyday of the showbands – with their fusion of Maoritanga, pop melody, rhythm and humour – the era's legacy was a pivotal moment in the renaissance of te reo.

Gerry Merito and Howard Morrison, early in the
Quartet's rise. Lou Clauson Collection, PA1-f-192-08-05,
Alexander Turnbull Library, Wellington

Urewera. All the other children at the Huiarau Native
School spoke Maori as their first language, and Morrison
worked to catch up in the playground. While milking the
family cows he would amuse himself by practising his
singing, and the batteries on the family radio were saved for
Thursday nights, when the *Lifebuoy Hit Parade* went to air.
'I would mimic whoever was singing, male or female. I knew
all the hit parade songs by heart. More than that, it gave me
a sort of subconscious knowledge of what people wanted to
listen to. And what the majority of people still want to listen
to is middle-of-the-road popular.'[284]

Morrison started secondary school as a boarder at Te
Aute College in Hawke's Bay. There he came under the
influence of his first two musical mentors, Canon Wi Huata
and Reverend Sam Rangiihu. Besides their inspirational
spirituality and musicianship, they were entertainers. 'Rev
Rangiihu in particular would always relax his audience
and put them at their ease with humour and timing. Then
when he sang "straight" you appreciated his vocal qualities
all the more.'[285] (In 1959, at the instigation of Reverend
Billy Graham, Huata and Rangiihu were instrumental in
writing 'Whakaaria Mai': Maori lyrics to the melody of
'How Great Thou Art'.)[286]

Morrison left high school at sixteen; the Whakatu
freezing works in Hastings offered 'the highest school
of learning'. It was during this year that he began
singing seriously, in public. With two friends, Morrison
entertained the other freezing workers – 'we'd sing at the
drop of a hat' – and he was invited to join the Kohupatiki
church choir in Hastings. Through this he became
reacquainted with the Whatarau family, whose young
daughters Isobel and Virginia had performed at Te Aute.
Morrison and the Whatarau daughters joined the Awapuni
Concert Party, which then embarked on a tour of the South
Island. He also joined the Whatarau sisters as part of the
Clive Trio, replacing Kahu Pineaha who had decided to
try a solo career. At the time the Trio was 'hot, very hot in
Maoridom', and Morrison learnt how to lead a song, sing
in harmony, and work out arrangements to emulate styles
such as Spanish, Latin American or Maori. He listened
keenly to vocal groups such as the Mills Brothers, the Ink
Spots and the Four Aces. Mario Lanza was at the height of
his popularity with a 'crossover' approach and, with his
love of Neapolitan music, Morrison 'fashioned myself on
him and I used to call myself Mario Maori Lanza'.[287]

The Awapuni Concert Party was well-rehearsed
and 'ahead of its time. We were the first group to mix

them songs they had learnt in Italy: 'O Sole Mio', 'Come
Back to Sorrento'. 'So my introduction to music – as in
music outside of the culture which I was brought up with –
was Neapolitan', said Morrison.[282]

Everyone seemed to sing, and the other music Morrison
especially enjoyed were the hymns learnt in church and
Bible class. 'It was a communal spirit in those days because
there weren't any other distractions and everything was
family orientated.' After a Sunday lunch the extended
family would get together to sing more popular songs, the
mornings having been devoted to hymns, sung in Maori.
'That's when I started to hear harmonies which really
attracted me.'[283]

Shortly afterwards Morrison's father, Temuera, a field
officer with the Maori Affairs Department, was transferred
to the bush settlement Ruatahuna in the heart of the

contemporary music with traditional cultural music – a practice at the time considered heresy.' Among the songs was 'Hoki Mai', learnt from East Coast Maori. The first half of an Awapuni show would be traditional, with the singers in piupiu; in the second half, the Clive Trio would star, with the Whatarau sisters in ball gowns and Morrison in a suit and bow-tie, singing modern pop songs.

His father promoted a show for the Clive Trio in Rotorua, but shortly afterwards he was diagnosed with leukaemia; he died aged 45 on New Year's Eve, 1954. The family was shattered, and so Morrison stayed in Rotorua rather than return to Hawke's Bay. This led to him meeting a character who would play a crucial role in his future.

It was during a long spell confined to bed that Gerry Merito got his first guitar. Between the ages of eight and fifteen, Merito spent years in Gisborne and Whakatane hospitals because of a bone disease in his leg. He was left with a permanent limp, but two nurses changed his life when they gave him an acoustic guitar.

Back home in Taneatua, Merito and his family sang together each night after dinner. He remembered his grandmother, 'sitting cross-legged, smoking a pipe and wearing an old straw hat. She would break into "My Bonnie" knowing all the words but not being able to speak the language.'[288]

The only electricity was in the cowshed, so that was where Merito tuned in to Uncle Tom's Friendly Road Choir, and heard 'people my age, and they were harmonising. I couldn't believe it – I thought only Maori harmonised'.

An aunt showed Merito three chords on the guitar, and how to strum; anything else, he learnt from listening to country music on the radio. His aunt's style of strumming was flamenco-influenced, with her fingers stroking 'all the strings, right across the guitar'. Merito used this style in the Quartet, and later developed his own style, plucking the top string down with his thumb, while bringing the bottom strings up. 'So you had that bass sound all the time. I realised very early that this guitar is only to enhance the voices, not to drown them out.' The virtuosic American guitarist Arthur 'Guitar Boogie' Smith was also an inspiration.[289]

Merito went to Rotorua to start an apprenticeship as a refrigeration engineer. He joined a concert party, and inevitably he and Morrison kept meeting each other. Merito saw Morrison performing at a talent quest with his sister, and was impressed by their professionalism:

'It sounded like opera to me but it was just a duet: they had been singing for some time.'[290]

Morrison remembered seeing Merito play at a family gathering: 'I couldn't get over how strong an acoustic guitar player he was. We started singing together and I realised here was someone who could accompany me.'[291] Morrison formed the Ohinemutu Quartet, and promptly won £250 at George Tollerton's Search for the Stars talent quest in Hamilton.[292] They avoided ballads and excited the audience with a medley of hits from the emerging genre, rock'n'roll: '*Get out of the kitchen, and rattle those pots and pans*', recalled Morrison. 'It went over gang-busters.'[293]

In another talent quest, at the Rotorua Soundshell, it was Merito who won, performing 'Guitar Boogie'. Morrison approached him about an idea he had: to form a group and 'copy what the Mills Brothers and the Ink Spots were doing', said Merito. 'We started imitating these groups with the oo-wahs and the wop-diddy-wops in the background, and I realised, "By golly, I can sing". So from there it grew.'[294]

Soon Morrison and Merito were working together on a survey gang in the bush, and part of the routine was singing around the campfire at night; they also sang at parties after rugby. Pubs still closed at six o'clock in the evening, so Merito would take his guitar along and the members' lockers would open up: 'Beers would be put in front of us and we'd stay there all night.'[295]

The singing ventures evolved into a regular quartet. 'Gerry was the anchor with me, we just used the relatives that were around at the time.' Merito was the only non-Morrison in the original quartet that featured Howard, his brother Laurie and their cousin John. 'All Morrisons and an alien from Tuhoe country', he joked.[296]

A mentor in this early period was Morrison's mother Kahu, a talented soprano herself. From the age of sixteen she had sung professionally, and as a young adult she toured with Rotorua's Whakarewarewa Maori Concert Party.[297] She encouraged their pop ambitions, smartened them up with cummerbunds and bow-ties, and lined the Quartet up for an inspection in her lounge before they headed out to a performance. Kahu Morrison also ensured they did not forget the Maori music with which they had grown up.[298]

They began doing one-off shows in the Bay of Plenty and Waikato before Auckland promoter Benny Levin saw them at Rotorua's Ritz Hotel in 1956. The rock'n'roll medley was part of their act, just as it was starting to

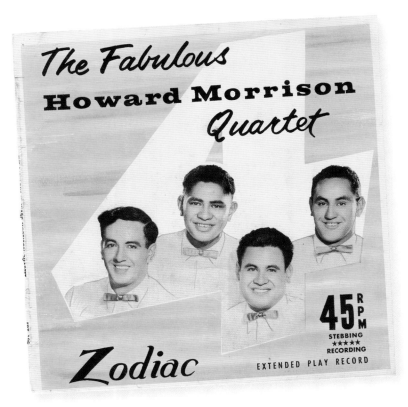

The original group on *The Fabulous Howard Morrison Quartet*, released in 1958. From left, Laurie Morrison, Gerry Merito, Howard Morrison and John Morrison. RNZ Music Library, Wellington

explode, so Levin invited them to join a variety show at the Auckland Town Hall. The fee was £8, with no accommodation provided, so the Quartet drove back to Rotorua that night.[299]

The fees soon increased, as the gigs quickly got more prestigious. Warming up the audience for a jazz concert at the Auckland Town Hall, the Quartet sang light 1950s pop and performed impressions of Nat King Cole, Jerry Lewis and others. 'We were no more jazz performers than the Neophonic is an indigenous cultural group', recalled Morrison, 'but, maybe because we were in such a contrast to the rest of the programme, we brought the house down.' That was exactly the reaction of Jim Warren to this concert:

> The Howard Morrison Quartet is the most appealing group to perform in this city in many a long day. Leader Howard Morrison has a friendly, uninhibited personality and a fine lead voice, with the ability to impersonate the current pop vocalists from Presley down – if you can go down . . . . Their popularity lies in the fact that they present the pops straight from the record, which is always the way the crowd like it.

But this alone does not account for their success. They have good appearance, charm and that certain Maori touch which immediately puts their audiences in a good humour.[300]

Levin then introduced them to Eldred Stebbing, with a view to recording the group. But first, they had to decide on a name. Morrison remembered going through the various options with the group – the Morrison Family, the Ohinemutu Quartet – when Stebbing took him aside and said, 'Look, you're the lead, you're the main man. I suggest you call it the Howard Morrison Quartet. Because if and when the quartet breaks up, there will always be Howard Morrison, entertainer and performer.'

Morrison then went back to the group. 'Gerry was my mate and I didn't have to worry about him. I was more worried about the other two.' In the event, his cousin John and his brother Laurie just said, 'Yeah, very good!'[301]

Stebbing took his portable Grundig tape-recorder down to Rotorua and recorded an EP with the newly named Howard Morrison Quartet. The first singles – released on 78s and 45s – were a mix of popular songs and Maori favourites, later recorded at Stebbing's Saratoga Avenue studio in Auckland. 'There's Only One of You'/'Big Man' was followed by 'Hoki Mai'/'Po Kare Kare Ana', and it was 'Hoki Mai' that provided them with an immediate, breakthrough hit. The Quartet had transformed the song from its origins as the country dirge 'Gold Mine in the Sky' that became Henare Waitoa's lament 'Tomo Mai'. It now had an irresistible upbeat Pacific swing:

> Hoki mai e tama ma ki roto, ki roto
> I nga ringa e tuwhera atu nei
> (A hi! Aue! Aue!)
> Kei te kapakapa mai te Haki, te Haki
> Ingarangi runga o Tiamana e

On the day 'Hoki Mai' came out, Morrison saw a queue outside a Rotorua record store. The song was playing on a speaker above the pavement; the crowd was already singing along.[302] 'Hoki Mai' quickly became a massive hit, but some Maori were upset that the Quartet had not given the song the respect it deserved for its place in Maori Battalion history.

'The LP recording of the Howard Morrison group of Rotorua has popularised this song throughout the country', Koro Dewes wrote in 1974. 'At present the wrong words are on the lips of the majority. Despite some disappointment for this state of affairs, the efforts of such groups will perpetuate and popularise some of the most significant modern Maori song–poetry and dance–poetry.'[303]

Morrison said the Quartet's spirited interpretation was appropriate for an inspirational song that 'encouraged the Maori Battalion troops to go forth and valiantly hold the values of their people – but to come home'. But some on the East Coast were offended that the Quartet had not realised the song's significance. 'At that time I was rather ignorant about the sanctity of the words. It became a hit because everybody was singing that song at parties before we even recorded it.'[304]

On a handshake agreement, Levin put a great deal of work into getting the Quartet established. He recalled that Morrison was reluctant to enter into a formal arrangement. 'I think he was wary of the Pakeha thing, and not used to being bound down by contracts.' But any tours the Quartet did were through Levin. 'It was just mutual trust on both parts.'[305]

The Quartet was invited to Melbourne for a six-week season at the Chevron Hotel, making its own way there, breaking even at £60 a week, and rapidly improving as performers. An American musician taught them about choreography, pacing, comic timing, stage patter and how to bow together.

Returning to New Zealand, Morrison was fired up by the Australian visit: by the potential revealed by television, the stage finesse they had witnessed, the New Zealand bookings that now stretched to Christmas and the possibility of going to the US at the invitation of the Platters' Buck Ram. He saw the diversity of the Quartet's material as one of its major assets: although they had a credible rock'n'roll single with 'Gum Drop', it had to take its place alongside standards, Maori favourites, country and pop. 'Every dog in the street is barking rock'n'roll', Morrison told *Joy*. 'I'm not really sold on rock'n'roll . . . . whatever one feels about it they've got to admit that it's the beat that changed a generation.' The acts that got there first – such as Bill Haley, Elvis Presley or Johnny Devlin – would last. 'But then everyone jumps on the bandwagon and it gets cheap. So we don't pursue rock'n'roll to any extent; if we did we would be just like any other group.'[306]

Morrison was keen for the Quartet to have a permanent lineup. He and Merito were still surveying; John Morrison's replacement Tai Eru was farming, and Laurie Morrison was taking leave from his engineering job. Levin

suggested a national tour, offering £200 per week; it was time to get serious.

Eddie Howell and teachers' college student Wi Wharekura replaced Laurie Morrison and Tai Eru. The Quartet was well known in the North Island by this stage, but the ten-week national tour was gruelling – all their travel was on public transport – and ambitious. The Howard Morrison Rock'n'Pop, Big Beat Stage Show had a strong lineup of acts, but it struggled to get full houses through the South Island. Although the northern leg made up the losses, with overheads of £10,000 Levin came out of it only £100 in profit, and deeply disillusioned.[307]

In 1960 a parody song written during the tour took them to another level altogether. Merito recalled that he and Morrison were sharing a dressing room before a concert, discussing British skiffle star Lonnie Donegan's current hit, a cover of Johnny Horton's 'Battle of New Orleans'.

'I said, "Listen to that – what the heck's good about that? It'd be pretty good if the battle was here . . . . the Wellington battle or the Waikato battle, whatever." And the wheels started rolling and between us the idea evolved.'

Merito thought that the song should begin at 1840, and it needed a place name that fitted the rhythm. 'I said, "What about *Tea K'watta*?" And Howard said, "No – you can't do that, it's *Te Kauwhata*." I thought, too bad, we'll just call it *Tea K'watta*.

'Big mistake. I got the blame for everything. I got murdered. I said, mate, if I could have fit Taneatua in, I wouldn't have worried about Te Kauwhata!'[308]

Morrison's introduction was spoken: 'This here's a story about the battle of the Waikato. Which was *fit* between the British, of course, and the Horis . . . .' When writing 'The Battle of Waikato' Merito stayed close to the 'New Orleans' song. The battle was now set in 1840, with Te Kooti as the protagonist; 'the mighty Mississip' became 'the mighty Waikato' – and the soldiers' meal of bacon and beans changed to pork and puha. As a parody, publishing royalties went to the original writer. But if Merito had any regrets about relinquishing the rights to his compositions, he shrugged them off. 'I always sold what I wrote,' he recalled in 2007. 'You know, I didn't want any mucking around.'

Eldred Stebbing recorded the song in concert at the Auckland Town Hall, and it was an instant hit, selling over 25,000 copies.[309] Up to that point the Quartet's recordings had been cover versions, in many genres, and always competing with the original. The parodies, starting with 'The Battle of Waikato', changed that. 'One thing we had in our favour on the New Zealand market was that we had an undeniably down-home, Maori sense of humour', recalled Morrison.[310] 'The Battle of Waikato' captured the humour and crossover appeal of the group; the Howard Morrison Quartet had found its own voice.

20,000 Fans Scream More!
Last month, in Auckland, New Zealand rock'n'pop came of age. Twenty thousand fans jam-packed the Western Springs Stadium for a mammoth outdoor concert starring top local recording personalities and, two weeks later, over twelve thousand packed into the Epsom Showgrounds for another night of big beat music.
Cinema, Stage and TV, 1 March 1960

A 'cavalcade of New Zealand recording stars' is how the big, outdoor variety show at Western Springs Stadium, Auckland, on 24 January 1960 was billed. Never before had such a strong lineup of local pop acts shared a stage. Several competing Auckland record companies had joined forces to present the show, which was part of Auckland's anniversary weekend carnival. The Howard Morrison Quartet topped the bill, which also featured the Keil Isles, Ronnie Sundin, Vince Callaher, Kahu Pineaha, Daphne Walker, Merv Thomas and His Dixielanders, mimic Don Linden, female impersonator Noel McKay and many others; master of ceremonies was Benny Levin, all for 2/6 for adults and a shilling for children.

The Howard Morrison Quartet demonstrated its 'slick stagecraft and harmonising', wrote one review; Ronnie Sundin had the bobbysoxers swooning to his 'high-octane delivery of such swinging items as "Waltzing Matilda"', while the Keil Isles and Red Hewitt's Buccaneers 'did their best to wreck the sound systems'.[311] Civic authorities were surprised by the success of the evening, especially in the way that 20,000 'jeans-clad teenagers' dispersed peacefully after the last downbeat faded.[312]

Morrison walked into a Rotorua store one day in 1959 and saw a suave salesman demonstrating his only product: Electromet frypans. The salesman saw him among the crowd of women and said, 'Here in your midst is your own very talented Howard Morrison. Now this guy and his group, they are really going to go places. And I am going to be their manager!'[313]

Harry Miller told a different story. He spotted Morrison at Bob Sell's Colony restaurant in Auckland, watching the floor show before the Quartet went on. He moved in with a pitch to manage the band.

For Miller, this would be his first foray into show business. He later described his association with the Quartet as being of 'epochal significance' in his life; it was momentous for both parties. The shopfloor demonstration over, Miller gave Morrison his 'most winning manner'. He knew of Morrison's reluctance to sign with a manager or agent, but said he had a new record company, and was offering the Quartet the chance to come in on the ground floor. As his first local artists, they would get his full attention for promotion: records, concerts, radio, television (which was just about to start transmission in Auckland).

Morrison recalled that 'Harry was plausible, very plausible. He was also an intimidating bugger; he'd come right up to your nose to talk to you. But the man couldn't be denied.'[314] Miller recalled Morrison saying, 'You'll have to convince the boys.' He then played his trump card: he would guarantee the group £2500 worth of work a year. To convince Morrison he was genuine, he signed over the ownership of his shiny, second-hand Jaguar Mark 7. 'It was on a piece of paper', said Morrison. 'I suppose I could have asked for the ownership papers as a guarantee. But I liked his style. I suspect that, one, he never had the money and, two, the car was still being paid off.'[315]

They shook hands on a deal: Miller would get 10 percent of their earnings up to a certain amount. Above that, it would be 20 percent; in the event, Miller's cut never went below 20 percent.

He hit the ground running, booking the Quartet into as many clubs as he could: the Sorrento, St Sep's, the Arabian, the Colony – sometimes up to four shows a night. 'Then we'd drive back to Rotorua', recalled Morrison. 'We were very square. No drink, just do the business, enjoy, don't hang around.'[316]

The Quartet was now in its most famous configuration, with new members Wi Wharekura and Noel Kingi. They all moved to Auckland, with wives and children – Kingi was the only member still single – and settled as a group into a big house in Penrose. 'It was probably hardest on the wives', said Morrison. 'Every young married woman wants to be mistress of her own home, her kitchen . . .'. Merito: 'Four bedrooms, three wives, two children and one shared kitchen. But I've spoken to the girls and they said, "No we got on like a house on fire." It was us, not them.'

The entrance of Harry M. Miller also meant the exit of Eldred Stebbing and Benny Levin. Morrison said that Levin encouraged them to sign with Miller as, disillusioned by the South Island tour, Levin was about to quit the music business and buy into a takeaway bar. It was a crazy idea, he later said of Benny's Tavern, 'but I made good hamburgers'. Unfortunately, the inner-city clientele was disappearing as factories and boarding houses closed down, and Levin's health – and savings – suffered. Within ten months he had sold the lease and was back as a promoter and dance-band leader.

Morrison asked Levin what he thought of Miller: 'I said I knew him very well, we used to go to Hebrew School together, because Harry was Jewish . . . . Harry could do anything.' When Morrison said Miller was offering a management contract, £30 a week whether they worked or not, and a house in Auckland, Levin replied, '"Take it. You'd be crazy not to take it." And I gave away the whole thing at that time. Who was to know what was going to happen?'[317]

The Quartet did not have a written recording contract with Stebbing, who was understandably upset that Zodiac was losing its biggest artists. 'This is where business can trample on sentiment and even on what you may feel is morally right', recalled Morrison. He was embarrassed about the decision, and when confronted by an 'incensed' Stebbing, 'I had to sort of be strong and say, "Well that's the way it is, Eldred: it's a business thing and not personal." It caused me a lot of pain.'[318]

Knowing he was about to lose the Quartet, Stebbing increased the promotion of his records by the group, which only helped lift its profile and benefit Miller, who said, 'I inherited their burgeoning popularity.'[319] To add insult to injury, Miller got the band to re-record its current hit for Zodiac, 'The Battle of Waikato', so that he could release it on his new La Gloria label.

Stebbing took Miller to court. 'Harry never knew anything about copyright, that didn't come into it. But it ended up with Harry having to go down to the city destructor and about 15,000 of them were put into the fire.'[320]

Any setback was only temporary. Miller's next brainwave was to approach Kerridge-Odeon to suggest they go as partners in a national theatre tour called the Showtime Spectacular. The Quartet would be top of a bill that featured rock'n'roll as well as traditional pop performers. With television beginning to make an impact on cinema attendance, Sir Robert Kerridge liked the idea: he would supply the theatres, Miller would supply the artists. Expenses – and profits – would be split down the middle. Miller then went to the National Film Unit to suggest the Quartet should be filmed performing several songs; the Quartet would do it for free, but the clips could be used as shorts in the cinemas. With Kerridge-Odeon co-promoting the Showtime Spectacular tour, the film clips were given plenty of exposure. And to complete the trifecta, Miller had an idea that became the Quartet's next hit.

The All Blacks were then embroiled in a controversy about their planned tour of South Africa: at the request of the host side, there were to be no Maori players in the team. The 'No Maori, No Tour' protests were under way, and while driving the Quartet down to Wellington in his Jaguar, Miller suggested a parody on the issue might be popular. 'Just to amuse him, we came up with some bullet points for the lyrics', recalled Morrison. 'Gerry had a really instinctive talent as a lyricist.'[321] According to Miller, Lonnie Donegan's latest hit 'My Old Man's a Dustman' came on the car radio, and the title presented itself: 'My Old Man's an All Black'. Merito, who wrote most of the words, claimed that no political statement was intended, and the song begins as a good-natured comedy, poking fun at the Scottish, soccer and basketball. But as it progresses, 'All Black' makes its acerbic point, albeit with a smile.

> I say, Gerry my boy, I believe they gave your old man a trial
> Yes that's right Howard – but they didn't tell him it was a
>   dog trial . . . .
> I say, Gerry my boy, I suppose your old man's a little
>   disappointed his mates left him behind
> Well actually Howard, he wasn't 'craven' to go . . .

The multi-cultural coda is spat out like the climax of a haka; the barbed final line was written by Morrison:

> Tahi rua taniwha, they won't take my old papa
> Be bop a lula, give 'em pork and puha
> Fee fee fi fi, fo fo fum – there's no Horis in that scrum.

By the time the Jaguar returned to Auckland, the song was finished. Thirty years later, Miller said, 'Sung by a group of Maoris with a sense of tongue-in-cheek fun it was a lyric which made an effective social protest on one level and a bouncy amusing satire on another.'[322]

The issues were complex. Morrison's father had been a Maori All Black alongside George Nepia, while his mother was later part of the official Maori welcome to the Springboks' visit to Rotorua in 1965. ('Things were different then', she recalled in 1992. 'We didn't use to worry so much about that.') And Gerry Merito joked that the few Maori players who were eligible, 'weren't good enough to go'.[323]

But when the Quartet performed 'My Old Man's an All Black' on tour, it was an immediate winner with audiences. Miller began taking advance orders for a record that did not yet exist. It needed to be recorded, and quickly. The first chance to record it was during a concert in the Pukekohe Town Hall. Ironically Pukekohe would soon attract national notoriety for having a barber shop whose proprietor refused to give a Maori a haircut.[324]

The acoustics were unforgiving, the equipment primitive – a plastic microphone, a portable Philips tape-recorder – and the Quartet had already performed several encores of the song when Miller walked out on stage. He told the audience they were about to become part of an historic event: the recording of the Quartet's latest hit. After a few takes, the audience was getting restless – many of them were farmers who had been up before dawn – so Miller 'made an executive decision: Lock the doors. They're going to have to sit there until we get it right.'

Morrison: 'That's his story, not quite the truth, but it makes good press, I guess.'[325]

Miller went out again and 'made an impassioned speech, in which I appealed to their social conscience, sense of nationalism, and anything else I could think of'. Two hours and eleven takes of the song later, Miller was satisfied he had a recording he could sell: the first take was the best. Adding to the atmosphere was the audience's enthusiasm – which dimmed a little as the impromptu session got close to midnight – and a referee's whistle. Ten days later, 'My Old Man's an All Black' was in the stores, where it sold 60,000 copies, said Miller. 'Thank you, Pukekohe.'[326]

Harry Miller had everything in place: a hit song, a promotional film clip in picture theatres, a national tour booked. The Howard Morrison Quartet was reaching a level of popularity unprecedented in New Zealand entertainment. The Showtime Spectacular tour of 1960 was expected to run for five weeks; in fact it lasted for nineteen. Opening night was at the St James Theatre in Wellington. As the curtain went up, recalled Miller, 'The nerves in my spine tingled as I stood at the back of the theatre and absorbed the fact that I had created a hit show. I had created a hit show – my first.'

With the Morrisons at the top of the bill, I had a young Rarotongan singer, Antoni Williams, who had immense appeal to women; Patti Brittain, an Australian singer built like a smaller version of Sabrina; Rama White, a Maori version of Tessie O'Shea who sent audiences into hysterics by the way she wobbled her belly when she sang and whom I billed as 'sixteen stone and a ton of fun'; Noel McKay, a beanpole female impersonator, married to a lady who looked rather like Liberace; Claude Papesch, a blind musician who played tenor sax and piano like a virtuoso; a talented vocal backing group called the Tremellos; and John Daley . . . who appeared as compère-comedian. [327]

As the audience from the 6.00 pm show left the theatre, it merged with those arriving for the 8.30 pm show, stopping the traffic and trams on Courtenay Place. Also leaving the theatre were Miller and the Quartet, about to have a quick Chinese meal. Above the marquee Miller had arranged a billboard, showing massive cartoon headshots of the Quartet.

'Look at that', Miller said to the group. 'It's big, eh?'
'Yes', replied Morrison, 'it's big, Harry, it's fantastic . . . '.
'Well your bloody heads are bigger than that', said Miller. 'Now get back to work.'[328]

Morrison, taken aback, later agreed that 'we were getting carried away. The ego had plenty of food, our vanity was well nourished.' Family life was getting neglected, and he later realised that while entertaining full houses was enjoyable, the Quartet was not receiving anything like a fair cut of the pie. They were earning £200 a week, a vast improvement on the £15 they had recently been getting, but they were the headliners of a hit tour, doing two shows a day, and three on Saturdays. Miller found himself 'virtually ankle-deep in money . . . . imagine what it felt like suddenly to have £20,000.' Almost over-crowded with talent, the Showtime Spectaculars became his cash-cow for the next three years, 'a roadshow which could do no wrong. I could always rely on it to replenish the coffers.'[329]

The next four years were a blur of touring, buses, NAC planes, stages, town halls, hotels and many rushed recording sessions. On Miller's La Gloria label between 1960 and 1962, they released 28 singles, eight EPs and eight albums. The recordings may have been more primitive than those done by Stebbing for his Zodiac label, but the arrangements became more sophisticated thanks to Robert Walton, who in 1960 and 1961 was also musical director and pianist on their tours. When Rim D. Paul of the Quin Tikis took over, he encouraged them to bracket their hits as medleys and to vary the harmonies; Merito in particular was keen to emulate the unison singing of the Beatles.[330]

Morrison mostly took the lead, with Wharekura singing alto and Kingi the deep bass. But leading from behind was Merito, as the comic foil and with the guitar strum that launched countless singalongs. 'Gerry was the driving force in harmonies', said Morrison. 'He could go anywhere, take any part; his pitch was absolutely marvellous.'[331] Merito praised Morrison's infectious energy for lifting the group up when they felt lacklustre or were out of sorts. 'His voice? Well, I don't think there was anyone to compare with him in our day. He was out on his own.'[332]

The evolution of the Quartet can be seen in the songs they chose to perform and record. At first, their audience expected covers of overseas hits, and Maori popular favourites. Of the latter, 'Pokarekare' was more Mills Brothers than Everly Brothers, 'Hoki Mai' the ultimate singalong, and 'Haere Ra E Hine' was played straight.

The Showtime Spectacular tour, 1961. Back, from left: Trevor King, Bob Paris, Jon Zealando, Don Frearson, Dave Adams, Brian Biddick, Bruce King, Kim Kreuger, Stan Wineera, Robert Walton, Toni Williams. Front: Brian Lehrke, Gerry Merito, Howard Morrison, Noel Kingi and Wi Wharekura. Trevor King collection

Like Elvis, they could sing anything, and would. Otherwise, perennials such as 'Marie' and 'Deep Purple' were intermingled with country ('Sixteen Tons', 'Tumbling Tumbleweeds', 'Ghost Riders in the Sky'), Italian-style pop ('It's Now or Never', 'My Prayer'), standards ('Begin the Beguine', 'I Love Paris'), spirituals ('When Jesus Was Born', 'Swing Low Sweet Chariot'), light rhythm'n'blues ('Gum Drop', 'Short Fat Fanny'), English and Irish pop ('White Cliffs of Dover', 'Danny Boy') and earnest coffee-house folk ('Michael Row the Boat', 'Where Have All the Flowers Gone?'). There was even an album for mothers, called *Always*.

And always there was humour, at first as spoofs or impressions: 'Smoke Gets in Your Eyes', as sung by the Splatters; 'Because of You' with walk-on parts by Jimmy Cagney, James Stewart, Jerry Lewis and the Ink Spots. *'You've heard of Johnnie "Cry Baby" Ray? Here's the Maori Stingray . . .'.*

Then the parodies, just four of them, but they made the group unique. 'It wasn't until we released "The Battle of Waikato" and "My Old Man's an All Black" that we felt we were doing something of our own', said Morrison in 1961. 'The words, at least, were original.'[333] Next came 'Mori the Hori' and 'George, the Wild(er) New Zealand Boy'. 'Mori the Hori' was perhaps one parody too many; the idea to base it on 'Ahab the Arab' came from a fifteen-year-old fan, Trevor Holmes. Then Morrison presented it to the others: 'I had this look of anticipation on my face, waiting for a wave of yeah, yeah, yeahs. When the boys weren't impressed at all with the idea I said, Okay, I'll write it myself.'

Recorded live in the Taihape town hall – with segues into 'The Locomotion' and a haka (*'Let's do the haka-motion, like we did the last summer'*), it was another hit. But Morrison could feel from the group's initial response that something was fading.[334]

On Australia's Tivoli circuit, they performed three non-Maori songs every night for seventeen weeks, the strict, old-school theatre discipline sharpening their professionalism. Morrison began to share the role of lead vocalist with the others, which 'probably staved off a passive revolt within the group . . . . they'd become a bit tired of being backing singers.'[335]

But their bonds were strong: a private language developed amongst the Quartet, evolving from the techniques learnt from the New Zealand magician Jon Zealando. As their support act, Zealando used to make his ventriloquist's doll speak without moving his lips, and the Quartet copied him from the side of the stage. Boy became *doy*: Hello doy – hello boy. *Cher!* – that's good! *Twer* meant a woman, from 'her'; 'heed' or 'sheed' meant a man or woman was worth talking to, 'heed not' meant don't get involved.[336]

Entertainer Simon Meihana toured with the Quartet as a warm-up act before he became part of Lou and Simon. He noticed their different characters: the down-to-earth Merito, who 'made the Quartet', the educated Wi Wharekura, Noel Kingi 'you couldn't get boo out of'. And Morrison himself: a driven leader and hard task master, constantly rehearsing the act. Recalled Meihana, 'Even his mother Kahu said, "I'm feeling a bit sad for my son. He is being a bit hard on the musicians and his friends."'[337]

Offers to perform in the US and Europe came in regularly, but Morrison turned them down, worried about the personal cost on their families. He also became disturbed by Miller's business approach when he realised that Miller was still taking his 20 percent management fee on top of his earnings as a promoter of their tours.

At a 1963 appearance in front of the Queen at a Royal Command Performance in Dunedin, Morrison met the veteran South Island promoter Joe Brown. When the Quartet parted company with Miller, the family-oriented Brown became their new manager, in a handshake agreement. He included them in the bill of his national Miss New Zealand tours, then at their peak of popularity.[338]

But they were running out of challenges and, with the big entourages on the Miss New Zealand tours – a busload of beauties, plus the Quartet and other entertainment – their families could no longer accompany them. Whereas Merito and Kingi liked to party after hours, Morrison and Wharekura didn't drink. 'I felt my discipline was being treated by the others as school-teacherish', recalled Morrison. There were 'rumblings of discontent' within the group about their roles, and from their families about all the time spent away.[339]

During 1964 Howard Morrison felt that the Quartet's time had come. They had achieved all their aspirations, and it was time to ease the burden of those back home. Morrison was about to turn 29, and his wife Kuia was expecting their third child. Merito had four children, and Wharekura had two. Noel Kingi was still 'single and fancy free'.[340]

'We had all that experience behind us; we had served our apprenticeship', Morrison recalled in 2001. 'So I had no qualms about saying to the group, I think it's time to break up, while we're on top. No reunions, just go and do our own things. If I take on engagements for the Quartet, we continue to alienate ourselves from our domestic responsibilities.'[341]

The Quartet was in a Sydney hotel when he told the others. 'In the elevator – it seems a bit cold now, when I think about it – I said, "I think it's time to break up." And there was no negative reaction to that.'

The final tour of the Howard Morrison Quartet in Spring 1964 was a huge event, 'like a long, ongoing party', recalled Morrison.[342] At the final Auckland show on 9 December, the Town Hall was 'packed to the gunnels'. The mayor Sir Dove Myer-Robinson came on stage and said the Quartet's break-up was an 'unnatural disaster'. Morrison: 'That was a really stunning statement. People stood up and cheered. There were tears from the audience. Not from us, of course, we're professionals. We just had to blow our noses a few times on our shirt sleeves.'[343]

The final song was 'Now is the Hour'. To Morrison, the Auckland farewell was more moving than the actual final show in Rotorua's Regent theatre a month later, which 'wasn't a goose-bump show, it was just a show'.[344]

Before they went on, Morrison said backstage, 'There'll be no nostalgia in the songs we sing. This will be treated as just another show.'[345] The Quartet wore its off-white tuxedos in the first half, its blue tuxedos in the second. Among their many hits performed that night, one was conspicuous by its absence: 'My Old Man's an All Black'.

Afterwards, recalled Morrison, they went through their usual routine in their shared dressing room. 'We stood in a row, as we normally did after a good show. I would be in front, clapping my hands, and the boys would be patting one another on the back and patting me on the back . . . . We just said "Cher!", shook hands and went out of the dressing room into the dark to make our separate ways home. No farewell party, no hullaballo.'[346]

Gerry Merito remembered it differently. 'We never shook hands, we never said hooray. I went to Howard's room. It was empty. I went to Noel's room and he must have left in his suit, as if he couldn't get out the door quick enough.

'I never thought the Quartet would break up. I didn't really believe it, so I had no ambitions, and nothing planned. I had four kids to worry about . . . . There must have been a lot of pressure towards the end for Howard. The other boys

In 1966 Gerry Merito's only solo album, *I Must Have Been a Beautiful (Baby) Spaceman* followed the Quartet's repertoire of comedy, parodies, topical and Maori songs. Impact Records/RNZ Music Library, Wellington

sort of went with the flow. They ran with the hounds and hunted with the hares. The pressure on Howard would have lifted off, but I didn't have that feeling. I just thought, What now? It wasn't a frightening feeling. I had a pocket full of money, and no ambitions. And people's memories.'[347]

Morrison was later rueful that 'in pursuit of the market', the Quartet's 'respect for the language and the culture wasn't always what it should have been'. But 40 years after their heyday, he could see there was also much to be proud of: the Quartet pioneered so many areas of the music industry. And it was 'accepted nationally, without being branded as *The Howard Morrison Quartet: Maori*. It was just the Howard Morrison Quartet, embraced by New Zealand. And we were able to bring Maori culture to the white, Pakeha majority. So the Maori part of us, we didn't have to beat our chests about. It just came out naturally.'[348]

1964: A TWIST IN TIME

Sitting on the bank at the Bowl of Brooklands for each *Showtime Spectacular* tour in the early 1960s was the Prime family from Hawera. A young Maori boy, already a good singer but with ambitions to become an *entertainer*,

Merv Thomas (with trombone) and His Dixielanders fanfare the movie *Pepe*, Queen Street, Auckland, 1961. Doig Photography/Merv Thomas collection

enjoyed vocalists such as the Clive Trio and Rama White. But one act in particular he watched with intense concentration. 'I used to sit there dreaming, thinking *that's* what I want to be', recalled Dalvanius Maui Prime. 'The Howard Morrison Quartet, they were incredible entertainers. Maori had their mega heroes. But the thing about the Quartet was there were all these Pakeha people getting into it as well.' He realised it could be done: Maori, singing in Maori, to a huge mainstream audience.[349]

As the Quartet's success escalated, the music industry evolved and re-organised itself for a new era in which pop groups would take over. In Auckland during 1961, there was fierce competition between the Orange Ballroom and a usurper around the corner on Symonds Street: the Oriental Ballroom. The Chinese community had bought the old State theatre and remodelled it into an upmarket cabaret. The bands hired to play during the week – and

the dance policies – illustrate the transition. Wednesdays were '50/50' nights, with music by the Al Paget Sextet and the dances equally split between ballroom style and jiving. Thursdays at the Oriental featured Merv Thomas and His Dixielanders; on Fridays, Bernie Allen conducted an ambitious eighteen-piece band. Even Bill Sevesi was enticed away from his long residency around the corner at the Orange.[350] But within three months Sevesi had been wooed back, and Thomas and Allen's bands were gone. 'The guitar bands have taken over the local scene more than somewhat', reported Warren.[351]

Meanwhile, Christchurch teenagers were enjoying the rivalry between its two leading bands. Max Merritt and the Meteors could rely on its dedicated fan base, which at its peak included 1200 members of the Teen Agers Club. Ray Columbus and the Invaders' frontman was such a showman the group had been given its own music

BLUE SMOKE

television series, *Club Columbus*. The two bands needed to strike out for more lucrative territory.

'It's legend now', Ray Columbus said in 2009, 'but promoters would come to town and catch our shows at the Plainsman and offer us deals to go to Auckland.' One night in 1962, the Howard Morrison Quartet was topping the bill at the Majestic, and the theatre manager Trevor King told them about the Invaders. 'So Howard came over after their show and caught ours', said Columbus. 'He talked me into going to Auckland – he said we'd "kill them" up there – so we took one of the offers and he was right. We were the toast of the Queen City.'[352]

The Invaders and Meteors struck Auckland almost simultaneously in December 1962, 'just prior to the Beatles' rise and the Shadows' decline'.[353] Auckland's rock'n'roll venues had proliferated in the years since Devlin arrived, and these two polished, energetic, R&B savvy visitors from Canterbury arrived as the advance guard of the beat boom.

In the same month, the popular Louis Prima act developed by Merv Thomas, with Marlene Tong and the Prophets, came to an end when promoter Philip Warren signed the popular Keil Isles for a £10,000 contract for 12 months.[354] The entertainment advertisements in the *Auckland Star* show the 1963 nightlife economy to be

buoyant, plus a generational shift. New clubs catered for young audiences: the Monaco on Federal Street, the Shiralee on Customs Street (run by Eldred Stebbing, it was later called the Galaxie), the Top 20 in Durham Lane. The drawcards at these venues were rock'n'roll groups: the Keil Isles, the Meteors, the Invaders, the Kavaliers, the Playboys (up from Christchurch, with Phil Garland and Diane Jacobs/Dinah Lee), the Embers double-billed with the Maori showband the Quin Tikis.[355] Al Paget ended an era when he said farewell to the North Shore at the Bayswater, but some in the old guard carried on: Bill Sevesi at the Orange, the Maurie Antony Sextet with 'tuneful dancing' at St Sep's.

What connected the two subcultures was not just a support act (the Convairs, a folk trio, which many of the clubs shared on the same night). Each advertisement emphasised dancing, and the opportunity to try the latest styles. At St Sep's, Reona Morris hoped to beat her own world record at the limbo, while at the Jive Centre the Nitebeats introduced a new dance from Europe, the tamouré twist. A doomed novelty in early 1962 was the beach dance, not just because participants needed to wear beach gear. Its timing was wrong. Like everywhere else in the Western world, the twist swept New Zealand's dance floors.[356]

During the twist boom, Wellington's Blockbusters released 'Twisters Twist' as a cardboard single to promote a shoe manufacturer. Phono 2904 Lc, Alexander Turnbull Library, Wellington

The dance was as simple as the song. Chubby Checker, its evangelist, said: 'Just pretend you're wiping your bottom with a towel as you get out of the shower, and putting out a cigarette with both feet.'[357] In Auckland, the twist received its first prominent exposure in January 1962, when a young American couple from a visiting cruise ship gave a 'frenzied preview' at the Oriental Ballroom. According to Phil Warren, it brought the other 600 dancers to a standstill, while they watched open-mouthed. 'If they want to twist, they can twist', he said at a demonstration held at the Fred Astaire dance studio. *Truth* went along with the hype: 'Some of the improvisations are hot. Some, it is alleged, verge on the obscene.'[358]

The NZBS decision – in its dying days before becoming a corporation on April Fool's Day, 1962 – that Checker's version of 'The Twist' was too noisy to get radio play gave the Keil Isles a windfall when they recorded their own rendition. The group followed with sequels – 'Twisting New Zealand Way', 'Twist It Up', 'Twist and Freeze' – and many other New Zealanders tried to cut in on the dance. The Don Ball Orchestra offered the 'Boogie Twist', Fia Chaplin wanted to 'Twist With the Yeti', Tommy Kahi multi-tracked the 'Twist Train Boogie', Tony and the Initials tried flattery with 'Mr DJ Twist' and then 'Twistin' Time' (written by the versatile Sam Freedman), while Bob Paris and the Peppermints branded theirs the 'Paris Twist'. The Blockbusters' 'Twisters Twist' was released as a square cardboard single to promote a footwear company. But clearing the floor on this cluttered dance card was 'Poi Poi Twist', in which Rim D. Paul and the Quin Tikis deliver a statement of rangatiratanga and an irresistible piece of pop. After a stately a cappella opening of 'E Aue', with exuberant boogie piano and honking saxophone, Paul insists:

> It's a Maori melody
> Come along and twist with me
> Poi poi and twist the night away . . . .[359]

Although many of the popular musicians who had begun performing in the swing era were just turning 40, their world was being eclipsed by a younger generation with guitars and amplifiers. The New Zealand recording industry was producing a wave of local releases unseen since the first flurry after 'Blue Smoke'. Although most of these singles did not threaten the imported competition, companies such as Viking and Zodiac seemed to be able

to survive with sales averaging about 1000, plus the occasional hit.

The swing, jazz and dance-band musicians who had prospered and kept New Zealand couples entertained from the 1930s to the 1950s had been served early redundancy notices. With their audience, they may have been bewildered, sidelined and even offended by rock'n'roll, but they got some kind of reward in the early 1960s when their heroes started to arrive on concert tours. For the first time since the 1920s, international acts began touring on a regular basis, and they came like an armada. Visitors in the mid-1950s such as the Ted Heath Band and Winifred Atwell were influential. Then, after a dry spell, the early 1960s saw a virtual flood: the Dave Brubeck Quartet, Ella Fitzgerald, Pete Jolly and Ralph Pena, Oscar Peterson, the Modern Jazz Quartet, Sarah Vaughan, Dizzy Gillespie, Eddie Condon, Thelonious Monk, and the biggest name of the century, Louis Armstrong.

Jazz fans greeted them exuding unconcealed awe: tootling dixie combos and Maori welcoming parties at the airports, extensive press coverage, formal receptions, informal parties where locals such as Crombie Murdoch and Marlene Tong impressed the visitors. The encounter with Vaughan and Gillespie was fractious; to the horror of the local backing bands, which included many of New Zealand's top players of the day, there were no music charts provided. Vaughan's pianist, Roland Hanna, saved her set by putting the New Zealand rhythm section – George Campbell and Don Branch – through hours of rehearsals. But Gillespie was arrogant and unhelpful, leaving the musicians disillusioned and his audiences disappointed. Lew Campbell's fourteen-piece band, hired to back Gillespie, was abandoned, leaving just Campbell's quartet as the accompaniment. After the 6.15 pm concert, Gillespie insisted on appearing with Vaughan's trio for the 8.30 pm show. 'The transformation was astounding', reported Ray Harris. Gillespie showed his satisfaction by doubling his time on stage to twenty minutes.[360]

'I think he had really inflated ideas about himself', recalled Lew Campbell. '"I'm Dizzy Gillespie, everybody knows me and they know my stuff." But he was quite wrong. He was in New Zealand, for goodness sake.'[361]

The visits of the Dave Brubeck Quartet were happier. The Maori welcome at Wellington airport for his first tour in 1960 inspired Brubeck to write 'Maori Blues', a 6/4 piece on his *Time Further Out* album. After their second

Above: Louis Armstrong touches down at Whenuapai airport, Auckland, 1963. Jim Warren collection

Top left: Jazz aficionado Ces Howard-Smith welcomes Winifred Atwell to Auckland, 1955. Bennie Gunn collection

Bottom left: Dave Brubeck with some of the Auckland jazz players who supported him, 1960. From left, Crombie Murdoch, George Campbell, Dave Brubeck, Lew Campbell, Bernie Allen, Neville Blanchet, Don Branch. Bernie Allen collection

visit in 1962, the quartet's bass player Eugene Wright stayed behind in Wellington to record an album of his own pieces. On *The Wright Groove* a trio of New Zealanders accompanied him: Lew Campbell on piano, saxophonist Laurie Lewis and Don Branch on drums. Overseeing the sessions was Bob Bothamley. Though the New Zealand musicians were unprepared and sceptical about the material, Wright was enthusiastic. 'The feeling was there and it was well played', he said. 'Actually you'd think that these were American musicians.'[362]

In the same period, rock'n'roll acts began to visit with similar frequency. Phil Warren promoted a groundbreaking show in 1959: Johnny Cash and Gene Vincent. Many other acts soon followed; some were at the height of their fame (Cliff Richard, Helen Shapiro,

Ben E. King), others had peaked (Johnnie Ray, Chubby Checker). Most arrived with just a minder, and perhaps a musical director who hired a local backing band. Here, the two camps shared stages: the rock'n'roll musicians and the old school, reading dots, sharing stories, grumbling about promoters.[363]

The small inner-city club scene could only thrive while costs were low. This was helped by the rundown buildings, pegged for demolition, with cheap rents for those who wanted to open a club. Also, the early 1960s was the last era in which entertainment options were not affected by television. As the wooden cabinets appeared in more homes, cinemas and nightclubs found their older customers were increasingly reluctant to go out, especially while hotel drinking hours still finished at sunset.

The biggest change came in 1963–64 with the sensational success of the Beatles. Working musicians unable to comb their hair forward found that 'no one wanted saxophones, trumpets and pianists any more'.[364] Record companies sought groups that sounded like the Beatles, and the variety of musical styles decreased. Sales of guitars boomed, and while many stayed under beds, aspiring young musicians now had different goals. At dances and social functions, amplified small combos could provide music at less expense.

Dance-band stalwart Ken Avery found many of his fellow musicians 'put away their saxophones and trumpets during the guitar band craze and unfortunately never got them out again'. When the opening hours of licensed premises were extended to 10.00 pm in 1967, Avery found that this was no help to his cohorts. While hotels started hiring bands, they were usually rock bands; if cocktail music was required, only a pianist and rhythm section were needed. 'Beatles and beer in that order ruined the New Zealand dance band business', he said. Although Avery approved of 10.00 pm closing, he remembered 'with some affection' the more restrictive regime –

> . . . when all the Wellington musicians would gather for drinks between five and six o'clock at the Forester's Arms Hotel. There could be up to 30 or 40 of us. If you needed a drummer or pianist to play that night, you only had to ask around the bar. We all went home quite merrily at 6.00 pm, had our evening meals, showered, changed into evening clothes and set out for our various dance band jobs. Ten o'clock closing spelt the end of a lot of worthwhile evening activities. An office with, say, 50 staff might organise an evening social and dance. Wives, sweethearts and friends would be invited, a small hall and band would be hired and everyone would have an enjoyable time . . . . Once 10 o'clock closing came in, these social evenings seemed to fade away and were replaced with a gathering for drinks at a hotel.[365]

The Beatles' influence was all-pervasive. After the heyday of the twist, couples no longer needed to dance together, so formal dance steps and strict tempos faded. The repertoire of songs required for these dances did too, though – in the spirit of the breeze and the Charleston – occasional song-specific novelties appeared in future years, such as the hustle and line dancing. To jazz musicians, songs were standards to be interpreted, while in rock music 'cover bands' became a term of derision. The talents of

Lennon and McCartney had another long-term spin-off: acts were expected to write and perform their own songs. The dedicated songwriters who stayed in the background – such as Sam Freedman – became the exceptions.

Watching the world they had enjoyed for decades disappear, many established musicians and the media were dismissive of the Beatles. Avery quotes a music store manager whose informants told him the band had a stable of songwriters on its payroll. *Listener* editor Monte Holcroft hoped to understand the Beatles' attraction by listening through a young person's ears. He almost succeeded, but declared, 'It is our hope and indeed firm intention that, having heard the Beatles once, we shall not hear them again.' Luck played a great part in the group's success, he suggested; it 'could have fallen just as easily on the Katipos or the Huhus, if those groups existed'.[366]

Jim Warren seemed bemused by the response to the group during their June 1964 tour, the screaming fans and 'intense, bally-hoo' media coverage. 'Although their music has little appeal for the musician or the older concert-goer, their act is a completely clean and healthy one and the kids certainly got a great charge from them.'[367] Howard Morrison expressed disdain towards the Beatles' phenomenon, but – for Harry Miller's La Gloria label – seized the opportunity to write and record a parody, 'I Want to Cut Your Hair': 'In your Beatle wig/oh I do not dig/the shaggy hair you wear . . .' (credited as backing band were the Huhus).[368] Phil Warren opened a teenage club called the Beatle Inn on Auckland's Little Queen Street (which later disappeared under the Downtown Centre). With an R18 entrance policy – no one *over* 18 was permitted – the club ran successfully for several years. The resident band, playing appropriate covers, was called the Merseymen; it was led by Bob Paris and included 'Jett Rink' (journalist Dylan Taite) on drums.[369] Tommy Adderley adjusted his Birmingham accent to be more Liverpudlian and recorded an Ann-Margret song called 'I Just Don't Understand' for Viking. To his surprise – 'it out-Scoused a lot of Scouse records' – he received airplay in New Zealand and found himself in the *Cashbox* Top 100 in the US, and with a No 2 hit in Canada – behind the Beatles' 'A Hard Day's Night'.[370]

Public broadcasting also responded to the increased energy in popular music. In the late 1950s, the NZBS's hesitant support of local pop talent had been felt across the industry. Eldred Stebbing found it difficult to get airplay for his Zodiac releases.[371] Television may have made the

The Beatles meet the Maori Hi-Five, Hong Kong, 9 June 1964. From left: Paul McCartney, Wes Epae, John Lennon, Kawana Pohe, Paddy Te Tai, George Harrison, Rob Hemi, Solomon Pohatu, and the local booking agent Frankie Blair. In front: assistant manager of the Hotel Escalante. Ringo Starr was absent due to tonsillitis. Fairfax Media Sundays Archive

old ballrooms echo but – combined with its commercial radio service – for nearly fifteen years from the mid-1960s the NZBC's commitment to local popular music was strong and its influence positive. Initiatives such as Kevan Moore's *C'mon* television series and commercial radio's Loxene Golden Disc awards helped the local pop music industry achieve its boom years, in record and ticket sales – and airplay.

But to those who came of age listening to pre-war Louis Armstrong 78s, dancing to Epi Shalfoon, or could recall the thrill of Artie Shaw's visit, an inevitable ennui was understandable. In 1963 Jim Warren, in demand as a trumpeter since the 1930s – and uncle of the entrepreneur known as Phil – indulged in some reflection. He observed that after Christmas each year, 'the Big Sag sets in and lips get soft, fingers are not so supple and if there are no jobs,

who cares? There is always the beach and the fishing lines and the boats.'

Practice tends to be forgotten and there's that strange but pleasant feeling of sitting at home with a few friends with a few bottles, or just sitting.

Television. Now there's something to while away the time, but after a period the old itch comes along and the realisation that the phone may ring and you'll be packing the horn in the back of the car and off to slay a job. So reluctantly but sensibly you start again on the long notes, the exercises and the scales and gradually you find that the old skill comes slowly back.

Rehearsal bands offered some solace, said Warren, and enthusiasts from a younger wave of local jazz musicians

– Bernie Allen and Wayne Senior – had established just the group. Most of the players were in their 20s, without many outlets for a blow.

'Auckland is now practically a 100 percent guitar town, and little groups like this are so important for reed and brass players. For, who knows, one of these days there may be a big band job in the town hall – and some of the oldsters aren't going to be blowing for ever.'[372]

An English band in the 1990s went by the name Pop Will Eat Itself. That's the nature of the business. The music keeps changing while the dominant market – hormonal teenagers, courting couples – is constantly rejuvenated, carving out its own identity. The music and musicians of an earlier era may seem rejected, by all but nostalgists and historians, but the connections between generations are in fact strong. Eldred Stebbing provides a link between Artie Shaw's visit and Dave Dobbyn; Jim Warren between Ted Croad and Johnny Devlin; Don Richardson between the Kiwi Concert Party and 'St Paul', the 1969 hit he arranged for Shane.

In 2007 the record industry created a 'music hall of fame' that seems destined to choose as its inductees only musicians from the rock era – while Eldred Stebbing was still alive, and Bill Sevesi still performing. In the 2000s, New Zealand music has enjoyed support from the public and media unseen since the boom years of the late 1960s and early 1970s, when it had the support of television shows such as *C'mon* and *Happen Inn*, and radio. Then, Broadcasting and local music worked together, but ironically the factor that finally broke the conservatism of New Zealand radio – the arrival of pirate, and then private, stations – would also bring competition that resulted in local music being left in the cold. A cultural cringe developed in many crucial quarters, especially radio, thanks in part to playlists that took their lead from US radio consultants. In the 1990s, government funding initiatives finally brought New Zealand voices back to its broadcasting media – which had generally been supportive in the years covered by this book – albeit often in homogenous international styles.

As much as each new generation likes to think it reinvents popular music, their contribution is only one step in an evolution. For well over a century, the popular music baton has been passed, taking detours and always absorbing influences. From the visiting Fisk Jubilee Singers and Hawaiian troupes before the First World War, to the Howard Morrison Quartet that concludes this story, the connections exist – and continue. The success of the Quartet and Johnny Devlin established the modern popular music industry, but their careers were built on those they replaced.

As to the music itself, popular music of the past century is derivative: that is the nature of market-oriented art. The enthusiasm with which changes in popular music in the US were adopted globally can be seen as cultural imperialism or cultural appropriation. Or, as give and take: they give, we take. We may have adopted the game of rugby from Britain, for example, but see nothing unusual in the fact that for many decades our players were the world's best. So it is to be expected that our musicians can excel at a borrowed art form and turn it into something unique.

It happened in 1983 when Dalvanius and the Patea Maori Club's 'Poi E' mixed break beats and kapa haka. It happened in 1996, when OMC's 'How Bizarre' blended mariachi horns with a distinctively Pacific swing. These songs referenced the past and combined their influences into something that could only come from New Zealand.

Opposite: Save the last dance for me: a jiving couple, somewhere in New Zealand, down the hall on a Saturday night. 'Rock'n'roll', *NZ Herald*/Auckland War Memorial Museum neg. H1998

NOTES

ONE WELCOME TO THE JAZZ AGE

1 Geoffrey W. Rice, *Black November*, Canterbury University Press, Christchurch, 2nd edn, 2005, p. 75.
2 Ida Reilly, quoted in Rice, *Black November*, p. 95.
3 *NZ Observer*, 12 November 1918.
4 Rice, *Black November*, pp. 119–20.
5 *NZ Herald*, 15 November 1918.
6 *Dominion*, 13 November 1918.
7 *Dominion*, 13 November 1918.
8 Geoffrey Rice, conversation with Chris Bourke, December 2009.
9 John MacGibbon, *Piano in the Parlour*, Ngaio Press, Wellington, 2007, p. 99.
10 Winston McCarthy, *Listen! It's a Goal!*, Pelham, London, 1973, pp. 19–20.
11 'Our Future – New Zealand', *Talking Machine News*, January/February 1919, p. 314.
12 MacGibbon, *Piano in the Parlour*, pp. 71–72; *Come Inside* revue programme, Grand Opera House, Wellington, 3 June 1918, Eph-B-Variety-1918-Efl, ATL.
13 Bruce Anderson, *Story of the New Zealand Recording Industry*, self-published, Wellington, 1984, p. 20.
14 As quoted in John Mansfield Thomson, *The Oxford History of New Zealand Music*, Oxford University Press, Auckland, 1991, p. 163.
15 T. Lindsay Buick, *The Romance of the Gramophone*, Ernest Dawson, Wellington, 1927, p. 60.
16 *The History of Recording in New Zealand: 1. Beginnings*, www.natlib.govt.nz; Anderson, *Story of the New Zealand Recording Industry*, pp. 1–3; MacGibbon, *Piano in the Parlour*, p. 97.
17 Anderson, *Story of the New Zealand Recording Industry*, p. 5.
18 Bryan Staff and Sheran Ashley, *For the Record: A History of the Recording Industry in New Zealand*, David Bateman, Auckland, 2002, p. 30.
19 *The History of Recording in New Zealand: 1. Beginnings*; Brian Salkeld, 'The Dancing Decade 1920–1930', *Stout Centre Review*, August 1992, p. 7.
20 Peter Downes, *Top of the Bill*, Reed, Wellington, 1979, pp. 49–59.
21 *NZ Theatre and Motion Picture*, 15 March 1921, p. 26.
22 Salkeld, 'The Dancing Decade 1920–1930', p. 3.
23 Wilton Baird, 'As It Was in the Beginning', *NZ Radio Record*, 17 June 1938, p. 13.
24 Igor Stravinsky, who was demonstrating this at the time in *Le Sacre du Printemps* (1913) and *Histoire du Soldat* (1918).
25 *Evening Post*, 25 November 1901, p. 4.
26 *Evening Post*, 3 May 1912, p. 4; 14 January 1914, p. 2.
27 John Whiteoak, '"Jazzing" and Australia's First Jazz Band', *Popular Music*, vol. 13, no. 3, 1994, p. 280.
28 *NZ Herald*, 12 June 1918, p. 6.
29 *Sun* (Sydney), 30 June 1918.
30 *Grey River Argus*, 8 July 1919, p. 4. Among Weir's other hits were 'When You Go Out Walking' (performed by music hall queen Violet Lorraine) and 'Loved One at Last'. He was later musical director of the Smart Set Diggers, an Australian troupe.
31 *Dominion*, 14 August 1919, p. 4.
32 *Dominion*, 18 August 1919, p. 5.
33 James J. Nott, *Music For the People: Popular Music and Dance in Interwar Britain*, Oxford University Press, Oxford, 2002, p. 129.
34 Bruce Johnson, *The Oxford Companion to Australian Jazz*, Oxford University Press, Melbourne, 1987, p. 10.
35 Programme, His Majesty's Theatre, Wellington, 28 June 1915, Eph-B-Variety-1915-Efl, ATL; Walter Sinton, 'Very Sad Goodbye to the Old Princess', *Evening Star* (Dunedin), 28 December 1974, p. 11.
36 Walter Sinton, *Evening Star*, 11 November 1975, p. 11.
37 *NZ Herald*, 12 June 1918, p. 5.
38 *NZ Herald*, 15 June 1918, p. 12.
39 [John Mansfield Thomson], 'Music in the Dark', *NZ Listener*, 22 February 1957, p. 7; the song was from the 1917 Rudolf Friml musical *You're in Love*.
40 *Northern Advocate*, 28 August 1975; *NZ Herald*, 2 May 1998, p. A10.
41 Bruce W. and Selwyn P. Hayward, *Cinemas of Auckland 1896–1979*, Lodestar Press, Auckland, 1979, p. 2.
42 Gordon Ingham, *Everyone's Gone to the Movies: The Sixty Cinemas of Auckland*, Minerva, Auckland, 1973, p. 14.
43 Clive Sowry, 'Hayward, Henry John 1865–1945', *Dictionary of New Zealand Biography*, updated 22 June 2007 (http://www.dnzb.govt.nz/); P. A. Harrison, *The Motion Picture Industry in New Zealand 1896–1930*, MA thesis, Auckland University, 1974, p. 65.
44 Thomson, *The Oxford History of New Zealand Music*, p. 158.
45 Harrison, *The Motion Picture Industry in New Zealand*, p. 65.
46 Jim Sullivan, 'Music for the Silent Movies – Violet Capstick', in Jim Sullivan (ed.), *Canterbury Voices: First-hand Memories of Canterbury's Past*, Hazard, Christchurch, 2007, pp. 52–57.
47 Margaret Fahey interview, *Spectrum* documentary 214A, 'A Piano For All Seasons', produced by Jack Perkins, Radio New Zealand, 1 January 1977.
48 Sullivan, 'Music for the Silent Movies – Violet Capstick'.
49 Vern Wilson, oral history interview by Patricia French, 3 August 1984, Auckland Central City Library, # 90-OH-007-1-10.
50 Advertisement, *Evening Post*, 29 September 1913, p. 2.
51 [Thomson], 'Music in the Dark'.
52 J. M. Thomson, 'Austin, Louis Daly Irving 1877–1967', *Dictionary of New Zealand Biography*, updated 22 June 2007 (http://www.dnzb.govt.nz/).
53 Redmer Yska, *Wellington: Biography of a City*, Reed, Auckland, 2007, p. 129.
54 Pat Lawlor, *Confessions of a Journalist*, Whitcombe & Tombs, Christchurch, 1935, pp. 87 and 252.
55 Lawlor, *Confessions of a Journalist*; Kerry Howe, *Singer in a Songless Land: A Life of Edward Tregear*, Auckland University Press, Auckland, 1991, p. 198; Chris Brickell, *Mates & Lovers: A History of Gay New Zealand*, Godwit, Auckland, 2008, p. 106; Peter Kitchin, 'Head Turner', *Dominion Post*, 20 January 2007, p. E8.
56 Whiteoak, '"Jazzing" and Australia's First Jazz Band', p. 282.
57 Dennis O. Huggard (ed.), *The Thoughts of Musician Desmond 'Spike' Donovan*, New Zealand Series No. 5, Dennis O. Huggard, Henderson, 1998, p. 26.
58 Ronald Pearsall, *Popular Music of the 20s*, David & Charles, Vancouver, BC, pp. 55-56.
59 Pearsall, *Popular Music of the 20s*, p. 59.
60 *Timaru Herald*, 8 February 1921 and 4 March 1921; Johnny Williams file, MS-Papers-9018-50, Dennis Huggard Archive (DHA), ATL; Diana Rhodes (ed.), *With My Camera for Company*, Hazard, Christchurch, 2003, p. 143.
61 Sandra Potter, 'The Man Who Formed Auckland's First Jazz Band!', *NZ Woman's Weekly*, 15 November 1971, p. 19; Huggard, *The Thoughts of Musician Desmond 'Spike' Donovan*, p. 8.
62 Nott, *Music For the People*, p. 128; Jim Godbolt, *A History of Jazz in Britain, 1919–1950*, Northway, London, 2005, pp. 8–11.
63 Henry Shirley, *Just a Bloody Piano Player*, Price, Auckland, 1971, p. 53. Australia received its first ODJB disc in 1921 – 'Lazy Daddy': see Johnson, *The Oxford Companion to Australian Jazz*, p. 9.
64 Laurie Lewis, *Arthur and the Nights at the Turntable: The Life and Times of a Jazz Broadcaster*, K'vrie Press, Wingen, NSW, 1997, p. 32.
65 George Whitnall Snow, in Huggard (ed.), *The Thoughts of Musician Desmond 'Spike' Donovan*, p. 23.
66 Walter Smith, 'From the Leaves of an Old Family Bible', *Te Karere*, May 1941, p. 658.
67 Taina W. Josephs ('formerly Diane [sic] Greening'), letter to Spike Donovan, MS 1451 85/29, Auckland Museum. Saxophones were heard in New Zealand brass band circles from at least the 1880s, and in vaudeville from 1900: *Christchurch Star*, 20 March 1884, p. 2; *Wanganui Chronicle*, 28 September 1888, p. 2; *Otago Witness*, 3 October 1900, p. 55.
68 Walter Smith, leader, saxophone, mandolin and guitar; Thompson Yandall snr, banjo; Lew Munro, piano; Arthur Adams, drums; Sydney David Kamau, saxophone.
69 Vern Wilson, oral history interview by Patricia French.
70 Gus Sorenson, 'Strings Are His Business', *NZ Woman's Weekly*, no date, c. 1952, p. 14.
71 *NZ Radio Record*, 12 August 1927, p. 8.
72 Huggard (ed.), *The Thoughts of Musician Desmond 'Spike' Donovan*, p. 21.
73 *NZ Herald*, 31 December 1929.
74 Jimmy Higgot, interviewed by Geoffrey Totton, 27 April 1987.
75 Huggard (ed.), *The Thoughts of Musician Desmond 'Spike' Donovan*, p. 24; Jimmy Higgot, interviewed by Geoffrey Totton.
76 Taina W. Josephs, letter to Spike Donovan.
77 Huggard (ed.), *The Thoughts of Musician Desmond 'Spike' Donovan*, p. 24.
78 'Dixie Jubilee Singers', *NZ Herald*, 5 January 1925, p. 14; 6 January 1925, p. 9; Max Cryer, *NZ Herald*, 12 October 1989, p. 2:1.
79 Sorenson, 'Strings Are His Business'.
80 Huggard (ed.), *The Thoughts of Musician Desmond 'Spike' Donovan*, pp. 46, 49, 51.
81 Shirley, *Just a Bloody Piano Player*, pp. 53–56.
82 Shirley, *Just a Bloody Piano Player*, p. 47; Potter, 'The Man Who Formed Auckland's First Jazz Band!', p. 19.
83 Shirley, *Just a Bloody Piano Player*, p. 53.
84 Owen Shaw, 'A Pioneer Among the Music Makers', *NZ Herald*, 13 May 1981, p. B1.
85 Potter, 'The Man Who Formed Auckland's First Jazz Band!'.
86 Potter, 'The Man Who Formed Auckland's First Jazz Band!'.
87 Huggard (ed.), *The Thoughts of Musician Desmond 'Spike' Donovan*, p. 51.
88 Potter, 'The Man Who Formed Auckland's First Jazz Band!'.
89 Advertisement, *NZ Truth*, 11 August 1923.
90 Spike Donovan explained the difference between venues: cabarets had tables and chairs, whereas dance halls had seating forms around the walls. Cabarets did not necessarily feature other entertainment; and many venues called cabarets were actually just dance halls (Huggard [ed.], *The Thoughts of Desmond 'Spike' Donovan*, p. 37).
91 Dick Scott, *Fire on the Clay: The Pakeha Comes to West Auckland*, Southern Cross, Auckland, 1997, pp. 84–92; Georgina White, *Light Fantastic: Dance Floor Courtship in New Zealand*, HarperCollins, Auckland, 2007, pp. 52–53; Graham W. A. Bush, *The History of Epsom*, Epsom & Eden District Historical Society, Auckland, 2006, pp. 23 and 188. Ethel Rayner's fortune came from meat-packing, and the Mt Eden mansion was later bought by arts patron James Wallace. The

Dixieland's building at 438 Queen Street revived its music connection in 1989 as the home of Real Groovy Records.

92   White, *Light Fantastic*, p. 51; *NZ Herald*, 21 October 1922, p. 6.
93   Huggard (ed.), *The Thoughts of Musician Desmond 'Spike' Donovan*, p. 10; *NZ Theatre and Motion Picture*, 1 May 1922, p. 12.
94   *NZ Observer*, 30 September 1922, p. 12; 6 January 1923, p. 13.
95   Squire Speedy, 'Early Entertainment in Milford' (http://www.speedy.co.nz/funmerchant/index.htm, accessed March 2010).
96   Besides Frost and Wilson, the quintet included trombonist Fred Swanberg, Ces Little on saxophone and Alby Green on drums: Dennis Huggard, 'Jazz in New Zealand', *Crescendo*, April 2004, p. 14; Vern Wilson, oral history interview by Patricia French.
97   Vern Wilson, oral history interview by Patricia French.
98   Report of the Committee of the Board of Health to Study Venereal Diseases, AJHR, 1922, H-31A, pp. 11–12.
99   'Modern Dances', *Press*, 30 August 1922, p. 8.
100 Walter Sinton, 'The Diggers Kept in Pace with Show Trends', *Evening Star*, 22 February 1975, p. 11.
101 'Mania for Dancing', *Press*, 28 November 1923, p. 5.
102 'Mixing Champagne and Cocktails in Cuddle Cubicles', *NZ Truth*, 5 August 1926, p. 7.
103 'Music in the Dominion', *Auckland Star*, Auckland Central City Library reviews scrapbook, 1922, p. 62.
104 Lindsay Brinsdon, 'True Jazz is "Down" in the Capital but Not Out', *Evening Post*, 11 June 1966, p. 29; unsourced advertisements, Eph-B-Cabot-Scrapbook-69, ATL.
105 *Fuller News*, 14 March 1925, p. 2, from an illustration in Andrew Bisset, *Black Roots, White Flowers: A History of Jazz in Australia*, ABC, Sydney, 2nd edn, 1987, p. 16.
106 Prompter, *NZ Observer*, 24 November 1923, p. 12.
107 *NZ Theatre and Motion Picture*, 1 January 1924, p. 45.
108 Bisset, *Black Roots, White Flowers*, p. 26.
109 *NZ Herald*, 3 December 1924, p. 15.
110 *NZ Herald*, 8 December 1924, p. 11.
111 Bisset, *Black Roots, White Flowers*, p. 22.
112 See chapter 5, Canaries and Cowboys: 1950s Pop Scenes, 'South Seas Rhythm'.
113 Shirley, *Just a Bloody Piano Player*, pp. 58–61.
114 Shirley, *Just a Bloody Piano Player*, p. 61.
115 'The Great Unknowns', *Tempo* (Australia), February/March 1939; Bissett, *Black Roots, White Flowers*, p. 49; Johnston, *The Oxford Companion to Australian Jazz*, p. 74.
116 Jack McEwen, 'Dance Music in Maoriland', *Australian Music Maker and Dance Band News (AMM)*, 1 December 1933, p. 41.
117 Bisset, *Black Roots, White Flowers*, p. 49.
118 Jack McEwen, 'Notes from New Zealand', *AMM*, November 1938.
119 *Spectrum* documentary 582, 'And Jim Played Banjo', produced by Alwyn Owen, Radio New Zealand, 1987; *AMM*, March 1963; 'Long-time Dance Pianist Dies', *Auckland Star*, 17 August 1977, p. 3.
120 *NZ Herald*, 12 August 1925, p. 14.
121 *NZ Observer*, 15 August 1925, p. 8.
122 *NZ Herald*, 12–19 August 1925.
123 *NZ Observer*, 22 August 1925, p. 6.
124 Peter Downes and Peter Harcourt, *Voices in the Air*, Methuen, Wellington, 1975, pp. 11–13; Patrick Day, *The Radio Years*, Auckland University Press, Auckland, 1994, pp. 39–40.
125 Downes and Harcourt, *Voices in the Air*, pp. 13 and 19.
126 Day, *The Radio Years*, p. 45.
127 The entrepreneurial Coutts was also a brewer, immortalised by the beer Kuhtze; his brewery later became the Taihape musicians' club. Coutts closed his station in 1928, moving to Auckland to concentrate on television: '2AQ (Taihape) Closes Down', *NZ Radio Record*, 2 November 1928, p. 25.
128 '2AQ (Taihape) Closes Down', *NZ Radio Record*; Day, *The Radio Years*, p. 40.
129 *NZ Radio Record*, 31 August 1928, p. 5.
130 Day, *The Radio Years*, p. 36; Downes and Harcourt, *Voices in the Air*, p. 16.
131 Day, *The Radio Years*, p. 47; *NZ Theatre and Motion Picture*, January 1924, p. 10; Nott, *Music for the People*, p. 218. 'Yes! We Have No Bananas' was an early example of savvy marketing: copies of the sheet music were distributed to band leaders to give away to their dancers, with bananas (Nott).
132 Walter Sinton, 'Dunedin Hosts a Magnificent Display', *Evening Star*, 8 March 1975, p. 11.
133 Sinton, 'Dunedin Hosts a Magnificent Display'. In the late 1920s, Hyman was working at the Bristol Piano Company in Wellington. He and a colleague at the firm, Basil Bird, were the first New Zealand-based musicians to have their bands' portraits printed on sheet music (*AMM*, December 1944).
134 Walter Sinton, 'Exhibition Top Place to Visit', *Evening Star*, 22 March 1975, p. 11.
135 *The Phono Record*, August 1926; Thomson, *Oxford History of New Zealand Music*, p. 165; Staff and Ashley, *For the Record*, p. 26.
136 Thomson, *Oxford History of New Zealand Music*, pp. 164–5.
137 Bruce Anderson, *EMI: Fifty Years in New Zealand*, EMI, Lower Hutt, 1976, p. 2.
138 Anderson, *Story of the New Zealand Record Industry*, p. 16.
139 *Auckland Sun*, 14 July 1928; *Evening Star*, 8 January 1977, p. 8; MacGibbon, *Piano in the Parlour*, p. 100; Thomson, *Oxford History of New Zealand Music*, p. 167.
140 Day, *The Radio Years*, pp. 60–61, 63, 74–75.
141 'When the Office Boy and His Pals Supplied a Dance Band', *NZ Radio Record*, 31 May 1935, p. 6.
142 *AMM*, December 1944; 'Early Radio in New Zealand', *NZ Radio Record*, 31 August 1928, p. 4.
143 Day, *The Radio Years*, pp. 75–76.
144 Downes and Harcourt, *Voices in the Air*, pp. 24–25.

145 *NZ Observer*, 25 August 1923, p. 12; 28 July 1923, p. 27; Walter Sinton, 'Spate of Plays . . . and the Springboks', *Evening Star*, 8 February 1975, p. 11.
146 *NZ Observer*, 11 January 1919, p. 6.
147 Nott, *Music For the People*, pp. 120–1.
148 Salkeld, 'The Dancing Decade 1920–1930', p. 4.
149 Among the acts on the bill were Togo ('the Miraculous Jap') and Mr and Miss Tree ('in an amazing demonstration of Musical Mentalism'): *NZ Theatre and Motion Picture*, 1 May 1922, p. 12.
150 'Harry G. Musgrove's Vaudeville Plans', *NZ Theatre and Motion Picture*, 1 February 1922, p. 34; Walter Sinton, 'Spate of Plays'; Katharine Brisbane (ed.), *Entertaining Australia: An Illustrated History*, Currency Press, Sydney, 1991, p. 192.
151 *NZ Theatre and Motion Picture*, 1 October 1924, p. 9.
152 *NZ Theatre and Motion Picture*, 1 May 1925, p. 17; 1 August 1925, p. 11.
153 'Where Are the Mummers of Yester Year?', *NZ Theatre and Motion Picture*, 1 November 1921, p. 36; 'Brilliant Vaudeville and Why We Are Getting It', *NZ Theatre and Motion Picture*, 1 November 1924, p. 8.
154 'Pokarekare' was first published by Apirana Ngata and Tomoana in 1919, though neither claimed to have composed the song; since then there has been no shortage of applicants. Allan Thomas, '"Pokarekare": An Overlooked New Zealand Folksong?', *Journal of Folklore Research*, vol. 44, nos 2/3, May–December 2007, pp. 227–37; Michele Hewitson, 'Pokarekare Mana', *NZ Herald*, 24 April 1999.
155 Another success with many fathers, 'Now is the Hour' and its contentious authorship feeds many lawyers: Terry Smyth, 'The Unsung Hero', *Sun-Herald* (Sydney), 13 December 2009, p. 6; Alan Sampson, 'Australians Claim Ownership of Famed Maori Farewell Ballad', *Dominion Sunday Times*, 16 August, 1992; Alan Sampson, 'Doubt Grows on Song Lyrics', *Dominion*, 18 August 1992.
156 Parlophone promotional booklet for its recordings made in Rotorua, 1927; liner notes, *Ana Hato raua ko Deane Waretini: Legendary Recordings 1927–49*, Kiwi Pacific.
157 Johannes C. Andersen, 'Maori Song and Music', *NZ Radio Record*, 3 February 1928, p. 2.
158 Alfred Hill, quoted in Thomson's *Oxford History of New Zealand Music*, p. 203.
159 Liner notes, *Ana Hato raua ko Deane Waretini*; Thomas, '"Pokarekare": An Overlooked New Zealand Folksong?'.
160 Liner notes, *Ana Hato raua ko Deane Waretini*.
161 'Maori Singers May Publicize NZ', *Auckland Star*, 8 August 1950, p. 4. After hearing the song in Rotorua, Fields' awareness of it was encouraged by singalongs with Nat Mouncey, a driver provided by the New Zealand government (*NZ Herald*, 20 January 1948).
162 Liner notes, *Ana Hato raua ko Deane Waretini*.
163 Alan Armstrong, 'Still Popular after Thirty Years', *Te Ao Hou*, 36, September 1961, p. 63; Mervyn McLean, *Maori Music*, Auckland University Press, Auckland, 1996, p. 320.
164 Armstrong, 'Still Popular after Thirty Years'; 'Pioneer Returns', *NZ Listener*, 20 March 1964, p. 10.
165 Armstrong, 'Still Popular after Thirty Years'; Rosemary McLeod, 'Ol' Brown Eyes', *North & South*, March 1989, p. 48; McLean, *Maori Music*.
166 Te Mauri Meihana, 'Maori Ear and Polynesian Throat', *NZ Radio Record*, 26 February 1937, p. 12.
167 *Levin Daily Chronicle*, 11 July 1930, quoted in liner notes, *The Tahiwis: Historic 1930 Recordings by Te Whanau Tahiwi*, Atoll CD A9801; National Library of New Zealand/Atoll, 1998.
168 Liner notes, *The Tahiwis*.
169 *Evening Post*, 19 and 21 July 1930.
170 Frank Broad, 'The Amateur Trials of the Early 1920s', *Auckland Star*, 23 February 1963.
171 Eddie Hegan, *No Choice*, Hodder & Stoughton, Auckland, 1980, p. 29.
172 Brisbane (ed.), *Entertaining Australia*; Hegan, *No Choice*, p. 29.
173 Not to be confused with Walter George's Sunshine Players, a professional troupe touring nationally for Fuller's from the 1910s.
174 Hegan, *No Choice*, pp. 31–33.
175 Hegan, *No Choice*, p. 45.
176 Hegan, *No Choice*, pp. 88, 165–8.
177 'JC Williamson presents Henry Santrey and His World Famous Orchestra', programme, Wellington, 1927, Eph-A-Variety-1927, ATL.
178 Julie Benjamin, 'Stuart, Bathia Howie 1893–1987', *Dictionary of New Zealand Biography*, updated 7 July 2005 (http://www.dnzb.govt.nz/).
179 *NZ Theatre and Motion Picture*, 15 January 1921, p. 11.
180 Hamish Keith, *New Zealand Yesterdays*, Reader's Digest, Sydney, 1984, p. 144.
181 'Steam Radio Leaves Studio B', *NZ Listener*, 2 September 1960, p. 4. The national emergency capabilities of 2YA were never tested, and required using 1YA and 3YA as relay stations: Peter Downes to Chris Bourke, 25 February 2010.
182 Downes and Harcourt, *Voices in the Air*, p. 35.
183 *NZ Radio Record*, 26 August 1927; 9 September 1927, p. 14.
184 Downes and Harcourt, *Voices in the Air*, p. 48.
185 Downes and Harcourt, *Voices in the Air*, p. 49.
186 Downes and Harcourt, *Voices in the Air*, p. 49; Staff and Ashley, *For the Record*, p. 26.
187 Salkeld, 'The Dancing Decade', pp. 10–11; *NZ Radio Record*, 2 September 1927, p. 11.
188 *NZ Theatre and Motion Picture*, 1 October 1925, p. 10; 2 November 1925, p. 11.
189 Walter Sinton, *Evening Star*, 6 November 1976, p. 10.
190 Walter Sinton, 'Empire's Glory Thrills Theatregoers', *Evening Star*, 4 December 1976, p. 10.
191 Sinton, 'Empire's Glory Thrills Theatregoers'.
192 Phyllis Bates, 'From the Charleston of 1925 to the Slow Foxtrot of 1935', *NZ Radio Record*, 9 August 1935, p. 62.

193 *NZ Herald*, 24 July 1926, p. 16; 'Dancing Taught by Radio', *NZ Radio Record*, 14 October 1927, p. 16; White, *Light Fantastic*, p. 58; *NZ Herald*, 5 November 1927.
194 Nott, *Music For the People*, p. 153.
195 Salkeld, 'The Dancing Decade', p. 3.
196 Bates, 'From the Charleston of 1925'.
197 'Modern Dancing', *Evening Post*, 29 November 1927, p. 5.
198 *Evening Post*, 23 April 1928, p. 2.
199 Phyllis Bates, 'Will You, Won't You, Join the Dance?', *NZ Truth*, 17 May 1928, p. 11; Wilton Baird, 'As It Was in the Beginning', *NZ Radio Record*, 17 June 1938, p. 13; Bisset, *Black Roots, White Flowers*, p. 27; Bates, 'From the Charleston', p. 62.
200 'Breeze (Blow My Baby Back to Me)', J. Albert & Son, Wellington, c. 1928; *Auckland Sun*, 18 July 1928.
201 *Auckland Sun*, 4–18 July 1928; 16 August 1928.
202 Bates, 'From the Charleston', p. 62; *Evening Post*, April 1928, as quoted in John Griffiths, 'Popular Culture and Modernity', *Journal of Social History*, vol. 41, no. 3, 2008, pp. 617–18; *NZ Truth*, 14 August 1930, p. 7.
203 Elsie Doyle, oral history interview by Patricia French, 13 December 1984, Auckland City Libraries.
204 Elsie Doyle, oral history interview by Patricia French.
205 Squire Speedy, *The Picturedrome Fun Merchant*, L. L. Speedy & Sons, Auckland, 1978, p. 22.
206 Jacqueline Ottaway, 'Ye Olde Pirate Shippe', *New Zealand Memories*, vol. 2, no. 10, 1997, p. 598.
207 *NZ Herald*, 8 September 1928, p. 17; 10 September 1928, p. 5.
208 Katherine Carr, 'On With the Dance', *Weekly News*, 6 September 1928, p. 60.
209 'The Country Dance: Old Steps Favoured', *Weekly News*, 5 January 1928, p. 21.
210 Griffiths, 'Popular Culture and Modernity', p. 620; *NZ Truth*, 14 August 1930, p. 7.
211 Letters from the City Engineers Department and the Traffic and Motor Inspectors' Office to the Town Clerk, 12 July 1928, 18 July 1928, 10 December 1929, Wellington City Archives.
212 'City Council's Decision: Indignation Expressed', *Press*, 2 October 1929, p. 10.
213 Shirley, *Just a Bloody Piano Player*, p. 56.
214 Some experimental short films were screened in Auckland in 1926, with crudely recorded sound and singing: Hayward and Hayward, *Cinemas of Auckland*, p. 17.
215 Frank Broad, 'When Musicians Worked Long and Got Little', *Auckland Star*, 6 October 1962.

TWO MOOD SWINGS: THE 1930S

1   'The Civic Theatre: Brilliant First Night', *NZ Herald*, 21 December 1929, p. 16.
2   Walter Sinton, 'Dunedin's Dream Come True', *Evening Star* (Dunedin), 5 February 1977, p. 10.
3   Walter Sinton, 'Fewer Stage Musicals After "Talkies" Arrived', *Evening Star*, 2 April 1977, p. 9.
4   Irene Gurr, 'The Community Sing', *Otago Before*, August 1995, pp. 6–11.
5   Gurr, 'The Community Sing'.
6   Michael Brown, '"And Everybody Sang" – Community Singing in Wellington, New Zealand', paper presented at New Horizons: New Zealand Folklore Symposium 2007, Victoria University of Wellington, 1 December 2007.
7   Brown, '"And Everybody Sang"'.
8   Gurr, 'The Community Sing'.
9   Dr Keith Barry, 'Radio and Talkies Have Done a Lot for Music', *NZ Radio Record*, 27 March 1936, p. 5.
10 *Spectrum* documentary 582, 'And Jim Played Banjo', produced by Alwyn Owen, Radio New Zealand, 1987.
11 'Dirty Work', *NZ Truth*, 24 September 1931.
12 'Natural Music: Plea for Preservation', *Dominion*, 10 April 1930, p. 10.
13 Frank Egerton, letter to Hon. de la Perrelle, 10 March 1931, IA 1 1/274, Archives NZ.
14 'Govt Bans Foreign Bands . . .', *Everyone's* (Sydney), December 1930, p. 12, IA 1 1/274, Archives NZ.
15 Jack McEwen, 'Dance Music in Maoriland', *AMM*, 1 December 1933, p. 41.
16 *Spectrum* documentary 582, 'And Jim Played Banjo'.
17 Bruce Johnson, 'The Advent of Swing', *Oxford Companion to Australian Jazz*, Melbourne, Oxford University Press, 1987, p. 14.
18 Sheila G. Marshall, 'Old Time Dances', *NZ Railways Magazine*, 1 May 1930, p. 60.
19 McEwen, 'Dance Music in Maoriland'.
20 'Dancing Time', *NZ Radio Record*, 11 August 1933, pp. 12–13; *AMM*, March 1934.
21 Jim Warren, interviewed by Chris Bourke, Auckland, July 2006.
22 Vern Wilson, oral history interview by Patricia French, 3 August 1984, # 90-OH-007-1-10, Auckland Central City Library.
23 Marcia Russell, 'Band on the Air', *NZ Listener*, 11 September 1982, p. 22.
24 Spike Donovan, in Dennis O. Huggard (ed.), *The Thoughts of Musician Desmond 'Spike' Donovan*, New Zealand Series No. 5, Dennis O. Huggard, Henderson, 1998, pp. 36–37; Russell, 'Band on the Air'.
25 Huggard (ed.), *The Thoughts of Musician Desmond 'Spike' Donovan*, p. 37.
26 Vern Wilson, oral history interview by Patricia French.
27 Chips Healy, in Russell, 'Band on the Air', pp. 22–23.
28 Andrew Bisset, *Black Roots, White Flowers: A History of Jazz in Australia*, ABC, Sydney, 2nd edn, 1987, p. 60.
29 Owen Shaw, 'Modest Maestro Right Out of Band-box', *NZ Herald*, 3 March 1979, p. 2:4; Vern Wilson, oral history interview by Patricia French; *AMM*, May 1935. Bert Peterson, Melbourne-born president of the New Zealand union, later said the Australians had been 'quite right, as the Auckland Union would do the same if the positions were reversed' (*AMM*, March 1947).
30 *AMM*, November 1936; Russell, 'Band on the Air', p. 23.
31 Jim Warren, interviewed by Chris Bourke.
32 Russell, 'Band on the Air', p. 23; *Tempo*, June 1955.
33 Peter Kitchin, 'When Life was a Cabaret, Old Chum', *Dominion Post*, 12 May 2007, pp. E10–11.
34 Jim Gower, interviewed by Chris Bourke, Upper Hutt, August 2006; Bob Barcham, interviewed by Chris Bourke, Titahi Bay, February 2008.
35 Jim Warren, in Tony Potter, 'Cheek to Cheek at the Orange', *Auckland Star*, 1 December 1984, p. B3.
36 *AMM*, August 1954; Huggard (ed.), *The Thoughts of Musician 'Spike' Donovan*, pp. 27–28. The second Peter Pan changed its name to Mainstreet around 1980.
37 *AMM*, August 1938; Huggard (ed.), *The Thoughts of Musician 'Spike' Donovan*, p. 38.
38 A. H. Walker, *Rangi-Mata-Rau: The Story of Pt Chevalier from 1861–1961*, Clancy & Herdman, Auckland, 1961, pp. 36–37; *AMM*, January 1937.
39 'Dance Halls', *Press*, 2 October 1929, p. 10.
40 Bill Gamble, 'Remember? You Danced Arm in Arm', *Christchurch Star*, 16 February 1981, p. 9.
41 Gamble, 'Remember?'; Bill Gamble, 'Strike Up the Music', *Christchurch Star*, 23 February 1981, p. 9.
42 Ron Williams, 'Nothing Like the Old Bands? Don't You Believe It!', *Joy*, 14 September 1959, p. 10.
43 Among these 'real fine combinations' were the bands of Miss Dorothy Brady (Rangiora), Mrs Ogilvie (Kaiapoi), Miss Alma McGrath (Southbrook), Miss Alice Wayland (Cust), Miss Moore (Christchurch), Mrs Breach (Waikuku), Mrs O'Shea (Woodend), Miss N. Bailey (Rangiora) and Miss Fitzgibbon (Loburn): *AMM*, May 1935.
44 Elsie Doyle (née Nixon), interviewed by Patricia French, 13 December 1984 (Auckland Central City Library oral history). Another woman musician prominent in Auckland was Marie Darby, a highly regarded swing pianist with Johnny Madden's band.
45 *AMM*, September 1937.
46 *AMM*, June 1938.
47 'All Talkie and No Picture', *NZ Truth*, 20 August 1931. The band was Epi Shalfoon, Jimmy Aspin and Tony Shalfoon on saxophones, Ron Knowles on banjo, Colin Castleton on sousaphone, Eric Munson on piano and Norman Steele on drums.
48 Epi Shalfoon file, MS-Papers-9018-41, DHA, ATL.
49 Neal Taylor, 'The Shalfoon Story', Shalfoon Dental, Auckland, 2003, p. 4; Reo Shalfoon, 'Shalfoon, Gareeb Stephen 1904–1953', *Dictionary of New Zealand Biography*, updated 7 July 2005 (http://www.dnzb.govt.nz/).
50 Ted Priestley, 'The Saga of Epi Shalfoon', Part One, *NZ Dancing News*, July 1959, p. 8.
51 Reo Sheirtcliff (née Shalfoon), 'Dancing in the Dark: A Memoir of Epi Shalfoon', *Music in New Zealand*, 11, Summer 1990–1991, p. 40; Ted Priestley, 'The Saga of Epi Shalfoon', Part Two, *NZ Dancing News*, August 1959, p. 11.
52 Unsourced clipping, 1930, Shalfoon file, DHA, ATL.
53 Priestley, 'The Saga of Epi Shalfoon', Part One.
54 E. J. Wansbone, 'New Zealand Personalities', *Jukebox*, October 1946.
55 Frank Gibson Sr, interviewed by Jim Sutton, Newstalk ZB, 1993.
56 Frank Gibson Sr, interviewed by Jim Sutton.
57 Priestley, 'The Saga of Epi Shalfoon', Part One, p. 12.
58 Reo Sheirtcliff, interviewed by Andrew Menzies, Auckland, 19 May 2002.
59 Huggard (ed.), *The Thoughts of Musician Desmond 'Spike' Donovan*, p. 62.
60 Huggard (ed.), *The Thoughts of Musician Desmond 'Spike' Donovan*, p. 62.
61 Huggard (ed.), *The Thoughts of Musician Desmond 'Spike' Donovan*, p. 62.
62 E. J. Wansbone, 'New Zealand Personalities'.
63 *AMM*, May 1950.
64 Reo Sheirtcliff, interviewed by Andrew Menzies.
65 Besides Epi Shalfoon on alto sax, the band was pianist Lloyd Sly; bass player Bob Ewing; on trumpets, Bobby Griffith and Nolan Rafferty; and Frank Gibson Sr on brushes. On the B-side, Reo's sister Glyn is in the vocal chorus with the band.
66 *AMM*, March 1952.
67 Sheirtcliff, 'Dancing in the Dark', p. 45.
68 Bert Peterson, 'Epi Shalfoon', *Te Ao Hou*, 5, Spring 1953, p. 19; Sheirtcliff, 'Dancing in the Dark', p. 45; Priestley, 'The Saga of Epi Shalfoon', Part One, p. 13.
69 Patrick Day, *The Radio Years*, Auckland University Press, Auckland, 1994, p. 321; J. H. Hall, *The History of Broadcasting in New Zealand: 1920–1954*, BCNZ, Wellington, 1980, p. 30; *NZ Radio Record*, 14 December 1934, p. 6. Day's figure of 8597 for 1930 appears to be a misprint, as Jack Leigh reports 'more than 70,000' licences by the end of 1931 ('Right Up With the Radio Times', *Auckland Star*, 12 December 1981, p. B5).
70 A. H. McLintock (ed.), 'New Zealand Broadcasting Service, 1936–62', *An Encyclopaedia of New Zealand*, 1966 (www.teara.govt.nz/en/1966/broadcasting-and-television/5).
71 Peter Downes and Peter Harcourt, *Voices in the Air*, Methuen, Wellington, 1975, p. 80; Day, *The Radio Years*, p. 211.
72 Day, *The Radio Years*, p. 136.
73 Leigh, 'Right Up With the Radio Times'.
74 'Head of Oldest Firm of its Kind', *NZ Radio Record*, 20 March 1936, p. 12.
75 Day, *The Radio Years*, p. 185.
76 The rest of the time was taken up with sports, drama, talks, news, weather, church services and children's sessions: Hall, *The History of Broadcasting in New Zealand*, p. 68.
77 Ken G. Collins, *Broadcasting: Grave and Gay*, Caxton, Christchurch, 1967, p. 74.
78 Len Barton, interviewed by Arthur Fryer, 1995, MS Papers-6996-6, ATL.
79 David Ricquish, 'The New Zealand Radio Dial 1930–31' (www.radioheritage.net/Story93.asp).

80   *NZ Radio Record*, 1 June 1934, p. 7.
81   *Press*, 8 January 1936, p. 6.
82   *NZ Radio Record*, 11 August 1933, p. 14.
83   *NZ Radio Record*, 20 April 1934, p. 6.
84   Laurie Lewis, *Arthur and the Nights at the Turntable: The Life and Times of a Jazz Broadcaster*, K'vrie Press, Wingen, NSW, 1997, pp. 52–67.
85   Also in 1937, Reg Shellam and Ian Powell began 'rhythm sessions' on 1ZM and 1ZB: Judy Kissin, 'Who Said Swing is Dying?', *NZ Woman's Weekly*, 13 June 1946, p. 8.
86   Les Andrews, *What a Laugh*, Gilchrist Holdings, Auckland, 1998, pp. 9 and 28.
87   Bill Hamer, 'Contribution to *Vanity*', pp. 63–65, Bill Hamer papers, MS-Group-1703, ATL.
88   Chris Bourke, 'Pearce, Arthur Fairchild 1903–1990', *Dictionary of New Zealand Biography*, updated 22 June 2007 (http://www.dnzb.govt.nz/).
89   Lewis, *Arthur and the Nights at the Turntable*, pp. 76–78, 164–9; Katherine Findlay, 'One More Time', *NZ Listener*, 2 July 1977, pp. 20–21.
90   Also known as 'Maori Tango', and recorded by Ellington three times, this piece was written by Willliam H. Tyers, an African-American composer. In 1908 it was the first US-written tango to be a hit. The title probably came from a desire to appear exotic rather than any actual or musical connection with the Pacific: Peter Downes, 'A Composer and His "Maori" Twins', *Crescendo*, 72, p. 16.
91   Murdoch Reilly, interviewed by Chris Bourke, 22 February 2007; Nick Bollinger, 'The Big Beat Goes On', *NZ Listener*, 17 January 1998, pp. 38–39.
92   'Barend Harris', *NZ Radio Record*, 12 February 1937, p. 12; Michael King, *Te Puea: A Life*, Reed, Auckland, 4th edn, 2003, p. 120.
93   'Neddo of 1ZB', *NZ Radio Record*, 5 February 1937, p. 12; *AMM*, June 1937.
94   'Jazz Merit List', *NZ Radio Record*, 3 April 1936, p. 20; 'Have Crooners Had Their Day?', *NZ Radio Record*, 27 November 1936, p. 16.
95   'In Bob Bothamley's Little Room', *NZ Listener*, 28 November 1941, p. 12.
96   'Notes from NZ', *AMM*, November 1932.
97   'Notes from NZ', *AMM*, August 1932; Anon, 'Minstrel Boys Now Play the Sax', *NZ Listener*, 12 September 1941, p. 7; Downes and Harcourt, *Voices in the Air*, p. 84.
98   Day, *The Radio Years*, pp. 180, 148, 184–5, 325–6.
99   Andrew Smith, 'Tex Morton and His Influence on Country Music in Australia', in Charles K. Wolfe and James E. Akenson (eds), *Country Music Annual 2002*, University Press of Kentucky, Lexington, 2002, p. 86.
100   Memo from T. J. Kirk-Burnnand to Mr Bothamley, 27 September 1937, AADL564, 139b, 3/1/16, Archives NZ.
101   Lewis, *Arthur and the Nights at the Turntable*, pp. 46 and 83.
102   *NZ Herald*, 20 and 26 October 1936, as quoted in Day, *The Radio Years*.
103   Ian Carter, *Gadfly: The Life and Times of James Shelley*, Auckland University Press, Auckland, 1993, p. 223.
104   James J. Nott, *Music for the People: Popular Music and Dance in Interwar Britain*, Oxford University Press, Oxford, 2002, p. 61.
105   Vern Wilson, oral history interview by Patricia French; Shaw, 'Modest Maestro'.
106   Shaw, 'Modest Maestro'; Peter Downes, 'Cheesman, Oswald Astley 1913–1985', *Dictionary of New Zealand Biography*, updated 22 June 2007 (http://www.dnzb.govt.nz/); Max Cryer in Cheesman's obituary, *NZ Herald*, 1 October 1985.
107   Henry Rudolph, oral history interview by Peter Downes, OHInt-0133/14, ATL.
108   Peter Downes has identified 28 October 1931 as the date 'Remembrance' was recorded in Sydney; Gil Dech remembered recording it three times, in 1925, 1936 and in the mid-1960s. Peter Downes, 'Dech, Gil 1897–1974', *Dictionary of New Zealand Biography*, updated 22 June 2007 (http://www.dnzb.govt.nz/).
109   John Parker, 'Famous Concert Pianist of Depression Days Dies in Wellington', *Evening Post*, 2 November 1974, p. 14.
110   Downes, 'Dech, Gil'; 'For Gil Dech, the Melodies Linger On and On', *Dominion*, 6 February 1973.
111   Touchstone, 'Meet Eric Mareo', *NZ Observer*, 23 November 1933, p. 16.
112   Shirley Hodsell Williams, 'Stark, Freda Beatrice 1910–1999', *Dictionary of New Zealand Biography*, updated 22 June 2007 (http://www.dnzb.govt.nz/).
113   J. G. McLean, 'Mareo the Enigma', *NZ Observer*, 2 July 1936, p. 7.
114   Charles Ferrall and Rebecca Ellis, *The Trials of Eric Mareo*, Victoria University Press, Wellington, 2002, p. 12.
115   McLean, 'Mareo the Enigma'; Spike Donovan, in Vern Wilson, oral history interview by Patricia French.
116   'The Man Who Brought Fame to Fred Astaire', *NZ Radio Record*, 8 March 1935, p. 6.
117   Gordon Mirams, *Speaking Candidly: Films and People in New Zealand*, Paul's Book Arcade, Hamilton, 1945, p. 5.
118   Wayne Brittenden, *The Celluloid Circus*, Random House, Auckland, 2007, p. 124.
119   'NZ Grabs One of Australia's Ace Melody Makers', *NZ Radio Record*, 2 October 1936, p. 17.
120   J. R. Allanson, 'Auckland Notes', *AMM*, August 1937 and January 1938; 'NZ Grabs One of Australia's Ace Melody Makers', *NZ Radio Record*.
121   The lineup was Ossie Cheesman, Jimmy Watters, Chips Healy, Nin Pitcaithly, Stan Hills and a twenty-year-old Jim Warren. The State Theatre later became the Oriental Ballroom.
122   Dunedin show reviewed by Neil Collins in *Country Music Spotlight*, 32, October/November/December 1960, p. 16.
123   'From Street Singer to Radio Star', National Broadcasting Service radio script, c. 1949.
124   Eric Watson, *Country Music in Australia*, Rodeo Publications, Kensington, NSW, 1976, p. 11.
125   'Singing Cowboy', *NZ Listener*, 21 October 1949, p. 7.
126   'His Records Sell Better Than Gracie Fields: But Hamilton Once Asked Tex Morton to Leave', unsourced 1939 clipping, Chris Bourke collection.
127   'Morton's First Music Found', *Daily Telegraph* (Sydney), 25 November 2003; Gordon Spittle, *Counting the Beat*, GP Publications, Wellington, 1997, p. 11.

128   Watson, *Country Music in Australia*, p. 13.
129   Watson, *Country Music in Australia*, p. 15. Goebel Reeves, the Texan writer of 'Hobo's Lullaby', claimed to have taught Jimmie Rodgers how to yodel.
130   Peter Doyle, *Echo and Reverb: Fabricating Space in Popular Music Recording*, Wesleyan University Press, Connecticut, 2005, p. 104.
131   Watson, *Country Music in Australia*, p. 16.
132   Graeme Smith, *Singing Australian: A History of Folk and Country Music*, Pluto Press, Melbourne, 2005, p. 88.
133   Gordon Spittle, 'Morton, Tex 1916–1983', *Dictionary of New Zealand Biography*, updated 7 April 2006 (http://www.dnzb.govt.nz/).
134   Andrew Smith, 'The Yodeling Cowgirls', in Wolfe and Akenson, *The Women of Country Music*, p. 191.
135   Gordon Spittle, *The Tex Morton Songbook*, GWS Publications, Auckland, 2008, p. 55; Bill Sevesi, interviewed by Chris Bourke, Mt Roskill, 1999; Tommy Kahi, oral history interview by Roger Watkins, 1996, ATL; Smith, 'The Yodeling Cowgirls', p. 100. In New Zealand, the 24 songs were released on Tasman, a label of Tanza's parent company, the Recording Corporation of NZ. Rodeo released them in Australia.
136   Poster for 1950 tour, Cabot Collection, ATL.
137   Eric Watson, *Country & Western Spotlight*, 28, October/November/December 1959, p. 24.
138   Max McCauley, interviewed by Chris Bourke, Gore, 31 October 2006.
139   Eric Watson, *Country & Western Spotlight*, 28. This performance became famous through its broadcast on the BBC and its inclusion on the LP *The Tex Morton Story*, Festival, 1959.
140   *The Australian*, 22 May 1976, p. 21.
141   'Singing Cowboy', *NZ Listener*, 21 October 1949, p. 7.
142   Jim Gower, interviewed by Chris Bourke; 'Tut Coltman on Tour', *Tempo*, September 1938.
143   Jim Gower, interviewed by Chris Bourke.
144   The touring band was Bob Girvan, sax; Alan Brown, drums; Noel Field, piano; Jim Gower, bass; Tiny McMahon, sax (replaced by Jim Creary); Ross Floyd, sax; Tut Coltman, leader and trumpet ('Tut Coltman on Tour', *Tempo*; Jim Gower, interviewed by Chris Bourke).
145   Nott, *Music for the People*, p. 164; Sid Colin, *And the Bands Played On*, Elm Tree Books, London, 1977, p. 77; *AMM*, December 1938.
146   'Top Entrepreneur Dies', *Otago Daily Times*, 25 August 1986; Rachel Elizabeth McDermott, *Entertaining Ideas: The Enterprises of Joe Brown*, HSOE [Hard School of Experience], University of Otago Department of History, 1998.
147   McDermott, *Entertaining Ideas*; *Otago Daily Times*, 7 November 1936, p. 15.
148   McDermott, *Entertaining Ideas*, p. 14; Calder Prestcott, interviewed by Chris Bourke, Dunedin, October 2006; *AMM*, August 1939.
149   McDermott, *Entertaining Ideas*, p. 14.
150   McDermott, *Entertaining Ideas*, p. 15.
151   Calder Prestcott, interviewed by Chris Bourke.
152   *AMM*, April 1938.
153   'Minstrel Boys Now Play the Sax', *NZ Listener*, 12 September 1941, p. 7.
154   Tony Potter, 'When Swing was King in Hillsborough', *Auckland Star*, 30 November 1986.
155   Unsourced letter to the editor, late 1930s, Paddi papers, PA Coll: 89, ATL.
156   *AMM*, March 1939.
157   Jim Gower, interviewed by Chris Bourke.
158   Unsourced advertisement, Paddi papers, PA Coll: 89, ATL.
159   Jim Warren and Jim Gower, interviewed by Chris Bourke; Don Richardson, interviewed by Chris Bourke, Wellington, February 2007; *AMM*, October 1938.
160   Jim Warren, interviewed by Chris Bourke. Jim Watters and Bert Peterson also played for the Americanadians during their long visit.
161   Williams, 'Nothing Like the Old Bands?'; Bert Peterson, *AMM*, December 1939; Sammy Lee file, MS-Papers-9018-50, DHA, ATL.
162   Gerard Oakes, 'Lee, Samuel (Sammy)', *Australian Dictionary of Biography*, Melbourne University Press, Melbourne, 2000, p. 74; Harry Stein, 'Whatever Happened to the Americanadians?', *Quarterly Rag*, 50, January 1989; Jim Warren, in Potter, 'Cheek to Cheek at the Orange'.
163   *New Zealand Tit-Bits*, 10 March 1926, p. 4.
164   'The Jitter-Bug is Coming', *NZ Radio Record*, 28 October 1938.

THREE MUSIC DECLARES WAR: 1939–1945

1   Ken G. Collins, *Broadcasting: Grave and Gay*, Caxton, Christchurch, 1967, p. 84.
2   *NZ Radio Record*, 1 September 1939, p. 38.
3   'Itch or Irritant?', *NZ Listener*, 20 October 1939, p. 16; 'Boomps-a-Daisy into Battle! New Marching Song is in Waltz Time', *NZ Listener*, 29 September 1939, p. 7.
4   'Hitting the Highspots', *NZ Listener*, 13 October 1939, p. 52; 'Songs of Two Wars', *NZ Listener*, 13 October 1939, p. 8; 'Auckland Notes', *Australian Music Maker and Dance Band News* (AMM), November 1939; 'Auckland Musicians Relax', *AMM*, December 1939.
5   'Songs of Two Wars', *NZ Listener*.
6   '"March of the Men of New Zealand": Locally Written Song Has Immediate Success From ZBs', *NZ Radio Record*, 1 September 1939, p. 3.
7   *AMM*, December 1939.
8   Bert Peterson, 'Peterson Bans Patriotic Pops', *AMM*, October 1941.
9   E. H. McCormick, memo to the under-secretary of Internal Affairs, 16 January 1946, WAII 2, Box 60, 343/2/24, Archives NZ.
10   Ivan Perrin, 'The Apple Song', published by Harry H. Tombs, Wellington, n.d. [1940]; Peter Downes and Peter Harcourt, *Voices in the Air*, Methuen, Wellington, 1975, p. 129; 'The Apple Song', *NZ Listener*, 29 March 1940, p. 47;

John MacKenzie and Theo Walters also recorded 'The Apple Song': 'John on the Jennings', *NZ Listener*, 29 September 1961, p. 9.

11 '1ZB's Record Request Session', *NZ Listener*, 8 December 1939, p. 48.
12 Ray Harris, interviewed by Chris Bourke, Seatoun, 2006.
13 John I. Spedding, 'MD Engaged for NZ Exhibition Cabaret', *AMM*, n.d. [1939]; Owen Shaw, 'Days of Dance Gigs Jingles and War', *NZ Herald*, 19 June 1982, p. 2:2.
14 Programme for Wellington Stage Employees' Sick & Benefit Society Annual Concert, 31 May 1925.
15 Spedding, 'MD Engaged'.
16 Walter Sinton, 'Pavlova!', *Evening Star* (Dunedin), 5 April 1975, p. 12; Walter Sinton, 'Dunedin Hosts a Magnificent Display', *Evening Star*, 8 March 1975, p. 11; Bert Peterson, 'Auckland' columns, *AMM*, November 1939 and December 1939.
17 Redmer Yska, *Wellington: Biography of a City*, Reed, Auckland, 2007, pp. 155–6.
18 Letter from J. Duigan to B. Freyberg, 15 April 1940, WAII, 8/0, Archives NZ.
19 Wira Gardiner, *Te Mura o te Ahi: The Story of the Maori Battalion*, Reed, Auckland, 1992, p. 29.
20 Patricia Grace, Irihapeti Ramsden and Jonathan Dennis (eds), *The Silent Migration: Ngāti Pōneke Young Māori Club 1937–1948*, Huia, Wellington, 2001, p. 161.
21 Meri Mataira in Grace et al., *The Silent Migration*, p. 166.
22 Nancy M. Taylor, *The New Zealand People at War: The Home Front, Vol. II*, Historical Publications Branch, Department of Internal Affairs, Wellington, 1986, p. 1202.
23 Trumpeter George Taylor had played with Ambrose's dance orchestra in London, and with Jimmy Dorsey in the US; and saxophonist/vocalist Ken Waldridge with Teddy Joyce's Orchestra (*AMM*, February 1940).
24 J. F. Cody, *28 (Maori) Battalion*, War History Branch, Wellington, 1956, pp. 12–13.
25 Mihi Edwards, *Mihipeka: Time of Turmoil – Nga Wa Raruraru*, Penguin, Auckland, 1992, pp. 112–13; 'Now is the Hour' by Clement Scott and Maewa Kaihau.
26 Jack Thornton, 'Ruru Karaitiana – Maori Songwriter', *The New Settler* [c. 1949], p. 17.
27 'Success in America: Dunedin Song Writer's "Blue Smoke"', *Otago Daily Times*, 5 April 1952, p. 11.
28 'Success in America', *Otago Daily Times*.
29 Regal Zonophone G24367; Bruce Anderson, *Story of the New Zealand Record Industry*, self-published, Wellington, 1984, p. 61.
30 Lyrics unavailable due to dispute between publishers.
31 Dennis O. Huggard (ed.), *The Thoughts of Musician Desmond 'Spike' Donovan*, New Zealand Series No. 5, Dennis O. Huggard, Henderson, 1998, pp. 30 and 54.
32 Huggard (ed.), *The Thoughts of Musician Desmond 'Spike' Donovan*, p. 54.
33 *AMM*, August 1936.
34 Jim Gower, interviewed by Chris Bourke, Upper Hutt, August 2006.
35 Vern Wilson, oral history interview by Patricia French, 3 August 1984, # 90-OH-007-1-10, Auckland Central City Library.
36 *AMM*, May 1938 and June 1938.
37 *AMM*, October 1938.
38 E. J. Wansbone, 'Jim Foley, Pianist', *Jukebox*, November 1946, p. 2.
39 *AMM*, April 1939 and May 1939. The recording group was Keith Harris, clarinet; Monty Howard, piano; Phil Campbell, trumpet; and Wally Ransom, drums.
40 Lew Campbell, interviewed by Chris Bourke, Sydney, 27 November 2006.
41 Shaw, 'Days of Dance Gigs Jingles and War'.
42 *AMM*, June 1940.
43 Shaw, 'Days of Dance Gigs Jingles and War'.
44 *AMM*, April 1940.
45 Bert Peterson, 'Quiet in Queen City', *AMM*, September 1940.
46 Walter Sinton, *Evening Star*, 4 August 1970, p. 22; 'Town Hall Dance', *Otago Daily Times*, 6 January 1942, p. 3.
47 *AMM*, March 1940.
48 *AMM*, April 1940 and December 1940.
49 J. H. Hall, *The History of Broadcasting in New Zealand 1920–54*, BCNZ, Wellington, 1984, p. 124; *AMM*, July 1941.
50 *AMM*, December 1941.
51 *Spectrum* documentary 95, *It's Nice to Be Back*, produced by George Blackburn, Radio New Zealand, 1 January 1974.
52 *AMM*, May 1940.
53 'Music for the Troops', *NZ Listener*, 17 May 1940, p. 48. Later in the war Hill became director of music for the RNZAF.
54 Ray Harris, interviewed by Chris Bourke, Wellington, August 1981 and July 2006.
55 Murray Marbeck, interviewed by Chris Bourke, Auckland, July 2006.
56 'In Bob Bothamley's Room', *NZ Listener*, 28 November 1941, p. 12.
57 'In Bob Bothamley's Room', *NZ Listener*.
58 Ian Carter, *Gadfly: The Life and Times of James Shelley*, Auckland University Press, Auckland, 1993, p. 240.
59 Downes and Harcourt, *Voices in the Air*, p. 137.
60 Carter, *Gadfly*, p. 221.
61 Laurie Lewis, *Arthur and the Nights at the Turntable: The Life and Times of a Jazz Broadcaster*, K'vrie Press, Wingen, NSW, 1997, pp. 119–20.
62 Collins, *Broadcasting: Grave and Gay*, p. 122.
63 Ray Harris, interviewed by Chris Bourke, Wellington, July 2006.
64 Henry Rudolph, oral history interview by Peter Downes, OHInt-0133/14, ATL.
65 Taylor, *The New Zealand People at War*, p. 1208.
66 'Making Music While Making War', *NZ Listener*, 12 February 1943, p. 10.
67 *Filmland*, August 1943, p. 10; Barry Hawkins, 'Early Master of the Mighty Wurlitzer', *Evening Post*, 22 February 1996; *Ohariu–Johnsonville News*, 3 June 1974.
68 'Elaine Moody Dies', *Evening Post*, 7 July 1983.
69 Ross Somerville, 'Schramm, Leo Paul 1892–1953', *Dictionary of New Zealand Biography*, updated 7 July 2005 (http://www.dnzb.govt.nz/).

70 *Northern Advocate*, 27 March 1961; *Western Leader*, 15 June 1995, p. 12; 'Mrs I. M. Midgley', undated clipping, Bios, ATL; *Northern Advocate*, 7 May 1980; *Gisborne Herald*, 27 August 1977.
71 Valerie Davies, *The Way We Were: Taranaki/Wanganui*, Moa Beckett, Auckland, 1994, p. 70.
72 Jim Warren, interviewed by Chris Bourke and Marama Warren, Auckland, July 2006.
73 'RNZAF Band Functions, 1937–44', AIR1 6/1/2 part 5, Archives NZ.
74 Memo to F. Jones, Minister of Defence, from personnel branch, RNZAF, 18 May 1942, AIR1 6/1/2 part 5, Archives NZ.
75 H. Gladstone Hill: programme to *Flying High* revue, April 1944; memo to Chief of Air Staff, 9 November 1942, AIR1 6/1/7, Archives NZ.
76 Jim Warren, interviewed by Chris Bourke.
77 Geoffrey Bentley, *RNZAF: A Short History*, Reed, Wellington, 1969, pp. 203–4.
78 Jim Warren, interviewed by Chris Bourke; *Flying High* revue programme, 1944.
79 'Flying High', *Evening Post*, 25 April 1944.
80 'She Helped Them Sing Their Troubles Away', *Auckland Star*, 23 October 1968, p. 21.
81 Walter Sinton, 'War: New Zealand Answers the Call', *Evening Star*, 5 May 1979, p. 10; 'They Closed the Shops', *NZ Listener*, 9 August 1940, p. 42; Walter Sinton, 'Fabulous War-time Efforts', *Evening Star*, 7 July 1949, p. 18.
82 Walter Sinton, '1939 – A Wonderful Year! But Disaster Looms Ahead', *Evening Star*, 1 April 1979, p. 8.
83 *Dominion*, 2 May 1940.
84 Mark Lindsay, *Being Grim and Gay: Dunedin Entertainment and Cultural Life, 1938–43*, BA (Hons) History thesis, University of Otago, Dunedin, 1984, p. 6. Australian baritone Peter Dawson toured the main centres for a series of Liberty concerts and broadcasts, with the NBS String Orchestra ('Peter Dawson Visits Us', *NZ Listener*, 15 May 1942, p. 32).
85 Noël Coward, quoted in Damien Wilkins, *When Famous People Come to Town*, Four Winds Press, Wellington, 2002, p. 40; *Dominion*, 30 January 1941, p. 4.
86 Collins, *Broadcasting: Grave and Gay*, p. 72; Downes and Harcourt, *Voices in the Air*, p. 125.
87 Eddie Hegan, *No Choice*, Hodder & Stoughton, Auckland, 1980, p. 117.
88 Dianne Haworth and Diane Miller, *Freda Stark: Her Extraordinary Life*, HarperCollins, Auckland, 2000, p. 109.
89 '£850 Raised: Noël Coward Concert in Wellington', *Dominion*, 31 January 1941, p. 12.
90 *Dominion*, 5 February 1941, p. 5.
91 *Dominion*, 22 April 1941, quoted in Grace et al., *The Silent Migration*, p. 180.
92 Grace et al., *The Silent Migration*, p. 187.
93 Mihipeka Edwards in Grace et al., *The Silent Migration*, p. 176.
94 Jock Phillips with Ellen Ellis, *Brief Encounter: American Forces and the New Zealand People 1942–1945*, Historical Branch, Department of Internal Affairs, Wellington, 1992, p. 9.
95 Denys Bevan, *United States Forces in New Zealand 1942–45*, Macpherson, Alexandra, 1992, pp. 370–1.
96 Edwards, *Mihipeka*, pp. 126–7.
97 Johnny Madden, interviewed by Alwyn Owen for *Spectrum* documentary 582, 'And Jim Played Banjo', produced by Alwyn Owen, Radio New Zealand, 1987.
98 Happi Hill obituary, *Press*, undated clipping, Rocky Don Hall collection.
99 Henry Rudolph, oral history interview by Peter Downes, OHInt-0133/14, ATL.
100 Report of Royal Commission on the Loss of Certain Vessels by Enemy Action and Alleged Leakage of Information, 21 March 1941, as quoted in Patrick Day, *The Radio Years*, Auckland University Press, Auckland, 1994, p. 266.
101 Bevan, *United States Forces in New Zealand 1942–45*, p. 359.
102 Harry Bioletti, *The Yanks Are Coming: The American Invasion of New Zealand 1942–1944*, Century Hutchinson, Auckland, 1989, p. 60; Lyall Laurent, interviewed by Geoffrey Totton, Auckland, 10 October 1987.
103 Bevan, *United States Forces in New Zealand 1942–45*, p. 359.
104 Bioletti, *The Yanks Are Coming*, p. 60.
105 Haworth and Miller, *Freda Stark*, p. 92.
106 '72 and Still Rocking', *Auckland Star*, 27 August 1980, p. 14.
107 Constitution and rules of the Orange Hall Society Incorporated, 1954, as quoted by Lisa J. Truttman in 'Orange Ballroom', on the Auckland City Council's *Heritage* website (http://www.aucklandcity.govt.nz/Council/services/heritage/pc217newton.asp).
108 Owen Shaw, 'Nights of Foxtrots and Madeira Cake', *NZ Herald*, 9 August 1980, p. 2:2.
109 Gordon Lanigan, letter to Dennis Huggard, 'Ted Croad' file, MS-Papers-9018-10, DHA, ATL.
110 Jim Warren, interviewed by Chris Bourke; Tony Potter, 'Cheek to Cheek at the Orange', *Auckland Star*, 1 December 1984, p. B3.
111 Potter, 'Cheek to Cheek at the Orange'.
112 Vern Wilson, oral history interview by Patricia French.
113 Tony Potter, 'When Swing was King in Hillsborough', *Auckland Star*, 30 November 1986.
114 Gerry Horsup in Potter, 'When Swing was King'.
115 *Auckland Star*, 15 August 1942, p. 6; Sandra Coney, *Every Girl: A Social History of Women and the YWCA in Auckland 1885–1985*, YWCA, Auckland, 1986, p. 231.
116 Bert Peterson, 'We, the Accused', *AMM*, September 1942.
117 Peterson, 'We, the Accused'; Alfred Fenn, letter, *Auckland Star*, 17 August 1942, p. 2.
118 *AMM*, May 1943.
119 Del Crook in Potter, 'When Swing was King'.
120 *Dominion*, 16 August 1943, p. 3; *AMM*, March 1943.
121 Coney, *Every Girl*, pp. 228–30.

122 Bioletti, *The Yanks are Coming*, p. 64.
123 Jennie Rowley Lees, *Franquin: Master Showman*, Currency, Sydney, 1997, p. 74; Joan Clouston, telephone conversation with Chris Bourke, March 2006.
124 Bioletti, *The Yanks are Coming*, p. 31; Phillips with Ellis, *Brief Encounter*, p. 56; Georgina White, *Light Fantastic: Dance Floor Courtship in New Zealand*, HarperCollins, Auckland, 2007, p. 112.
125 Bioletti, *The Yanks are Coming*, p. 64.
126 Jean Matekitewhawhai Andrews (née Budge), in Judith Fyfe (ed.), *War Stories Our Mothers Never Told Us*, Penguin, Auckland, 1995, pp. 84–85.
127 Eldred Stebbing, interviewed by Chris Bourke, Herne Bay, March 2004.
128 Bioletti, *The Yanks are Coming*, p. 64.
129 Phillips with Ellis, *Brief Encounter*, pp. 24 and 47; *Evening Post*, 18 August 1943, p. 6.
130 Tony Potter, 'Jam All Night, Sleep Half Day', *Auckland Star*, 13 January 1987, p. B1.
131 Bevan, *United States Forces in New Zealand 1942–45*, p. 127.
132 Jim Warren, letter to Chris Bourke, April 2009; Wansbone, 'Jim Foley, Pianist', p. 3.
133 Wansbone, 'Jim Foley, Pianist'; Jim Warren, interviewed by Chris Bourke.
134 Frank Broad, 'Well-known Artist's Indomitable Spirit', *Auckland Star*, 9 March 1963. L. C. M. Saunders would serve as the *NZ Herald*'s classical music critic for more than 50 years.
135 Lyall Laurent, interviewed by Geoffrey Totton.
136 Bevan, *United States Forces in New Zealand 1942–45*, p. 358.
137 Bert Peterson and Peter Sellers, 'Claude Thornhill Show in Auckland', *AMM*, August 1945. Thornhill himself did not visit; he had been invalided back to Pearl Harbour.
138 Bevan, *United States Forces in New Zealand 1942–45*, pp. 284–5.
139 Letter from R. G. Mason, secretary of Auckland RSA, to the Minister of Defence, 25 January 1944, AC1 310/11/4, Archives NZ.
140 Memos to Minister of Defence and Adjutant-General, 14–23 May 1945, AC1 310/11/4, Archives NZ.
141 Michael King, *Te Puea: A Life*, Reed, Auckland, 4th edn, 2003, pp. 235–7.
142 Bevan, *United States Forces in New Zealand 1942–45*, p. 368.
143 Thomas N. Parlon, interviewed by G. Kurt Piehler and Joyce Ann Milsaps, 17 April 2000 (OHI0029321), Center for the Study of War and Society at the University of Tennessee Department of History. Actually it was Gracie Fields who popularised 'Now is the Hour' in Britain and the States, though Bathie Stuart claimed to have been singing it during her lectures in the US since 1928 ('Tune of "Now is the Hour" Sung in US for 20 Years', *Dominion*, 22 January 1948, p. 8).
144 *AMM*, June 1943.
145 From US radio programme on Shaw.
146 Artie Shaw, from his autobiography *The Trouble with Cinderella*, Farrar, Straus & Young, New York, 1952, quoted in Dennis O. Huggard, *Artie Shaw in New Zealand – 1943*, New Zealand Series No. 15, Dennis O. Huggard, Henderson, 2008, pp. 6–8.
147 Dale Alderton, interviewed by Chris Bourke, Auckland, January 2007.
148 'Swing Music', *NZ Observer*, 4 August 1943, p. 10.
149 Mack Pierce, quoted in Huggard, *Artie Shaw in New Zealand*, p. 24.
150 Bert Peterson, 'Artie Shaw Makes History at Auckland!', *AMM*, September 1943.
151 Murray Warren, interviewed by Chris Bourke, Auckland, January 2007.
152 Don Richardson, interviewed by Chris Bourke, Seatoun, February 2007; Pat McMinn, interviewed by Chris Bourke, Mt Maunganui, November 2007.
153 Vern Wilson, oral history interview by Patricia French.
154 'Blues for Business But Beethoven for Pleasure', *NZ Listener*, 27 August 1943.
155 Telegram dated 11 August 1943 in Pearce papers, ATL; Lewis, *Arthur and the Nights at the Turntable*, p. 131.
156 'Artie Shaw's Big Band in Wellington', *Dominion*, 16 August 1943, p. 3.
157 Jack McNamara, 'Rosoman Reminisces', *Jukebox*, April 1947, p. 3; Huggard, *Artie Shaw in New Zealand*, p. 22.
158 Peterson, 'Artie Shaw Makes History at Auckland!'.
159 Huggard, *Artie Shaw in New Zealand*, p. 29.
160 Max Kaminsky, *My Life in Jazz*, Harper & Row, New York, 1963, p. 149.
161 'Americans' Gesture: Dance for New Zealanders', *Dominion*, 10 August 1943, p. 3.
162 Bert Peterson, 'New Zealand Girl Singer Praised by Peter Dawson', *AMM*, November 1942.
163 Bert Peterson, Auckland column, *AMM*, July 1940.
164 Bert Peterson, Auckland column, *AMM*, January 1941.
165 Bert Peterson, 'Auckland, and Points South', *AMM*, January 1944.
166 *AMM*, April 1942.
167 *NZ Listener*, 15 April 1955, p. 25; Tony Potter, 'She Still Has Time to Sing', *Auckland Star*, 31 March 1984, p. B3. The McMinns in Edgar Bendall's Collegians were not brothers of Pat McMinn.
168 Pat McMinn, interviewed by Chris Bourke.
169 Norton Hammond, letter to Pat McMinn, 4 June 1942.
170 Potter, 'She Still Has Time to Sing'.
171 Pat McMinn, interviewed by Chris Bourke.
172 *NZ Listener*, 1 July 1955, p. 25.
173 Pat McMinn, interviewed by Chris Bourke.
174 Christopher Moor, 'Sweetheart of the Forces', *NZ Memories*, No. 17, p. 133.
175 '"Roses" for Roseman [sic]', *Music Maker*, December 1941.
176 Peter Kitchin, 'Perfect Pitch Never Left Her', *Evening Post*, 10 December 2001.
177 'Clever Company: 2YA Camp Entertainers', *Dominion*, 6 November 1944, p. 3.
178 Anita Osborn (Ann Marston), interviewed by Chris Bourke, Christchurch, October 2006.
179 L. Robinson, 'Christchurch Spotlight', *Jukebox*, November 1946, p. 8.
180 Robinson, 'Christchurch Spotlight'.
181 Wellington newspaper advertisement, 19 May 1945, Dennis Huggard collection.
182 'A Girl from Detroit', *NZ Listener*, 4 May 1945, p. 11.
183 *Maestro*, 1 October 1946, p. 9.
184 'Fan Mail and Local Songs Show NZ Interest in Popular Music, Says Singer',

185 *Swing Session*, July 1948, DHA; *Jukebox*, October 1946.
186 'Fan Mail and Local Songs', unnamed Wellington newspaper.
187 'Christchurch News', *Jukebox*, October 1946, p. 5; when the Mayfair reopened, Charlie Patterson's eight-piece band included two pianos.
188 Anita Osborn, interviewed by Chris Bourke.
189 Tony Rex, *Kiwi Concert Party: October 1940–January 1954*, unpublished manuscript, Auckland War Memorial Museum; also at MS-Papers-5735, pp. 1–3, ATL.
190 Rex, *Kiwi Concert Party*, pp. 2–5.
191 Rex, *Kiwi Concert Party*, pp. 7–8.
192 Rex, *Kiwi Concert Party*, p. 6.
193 Peter Downes, *Top of the Bill*, Reed, Wellington, 1975, pp. 76–85; Rex, *Kiwi Concert Party*, pp. 18–22.
194 Rex, *Kiwi Concert Party*, p. 1.
195 Kirk-Burnnand used the pseudonym Russell Murray when Begg's published 'The Kiwis on Parade', WAII 2, box 60 343/2/24, Archives NZ.
196 'No Need to Make it Cheap', *NZ Listener*, 13 August 1943, p. 5.
197 Terry Vaughan, 'A Pedalpoint: The Kiwi Concert Party in North Africa', *Music in New Zealand*, 11, Summer 1990–91, pp. 35–37.
198 Helen Paske, 'When Men were Men . . . and Girls', *NZ Listener*, 4 November 1978, p. 20.
199 Terry Vaughan, *Whistle As You Go: The Story of the Kiwi Concert Party*, Random House, Auckland, 1995, p. 62.
200 Vaughan, *Whistle As You Go*, p. 63.
201 'Not Much Beer and Few Skittles – But a Lot of Fun', *NZ Listener*, 21 September 1945, p. 17.
202 'He Had to Lead a Band', *NZ Listener*, 3 August 1945, p. 6; 'Kiwis have Excellent Entertainment', *NZ Free Lance*, 8 September 1943.
203 AD1 345/1/1994, Archives NZ.
204 'No Need to Make it Cheap', *NZ Listener*.
205 Les Cleveland, 'Teacup Warriors', *NZ Books*, Spring 2009, p. 17; Les Cleveland, *Saturday Morning With Kim Hill*, Radio New Zealand, 24 April 2004.
206 Les Cleveland, 'Remember?', *NZ Listener*, 23 April 1973, p. 11; Cleveland, *Saturday Morning With Kim Hill*.
207 Les Cleveland, 'The Songs We Sang', *Joy*, 23 November 1959, p. 6.
208 Cleveland, 'Remember?'. 'Blue Smoke', although sung by troops during the war, was not yet recorded.
209 Les Cleveland, *The Great New Zealand Songbook*, Godwit, Auckland, 1991, p. 125; Cleveland, *Saturday Morning With Kim Hill*.
210 *Kiwi Songs*, collected by NZERS/MEF, University of Waikato Library, no date; Cleveland, 'The Songs We Sang', p. 6.
211 'No Need to Make it Cheap', *NZ Listener*; Cleveland, 'Remember?'; Rev. M. L. Underhill and others, *Chaplains*, Historical Publications, Wellington, 1950, p. 33.
212 Cleveland, 'Remember?'; Cleveland, *Saturday Morning With Kim Hill*.
213 Les Cleveland, *Dark Laughter: War in Song and Popular Culture*, Praeger, Westport, CT, 1994, p. 73; Cleveland, *Saturday Morning With Kim Hill*.
214 Geoff Chapple, 'Unseen Enemy', *Sunday Star*, 23 August 1992, p. C15.
215 *Evening Post*, 3 April 1945, p. 7, quoted in Taylor, *The New Zealand People at War*, p. 1213.
216 'Young People Made the Most Fun on VE-Day', *NZ Free Lance*, 16 May 1945, p. 5.
217 'VE Day Impressions', *NZ Woman's Weekly*, 17 May 1945, p. 1.
218 'VE Day Impressions', *NZ Woman's Weekly*, p. 5.
219 'VE Day Impressions', *NZ Woman's Weekly*, p. 5.
220 'The Final Celebrations: Happy Crowds', *Otago Daily Times*, 11 May 1945, p. 4.
221 'VE Day Impressions', *NZ Woman's Weekly*, p. 45.
222 'Rejoicing in Oamaru', *Otago Daily Times*, 18 August 1945, p. 4; Colin Dorsey, *Dance Bands of the 20th Century in North Otago*, Dorsey, Oamaru, 2001, p. 85.
223 'Milling Crowds', *NZ Herald*, 16 August 1945, p. 4.
224 'Milling Crowds', *NZ Herald*.
225 'The Return to Peace', *Otago Daily Times*, 16 August 1945, p. 6.
226 Monty Soutar, 'Maori War Effort Overseas in the Second World War', in Ian McGibbon (ed.), *The Oxford Companion to New Zealand Military History*, Oxford University Press, Auckland, 2000, p. 311.
227 Cody, *28 Maori Battalion*, p. 486.
228 Written in the nineteenth century, 'Gold Mine in the Sky' had been a hit in the 1920s for Carl T. Sprague and, more recently, Gene Autry.
229 Te Kapunga Matemoana Dewes, *Nga Waiata Haka a Henare Waitoa o Ngati Porou: Modern Dance-poetry by Henare Waitoa of Ngati Porou*, Masters thesis, Department of Anthropology and Maori, Victoria University of Wellington, 1974, p. 96.

FOUR THE BIRTH OF A RECORDING INDUSTRY: THE 1940S

1 Whai Ngata, 'Ngarimu, Te Moananui-a-Kiwa 1919–1943', *Dictionary of New Zealand Biography*, updated 22 June 2007 (http://www.dnzb.govt.nz/).
2 A/Ref 145/1/4, Upper Hutt City Council Archive.
3 Ruru Karaitiana, army personnel record; Jack Thornton, 'Maori Writes Hit Tunes', unsourced news clipping, c. 1951, Chris Bourke collection; Joan Kennett, interviewed by Chris Bourke, Palmerston North, December 2008.
4 Certificate of discharge 3062, New Zealand Military Forces.
5 Jack Thornton, 'Ruru Karaitiana, Maori Songwriter', *The New Settler*, n.d. [1950], p. 16.
6 *Maestro*, 1 September 1946, p. 15.
7 Bob Barcham, interviewed by Chris Bourke, Titahi Bay, February 2008. As a ten-year-old, novelist Patricia Grace saw Karaitiana in his uniform performing 'Blue

Smoke' at the Begg's piano: Patricia Grace, *Tu*, Penguin, Auckland, 2004, p. 285.

8   'Maori Composer's Song "Blue Smoke" Published in NZ', *Dominion*, 14 January 1948, p. 8; '"Now is the Hour", Gracie Fields' Popular "Hit", is Really "Swiss Cradle Song"', *Wanganui Herald*, 14 January 1948.

9   Allan Thomas, *Music is Where You Find It: Music in the Town of Hawera, 1946*, Music Books New Zealand, School of Music, Victoria University of Wellington, 2004, pp. 114–17.

10 HMV advertisement, *2ZB Pictorial Souvenir: 10th Anniversary*, April 1947, reproduced and reprinted in Bryan Staff and Sheran Ashley, *For the Record: A History of the Recording Industry in New Zealand*, David Bateman, Auckland, 2002, p. 39.

11 John Shears, interviewed by Chris Bourke, Auckland, 22 January 2007.

12 Bart Fortune, telephone interview with Rachel Barrowman, 7 September 1985; Bart Fortune, letter to Rachel Barrowman, 10 October 1985; Rachel Barrowman, *A Popular Vision: The Arts and the Left in New Zealand, 1930–1950*, Victoria University Press, Wellington, 1991, pp. 93–95, 117; Tim Beaglehole, *J. C. Beaglehole*, Victoria University Press, Wellington, 2006, pp. 309–10.

13 John W. Stokes, *The Golden Age of Radio in the Home*, Craigs, Invercargill, 2nd edn, 1998, pp. 61–65.

14 John Shears, interviewed by Chris Bourke; Bart Fortune, letter to W. H. (Fred) Green, 15 June 1946; Stokes, *The Golden Age of Radio in the Home*, p. 65.

15 'Hataitai's Radio Doctor Well Named', *Eastern Suburb News*, 17 October 1979; Stan Dallas, interviewed by Jim Sullivan, Radio New Zealand, 16 December 1994; Stan Dallas, interviewed by Gordon Spittle, 21 September 1992.

16 Columbus Recording Studios advertisement, *NZ Listener*, 8 October 1948, reproduced in Staff and Ashley, *For the Record*, p. 41; Bart Fortune, letter to W. H. Green, 15 October 1948.

17 'NZ Artists May Be Recorded', *Southern Cross*, 15 October 1948, p. 1.

18 Bart Fortune, letter to W. H. Green, 15 October 1948.

19 Stan Dallas, interviewed by Jim Sullivan.

20 Stan Dallas, interviewed by Gordon Spittle; 'Remember Way Back Before NZ Artists Cut Discs?', *Joy*, 16 May 1960, p. 10; John Shears, interviewed by Chris Bourke.

21 Bart Fortune, in Staff and Ashley, *For the Record*, p. 41.

22 Joan Kennett, interviewed by Chris Bourke.

23 John Shears, interviewed by Chris Bourke; Joan Kennett, interviewed by Chris Bourke; Pixie Williams, interviewed by Warwick Burke, 31 December 2002, and Jim Sullivan, 1991, Radio New Zealand.

24 All the musicians were credited on the label, with a ring-in: Carter's usual bass player Noel Robertson, who was ill when the sessions began. 'Everyone wanted their name on the record', recalled Carter. 'It wasn't what you got paid: it was a record with your name on it.' Jim Carter, interviewed by Chris Bourke, Nelson, October 2008.

25 John Shears, interviewed by Chris Bourke.

26 Pixie Williams, interviewed by Warwick Burke.

27 Stan Dallas, interviewed by Jim Sullivan.

28 Ken Avery, *Where Are the Camels? A Dance Band Diary*, p. 25; National Film Unit *Weekly Review*, 407, 24 June 1949.

29 'Tanza Discs Are Latest NZ Product', *Southern Cross*, 2 July 1949, p. 7.

30 J. K. Smith, *Off the Record*, J. K. Smith, Whangarei, 2001, p. 262; http://www.78rpm.net.nz/78s/madeinnz.htm; Bruce Anderson, *EMI: Fifty Years in New Zealand*, EMI, Lower Hutt, 1976, p. 3.

31 Ruth Brown, 'Mystery of the First NZ Pop Star', *Otago Daily Times*, 27 December 1994; Gordon Spittle, 'Out of the Blue', *Southern Skies*, November 1993, p. 56.

32 John Shears, interviewed by Chris Bourke.

33 Stan Dallas, interviewed by Jim Sullivan.

34 'Success in America', *Otago Daily Times*, 5 April 1952.

35 'Kiwi's Song Wins Sudden Fame', unsourced clipping, c. 1948, Ruru Karaitiana scrapbook.

36 'Success in America', *Otago Daily Times*; Joan Kennett, interviewed by Chris Bourke.

37 Joan Kennett, interviewed by Chris Bourke; Val Aldridge, 'Drifting Memories', *Dominion*, 9 November 2000, p. 20.

38 'Saddle Hill' b/w 'It's Just Because' was soon released on Tanza, credited to Pixie Williams with Ruru Karaitiana's Quavertones. '"Saddle Hill" Finds Favour with Audience', *Otago Daily Times*, 15 August 1951.

39 'Songwriter: "I am being hounded"', *NZ Truth*, 2 February 1955, p. 3.

40 Joan Kennett, interviewed by Chris Bourke; Ruma Karaitiana, conversation with Chris Bourke, October 2008.

41 Val Aldridge, 'Drifting Memories', *Dominion*, 9 November 2000, p. 20; Joan Kennett, interviewed by Chris Bourke.

42 Thornton, 'Ruru Karaitiana, Maori Songwriter'.

43 JAK [Jack Kelleher], 'Blue Smoke', *Dominion*, 17 December 1970, p. 15.

44 Tom Bolster, 'His "Idea" Led to NZ-made Records', *Auckland Star*, c. December 1949.

45 Among the Astor regulars were George Campbell, Neil Dunningham, Bob Ewing, Frank Gibson Sr, Bobby Griffith, Ray Gunter, Nancy Harrie, Derek Heine, Dick Hobday, Julian Lee, John MacKenzie, Crombie Murdoch and Jim Warren.

46 Stan Dallas, 'Remember Way Back Before NZ Artists Cut Discs?', *Joy*, 16 May 1960, p. 10.

47 Jim Warren, interviewed by Chris Bourke, Auckland, July 2006; Jim Mora, 'Mr Nice Guy', *Metro*, June 1993, p. 93.

48 Bolster, 'His "Idea" Led to NZ-made Records'.

49 Anderson, *EMI: Fifty Years in New Zealand*, p. 5. 'Buttons' sales: *Freedom: The National Weekly*, 7 September 1949, p. 10. Besides 'You Can in Yucatan', another 1949 Peach recording before his association with Tanza was the Knaves with 'He Holds the Lantern (While His Mother Chops Wood)' b/w 'Powder Your Face With Sunshine' (HMV LA-2). Also among the earliest local HMV releases (c. 1953) was Les Wilson with 'The Yodelling Cowboy' and John Parkin's 'Piano Medley' series.

50 Bolster, 'His "Idea" Led to NZ-made Records'; Smith, *Off the Record*; *AMM*, December 1949.

51 'The Unpredictable Business of Marketing Gramophone Records', *Dominion*, 23 August 1953, p. 8.

52 Martin Finlay, 'To Assist New Zealand Artists', *Here & Now*, March 1952, p. 3.

53 Murray Marbeck, in Staff and Ashley, *For the Record*, p. 44.

54 Eldred Stebbing, interviewed by Chris Bourke, Herne Bay, July 2006.

55 Radio Corp's closest Radio Centre shops were in High Street and Karangahape Road.

56 Bert Peterson, 'Record Rumpus in Auckland', *AMM*, January 1952.

57 Finlay, 'To Assist New Zealand Artists', p. 4.

58 Finlay, 'To Assist New Zealand Artists', p. 4.

59 Bert Peterson, 'Curious Controversy Continues', *AMM*, April 1952.

60 Finlay, 'To Assist New Zealand Artists', p. 4. The Duplicats was a vocal trio: Esme Stephens, her husband Dale Alderton and Ena Allen.

61 Stan Dallas, interviewed by Gordon Spittle.

62 Eldred Stebbing, interviewed by Chris Bourke, Herne Bay, March 2004.

63 Eldred Stebbing, interviewed by Chris Bourke, July 2006; Andrew Bisset, *Black Roots, White Flowers: A History of Jazz in Australia*, ABC, Sydney, 2nd edn, 1987, p. 96.

64 'The Magic of Sound', *Auckland Star*, 20 June 1967, p. 24.

65 'Music-hungry Country is Denied New Records', *Freedom: The National Weekly*, 7 September 1949, p. 10; Eldred Stebbing, interviewed by Chris Bourke, July 2006; 'The Magic of Sound', *Auckland Star*; Staff and Ashley, *For the Record*, p. 56.

66 Phil Gifford, 'Live Wireless', *NZ Listener*, 21 August 1982, p. 20.

67 Laurie Lewis, interviewed by Chris Bourke.

68 George Wood, 'NZ Offers Work For Only the Lucky Few', *Melody Maker*, 9 July 1949.

69 Wood, 'NZ Offers Work For Only the Lucky Few'; Dale Alderton, interviewed by Chris Bourke.

70 Harry Voice, interviewed by Chris Bourke, Christchurch, October 2006.

71 'Calder Prestcott of Dunedin', *Allegro*, November 1973, p. 15.

72 'Freddy Gore is New Zealand's No. 1 Dance Band Leader', *Tempo*, June 1948.

73 Others who 'went legit' included saxophonist-turned-clarinettist Pat Watters, violinist Fred Engels and bass player Johnny McNeilly: *AMM*, March 1947; *Tempo*, January 1952. From 1949 the NZBS began several years of deficit, partly due to the costs of the orchestra; by 1954 the deficit on the National Orchestra was £86,236: Patrick Day, *The Radio Years*, Auckland University Press, Auckland, 1994, p. 285. By comparison, the total cost of dance bands for the four main centres in 1950 was £9460; arrangements cost approximately £800 per annum in each centre: AADL 564, 444b 3/50/13, pt 1, Archives NZ.

74 Bert Peterson, 'Auckland News', *AMM*, April 1950.

75 Doug Caldwell, interviewed by Chris Bourke, Christchurch, October 2006.

76 The 1YA concerts were broadcast from its studios in Shortland Street and from 1ZB's Radio Theatre on Durham Street West (Gifford, 'Live Wireless'); Peter Downes, interviewed by Chris Bourke, Tawa, 25 October 2008; Crombie Murdoch, interviewed by Geoffrey Totton, 17 August 1987.

77 Gordon was accompanied by guitarists Dick Hobday, John Bradfield and Thompson Yandall.

78 DFT, 'Auckland's First Jazz Concert a Great Success', *Auckland Star*, 8 August 1950, p. 4. The concert was eventually released in 1994 as *Jazz Concert 1950* (Ode SODET 467).

79 *AMM*, November 1952; A. J. McCarthy, 'Dr Buckley's Bon Mot on Bebop Ban on Bechstein', *Northern Advocate*, 14 February 1953.

80 Photo in possession of Jim Gower; Jim Gower, interviewed by Chris Bourke, Upper Hutt, July 2006.

81 'New Band for 2YA', *NZ Listener*, 6 July 1945, p. 17.

82 Doug Gardner, 'Another Big Live "Jam" Session', *Swing!*, August 1942, p. 5.

83 *AMM*, April 1944.

84 Dale Alderton, interviewed by Chris Bourke, January 2007; *AMM*, June 1944.

85 F. O'Donoghue, memo to James Shelley, William Yates and Bob Bothamley, NBS memo, 22 December 1944, AADL564, 139b, 3/1/16, Archives NZ.

86 Newspaper advertisement, March 1945, Thérèse Gore collection.

87 In Taumarunui, Frances Fabish sang 'Why Don't You Fall in Love with Me', Joy Hamon 'I'll Get By', Mavis Hickton 'I'll Walk Alone', and Valerie Brown 'This is a Lovely Way to Spend an Evening': Taumarunui review clipping, paper unnamed, 3 February 1945, Thérèse Gore collection.

88 'New Band for 2YA', *NZ Listener*.

89 *AMM*, 20 July 1942.

90 'New Band for 2YA', *NZ Listener*.

91 Thérèse Gore, interviewed by Chris Bourke, Auckland, January 2007.

92 *Jukebox*, October 1946, p. 9.

93 *NZ Free Lance*, 11 September 1946.

94 'The Press Ball Gazette', invitation for New Plymouth Press Ball, c. 1951, Thérèse Gore collection; *AMM*, November 1951, February 1952.

95 *AMM*, October 1952.

96 Mike Nock, interviewed by Chris Bourke, Sydney, October 2006.

97 *Tempo*, June 1948.

98 Laurie Lewis, interviewed by Chris Bourke, Melbourne, November 2006.

99 Thérèse Gore, interviewed by Chris Bourke.

100 Clipping from unnamed Northland paper, c. 1966, Chris Bourke collection.

101 In 1946 there were three in Auckland alone – the Swing Club, the Rhythm Club and the Artie Shaw Club – plus clubs in Wellington, Hamilton, Whangarei, Te Kuiti and other centres. Dunedin's was called Little Nick's Swing Club. Meetings of the Wellington Swing Club were held in the hall above Nimmo's music store on Willis Street, directly opposite the Majestic Cabaret. Judy Kissin, 'Who Said Swing is Dying?', *NZ Woman's Weekly*, 13 June 1946, p. 8.

101 'Organisation of Swing-lovers', *NZ Free Lance*, 11 September 1946, p. 40; 'Wellington's First Jazz Concert', *AMM*, March 1951.
102 Owen Shaw, 'May I Have the Pleasure?', *NZ Herald*, 2 April 1977, p. 2:4.
103 Mary Throll, *The Scottish Nightingale: An Autobiography*, Wordsell Press, Pakuranga, 2003, pp. 60–61.
104 Duncan Stuart, 'Bless My Soul, It's . . . Rock'n'Roll', *Metro*, March 1986, p. 98.
105 Stuart, 'Bless My Soul'; Throll, *The Scottish Nightingale*, pp. 60–61.
106 *AMM*, Auckland columns, 1938–40; *Jukebox*, November 1946; 'In Tune with Dixie Days', *Auckland Star*, c. 1978, Dennis Huggard collection.
107 Pat McMinn, interviewed by Chris Bourke, Mt Maunganui, November 2007; Johnny Cooper, *Joy*, 24 November 1958, p. 10.
108 *Dominion*, 16 February 1949, p. 11.
109 Ian Mackay, *Broadcasting in New Zealand*, A. H. & A. W. Reed, Wellington, 1953, pp. 92–93.
110 NZPD, Vol. 283, p. 2452, as quoted by Day, *The Radio Years*, p. 317.
111 Day, *The Radio Years*, p. 318.
112 Day, *The Radio Years*, p. 318.
113 Mackay, *Broadcasting in New Zealand*, p. 99.
114 Peter Downes, interviewed by Chris Bourke.
115 'Brumas', 'Radio in New Zealand', *Cinema, Stage & TV*, September 1956, p. 33.
116 Peter Downes, conversation with Chris Bourke, 25 February 2010.
117 'Open Microphone', *NZ Listener*, 6 February 1953, p. 14; Wilton Baird, 'As It Was in the Beginning', *NZ Radio Record*, 17 June 1938, p. 13; Alan Armstrong, 'Still Popular After Thirty Years', *Te Ao Hou*, September 1961, p. 63. Most credit for the recording session belongs to their founder and manager, Rotorua solicitor Martin Hampson (*Dominion*, 10 May 1930, p. 22).
118 'Top Tunes from the ZBs', *NZ Listener*, 1 November 1946; 'Open Microphone', *NZ Listener*; Baird, 'As It Was in the Beginning'.
119 CBCH, '19 Years of Hit Parade', *NZ Listener*, 24 December 1965, p. 8.
120 Selwyn Toogood, interviewed by Gordon Spittle, 28 October 1992.
121 Murray Tanner, interviewed by Chris Bourke, Auckland, January 2007.
122 'ZB Hit Parade of 1952', *NZ Listener*, 22 August 1952, p. 15.
123 Justin du Fresne, interviewed by Chris Bourke, Wellington, February 2007.
124 Downes, quoted in Redmer Yska, *All Shook Up*, Penguin, 1993, p. 133.
125 *NZ Truth*, 30 March 1955, p. 7; *AMM*, January 1946.
126 Julian Lee, interviewed by Haydn Sherley, *Musical Chairs*, Radio New Zealand, 2000; Lee press biography, mid-1970s, RNZ Infofind.
127 Julian Lee, interviewed by Chris Bourke, Bowral, NSW, 27 November 2006.
128 Ken Catran and Penny Hansen, *Pioneering a Vision: A History of the Royal New Zealand Foundation for the Blind 1890–1990*, RNZFB, Auckland, 1992.
129 Walter Sinton, 'It was All "Style" Four Decades Ago', *Evening Star*, 3 February 1979.
130 DFT, 'Auckland's First Jazz Concert a Great Success', *NZ Herald*, 8 August 1950.
131 Alan Siddall, 'New Zealand News', *Tempo*, August 1952.
132 Julian Lee, interviewed by Haydn Sherley.
133 Among Lee's radio broadcasts was a series emulating his blind friend and collaborator George Shearing, with Lee on piano accompanied by a string section playing his own arrangements.
134 'Songs Our Mothers Never Taught Us', *NZ Listener*, 24 April 1952, pp. 6–7.
135 Peter Downes, interviewed by Chris Bourke.
136 Alwyn Owen, 'Confessions of a Programmer', *Memories*, August/September 2005, p. 13.
137 Dave Van Weede, interviewed by Chris Bourke, Auckland, January 2007.
138 John Shears, interviewed by Chris Bourke, Auckland, 22 January 2007.
139 Murdoch Riley, interviewed by Chris Bourke, Raumati, February 2008.
140 'The Hit(s) Parade', *NZ Listener*, 11 January 1957, p. 14.

FIVE CANARIES AND COWBOYS: 1950S POP SCENES

1 This presumably refers to New Zealand discs up against overseas versions of the same songs (*NZ Truth*, 14 October 1953, p. 26).
2 'Canaries Sing at Night', *NZ Listener*, 31 August 1951, p. 6.
3 *Jukebox*, August 1946.
4 'Canaries Sing at Night', *NZ Listener*.
5 'Mockin' Bird Hill' was also covered by Mavis Rivers for Tanza in 1951, and it was Southern Music's biggest sheet music success in New Zealand, with 30,000 copies sold. Redmer Yska, *All Shook Up*, Penguin, Auckland, 1993, p. 132; John Berry, '50 Years of Music', *NZ Herald*, 2 May 1981, p. 2:6.
6 'Popular Music from 1YA', *NZ Listener*, 5 November 1948, p. 15.
7 Dale Alderton, interviewed by Chris Bourke, Auckland, January 2007.
8 Pat McMinn, interviewed by Chris Bourke, Mt Maunganui, November 2007.
9 On this recording, the Astor Dixie Boys were George Campbell, Crombie Murdoch and Eddie Croad: *NZ Listener*, 14 April 1955, p. 25.
10 Stan Dallas, 'Remember Way Back Before NZ Artists Cut Discs?', *Joy*, 16 May 1960, p. 10.
11 Jim Mora, 'Th' Gals', *Metro*, June 1993, p. 95.
12 Mavis Rivers, interviewed by Chris Bourke, Wellington, 14 March 1990.
13 Mavis Rivers, interviewed by Chris Bourke.
14 Tommy Kahi, oral history interview with Roger Watkins, 17 November 1993, OHInt-0485-23, ATL.
15 'Mavis Singing', *NZ Listener*, 11 September 1959, p. 3.
16 Bill Hamer, 'The Tanza Saga: The Story of New Zealand's Pioneer Record Label', monograph at MusLib, P Box, q780, HAM 1992, ATL; published in *Australian Music & Record Review*, October 1992.
17 Mavis Rivers, interviewed by Chris Bourke.
18 Mavis Rivers, press biography, c. 1982 (RNZ Infofind); used by Robyn Welsh, 'Mavis and Matt: The Start of Something Great', *NZ Woman's Weekly*, 26 September 1983, p. 12.
19 Shane Rivers, 'Rivers, Mavis Chloe 1929–1992', *Dictionary of New Zealand Biography*, updated 7 April 2006 (http://www.dnzb.govt.nz/).
20 Graeme Kennedy, 'Fame and Wealth . . . But Mavis is Still an Island Girl', *8 O'Clock*, 16 April 1977, p. 43; Mavis Rivers, interviewed by Chris Bourke.
21 Roger Dick, 'A Preliminary New Zealand song index 1950–1985', ATL ref. 2000-199-1/15.
22 'A Swinging Jingle that Never Dies . . .', *Auckland Star*, 22 March 1975, p. 20.
23 'Girls Who Make Local Records Popular', *NZ Truth*, 14 October 1953, p. 26; 'En-Zedders On Record', *Record Monthly*, 1 April 1957, p. 23.
24 *AMM*, August 1953.
25 Tony Potter, 'The Final Note From a Leading Musical Light', *Sunday Star-Times*, 8 October 2000.
26 Nancy Harrie, interviewed by Jim Sutton, Newstalk ZB, c. 1999.
27 Nancy Harrie, interviewed by Jim Sutton.
28 *AMM*, July 1954.
29 Nancy Harrie, interviewed by Jim Sutton.
30 Edith Teague, 'Nancy Harrie, Two Hands in Harmony', *NZ Woman's Weekly*, 9 August 1951, p. 11; Wally Ransom, liner notes to *The Colourful Piano of Nancy Harrie* (Zodiac ZLP 1016); 'Nancy Harrie: TV Star Viewers Never See', *NZ Herald*, 19 November 1970, p. 1:11.
31 'Nancy Harrie: TV Star Viewers Never See', *NZ Herald*.
32 'Auckland News', *AMM*, April 1953.
33 John Shears, interviewed by Chris Bourke, Auckland, 22 January 2007; *AMM*, April 1953.
34 George Fraser, *Seeing Red: Undercover in 1950s New Zealand*, Dunmore Press, Palmerston North, 1995, p. 71.
35 JCR, 'Knavish Tricks', *NZ Listener*, 27 January 1950.
36 'Farewell to Auckland's Knaves', *NZ Listener*, 22 May 1953, p. 25.
37 'Some Modern Singing', unsourced newspaper clipping, Dennis Huggard collection: Knaves.
38 'Farewell to Auckland's Knaves', *NZ Listener*; 'Knaves Disbanding', *AMM*, July 1953.
39 Jim Mora, 'Mr Nice Guy', *Metro*, June 1993, p. 93.
40 'En-Zedders On Record', *Record Monthly*, 1 March 1957, p. 27.
41 Fraser Daly, interviewed by Jim Sutton, Newstalk ZB, 8 November 1998.
42 Barney Erickson, interviewed by Suzanne Ormsby, *Te Reo Puoro Maori Mai I Mua Tae Noa Mai Ki Inaianei, The Voices of Maori Music, Past Present and Future: Maori Musicians of the 1960s*, MA thesis, University of Auckland, 1996, p. 162.
43 Andrew Bisset, *Black Roots, White Flowers: A History of Jazz in Australia*, ABC, Sydney, 2nd edn, 1987, p. 102.
44 *AMM*, September 1938; *Jukebox*, August 1946; Berry, '50 Years of Music'; John Berry, 'Soap, Songs or Sheet Music – Wally Sells It', *Auckland Star*, 25 February 1961; Eldred Stebbing, interviewed by Chris Bourke, Auckland, July 2006.
45 'Latin Rhythms; Japanese Pops', *NZ Listener*, 19 May 1961; 'Chicka-Boom-Chick', *NZ Listener*, 3 March 1950, p. 6; concert programme, 16 June 1955, Dennis Huggard collection.
46 *Joy*, 17 August 1959, p. 10.
47 Murdoch Riley, interviewed by Gordon Spittle, 7 October 1992; and by Chris Bourke, Raumati, 22 February 2008.
48 Ken Avery, *Where Are the Camels? A Dance Band Diary*, Clare Avery, Wellington, 2010, p. 38.
49 *Allegro*, June 1953, p. 11.
50 OJ, 'The Fans Liked It – Every Minute of It', *Evening Post*, 13 December 1954.
51 Tony Potter, 'Jam All Night, Sleep Half Day', *Auckland Star*, 13 January 1987, p. B1.
52 Laurie Lewis, interviewed by Chris Bourke, Sydney, November 2006.
53 *Auckland Star*, 9 and 23 January 1960.
54 Jim Warren, *AMM*, May 1957.
55 Merv Thomas, interviewed by Chris Bourke, Auckland, May 2007.
56 Mora, 'Mr Nice Guy', p. 93.
57 Duncan Campbell, 'Live Jazz Lives Again', *NZ Listener*, 8 October 1994, p. 43.
58 Richard Wolfe, 'The Quiet Man at the Piano', *Music in New Zealand*, Autumn 1993, p. 42; Crombie Murdoch, interviewed by Geoffrey Totton, Auckland, 17 August 1987.
59 Anon, '"Bop" in Place of Chopin', *NZ Observer*, 21 July 1954, p. 8.
60 Wolfe, 'The Quiet Man at the Piano'; Murdoch Riley, interviewed by Chris Bourke.
61 Stan Dallas, interviewed by Gordon Spittle, 21 September 1992.
62 Pat McMinn, interviewed by Chris Bourke.
63 Stan Dallas, interviewed by Gordon Spittle.
64 Mora, 'Mr Nice Guy', p. 93.
65 Mora, 'Mr Nice Guy', p. 93.
66 Bruce Morley, 'Recordings', *Music in New Zealand*, Summer 1994–95, p. 64.
67 Letter, *Jukebox*, December 1946, p. 18.
68 Jack McNamara, 'Rosoman Reminisces', *Jukebox*, April 1947, p. 2; 'Bop in Town Hall Concert Chamber', *Southern Cross*, 18 December 1950.
69 Dale Alderton, interviewed by Chris Bourke.
70 'Jazz Storms the Town Hall', *Evening Post*, 11 November 1952.
71 *AMM*, May, June and August 1950; Jim Warren, interviewed by Chris Bourke, Auckland, July 2006.
72 'Tolerant Enthusiast', *NZ Listener*, 3 March 1950, p. 24; Don Richardson, interviewed by Chris Bourke, Seatoun, February 2007.
73 *NZ Herald*, 17 January 1955; *NZ Truth*, 25 September 1954; Eldred Stebbing, interviewed by Chris Bourke, Herne Bay, March 2004.
74 John Shears, letter to Chris Bourke, 16 January 2007. HMV's parent company, EMI in Britain, had just acquired 96 percent of Capitol's stock. Besides Capitol and its

own discs, HMV (NZ) Ltd was now distributing Beltona, Brunswick, Columbia, Decca, London, MGM, Odeon, Parlophone, Regal Zonophone and Vogue (*Tempo*, February 1955).

75 'Nat "King" Cole Was a Shy Young Soul', *NZ Listener*, 4 February 1955, p. 7; Mike Nock, interviewed by Chris Bourke, Sydney, 26 November 2006; Bob Ewing, interviewed by Andrew Menzies, Auckland, 24 May 2002 (from Menzies' Victoria University of Wellington essay 'The stylistic evolution of jazz in Auckland, 1912–August 1950', Chris Bourke collection.

76 Gordon Spittle, 'Play It Again, Sam', *Southern Skies*, February 1993, p. 40; Mac McKenzie, 'Sam Freedman', *NZ Hawaiian Steel Guitar Association Gazette* (*NZHSGA Gazette*), August 2005, p. 11.

77 The advertisement was a re-recording, with 70-year-old Daphne Walker once again the vocalist: Janine Burgess, 'Haere Mai . . . Sam's Old Song is Ka Pai', *Horowhenua–Kapiti Chronicle*, 5 October 2000, p. 1.

78 George Kanahele, quoted in Peter Doyle, *Echo and Reverb: Fabricating Space in Popular Music Recording 1900–1960*, Wesleyan University Press, Middletown, CT, 2005, pp. 122–3.

79 *Evening Post*, 27 May 1911, p. 2; *NZ Truth*, 3 June 1911. Sometimes spelt Ka'ai, George Kanahele prefers Kaai.

80 *Evening Post*, 5 June 1911, p. 2; George Kanahele, *Hawaiian Music and Musicians: An Illustrated History*, University of Hawai'i Press, Honolulu, 1979, p. 193.

81 The *New York Times* review, as quoted in Kanahele, *Hawaiian Music and Musicians*, p. 45.

82 *NZ Theatre and Motion Picture*, 1 July 1924, p. 9.

83 Henry A. Peelua Bishaw, *The Albert Ukulele Hawaiian Guitar*, Albert's, Sydney, 1919, p. 3; *Evening Post*, 5 June 1911, p. 2. Bishaw also used the first name Herman.

84 Dennis O. Huggard (ed.), *The Thoughts of Musician Desmond 'Spike' Donovan*, New Zealand Series No. 5, Dennis O. Huggard, Henderson, 1998, p. 24.

85 Walter Smith, 'From the Leaves of an Old Family Bible', *Te Karere*, May 1941, p. 658; Walter Smith, 'On!! New Zealand' sheet music, Aloha Publishing, Auckland, 1924.

86 *Northern Advocate* review, from Michael King, *Te Puea: A Life*, Reed, Auckland, 4th edn, 2003, p. 120.

87 Zonophone advertisement, *Dominion*, 12 April 1924; Catalogue *No. 7*, Farmers Trading Company, Auckland, 1925, Eph-B-Retail-FTC-1925, ATL.

88 *NZ Theatre and Motion Picture*, 1 May 1925, p. 23; 1 June 1925, p. 10.

89 Ernest Kaii's [*sic*] Hawaiian Troubadours' programme, Grand Opera House, Wellington, 12 November 1927, Eph-A-Variety-1927, ATL; 'Stanley McKay's Gaieties', *New Zealand Sporting and Dramatic Review*, 7 April 1938, p. 1.

90 'Are You There, Rarotonga?', *NZ Radio Record*, 31 May 1929, p. 8.

91 Jackey and Rebecca Coyle, 'Aloha Australia: Hawaiian Music in Australia 1920–1955', *Perfect Beat*, January 1995, p. 33.

92 'Yaaka Hula' in New Zealand: Graham Reid, recalling an anecdote of his musician father, Bisset, *Black Roots, White Flowers*, p. 21; Brian Salkeld, 'The Dancing Decade 1920–30', *Stout Centre Review*, August 1992, p. 7. A Zonophone advertisement from 12 April 1924 includes the Hawaiian Guitars' disc 'Moe Uhane Waltz' b/w 'Hawaii I'm Lonesome for You', BA/ATL.

93 Coyle and Coyle, 'Aloha Australia', pp. 41–42.

94 Listeners imagined that the oscillations in the shortwave signals were ocean waves rolling up Waikiki Beach. When radio reception improved, there were complaints, so a microphone was placed by a beach to capture the surf as a sound effect: Doyle, *Echo and Reverb*, pp. 120–6; Kanahele, *Hawaiian Music and Musicians*, pp. 112–13.

95 Coyle and Coyle, 'Aloha Australia', pp. 37–39.

96 Robin Hyde, 'On the Road to Anywhere', *NZ Railways Magazine*, 1 April 1935, reprinted in Gillian Boddy and Jacqueline Matthews (eds), *Disputed Ground: Robin Hyde, Journalist*, Victoria University Press, Wellington, 1991, p. 318.

97 *AMM*, August 1938 and September 1938.

98 PC4 4297 and PC4 4623, Archives NZ; 'Heritage: Bunny Milne', *NZHSGA Gazette*, February 1998.

99 *AMM*, October 1944

100 Mati, a Tahitian, had been performing in Auckland since the early 1930s.

101 Mac McKenzie, 'Heritage: Gus Lindsay', *NZHSGA Gazette*, February 1997.

102 Mac McKenzie, 'Heritage: Mati Hita', *NZHSGA Gazette*, August 1997.

103 Mac McKenzie, 'The Pathfinders', *NZHSGA Gazette*, February 2005.

104 Jim Carter, interviewed by Chris Bourke, Nelson, October 2008.

105 Lorene Ruymar, *The Hawaiian Steel Guitar and its Great Hawaiian Musicians*, Centerstream, Anaheim Hills, CA, 1996, p. 44.

106 Sam Sampson, 'South Sea Island Magic: Bill Sevesi and the Auckland Music Scene', *Perfect Beat*, July 1998, p. 36.

107 Mac McKenzie, 'Sad News: Bill Wolfgramm', *NZHSGA Gazette*. November 2003.

108 *NZ Listener*, 15 July 1955, p. 28.

109 Wolfgramm recorded another version of 'Fijian Holiday' with Daphne Walker for Stebbing in 1953.

110 Mac McKenzie, 'Bill Wolfgramm: The Man Behind the Music', *NZHSGA Gazette*, November 2003.

111 *NZ Listener*, 15 July 1955, p. 28.

112 *Tempo*, January 1956.

113 McKenzie, 'Sad News: Bill Wolfgramm'.

114 'En-Zedders on Record', *Record Monthly*, 1 November 1956, p. 17.

115 Gordon Spittle, 'Play it Again, Sam', *Southern Skies*, February 2003, p. 40; Middlebrow, 'On the Air', *NZ Truth*, 10 September 1955.

116 Daphne Walker, interviewed by Jim Sutton, Newstalk ZB, 16 December 2001.

117 Bill Sevesi, interviewed by Jim Sutton, Newstalk ZB, 16 December 2001.

118 Daphne Walker, interviewed by Jim Sutton.

119 Murdoch Riley, interviewed by Gordon Spittle.

120 'En-Zedders on Record', *Record Monthly*, 1 November 1956, p. 17.

121 Mac McKenzie, 'Bill Sevesi QSM', *NZHSGA Gazette*, November 1998; Sampson, 'South Sea Island Magic', p. 21.

122 Bill Sevesi, interviewed by Jim Sutton.

123 Bill Sevesi, interviewed by Jim Sutton; Gordon Spittle, *The Tex Morton Songbook*, GWS Publications, Auckland, 2008, p. 55; Sampson, 'South Sea Island Magic', p. 26.

124 Also in this band were Ray Gunter on guitar and Lloyd Sly on piano accordion.

125 Bill Sevesi, interviewed by Jim Sutton.

126 Bill Sevesi, interviewed by Jim Sutton.

127 McKenzie, 'Bill Sevesi QSM'; Chris Williams, 'Bill Sevesi and His Polynesian Memories', *Metro*, May 1990, p. 125.

128 McKenzie, 'Bill Sevesi QSM'.

129 *NZ Herald*, 11 September 1928, p. 13; *Auckland Sun*, 25 August 1928, p. 16; *NZ Herald*, 5 September 1928, p. 20.

130 Garth Gibson, 'A History of Country Music in New Zealand', part one, *Country & Western Spotlight*, new series 3, June 1975, pp. 3–4.

131 Jack Riggir, oral history interview by Kerry Stevens, Putaruru, 9 May 1984, OHColl-0133, ATL.

132 Bruce Anderson, *Story of the New Zealand Recording Industry*, self-published, Wellington, 1984, p. 60.

133 Graeme Smith, 'Australian Country Music and the Hillbilly Yodel', *Popular Music*, vol. 13, no. 3, 1994, p. 297; www.nashvillesongwriters foundation.com/p-s/carson-j-robison.aspx.

134 Smith, 'Australian Country Music and the Hillbilly Yodel', pp. 303–4.

135 John I. Spedding, Dunedin column, *AMM*, September 1939.

136 Garth Gibson, 'Spotlight on Les Wilson', *Country & Western Spotlight*, 5, March 1956, p. 3.

137 *NZ Listener*, 15 March 1940, pp. 49 and 53; *AMM*, August 1941.

138 Happi Hill obituary, *Press*, no date, Rocky Don Hall collection.

139 'From Way Out West', *NZ Listener*, 10 April 1941, p. 7.

140 Happi Hill obituary; J. K Smith, *Just for the Record: A Discography of Vinyl Recordings by New Zealand Recording Artists from 1949 to 2000*, J. K. Smith, Whangarei, 3rd edn, 2001, pp. 102 and 233.

141 Rocky Don Hall, interviewed by Chris Bourke, Levin, October 2008.

142 'Sisters Tune Up', *Christchurch Star*, undated clipping from 1990s, Chris Bourke collection; 'The Canadian Sisters', *Country & Western Spotlight*, c. 1974, p. 14.

143 Chris Bourke, 'Pearce, Arthur Fairchild 1903–1990', *Dictionary of New Zealand Biography* (http://www.dnzb.co.nz); Pearce papers, MS-90-327-20, ATL.

144 Stan Dallas, *Joy*, 16 May 1960, p. 10; Stan Dallas, interviewed by Gordon Spittle; *NZ Listener*, 1 April 1955, p. 24; Bill Hamer, 'The Tanza Saga: The Story of New Zealand's Pioneer Record Label', monograph at MusLib, P Box, q780, HAM 1992, ATL, published in *Australian Music & Record Review*, October 1992.

145 'I'll Serenade a Star', words and music by Sam Freedman, Maoriland Publications, Wellington.

146 Nola (Hewitt) McCrorie, *Maple on the Hill: The True Story of the Tumbleweeds*, unpublished monograph, Chris Bourke collection.

147 McCrorie, *Maple on the Hill*.

148 *Country Music*, 19, 1976, p. 12 (a reprint of a 1957 *Record Monthly* profile); McCrorie, *Maple on the Hill*.

149 Colin McCrorie, interviewed by Chris Bourke, Dunedin, October 2006.

150 *Maple on the Hill*, a documentary by Stephen Latty, 1988.

151 *Country & Western Spotlight*, 26; Emily Flynn, 'Best Western', *NZ Listener*, 10 December 1988, p. 39; Roy Colbert, 'Wilson, Colin James 1922–1993', *Dictionary of New Zealand Biography* (http://www.dnzb.govt.nz).

152 *NZ Truth*, 19 May 1954, p. 24.

153 Ron Hayward, letter to Chris Bourke, 26 January 2010.

154 2ZM was later re-named 2XM, and existed until 1963.

155 Eric Watson, *Country Music in Australia, Volume Two*, A Cornstalk Book, Angus & Robertson, Sydney, 1983, pp. 7–11; Doyle, also quoting Watson, in *Echo and Reverb*, pp. 104–5.

156 *Country & Western Spotlight*, 43 September 1963, p. 10.

157 Andrew Smith, 'The Yodeling Cowgirls', in Charles K. Wolfe and James E. Akenson (eds), *The Women of Country Music: A Reader*, University Press of Kentucky, Lexington, 2003, p. 198.

158 'Music by New Zealanders', *NZ Listener*, 26 July 1957, p. 27.

159 Gibson, 'A History of Country Music in New Zealand'.

160 Gibson, 'A History of Country Music in New Zealand'.

161 As quoted by Gibson in *Country & Western Spotlight*, 1, November 1955, p. 5.

162 *Country & Western Spotlight*, 13, November 1956, p. 4.

163 Les Wilson Show poster, 1960: Eph-C26756, ATL.

164 Victoria Clark, 'Mates in Music and Song', *NZ Herald*, 11 April 1984.

165 Jack Riggir, oral history interview by Kerry Stevens.

166 Archive 1XH radio clip in the Jack Riggir oral history interview by Kerry Stevens.

167 Eldred Stebbing, letter to Jack Riggir, 13 April 1951, Riggir, AJ: MS 84-020-1, ATL.

168 Jack Riggir, oral history interview by Kerry Stevens; Ron Hayward, interviewed by Chris Bourke, Stratford, 3 November 2007.

169 Peter N. Temm, '"Smiling Billy" Calling!', *NZ Woman's Weekly*, 2 August 1951, p. 11.

170 'Government Invades Professional Dancing Field', *NZ Truth*, 6 June 1951, p. 18.

171 'Dunedin Led Dominion in Field of Impromptu Square Dancing', *Otago Daily Times*, 12 March 1955, p. 6.

172 John Cooke, 'Introducing the Luke Simmons Story', *Country & Western Spotlight*, 18, April/May/June 1958, p. 9.

173 *Country & Western Spotlight*, 7, April/May/June 1958, p. 7.

174 Lee was appointed Stebbings' musical director in approximately September 1952 (Dennis O. Huggard, 'Introduction', *The Stebbing Catalogue*, New Zealand Series No. 3, Dennis O. Huggard, Waitakere, 4th edn, 2008, p. 3).

175 Garth Gibson, *Country & Western Spotlight*, 19, July/August/September 1957, p. 20.
176 Barton's Follies poster, 1950: Eph-C23938, ATL.
177 Gibson, *Country & Western Spotlight*.
178 Tex Morton guitar advertisement, *NZ Listener*, 27 January 1950, p. 35.
179 Rex Franklin, interviewed by Jim Sutton on 1ZB, 28 March 1999.
180 Rex Franklin, interviewed by Jim Sutton.
181 Rex Franklin, interviewed by Jim Sutton. The Ruahine Ramblers went on to make several discs with the singers Doug Rider and Paul Jarrett.
182 Rex Franklin, liner notes to CD, *A Real New Zealand Cowboy Song* by Rex and Noelene Franklin (Bear Family BCD16228, Germany, 1999).
183 Noelene Franklin, interviewed by Jim Sutton on 1ZB, 28 March 1999.
184 Noelene Franklin, interviewed by Jim Sutton.
185 This debut 78 featured the songs Hank Snow made popular: 'Would You Mind'/'I Wonder Where You Are Tonight' (Tanza Z300).
186 Rex Franklin, interviewed by Jim Sutton.
187 Rex Franklin, interviewed by Jim Sutton.
188 Sarah Gault, 'Country Music Duo Look to New Horizons with Deal', *Daily News* (New Plymouth), 4 March 1999, p. 4.
189 Johnny Cooper, interviewed by Gordon Spittle, 5 October 1992; Johnny Cooper on *Spectrum* documentary 785, 'A Rock Pioneer', produced by Jerome Cvitanovich, Radio New Zealand, 1993.
190 The Range Riders were Will Lloyd-Jones, bass; Don Aldridge, steel guitar; Ron James, piano accordion; and Cooper and Gatfield on acoustic guitars.
191 Gordon Spittle, 'Johnny Cooper: The Original Maori Cowboy', *Music in New Zealand*, 24, Autumn 1994, p. 43.
192 Johnny Cooper, interviewed by Gordon Spittle.
193 *Country & Western Spotlight*, 5, March 1956, p. 1.
194 *Country & Western Spotlight*, 1, November 1955, p. 4.
195 *Country & Western Spotlight*, 2, December 1955, p. 1.
196 *Country & Western Spotlight*, 7, May 1956; 13, November 1956.
197 *Country & Western Spotlight*, 8, June 1956.
198 *Country & Western Spotlight*, 10, August 1956; 18, April 1957.
199 *Country & Western Spotlight*, 49, March 1965, p. 24.
200 *Country & Western Spotlight*, 27, July/August/September 1959, p. 20; Max McCauley, interviewed by Chris Bourke, Gore, October 2006.
201 Garner Wayne, interviewed by Jim Sutton, Newstalk ZB, 1999.
202 Jack Leigh, 'New "Innings" for Old MCC', *Auckland Star*, 14 September 1974, p. 2:8.
203 Josie Harbutt, 'The Sheltering Island', *Planet*, 13, Winter 1994, p. 12.
204 Tautoko Morehu, 'The Maori Community Centre', *Te Maori News*, October 1992, p. 3.
205 Mervyn McLean (ed.), *Catalogue of Radio New Zealand Recordings of Maori Events, 1938–1950*, Archive of Maori and Pacific Music, Anthropology Department, University of Auckland, Auckland, 1991, p. 133.
206 Michael King, *The Penguin History of New Zealand*, Penguin, Auckland, 2007, p. 404.
207 Ian Pool, *Te Iwi Maori: A New Zealand Population Past, Present & Projected*, Auckland University Press, Auckland, 1991, p. 157.
208 Joan Metge, *A New Maori Migration*, Athlone Press, London, 1964, p. 228.
209 'Where Maoris Meet', *Weekly News*, 26 January 1949, p. 7.
210 Onlooker, 'Platters Sing with Maori Group', *Joy*, 27 April 1959, p. 8.
211 Gerry Merito, interviewed by Chris Bourke, Cambridge, 4 November 2007.
212 Leigh, 'New "Innings" for Old MCC'.
213 'Auckland's Community Centre', *Te Ao Hou*, September 1962, p. 25.
214 'Auckland's Community Centre', *Te Ao Hou*, p. 25
215 Simon Meihana, interviewed by Suzanne Ormsby, see Ormsby, *Te Reo Puoro Maori Mai I Mua Tae Noa Mai Ki Inaianei*, p. 126.
216 Ormsby, *Te Reo Puoro Maori Mai I Mua Tae Noa Mai Ki Inaianei*, p. 126.
217 'Auckland's Community Centre', *Te Ao Hou*, p. 29.
218 *AMM*, October 1958.
219 Gerry Merito, interviewed by Chris Bourke.
220 Simon Meihana, interviewed by Suzanne Ormsby; see Ormsby, *Te Reo Puoro Maori Mai I Mua Tae Noa Mai Ki Inaianei*, p. 126.
221 Leigh, 'New "Innings" for Old MCC'.
222 Ben Tawhiti, interviewed by Suzanne Ormsby; see Ormsby, *Te Reo Puoro Maori Mai I Mua Tae Noa Mai Ki Inaianei*, p. 185.
223 Andrew Tumahai, 'Boy is What They Call Me, But My Real Name is Charlie', *Te Maori News*, January 1996, p. 5.
224 Ormsby, *Te Reo Puoro Maori Mai I Mua Tae Noa Mai Ki Inaianei*, p. 72.
225 John Berry, 'Maori Entertainers in Auckland', *Te Ao Hou*, June 1959, p. 53.
226 Berry, 'Maori Entertainers in Auckland'.
227 Jim Warren, *AMM*, May 1959.

SIX SUNSETS AND SUNRISES: INTO THE 1960S

1 'Glamour Girl With Her Mind on the Job', *Joy*, 7 December 1959, p. 3.
2 *NZ Listener*, 10 November 1950, p. 5.
3 *NZ Listener*, 7 March 1952, p. 19; 24 April 1952, p. 6.
4 Redmer Yska, *All Shook Up*, Penguin, Auckland, 1993, p. 129.
5 To the establishment, bodgies were surly, slovenly youths of dubious morality who hoped to emulate Marlon Brando's character in *The Wild One* ('What are you rebelling against, Johnny?', 'Whaddaya got?'). Widgies were their female companions.
6 Christine Mintrom, *Tommy Adderley 1940–1993*, iUniverse, Lincoln, Nebraska, 2003, p. 34.
7 Tommy Adderley, interviewed by Gordon Spittle, 11 August 1992.
8 Tommy Adderley, interviewed by Eric Gerritsen, *Music in New Zealand*, Autumn 1989, p. 12.
9 'Moral Delinquency Said to Be Widespread', *NZ Truth*, 14 July 1954, p. 9; Yska, *All Shook Up*, p. 68.
10 Yska, *All Shook Up*, p. 82.
11 *Report of the Special Committee on Moral Delinquency in Children and Adolescents*, Government Printer, Wellington, 1954, 3: Broadcasting.
12 NZBS Standards Recordings Purchasing Committee decision ledger, RNZ; committee memos, RNZ Sound Archives.
13 NZBS Standards Recordings Purchasing Committee decision ledger, RNZ; committee memos, RNZ Sound Archives.
14 Mazengarb hearings, 9 August 1954, as quoted in Yska, *All Shook Up*, p. 137; Tony Hopkins, interviewed by Gordon Spittle, 18 September 1992; NZBS Standards Recordings Purchasing Committee decision ledger, RNZ.
15 Letters to the editor, *NZ Herald*, 19 January to 1 February 1955; Yska, *All Shook Up*, pp. 154 and 176.
16 NZBS Standards Recordings Purchasing Committee decision ledger, RNZ; committee memos, RNZ Sound Archives.
17 Moliere, 'Who Is Radio's Ban Man?', *NZ Observer*, 11 August 1954, p. 12.
18 Peter Downes, interviewed by Chris Bourke, Tawa, October 2008.
19 Max Merritt, 'Rock's In – Rock's Out', *Joy*, 7 June 1960, p. 10.
20 Middlebrow, 'On the Air', *NZ Truth*, 24 August 1955, p. 26.
21 Dave Van Weede, interviewed by Chris Bourke, Auckland, 23 January 2007.
22 Johnny Cooper, interviewed by Gordon Spittle on 5 October 1992; also on Radio New Zealand and Radio Pacific, Chris Bourke collection.
23 Dave Van Weede, letter to Dennis Huggard, 13 January 2010.
24 The band was: Ken Avery on tenor sax, Jim Carter using a Spanish acoustic guitar fitted with a pickup, Slim Dorwood on bass, Bob Barcham piano and Vern Clare drums. (Ken Avery, *Where Are the Camels? A Dance Band Diary*, p. 32; Don Aldridge, interviewed by Gordon Spittle, 23 September 1992).
25 Middlebrow, 'On the Air', *NZ Truth*, 31 August 1955, p. 24; 7 September 1955, p. 26.
26 Johnny Cooper on *Spectrum* documentary 785, 'A Rock Pioneer', produced by Jerome Cvitanovich, Radio New Zealand, 1993.
27 Johnny Devlin, interviewed on Radio Pacific, 1990.
28 *NZ Herald*, 7 September 1955, p. 20.
29 *NZ Herald*, 20 September 1955, p. 16.
30 Tony Hopkins, interviewed by Chris Bourke, Piha, January 2001.
31 Ray Columbus, letter to Chris Bourke, July 2009.
32 Gordon Spittle, 'Duke of Jukeboxes', *Southern Skies*, April 1995, p. 54; Yska, *All Shook Up*, p. 134.
33 Sonny Day, interviewed by Gordon Spittle, 4 August 1992.
34 Laurie Lewis, *Arthur and the Nights at the Turntable: The Life and Times of a Jazz Broadcaster*, K'Vrie Press, Wingen, NSW, 1997, pp. 206, 209, 212.
35 Arthur Pearce, *Western Song Parade* scripts, MS Papers 90-327-13 to 90-327-20, ATL; programme # 55, 2YD, 26 January 1956.
36 Lewis, *Arthur and the Nights at the Turntable*, p. 212.
37 Arthur Pearce, *Western Song Parade* scripts, programme # 56, 2YD, 2 February 1956. Such was his enthusiasm for Presley, he even played 'Milk Cow Blues Boogie' on *Rhythm on Record*, reasoning that as blues, it was connected with jazz. Laurie Lewis listened 'with astonishment. This was probably the only occasion when the listening jazz fans were unanimous in their rejection of one of Arthur's choices' (Lewis, *Arthur and the Nights at the Turntable*, p. 212).
38 Lewis, *Arthur and the Nights at the Turntable*, p. 212; Murdoch Riley, interviewed by Chris Bourke, 22 February 2008.
39 Stan Dallas, interviewed by Gordon Spittle, 21 September 1992.
40 Harry Voice, interviewed by Chris Bourke, Christchurch, October 2006; Don Branch, in *The Drum Scene: Auckland*, a 1963 monograph by Bruce Morley, p. 17 (ATL).
41 Lew Campbell, interviewed by Chris Bourke, Sydney, 27 November 2006.
42 Laurie Lewis, interviewed by Chris Bourke, Melbourne, 1 December 2006.
43 *NZ Herald* advertisements, 24 November 1955.
44 Programmes, Festivals of Jazz, 1955–1957 (Don Richardson scrapbook).
45 'Jazz Night', *NZ Listener*, 28 October 1955, p. 8.
46 HMV's Fred Smith, in John Dix, *The History of New Zealand Rock'n'Roll*, Department of Education, Wellington, 1986, p. 8; Peter J. Read, *Blue Suede Gumboots? The Impact of Imported Popular Culture in New Zealand in the 1950s*, MA History thesis, University of Otago, 1990, p. 25.
47 *Auckland Star*, 13 January 1956, p. 13.
48 *Tempo*, November 1955; Dennis Huggard, *The Tanza Catalogue*, New Zealand Series, booklet one, Dennis O. Huggard, Glendene, 5th edn, 2005, p. 42; John K. Smith, *Just for the Record*, John K. Smith, Whangarei, 2001, p. 43.
49 *Dominion* and *Evening Post*, 17 May 1956.
50 'Jazz Star Has No Fears About "Rock An' Roll"', *Evening Post*, late September 1956.
51 Letters to the editor, *Evening Post*, 1955–1956; B. O. Peterson, letter to Vern Clare, 7 December 1955 (Don Richardson scrapbook); L. D. Austin, letter to the editor, *Evening Post*, 13 December 1956.
52 *NZ Truth*, 9 October 1956, p. 22.
53 Yska, *All Shook Up*, p. 109.
54 Wayne Brittenden, *The Celluloid Circus: The Heyday of the New Zealand Picture Theatre*, Auckland, Random House, 2009, pp. 35 and 63.
55 Graham Dent, interviewed by Roger Watkins, 24 November 1992, oral history OHC-005013, ATL; *Auckland Star*, 24 September 1956, p. 4.
56 Graham Dent, interviewed by Roger Watkins.
57 *NZ Herald*, 28 September 1956, p. 20; 29 September 1956, p. 20; 5 October 1956, p. 24; Graham Dent, interviewed by Roger Watkins.

58   For example, Jazz at the Opera House brought 'rock'n'roll in the flesh for the first time at New Plymouth' on 18 April 1956; Wellington's sixth Festival of Jazz on 14 May featured Johnny Cooper; and a Benny Goodman/Glenn Miller tribute concert at Auckland Town Hall in August featured pianist and promoter Benny Levin singing with 'Queen of the rock'n'roll', Ngaire Gedson, plus a band called the Rock and Rollers (*Tempo*, August 1956).

59   The band was drummer Frank Gibson, trumpeter Bob Griffith, trombonist Neil Dunningham, Scottish pianist Don Grant, saxophonist Pem Sheppard, bassist Bob Ewing and vocalist Steve Shaw; *Auckland Star*, 3 October 1956, p. 23; Merv Thomas, interviewed by Chris Bourke, Auckland, 25 May 2007.

60   Duncan Stuart, 'Bless My Soul, It's . . . Rock'n'Roll', *Metro*, March 1986, p. 98.

61   Bruce Kaplan, 'They Flock to Rock at Dave's Jive Centre', *Joy*, 2 March 1959, p. 21.

62   Stuart, 'Bless My Soul'.

63   'For Old Times – A Noise Shop', *Auckland Star*, 17 March 1978, p. 6; *NZ Herald*, 11 October 1956, p. 20.

64   Interview with Bernie Allen, *Allegro*, August 1974, p. 7.

65   Gibson's second band was Bernie Allen, saxophone; Jack Shanks, piano; Merv Thomas, trombone; Dave Foreman, trumpet; Frank Gibson, drums (Merv Thomas, interviewed by Chris Bourke); *NZ Herald*, 24 October 1956.

66   Lou Clauson, interviewed by Marty Duda, Radio New Zealand, 2009; *Papakura Ribbon*, 24 October 1956.

67   'For Old Times – A Noise Shop', *Auckland Star*.

68   Merv Thomas, interviewed by Chris Bourke.

69   Kaplan, 'They Flock to Rock . . .'; 'Rock & Roll', *NZ Listener*, 9 November 1956, p. 9; *Otago Daily Times*, 13 November 1956, p. 12.

70   *Otago Daily Times*, 3 November 1956, p. 1.

71   *Southern News*, 25 October 1956, p. 12, as quoted in Read, *Blue Suede Gumboots?*, p. 95.

72   *Southern News*, 22 November 1956, p. 12.

73   'Rock and Roll at Town Hall', *Evening Post*, 29 November 1956.

74   Laurie Lewis, interviewed by Chris Bourke.

75   FH, *Dominion*, 18 December 1956, p. 13.

76   *Music Maker*, December 1956.

77   *Tempo*, October 1956.

78   Jon Stratton, *The Young Ones: Working-Class Culture, Consumption and the Category of Youth*, Black Swan Press, Perth, 1992, p. 142. The musical accompaniment was the Sorrento Orchestra led by Allan Levitt, an English multi-instrumentalist and former member of the Joe Loss Orchestra who had arrived in New Zealand in 1955.

79   Stratton, *The Young Ones*, p. 142.

80   'The Experts Get Really Hep', *Evening Post*, 13 March 1957, p. 16.

81   Don Richardson, interviewed by Chris Bourke, February 2007.

82   'Rocked to Rest After 49 Hours', *Otago Daily Times*, 12 July 1957, p. 5; 'Rocked Round the Clock', *NZ Woman's Weekly*, 1 July 1955, p. 6.

83   *Otago Daily Times*, 8 January 1963, p. 7; and 19 May 1958, p. 5.

84   Rachel Elizabeth McDermott, *Entertaining Ideas: The Enterprises of Joe Brown*, HSOE [Hard School of Experience], University of Otago Department of History, 1998.

85   *Otago Daily Times*, 19 May 1958, p. 5, quoted by McDermott, *Entertaining Ideas*.

86   'Rock'n'Roll Party in Hastings Cemetery', *Dominion*, 16 April 1958.

87   'Rock'n'Rollers Nearly Break Up Sunday Concert', *Dominion*, 29 May 1957; 'Rock'n'Roll Inquest', *NZ Truth*, 23 July 1957.

88   *Otago Daily Times*, 20 April 1959, p. 5; *Otago Daily Times*, 9 June 1958, p. 1 – as quoted in Read, *Blue Suede Gumboots?*, p. 118.

89   'Four Thousand Feet "Rocked" the Town Hall', *Dominion*, 21 February 1957.

90   Bernie Allen, interviewed by Chris Bourke, Auckland, May 2007; 'Mass Hysteria Due to Rock'n'Roll Men', *Evening Star*, February 1957.

91   'Rock an' Roll at the Opera House', *Manawatu Evening Standard*, 26 March 1957.

92   Johnny Devlin, interviewed by Chris Bourke, August 2006; John Baker, liner notes to Johnny Devlin, *How Would 'Ya Be* (Ode CD, 2007); Johnny Devlin, interviewed by Eric Frykberg, Radio New Zealand, 2003.

93   Johnny Devlin, interviewed by Gordon Spittle, 29 October 1992.

94   Johnny Devlin, interviewed by Chris Bourke.

95   Interviews with Johnny Devlin and Colin King by Chris Bourke; Tommy Kahi, oral history interview by Roger Watkins, 17 November 1993, ATL; John Baker, liner notes to Johnny Devlin, *How Would 'Ya Be*.

96   Alan Loney, interviewed by Chris Bourke, Melbourne, November 2006.

97   Turntable, 'Jazz Festival Could Be Misleading', *Evening Post*, 13 August 1957.

98   Johnny Devlin, interviewed by Jim Sutton, Newstalk ZB, 1998.

99   Johnny Devlin, interviewed by Chris Bourke.

100   Johnny Devlin, interviewed by Gordon Spittle.

101   Johnny Devlin, interviewed by Jim Sutton, Newstalk ZB.

102   Merv Thomas, interviewed by Chris Bourke.

103   Dave Van Weede, interviewed by Chris Bourke; Phil Warren, interviewed by Jim Sutton, Newstalk ZB, 1998.

104   *Joy*, 2 March 1959, p. 12.

105   Johnny Devlin, interviewed by Chris Bourke; and by Eric Frykberg; *NZ Woman's Weekly*, 9 February 1959.

106   'Carol Has Nearly as Many Fans as Johnny Does', *Joy*, 2 March 1959, p. 12.

107   Tony Hopkins, interviewed by Chris Bourke.

108   'Carol Has Nearly as Many Fans as Johnny Does', *Joy*.

109   'Rock'n'Roll Singer a "Nice Young Man"', *Press*, 10 January 1959, p. 4.

110   Johnny Devlin, interviewed by Chris Bourke; by Gordon Spittle; John Baker, liner notes to Johnny Devlin, *How Would 'Ya Be*.

111   'Rockin' that Man', *NZ Woman's Weekly*, 23 March 1959, p. 9; Phil Warren, interviewed by Jim Sutton.

112   'Rockin' that Man', *NZ Woman's Weekly*.

113   *Cinema, Stage and TV*, November 1959, p. 39; December–January 1959–60, p. 21; March 1960, p. 50.

114   'Rock'n'roll Singer a "Nice Young Man"', *Press*, 10 January 1959, p. 4.

115   Middlebrow, 'It's a Long Time Dying', *Joy*, 6 April 1959, p. 10.

116   Don Richardson, 'It's a Slow Knock for the Rock', *Joy*, 27 October 1958, p. 10.

117   Rod Stone, at Andy Shackleton's website commemorating early Wellington rock'n'roll bands (www.ashack.co.nz).

118   Mike Nock, interviewed by Chris Bourke, Sydney, 26 November 2006.

119   Gordon Campbell, 'Rock Around the Two Half-hours', *NZ Listener*, 8 May 1982, p. 14.

120   *Weekly News*, 3 September 1958, p. 23.

121   Nell Hartley, 'Somewhere to Go', *Weekly News*, 3 September 1958, p. 5.

122   Max Merritt, 'Rock's In – Rock's Out', *Joy*, 7 June 1960, p. 10.

123   Megan Ritchie, *Shaken, But Not Stirred? Youth Cultures in 1950s Auckland*, MA History thesis, University of Auckland, 1997, pp. 47–48.

124   Bruce Kaplan, 'The Bob Paris Story', *Joy*, 16 February 1959, p. 8; Bob Paris, interviewed by Gordon Spittle, 6 August 1992. The original Bob Paris Combo featured Bill Fairs, saxophone; Keith McMillan, drums; and Gene Blazer, bass; Dunningham added Ian Lowe, guitar; pianist Bob Anderson; and Samoan-born, eighteen-year-old vocalist Desma.

125   Bob Paris, interviewed by Gordon Spittle; Roger Watkins, *Hostage to the Beat: The Auckland Scene 1955–1970*, Tandem, Auckland, 1995, p. 24.

126   Cees Klop, liner notes, *The Keil Isles: Early Rock & Roll from New Zealand, Vol. 1 & 2* (Collector Records, CLCD 7753/A/B); Watkins, *Hostage to the Beat*, p. 86.

127   Watkins, *Hostage to the Beat*, pp. 59–60.

128   Red Hewitt, interviewed by Jim Sutton, Newstalk ZB, 1999; 'Red Hewitt', *NZ Country Music Magazine*, March 1994, pp. 4–5.

129   'Red Hewitt', *NZ Country Music Magazine*.

130   'From Youth-Club Beginnings', *Joy*, 11 May 1959, p. 10; Roger Watkins, *When Rock Got Rolling: The Wellington Scene 1958–1970*, Hazard Press, Christchurch, 1989, pp. 62, 69–71.

131   Rod Stone, at Andy Shackleton's website (www.ashack.co.nz); Watkins, *When Rock Got Rolling*, p. 37.

132   Allen Quennell, interviewed by Geoffrey Totton, 14 April 1987, ATL; liner notes, *Early Rock & Roll From New Zealand, vol. 5 & 6*, Collector Records CLCD 7755/A/B, p. 14; Neil McKelvie, *45 South in Concert*, Southland Musicians' Club, Invercargill, 2006, p. 152.

133   Max Merritt, interviewed for *Musical Chairs*, Radio New Zealand, 2003.

134   Kate Preece, 'Sounds Like Us', *Avenues*, May 2009, p. 27.

135   *Spectrum 1288, Where Were You in '62?*, produced by Gerard Duignan, Radio New Zealand, 2002; Phil Garland, *Faces in the Firelight: New Zealand Folksong and Story*, Steele Roberts, Wellington, 2009, pp. 17–19; Preece, 'Sounds Like Us', p. 28.

136   Preece, 'Sounds Like Us'; John Dix, *Stranded in Paradise*, Paradise Publications, Wellington, 1988, pp. 41–42.

137   Merritt, 'Rock's In – Rock's Out'.

138   Mary Throll, *The Scottish Nightingale*, Wordsell Press, Auckland, 2004, pp. 62–63; John Berry, *Seeing Stars*, Seven Seas, Wellington, 1964, pp. 85, 95–97.

139   Philip English, 'Rock'n'roll Pioneer Kept Teens Dancing', *NZ Herald*, 23 July 2002, p. A9; Kaplan, 'They Flock to Rock . . .'.

140   Harry M. Miller, *My Story*, Macmillan, Melbourne, 1983; Berry, *Seeing Stars*, pp. 84–86; Bryan Staff and Sheran Ashley, *For the Record*, David Bateman, Auckland, 2002, pp. 69–74.

141   Toni McRae, 'Benny Levin: the Show Goes On', *Sunday Star*, 27 December 1992.

142   *AMM*, July 1958.

143   Peter Calder, 'Benny Levin: Showman Extraordinaire', *NZ Herald*, 5 July 1993, p. 1:9.

144   Chris Bourke, 'Phil Warren, Impresario', *NZ Listener*, 9 February 2002; John Berry, 'A Quick Tempo Success', *Auckland Star*, 20 February 1965, p. 15; Tony Potter, 'Entrepreneur and Ace of Many Clubs', *Sunday Star-Times*, 27 January 2002; Phil Warren, oral history interview by Roger Watkins, 25 January 1992 (ATL OHA 2095).

145   Noad in *Electrical and Radio Trader*, May 1957, as quoted in Staff and Ashley, *For the Record*, pp. 58–59.

146   HMV advertisement, *NZ Listener*, 8 February 1957, p. 4.

147   Noad in *Electrical and Radio Trader*, May 1957.

148   *Evening Post* advertisements, May/June 1958, Bruce Anderson scrapbooks, FMS-Papers-5277-01, ATL; Staff and Ashley, *For the Record*, pp. 59–60.

149   Tommy Adderley, interviewed by Gordon Spittle, 11 August 1992; Murray Marbeck, interviewed by Chris Bourke, Auckland, July 2006; 'Copyright Holdups', *Joy*, 6 April 1959, p. 10. When the stage version of *My Fair Lady* finally reached Auckland in 1961, its season lasted six months and played to 640,000 people at His Majesty's Theatre (*NZ Herald*, 17 August 1961).

150   In 1957, for example, besides the Columbus and HMV stores, a record buyer in downtown Wellington could visit The Record Shop, Discville at Fears, Dixon Maddevers, the Record Grotto and Coffee Bar at Gurney's Electric Company, James Smith's, the Record Bar in the DIC and two branches of the Lamphouse. *Evening Post* advertisements, 1957–58, Bruce Anderson scrapbooks, FMS-Papers-5277-01, ATL.

151   *Tempo*, October 1956; *AMM*, October 1946; Jim Warren, interviewed by Chris Bourke, Auckland, July 2006.

152   *Truth*, 18 February 1958, p. 26; 1 April 1958, p. 26.

153   *Auckland Star*, May 1958, as quoted in David McGill, *Kiwi Baby Boomers*, Mills, Lower Hutt, 1989, p. 149. As there were no systematically compiled record sales charts in New Zealand until 1975, any reference to chart success is unreliable; it often just means the in-house chart of a regional radio station, reflecting the popularity of songs among their listeners, or charts compiled from the votes of fans (as in the *Listener* hit parade, which began in 1966).

154 Murdoch Riley, interviewed by Chris Bourke.
155 Murdoch Riley, interviewed by Chris Bourke.
156 Staff and Ashley, *For the Record*, pp. 74–76; Murdoch Riley, interviewed by Chris Bourke.
157 HMV 78 rpm collection, RNZ Sound Archives, Christchurch.
158 Dave Van Weede, interviewed by Chris Bourke.
159 Lotus was originally owned by Tasman Vaccine Laboratories. Nick Bollinger, 'The Golden Years of HMV: An Interview with Frank Douglas', *Music in New Zealand*, Autumn 1992, pp. 52–53; Bruce Anderson, *EMI: Fifty Years in New Zealand*, EMI, Lower Hutt, 1976, p. 4.
160 Bollinger, 'The Golden Years of HMV'.
161 Watkins, *When Rock Got Rolling*, p. 103; Bollinger, 'The Golden Years of HMV'.
162 Bill Cate, oral history interview by Roger Watkins, National Library OH MSC 5038.
163 Spencer Leigh, 'Pre-Fab Britain', *Record Collector*, August 2006, pp. 65–80; Elijah Wald, *How the Beatles Destroyed Rock'n'Roll: An Alternative History of American Popular Music*, Oxford University Press, New York, 2009, pp. 85–89.
164 'Rock-and-Roll Song About Resuscitation', *Evening Post*, 1 March 1957; Johnny Cooper, Radio New Zealand interview for *Musical Chairs*, 2001.
165 Advertisement, *Evening Post*, 9 September 1957, p. 2.
166 Murdoch Riley, interviewed by Gordon Spittle, 7 October 1992; 'Pop Singer at 16 is On Crest of Wave', *Evening Post*, 5 February 1960, p. 16.
167 'The Boy With the Voice', *Playdate*, June 1960, p. 52.
168 *Joy*, 29 June 1959, p. 10.
169 *Joy*, 1 December 1958, p. 10.
170 Bill Cate, oral history interview by Roger Watkins, OH MSC 5038, ATL; John King, 'Bill and Boyd Have Fallen on Their Feet', *Joy*, 7 June 1960, p. 4; Smith, *Just For the Record*, pp. 16–17.
171 Bernie Allen, interviewed by Chris Bourke, Auckland, May 2007.
172 Bennie Gunn, *57a or Tales of a Musicians' Hangout*, Talisman Press, Auckland, 1993, pp. 28–29.
173 Alwyn Lewis, *Join 'Em on the Riff*, K'Vrie Press, Wingen, NSW, 1996, p. 38; *AMM*, March 1955; Bruce Morley, *The Drum Scene: Auckland*, self-published monograph, ATL, 1963.
174 Mike Nock, interviewed by Chris Bourke.
175 Sy Bluhm, Jazz Action Society newsletter, Sydney, May 1994, Jamieson file, DHA, ATL; Lew Campbell, interviewed by Chris Bourke.
176 Jamieson moved to Australia in 1968, and was similarly influential until his death in 1994: Sy Bluhm, Jazz Action Society newsletter.
177 Rob MacGregor, *Around NZ in Eighty Cups*, Penrose Printing, Auckland, 1960, pp. 79–80.
178 Des Dubbelt, 'On the Town', *Playdate*, May 1960, p. 53.
179 John Berry, 'He's Top of the Auckland Nightclub Tree and Still Climbing', *Joy*, 3 August 1959, p. 5.
180 Millie Bradfield, interviewed by Suzanne Ormsby, in Suzanne Ormsby, *Te Reo Puoro Maori Mai I Mua Tae Noa Mai Ki Inaianei, The Voices of Maori Music, Past Present and Future: Maori Musicians of the 1960s*, MA thesis, University of Auckland, 1996, p. 118.
181 Mahora Peters with James George, *Showband! Mahora and the Maori Volcanics*, Huia, Wellington, 2005, p. 36.
182 *Tempo*, March 1955; *AMM*, November 1958; Jo Jules, *A Passion for Jazz: The Christchurch Scene Then and Now*, School of Performing Arts, Christchurch, 2009, p. 56.
183 Carol Cromie, 'The Jazz Singer', *NZ Listener*, 9 July 1988, p. 27; Judy O'Connor, 'Tribute to Maori from Onehunga', *Press*, 27 July 1988.
184 Cromie, 'The Jazz Singer'.
185 Anon, 'Ricky's Audience Screamed for More Songs', *NZ Herald*, 14 October 1967, p. 2:6; Rebecca Scott, 'Sydney Mourns Jazz Great's Death', *Sunday Star-Times*, 5 June 1988.
186 Millie Bradfield, interviewed by Suzanne Ormsby, in Ormsby, *Te Reo Puoro Maori Mai I Mua Tae Noa Mai Ki Inaianei*, p. 119.
187 Millie Bradfield, interviewed by Suzanne Ormsby, in Ormsby, *Te Reo Puoro Maori Mai I Mua Tae Noa Mai Ki Inaianei*, p. 119.
188 Bruce Kaplan, interviewed by Chris Bourke, Melbourne, 1 December 2006.
189 Watkins, *Hostage to the Beat*, p. 138.
190 Cromie, 'The Jazz Singer'.
191 Millie Bradfield, interviewed by Suzanne Ormsby, in Ormsby, *Te Reo Puoro Maori Mai I Mua Tae Noa Mai Ki Inaianei*, pp. 116–19; John Berry, 'Switch in Plans by Singer', *Auckland Star*, 12 September 1961; *AMM*, May 1964.
192 Jim Warren, *AMM*, September 1962. Besides vocalist Tong, the band featured Merv Thomas on trombone and tuba; Bernie Allen on reeds, flute and arrangements; Morrin Cooper on trumpet; Stu Parsons on sax; Lyall Laurent, piano; Bernie Hansson, bass; and Brian Spence, drums.
193 *Auckland Star*, 17 April 1963; *NZ Herald*, 21 February 1963.
194 Watkins, *Hostage to the Beat*, p. 169.
195 Yska, *All Shook Up*, p. 74; 'Protest Over Police Suspicions', *NZ Herald*, 23 October 1963.
196 '"House of Jazz" Tenant Before Court', *NZ Truth*, 13 December 1960, p. 58; Pat Lawlor, *Confessions of a Journalist*, Whitcombe & Tombs, Christchurch, 1935, p. 88.
197 Tommy Adderley, interviewed by Erik Gerritsen, *Music in New Zealand*, Autumn 1989, p. 13; Tommy Adderley, *Musical Chairs* documentary, RNZ, 2003.
198 *AMM*, May 1964.
199 *Jazz (for Listening) Wellington* (Philips PL08751, 1962) and *Private Party – Guests Only* (Kiwi SLC35, 1966).
200 Redmer Yska, *New Zealand Green: The Story of Marijuana in New Zealand*, David Bateman, Auckland, 1990, pp. 71–72; Neil Harrop, at Andy Shackleton's website (www.ashack.co.nz).
201 *AMM*, July 1962.
202 Yska, *New Zealand Green*, p. 72.
203 'Martin – Life and Soul of Club', *Christchurch Star*, 23 October 1982; Doug Caldwell, interviewed by Chris Bourke, Christchurch, October 2006.
204 Tommy Kahi, oral history interview by Roger Watkins, ATL; Doug Caldwell, interviewed by Chris Bourke; Pat Neho, 'A Musician Has to Experiment to Progress', *Joy*, 28 September 1959, p. 10; Jules, *A Passion for Jazz*, pp. 32 and 40.
205 Doug Caldwell, interviewed by Chris Bourke.
206 Michael Brown, *There's a Sound of Many Voices in the Camp and On the Track: A Descriptive Analysis of Folk Music Collecting in New Zealand, 1955–1975*, MA thesis, Victoria University of Wellington, 2006, p. 22.
207 Alan Mulgan, 'A Nation's Songs', *New Zealand Magazine*, March/April 1941, pp. 19–21.
208 Pat Sunde, 'Folk-song Scene – NZ', *Fernfire*, September 1966, pp. 16–19; Mike Harding, *When the Pakeha Sings of Home*, Godwit, Auckland, 1992, pp. 4–5.
209 Brown, *There's a Sound of Many Voices in the Camp and On the Track*, pp. 28–29, 35, 47–56 and 66–67; Joy Lee, 'His Hitch-hikes Prove NZ has Own Folk Songs', *NZ Woman's Weekly*, c. 1959, Chris Bourke collection.
210 'Gold-medal Balladeer', *NZ Listener*, 16 August 1957, p. 9; 'Wandering Minstrel', *NZ Listener*, 12 July 1957, p. 7; 'Clauson Comes Back', *NZ Listener*, 26 March 1959, p. 3.
211 'Cazna Gyp' was Anzac backwards and 'guard your property'. In 1961 Bob Edwards and Neil Roberts co-wrote 'Sticky-Beak the Kiwi', a Christmas hit for fourteen-year-old Julie Nelson that year: *Sunday Star-Times*, 27 December 1998, p. A7; David Dell, conversation with Chris Bourke, 8 August 2006; 'Wandering Minstrel', *NZ Listener*.
212 Rosemary Vincent, 'Think of Adding Another to Auckland's Coffee Bar Jungle', *Hit Parade*, 1962, p. 14.
213 Michael Stuart, 'Making of the Monde Marie', *Evening Post*, 28 August 1996, p. 23; Karl du Fresne, 'Glory Days at the Monde Marie', *Evening Post*, 13 July 2000, p. 5; 'Folk Song of *Your* Generation Given an Airing', *Joy*, 20 July 1959, p. 16; Vernon Wright, 'Untrained Voices Best for Folksinging', *Joy*, 11 April 1960, p. 10.
214 Peter Cape, 'Monde Marie', from Roger Steele, *An Ordinary Joker: The Life and Songs of Peter Cape*, Steele Roberts, Wellington, 2001, p. 81.
215 Du Fresne, 'Glory Days at the Monde Marie'; Brown, *There's a Sound of Many Voices in the Camp and On the Track*, p. 23.
216 Garland, *Faces in the Firelight*, pp. 17–21.
217 'The Maori Flute' appeared on Inia Te Wiata's EP [*sic*] *The Maori Flute* (Kiwi EA120, 1966).
218 Peggy Haworth, 'Synopsis of Life of Willow Macky', unpublished, 2006, Chris Bourke collection; 'Willow Macky', *Aprap*, June 2005, p. 10; Robin Nathan, 'Willow Macky: Balladeer for a New Country', *Music in New Zealand*, Spring 1994, pp. 37–43.
219 Nathan, 'Willow Macky', p. 38.
220 'Little Money Made By NZ Composers', *Evening Post*, 6 April 1957.
221 'A Teacher of Music in the Modern Manner', *Joy*, 13 June 1960, p. 10.
222 'Paekakariki and Beyond', *NZ Listener*, 18 October 1957, p. 20.
223 Avery, *Where Are the Camels? A Dance Band Diary*, p. 24.
224 Ken Avery, *The Ken Avery Songbook*, Ken Avery, Wellington, c. 1975, p. 2.
225 'Tea at Te Kuiti' by Ken Avery (Crown Music Pty, Australia); Ash Burton's backing band the Nightcaps included Bill Hoffmeister on ukulele and Terry Crayford on piano and bass (Avery, *Where Are the Camels? A Dance Band Diary*, p. 102).
226 Sam Freedman, interviewed by Gordon Spittle, 29 September 1992.
227 Sam Freedman, interviewed by Gordon Spittle; 'Little Money Made By NZ Composers', *Evening Post*.
228 Sam Freedman, interviewed by Gordon Spittle.
229 Eddie O'Strange, 'Unsung Songwriter Signs Off', *Dominion Post*, 26 June 2008, p. B7.
230 Steele, *An Ordinary Joker*; Gordon Spittle, *Counting the Beat*, GP Publications, Wellington, 1997, pp. 37–39.
231 James Hartstonge, unpublished memoir, ATL, pp. 216–17; he was later concert manager of the NZSO for a period.
232 Justin du Fresne, interviewed by Chris Bourke, Wellington, February 2007; 'On With the Dance', *NZ Listener*, 24 May 1957, p. 5.
233 Bas Tubert, 'The Rock's Good But Nix the Gimmix', *Joy*, 3 November 1958, p. 10.
234 'Radio Jubilee Today, and an Old Hand Remembers', unsourced clipping, Auckland scrapbooks, June 1972, p. 204 (Auckland Central City Library).
235 Stuart, 'Bless My Soul', p. 100; Eldred Stebbing, interviewed by Chris Bourke, March 2004; Bill Francis, *ZB: The Voice of an Iconic Radio Station*, HarperCollins, Auckland, 2006, p. 127; Berry, *Seeing Stars*, p. 55.
236 Calder Prestcott, interviewed by Chris Bourke, Dunedin, October 2006; Don Richardson, interviewed by Chris Bourke. Mention should be made of Bothamley's equally committed assistant in Auckland, pianist Don Patton.
237 Doug Caldwell, interviewed by Chris Bourke.
238 *AMM*, November 1962.
239 Lewis, *Arthur and the Nights at the Turntable*, p. 266.
240 Ray Harris, 'We'll Remember You, Bob', *NZ Listener*, 15 July 1966.
241 Johnny Douglas, interviewed by Chris Bourke, Wellington, 31 January 2008.
242 Bernie Griffin, 'Bas Tubert: Intrepid Reporter', *NZ Listener*, 11 June 1988, p. 38.
243 Peter Downes and Peter Harcourt, *Voices in the Air*, Methuen, Wellington, 1976, p. 164.
244 Bernie Griffin, 'Bas Tubert: Intrepid Reporter'.
245 Warren Barton, 'Let's Play It Again, Cham', *Dominion Post*, 1 January 1997, p. 9.
246 Kerry Stevens, conversation with Chris Bourke, Auckland, 2001.
247 Neville Chamberlain, quoted in Downes and Harcourt, *Voices in the Air*, p. 165.
248 'Lou Parun, Cham the Man: Radio Pioneer', *Dominion Post*, 1 March 2007.
249 Catch phrases listed on Andy Shackleton's website (www.ashack.co.nz).
250 Johnny Douglas, interviewed by Chris Bourke; Katharine Brisbane (ed.),

251 Godfrey Gray, *33 Years Behind the Mast: Recollections of a Career in New Zealand Broadcasting*, unpublished memoir, ATL, p. 2. Gray was an operator on the *The Sunset Show*.
252 Justin du Fresne, interviewed by Chris Bourke.
253 CBCH, '19 Years of Hit Parade', *NZ Listener*, 24 December 1965, p. 8.
254 *Variety*, July 7, 1954.
255 *Monthly Film Bulletin*, August 1954, p. 117.
256 Jack Leigh, 'Band Erupts for Old Troupers', *NZ Herald*, 3 May 1997, p. G:5.
257 'Maori Showbands', Te Papa on-line exhibition, 2005 (www.maorishowbands.co.nz, accessed 12 March 2010).
258 Ans Westra, 'Henare Gilbert Comes Home Again', *Te Ao Hou* 39, June 1962, p. 2.
259 Rob Hemi, interviewed by Suzanne Ormsby in 1996, in Ormsby, *Te Reo Puoro Maori Mai I Mua Tae Noa Mai Ki Inaianei*, p. 193. Ward-Holmes later became an agent in Canada.
260 'Maori Showbands', Te Papa on-line exhibition.
261 Stuart, 'Bless My Soul', p. 101.
262 Stuart, 'Bless My Soul', p. 101.
263 Hemi, in Ormsby, *Te Reo Puoro Maori Mai I Mua Tae Noa Mai Ki Inaianei*, p. 191.
264 Hemi, in Ormsby, *Te Reo Puoro Maori Mai I Mua Tae Noa Mai Ki Inaianei*, p. 191.
265 'Maori Showbands', Te Papa on-line exhibition.
266 Watkins, *When the Rock Got Rolling*, p. 44.
267 Rob Hemi, in Ormsby, *Te Reo Puoro Maori Mai I Mua Tae Noa Mai Ki Inaianei*, p. 142.
268 Lloyd Ashton, 'Showband!', *Mana*, December 2004/January 2005, p. 15.
269 The Hi-Five left for Australia with a new lineup: Rob Hemi, Solomon Pohatu, Kawana Pohe, Harata (Charlotte) Pohe, Wes Epae, Paddy Te Tai and Tuki Witika.
270 Shot in England and released in 1962, the film also featured Inia Te Wiata (as a chief, again) and former Brown Bomber Henare Gilbert.
271 'Hi-Fives Live Right Up to Reputation', *NZ Herald*, 4 March 1963, p. 1:3.
272 Bruce Morley, 'The Launching of Nga Matua', *Music in New Zealand*, 21, Winter 1993, pp. 39–40.
273 Gerry Merito, interviewed by Chris Bourke, Cambridge, 4 November 2007.
274 Peters with George, *Showband*, p. 38.
275 Tapu Misa and Dale Husband, 'You Are a Part of Me', *Mana*, June/July 2002, p. 27.
276 Barney Erickson, in Ormsby, *Te Reo Puoro Maori Mai I Mua Tae Noa Mai Ki Inaianei*, p. 162.
277 Erickson, in Ormsby, *Te Reo Puoro Maori Mai I Mua Tae Noa Mai Ki Inaianei*, p. 162.
278 Peters with George, *Showband*, p. 40.
279 Gugi Waaka, quoted in Misa and Husband, 'You Are a Part of Me', p. 27.
280 'Maori Volcanics are "Wild"', in Peters with George, *Showband!*, p. 90.
281 Pauline Ray, 'A Royal Homecoming', *NZ Listener*, 20 November 1982, p. 14.
282 Howard Morrison, interviewed by Caitlin Cherry for Radio New Zealand, 2001; Howard Morrison with John Costello, *Howard*, Moa Beckett, Auckland, 1992, p. 19.
283 Howard Morrison, interviewed by Caitlin Cherry.
284 Morrison and Costello, *Howard*, p. 27.
285 Morrison and Costello, *Howard*, p. 32.
286 Richard Spence, *Whakaaria Mai: The Biography of Canon Wiremu Wi te Tau Huata*, Dunmore Press, Palmerston North, 1994, p. 198.
287 Howard Morrison, interviewed by Caitlin Cherry.
288 Gerry Merito, interviewed by Chris Bourke.
289 Smith was famous for the song that gave him his nickname, and also for writing 'Feudin' Banjos', later a hit as 'Duelling Banjos'.
290 Gerry Merito, interviewed by Warwick Burke for Radio New Zealand, 1999.
291 Morrison and Costello, *Howard*, p. 43.
292 Berry, *Seeing Stars*, p. 38. This sextet featured Morrison's cousins John and Terry, Gary Rangiihu, Chubby Hamiora and future Quartet singer Wi Wharekura on guitar.
293 Howard Morrison, interviewed by Caitlin Cherry.
294 Gerry Merito, interviewed by Warwick Burke.
295 Gerry Merito, interviewed by Warwick Burke.
296 Howard Morrison, interviewed by Caitlin Cherry; Gerry Merito, interviewed by Warwick Burke.
297 Catherine Watson, 'Kahu Morrison: Kuia', *Listener & TV Times*, 18 May 1992, p. 15; in the mid-1960s, Kahu Morrison recorded Maori songs for Zodiac and Viking.
298 Gerry Merito, interviewed by Chris Bourke.
299 Benny Levin, in Costello and Morrison, *Howard*, p. 62; Gerry Merito, interviewed by Warwick Burke and by Chris Bourke.
300 Jim Warren, 'Auckland News', *AMM*, May 1958.
301 Morrison and Costello, *Howard*, p. 64.
302 Morrison and Costello, *Howard*, pp. 65–66.
303 Te Kapunga Matemoana Dewes, *Nga Waiata Haka a Henare Waitoa o Ngati Porou: Modern dance-poetry by Henare Waitoa of Ngati Porou*, Department of Anthropology and Maori, Victoria University of Wellington, 1974, p. 96.
304 Howard Morrison, interviewed by Caitlin Cherry.
305 Benny Levin, oral history interview, OH-A-2086, ATL.
306 Vern Whitehead, 'Howard Morrison Quartet Crazy About TV', *Joy*, 31 August 1959, p. 5.
307 Also on the bill were the Bob Paris Combo, Hiria Moffat, Danny Robinson, Eddie Howell: Programme, Eph-A-Cabot-Music-1959, ATL; Vern Whitehead, 'Howard Morrison Quartet Crazy About TV'.

308 Gerry Merito, interviewed by Chris Bourke.
309 Eldred Stebbing, oral history interview with Roger Watkins, 3 February 1993, OHA-2093.
310 Morrison and Costello, *Howard*, p. 67.
311 '20,000 Fans Scream "More!"', *Cinema, Stage and TV*, 1 March 1960, p. 32.
312 *NZ Herald*, 25 January 1960; *Auckland Star*, 25 January 1960.
313 Morrison and Costello, *Howard*, p. 67.
314 Morrison and Costello, *Howard*, p. 68.
315 Morrison and Costello, *Howard*, p. 68.
316 Stuart, 'Bless My Soul', p. 101.
317 Benny Levin, oral history interview.
318 Morrison and Costello, *Howard*, p. 71.
319 Harry M. Miller, as told to Dennis O'Brien, *Harry M Miller: My Story*, Macmillan, Melbourne, 1983, p. 59.
320 Eldred Stebbing, oral history interview with Roger Watkins.
321 Howard Morrison, interviewed by Caitlin Cherry.
322 Miller, *My Story*, p. 63.
323 Watson, 'Kahu Morrison: Kuia', pp. 15 and 18; Gerry Merito, interviewed by Chris Bourke.
324 'Sorry, mate, but we don't cut hair for Maoris', *NZ Truth*, 3 October 1961.
325 Howard Morrison, interviewed by Caitlin Cherry.
326 Miller, *My Story*, p. 64.
327 Miller, *My Story*, p. 62. Actually, he billed White as 'twenty stone and a ton of fun' – advertisement in Peter Downes, *Top of the Bill*, Reed, Wellington, 1979, p. 87.
328 Gerry Merito, interviewed by Jim Sutton, Newstalk ZB; Morrison and Costello, *Howard*, p. 75; Howard Morrison, interviewed by Caitlin Cherry.
329 Miller, *My Story*, pp. 66 and 81.
330 Gerry Merito, interviewed by Chris Bourke.
331 Morrison and Costello, *Howard*, p. 95.
332 Morrison and Costello, *Howard*, p. 115.
333 'Four Up', *NZ Listener*, 20 October 1961, p. 7.
334 Morrison and Costello, *Howard*, p. 105.
335 Morrison and Costello, *Howard*, p. 95.
336 Gerry Merito, interviewed by Chris Bourke; Morrison and Costello, *Howard*, p. 113.
337 Simon Meihana, interviewed by Sharon Ormsby, in Ormsby, *Te Reo Puoro Maori Mai I Mua Tae Noa Mai Ki Inaianei*, pp. 128–9.
338 Morrison and Costello, *Howard*, p. 95.
339 Morrison and Costello, *Howard*, p. 105.
340 Howard Morrison, interviewed by Caitlin Cherry.
341 Howard Morrison, interviewed by Caitlin Cherry.
342 Morrison and Costello, *Howard*, p. 109. Also on the bill were Toni Williams, Anne and Jimmy Murphy, the Nick Smith Combo and Jim McNaught: *NZ Truth*, 29 September 1964, p. 52.
343 Howard Morrison, interviewed by Caitlin Cherry.
344 Howard Morrison, interviewed by Caitlin Cherry.
345 Contemporary review reproduced in Morrison and Costello, *Howard*, p. 110.
346 Morrison and Costello, *Howard*, p. 111.
347 Gerry Merito, interviewed by Chris Bourke.
348 Howard Morrison, interviewed by Caitlin Cherry.
349 Dalvanius Maui Prime, interviewed by Chris Bourke, Auckland, 12 February 2000.
350 *AMM*, October 1961.
351 *AMM*, December 1961.
352 Preece, 'Sounds Like Us', p. 28.
353 Watkins, *Hostage to the Beat*, pp. 109–10; Dix, *Stranded in Paradise*, p. 41.
354 *AMM*, December 1962.
355 The Embers was a virtual super-group, with former members of the Buccaneers and the Devils, and became an early vehicle for pianist/band leader Mike Perjanik and guitarist Doug Jerebine (Watkins, *Hostage to the Beat*, p. 53).
356 *Auckland Star* entertainment page advertisements, 1963; *AMM*, March 1962.
357 Wald, *How the Beatles Destroyed Rock'n'Roll*, p. 215.
358 'Twist – Exotic (Some Say Erotic) – Dance Craze is Here At Last!', *NZ Truth*, 16 January 1962, p. 6.
359 'Poi Poi Twist', Rim D Paul with the Quin Tikis, 1963 (Zodiac Z451138). Dalvanius and Herbs both revived the 'E Aue' introduction idea in the 1980s.
360 Ray Harris, 'Sarah Vaughan & Dizzy Gillespie', *NZ Listener*, 18 November 1960, p. 9.
361 Lew Campbell, interviewed by Chris Bourke.
362 'He's Got Rhythm', *NZ Listener*, 8 June 1962, p. 7; Eugene Wright, *The Wright Groove*, 1962 (Philips P08755L).
363 In the backing band of Helen Shapiro, for example, were pop guitarists Peter Posa and Bob Paris, plus jazz players George Campbell, Colin Martin, Brian Smith, Bernie Allen and Derek Neville (*AMM*, November 1962).
364 Avery, *Where Are the Camels? A Dance Band Diary*, p. 30.
365 Avery, *Where Are the Camels?*, p. 92.
366 Monte Holcroft, 'Yeh! Yeh! Yeh!', *NZ Listener*, 13 December 1963.
367 *AMM*, August 1964.
368 *The Beatles Inside NZ* documentary, Ninox Films, Wellington, 1994, F22312, New Zealand Film Archive.
369 Phil Warren, interviewed by Mike Turner for *The Tonight Show*, Radio New Zealand, June 1984.
370 Tommy Adderley, interviewed by Roger Watkins, 1992, as quoted in Mintrom, *Tommy Adderley 1940–1993*, pp. 4–5.
371 Eldred Stebbing, interviewed by Chris Bourke, 2004.
372 Jim Warren, 'New Zealand Message', *AMM*, April 1963.

SELECT BIBLIOGRAPHY

Anderson, Bruce, *Story of the New Zealand Recording Industry,* self-published, Wellington, 1984.

Australian Dance Band News, 1932–1933, which became *Australian Music Maker and Dance Band News,* 1933–1940, then *Music Maker, incorporating Australian Music Maker and Dance Band News,* 1940–1972. Sydney. [*AMM* in endnotes]

Avery, Ken, *Where Are the Camels? A Dance Band Diary,* Clare Avery, Wellington, 2010.

Berry, John, *Seeing Stars,* Seven Seas, Wellington, 1964.

Bollinger, Nick, *100 Essential New Zealand Albums,* Awa Press, Wellington, 2009.

Bisset, Andrew, *Black Roots, White Flowers: A History of Jazz in Australia,* ABC, Sydney, 2nd edn, 1987.

Brown, Michael, *There's a Sound of Many Voices in the Camp and On the Track: A Descriptive Analysis of Folk Music Collecting in New Zealand, 1955–1975,* MA thesis, Victoria University of Wellington, 2006.

Cleveland, Les, *The Great New Zealand Songbook,* Godwit, Auckland, 1991.

Day, Patrick, *The Radio Years,* Auckland University Press, Auckland, 1994.

Dix, John, *Stranded in Paradise: New Zealand Rock'n'Roll 1955–1988,* Paradise Publications, Wellington, 1988.

Dorsey, Colin, *Dance Bands of the 20th Century in North Otago,* Colin Dorsey, Oamaru, 1991.

Downes, Peter, and Peter Harcourt, *Voices in the Air,* Methuen, Wellington, 1975.

Downes, Peter, *Top of the Bill,* Reed, Wellington, 1979.

Gilkison, Alistair, *Archive of New Zealand Sheet Music,* self-published, Lower Hutt, 2006.

Gunn, Bennie, *57a or Tales of a Musicians' Hangout,* Talisman Press, Auckland, 1993.

Hardie, Richard, and Allan Thomas, *Jazz Aotearoa: Notes Towards a New Zealand History,* Steele Roberts, Wellington, 2009.

Harding, Mike, *When the Pakeha Sings of Home,* Godwit, Auckland, 1992.

Hegan, Eddie, *No Choice,* Hodder & Stoughton, Auckland, 1980.

Huggard, Dennis O. (ed.), *The Thoughts of Musician Desmond 'Spike' Donovan,* New Zealand Series No. 5, Dennis O. Huggard, Henderson, Auckland, 1998.

Huggard, Dennis O., *The Tanza Catalogue,* New Zealand Series, booklet one, Dennis O. Huggard, Glendene, Auckland, 5th edn, 2005.

Huggard, Dennis O., *Jazz Records of New Zealand 1930–1980,* New Zealand Series No. 4, Dennis O. Huggard, Glendene, Auckland, 2005.

Huggard, Dennis O., *The Stebbing Catalogue,* New Zealand Series No. 3, Dennis O. Huggard, Waitakere, Auckland, 4th edn, 2008.

Jules, Jo, *A Passion for Jazz: The Christchurch Scene Then and Now,* School of Performing Arts, Christchurch, 2009.

Lewis, Laurie, *Arthur and the Nights at the Turntable: The Life and Times of a Jazz Broadcaster,* K'vrie Press, Wingen, NSW, 1997.

MacGibbon, John, *Piano in the Parlour,* Ngaio Press, Wellington, 2007.

McKelvie, Neil, *45 South in Concert,* Southland Musicians' Club, Invercargill, 2006.

Mora, Jim, 'Mr Nice Guy', *Metro,* June 1993, p. 93.

Mora, Jim, 'Th' Gals', *Metro,* June 1993, p. 95.

Morrison, Howard, with John Costello, *Howard,* Moa Beckett, Auckland, 1992.

Nott, James J., *Music for the People: Popular Music and Dance in Interwar Britain,* Oxford University Press, Oxford, 2002.

Ormsby, Suzanne, *Te Reo Puoro Maori Mai I Mua Tae Noa Mai Ki Inaianei, The Voices of Maori Music, Past Present and Future: Maori Musicians of the 1960s,* MA thesis, University of Auckland, 1996.

Peters, Mahora, with James George, *Showband! Mahora and the Maori Volcanics,* Huia, Wellington, 2005.

Read, Peter J., *Blue Suede Gumboots? The Impact of Imported Popular Culture in New Zealand in the 1950s,* MA History thesis, University of Otago, 1990.

Sheirtcliff, Reo, 'Dancing in the Dark: A Memoir of Epi Shalfoon', *Music in New Zealand,* 11, Summer 1990–1991, Music in New Zealand, Auckland, 1990.

Sinclair, Lex, *Take Me Back to Yesterday Once More: A History of Musicians, Dance Bands and Country Music in South Canterbury, 1920s–1970s,* Lex Sinclair, Timaru, 2002.

Smith, John K., with Colin M. Linwood, *Just for the Record: A Discography of Vinyl Recordings by New Zealand Recording Artists from 1949 to 2000,* John K. Smith, Whangarei, 3rd edn, 2001.

Spittle, Gordon, *Counting the Beat,* GP Publications, Wellington, 1997.

Spittle, Gordon, *The Tex Morton Songbook,* GWS Publications, Auckland, 2008.

Staff, Bryan, and Sheran Ashley, *For the Record,* David Bateman, Auckland, 2002.

Steele, Roger, *An Ordinary Joker: The Life and Songs of Peter Cape,* Steele Roberts, Wellington, 2001.

Stuart, Duncan, 'Bless My Soul, It's . . . Rock'n'Roll', *Metro,* March 1986, pp. 96–103.

Thomas, Allan, *Music is Where You Find It: Music in the Town of Hawera, 1946,* Music Books New Zealand, School of Music, Victoria University of Wellington, 2004.

Thomson, John Mansfield, *The Oxford History of New Zealand Music,* Oxford University Press, Auckland, 1991.

Vaughan, Terry, *Whistle As You Go: The Story of the Kiwi Concert Party,* Random House, Auckland, 1995.

Watkins, Roger, *When the Rock Got Rolling: The Wellington Scene, 1958–1970,* Hazard, Christchurch, 1989.

Watkins, Roger, *Hostage to the Beat: The Auckland Scene 1955–1970,* Tandem, Auckland, 1995.

White, Georgina, *Light Fantastic: Dance Floor Courtship in New Zealand,* HarperCollins, Auckland, 2007.

Yska, Redmer, *All Shook Up,* Penguin, Auckland, 1993.

INDEX

1	*Lifebuoy Hit Parade* poster	34	Howard Morrison Quartet
2	Crombie Murdoch	35	Marlene Tong
3	Ronnie Sundin	36	Jean McPherson
4	Walter Smith	37	Gerry Merito
5	Art Rosoman	38	Ossie Cheesman
6	Alan Brown, Jack Roberts and Jim Gower	39	2ZB's Carol Sanders and US Marine
7	Dinah Greening	40	Howard Morrison
8	Dean Waretini and Ana Hato	41	Showtime Spectacular tour, 1961
9	Mavis Rivers	42	Melody Maids of Okato
10	Jimmy Long	43	Solitaires' clarinettist, Christchurch
11	The Convairs	44	Henry Rudolph
12	Peter Logan and His Hawaiians	45	Bob Parrish
13	Peter Posa and White Rabbit	46	Claire Kennedy
14	Southern Dixieland Band	47	Johnny Devlin
15	Max McCauley	48	Clive Laurent
16	Cheryl and Lynn Apaapa	49	A Dunedin harmonica quintet and guitarist
17	Marion Waite	50	Lauri Paddi Band
18	Eddie Croad	51	Joe Papesch
19	Bill Hoffmeister's 2YA Orchestra	52	Mavis Rivers
20	Sunbeams guitarist	53	Tommy Kahi
21	Excelsior Piano Accordeon Band	54	Ruru Karaitiana
22	Ray Paparoa	55	Hawaiian Serenaders with Heather Douglas
23	Garner Wayne	56	Bernie Allen
24	Toni Williams and Howard Morrison	57	Len Hawkins Radio Band
25	Epi Shalfoon	58	Jim Watters
26	Peter Posa	59	Len Hawkins
27	Anania Amohau, 'Maori Battalion Marching Song'	60	Alan Dunnage
28	Tai Paul and His Pohutu Boys	61	Mavis Rivers
29	Amiria and Henare Waitoa	62	Lou Clauson, Tex Morton, Simon Meihana
30	*Tex Morton Song Album*	63	Musical group, Wanganui
31	Ron Hayward	64	Johnny Cooper and His Range Riders
32	Johnny Devlin	65	Pete Sinclair, Ricky May and Lou Pryme
33	Dudley Wrathall	66	The Knaves with Thomson Yandall